The Ripple Effects of Environmental Policies:

Economic, Financial, and Institutional Perspectives

Mohieddine Rahmouni
King Faisal University, Saudi Arabia

IGI Global
Scientific Publishing
Publishing Tomorrow's Research Today

Published in the United States of America by
IGI Global Scientific Publishing
701 East Chocolate Avenue
Hershey, PA, 17033, USA
Tel: 717-533-8845 | Fax: 717-533-7115
Website: https://www.igi-global.com E-mail: cust@igi-global.com

Library of Congress Cataloging-in-Publication Data

Names: Rahmouni, Mohieddine, 1977- editor
Title: The ripple effects of environmental policies : economic, financial, and institutional perspectives / edited by Mohieddine Rahmouni.
Description: Hershey : IGI Global Scientific Publishing, 2026. | Includes bibliographical references and index. | Summary: "This book advances scholarly and policy understanding of the indirect, systemic, and often unintended consequences of environmental regulation. While much of the existing literature concentrates on direct environmental effectiveness or short-term compliance costs, this volume provides a holistic and interdisciplinary framework for evaluating how environmental policies propagate through economic systems, financial markets, and institutional structures"-- Provided by publisher.
Identifiers: LCCN 2026005284 (print) | LCCN 2026005285 (ebook) | ISBN 9798337389981 hardcover | ISBN 9798337389998 paperback | ISBN 9798337390000 ebook
Subjects: LCSH: Environmental law--Economic aspects--Mexico | Renewable energy sources--Law and legislation--Mexico | Clean energy industries--Finance--Law and legislation--Mexico | Sustainable development--Law and legislation--Mexico | Environmental policy--Economic aspects | Environmental policy--China
Classification: LCC KGF3421 .R57 2026 (print) | LCC KGF3421 (ebook)
LC record available at https://lccn.loc.gov/2026005284
LC ebook record available at https://lccn.loc.gov/2026005285

British Cataloguing in Publication Data
A Cataloguing in Publication record for this book is available from the British Library.

Table of Contents

Detailed Table of Contents

Environmental policy affects economic growth, incentives, and the structural composition of economies, functioning not merely as a regulatory instrument but as a transformative macroeconomic force. By generating price, risk, and behavioral signals, environmental policies influence firms, households, and financial markets through multiple transmission channels, including productivity, innovation, capital allocation, and social distribution. While transition costs may temporarily reduce output in carbon-intensive sectors, long-term productivity gains can emerge through improved energy efficiency, process innovation, and shifts toward higher-value activities. Stringent environmental regulations often stimulate research and development in low-carbon, energy-efficient, and circular-economy technologies, thereby mitigating abatement costs and supporting sustainable growth. Financial markets respond through changes in asset valuation, credit availability, risk premia, and portfolio composition as sustainability standards and disclosure mandates reshape investor expectations.

The environmental policy has now become a strategy aimed at economic, financial and institutional change and not just another regulatory device. In this chapter, the

It employs carbon price trajectories, emissions scopes, intensity metrics, internal carbon pricing, and result indicators such as cost of capital to assess policy stringency and business vulnerability and responsiveness, therefore rendering policy signals decision-useful. It demonstrates how disclosure mandates and assurance mitigate information asymmetry, facilitating systematic repricing, capital reallocation, and macroprudential supervision of climate-related risks during the net zero transition.

The international trade architecture is shifting from a focus on pure economic growth to global emissions mitigation, primarily to combat carbon leakage. By utilizing instruments like the Carbon Border Adjustment Mechanism (CBAM) and integrating environmental provisions into trade agreements, green production standards are harmonized to protect climate goals from policy asymmetries. This transition is systemically transmitted through Global Value Chains (GVCs), where multinational transparency demands drive the adoption of environmental standards in developing nations. Ultimately, the synergy between carbon pricing, legal clauses, and GVC connectivity shifts the global paradigm from cost efficiency to sustainability, fostering transnational decarbonization and inclusive green growth.

The chapter examines the effects of the EU's application of the Carbon Border Adjustment Mechanism (CBAM) on the Western Balkan countries, whose economies rely significantly on exports of goods produced with high levels of greenhouse gas emissions. The potential impact of CBAM on these countries is assessed across 35 product groups by comparing several indicators (absolute export volumes, the degree of dependence on the European market, significance for national exports, the existence of stable trade relationships, location and size of production facilities).

The chapter also assesses national initiatives related to the implementation of the EU climate policy principles, in particular the establishment of carbon pricing instruments, which may be taken into account in the calculation of CBAM costs. In addition, indicative CBAM costs for ten carbon-intensive products from Serbia are estimated, taking into account embedded and direct emissions, exports to the EU, and projected CBAM certificate prices.

This study examines the spatial spillover effects of environmental policy stringency, GDP per capita, and fossil energy consumption on the ecological footprint in EU–14 countries over the period 1990–2020 using spatial econometric techniques. The results reveal strong and positive spatial dependence in the ecological footprint, indicating significant cross-country spillovers. Environmental policy stringency is found to reduce the ecological footprint both directly and indirectly, while fossil energy consumption and GDP per capita increase environmental pressure through significant domestic and spillover effects. Notably, indirect effects dominate direct effects, highlighting the critical role of regional interdependence in shaping environmental outcomes. These findings demonstrate that environmental policies generate ripple effects beyond national borders and emphasize the necessity of coordinated environmental and energy policies, increased investment in renewable energy, and strategies to decouple economic growth from fossil fuel dependence across the EU–14 region.

The examination of green public expenditure is highly important and this cannot be studied as an individual factor where in healthcare financing and welfare measures also should be embedded to understand this interdependent concept which will provide details about current budgetary pressures and also futuristic fiscal capacity. By exploring about the fiscal transmission channels through short, medium and long-term aspects, this chapter would study the static budgetary analysis by capturing the dynamic interactions throughout the environmental spending and reduced health care costs. This chapter also integrates the welfare economics towards the fiscal analysis

paper presents a causal framework that explains how SRI capital starts to generate actual impact while it identifies policy changes that will enhance organizational responsibility and operational efficiency.

The work tries to investigate the role of institutions for achieving green economic growth for the Chinese economy by considering the period from 1996- 2021. Besides institutional factors, foreign direct investment, renewable energy consumption, and expenditure on research and development also are considered. The results from the Bounds test show a high degree of long-term relationship. The research investigates the overall impact of governance on green growth and the individual impact of each of the governance indicators. For institutional quality, a positive impact on green economic growth is observed. Within institutional quality it is seen that barring rule of law and control of corruption, all other variables show a positive impact on our dependent variable. With respect to Foreign direct investment it is seen that the impact is negative which means the Pollution haven hypothesis is upheld for Chinese economy. For renewable energy consumption and expenditure incurred on research and development the impact yet again is positive.

Environmental policies have evolved from narrow regulatory tools to key instruments of economic governance, affecting resource-dependent economies by influencing extractive sectors, revenue systems, and governance. This chapter introduces the Governance Ripple Framework, viewing environmental policies as institutional shocks that cause sequential fiscal, institutional, and equity effects. Using a qualitative–comparative approach, it analyzes Nigeria, Indonesia, and Chile, illustrating that

Preface

DESCRIPTION

Over the past three decades, environmental policies have become central instruments of economic governance as governments respond to climate change, environmental degradation, and increasing resource scarcity. Policy tools such as carbon pricing, emissions standards, green subsidies, and conservation regulations have expanded rapidly in scope and ambition at both national and international levels. While these instruments are primarily designed to achieve ecological objectives, a growing body of research demonstrates that their consequences extend well beyond environmental outcomes, generating complex and interconnected economic, financial, and institutional effects.

The Ripple Effects of Environmental Policies: Economic, Financial, and Institutional Perspectives responds to the need for a systematic and interdisciplinary examination of how environmental policies interact with economic systems, financial structures, and institutional arrangements at national and global scales. By integrating insights from environmental economics, finance, public policy, and institutional analysis, it provides a comprehensive framework for understanding how environmental interventions propagate through economies and societies. Covering topics such as capital reallocation, healthcare financing, and renewable energy, this book is an excellent resource for academicians, researchers, graduate and postgraduate students, policymakers, government officials, financial market professionals, and more.

COVERAGE

The many academic areas covered in this publication include, but are not limited to:

- Capital Reallocation
- Carbon Pricing
- Emissions Trading Systems (ETS)
- Environmental Policies
- Environmental Regulations
- Financial Markets
- Green Finance
- Healthcare Financing
- Natural Resource Institutions
- Public Expenditure
- Renewable Energy
- Socioeconomic Equity
- Sustainability

Acknowledgment

Funding: This work was supported by the Deanship of Scientific Research, Vice Presidency for Graduate Studies and Scientific Research, King Faisal University, Saudi Arabia [Grant No. KFU260984].

Introduction

Environmental policy has evolved from a narrow regulatory tool aimed at correcting environmental externalities into a central driver of economic restructuring, financial market transformation, and institutional reform. In an era defined by climate risks, energy transitions, and sustainability imperatives, environmental policies generate ripple effects that extend far beyond environmental outcomes. They influence capital allocation, reshape trade patterns, redefine fiscal priorities, alter governance structures, and transform development trajectories. Understanding these multidimensional effects is essential for designing coherent and effective policy frameworks.

The Ripple Effects of Environmental Policies: Economic, Financial, and Institutional Perspectives brings together diverse scholarly contributions to examine how environmental policy operates as a systemic shock that propagates across economic systems. Rather than treating environmental regulation as an isolated intervention, this volume conceptualizes it as a structural force that generates sequential and interconnected impacts across markets, institutions, and societies.

From an **economic perspective**, environmental policies influence productivity, innovation incentives, sectoral composition, and long-term growth dynamics. Carbon pricing, regulatory standards, and fiscal instruments alter relative prices, shift comparative advantages, and accelerate structural transformation toward low-carbon production systems. These mechanisms shape not only domestic economic performance but also international competitiveness and global value chains.

From a **financial perspective**, environmental policy signals are increasingly embedded in asset pricing, credit markets, investment strategies, and risk management frameworks. Carbon pricing mechanisms, disclosure mandates, and sustainability standards reshape investor expectations, affect risk premia, and redirect capital toward renewable energy, clean technologies, and climate-resilient infrastructure. Financial markets thus act as transmission channels through which environmental policies amplify or moderate economic adjustment processes.

From an **institutional perspective**, the effectiveness of environmental policies depends critically on governance quality, regulatory coherence, and administrative capacity. Institutional arrangements determine whether policy ambitions translate into inclusive growth, equitable distributional outcomes, and sustainable development pathways. In resource-dependent economies and emerging markets alike, governance structures mediate the fiscal, social, and developmental consequences of environmental reform.

The chapters in this volume collectively explore these dimensions through theoretical analysis, empirical investigation, comparative case studies, and policy evaluation. They examine carbon pricing systems, financial stability implications, trade spillovers, fiscal trade-offs, sustainable investment instruments, and governance transformations across different regional contexts. Together, they demonstrate that environmental policies do not operate in isolation; they reshape interconnected economic and institutional ecosystems.

By integrating economic theory, financial market analysis, and institutional governance perspectives, this volume provides a comprehensive understanding of how environmental policies generate ripple effects across multiple layers of the global economy. It offers insights for policymakers, scholars, financial practitioners, and institutional leaders seeking to navigate the transition toward sustainable and inclusive development.

In doing so, the book contributes to a broader recognition: environmental policy is no longer peripheral to economic governance—it is central to the architecture of twenty-first-century development.

Chapter 1

The Ripple Effects of Environmental Policy Economic Growth, Innovation, Finance, and Just Transitions in a Low-Carbon Economy

Amit Verma
http://orcid.org/0000-0002-9283-7873
Kalicharan PG College, Lucknow, India

Aarti Chopra
http://orcid.org/0000-0002-9068-0155
Poornima University, Jaipur, India

Vikas Singh
Motilal Nehru National Institute of Technology, Allahabad, India

Shrish Kumar Tiwari
Central University of Gujrat, India

ABSTRACT

Environmental policy affects economic growth, incentives, and the structural composition of economies, functioning not merely as a regulatory instrument but as a transformative macroeconomic force. By generating price, risk, and behavioral signals, environmental policies influence firms, households, and financial markets

DOI: 10.4018/979-8-3373-8998-1.ch001

through multiple transmission channels, including productivity, innovation, capital allocation, and social distribution. While transition costs may temporarily reduce output in carbon-intensive sectors, long-term productivity gains can emerge through improved energy efficiency, process innovation, and shifts toward higher-value activities. Stringent environmental regulations often stimulate research and development in low-carbon, energy-efficient, and circular-economy technologies, thereby mitigating abatement costs and supporting sustainable growth. Financial markets respond through changes in asset valuation, credit availability, risk premia, and portfolio composition as sustainability standards and disclosure mandates reshape investor expectations.

1. INTRODUCTION: CENTRAL CONTRIBUTION, SCOPE, AND ORGANIZING LOGIC

1.1 Why Environmental Policy Is Now a Systemic Economic Intervention

Environmental policy has transformed from a pollution-control mechanism to a structuring force of contemporary economies. Traditionally, environmental regulation has been perceived as a corrective policy instrument designed to internalize externalities within certain sectors. Nowadays, though, climate and environmental policies are economy-wide governance regimes that shape production patterns, capital allocation, technology pathways, demand for labor and international competitiveness. This evolution speaks volumes about the magnitude and duration of today's environmental woes. Carbon prices, emissions standards, green industrial strategies, climate-related financial disclosure regulations and transition-orientated labor policies are not discipline specific rules for the regulated firms alone; they change relative prices across entire production systems, expectations about future profitability and therefore the direction of structural change. And in doing so environmental policies not only affect the nature of compliance behavior, but also influence investment horizons, innovation pathways and institutional change. Environmental policy is in this respect a systemic economic intervention. It functions via long term shifts to incentives, expectations and governance systems and has outcomes that evolve over time and flow across sectors. It is not a single regulatory jolt but an ongoing reorientation of the form of economic organization.

In this background, the aim of this chapter is not to present a complete literature review. Rather, it provides an integrative synthesis and conceptual structure which will make clear how environmental policy makes economy-wide ripples. The chapter synthesizes the diverse strands of growth theory, innovation economics, financial economics, labor market analysis and political economy into an integrated analytical framework. Through placing synthesis above enumeration, the chapter extends insights into how environmental ambition operationalizes as structural economic change (Perman, 1994).

1.2 Central Analytical Contribution

The main contribution of this chapter is the construction of an integrated ripple-effect framework which in relativizes these literatures and places them into coherent pathways and impacts on growth, innovation, finance, and labor markets. A great deal of the literature treats the economic impact of environmental policy measures as separate cases. Growth studies deal with output and productivity effects; innovation research analyses induced technological change; financial analysis addresses risk repricing and asset valuation, while labor market research is concerned with employment and distributional effects. Even though each 'arm' given contributes significant information, these domains are not independent of each other which is completely hidden by their detachment building three distinct strands (Popp, 1997).

This chapter endeavours to partially fill that gap by suggesting a multi-stage transmission system model of environmental policy. Policy instruments create price signals and credibility effects that drive firm and investor actions. These responses affect the dynamics of innovation and diffusion, which are then reflected in capital allocation and financial risk. Capital relocation shifts patterns of labour demand among sectors and regions, with distributional implications. Labour and distributional outcomes also circularly feed into political legitimacy and policy durability, affecting future expectations and investment decisions. Hence, the economy-wide effects of environmental policy arise from those linked mechanisms rather than from disconnected sectoral responses. Regulation of the environment is thus not framed as an isolated intervention with discrete affects, but as a driver of structural transformation that has through identifiable and interlinking channels general effects on economic systems (Jaffe & Palmer, 1997).

1.3 Conceptual Framing of "Ripple Effects"

Operationalization of "ripple effects" A structured sequence of interconnected transition stages is adopted to enable analytical distinction (then referred to as ripple effect for simplicity's sake). "Ripple effects" refer to multistage processes when environmental policy affects economic impacts beyond the directly regulated areas through price signals, expectancy formation and innovation responses, financial reallocation and labor changing.

These ripple effects can be thought of like a domino effect:

1. Policy tool (e.g., carbon price, standard, disclosure)
2. The price, cost constraint or the credibility signal of costs and expected returns
3. Corporate and investor response: From changed production, investment, or portfolio choices
4. Innovation and diffusion dynamics that compete for R&D and technology adoption
5. Reallocate capital and reprice risk across financial markets
6. Labour re-allocation and distributional implications across sectors and regions
7. Macroeconomic and trade spillovers on inflation, competitiveness and between borders flows
8. Endogenous political economy feed-back to policy stability, and expectations for the future

While they are presented linearly, these phases interact iteratively. Repricing allows the financial market to speed up innovation through reduced cost of capital for clean technology. Labour displaced without sufficient transitional support may lack political acceptability, eroding policy credibility and investment decisions. Imbalance feedback loops emphasize the systemic nature of environmental policy effects. This organized framing classifies the effects of indirect and feedback effects. Direct effects are those of immediate compliance costs and sectoral adjustments. Indirect mechanisms include innovation, diffusion, and capital flows. Feedback effects occur when the resulting distributions and political responses change policy credibility and economic expectations. These operations compose the ripple-effect architecture that drives the analysis through this chapter (Porter & van der Linde, 1995).

By providing a unified conceptual framework from the outset, it helps to create a structured set of tools to help understand how environmental policy works with growth, innovation, finance, labour markets and just transition considerations. This intra-industry ripple-effect framework is developed as a theoretical vehicle that provides an umbrella for the following empirical and industry-level discussion. Instead of regarding economic growth, technology change, financial markets and labor mobility as isolated or loosely coupled topics, the conceptual anatomy reveals that they are structurally interwoven. In so doing, the chapter furthers coherence among thematic contributions and illuminates how the ecological ambition potentially metamorphoses into systemic economic change. It places environmental policy, not as an external restraint denying economic activity but as a key driver of how long-term structural transformation becomes manifest in a low carbon economy (Pizer, 2002).

2. CONCEPTUAL FOUNDATIONS AND ANALYTICAL FRAMEWORK

2.1 Environmental Policy Instruments Mapped to Transmission Channels

Environmental regimes may vary widely according to the shape, structure and content of their policy design, enforcement and economic implications. Without a classification scheme, studies are prone to turning into independent conversations of growth, innovation, finance and labor effects without analytical focus. Here we systematically map policy instruments to their leading economic transmission channels so as to disentangle mechanism-specific effects and avoid scattering the discussion. A classification of environmental policy instruments based on their predominant economic transmission mechanism, and corresponding economic effects is shown in Table 1. The table is a reference point that helps explain how different policy instruments 'switch on' different, but related, channels in the economy. Market-based instruments including carbon tax and emissions trading system (ETS) work mainly via price signals and the internalization of costs. Through increasing the marginal cost of carbon-intensive activities, they stimulate firms to restructure their input use and production techniques. Transmission is based mainly through relative price movements that lead to increases in productivity and sectoral shifts (Delvaux & Leuven, 2005).

Table 1. Classification of Environmental Policy Instruments and Economic Transmission Channels

Policy Instrument Category	Examples	Primary Economic Transmission Channel	Key Economic Effects
Market-Based Instruments	Carbon tax, Emissions trading schemes	Price signals and cost internalization	Resource reallocation, efficiency gains
Regulatory Instruments	Emission standards, technology mandates	Compliance-driven production adjustment	Structural change, productivity shifts
Innovation & Industrial Policy	Green subsidies, R&D incentives	Technological innovation and diffusion	Endogenous growth, cost reduction
Financial & Disclosure Policies	ESG disclosure, climate stress testing	Capital allocation and risk repricing	Green investment, financial stability
Labor & Social Policies	Reskilling programs, transition support	Employment adjustment and income redistribution	Equity, workforce resilience

Regulatory tools such as emission standards and technology mandates operate through production adjustments driven by compliance. Instead of using prices alone for coordination, they enforce quantitative, or performance-based constraints. These instruments typically induce structural changes as firms are forced to switch production techniques, retire old capital and adopt cleaner processes. Innovation and industrial policy measures, i.e. green subsidies and R&D incentives, work through the innovation/diffusion channel. They reduce the financial costs of CTLs' development and diffusion, induce directed technological change and speed up endogenous growth mechanisms. Financial and disclosure rules e.g. ESG disclosure requirements, climate stress tests mainly affect capital allocation and repricing of risks. They redefine investor behaviour and direct investment flows towards sustainable sectors by increasing transparency and incorporating climate-related risks in financial decision making, contributing to furthering financial stability and green investment (Sneeringer, 2009).

Labor and social policies, comprising retraining schemes and transition assistance measures, work through the channels of employment adjustment and income redistribution. These instruments reduce adjustment costs, make the workforce more resilient, and contribute to the equity of structural transformation. Through such a type of policy instrument construction, Table 1 gives a mechanism-based framework that connects the design of policies to economic channels and transmission mechanism. In the text, sections published later they refer to Table 1 in order to ensure analytical consistency and prevent treating policy sectors as separate thematic boxes.

2.2 Integrated Theoretical Lenses

To comprehend the sociocultural consequences of digital technologies, it is necessary to integrate theoretical perspectives into larger settlements and avoid using any single framework in an isolated manner. Environmental policy affects economic systems by ways that are analoguesly explained both by growth theory, innovation theory, institutional economics and political economy. Table 1–Revenue versus Efficient Environmental Regulation From the neoclassical growth point of view, so-called efficient environmental regulation can entail short-run adjustment costs because it raises production costs or attracts resources away from traditional capital accumulation. But long-term effects hinge on substitution opportunities, technological adjustment and capital redeployment. Thus, the size and smoothness of growth effects are contingent on how well the economy can adapt (Borck & Coglianese, 2009).

Endogenous growth theory and models of directed technical change also suggest that policy-induced changes in relative prices can redirect the direction of innovation. Regulation may thus act to induce R&D in cleaner technologies and thereby shift the direction of technological change, with implications for long-run productivity growth paths. Innovation thus is not exogenous, but policy-sensitive. Institutional economics emphasizes the role of credibility, enforcement power and quality of governance. Policy communications affect investment beliefs, but only to the extent that they are deemed credible and durable. Poor enforcement, policy flip-flops or incoherent governance structures erode the linkage of price and disclosure signals into longer-run investment (Johnstone et al., 2009).

Numerous political economy lenses focus on distributive effects and legitimacy. Who benefits and who loses from environmental policies varies among sectors, regions and income groups. These distributional effects shape public support as well as the political durability and credible of future policies. In this way, political economy dynamics also feed back into investment expectations and innovation responses. The expansion of these theoretical frameworks makes it possible to conceive environmental policy not simply as a regulatory constraint but as a systemic instrument, whose economic effects are determined by: The degree of credibility of institutions; The capacity for technological adaptation; Reaction to demands coming from the capital markets and citizens.

2.3 Ripple-Effect Transmission Channels: The Unifying Schematic

For the purpose of operationalizing the notion of ripple effect, this chapter identifies four central transmission channels that orientate the analysis and are referred to throughout:

1. Innovation channel: The direction and intensity of R&D depends on the environmental policy, which in turn determines technological trajectories and productivity.
2. Expectations and uncertainty duct: Policy credibility (predictability) influences long-horizon investment (and capital commitment).
3. Financial restructuring channel: Risk pricing and asset price revaluations reallocate capital into low-carbon sectors and out of high-carbon assets.
4. Labor reallocation channel: Structural change changes the composition of employment, demand for skills and distribution of income (Ambec et al., 2010).

Figure 1. Integrated Ripple-Effect Framework of Environmental Policy

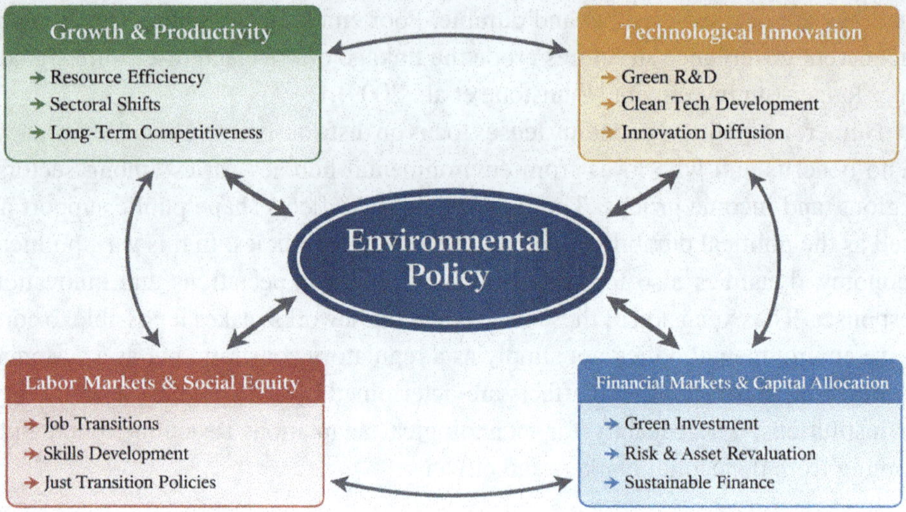

These channels are visually integrated in the Integrated Ripple-Effect Framework of Environmental Policy (see Figure 1). Figure 1 serves as the analytical core for the chapter. In so doing, it highlights the manner in which policy tools produce price and credibility signals that affect innovation, financial and labor outcomes -- mediated through dynamic linkages among these realms. The schematic emphasizes that the ripples aren't linear so much as circular. Policy-driven innovation, for instance, may lower long-term costs and thus affect financial valuations and labor adjustments. On the other hand, weak labor adjustment can also lead to a loss of political backing and erosion of policy credibility and innovation incentives. Returning to Figure 1 at the beginning of each section also encourages consistency throughout the chapter and with cross-body-system interactions, rather than being separate topical discussions (Haščič et al., 2010).

2.4 Transitional Bridge to the Growth Analysis

The growth implications of environmental policy arise through the interaction of the four transmission channels discussed above. Short-run adjustment costs may be large when capital and labor markets are inflexible, institutions are frail or policy signals not credible. We find that compliance costs and factor reallocation frictions can lead to a temporary decline in output growth under such circumstances. Long-term gains, however, are easier when innovation is faster or when capital reallocates actively and well, when financial markets price risks fluidly, labor institutions are supportive of adaptation. As such, the growth consequences are not simply a function of which policy is applied but also how well innovation, finance and labor adjustment mechanisms work together over time. The next section extends this framework to analyze the role of these channels in short-run adjustment dynamics and long-run structural growth paths (Aldy & Pizer, 2011).

3. ENVIRONMENTAL POLICY AND ECONOMIC GROWTH DYNAMICS

3.1 Growth–Environment Relationship Reframed as Time-Horizon Dependent

The deep discussion around environmental policy and growth have long been defined in binary terms: Either regulation implies a trade-off that stalls the economy's growth or it produces a "win-win" from incentivizing innovation and efficiency. This dichotomy focuses less attention on the temporal nature of adjustment. A more analytically reliable approach differentiates between short-run and long-run dynamics, acknowledging that whether costs or benefits dominate is a matter of time frame as well as institutional capacity and policy design.

Over the short run, environmental policy may lead to adjustment costs and frictions to firms and households as they become accustomed to the new set of restrictions. Capital (hence, capital stock) labor assignment and production technology are not instantly mobile. You might get transitional inefficiencies and temporary falls in output, as well as reallocation pressures. Over the long run, productivity dynamics are determined by innovation, diffusion and capital reallocation toward cleaner and possibly more productive sectors. The long-run effect of environmental policy relies on how well they work in practice, induced innovation as well as capital reallocation and labor adjustment. When policy sequencing is credible and institutions are facilitative, productivity enhancing structural transformation can counter this or outweigh these initial adjustment costs (Aldy & Pizer, 2011).

Accordingly, growth responses should be considered time-structured rather than as static trade-offs. Dynamics of short-run frictions play off with long-run innovation-driven gains to arrive at the growth path as a whole.

Figure 2. Environmental Policy Intensity and Long-Run Growth Trajectories

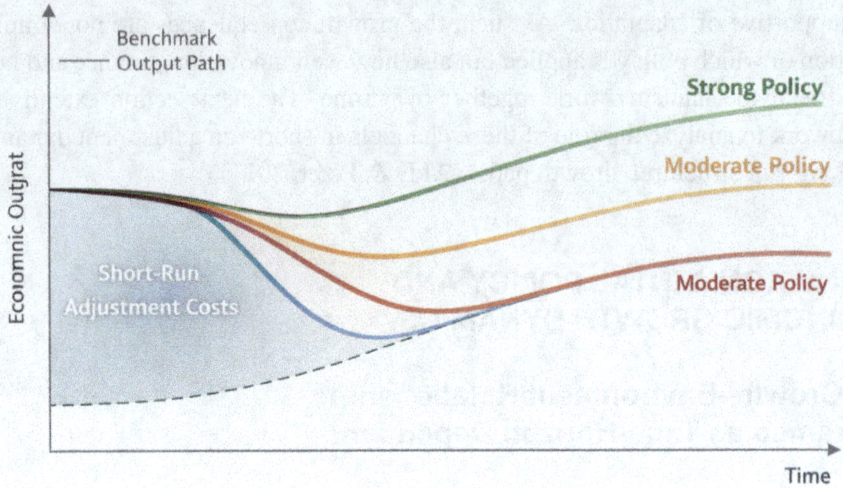

3.2 Short-Run Adjustment Costs: Conditions, Magnitudes, and Transmission

Short-term adjustment costs These come about because, in practice, environmental policy often demands changes to existing capital stocks and production processes as well as employment patterns. These costs are passed through multiple channels. The first is that enterprises may need to make capital retrofitting investments in or prematurely retire physical assets, especially for carbon-intensive industries. Stranded physical capital – when infrastructure that used to make economic sense under previous regulative regimes becomes valueless under the new regime, could weaken balance sheets and temporarily slow investment down while they are being repaired. Second, companies might find that they need to scale back their output temporarily while production systems are restructured. Compliance adaptations could include downtime for installations, supply chain reconfiguration or temporary inefficiencies. Third, direct abatement costs -- such as reporting and monitoring technology investments and emissions-control equipment—may raise operating costs at least in the short run. Fourth, environmental legislation might create labor displacement in high-emission industries, especially when industry is skill-specific and not as easily reabsorbed immediately. Loss of jobs in such carbon-intensive activities as fossil fuel extraction, traditional power generation and energy-intensive manufacturing could create pockets of income loss (Rausch et al., 2011).

Finally, due to financial constraints, technology upgrading may not be rapid. Firms with higher costs of compliance to other markets could face stricter credit conditions, particularly if financial markets re-price transition risks. Restrictions to the flow of capital causes slow adjustment and magnify short-term output impacts.

Short run costs are likely to be the dominant factor under certain conditions:

1. Policy shocks with little warning, which squeeze out the adjustment period.
2. A lack of credit with which to finance demand for cleaner technology, and the high cost of that same capital to hamper investment in it.
3. Limited labor mobility and little social-protection, leading to a longer duration of unemployment and loss of income.
4. Policy uncertainty or flip-flops that makes it more difficult for investors to look out and lock in, resulting in a capital freeze (low R).

In such a case, adjustment costs can dominate innovation benefits in the short-run and lead to quantifiable albeit typically transitory decreases in output growth.

3.3 Long-Run Growth Dynamics: Conditions for Dominance

Long-term growth prospects are determined not simply by the costs of compliance alone, but through linkages between innovation, capital allocation and institutional adjustment. Environmental policy can influence the direction of technological change, speed up diffusion of cleaner production techniques, and reallocate resources towards more productivity-enhancing endeavors.

Structural drivers to long-term growth dynamics There are four structural drivers underneath long run growth dynamics:

1. Continuous induced innovation, whereby policy signals reroute R&D towards low-carbon technologies and resource productivity.
2. Diffusion and scale economies, that is, how unit cost of different technologies decreases as clean technologies are more widely adopted and production scales increase.
3. Flow of capital into cleaner, more productive sectors, supported by repricing of financial markets and risk- adjusted investment flows.
4. Public investment and supportive institutions, such as infrastructure and education and credible regulatory sequencing (Acemoglu et al., 2012).

5. Long-term gains are likely to come when these mechanisms are mutually reinforcing. The following explicit formulation of the domination condition can be made:

Credible policy path + supportive innovation supply-infrastructure + working financial systems + adaptable labor institutions → productivity benefits from the long-run probably will outweigh short-run adjustment costs.

If policy credibility reduces uncertainty, then innovation incentives are durable. Diffusion is faster when financial markets allocate capital well. The key to social sustainability in a time of structural change is when labor institutions support retraining and mobility. In those settings, environmental policy is a driver of productivity-enhancing change rather than being in the way of growth.

3.4 Evidence Synthesis

Table 2 Summary of the empirical findings on environmental policy and economic growth (refer to Table 2). Instead of describing the studies, this table compiles evidence across time scales and methodological techniques.

Table 2. Summary of Empirical Studies on Environmental Policy and Economic Growth

Study Focus	Methodology	Key Findings
Cross-country growth analysis	Panel regressions	Short-run costs, neutral to positive long-run growth
Sector-level productivity	Industry panel data	Productivity gains in green sectors
Innovation-driven growth	Patent-based analysis	Strong regulation stimulates clean innovation
Non-linear effects	Threshold models	Growth effects depend on policy intensity
Institutional interaction	Governance-adjusted models	Strong institutions amplify positive outcomes

The evidence can be classified by three levels:

Time horizon: Even short-run analyses tend to find only modest transition costs of compliance and industry decline. Long-run studies, especially those adding innovation dynamics, frequently report persistent neutral or even positive productivity effects after reallocations and technological adjustments have taken place.

Outcome metric: Some studies consider changes in the level of GDP; while others look at growth rates, or productivity at sector or firm level. Despite some variation across scenarios and across the two models, aggregate GDP effects are generally small compared to arises for sectoral productivity response – particularly in green sectors.

Heterogeneity: The growth impacts also depend on policies and institutions, financial development and composition of sectors. Long-term gains will only be made in economies that have robust innovation systems and credible governance systems.

Organizing the empirical literature in this way highlights that patterns of growth are contingent and not general. There is no support for an issue-salience tradeoff story. The evidence indicates horizon-dependent but institutionally contingent effects (Aghion et al., 2012).

3.5 Structural Change as the Main Growth Pathway

Environmental policy generally has a greater impact on the structure of production by industries than it does on overall growth. Cuts to high-carbon sectors and growth in clean technology industries transform industrial structures, supply chains and regional patterns of production. Aggregate GDP can look stable while seismic restructuring is taking place. Structural change is thus the main channel through which environmental policy affects long-term productivity. In addition, cleaner industries tend to have higher levels of innovation intensity, knowledge spillovers and learning effects. And if investment and labor migrate to these sectors, economywide productivity could increase.

This change of structure is directly related to the dynamics of innovation. Targeted technological progress and rapid growth determine whether nascent sectors can reach scale and cost-competitiveness. Structural change can occur gradually and disruptively if it is not accompanied by sustained innovation and diffusion. With them, redistribution is a part of long-run growth. The following section thus considers how environmental policy influences innovation paths and diffusion patterns, which are what in turn make structural transformation growth retardant as opposed to adjustment-led. The evidence in Table 3 further highlights that innovation intensity, skill requirements, and capital needs vary significantly across sectors, reinforcing the importance of tailored policy design rather than uniform regulatory approaches (Martin et al., 2012).

Table 3. Innovation Responses to Environmental Policy across Industries

Industry	Policy Pressure	Innovation Response	Economic Implications
Energy & Utilities	High carbon pricing, emission caps	Renewable energy adoption, grid innovation	Lower emissions, long-term cost stability
Manufacturing	Efficiency standards, emission limits	Process optimization, cleaner production	Productivity gains, competitiveness
Automotive	Fuel economy & emission norms	Electric vehicles, hybrid technologies	Market restructuring, new value chains
Chemicals	Hazardous substance regulation	Green chemistry, material substitution	Risk reduction, compliance-driven innovation
Construction	Energy efficiency codes	Green building materials, smart design	Lifecycle cost savings, sustainability branding

4. INNOVATION UNDER ENVIRONMENTAL REGULATION: INDUCED INNOVATION, DIFFUSION, STRUCTURAL TRANSFORMATION

4.1 Differentiating Innovation Mechanisms

Technological change under environmental regulation is not a uniform process. To discern the theoretical foundations of technological change in long-term growth and structural transformation, a distinction among three interrelated (but conceptually distinct) mechanisms must be made: induced innovation, diffusion effects, and structural transformation. Environmental policy may work through induced innovation as it changes relative prices and expected rates of return, thereby changing the pattern of investment in research and development activity. When inputs that are carbon-intensive rise in cost or are regulated, firms have an incentive to invent cleaner technologies, more efficient enterprises and even new materials. Innovation becomes policy-led rather than market-dominated (Pindyck, 2012).

Diffusion benefits are incurred through the diffusion and expansion of clean technologies across industry, location, and sector. Whereas invention creates new technology choices, diffusion is what determines whether or not it translates into economy-wide productivity gains. The diffusion process requires access to finance, regulation that ensures demand certainty, compatible infrastructure and institution capacity. Structural transformation is...the larger change in the reconfiguration of value chains, sectoral composition and industrial organization over time. Industries grow or decline, supply chains reorganize, and comparative advantages change as clean technologies mature and diffuse. So perhaps this so-called structural change is just macro for continuing innovation and its diffusion.

By distinguishing among these mechanisms, the analysis steers clear of the fallacy of treating creative action as a monolithic result and locates it in an evolving process that connects policy arrangements to long-term economic transformation (Goulder & Schein, 2013).

4.2 Induced Innovation: Micro Foundations and Policy Design

The microeconomic logic of induced innovation is simple yet powerful. The marginal cost of pollution-intensive production is raised by environmental regulation. This new relative price induces new markets for cleaner substitutes and increases the expected return to research in low-carbon technologies. Firms react by investing in process innovation (e.g. increasing efficiency and reducing emissions) or product innovation (i.e. developing alternative products and technologies).

The process of induced innovation takes place in a number of steps:

Regulation → higher relative price of pollution → cleaner substitutes become more profitable → reallocation of R&D investment → technological change.

Nevertheless, induced innovation does not happen automatically. Several conditions determine its effectiveness:

Predictable and credible policy signals: Investment on long horizon R&D must feel secure in continued stringency of regulation. Policy reversals or lack of certainty erode these incentives for continued innovation.

Sufficient stringency: Faint or normative regulation may not matter much to the expected returns. Innovation reactions scale with regulatory strength, especially when companies expect standards to be progressively strengthened.

Absorptive capacity: Bludgeoning won't work It will take capabilities, managerial talent and supply-chain integration for firms to be able to transform regulatory pressure into technological innovation. Lacking proper human capital and organizational capability, regulatory push can lead to regulation-induced compliance rather than innovation (Griggs et al., 2013).

Under these circumstances, environmental policy is a catalyst for induced technical change by which the course of productivity growth is redirected towards environmentally friendly cleaner and more efficient systems.

4.3 Innovation Pathways and Feedback Mechanisms

Figure 3 breaks down the innovation process into interrelated section. The direction of R&D is altered by policy, shifting research investment towards low-carbon technologies and more efficient processes. This reorientation of knowledge production and industrial opportunities. The second of these is the interplay between innovation and learning by-doing/cost-curve dynamics. As we have seen, the longer clean technologies develop, the less they cost per unit. Cost-savings will increase competitiveness, driving uptake and additional investment. Third, innovation is endogenously affected by the feedback from financial and labor markets. The availability of capital determines the possibility for tactics to grow new technologies. High second-best subsidies speed up commercialization and diffusion while credit constraints retard the pace. Likewise, the supply of skilled labor affects the pace at which firms can learn and improve upon new technologies (Anderson et al., 2014).

Figure 3. Environmental Regulation and Green Innovation Pathways

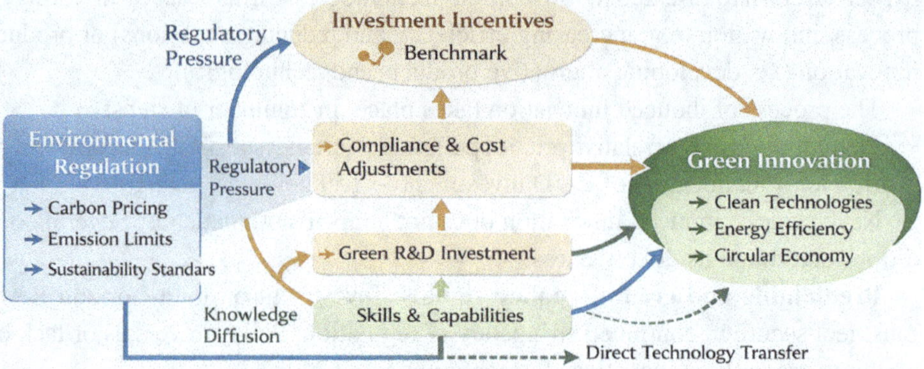

Figure 3 consequently reveals the fact that innovation is situated in a wider context of financial conditions and labor. Regulatory pressure is not enough, and the innovation process depends on accompanying organizational and market reactions.

4.4 Diffusion as the Conversion of Innovation into Productivity

Induced innovation creates new technologies, but diffusion values whether these innovations translate into economy-wide productivity gains. Diffusion is the scale-increasing vehicle that transforms localized invention into broad efficiency improvement. Diffusion channels and diffusion barriers are classified in Table 4. The table offers a systematic summary of the impact of various institutional and market conditions on the diffusion of clean technology. Market penetration is influenced by demand encouragement and price competitiveness. Carbon pricing or strong performance standards can incentivize adoption but high initial costs may limit the willingness of manufacturers without access to capital to invest (Cohen & Tubb, 2015).

Table 4. Green Technology Diffusion Channels and Barriers

Diffusion Channel	Key Actors	Facilitating Factors	Major Barriers
Market-based diffusion	Firms, consumers	Cost reductions, demand incentives	High upfront costs, market uncertainty
Policy-driven diffusion	Governments, regulators	Subsidies, standards, mandates	Policy instability, weak enforcement
Financial diffusion	Banks, investors, funds	Green finance, risk-sharing instruments	Capital constraints, risk aversion
Knowledge spillovers	Universities, R&D labs	Collaboration, open innovation	Intellectual property restrictions
International transfer	Multinationals, global institutions	FDI, technology licensing	Institutional gaps, absorptive capacity

Policy diffusion depends on regulatory clarity and implementation. Predicted, solid standards and enforcements lead to predictable markets economics; unstable or inadequately enforced requirements lead to reduce the reward of adoption. Monetary spread is shaped taking into account the access to green money and risk mutualization. Investment will by stymied if investors are risk-averse to new and clean technologies. Spillovers can occur in collaboration, networks or open innovation systems. But the transfer of knowledge can be hampered by intellectual property constraints or limited institutional connections. Technology is transferred internationally through FDI, licensing and trade. But diffusion across borders is contingent on absorptive capacity, which includes technical knowledge and institutional backing. Spillovers, therefore, link innovation and macroeconomic performance. Without successful disseminating mechanisms, innovation will be restricted to specific sectors and thus its aggregate growth impact remains constrained (Sinn, 2015).

4.5 Industry Heterogeneity and Strategic Firm Responses

Innovative reactions to environmental policy by industry differ greatly. Sector-Specific Innovation Patterns and Strategic Responses The sector-specific levels of innovation and strategic responses are summarized in Table 3. In some industries, such as energy-intensive manufacturing, the focus is almost entirely on optimizing processes to make existing production frameworks more efficient and less carbon intensive. Others, like renewable energy and electric mobility are focusing on product innovation, creating new technologies and business models from scratch.

Table 3 shows the relative efficacy of policy instruments in various settings. Market-based instruments can push through modest efficiency improvements in mature sectors, whereas focused subsidies and R&D incentives could prove more effective for fledgling technology fields. Industry mix also has labor and financial implications. Industries that prioritize product innovation are more likely to reflect high-skilled, large initial cost investments and generate greater dependence on specialized financing resources and sophisticated human capital. On the other hand, process improvement may involve retraining and some level of capital upgrading in enterprises. Acknowledging these sectoral distinctions become critical for coherent policy making. Broad regulatory approaches can have differing innovation effects if they do not consider industry-special technological paths and constraints (Calel & Dechezleprêtre, 2016).

4.6 Innovation, Finance, and Labor as Co-Determined Processes

The next air will not invent itself in a vacuum independent of financial and labor systems. Expected returns contribute to perceptions of risk and the valuation of assets in financial markets. Institutions of the financial markets, by their power to allocate capital, in reciprocal exert their pressure on innovative businesses with different costs of acquiring this capital. Promising technology could miss out on scaling if it doesn't have sufficient funding attached (Dechezleprêtre & Sato, 2017).

In turn labor markets also determine the rate, and inclusiveness of technological restructuring. The concentration of skilled workers affects the rates of adoption and layoffs in declining sectors have an impact on the political support and social stability. Innovation, finance and labor are then co-determined. Regulatory signals set technology on a new path, but the final economic outcome depends on the extent that financial systems facilitate scaling and labor institutions support adaptation. This holistic view serves as the basis for analyzing financial reallocation mechanisms in the next section and labor market dynamics in the following section, so that they are conceived as connected dimensions of structural transformation, rather than being erroneously studied in separate policy silos (Stiglitz et al., 2017).

5. FINANCE, CAPITAL REALLOCATION, AND CLIMATE-RELATED FINANCIAL DYNAMICS

5.1 Environmental Policy as a Financial Signal

Environmental policy is not just a regulatory constraint, but it's also an enormous financial signal that changes people's expectations and risk assessments and statement valuations. Financial markets are by their nature forward-looking and thus shifts in policy influence investors' behavior long before production systems physically shift. The channels through which policy influences finance are numerous and interconnected. The first is that environmental policy changes expectations about future regulation and demand. The credible commitment to decarbonization implies a lowering in the demand for carbon-emitting assets over the long term and an increase in the potential of clean technologies. It is on such expectations that investors base contribution values by adjusting projected cash flows and discount rates (Battiston et al., 2017).

Second, policy triggers risk repricing notably for transition and physical risks. Transition risks include regulatory stringency, technological substitution and changing consumer preferences, while physical risks are about climate-related damage and disruption. When they expect more stringent regulations or increased carbon pricing, the perceived risk of fossil-fuel-dependent companies rises and their assets are devalued. Third, improved disclosure and quality of information regarding risks (e.g. climate-related financial reporting standards) contributes to reducing the asymmetry in information and thus the risk. Clear reporting of exposure to climate risks and transition strategies accelerates the sorting and differentiation of companies.

Fourth, prudential standards and stress testing incorporate climate risk into supervisory frameworks. Banks have to price vulnerability under climate-related scenarios into capital allocation and lending. Fifth, reclassification driven by taxonomy and portfolio mandates expand the definition of what is considered sustainable or transitional asset. Asset managers and institutional investors are shifting portfolios with climate objectives at the fore, guiding capital flows (Deschênes, 2018).

Through these channels, environmental policy remolds the financial behavior ahead of real-economy change coming into play, so the finance becomes a key transition link in this sanitized ripple-effect mode.

5.2 Capital Reallocation Effects: The Financial Transmission Mechanism

Figure 4 is an analytical workhorse, depicting the chain from regulatory action to macroeconomic effects. The transmission starts with a policy signal, say carbon pricing or disclosure. Such a signal shifts investor beliefs and leads to revaluation of asset markets. "Fossil fuel assets that are carbon intensive could be discounted because of excessive future costs or regulatory risk; and conversely, the price of clean tech companies may well go up."

Figure 4. Capital Reallocation Effects of Environmental Policy in Financial Markets

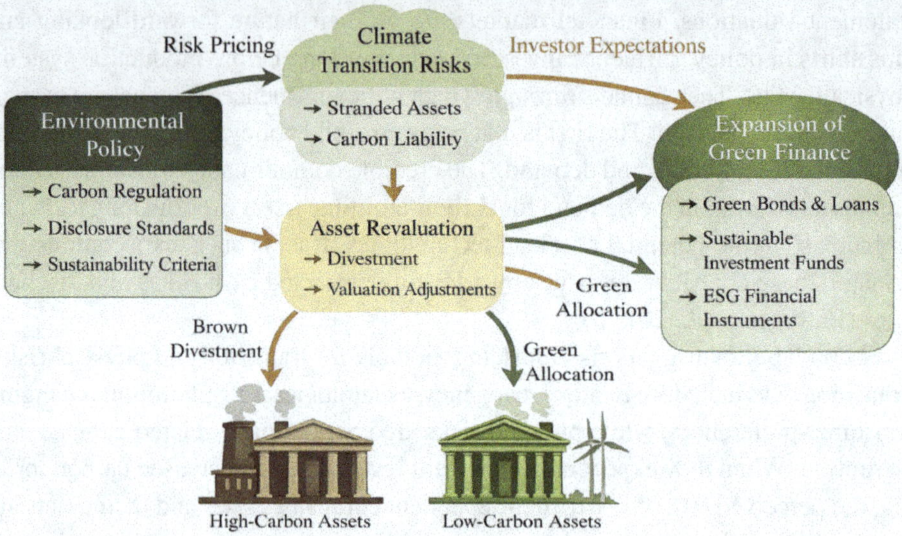

Valuation shifts drive changes in the portfolio, as investors rebalance their portfolios to reflect the new risk-return trade-offs. Such re-allocation alters the cost of capital across industrial sectors: companies which are viewed as being aligned with low-carbon transition experience reduced financing costs, while carbon-intensive firms suffer from higher borrowing rates and limited availability of funds. Fluctuations in the price of capital affect investment and innovation. Falling finance costs drive an acceleration of expansion and technology scaling within green sectors, strengthening the innovation dynamics considered earlier. On the other hand, disinvestment in high carbon industries may create an investment squeeze and structural shrinkage. Figure 4 therefore illustrates that financial markets are an amplifier of policy signals, speeding up the capital reallocation and determining the speed of structural transformation (Ells, 2018).

5.3 Policy Instruments and Financial Market Responses

Different market reactions are the result of different environmental policy instruments. Table 5 summarizes the comparison between categories of policies and market responses (see Table 5). The table distinguishes between repricing, disinvestment, new issuance and prudential de-risking mechanisms. Some are instantaneous market responses, in the form of rapid re-jigging of share and bond prices after regulatory announcements. Companies with large carbon asset exposure will value adjustment as investors expect cash flows to be revised (Kahn et al., 2019).

Table 5. Environmental Policy Instruments and Financial Market Responses

Policy Instrument	Targeted Financial Channel	Market Response	Systemic Implications
Carbon Pricing	Asset valuation & risk pricing	Repricing of carbon-intensive assets	Stranded asset risk, capital shift
Climate Disclosure Rules	Information transparency	Improved risk assessment by investors	Lower information asymmetry
Green Taxonomies	Investment classification	Increase in sustainable investment flows	Standardization of green finance
Prudential Regulation	Bank capital allocation	Reduced exposure to high-carbon sectors	Financial stability enhancement
Green Bond Incentives	Debt markets	Expansion of green bond issuance	Lower cost of capital for green projects

Other actions entail portfolio reallocation and divestment, for example when exclusion criteria or climate-aligned mandates are adopted by institutional investors. These changes are capable to slowly alter the allocation of capital across sectors. Policy instruments can also encourage new issuance such as green bonds and sustainability linked financing, redirecting new capital towards low-carbon investments.

Further, prudential regulation and supervisory stress testing incentivizes de-risking behavior that will induce financial firms to reposition their exposure to climate-exposed assets over multi-year horizons. Organizing these responses in a systematic format, Table 5 provides some insights into the way environmental policy affects financial markets via fast repricing mechanisms and slow changes in structural allocations.

5.4 Financial Stability, Stranded Assets, and Systemic Risk

Although one can't do without the reallocation of capital needed for structural transformation, fast repricing is systemic risk. The key challenge is that sudden changes in the values of assets can magnify fragility through interrelated balance-sheet channels. Table 6 lists climate-related financial risks and their respective countermeasures (see Table 6). The chain starts with transition risk, which could precipitate asset write-downs for carbon-intensive firms. When collateral values fall significantly, balance sheets are weakened and the resulting credit tightening follows. When purchasing slows, economic activity slows with it because investment becomes narrower and there ends up being less credit available. And those dynamics can play out in terms of wider financial instability (Engle et al., 2019).

Table 6. Climate-Related Financial Risks and Mitigation Tools

Risk Category	Description	Affected Financial Sector	Mitigation Tools
Transition Risk	Policy, technology, and market shifts during low-carbon transition	Banks, equity & bond markets	Carbon stress testing, portfolio diversification
Physical Risk	Losses from climate-related disasters and extreme events	Insurance, infrastructure finance	Climate insurance, resilience investment
Liability Risk	Legal claims related to climate damage or non-compliance	Corporate finance, insurers	Disclosure standards, legal risk assessment
Market Risk	Asset price volatility linked to climate news and regulation	Capital markets, asset managers	Dynamic risk pricing, hedging strategies
Systemic Risk	Cascading financial instability due to climate shocks	Financial system as a whole	Macroprudential regulation, green capital buffers

Physical threats, for instance climate related catastrophes are also causing asset losses and insurance-industry stress. These pressures may be amplified with exposure to transition risk and spread through linked financial networks. Yet macroprudential instruments and stress test frameworks do not need to be mere checks in the boxes, but can even other than counter-cyclicals act as stabilizers. By anticipating climate-driven shocks and promoting a gradual re-pricing of exposures, supervisors can temper the impact of sudden corrections and contribute to less systemic risk. Thus, financial regulation has two functions: one is to help redirect capital toward sustainable sectors and the other is to protect against threats to financial stability that can arise during the transition.

5.5 Integration of Finance, Innovation, and Labor

Financial markets are tightly linked to technology and labour adjustment. The diffusion of clean technologies is directly affected by the cost and availability of capital. Ceteris paribus, cheaper financing speeds up commercialization and scaling; credit constraints slow it down. Financial systems also impact transitions of work, especially in places that rely on carbon-intensive sectors. The availability of credit for the SME sector in transition areas this is supports diversification and job creation. Public and private mechanisms of financing could be used for reskilling programs, infrastructure retooling, or regional renewal.

Conversely, innovation influences finance. As technology changes the anticipated profitability, financial markets revaluation applies differently to incumbents and entrants. The rise of new models of risk and strategies for investment, specifically tailored to evolving technology settings. These nexuses show that finance is not an isolated policy level but a central pivot in the ripple-effect architecture. Innovation outcomes are sensitive to financial conditions, and workers' adjustment depends on investments flowing and regional credit access (Pattillo et al., 2019).

5.6 From Capital Reallocation to Labor Adjustment

Shifting capital out of high-carbon assets is certain to create locally concentrated economic upheaval. Investment and employment shrink in the areas relying on fossil fuel extraction, carbon-intensive production or outdated infrastructure. These localized impacts can create social and political pressures which may affect the durability of policies. The flight of capital also has a direct impact on labor force and regional equity. These impacts must be addressed through integrated just transition frameworks that harmonize finance, industry and labor policy. In the next section we consider how labor markets accommodate – or resists – structural change and with what distributional consequences, which then influences the long-run sustainability of environmental-policy driven transformation (Markkanen & Anger, 2019).

6. LABOR MARKETS, DISTRIBUTIONAL IMPACTS, AND JUST TRANSITIONS

6.1 Labor Impacts as an Endogenous Outcome of Innovation and Finance

Labor market results should not be seen as an area of policy that is separate and/or secondary. Change in employment is the social expression of such structure change, which is a result of innovation, capital redeployment and regulatory signs. When the environmental policy redirects technological development and capital flows it will also change sectoral employment patterns, skill requirements and income distribution. Thus, labor reallocation is endogenous to the innovation and financial channels discussed earlier.

The direct one-dimensional primary labor effects of environmental transition can be categorized in the four following, closely interconnected dimensions. First, sectoral reallocation happens when jobs shrink in industries that are carbon-intensive and grow in low-carbon sectors. Second, skill-biased demand shifts arise as clean technology industries frequently rely on greater technical knowledge, digital skills and engineering know-how than traditional ones. Third, clustering effects can emerge at regional level in locations where extraction of fossil fuels or heavy and energy intensive manufacturing are concentrated. Fourth, wage and inequality differential dynamics arise as workers in growing sectors can obtain higher wages, while for displaced one's income loss or grown time of being unemployed may occur (Bolton & Kacperczyk, 2019).

By conceptualizing labor effects as conditional on innovation paths and capital allocation, the analysis underscores that employment is conditioned upon the general ripple-effect structure, rather than regulated environmental alone.

6.2 Employment effects: decomposition and heterogeneity

Impacts on employment of environmental policy are diverse between sectors and the time periods. Job losses in other fossil-fuel-reliant industries — think of coal mining, oil production and conventional power generation — can also be very severe and rapid, especially when capital is withdrawn at the same time as regulations are tightened. Because these industrial activities frequently locate geographically in clusters, job losses may produce local economic hardship. As shown in **Table 7**, environmental policy affects financial markets through multiple causal pathways, including expectation formation, disclosure-driven capital reallocation, and the emergence of stranded asset risks (Krueger et al., 2020).

Table 7. Environmental Policy Instruments and Financial Transmission Mechanisms

Policy Instrument	Primary Financial Channel	Financial Market Response	System-Level Implication
Carbon pricing / emission caps	Expectations and asset valuation	Repricing of carbon-intensive assets	Transition risk exposure
Climate disclosure rules	Information transparency	Capital reallocation toward low-carbon assets	Reduced information asymmetry
Technology standards	Investment incentives	Shift in portfolio composition	Sectoral rebalancing

Policy Instrument	Primary Financial Channel	Financial Market Response	System-Level Implication
Fossil fuel subsidy removal	Profitability and cash flows	Asset devaluation	Stranded asset risk
Climate stress testing	Risk management practices	Portfolio adjustment	Financial stability enhancement

In contrast, employment in renewables, energy efficiency services, green manufacturing and supply chains is generally spread more broadly across regions and companies. These often require skill-specific jobs, and rely on a supportive investment in infrastructure, technology and training. Even if the net employment effects can be shown to be zero or positive in the aggregate (over some time frame), there is little reason to expect that job creation will replace jobs lost, either in a geographically concentrated area or within any predictable amount of time.

One of its biggest challenges is a mismatch in skills. Workers are not automatically transferred into new sectors. Inequality in technical requirement, educational background and geographical location constrain mobility. Without specific retraining and mobility assistance, transition can create permanent unemployment and wage scarring (Ilhan et al., 2020).

The employment effects are constructible in sectoral, skill and regional terms rather than being read out from aggregate job figures.

6.3 Consequences for Employment by Sector and Skills

Table 8: Employment and skill impacts across carbon-intensive, green sectors (see Table 8). The table offers a systematic summary of how environmental transition alters the pattern of the labor demand and it emphasizes which mechanisms are most relevant from a policy perspective.

Four dimensions stand out as significant. In the first place, mismatch risk partakes differently across sectors. Because carbon-intensive industries tend to have occupation-specific skills that do not transfer well, the transition can be challenging. Second, the retraining potential relies on similarity of skill sets and on promotional opportunities in new occupational branches. Third, the green TTB is affected by the speed at which capital can be invested and projects developed. Fourth, local resilience constraints affect whether economies diversify or remain locked in to declining sectors (Hale, 2020).

Table 8. Employment and Skill Impacts across Carbon-Intensive and Green Sectors

Sector Type	Employment Trend	Skill Demand Shift	Policy Implications
Carbon-Intensive Sectors	Job contraction and layoffs	Decline in routine and fossil-fuel-specific skills	Need for transition support and income protection
Renewable Energy	Rapid job creation	High demand for technical and engineering skills	Investment in vocational and technical training
Energy Efficiency Services	Moderate job growth	Demand for retrofit and digital skills	Upskilling programs for existing workforce
Green Manufacturing	Structural employment expansion	Advanced manufacturing and automation skills	Industrial policy and skill alignment
Environmental Services	Stable to growing employment	Interdisciplinary and regulatory compliance skills	Education–industry collaboration

By characterizing work dynamics in this way, Table 8 helps to illustrate that labor outcomes are not determined simply by environmental regulation but rather by structural forces. The success of labor market adjustment is contingent on policy coordination and the capacity of institutions.

6.4 Distributional and Regional Impacts

The distributive implications of environmental policy are complex, and there is a need for analytic clarity in order to focus on the major economic mechanisms. Four mechanisms warrant particular attention.

There are several ways in which households can be affected by energy price pass-through and other related mechanisms and policy actions: First, it can influence disposable income, especially for lower-income groups with relatively high shares of expenditure on energy. In the absence of mitigation, carbon pricing could be regressive in the shorter run.

Second, localized employment shocks in carbon-reliant regions may erode regional tax bases, reduce the provision of public services and increase geographic inequality. Centralized job losses can also have multiplied effects in local economies (Ojo & Delaney, 2021).

Third, the skill-biased character of transition can generate wage dispersion. Workers with high levels of skills may see higher wages in growing clean tech industries while the reverse holds for displaced workers.

Fourth, institutional buffers such as social protection systems and active labor market policies are crucial against inequality. Plus, income support, retraining programs and job-matching services that would ease transitions and boost mobility (Parry et al., 2021).

Concentrating on these prioritized mechanisms helps to demystify how the distributional effects combine both innovation and finance. In the absence of adequate institutional buffering, inequality can erode political support for environmental policy — compromising long-term credibility.

6.5 Just Transition as an Instrument of Policy Design

The framework of a just transition brings together labor, socio- and territorial policies with environmental strategy. Aligning with TLTs: policy instruments for a just transition Table 9 presents an overview of the policy instrument family that may support fair transition processes (cf. Instead of treating these tools as secondary options, however, the table is intended to frame them as part and parcel with good policy design.

Table 9. Policy Instruments Supporting Just Transitions

Policy Instrument	Target Group	Objective	Expected Outcomes
Active Labor Market Policies	Displaced workers	Facilitate reemployment and reskilling	Reduced unemployment duration
Reskilling & Training Programs	Low- and mid-skilled workers	Skill transition to green jobs	Improved employability
Income Support Schemes	Affected households	Mitigate income shocks	Social protection and stability
Regional Development Funds	Carbon-dependent regions	Economic diversification	Balanced regional growth
Social Dialogue Mechanisms	Workers, employers, governments	Inclusive transition governance	Equitable policy outcomes

Income compensatory institutions, i.e. unemployment insurance and wage subsidies or wage insurance, stabilize aggregate demand and political support during adjustment. As well, retraining skills and education programs promote the diffusion of innovation and flexibility of labour force supply consistent with new technological opportunities. Regional aid funds and infrastructure spending mitigate geographical divergence by promoting economic diversification in the lagging regions. Social dialogue and participatory governance reduce opposition, facilitate targeting of policies and can prevent contentious issue-formation, which in turn increase the legitimacy.

The package logic in Table 9 thus reinforces the point that labor policy is not external to environmental strategy, but important for securing policy longevity and enabling cost effective structural change.

6.6 Labour Adjustment Dynamics and Feedback Effects

The transition of the labor environment is depicted in Figure 5, to describe the process by which labor adjusts under environmental change. In Figure 5, we show the employment changes being connected with political and economic feedback loops.

Figure 5. Labor Market Adjustment under Environmental Policy Transitions

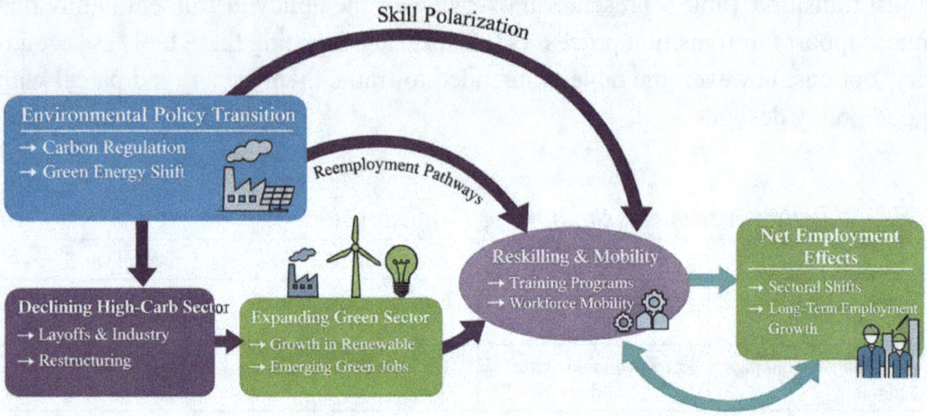

Poorly handled labor adjustment can produce the same political kickback in localized unemployment and wage reduction. Policy Sector political resistance can reverse or dilute policy, heightening regulatory uncertainty. Increased uncertainty undermines investor sentiment, which suppresses innovation and capital redeployment. Slower innovation erodes productivity gains, amplifying economic pressure (Stern & Stiglitz, 2021).

On the other hand, well-functioning labor default institutions enhance policy credibility and investment stability. Governments can maintain a long-term regulatory commitment by minimizing transition-related suffering, thereby entrenching incentives for innovation and financial stability.

Figure 5 thus indicates that labor dynamics are intertwined in larger organizational loops that define the success of environmental transitions.

6.7 Labor Markets, Macroeconomic Stability, and Trade

The macroeconomic stability and competitive position of a country depends on its labor market performance. Substantial job loss may lower aggregate demand and erode regional tax bases, imposing negative effects on fiscal capacity. Long-term unemployment could also affect the dynamics of wages and inflation (Stevis et al., 2021).

Internationally, competitiveness in emerging clean technology sectors is also determined by labor costs and skill availability. Successful, retraining of workers and investment attraction might enhance export capacity of regions, while areas with persisting adjustment problems might face relative decline.

Hence, labor shocks and distributional results link directly to macroeconomic spillovers and trade patterns. Incorporating labor into the design of environmental policies is hence not only a matter of social justice: it is also crucial for macroeconomic stability and competitiveness in a low-carbon economy (Skea et al., 2022).

7. MACROECONOMIC STABILITY, TRADE, AND GLOBAL SPILLOVERS

7.1 Inflation and Competitiveness: Short-Run and Long-Run Dynamics

Environmental policy affects the stabilization of macro-economy through price mechanism, production costs and international competition. Time-dependent framework is required to separate short-run inflationary pressures and long-run productivity impact.

In the near term, cost pass-through from higher energy prices and compliance costs may add to upward price pressure. Carbon pricing and emissions standards can raise the variable input cost of energy-neutralizing industries (in various ways that will be discussed) and increase total output prices, which are passed to final users depending on market structure and output demand elasticities. The distributional implications of such price changes depend on household, and energy outlays are a greater percentage of consumption for lower income families. Moreover, competitive pressures may increase where local firms experience higher regulations costs compared to foreign competitors in less regulated environs (Alexandra-Gabriela, 2022).

However, over time, as innovations and more efficient production practices become known, those cost increases can be largely offset. Unit energy intensity decreases as cleaner technologies are scaled up and as learning effects bring down production costs. The higher energy efficiency and interfuel substitution reduce exposure to fossil fuel price movements, which gradually drains the inflationary result. Hence, macroeconomic stability relies on whether innovation and capital reallocation channels develop sufficiently to offset short-run adjustment costs.

7.2 Leakage and Border Adjustments

Leakage Task Force Carbon leakage is the phenomenon that domestic production and associated emissions are replaced by imports from other countries not tightly regulated for environmental concerns. Leaks can occur via repositioning of trade, diversion of investment or changes in global supply chains. From an international macroeconomic standpoint, both environmental effectiveness and domestic efficiency are being compromised due to leakage as economic activity is displaced with no abatement in the world.

Policy measures against leakage comprise border carbon adjustments (BCAs), which impose a carbon related charge on imported goods equal to domestic carbon pricing. These measures seek to create an equal competitive environment as well as to secure environmental sustainability by deterring displacement (Ren et al., 2022),

Yet border measures add analytical and political complexity. They can lead to trade disputes; they may question the compatibility with international trade law and create a relatively high load for developing countries with marginal administrative and technical resources available. In addition, BCAs can change the structure of global value chains and impact export-oriented economies and comparative advantage.

An analytical approach to leakage also needs to acknowledge both ecological and equity concerns. Border measures may provide a remedy for competitive distortions, but have to be shaped carefully to not increase development disparities.

7.3 International Spillovers: Structured Synthesis

Environmental policy causes international spillovers that transmission abroad national economic adaptations. Table 10 main spill-over channels and macroeconomic implications (see Table 10). The table framework overflows into five interrelated domains.

Table 10. International Spillover Effects of Environmental Policies

Spillover Channel	Affected Dimension	Key Implications
Cost pass-through	Inflation	Short-term price pressures
Competitiveness	Trade performance	Export and market share shifts
Carbon leakage	Emissions	Relocation of production

Spillover Channel	Affected Dimension	Key Implications
Border adjustments	Trade policy	Trade diversion and disputes
Climate finance	Development	Mitigation of inequality

The first is inflationary pass-through via international commodity markets if big economies enact carbon pricing or directly limit availability of coal. Global energy price variations may impact the import-dependent countries.

Second, "endogenous" competitiveness adjustments occur when regulatory asymmetry changes trade patterns and the comparative advantage of one country relative to another. Cost differentials may result in industries moving or supply chains being reconfigured.

Third, leakage effects shift the priority point of emissions and production geographically, potentially undermining effectiveness if not mitigated.

Fourth, border measures like BCAs alter trading patterns and investment incentives, affecting global supply chains.

Fifth, the deployment and impacts of climate finance affect the flow of capital to emerging and developing economies, influencing their ability to invest in low-carbon technology and adapt to regulatory changes.

In defining spillovers in this way, Table 10 highlights that macroeconomic and trade-related spillover effects are a key purpose of the architecture for transmitting ripple effects, rather than tangential features (Adeneye, 2023).

7.4 Cross-Border Spillover Dynamics

The Cross-Border Spillovers of Environmental Policy (Fig 6) visually illustrates how the stringency of domestic policy impacts on global economic structures. Figure 6 describes the sequence from a nation taking regulatory action to international effects.

Figure 6. Cross-Border Spillovers of Environmental Policy

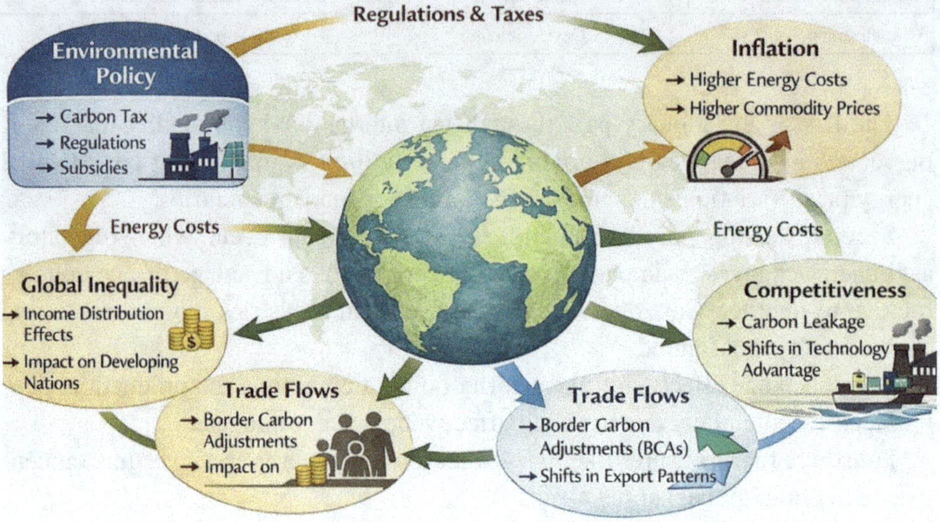

Increased domestic policy tightening can lead to a restructuring of the global supply chain, as businesses change sourcing and production locations to control cost and exposure to regulatory requirements. These regional rebalancing's have direct impact on cross-border capital flows—investment is redirected to regions with better regulation or policy environments.

Capital reallocation combines with variations in institutional capabilities and technology readiness to contribute to development disparities. Economies with sound innovation systems and access to finance will potentially receive investment and technology upgrades, while countries that lack absorptive capacity may become marginalized.

Therefore, Figure 6 indicates that environmental policy of leading economies create second-best ripple effects through the trade, finance and development channels motivating coordinated governance strategies (Genc & Kosempel, 2023).

7.5 Development and Equity in Global Change

Questions of development and equity are at stake in the world dimension to environmental transition. Several mechanisms warrant particular attention.

Financing and technology transfer are both core to ensuring that developing economies can join in low-carbon transformation. In the absence of low-weight capital and knowledge spill-overs, regulatory asymmetries could rise productivity gaps.

Absorptive capacity restrictions, in terms of technology know-how and institutional infrastructures limit the ability of some countries to apply advanced clean technology. Building capacity of institutions and governance structures for education systems, research becomes important for equitable engagement (Seck et al., 2023).

The burden of adjustment under a joint implementation efficiency standard could differ in an asymmetrical manner across developing countries, both in terms of country exposures to border carbon adjustments and trade tensions when export sectors tend to be more carbon-intensive. They can have a chilling effect in terms of the cost associated with compliance beyond what a county can adapt to quickly.

Global collective climate finance mechanisms – multilateral funds and concessional financing – can help to reduce inequities by promoting infrastructure construction, technological upgrading and the building up of institutions. Global spillovers are managed efficiently with the help of international cooperation (Taylor et al., 2023).

7.6 Governance and Policy Coherence on the Handling of Spillovers

The macroeconomic and international spillovers noted above point to the importance of a coherent policy framework and institutional coordination. Environmental policy cannot be considered as something that is designed in a vacuum and without taking into account trade policy, financial regulation and economic development. Ensuring the positive spillovers may require coherence across domestic and global regimes.

The management of spillover relies on credible sequencing, if possible transparent communication and co-ordinate schemes that tackle competitiveness and fairness concerns in parallel. In the absence of coordinated governance, spillovers could also create unintended economic volatility, trade disputes or political resistance to weaken the policy durability.

This analysis underlines that macroeconomic stability and global equity cannot be decoupled from environmental ambition. The next section accordingly explores how governance architecture and policy-design trade-offs can be designed to better undertake ripple management across growth, innovation, finance, labor and trade dimensions (Helleiner et al., 2024).

8. POLICY DESIGN, GOVERNANCE, COORDINATION, AND TRADE-OFF MANAGEMENT

8.1 Policy Coherence and Sequencing

The successful evolution of the environment demands policy coherence and careful sequencing. Coherence means convergence across climate, industrial, fiscal, social and economic policies. Ripples, in the form of unnecessarily instability, may spread when there is climate regulation without accompanying industrial support, financial oversight and labour adjustment arrangements. In contrast, there are complementarities across the innovation-finance-labour positive transmission channels strengthened by coherent policy frameworks (Ranasinghaarachchi, 2024).

Sequencing" refers to what is the issue of timing and instrumental order, in this case for instruments that avoid adjustment costs but sustain long-term credibility. Infrastructure, research capacity and workforce skills are three investment targets of the necessary early stages that could prepare the economy for structural shift. When adaptive capacity is increasing, tightening emissions standards or implementing carbon pricing will cause less of a shakedown. This sequencing distills some of the short-run frictions, while maintaining credible long-run signals about policy. A policy escalation when the time is right also signals to investors that policymakers have staying power, and enables firms and workers to adjust incrementally rather than abruptly (Adeyemi et al., 2025).

8.2 Governance Architecture as a Control Network

Coping with ripple effects require a mode of governance that would function as an adaptive control system rather than merely as a static regulative structure. The Governance Architecture for Managing Policy Ripple Effects framework (see Figure 7) clarifies the fact that policy space is a function of institutional design which in turn influences economic outcomes. Figure 7 provides a conceptual view of governance as an integrated process covering the monitoring of economic responses, (judging about) unintended effects and dynamic adjustment of the site-governance instruments.

Sound governance includes strong monitoring and enforcement capacity that act as a backstop to ensure that regulatory signals translate into action. When it comes to both price signals and disclosure requirements, without credible enforcement, they have less bites (Cheng, 2025).

We must also have in governance, adaptive feedback loops. Economic environment is developing with the progress of innovation and capital flows. Policy environments that include regular review and adjustment can recognize new threats as well as opportunities (Febriyanti, 2025).

There must be coordination between federal, state and local agencies. Climate policy cuts through trade policy, financial oversight, regulation of labor markets and regional development. Decentralization and the fragmentation of government undermine coherence; more to the point, they elevate adjustment costs.

Lastly, disclosure and credibility devices help boost investor and household confidence". "Such communication of the long-term objectives helps to lessen uncertainty, facilitates capital allocation and anchors expectations.

Figure 7. Governance Architecture for Managing Policy Ripple Effects

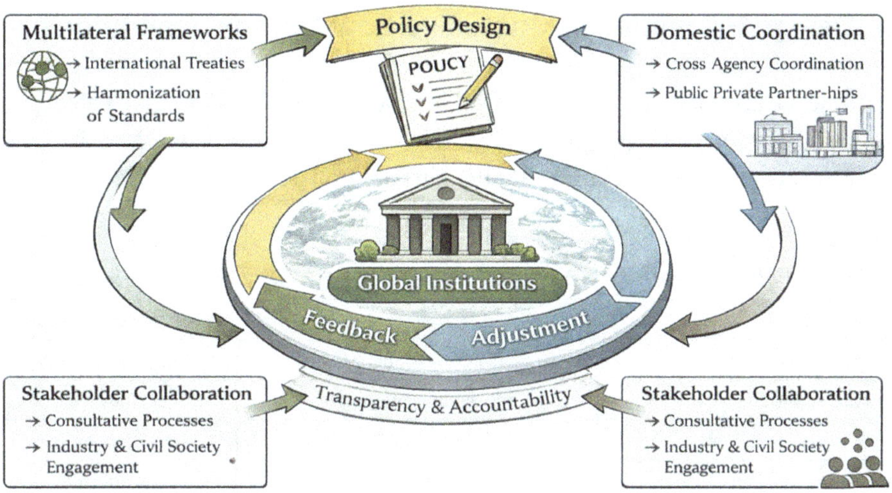

For this reason, Fig. 7 situates governance as the institutional infrastructure that directs ripple effects productively rather than destabilizing.

8.3 Political Economy Constraints on the Transmission Chain

Political economy the political economy dimension is included within the ripple-effect framework rather than being external constraints. Uncontrolled distributive effects can generate opposition, which loops back into the stability of policy. The dynamic can be summarized or sequenced: distributional pain gives rise to political resistance; resistance leads to policy volatility; volatility breeds uncertainty; uncertainty undermines investment incentives; reduced investment slows the growth of innovation and productivity (Kaushiva, 2025).

Those with vested interests in carbon-dominated industries may mobilize to block tougher regulations, particularly in areas without diverse economies which are reliant on legacy industries. Likewise, when households are hit by rising energy prices without any compensatory measures to ensure support they will withdraw their political support. These reactions can be detrimental to sequencing and can erode the credibility of policy.

Economic policymaking is forced to be political in the mechanism chain, and policy design requires controlling effectively two mechanisms— both economic and social transmission channels at the same time (Nawn, 2025).

8.4 Design Principles for Inclusive Low-Carbon Transitions

Table 11 presents an overview of policy design principles to give effect to the governance framework (see Table 11). The table serves as a scaffold for policy implications; that is, the conceptual insights are translated into concrete guidance.

Table 11. Policy Design Principles for Inclusive Low-Carbon Transitions

Design Principle	Description	Expected Outcome
Policy coherence	Alignment across policy domains	Reduced conflicts
Gradual sequencing	Phased implementation	Lower adjustment costs
Institutional credibility	Stable and predictable regulation	Investment confidence
Monitoring and enforcement	Robust compliance systems	Policy effectiveness
Stakeholder engagement	Inclusive participation	Political legitimacy

The policy coherence that climate actions are 'backed up' by industrial strategy, fiscal support, financial regulation and social protection. Step by step sequencing in decision making balancing ambition with adaptation potential. Institutional integrity, if anything, is an aid to investment stability and long-range decision making. Termination of services the plant Inspection company co. has the right to terminate provision of services should the contractor persistently or in a serious way neglect his obligation but without preventing always good from fulfilling contractual and legal duties Monitoring and enforcement Ensuring that regulatory objectives are implemented on a basis is paramount. Involving stakeholders, such as social dialogue and participatory governance, is found to decrease resistance and increase the targeting of policies ("Carbon pricing and emissions trading systems," 2025).

The latter two principles together form a framework for the development of environmental policy that channels ripple effects towards positive results instead of instability.

8.5 Managing Core Policy Trade-Offs

Transition is never about a win-win; trade-offs will always be there and we have to take an integrative approach to address these, not simply react with more demand for the planet. From the ripple-effects perspective a number of aggregate trade-offs are evident.

The first tradeoff is that between ambition and the costs of adjustment. Quick, tough policy could speed the pace of decarbonization but heighten short-term disruption. Some combination of management levers – slow sequencing, early complementarity investments in innovation and skills, transition support instruments can be used.

The second trade-off is between competitiveness and preventing leakage. If domestic regulation is intense, firms would be at a disadvantage in comparison with jurisdictions with lax standards. Weaknesses can be addressed with border measures and coordinated international frameworks, although these need to be weighed against considerations of equity and trade (Wirdyansyah, 2025).

The third tradeoff is between financial stability and rapid repricing. Rapid revaluation of assets by Swift might speed up capital redistribution with a risk of increasing system-wide leverage. Prudential regulation, climate stress testing and transition planning can help to cushion the adjustment.

The fourth conflict is between efficiency versus equity. Market-based instruments deliver allocative efficiency but distributional impact can erode political support. Efficiency can be balanced with fairness using revenue recycling, compensation distribution and social protection programmes.

The fifth dilemma is between technology neutrality and targeted support. Price-neutral policies incentivize wide areas of innovation, whereas mission-oriented industrial strategies speed up particular ones. Middle ground could blend portfolio incentives with targeted support for sectors with higher potential (Sciuchina, 2026).

Policy instruments to address each of these trade-offs include sequencing and complementing public investment, social safety nets, risk-sharing financial instruments and institutional reforms. Being explicit about the trade-offs make policy more transparent and less prone to backfiring (Linden et al., 2026).

8.6 From Governance to Future Research

The governing challenges identified here highlight voids in existing models of analysis and evidences. The integrated modeling frameworks which include innovation dynamics, financial stability considerations, labor adjustment mechanisms and political feedback loops are still largely absent. Network approaches can allow for a comprehensive exploration of interdependencies between sectors and regions and behavioral analysis may be able to reveal how expectations and perceptions impact the acceptance of policy.

Filling these research gaps is indispensable for the improvement of governance and policies in favor of environmental transitions. It is to these next steps in potential research that the following section turns, as it offers future research agendas to extend this end of chapter integrative framework (Stern, 2008).

9. FUTURE RESEARCH DIRECTIONS AND EMERGING ISSUES

9.1 Integrated Macro–Climate–Finance–Labor Modeling

The concept of a ripple-effect model proposed in this paper emphasizes the requirement for such integrated models that can describe interactions across domains. Standard macroeconomic models typically represent the environmental policy as an exogenous shock in aggregate production, financial market models decouple the risk repricing from real sector adjustment and labor force or employment models neglects technological and capital dynamics. Future investigations will need to extend beyond such fragmentary analyses.

A unified modeling approach would be characterized by heterogeneous firms and households – with different levels of capital intensity, access to regulation, skill composition and consumption patterns – in a special general equilibrium. The distributional effects of the shock and the sectoral reactions cannot be accounted for in representative-Agent models (World Bank, 2024).

Models would also need to contain sectoral input-output networks, in order to follow how cost changes and innovations propagate via supply chains. Ripple effects might be enhanced or diminished by network features and possible substitutability's (Stern, 2008).

Financial accelerator mechanisms are necessary to capture how asset repricing affects the extent of credit provision, the dynamics of investment and macroeconomic volatility. Risk and balance-sheet effects of transitions have to be considered together with production decisions.

Future research needs to better model the spatially concentrated labor shocks, e.g., at the regional level where most fossil fuel minerals are found, and to consider how regional multipliers impact on aggregate demand and fiscal capacity.

Lastly, models need to incorporate policy credibility and expectations dynamics. Looking ahead behavior under uncertainty governs the timing of investments, the intensity of innovations and the allocation of capital. Reflecting expectation formation and credibility constraints in macro–climate models is essential to describe the complete transmission structure.

Construction of such integrative platforms would facilitate an enhanced more realistic assessment of trade-offs, sequencing strategies and distributional impacts for policy-makers.

9.2 Characteristics of Ripple Effects and Their Measurement and Estimating

In order to progress empirical understanding, better instruments for measurement are needed. Contemporary assessment methodologies tend to be narrow and place undue emphasis on emissions reductions or total effect on GDP rather than intermediate transmission effects.

Research must establish equivalent measures of policy credibility and uncertainty, perhaps in the form of indicators that measure rule stability, enforcement quality, and investor sentiment. These measures would show how institutional signals affect where capital is channeled and what is innovated (UNFCCC, 2015).

We also need to be able measure where innovation is heading and how quickly innovations are being diffused. Patent categories, trends in R&D investment, and adoption rates of technologies might be further cleaned up to separate marginal improvements from transformative changes. Tracking diffusion across regions and sectors would reveal whether the new's reaching parts that matter.

A second priority is to create transition-risk and re-pricing trajectories indicators. Information on asset write-downs, differences in the cost of capital, and portfolio reallocation can be quantified by harmonized cross-country indicators.

Measures of the quality and equity of labor adjustment, as well as outcomes such as duration until re-employment, wage recovery, regional income convergence, and use of retraining programs are also important. In the absence of common metrics, we lack a sufficient assessment of just transition policies.

Symptomatic dimension measurement on a systematic basis would facilitate cross-jurisdictional comparisons and evidence-based policy development (Unruh, 2000).

9.3 Behavioral and Institutional Realism

Economic transformation is not just about prices and rules, but also fairness, confidence in institutions, and social conversation. Future research in environmental policy should be of an institutional and behavioral realist nature.

Public acceptance of carbon pricing and regulation is influenced by the perceived fairness of cost distribution. If they see policies as unfair, compliance and political survivability could suffer. Trust in institutions determines if policy signals are considered as credible and firms' decisions to invest in long-term innovation.

There is a need for studies to investigate the impact of social dialogue mechanisms such as stakeholder consultation and participatory governance on adoption and implementation outcomes. Behavioral reactions to incentive schemes, forms of communication and the design of revenue recycling are also deserving of further systematic investigation.

Behavioral perspectives integrated with labor and distributional mechanisms would provide insights into how the dynamic political economic feedback loops operate within ripple-effect infrastructure (World Bank, 2010).

9.4 International Coordination Research Priorities

With the climate and trade spillovers that are cross-affecting each other, future studies need to deal with international coordination issues. One area of priority is the development of mechanisms to allocate climate finance. It is important to understand the role of multilateral funds and concessional lending facilities in influencing technology adaptation and infrastructure investment to achieve a just transition in developing countries.

Research must also examine the impact of technology transfer and absorptive capacity programs by determining institutional frameworks which contribute to successful diffusion. Cross-country comparisons can inform what it is about education systems, quality of governance and financial development attitudes that result in different outcomes.

Another priority on the agenda is to assess CBAM-equity arrangements by studying how border measures can be designed for leakage prevention while securing development fairness. Moreover, evidence as to the impact on trade, administrative feasibility and legal compatibility would inform a more sophisticated policy design (Xhindole et al., 2025).

Promoting these research priorities can also help to further refine the integrated framework proposed in this chapter, and to underpin governance strategies for regulating the economic, financial, labor and trade knock-on effects of environmental transition.

10. CONCLUSION: SYNTHESIS, OVERARCHING LESSONS, AND STRUCTURED POLICY IMPLICATIONS

10.1 Restated Contribution and Framework

We have developed in this chapter a unified framework for analysis of how environmental policy influences ripples throughout the economy through multiple interlinked transmission channels. Instead of seeing growth, innovation, finance, labor and trade as perpendicular or separate spaces (and much less in the abstract multi-dimensional matrix dubbed "Knowledge Based Economy") they are depicted as part of a unified landscape based on Marcelo Resende's ripple-effect scheme. The chapter cuts across hitherto disparate literatures by making systematic the translation and transmission of policy signals through innovation systems, financial markets, labour structures and macroeconomic dynamics.

The most significant insight is to show that environmental policy is functioning as a systemic economic intervention. It does not only impact the regulated sectors, but it also applies for expectations downstream of them; capital allocation upstream from them; technology direction, social distribution. The unified model sheds light on the fact that the results are not only due to the nature of policy stringency, but to the interrelation of credibility, institutional capacity, financial stability and labor adaptability. In doing so, the chapter recasts environmental policy from a limited instrumental regulatory mechanism to an integrated transformation strategy.

10.2 Key Synthesized Insights

A few overarching observations arise from the combined analysis.

First, growth impacts are time-structured. The costs of adjustment in the short-run are real but contingent – involving capital retrofitting, labor displacement and compliance frictions. But that long-run growth depends on induced innovation, diffusion and the ability of financial and labor systems to facilitate reallocation. Long-term productivity gains can outweigh the transitional ones when policy credibility and institutional coherence are high.

Second, innovation is multi-dimensional. Induced innovation, diffusion and structural change need to be interpreted as separate yet interdependent processes. The innovation pathway schematic (Figure 3) and the diffusion synthesis (Table 4) both emphasize that diffusion is the key link between localized invention and economy-wide increases in productivity. Without successful diffusion, innovation is sectorally contained and the growth gain would be diluted.

Third, finance is an intermediary and not a byproduct of environmental change. Figure 4 depicts the asset repricing and capital reallocation that are driven by policy credibility and disclosure mechanisms, Table 5–Table 7 present structured responses across instruments that influence both innovation scaling and financial stability. Financial systems speed up or slow down the rate of structural change, which makes good prudential design essential for successful transition.

Fourth, political feasibility is driven by the labor market – and justice transition frameworks. Job reallocation, skill biased demand shifts and regional concentration effects are interacting directly with innovation and finance. The labor adjustment schematic and employment synthesis (see Figure 5, Table 8–Table 9) show how unmanaged labor shocks may erode policy commitment while thoughtful transition-aid bolsters credibility and social sustainability.

Fifth, international spillovers require coordination. Trade channels, carbon leakage, border measures and climate finance allocation inform global equity and domestic political constraints (see Figure 6; Table 10). One jurisdiction's environmental policy has global supply chain and capital flow implications that require collaborative governance arrangements.

Taken together, these findings strengthen the conceptualization of environmental transition as a system. The phenomena of ripple effects is a complex, iterative and interconnected set of permutations that must be managed holistically.

10.3 Closing Integrative Statement

Environmental policy works best — and delivers stronger economic and social sustainability performance — when it is designed as an integrated system to manage those kinds of ripple effects across innovation, finance, labor and trade. The treatment of environmental regulation as an independent constraint linked simply to sectoral compliance fails to capture the interactions between the mechanisms through which the long-run determines itself. A systemic governance orientation based on credible sequencing, institutional readiness and inclusive transition frameworks enables environmental ambition to dovetail with macroeconomic stability, financial resilience and social equity.

REFERENCES

Acemoglu, D., Aghion, P., Bursztyn, L., & Hemous, D. (2012). The environment and directed technical change. *The American Economic Review*, *102*(1), 131–166. DOI: 10.1257/aer.102.1.131 PMID: 26719595

Adeneye, Y. (2023). Climate finance research: A thematic review and directions for the future. Social and Environmental Accountability Journal, 1–4.

Adeyemi, F., Jempeji, A.-B., Olaniran, A., Taliat, M., & Adeleke, A. (2025). Climate risks and financial stability: A global evidence. *Finance Research Open*, *1*(3), 100032. DOI: 10.1016/j.finr.2025.100032

Aghion, P., Dechezleprêtre, A., Hemous, D., Martin, R., & Van Reenen, J. (2012). Carbon taxes, path dependency and directed technical change: Evidence from the auto industry. *Journal of Political Economy*, *124*(1), 1–35. DOI: 10.1086/684581

Aldy, J. E., & Pizer, W. A. (2011). The competitiveness impacts of climate change mitigation policies. *Journal of the Association of Environmental and Resource Economists*, *2*(4), 1–29. DOI: 10.1086/683305

Alexandra-Gabriela, M. (2022). General requirements exposure draft: Comments about responsible reporting. *Revista Economica (Sibiu)*, *74*(2), 22–29. DOI: 10.56043/reveco-2022-0013

Ambec, S., Cohen, M., Elgie, S., & Lanoie, P. (2010). The Porter hypothesis at 20: Can environmental regulation enhance innovation and competitiveness? CIRANO Working Papers, 7. DOI: 10.2139/ssrn.1682001

Anderson, S. T., Kellogg, R., & Salant, S. W. (2014). Hotelling under pressure. SSRN Electronic Journal. DOI: 10.2139/ssrn.2537827

Battiston, S., Mandel, A., Schuetze, F., & Visentin, G. (2017). A climate stress-test of the financial system. *Nature Climate Change*, *7*(4), 283–288. DOI: 10.1038/nclimate3255

Bolton, P., & Kacperczyk, M. (2019). Do investors care about carbon risk? SSRN Electronic Journal. DOI: 10.2139/ssrn.3398441

Borck, J., & Coglianese, C. (2009). Voluntary environmental programs: Assessing their effectiveness. *Annual Review of Environment and Resources*, *34*(1), 305–324. DOI: 10.1146/annurev.environ.032908.091450

Calel, R., & Dechezleprêtre, A. (2016). Environmental policy and directed technological change: Evidence from the European carbon market. *The Review of Economics and Statistics*, *98*(1), 173–191. DOI: 10.1162/REST_a_00470

Carbon pricing and emissions trading systems: Legal mechanisms for reducing greenhouse gas emissions. (2025). [Source details not provided].

Cheng, J. (2025). Climate change: Impacts on the global economy. Highlights in Business. *Economics and Management*, *64*, 116–123. DOI: 10.54097/x97r9877

Cohen, M., & Tubb, A. (2015). The impact of environmental regulation on firm and country competitiveness: A meta-analysis of the Porter hypothesis. SSRN Electronic Journal. DOI: 10.2139/ssrn.2692919

Dechezleprêtre, A., & Sato, M. (2017). The impacts of environmental regulations on competitiveness. *Review of Environmental Economics and Policy*, *11*(2), 183–206. DOI: 10.1093/reep/rex013

Delvaux, B., & Leuven, K. (2005). The EU greenhouse gas emission allowance trading directive. *Environmental Law Review*, *7*(1), 63–68. DOI: 10.1177/146145290500700104

Deschênes, O. (2018). Environmental regulations and labor markets. *IZA World of Labor: Evidence-Based Policy Making*. Advance online publication. DOI: 10.15185/izawol.22.v2

Ells, K. (2018). The tragedy of the commons. In [Book/source details not provided]. DOI: 10.4324/9781315640051-24

Engle, R. F., Giglio, S., Lee, H., Kelly, B., & Stroebel, J. (2019). Hedging climate change news. SSRN Electronic Journal. DOI: 10.2139/ssrn.3422236

Febriyanti, D. (2025). Green jobs and employment growth: Global analysis of policy impacts and investment trends. In [Proceedings/source details not provided]. DOI: 10.2991/978-94-6463-758-8_164

Genc, T., & Kosempel, S. (2023). Energy transition and the economy: A review article. *Energies*, *16*(7), 2965. DOI: 10.3390/en16072965

Goulder, L. H., & Schein, A. R. (2013). Carbon taxes versus cap and trade: A critical review. *Climate Change Economics (Singapore)*, *4*(3), 1350010. Advance online publication. DOI: 10.1142/S2010007813500103

Griggs, D., Stafford Smith, M., Gaffney, O., Rockström, J., Öhman, M., Shyamsundar, P., Steffen, W., Glaser, G., Kanie, N., & Noble, I. (2013). Sustainable development goals for people and planet. *Nature*, *495*(7441), 305–307. DOI: 10.1038/495305a PMID: 23518546

Hale, T. (2020). Catalytic cooperation. *Global Environmental Politics*, *20*(4), 73–98. DOI: 10.1162/glep_a_00561

Haščič, I., de Vries, F., Johnstone, N., & Medhi, N. (2010). Effects of environmental policy on the type of innovation. OECD Journal: Economic Studies, 1–18. DOI: 10.1787/eco_studies-v2009-art2-en

Helleiner, E., DiLeo, M., & Klooster, J. (2024). Financial technocrats as competitive regime creators: The founding and design of the Network for Greening the Financial System. *Regulation & Governance*, *19*(3), 901–916. Advance online publication. DOI: 10.1111/rego.12629

Ilhan, E., Sautner, Z., & Vilkov, G. (2020). Carbon tail risk. *Review of Financial Studies*, *34*(3), 1540–1571. DOI: 10.1093/rfs/hhaa071

Jaffe, A. B., & Palmer, K. (1997). Environmental regulation and innovation: A panel data study. *The Review of Economics and Statistics*, *79*(4), 610–619. DOI: 10.1162/003465397557196

Johnstone, N., Haščič, I., & Popp, D. (2009). Renewable energy policies and technological innovation: Evidence based on patent counts. *Environmental and Resource Economics*, *45*(1), 133–155. DOI: 10.1007/s10640-009-9309-1

Kahn, M. E., Mohaddes, K., Ng, R., Pesaran, M. H., Raissi, M., & Yang, J.-C. (2019). Long-term macroeconomic effects of climate change: A cross-country analysis. IMF Working Papers. DOI: 10.5089/9781513514598.001

Kaushiva, A. (2025). Green economic transition and green skills: A pathway for sustainable development. *Shanlax International Journal of Economics*, *13*(3), 71–78. DOI: 10.34293/economics.v13i3.8611

Krueger, P., Sautner, Z., & Starks, L. T. (2020). The importance of climate risks for institutional investors. *Review of Financial Studies*, *33*(3), 1067–1111. DOI: 10.1093/rfs/hhz137

Linden, J., O'Donoghue, C., & Sologon, D. (2026). Modelling distributional impacts of carbon taxation: A systematic review and meta-analysis. arXiv. https://doi.org//arXiv.2601.07713DOI: 10.48550

Markkanen, S., & Anger, A. (2019). Social impacts of climate change mitigation policies and their implications for inequality. *Climate Policy*, *19*(7), 1–18. DOI: 10.1080/14693062.2019.1596873

Martin, R., de Preux, L. B., & Wagner, U. J. (2012). The impact of a carbon tax on manufacturing: Evidence from microdata. *Journal of Public Economics*, *117*. Advance online publication. DOI: 10.2139/ssrn.1367149

Nawn, N. (2025). Addressing climate-related financial risks. In [Book/source details not provided]. DOI: 10.4324/9781003589709-10

Ojo, D. D., & Delaney, M. (2021). Regulating climate risks and liability risks: Breaking the tragedy of the horizon, climate change and financial stability. [Source details not provided].

Parry, I. W. H., Black, S., & Roaf, J. (2021). Proposal for an international carbon price floor among large emitters. *Staff Climate Notes*, *001*(1), 1. Advance online publication. DOI: 10.5089/9781513583204.066

Pattillo, C., Mauro, P., Parry, I., Baunsgaard, T., Gbohoui, W., Lam, R., Mylonas, V., Raissi, M., Shah, A., & Shang, B. (2019). *IMF fiscal monitor: How to mitigate climate change (October 2019)*. International Monetary Fund.

Perman, R. (1994). The economics of the greenhouse effect. *Journal of Economic Surveys*, *8*(2), 99–132. DOI: 10.1111/j.1467-6419.1994.tb00096.x

Pindyck, R. S. (2012). The climate policy dilemma. *Review of Environmental Economics and Policy*, *7*(2), 219–237. Advance online publication. DOI: 10.1093/reep/ret007

Pizer, W. A. (2002). Combining price and quantity controls to mitigate global climate change. *Journal of Public Economics*, *85*(3), 409–434. DOI: 10.1016/S0047-2727(01)00118-9

Popp, D. (1997). Induced innovation, energy prices, and the environment. [Source details not provided].

Porter, M. E., & van der Linde, C. (1995). Toward a new conception of the environment-competitiveness relationship. *The Journal of Economic Perspectives*, *9*(4), 97–118. DOI: 10.1257/jep.9.4.97

Ranasinghaarachchi, N. (2024). IFRS S2: Climate-related disclosures—Governance & strategy [Report].

Rausch, S., Metcalf, G. E., & Reilly, J. M. (2011). Distributional impacts of carbon pricing: A general equilibrium approach with micro-data for households. *Energy Economics, 33*, S20–S33. DOI: 10.1016/j.eneco.2011.07.023

Ren, S., Yang, X., Hu, Y., & Chevallier, J. (2022). Emission trading, induced innovation and firm performance. *Energy Economics, 112*, 106157. DOI: 10.1016/j.eneco.2022.106157

Sciuchina, N. (2026). Legal aspects of sustainable employment in the green transition of the labor market. Revista Moldovenească de Drept Internaţional şi Relaţii Internaţionale, 21, 47–56. DOI: 10.61753/1857-1999/2345-1963/2026.21-1.04

Seck, G., Parajuli, B., & Casals, X. (2023). IRENA world energy transitions outlook 2023 (Vol. 2). DOI: 10.13140/RG.2.2.10445.65768

Sinn, H.-W. (2015). The green paradox: A supply-side view of the climate problem. SSRN Electronic Journal. DOI: 10.2139/ssrn.2621998

Skea, J., Shukla, P. R., Reisinger, A., Slade, R., Pathak, M., Al Khourdajie, A., van Diemen, R., Abdulla, A., Akimoto, K., Babiker, M., Bai, Q., Bashmakov, I., Bataille, C., Berndes, G., Blanco, G., Blok, K., Bustamante, M., Byers, E., Cabeza, L., & Winkler, H. (2022). Summary for policymakers. In *Climate change 2022: Mitigation of climate change. Contribution of Working Group III to the Sixth Assessment Report of the Intergovernmental Panel on Climate Change*. Cambridge University Press., DOI: 10.1017/9781009157926.001

Sneeringer, S. (2009). A question of balance: Weighing the options on global warming policies. *Global Environmental Politics, 9*(1), 146–147. DOI: 10.1162/glep.2009.9.1.146

Stern, N. (2008). The economics of climate change: The Stern review. *The American Economic Review, 98*(2), 1–37. DOI: 10.1257/aer.98.2.1

Stern, N., & Stiglitz, J. E. (2021). The social cost of carbon, risk, distribution, market failures: An alternative approach. SSRN Electronic Journal. DOI: 10.2139/ssrn.3785806

Stevis, D., Krause, D., & Morena, E. (2021). Towards a just transition for all: Lessons from the pandemic. [Source details not provided].

Stiglitz, J. E., Stern, N., Duan, M., Edenhofer, O., Giraud, G., Heal, G., La Rovere, E., Moyer, E., Mari Pangestu, P., Shukla, P., Sokona, Y., & Winkler, H. (2017). Report of the High-Level Commission on Carbon Prices. DOI: 10.13140/RG.2.2.26038.09288

Taylor, P., Bays, J., Bradshaw, M., Webb, J., Britton, J., Bolton, R., Chaudry, M., Qadrdan, M., Wu, J., Anable, J., Brand, C., Rattle, I., Gailani, A., Bell, K., Poulter, H., Halliday, C., Shepherd, A., Watson, S., Lovett, A., & Hastings, A. (2023). Review of energy policy 2023. DOI: 10.5286/UKERC.EDC.000967

UNFCCC. (2015). *Paris agreement*. United Nations.

Unruh, G. C. (2000). Understanding carbon lock-in. *Energy Policy*, *28*(12), 817–830. DOI: 10.1016/S0301-4215(00)00070-7

Wirdyansyah, D. (2025). Carbon Border Adjustment Mechanism (CBAM) and its implications for developing economies: A systematic literature review. *Indonesian Journal of Energy*, *8*(2), 162–176. DOI: 10.33116/ije.v8i2.292

World Bank. (2010). *World development report 2010: Development and climate change*. World Bank.

World Bank. (2024). *State and trends of carbon pricing 2024*. World Bank.

Xhindole, C., Tarquinio, L., & Sierra-García, L. (2025). Climate change and Task Force on Climate-related Financial Disclosures (TCFD) reports: A comparison between Italy and Spain. *Journal of Accounting & Organizational Change*, *21*(7), 1–28. DOI: 10.1108/JAOC-05-2024-0172

Chapter 2
From Regulation to Transformation–Economic and Institutional Pathways of Environmental Policy

S. Aarthi
http://orcid.org/0009-0006-9064-2091
Marwadi University, Rajkot, India

R. N. Ravikumar
http://orcid.org/0009-0009-3705-1681
Marwadi University, Rajkot, India

ABSTRACT

The environmental policy has now become a strategy aimed at economic, financial and institutional change and not just another regulatory device. In this chapter, the authors discuss how environmental regulation, market-oriented instruments and co-ordinated policy frameworks redefine the structure of production, investment behavior, labour market, and governance structures. Treating the environmental policy as an endogenous factor, the analysis defines its impact on the dynamics of innovation, reallocation of capitals, and the structural economic change. Another crucial aspect highlighted in the chapter is the relevance of institutional quality and multi-level governance in the process of converting regulatory ambition into long term inclusive, and sustainable development outcomes.

DOI: 10.4018/979-8-3373-8998-1.ch002

1. INTRODUCTION

Environmental policy has grown to become a much more inclusive regulatory tool within the confines of pollution control to a more pivotal tool in determining economic restructuring, financial practices and institutional transformation. Even though the traditionally viewed regulation as a constraint on economic activity, as recent experience has revealed, environmental actions may in fact influence the way innovation occurs, the direction of money flows, and the governance of an organization. This change is especially noticeable in circumstances of an increased risk of climate, accelerated technological change, and incremental financial integration. The originality of the chapter is that it views environmental policy as an explicit endogenous determinant of systemic change, and not an ameliorative or supportive policy domain. In contrast to current integrative policy models that tend to look at the economic, financial, or institutional aspects separately, this chapter constructs a coherent analyst perspective that follows the formation of regulatory ambition, market-related instruments, and quality of governance that have a united influence on long-term growth trends, financial stability, and social adjustments. Environmental policy is therefore seen not so much as a reaction to market failure, but also as a kind of strategic message that restructures expectations, incentives and coordination within the economic systems (Acemoglu et al., 2010). This chapter develops a unified system of policy design and structural results by incorporating the economic theory, sustainable finance, and institutional governance. It shows that environmental regulation can impact the productivity pattern, shift the flow of financial risks and investment and transform both labor markets due to innovation and skill distribution, but that depends crucially on institutional capacity and policy credibility. Through this, the chapter adds a consistent analytical spectacle to the interpretation of environmental policy as a transformational process of various economic settings.

1.1 From Compliance to Systemic Transformation

Environmental policy first developed as a corrective regulatory reaction to apparent environmental degradation, concerned mostly with emission limits, technology standards and compliance regulation. These initial frameworks were mostly reactive systems in nature that aimed to curb negative externalities without necessarily changing the economic systems. With time, the objectives of policies were broadened since the environmental issues became intricate and entangled with the other developmental objectives. Instruments like carbon pricing, trade permits and green subsidies that are market-based became an example of move towards incentive-based approaches and where firms should internalize the environmental costs whilst having freedom of choice in compliance strategies (Ivahnenko et al., 2025). In more recent times, the environmental policy has been placed as a driver of systemic change, which affects the systems of innovation, the competitiveness of industry, and the dynamics of the labor market. This change is a sign of the realization that regulatory indicators are important in determining expectations, investment horizons, and technology direction. The new form of environmental policy has therefore ceased to be merely a matter of compliance and has shifted towards a proactive mode of guiding the economies towards a low-carbon and resource efficient course of action with repercussions that spans the production networks, finance and the institutional structure (Cui et al., 2022). The figure 1 shows the development of the environmental policy between the first level of compliance with the regulations to the use of market-based tools to transform the sphere to the systemic level which impacts the systems of innovations and competitiveness of industries and the dynamics of labor markets.

Figure 1. Evolution of Environmental Policy Instruments

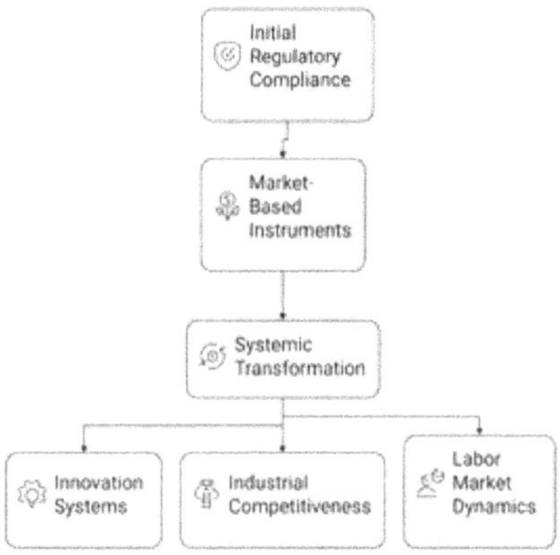

1.2 Integrating Economic, Financial, and Institutional Dimensions

Considering the aspect of the environmental policy using one disciplinary perspective is likely to underrate its transformational potential and unforeseen consequences. One of the aspects emphasized by economic perspectives is how stringency of policy changes relative prices, productivity, and sectoral composition but they tend to ignore financial constraints and institutional capacity. Financial views demonstrate the impact of environmental regulation to risk assessment, capital allocation, and valuation of assets especially in the context of increasing understanding of climate-related financial risk and stranded assets (Bárcena-Ruiz & Garzón, 2022). Institutional perspectives on the other hand stress on the quality of governance, the credibility of enforcement and well-coordination within the working areas of policy and execution powers. The combination of these dimensions allows having a more holistic perception of the functioning of the environmental policies in practice, as opposed to how they exist separately. Economic incentives demand financial systems that can direct investment to be on sustainable activity and institutional structures define consistency, transparency, and flexibility of policy. The relationship between these factors determines the pace, distribution and sustainability of transformational results (Steinebach, 2022). The synthesis of analysis thus offers greater understanding of the conditions in which the environmental policy can be used to pursue efficiency, stability and the equity goals at the same time.

1.3 Structure and Contributions of the Chapter

This chapter is organized in such a way that it analytically discusses how the environment policy can be used as a source of economic and institutional change. After the introduction, the background section places the current environmental policy in terms of its history and theory. The chapter is then focused on analysis with clear research objectives. The paper outlines a conceptual model that explains how policy instruments, economic mechanisms, financial systems and institutional structures interact. The methodology section describes the analysis mode used and a literature review is given in accordance with the objectives. Real-life transformation pathways and governance issues are demonstrated with the help of recent case studies. The discussion and findings section brings together the observations in the economic, financial and institutional levels. The future research directions point to questions and gaps in the empirical research, and managerial implications convert the policy understanding into the strategic advice of the firms and other financial participants. The chapter ends with another restatement of environmental policy as dynamic and endogenous process that determines sustainable development paths.

2. BACKGROUND TO THE STUDY

The context to this research is based on the increased understanding that environmental policy does not exist as a separate regulatory intervention, but as an activity that exists in a complex economic and institutional environment. Conventional policy frameworks have viewed environmental goals as subsidiary to growth with environmental concerns being addressed either through solitary remedial action. Nevertheless, the increasing threat of climatic conditions, resource limitations, and international sustainability obligations have changed this opinion. Environmental policies have since overlapped with industrial policy, financial policy, labour markets and international trade (Ravikumar et al., 2025). Such contacts have been increased with economies facing large scale structural adjustment and technological change. The background section puts this shift into perspective by looking back at the evolution of environmental regulation throughout history, reflecting on the shifts in economic theory concerning regulation and growth and showing various emerging global issues that reexamine the priorities of policy. Such fundamental dynamics are very crucial to the interpretation of modern policy consequences and institutional reactions. The background provides the analytical foundation of how the environmental policy should be treated as a systemic force that can reorganize economic organization, structure of governance and a cross borders economic relations.

2.1 Evolution of Environmental Regulation

Environmental regulation that was originally formed by command-and-control methods, with a focus on the legal norms, permits and penalties in order to limit pollution and degradation of resources. These tools focused more on prediction of results and were frequently characterized by high compliance rates and low technology. With the continuing environmental issues, policymakers came up with market-based tools, which would help attain environmental objectives at a reduced cost. Emission trading, environmental taxation and subsidy reforms increased the policy toolkit and made environmental goals aligned to the economic incentives. Hybrid policy frameworks over time came into existence, which were a mixture of regulatory standards and market mechanisms and voluntary initiatives (Anwar et al., 2024). Recent events are indicators of an overdependence on mission-driven policies, government investment, and support of innovation to speed up structural change. This social developmental process can be seen as a slow move towards a less restraining approach of policy-making. The widening set of tools indicates an increasing realization that environmental issues need concerted action between production systems, financial markets and systems of governance and no single regulatory solutions. Table 1 Summary The evolution of command-and-control regulation into market-based and transformational policy tools.

Table 1. Evolution of Environmental Policy Instruments

Policy Phase	Dominant Instruments	Primary Objective	Economic Implication
Early regulation	Emission standards, permits	Pollution control	Compliance cost focus
Market-based phase	Taxes, tradable permits	Cost-efficient abatement	Price signal creation
Innovation-oriented phase	Subsidies, R&D support	Technological change	Productivity enhancement
Transformational phase	Integrated policy mixes	Structural transition	Long-term growth realignment

2.2 From External Constraints to Endogenous Drivers

Economic thought has been thoroughly changed with an absolute shift in the conceptualization of environmental regulation. The initial models considered the environmental policy to be an external limitation whereby it decreased efficiency and competitiveness by raising the cost of production. This School of thought focused on trade-offs between the environment and economic development. Recent theoretical and empirical studies dispute this perception by putting environmental policy in the context of it being an endogenous source of innovation, productivity, and structural change. The regulatory stringency has the ability to drive technological progress through re-incentivizing and re-rewarding the expectations that result in cleaner processes in production and new markets (Bohringer & Lange, 2003). This change is in line with evolutionary and endogenous growth theories that focus on learning and knowledge spillovers and institutional feedback. It is becoming more obvious that environmental policy impacts long-term growth trends as opposed to creating short-term costs. This reframing is in favour of the opinion that well-crafted policies may result in improving competitiveness, and also they may promote the goals of sustainability, when the necessary financial and institutional conditions are found complementary.

2.3 Climate Risk, Sustainability Transitions, and Governance

The modern world environment has enhanced the transformative purpose of environmental policy. Climate change poses systemic risks on the economic stability, financial market and social welfare of the regions. Sustainability transitions entail massive re-distribution of capital, labour and technology pushing governance systems to unprecedented levels (Aarthi et al., 2025). Meanwhile, globalization makes it difficult to implement policies due to trade across the borders, investment, and global value chains. International spillovers are increasingly caused by environmental regulations which are affecting competitiveness and policy diffusion across boundaries (Simpa et al., 2024). The issues of governance can be explained by the necessity to facilitate action among a variety of levels of authority and prevent the fragmentation and capture of regulations. The above dynamics indicate the value of the institutional capacity, transparency and international cooperation. Environmental policy is therefore incorporated in an international environment that is marked by ambiguity, interdependence and distributional tensions. It is important to understand such a context when considering the efficacy and openness of policy-based pathways of transformation.

3. RESEARCH OBJECTIVES

The purpose that this chapter is guided by is the systematic study of environmental policy as an economic, financial, and institutional transformation initiative. Instead of perceiving regulation as a fixed constraint, the aims focus on its dynamic aspect of reforming the production systems, market practices, state forms, and long-term development paths. The research objectives correspond to the analytical focus of the chapter and facilitate an extensive assessment of the policy effectiveness in a variety of aspects.

- To examine the pathways through which environmental policies induce structural economic transformation, including changes in productivity, sectoral composition, and innovation dynamics.
- To analyze the effects of policy stringency on financial markets, with particular emphasis on capital allocation, risk assessment, and investment behavior under sustainability and climate-related risks.
- To assess labor market responses to environmental regulation, focusing on employment reallocation, skill transitions, and distributional implications across regions and sectors.
- To evaluate the role of institutional quality, governance capacity, and regulatory credibility in enabling or constraining long-term policy effectiveness.
- To explore the interaction between domestic environmental policies and international economic linkages, including trade competitiveness, investment flows, and cross-border policy spillovers.

4. CONCEPTUAL MODEL

The conceptual model views the environmental policy as an endogenous and dynamic force, which influences the economic, financial, and institutional structure. The model does not view regulation as an outside intervention, but rather as signals, which work to modify expectations, incentives and coordination of economic actors. The transmission of these signals goes through the main transmission channels which include the innovation systems, financial markets and labor markets and the end effect is structural changes in the pattern of production, the flow of investments, and the composition of the labor force. The model also appreciates that the outcome is not predetermined, but through institutional quality and governance arrangements (Sang et al., 2025). The ability to enforce, the trustworthiness of the policy, and its coordination at different governance levels defines either success of transforming regulatory ambition to enduring change or shorter modification. Through a combination of these factors, the model incorporates a relationship between the policy design, the market reactions, and the institutional situations. This framework allows considering the environmental policy in a holistic perspective and how it can effectively influence growth, competitiveness, financial stability, and social inclusion (Bai & Yang, 2016). It also offers a systematic point of attachment of theoretical knowledge, empirical evidence and case study, making the parts on analysis of the chapter work in unison.

The conceptual model provides a direct guide on the illustrations that are done empirically in the ensuing case studies. In Case Study I, the operationalization of the innovation as well as the production-side transmission channels involves the flow of policy-based industrial policies into the manufacturing scale-up, coordination of investments, and workforce adaptation. Case Study II represents transmission channel through financials, showing the way in which the supervisory expectations, disclosure requirements and collateral structure reorganise the risk pricing and capital allocation. Combined, the cases offer actual examples of the mechanisms of the core of the model and underline the moderating power of the institutional capacity as a focus of the framework. Table 2 Shows the key elements and interconnections within the conceptual framework, associating the policy instruments to the economic, financial, and institutional outcomes.

Table 2. Policy–Market–Institution Linkages

Component	Role in the Model	Expected Outcome
Environmental policy instruments	Policy signal generation	Investment and behavior change
Economic systems	Production and sectoral response	Structural reallocation
Financial systems	Risk pricing and capital allocation	Green investment scaling
Institutions	Governance and enforcement	Policy credibility and durability

4.1 Environmental Policy as an Endogenous Driver

The conceptualization of the environmental policy is an endogenous force, and it actively transforms economic structures instead of putting a limitations on them. The regulatory action, instruments based on markets and public investments change relative prices and expectations, which makes a difference in the firm behavior and long-term planning. The changes have impacts on technology adoption, capital intensity and sectoral specialization. In the long term, the incentives created by policy trigger a faster growth of the low-carbon and resource-efficient operations coupled with the rapid deterioration of environmentally intensive industries. The structural change is a result of a cumulative change in production networks, supply chains, as well as consumption patterns (von Malmborg, 2025). The endogenous view puts more emphasis on feedback, of which earlier policy interventions encourage innovation and learning that support transformation processes. The approach goes beyond the fixed cost-benefit interpretations and focuses on transition risks, path dependency and opportunity creation. The policy towards the environment thereby gets inculcated within the development processes and decides economic courses through a constant engagement with the market forces and institutional retaliation.

4.2 Innovation, Finance, and Labor Market Channels

The main channels through which the environmental policy impacts are conveyed throughout the economy are innovation, and financial systems, and labor markets. Innovation reacts to the regulatory signals by targeting the research and development to less pollutant technologies and production processes. The financial markets convert policy expectations to risk perception change, asset valuation change and capital allocation change which impact investment decisions in the various sectors. Criteria related to sustainability are increasingly defining lending, portfolio structures, and long-term financing structures (R. N. Ravikumar et al., 2025). The economic structures change with changes in the employment demand and requirements of skills and geographical movements within the labor markets.

These processes go hand in hand, with innovation needs to be funded, and labor reorganization is contingent upon investment patterns and technological change. The rate and direction of change is predetermined by the effectiveness of these channels to policy signals. Their interaction is crucial to the evaluation of the efficiency and distributional implications of environmental policy-based transformation (Adelekan et al., 2024). Table 3 Maps environment policy as an environmental policy is the driver of structural change that works via innovation, finance, and labor markets.

Table 3. Environmental Policy Transmission Mechanisms

Transmission Channel	Key Mechanism	Transformation Effect
Innovation systems	R&D redirection	Clean technology diffusion
Financial markets	Risk revaluation	Capital flow reallocation
Labor markets	Skill adjustment	Workforce transition
Supply chains	Input substitution	Emissions intensity reduction

4.3 Institutional Quality and Multi-Level Governance

The efficiency of environmental policy and mechanism of transmission is moderated through institutional quality and governance setup. Strong institutions create credibility in the policy, decrease uncertainty and long-term investment decisions are made. The ability to enforce the rules, the opportunity to be transparent and accountable will affect the compliance behavior and reduce regulatory arbitrage. The multi-level governance structures assist in the coordination of the national, regional, and local authorities and allow aligning the policy to conditions on the sectoral and territorial levels. Nonetheless, the implementation could be undermined by disjointed governance by having overlapping mandates and disparate incentives. Technological lock-in can also be coupled with institutional inertia and vested interest hindering the adaptation and supporting technological lock-in (Mathieu, 2023). The effective governance in a balance between the variance and rigidity enables policies to change in response to the economic feedback and technological advancement. The moderating levels of the institutions underline the fact that one and the same policy instruments may produce different results in different situations, basing on the qualities of governance and administrative capacities. The institutional design thus comes into the limelight of ensuring that the regulatory ambition is converted into the structural transformation.

5. RESEARCH METHODOLOGY

The research methodology uses integrative approach of analysis that involves bringing together economic and institutional approach to analyzing the transformative role of environmental policy. Instead of focusing on one empirical approach, the methodology focuses on conceptual synthesis and comparison analysis to involve intricate interactions among systems. It is a suitable method of measurement in multi-dimensional results like structural change, financial reallocation and governance effectiveness. The discussion is based on the existing theoretical models, policy reviews, and results of studies focused in various economic settings. The synthesis of insights across studies and the determination of common patterns, mechanisms as well as constraints is conducted by employing qualitative methods (Patil & Vonk, 2025). The discussion of context-related dynamics and difficulties of policy implementation is also supported by the use of comparative case analysis. The methodology places the emphasis on analytical consistency and interpretive richness rather than the causal approximation, and it allows approaching transformation processes in a far more sophisticated manner. There are data availability limitations, generalizability limitations, and temporal limitations which are explicitly mentioned to guarantee transparency and analytical rigor.

5.1 Integrated Economic and Institutional Framework

The analytical framework combines the economic mechanisms with the institutional analysis in order to make the analysis of the full scope of effects of environmental policies. Economic analysis is concerned with incentives, market reactions and structural adjustment mechanisms, and institutional analysis deals with the capacity to govern, the credibility of regulatory responses as well as coordination mechanisms (Wang et al., 2023). This integrated model appreciates the fact that the economic results are not only based on policy formulation, but also on the institutional context within which the policies are applied. The model enables the analysis of the feedback mechanism between regulation, innovation, monetary conduct, and adjustment of the labor market. It also takes into consideration the heterogeneity within and between sectors and regions, which implies the variation in the institutional arrangements and policy exposure (Zhang & Bi, 2023). The framework facilitates the consideration of transformation pathways on economic and institutional levels and prevents reductionist perspectives on policy effects.

5.2 Qualitative Policy Synthesis and Case Analysis

Qualitative synthesis is employed in the research to integrate the findings of policy reports, empirical research and comparative research. The method enables the identification of recurring processes and contingent factors of the policy outcomes. Comparative cases analysis is used to demonstrate that different outcomes may be attained in the same policy objective because of various institutional and economic situations. The cases will be selected based on policy tools diversity, regime systems as well as development stages (Green & Koebele, 2025). Synthesis assigns significance to similarity and dissimilarity between cases and emphasizes the impact of the institutional capability and financial system in affecting the paths of transformation. It is one approach that brings out the encouragement of theory-based interpretation but with the basis of real-life policy experience. The most appropriate type of synthesis is qualitative when it comes to describing interactions, which are complex, as well as long-term dynamics that cannot be easily separable with a strictly quantitative method.

5.3 Scope, Assumptions, and Methodological Limitations

The macroeconomic, financial, labor, and institutional aspects of environmental policy are examined in the framework without any sector-specific technical modelling. The research presupposes rational behaviour of policy responses in circumstances of limited information and institutional factors. Although the methodology can be used to achieve general comparative understanding, it fails to determine causal relationships and measure specific magnitudes of effects. Interpretation of these data may be biased by data limitations and change in policy reporting (Zhang et al., 2023). The temporal dynamics are conceptualized instead of being estimated longitudinally. Irrespective of these shortcomings, the methodology adopted offers a sound conceptual framework of the transformation processes and the establishment of main enabling conditions. The clear recognition of assumptions and limitations increases the transparency and allows interpreting the findings in an informed manner.

6. LITERATURE REVIEW

The environmental policy literature is moving towards regarding regulation as a source of economic change as opposed to a hindrance to economic growth. Analytical efforts have been made to understanding early on the existence of efficiency losses, and compliance costs, usually on a trade-offs basis between environmental protection and competitiveness. The more recent contributions assume dynamic visions that emphasize the effects of learning, incentives to innovate and structural redistribution as caused by policy interventions (Vongpatchim et al., 2025). In economic, financial, and institutional aspects, the literature agrees in a discussion that policy results are based on interaction influences between market reactions, governance capacity, and global economic integration. This part is a synthesis of important thematic lessons in line with the objectives of the chapters with focus on productivity dynamics, financial reallocation, and institutional spillovers without being limited to narrow disciplinary scopes.

6.1 Environmental Policy and Structural Economic Change

The literature on the issue of the impact of environmental policy on productivity indicates a transformation in the short-term approach to costs to the long-run dynamic analysis. Although preliminary regulation can increase the adjustment costs, an increasing number of studies point to the fact that properly designed policies can trigger technological modernization and resourcefulness. Increases in productivity are commonly associated with innovation processes elicited by regulatory signals that inspire firms to implement more clean processes and invest in new capabilities (Farooq & Khoshnaw, 2025). The structural economic change appears when the industries with lower environmental intensity grow, whereas the activities with high carbon and resource intensity decrease. The reallocation process transforms the composition of the industrial world and changes the comparative advantages between the regions. Heterogeneity in results is also highlighted in the literature, where it is stated that productivity effects are heterogeneous in terms of policy stringency, sectoral exposure and complementary investments (Huliselan, 2025). Notably, the environmental policy has come to be seen as defining growth patterns by means of cumulative innovation and learning, as opposed to generating one time efficiency impacts.

6.2 Climate Risk and Asset Valuation

The literature of financial market emphasizes the influence of the environmental policy in the redefinition of risk perceptions and capital allocation. The regulatory signals also have an impact on how the financial institutions determine long term risks in climate change, technological transition and regulatory uncertainty. Environmental policy has an impact on the asset valuation because it influences the expected returns in the carbon-intensive industries and makes sustainable investments more appealing. This process plays a role in redistribution of capital to low-carbon technologies and infrastructure (Ererdi & Güneren Genç, 2025). Possible origin of financial instability, such as stranded assets and sudden valuation changes are also found in the literature. The rising level of integration of sustainability requirements in the decision making in investment indicates the interdependence that has been increasing between the environmental regulation and the financial stability (Wibowo et al., 2025). All these dynamics highlight the role of financial systems in enhancing or suppressing transformation brought about by policies, based on the depth of the market, quality of disclosure and consistency of regulations.

6.3 Institutions, Governance, and Policy Spillovers

The literature on institutional and governance aspects highlights that the capacity to implement, credibility and coordination of environmental policy are crucial factors on effective environmental policy. Strong institutions increase compliance and decrease the uncertainty that allows firms and investors to react to the policy signals with certainty. Such multi-level governance arrangements make it possible to align national goals and local realities and create the dangers of fragmentation and regulatory conflict (Armiento & Villa, 2025). The literature also identifies the international aspect of the environmental policy, in that the domestic regulations create spillovers in terms of trade, investment, and global value chains. The policy diffusion takes place when jurisdictions start using similar tools whereas competitiveness issues arise when the stringency of regulations in different countries is different. Efforts to control these spillovers are seen in the border control measures and environmental provisions in trade agreements. All in all, the literature has depicted environmental policy as enshrined in institutional and internationalized settings which defines its scope and its constraints.

7. CASE STUDIES

The section gives two additional, more recent, policy-relevant case examples to illustrate how the environmental policy transforms to non-compliance-based regulation to more comprehensive economic and institutional change. The former scenario is preoccupied with industrial change and green innovation that proves that policy formulation can remodel the technology utilization, manufacturing capacity and skill formation with reference to the orchestration of regulatory and investment indicators. The second is the financial-system responses on climate-related regulation, which demonstrates the impact of the supervisory expectation, disclosure laws and incorporation of climate risks on credit provision, collateral practice and modalities of stress testing (R. N. Ravikumar & Aarthi, 2025b). The cases are pooled to, respectively, reflect the policy created structural change to the real-economy activity and the accompanying change to the financial management and risk pricing. The cross-case synthesis then compares the transmission mechanisms and identifies the stability, swiftness and widely distributed transformation outcome across industries and jurisdiction as being defined by the quality of institutions and coordination at multiple tiers. A comparative summary of the case studies used, policy focus, scope, and results is provided in Table 4.

Table 4. Summary of Policy-Driven Case Studies

Transmission Channel	Key Mechanism	Transformation Effect
Innovation systems	R&D redirection	Clean technology diffusion
Financial markets	Risk revaluation	Capital flow reallocation
Labor markets	Skill adjustment	Workforce transition
Supply chains	Input substitution	Emissions intensity reduction

7.1 Case Study I: Policy-Driven Industrial Transformation

The most recent such policy-based industrial change has been the move of the European Union to industrialize domestic clean-technology production via the Net-Zero Industry Act (NZIA), which is an industrial pillar of the overall Green Deal Industrial Plan. The NZIA creates a strategic model to scale up manufacturing the important net-zero technologies and minimise the bottlenecks which limit deployment. The aim to achieve a significant portion of domestic production of annual deployment requirements by 2030 and steps to accelerate the permitting process, enhance access to capital, and facilitate skills training of clean-tech value chains is a key characteristic. Practically, the tool connects the ambition of the environment and industrial competitiveness through reducing administrative hustle, enhancing policy confidence over investing in batteries, solar, wind, hydrogen-related technologies, and carbon capture (Xie & Wang, 2022). The interaction between regulation and policy of innovation is depicted in the case: the policy of faster permitting eases tensions with the policy of industrial targets and diffusion constrained by the provision of funding and skills (R. N. Ravikumar & Aarthi, 2025c). The compliance is thus not the sole transformation pathway which would be geared towards reorganizing production systems, supply chains, and the labor demand to base on the priorities of net-zero deployment (Eissa & Zaki, 2023). The figure 2 depicts the translation of the Net-Zero Industry Act of the EU strategic environmental ambition into tangible industrial, financing, and skills actions to magnify the manufacturing and competitiveness of clean-technology.

Figure 2. EU's Net-Zero Industry Act Implementation Framework

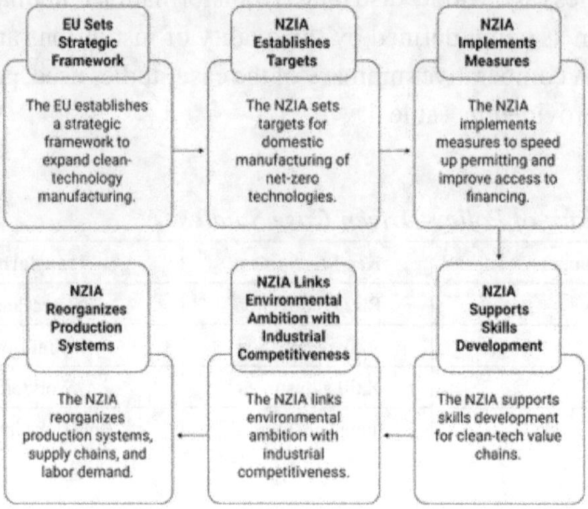

7.2 Case Study II: Financial System Responses to Climate Regulation

The latest and more practical response of the financial-system has been the increased integration of climate-related risk into the practices of the supervisory and monetary-policy-related by the European Central Bank. At the supervisory tier, the climate risk is becoming an increasing credit-relevant, and the climate factors are incorporated in stress-test extensions and the related analytical frameworks that form a relationship between transition risks and physical risks and how the type of exposure of banking entities to non-financial ones. At the same time, regulatory disclosure structure is expanding the information foundation based on which markets and overseers are acting to carry out risk assessment (Ravikumar & Aarthi, 2025). The initial category of covered companies has to utilize the regulations offered by Corporate Sustainability Reporting Directive (CSRD) and present the report during the financial year of 2024 and be released in the year 2025, which strengthens the standardized sustainability reporting as an input in the process of valuing and credit (Deng et al., 2022). Straussing has changed to operational levers: a climate factor will be announced to be operationalized in ECB lending operations as early as in the second half of 2026 and may affect collateral treatment of assets containing climate risks and incentives on the banks to better handle climate risks and alignment of their portfolios. In this instance, it can be seen that the financial transformation has been achieved through the disclosure channels, the supervising channels and collateral channels that cumulatively reshape the manner in which risks are priced and the distribution of capital. As shown in figure 3, the European central bank presents the climate risks in the supervision, stress tests, disclosure, collateral treatment and lending processes, in order to influence the financial stability and the behaviour of banks.

Figure 3. ECB Climate Risk Integration Framework

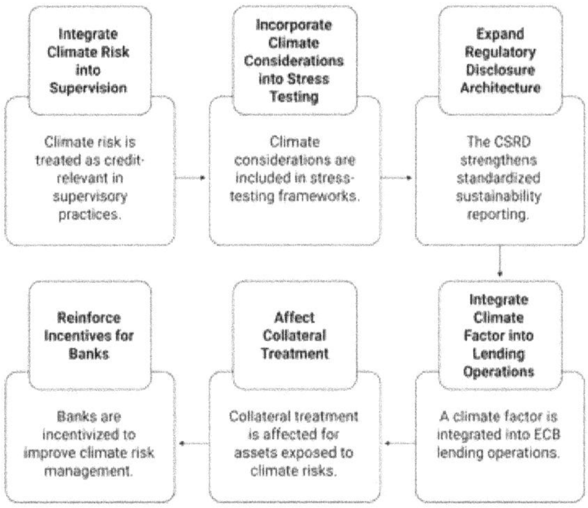

7.3 Comparative Economic and Institutional Outcomes

Cases In both instances, the environmental policy is implemented with a mixture of expectation, coordination, and credibility and not solely on compliance. The industrial example highlights structural change of the real economy through the allowance of scale of production, targeted manufacturing scale, and skills creation, which alleviate frictions during adoption and enhance Generalization of innovation. The financial case focuses on the re-pricing of risk by using standardized disclosure, as well as, by integrating climate risk in their supervision and prospective changes in collateral-policy that is going to affect the incentives and capital allocation of the banks. Institutions Both cases emphasize the role of the implementation capacity and multi-level congruence: industrial change requires smooth administrative performance and stable industrial-policy alignment and financial change requires supervisory quality and credible disclosures and effective risk-management requirements (Mu et al., 2021). Combined with the above, the cases reveal that transformation thrives best when policy tools in the real economy and in finance are supporting and reinforcing each other as well as being accompanied by credible governance structures (R. N. Ravikumar & Aarthi, 2025a). Table 5 Comparison of sectoral effects, financial reactions, and governance situations in the case studies.

Table 5. Comparative Economic, Financial, and Institutional Outcomes

Dimension	Case Study I	Case Study II
Economic impact	Sectoral restructuring	Investment reprioritization
Financial response	Public–private funding	Risk-based valuation
Institutional role	Permitting and coordination	Supervisory enforcement
Transformation speed	Medium to long term	Short to medium term

8. RESULTS AND DISCUSSION

The findings based on the case studies demonstrate that environmental policy can serve as a systemic driver of change in the cases when the regulatory ambition is coordinated with industrial strategy, financial governance and institutional capacity. It has been demonstrated that policy instruments do not work alone but their effectiveness is determined by the interaction of the factors of economic incentives, financial reactions and mechanisms of governance. The industrial policy frameworks associated with the environmental targets can boost sectoral redistribution and diffusion of innovations, whereas the financial regulation can convert long-term climate targets into the current investment and risk-taking decisions. Meanwhile, institutional circumstances determine the pace and inclusion of a change process. There are coordination gaps, administrative capacity, and credibility constraints which may strengthen desired results or undermine them (Listyarini & Warlina, 2017). The argument points to the fact that the environmental policy inspires its most effective effects when it is approached as a dynamic and integrated process, not as a rigid system of rules. These discoveries support the opinion that results of transformation are dependent on the supplementary fields of policy and institutional preparedness.

8.1 Economic and Sectoral Effects of Environmental Policy

Evidence in the case shows that the instruments of environmental policies have a pronounced economic and sectoral effect in the form of restructuring the incentives of production and competition. Industrial structures based on policy promote the growth of low-carbon and clean-technology industries and hastens the relative decadence of activities that are environmentally intensive. Certainty and efficiency in regulations lower the amount of time spent on investments making firms able to scale production and adopt new technologies at an accelerated pace. These dynamics help in sectoral reallocation to activities that are in line with long-term sustainability objectives (Bianco, 2018). Meanwhile, the distribution of adjustment costs is not balanced, with the traditional sectors experiencing more challenges with the transition. The findings indicate that the environmental policy can have an impact not only on the speed of structural transformation but also its orientation, promoting an innovation-intensive and capital-deep sectors. Collected together with a supportive industrial policy, environmental regulation can only lead to productivity-inducing transformation as opposed to the overallized cost hiking. The policy coherence and the presence of supportive mechanisms complementary to each other thus determine sectoral impacts.

8.2 Financial Stability and Labor Market Transitions

According to the results of the financial-system case, environmental regulation has begun to impact financial stability more and more, and investment behaviour by redistributing risks and altering valuations by disclosures. The expectations on climate-related reporting and supervision have changed the way financial institutions evaluate the credit risk and portfolio exposure and promote capital flows to lower-risk, sustainability-oriented assets. Such changes affect the way investment is carried out in various sectors, which strengthen the real-economy change brought about by industrial policies (Vitali et al., 2013). These investment patterns are reflected in labor market transformations where jobs are being created in clean-technology and other service-providing industries and lost in carbon-intensive jobs. The findings indicate the increasing pressure on the new sets of skills and the rising significance of workforce mobility and retraining. These transitions will increase the regional and social inequalities unless they are properly adjusted. On the whole, the data points to the idea that financial regulation and the labor market functioning is an amplifier of the environmental policy, defining the stability outcomes and distributional influence.

8.3 Institutional Constraints and Adaptive Capacity

According to the discussion, the outcome of environmental policies is highly conditional on the institutional factors. Good governance systems lead to increased credibility and less uncertainty as firms and financial players can react effectively to policy signals. On the other hand, divided authority, bureaucracy, and lack of uniformity in enforcing change undermine the transformation channels. The problem of coordination is especially pronounced in a multi-level government environment, in which overlapping roles may slow down the implementation process and diffuse the impact of policies. Adaptive capacity is found as a fundamental factor in success in the long run, where the institutions have to change regulatory frameworks with technological change and economic feedback (Yin et al., 2023). The case studies demonstrate that policies that have a flexible implementation mechanism, and accountability structures will have a longer-lasting outcome. Institutional constraints are thus a key reason behind the difference in economic and financial responses that are manifested in different environments. The proper environmental policy needs not only ambitious design but also governance systems that are able to learn, coordinate and adapt in time.

9. FUTURE RESEARCH DIRECTIONS

The future studies are needed to further insight into the part of the environmental policy as a long-term factor of economic and institutional change. Although the current literature offers important information regarding short- to medium-term effects, significant gaps exist in the description of dynamic adjusting processes and structural performance in the long-term perspective (Xiao et al., 2022). The development of new policy framework and the changing financial regulations provides new possibilities of empirical research, especially when the standardized sustainability data are more provided. Heterogeneity at regional, sectoral, and institutional locations should also be the focus of further studies, since the channels of transformation are local (Bretschger, 2019). The progressive advancement of the methodological approaches that combine the economic, financial, and governance aspects will become the key to the enhanced policy evaluation and development. This paragraph presents some of the major research priorities, which can facilitate stronger evidence on productivity, equity, and international coordination in implementing the environmental policies.

9.1 Policy Stringency and Long-Term Growth

Measuring the long-term productivity and growth impact of the stringency of environmental policy should form the focus of future research. Current empirical studies tend to focus on short-term cost implications or single cases of innovation and the long-term implications of these processes are not well-known. The longitudinal analyses would be required to capture the learning impacts, technology adoption and time-lapse capital reallocation. Sustainability reports and company-level reporting can facilitate better data availability that can be used in order to measure the impact of regulatory signals on investment and efficiency more accurately (Hourcade et al., 2012). Other studies must also be carried out on non-linear effects, thresholds, and transition phases as it is appreciated that productivity responses might change at different stages of policy implementation. An insight into the circumstances where the environmental policy improves or limits growth has continued to feature prominently in solving the debate between competitiveness and sustainability.

9.2 Distributional and Regional Equity

Future studies should incorporate both the distributional and regional equity in the environmental policy analysis. Regions and social groups have been impacted by the structural transformation but in a dissimilar manner depending on the industrial structure, movement of labor, and the ability to establish institutions. The granularity of the studies is needed to determine these changes of employment transitions, income effects and availability of new opportunities by the territories (Fan & Liang, 2025). The effectiveness of compensatory policies like retraining programs, place-based development policies and fiscal redistribution should be researched. The correlation of environmental policy assessment with social and regional statistics can be utilized to detect trade-offs and synergies among efficiency and equity goals. These dimensions form the basis of the need to address the policies that can support political interest and foster the inclusive change.

9.3 Cross-Border Spillovers and Coordination

Trade, investment and global value chains are growing to produce cross-border spillovers of environmental policies, although there is limited empirical research to date. Future studies are required to study the implications of the variation of the stringency of policy on competitiveness and relocation choice and diffusion of the policy across the jurisdiction. The relationship between domestic regulation and international coordination mechanisms, such as border measures and sustainability provisions in trade agreements, should be paid more attention to. Multi-country and comparative studies have the potential to enhance the knowledge of the coordination effectiveness in reducing leakage risks and facilitating convergence (Zarnic et al., 2010). The consolidation of empirical research on spillovers will help to make international policy-making more consistent and will decrease the tension between the ambition to have the environment and integration of the economy.

10. MANAGERIAL IMPLICATIONS

The implications of the findings of this chapter are significant in regards to managerial decision-making in firms, financial institutions as well as organizations which are involved in regulated environments. The environmental policy is growing to influence the markets situation, investment perspectives and operational risks in such a way that it is the proactive strategic adaptation and not reactive compliance (Shafizadeh, 2024). Managers should read regulatory signals as long run structural change, which is affecting competitiveness, cost structures and workforce requirements. The appropriate responses require an in-built sustainability factor in the strategic planning, financial planning, and human resource development. The managerial implications stated in this section show how organizations can match strategy, finance and workforce planning with the dynamic environment and regulatory environment.

10.1 Strategic Adaptation to Policy Signals

Business entities must be able to respond to the environmental policy indicators that transform markets and competitiveness. The stringency of regulation affects technology decisions, supply chain structure and when to invest. Managers predicting policy paths are able to get first-mover benefits by investing in more clean processes and innovative capacity. Strategic adaptation entails entrenching the concept of sustainability in corporate strategy as opposed to it being a compliance function. The companies are also forced to deal with transition risks of old assets and changing consumer tastes (Shen, 2024). The consistency between product portfolios and operational practices and long-term environmental goals promotes resiliency and competitiveness in more and more controlled markets. Table 6 Summarizes the findings in policy, firm, financial institution, and labor system implications of the findings.

Table 6. Policy, Managerial, and Institutional Implications

Stakeholder	Key Implication	Strategic Response
Policymakers	Need for coordination	Integrated policy design
Firms	Regulatory foresight	Strategic innovation
Financial institutions	Climate risk exposure	Sustainable finance integration
Workforce	Skill shifts	Reskilling and training

10.2 Financial Decision-Making under Climate Risk

Sustainability requirements and risk assessment in respect to climate are becoming dominant in the financial decision-making process. Managers need to include regulatory disclosures, risk pricing and financing conditions in capital budgeting and investment appraisal. Finance is increasingly being pegged on plausible sustainability performance and reporting. Climate risk should be incorporated in financial planning to enable the accurate valuation of assets and liabilities. Companies that match financial strategies to the changing regulatory and market anticipations are in a better position to raise capital and deal with uncertainty. This change necessitates a more coordinated approach to financial management, risk governance, as well as sustainability functions (Wang et al., 2018). The figure demonstrates that the sustainability criteria, climate risk assessment, regulatory disclosures, and risk pricing are incorporated into the primary financial decision-making processes like asset valuation, capital budgeting, and investment appraisal.

Figure 4. Financial Decision-Making under Climate Risk

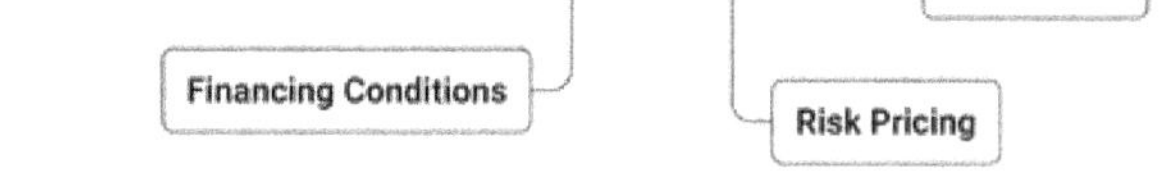

10.3 Workforce Planning and Reskilling

Implication of environmental policy induced change The change in environmental policy has far reaching effects on the way workforce is planned and the organization of work is designed. The change in demand of the skills will be brought by the technological changes and industry redistribution that managers should expect (Maund et al., 2018). Reskilling and ongoing learning should be invested in to facilitate the adjustability and productivity of the workforce. Organizational change entails redesigning of jobs, processes, and rewards to facilitate sustainability and innovation goals. The cost of adjustment can be decreased and the engagement of the employees improved when firms manage the labor transitions actively. The strategic workforce planning then emerges as a very important element of long-term organizational resilience amidst the environmental and regulatory change.

11. CONCLUSION

The environmental policy has changed its systems as a narrow-defined control mechanism to a key instrument in the formation of economic systems, financial systems and institutional forms of control. The discussion shows that properly crafted policy tools can affect the dynamics of productivity, reallocation within the sector as well as the channel of innovation by changing relative prices, expectations, and investment incentives. Financial systems are of particular importance in converting regulatory ambition into workable results by modifying risk assessment, capital distribution and asset valuation, strengthening real-economy change in addition to increasing fresh stability anxieties. These changes are also manifested in labor market adjustments, where employment reallocation and skills requirements are changing, and require workforce adaptive approaches. Governance capacity, credibility and coordination make the difference in turning policy intentions into lasting results as the institutional quality turns out to be a critical determinant of whether the intentions are converted into the policy results. Environmental policy should therefore be regarded as a dynamic and endogenous process as opposed to a set of rules which by definition are subject to feedback processes involving regulation, market and institution. It relies on its transformative potential that can be achieved through adaptive design, cross-domain coherence, and its sensitivity to technological and economic change.

Policy wise, these results emphasize the necessity of incorporating all the environmental goals with the industrial policy, financial policy and social policy to control transition risk and distributional impacts. A sustainable growth and financial stability can be achieved with the support of the effective environmental policy and the encouragement of social inclusion, though development of the mechanisms to cover the adjustment costs and territorial imbalance is necessary. On balance, it can be concluded that the chapter shows that the environmental policy is the most effective when perceived as an endogenic and adaptive pivotal of transformation woven into the economic, financial, and institutional systems. It influences its growth, financial stability, and labor adjustment based on the consistent policy design, reputable governance, and coordination among areas. The chapter offers an analytical contribution to comprehending sustainable transformational journeys in an ever more merged global economy by making environmental regulation seem more of a dynamic coordination, rather than the fixed constraint.

REFERENCES

Aarthi, S., Ravikumar, R. N., Sobirova, K., & Mamadiyarov, Z. (2025). Empowering a sustainable future through digital learning and the SDGs. In *Harnessing E-Learning to Create a Sustainable Future* (pp. 145–172). IGI Global Scientific Publishing., DOI: 10.4018/979-8-3373-0112-9.ch006

Acemoglu, D., Aghion, P., Bursztyn, L., & Hemous, D. (2010). The environment and directed technical change. SSRN *Electronic Journal*. DOI: 10.2139/ssrn.1668575

Adelekan, O. A., Ilugbusi, B. S., Adisa, O., Obi, O. C., Awonuga, K. F., Asuzu, O. F., & Ndubuisi, N. L. (2024). Energy Transition Policies: A global review of shifts towards renewable sources. *Engineering Science & Technology Journal*, *5*(2), 272–287. DOI: 10.51594/estj.v5i2.752

Anwar, S., Maulidiyah, D. R., Rusanti, E., & Mochlasin, M. (2024). Book review: Sustainable finance and ESG; risk, management, regulations and implications for financial institutions. *Rajagiri Management Journal*, *18*(1), 99–103. DOI: 10.1108/RAMJ-01-2024-246

Armiento, M., & Villa, A. (2025). 7. Energy transition and industrial competitiveness in the EU. In *Open Reports Series* (pp. 115–124). Open Book Publishers., DOI: 10.11647/obp.0499.07

Bai, Y., & Yang, X. (2016). The research on the economic effect of market-based environmental policy instruments. *Open Journal of Social Sciences*, *04*(04), 38–47. DOI: 10.4236/jss.2016.44006

Bárcena-Ruiz, J. C., & Garzón, M. B. (2022). Environmental policy instruments and ownership of firms. *Manchester School*, *90*(4), 385–408. DOI: 10.1111/manc.12412

Bianco, D. (2018). Environmental policy in an endogenous growth model with expanding variety. *Revue d'Économie Politique*, *127*(6), 1013–1028. DOI: 10.3917/redp.276.1013

Bohringer, C., & Lange, A. (2003). Economic implications of alternative allocation schemes for emission allowances. SSRN *Electronic Journal*. DOI: 10.2139/ssrn.423401

Bretschger, L. (2019). Malthus in the light of climate change. SSRN *Electronic Journal*. DOI: 10.2139/ssrn.3377220

Cui, B., Shui, Z., Yang, S., & Lei, T. (2022). Evolutionary game analysis of green technology innovation under the carbon emission trading mechanism. *Frontiers in Environmental Science, 10*, 997724. Advance online publication. DOI: 10.3389/fenvs.2022.997724

Deng, H., Li, C., & Wang, L. (2022). The impact of corporate innovation on environmental performance: The moderating effect of financing constraints and government subsidies. *Sustainability (Basel), 14*(18), 11530. DOI: 10.3390/su141811530

Eissa, Y., & Zaki, C. (2023). On GVC and innovation: The moderating role of policy. *Economia e Politica Industriale, 50*(1), 49–71. Advance online publication. DOI: 10.1007/s40812-022-00255-9

Ererdi, E., & Güneren Genç, E. (2025). Short-term costs and long-term benefits of environmental, Social, and governance performance on corporate credit ratings. *International Journal of Finance & Banking Studies (2147-4486), 14*(1), 90–97. DOI: 10.20525/ijfbs.v14i1.4014

Fan, H., & Liang, C. (2025). Effective government and regional technological innovation: Evidence from 284 cities in China. *Regulation & Governance, 19*(4), 1101–1121. DOI: 10.1111/rego.12649

Farooq, R. L., & Khoshnaw, A. Q. H. (2025). *The impact of financial independence on strategic decision- making: An analytical study of leaders' perspectives in public polytechnic universities of the Kurdistan Region*. Academic Journal of International University of Erbil., DOI: 10.63841/iue24550

Green, J. E., & Koebele, E. A. (2025). Coordinating school improvement: Understanding the impact of state implementation approach on coordination in multilevel governance systems. *The Review of Policy Research, 42*(2), 188–211. DOI: 10.1111/ropr.12612

Hourcade, J.-C., Pottier, A., & Etienne, E. (2012). The environment and directed technical change: Comment. SSRN *Electronic Journal*. DOI: 10.2139/ssrn.1991109

Huliselan, M. (2025). Environmental accounting and financial management: A strategic approach to corporate sustainability. *Journal of Economics and Management Scienties*, 164–170. DOI: 10.37034/jems.v7i3.106

Ivahnenko, I. S., Molodko, O. V., Shepeta, M. O., Pylypchuk, V. V., & Borodynia, V. V. (2025). The essence and evolution of organizational and managerial decisions in construction. *Building Production*, (80), 43–52. DOI: 10.36750/2524-2555.80.43-52

Listyarini, S., & Warlina, L. (2017). The development model of the policy alternatives in controlling air pollution in the Jakarta province, Indonesia. *International Journal of Environmental Sciences and Development*, *8*(7), 496–500. DOI: 10.18178/ijesd.2017.8.7.1003

Mathieu, E. (2023). Policy coherence versus regulatory governance. Electricity reforms in Algeria and Morocco. *Regulation & Governance*, *17*(3), 694–708. DOI: 10.1111/rego.12488

Maund, K., Gajendran, T., & Brewer, G. (2018). Key issues for implementation of environmental planning policy: Construction management practice. *Sustainability (Basel)*, *10*(7), 2156. DOI: 10.3390/su10072156

Mu, D., Ren, H., & Wang, C. (2021). A literature review of taxes in cross-border supply chain modeling: Themes, tax types and new trade-offs. *Journal of Theoretical and Applied Electronic Commerce Research*, *17*(1), 20–46. DOI: 10.3390/jtaer17010002

Patil, A., & Vonk, W. A. (2025). Stakeholder perspectives on EU regulatory frameworks: Navigating critical raw materials, battery innovation, and recycling challenges. *Open Research Europe*, *5*, 104. DOI: 10.12688/openreseurope.19634.1

Ravikumar, A. S., Kalandarov, A., Djumaniyazova, M., & Habib, M. (2025). A roadmap to a sustainable future. In *Advances in Computational Intelligence and Robotics* (pp. 267–302). IGI Global Scientific Publishing. DOI: 10.4018/979-8-3373-3017-4.ch010

Ravikumar, R. N., & Aarthi, S. (2025a). Climate data without borders. In *Cross-Border Cooperation in the Age of Climate Change* (pp. 61–90). IGI Global Scientific Publishing., DOI: 10.4018/979-8-3373-3972-6.ch003

Ravikumar, R. N., & Aarthi, S. (2025b). Green retrofitting of warehouses. In *Innovations in Green and Energy-Efficient Warehousing* (pp. 309–338). IGI Global Scientific Publishing., DOI: 10.4018/979-8-3373-3176-8.ch012

Ravikumar, R. N., & Aarthi, S. (2025c). Integrated cross-border renewable energy infrastructure for a green transition. In *Cross-Border Cooperation in the Age of Climate Change* (pp. 301–332). IGI Global Scientific Publishing., DOI: 10.4018/979-8-3373-3972-6.ch011

Ravikumar, R. N., Aarthi, S., Pardaev, J., & Shukla, P. (2025). Quantum computing for financial modelling. In *Quantum-Driven Financial Intelligence* (pp. 221–252). IGI Global Scientific Publishing., DOI: 10.4018/979-8-3373-2893-5.ch010

Ravikumar, & Aarthi, S. (2025). AI-driven climate resilience. In *Advances in Computational Intelligence and Robotics* (pp. 207–238). IGI Global Scientific Publishing. DOI: 10.4018/979-8-3373-5540-5.ch007

Sang, L. T., Ravikumar, R. N., Aarthi, S., & Ben, T. L. (2025). Optimizing sales and inventory performance using AI and business intelligence in POS environments. In *Advances in Computational Intelligence and Robotics* (pp. 259–290). IGI Global Scientific Publishing. DOI: 10.4018/979-8-3373-4392-1.ch011

Shafizadeh, H. (2024). Decision-making under uncertainty: How organizations adapt to environmental changes? *Journal of Resource Management and Decision Engineering*, *3*(1), 4–10. DOI: 10.61838/kman.jrmde.3.1.2

Shen, C. (2024). The impact of carbon emission trading system on ESG of agricultural enterprises: Evidence from 24 listed agricultural companies in China. *Transactions on Economics. Business and Management Research*, *5*, 46–58. DOI: 10.62051/ca4vcy22

Simpa, P., Solomon, N. O., Adenekan, O. A., & Obasi, S. C. (2024). Strategic implications of carbon pricing on global environmental sustainability and economic development: A conceptual framework. *International Journal of Advanced Economics*, *6*(5), 139–172. DOI: 10.51594/ijae.v6i5.1134

Steinebach, Y. (2022). Instrument choice, implementation structures, and the effectiveness of environmental policies: A cross-national analysis. *Regulation & Governance*, *16*(1), 225–242. DOI: 10.1111/rego.12297

Vitali, S., Tedeschi, G., & Gallegati, M. (2013). The impact of classes of innovators on technology, financial fragility, and economic growth. *Industrial and Corporate Change*, *22*(4), 1069–1091. DOI: 10.1093/icc/dtt024

von Malmborg, F. (2025). At the controls: Politics and policy entrepreneurs in EU policy to decarbonize maritime transport. *The Review of Policy Research*, *42*(5), 1243–1276. DOI: 10.1111/ropr.12609

Vongpatchim, P., Rangsungnoen, G., & Chainirun, P. (2025). Organizational management to achieve sustainable financial stability: A case study of the company in Thailand. *International Journal of Analysis and Applications*, *23*, 128. DOI: 10.28924/2291-8639-23-2025-128

Wang, D., Dong, L., & Mei, J. (2023). An advanced review of climate change mitigation policies in Germany, France, and the Netherlands. *Environmental Research Letters*, *18*(10), 103001. DOI: 10.1088/1748-9326/acf58f

Wang, R., Wijen, F., & Heugens, P. P. M. A. R. (2018). Government's green grip: Multifaceted state influence on corporate environmental actions in China. *Strategic Management Journal, 39*(2), 403–428. DOI: 10.1002/smj.2714

Wibowo, M., Setiawan, H., Dewianawati, D., Setiawan, E., & Judijanto, L. (2025). The role of ESG criteria in sustainable financial project scope management: A systematic literature review. *Jurnal Ilmiah Manajemen Kesatuan, 13*(6), 5115–5126. DOI: 10.37641/jimkes.v13i6.4048

Xiao, Z., Peng, H., & Pan, Z. (2022). Innovation, external technological environment and the total factor productivity of enterprises. *Accounting and Finance, 62*(1), 3–29. DOI: 10.1111/acfi.12779

Xie, S., & Wang, J. (2022). Evaluating the effect of China's carbon emission trading policy on energy efficiency of the construction industry based on a difference-in-differences method. *Advances in Civil Engineering, 2022*(1), 1–12. DOI: 10.1155/2022/6096435

Yin, X., Wang, D., Lu, J., & Liu, L. (2023). Does green credit policy promote corporate green innovation? Evidence from China. *Economic Change and Restructuring, 56*(5), 3187–3215. DOI: 10.1007/s10644-023-09521-9

Zarnic, Z., Varga, J., Labat, A., & Conte, A. (2010). What is the growth potential of green innovation? An assessment of EU climate policy options. SSRN *Electronic Journal*. DOI: 10.2139/ssrn.1728703

Zhang, G., & Bi, S. (2023). Inhibition or promotion: the impact of carbon emission trading on market structure: evidence from China. *Frontiers in Energy Research, 11*, 1238416. Advance online publication. DOI: 10.3389/fenrg.2023.1238416

Zhang, J., Tang, H., & Bao, M. (2023). Can environmental protection policies promote regional innovation efficiency: A difference-in-differences approach with continuous treatment. *Environmental Science and Pollution Research International, 30*(1), 1357–1373. DOI: 10.1007/s11356-022-22280-w

KEY TERMS AND DEFINITIONS

Climate-Related Financial Risk: Risks to financial stability arising from climate change impacts and transition to a low-carbon economy.

Environmental Policy: Government rules, incentives, and interventions designed to protect the environment and manage natural resources.

Financial Risk Reallocation: Changes in how financial markets assess and distribute risk due to environmental and climate-related policies.

Green Innovation: Development and adoption of technologies, processes, or products that reduce environmental impact.

Institutional Quality: The effectiveness of governance systems, including enforcement, transparency, and accountability.

Labor Market Transition: Movement of workers across sectors and occupations due to structural and technological change.

Market-Based Instruments: Policy tools such as taxes, tradable permits, and subsidies that use market signals to achieve environmental goals.

Multi-Level Governance: Coordination of policy across national, regional, and local levels of authority.

Policy Spillovers: Effects of environmental policies that extend beyond national borders through trade, investment, and global value chains.

Policy Stringency: The strictness and intensity of environmental regulations and standards imposed on economic activities.

Stranded Assets: Assets that lose value or become obsolete due to environmental regulation or technological change.

Structural Economic Change: Long-term shifts in the composition of an economy across sectors, technologies, and production systems.

Chapter 3
Carbon Pricing and Capital Reallocation:
A Comparative Case Study of Global Emissions Trading Systems and Financial Markets

K. Balaji
http://orcid.org/0000-0002-3065-3294
Christ University, Bengaluru, India

ABSTRACT

Carbon pricing has emerged as a central policy instrument for aligning financial markets with climate objectives. Emissions trading systems (ETS) increasingly act not only as environmental tools but also as powerful financial signals shaping global investment behavior. This chapter investigates how carbon pricing mechanisms influence capital reallocation in global financial markets through a comparative case study of major emissions trading systems, including the European Union Emissions Trading System (EU ETS), China's National ETS, and the California Cap-and-Trade Program. Methodologically, the chapter adopts a mixed-methods case study design integrating quantitative financial market analysis with institutional and policy review. Secondary data are drawn from carbon allowance markets, stock exchanges, sectoral investment flows, and ESG disclosures. The findings indicate that higher and more credible carbon prices are associated with a systematic reallocation of capital away from carbon-intensive assets toward renewable energy, clean technology, and low-carbon infrastructure.

DOI: 10.4018/979-8-3373-8998-1.ch003

1. INTRODUCTION

Climate change has emerged as one of the most significant systemic risks confronting the global economy, with far-reaching implications for production systems, financial markets, and long-term growth trajectories. In response, governments have increasingly adopted carbon pricing instruments to internalize the environmental externalities associated with greenhouse gas emissions and to align market incentives with climate mitigation objectives. Carbon pricing implemented through carbon taxes or emissions trading systems (ETS) represents a shift from purely regulatory approaches toward market-based environmental governance. Over the past two decades, these mechanisms have expanded rapidly across developed and emerging economies, reflecting growing recognition that climate policy is inseparable from economic and financial policy.

Emissions trading systems have consequently evolved beyond their original role as compliance mechanisms to become sophisticated economic and financial instruments. Mature markets such as the European Union Emissions Trading System (EU ETS) now exhibit features similar to commodity and financial derivatives markets, including futures trading, risk hedging, and speculative participation (Balaji, K. & PS.Rao, 2024). Newer systems, including China's national ETS and subnational schemes such as California's cap-and-trade program, further illustrate the growing integration of carbon pricing into broader financial architectures. This evolution has intensified the interaction between climate policy, corporate strategy, and financial market behaviour. Accordingly, this chapter aims to examine carbon pricing as a financial signal and to assess its effectiveness in redirecting capital through a comparative case analysis of major global emissions trading systems and associated financial market responses (Song et al., 2019). Despite the rapid expansion of carbon pricing regimes, existing scholarship has largely examined emissions trading systems (ETS) in isolation, focusing either on environmental effectiveness or short-term asset price responses without systematically analyzing how institutional design differences shape cross-market capital reallocation dynamics.

1.1. Research Gap and Rationale for Comparative Analysis

This chapter addresses that gap by advancing a comparative financial perspective that treats carbon pricing as a transmission mechanism linking regulatory credibility, market structure, and investor behaviour across jurisdictions. By comparing mature, emerging, and subnational ETS frameworks, the analysis reveals how variations in policy stability, market depth, and financial integration condition the magnitude and speed of asset repricing and capital shifts. Such cross-case evaluation uncovers structural patterns in climate–finance interaction that single-case studies cannot detect, particularly regarding the role of institutional design in amplifying or dampening investment reallocation. In doing so, the chapter contributes new insight into carbon pricing as a differentiated financial governance instrument rather than a uniform environmental policy tool.

2. THEORETICAL AND CONCEPTUAL FOUNDATIONS

Carbon pricing is fundamentally grounded in environmental economic theory, particularly the Pigouvian framework, which advocates pricing negative externalities to correct market failures. By attaching a monetary cost to greenhouse gas emissions, carbon pricing mechanisms transform environmental harm into a quantifiable economic variable that directly enters firms' production decisions, cost structures, and investment appraisals. In this sense, carbon prices operate not only as regulatory constraints but also as powerful economic and financial signals. Rising and credible carbon prices convey forward-looking information about regulatory stringency, transition risks, and long-term policy commitments, thereby influencing corporate strategies, investor expectations, and the relative attractiveness of assets across sector (Nelsons et al., 2012).

Capital reallocation theory provides an essential lens for understanding how such signals translate into shifts in investment flows. From a financial economics perspective, capital is continuously reallocated toward assets offering superior risk-adjusted returns. Climate policies alter this calculus by reshaping both expected cash flows and perceived risks (Balaji, K. 2023).. Carbon-intensive firms face higher operating costs, regulatory uncertainty, and potential asset stranding, leading to downward revisions in profitability expectations and upward adjustments in required rates of return (Dutta & Mitra, 2017).

This dynamic directly engages debates surrounding the Efficient Market Hypothesis (EMH). Under the semi-strong form of EMH, publicly available information—including climate policy announcements and carbon price movements should be rapidly incorporated into asset prices (Tu et al., 2019). The framework thus connects carbon pricing regimes, financial market responses, and investment flows, providing the analytical foundation for the comparative case analyses that follow(He & Ye, 2019; Liu et al., 2020).

2.1. Conceptual Framework Linking Carbon Prices, Risk Transmission, and Investment Flows

The conceptual framework presented in Figure 1 is grounded in the theoretical integration of environmental economics and climate-aware finance. It is developed to illustrate how carbon pricing mechanisms operate not merely as environmental regulatory tools, but as financial signals that reshape firm behaviour, investor expectations, and market-level risk perceptions. Prior to the transmission of these signals, financial markets are often characterized by partial pricing of climate-related risks, informational asymmetries, and continued capital concentration in carbon-intensive sectors. In this pre-intervention phase, asset valuations largely reflect conventional financial metrics, with limited systematic incorporation of transition risks, regulatory tightening, or long-term decarbonization pathways. The framework therefore begins with carbon pricing signals—such as allowance price movements, regulatory announcements, and policy credibility as the primary exogenous drivers capable of altering the informational environment of financial markets(Qiang et al., 2025).

Figure 1. Conceptual Framework Linking Carbon Prices, Risk Transmission, and Investment Flows

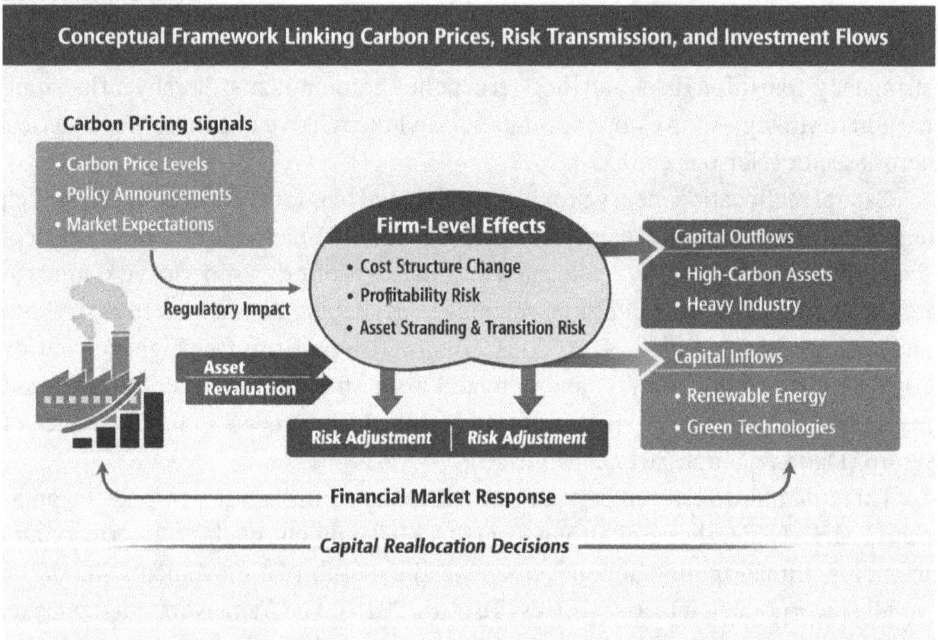

Source: Review of literature. Compiled by: Researcher.

As illustrated in Figure 1, carbon pricing signals are transmitted through regulatory and market channels to generate firm-level effects, including changes in cost structures, profitability expectations, and exposure to asset-stranding risks. These firm-level adjustments initiate a broader risk transmission process, reflected in asset revaluation, shifts in equity and credit risk premia, and evolving investor sentiment. Financial markets respond by repricing carbon-intensive and low-carbon assets, thereby activating capital reallocation mechanisms (Balaji, K. 2025d). The framework demonstrates how these processes result in capital outflows from high-emission sectors and capital inflows toward renewable energy, clean technologies, and sustainable infrastructure. This post-transmission phase highlights the emergence of climate-aware investment behaviour, where carbon prices influence portfolio construction, financing conditions, and strategic investment decisions (Tost et al., 2020).

2.2. Transmission Mechanism: From Carbon Price Signals to Capital Reallocation

Rising carbon prices operate through a clear economic and financial transmission mechanism rather than merely correlating with investment shifts. When carbon prices increase, regulated firms face higher compliance costs, either through purchasing additional allowances or investing in emissions-reduction technologies. These higher expected operating costs reduce projected future cash flows for carbon-intensive firms, leading investors to revise profitability forecasts downward. As a result, equity valuations decline, credit spreads widen, and the cost of capital rises for high-emission sectors. Simultaneously, low-carbon firms experience improved relative competitiveness, stronger growth expectations, and enhanced investor confidence, which lowers their cost of capital and increases access to financing. Financial institutions and asset managers, seeking superior risk-adjusted returns, rebalance portfolios away from carbon-intensive assets and toward renewable energy, clean technologies, and transition-aligned infrastructure. Over time, these pricing, valuation, and portfolio adjustments translate into observable capital reallocation from high-carbon to low-carbon sectors. Thus, carbon pricing influences investment not merely through regulatory pressure, but through systematic asset repricing, risk premium adjustments, and cost-of-capital differentials that reshape financial decision-making.

3. REVIEW OF CONTEMPORARY LITERATURE

3.1 Carbon Markets and Asset Price Responses

The early literature on carbon markets primarily focused on the efficiency and environmental effectiveness of emissions trading systems, particularly following the launch of the European Union Emissions Trading System (EU ETS) in 2005. Foundational economic analyses highlighted carbon trading as a cost-effective mechanism for emissions reduction and market-based environmental governance (Leroutier, 2022). As carbon markets matured, research attention increasingly shifted toward financial market responses. Studies began examining how carbon price movements affect stock returns, volatility, and sectoral performance, especially in energy-intensive industries. Empirical evidence from European markets suggests that carbon prices are systematically incorporated into equity valuations, with higher carbon costs negatively affecting the stock performance of utilities, cement, steel, and aviation sectors, while positively influencing renewable and clean technology firms(Li et al., 2021). Studies by (Yuan et al., 2018) demonstrate that the tightening of EU ETS rules and allowance scarcity led to significant revaluation of electricity producers and carbon-intensive firms (Balaji, K. 2025b).. More recent research incorporating global datasets finds that carbon pricing regimes influence cross-border capital flows and market risk premia, suggesting that emissions trading systems are increasingly embedded within global financial architectures (Xu et al., 2023).

3.2 Carbon Risk, Stranded Assets, and Firm Valuation

A parallel and rapidly expanding strand of literature conceptualises climate change as a source of systemic financial risk. Early warnings regarding "stranded assets" emphasised that fossil fuel reserves, carbon-intensive infrastructure, and related capital stock could lose economic value under stringent climate policies (Hall et al., 2016). This perspective catalysed extensive academic inquiry into the relationship between carbon exposure and firm valuation. Studies consistently report that firms with higher carbon intensity face valuation discounts, elevated cost of capital, and increased downside risk, reflecting markets' gradual incorporation of transition risks (Mitridati et al., 2021).

More recent research integrates climate risk into asset pricing models, demonstrating that carbon emissions act as a priced risk factor in equity markets (Gugler et al., 2021). Empirical evidence further shows that climate policy uncertainty and carbon price volatility significantly influence firm profitability expectations and credit conditions (Chai et al., 2025). These findings reinforce the view that carbon pricing does not merely affect operating costs but fundamentally reshapes how markets assess long-term corporate viability, thereby accelerating capital withdrawal from carbon-intensive business models (Balaji, K. 2025c).

3.3 ESG Integration, Green Finance, and Investor Behaviour

Since the mid-2000s, the rise of Environmental, Social, and Governance (ESG) investing has transformed the interface between sustainability and financial markets. Early contributions emphasized the ethical and reputational motivations behind socially responsible investing (SRI) (Aggarwal et al., 2009). Over time, ESG integration has evolved into a financially motivated strategy aimed at managing long-term risks and capturing sustainability-driven growth opportunities (Ohler et al., 2020).

Institutional investors reallocate portfolios toward low-carbon assets, renewable energy, and green bonds, particularly following climate policy announcements and carbon market reforms (Foramitti et al., 2021). The rapid expansion of green finance instruments—green bonds, transition bonds, sustainability-linked loans, and climate funds—further reflects the growing financialization of climate governance (Zhang et al., 2020). Research also indicates that firms with credible decarbonization strategies benefit from improved access to capital, lower financing costs, and enhanced investor confidence (Vrontisi et al., 2020).

3.4 Research Gaps and the Need for a Comparative Case Approach

Despite the richness of this literature, several gaps persist. First, much of the empirical evidence remains geographically concentrated on the EU ETS, limiting the generalizability of findings to emerging carbon markets such as China's national ETS or subnational schemes like California's cap-and-trade system (Deng et al., 2021). Second, existing studies often examine isolated financial indicators—stock returns, volatility, or emissions exposure without systematically integrating institutional design, market maturity, and financial transmission mechanisms. Third, there is limited comparative research exploring how differences in regulatory credibility, market depth, and financial development shape the strength and direction of capital reallocation under carbon pricing regimes. Furthermore, while carbon risk and ESG finance are widely studied, their interaction with concrete carbon pricing mechanisms remains underexplored.

4. GLOBAL EMISSIONS TRADING SYSTEMS: INSTITUTIONAL OVERVIEW

Emissions trading systems (ETS) represent the most prominent market-based instruments for operationalizing carbon pricing across jurisdictions. This section reviews three major ETS frameworks the European Union Emissions Trading System, China's National Emissions Trading Scheme, and the California Cap-and-Trade Program to establish the institutional context for the subsequent comparative financial market analysis(Zhang & Liu, 2019).

The selection of the European Union Emissions Trading System (EU ETS), China's National ETS, and California's Cap-and-Trade Program is guided by analytical, institutional, and financial relevance criteria rather than geographic convenience.

First, these systems represent three distinct models of carbon market governance: a mature supranational market-based system (EU ETS), a large-scale emerging hybrid system embedded within state-directed financial architecture (China ETS), and a subnational yet highly integrated regulatory model operating within advanced capital markets (California). Together, they capture variation in regulatory credibility, market depth, sectoral coverage, and financial integration, key variables shaping capital reallocation dynamics. Second, each case is embedded in financially significant jurisdictions with developed equity, bond, and energy markets, allowing observation of meaningful asset repricing and investment responses. Third, these systems differ in price levels, stability mechanisms, allocation rules, and institutional maturity, making them analytically comparable while enabling structured contrast. Other ETSs were not selected because they either remain in early developmental stages with limited financial depth, have narrow sectoral coverage, or lack sufficient market liquidity to generate observable capital market transmission effects. The chosen cases therefore, provide maximum variation across governance models while maintaining comparability in economic scale and financial relevance, strengthening the robustness of the comparative analysis.

4.1 European Union Emissions Trading System (EU ETS)

4.1.1 Structure and Regulatory Framework

The European Union Emissions Trading System (EU ETS), launched in 2005, represents the world's largest and most established carbon market. It operates under a cap-and-trade mechanism, where a cap is placed on total greenhouse gas emissions from covered sectors, and emission allowances are allocated or auctioned to participating entities. The system functions in multi-phase regulatory cycles, each introducing policy refinements to improve efficiency and emission reduction outcomes. The EU ETS covers power generation, manufacturing industries, aviation, and other energy-intensive sectors across member states. The regulatory framework is supported by strict monitoring, reporting, and verification standards, ensuring transparency and accountability. Over time, the system has transitioned from free allocation of allowances toward auction-based allocation to strengthen market efficiency and reduce excessive allowance supply.

4.1.2 Carbon Price Trends and Market Volatility

Carbon prices within the EU ETS have experienced considerable fluctuations since its inception. Initial phases witnessed low carbon prices due to oversupply of allowances and weak regulatory design. However, structural reforms, including the introduction of the Market Stability Reserve (MSR), have significantly improved price stability by adjusting allowance supply based on market conditions. In recent years, carbon prices have shown upward trends, reflecting stronger regulatory commitments and growing investor interest in climate-related assets. Despite improvements, the market remains sensitive to macroeconomic factors, energy price fluctuations, and policy announcements, which continue to influence carbon price volatility(Lee et al., 2020).

4.1.3 Sectoral Coverage and Emission Reduction Performance

The EU ETS covers a wide range of sectors, including electricity generation, heavy industries such as cement, steel, and chemicals, and intra-European aviation. The system has contributed substantially to emission reductions, particularly in the power sector, by incentivizing the transition from coal-based energy production to renewable energy sources. Empirical evidence indicates that regulated firms have increasingly adopted energy-efficient technologies and renewable energy investments to comply with emission caps. The system's sectoral coverage expansion has strengthened its overall environmental effectiveness and demonstrated measurable progress toward the European Union's climate targets.

4.1.4 Financial Market Integration and Investment Implications

The EU ETS has significantly influenced financial markets by creating a mature carbon trading ecosystem. Carbon allowances are now traded as financial assets through derivatives markets, including futures and options, facilitating risk management and investment diversification. The system has encouraged institutional investors to shift capital toward low-carbon technologies, renewable energy projects, and green financial instruments such as green bonds. Furthermore, the EU ETS has played a critical role in integrating climate risks into corporate financial decision-making, promoting long-term sustainable investment strategies.

4.2 China's National Emissions Trading System

4.2.1 Evolution from Pilot Programs to National Market

China's carbon market has evolved from regional pilot emissions trading programs introduced in 2013 to a national ETS launched in 2021. The pilot programs were implemented across major provinces and cities to test market design, regulatory mechanisms, and monitoring frameworks. Lessons learned from these pilots facilitated the development of a centralized national carbon trading system. China's ETS currently focuses primarily on the power generation sector, reflecting the country's high reliance on coal-based energy and its commitment to reducing carbon intensity.

4.2.2 Industrial Coverage Expansion

While the initial phase of China's ETS targets the power sector, the government has outlined plans to expand coverage to additional energy-intensive industries such as steel, cement, petrochemicals, and aviation. The gradual expansion strategy allows policymakers to strengthen regulatory infrastructure and ensure accurate emissions monitoring before incorporating additional sectors. The expansion of industrial coverage is expected to enhance market liquidity and improve emission reduction outcomes in the long term.

4.2.3 Capital Allocation and Innovation Effects

China's carbon market has begun influencing corporate capital allocation decisions, encouraging firms to invest in cleaner production technologies and renewable energy solutions. Carbon pricing signals have incentivized companies to adopt energy-efficient technologies, improve operational efficiency, and invest in research and development for low-carbon innovation. The ETS also supports China's broader industrial modernization goals by promoting sustainable economic transformation and reducing dependence on fossil fuel-intensive production processes.

4.2.4 Policy and Implementation Challenges

Despite significant progress, China's ETS faces challenges related to data transparency, limited sectoral coverage, and relatively low carbon price levels. Variations in regulatory enforcement across provinces and limited availability of reliable emissions data create monitoring and compliance difficulties. Additionally, ensuring market liquidity and maintaining investor confidence remain critical policy priorities. Strengthening verification mechanisms and expanding sectoral participation are essential for improving the effectiveness of China's carbon pricing system.

4.3 North American Carbon Markets

4.3.1 California Cap-and-Trade Program

The California Cap-and-Trade Program, introduced in 2013, represents one of the most comprehensive carbon markets in North America. The program covers power plants, industrial facilities, and transportation fuels, making it one of the broadest sectoral carbon pricing initiatives globally. California employs a combination of allowance auctions and free allocation to balance environmental objectives with economic competitiveness. The program has generated substantial revenue, which is reinvested into climate mitigation projects, renewable energy development, and environmental justice initiatives.

4.3.2 Regional Greenhouse Gas Initiative (RGGI)

The Regional Greenhouse Gas Initiative (RGGI) is a cooperative carbon trading program involving several north-eastern U.S. states, primarily targeting emissions from the power sector. RGGI focuses on reducing carbon emissions through a regional cap-and-trade mechanism supported by regular allowance auctions. The program has achieved notable emission reductions while generating revenue for energy efficiency programs and renewable energy investments. RGGI demonstrates the effectiveness of regional collaboration in climate policy implementation.

4.3.3 Chicago Climate Exchange (Historical Perspective)

The Chicago Climate Exchange (CCX), established in 2003, was one of the first voluntary carbon trading platforms in North America. Although the exchange ceased operations due to limited regulatory support and insufficient market demand, it played a significant role in pioneering carbon trading mechanisms and raising awareness about market-based climate solutions. The CCX provided valuable insights into voluntary carbon market dynamics and contributed to the development of future compliance-based carbon trading systems.

4.3.4 Cross-Border Linkages and Financial Integration

North American carbon markets have demonstrated increasing cross-border collaboration, particularly through the linkage between California's carbon market and Quebec's cap-and-trade system. These linkages enhance market liquidity, reduce compliance costs, and promote regulatory harmonization. Financial integration across carbon markets also facilitates the development of carbon derivatives and climate-related investment products, strengthening the role of financial institutions in supporting climate transition.

4.4 Emerging Carbon Markets

4.4.1. India's Carbon Credit Market Development

India has been progressively developing its carbon market infrastructure through initiatives such as the Perform, Achieve, and Trade (PAT) scheme and voluntary carbon credit trading mechanisms. The government is working toward establishing a comprehensive domestic carbon trading framework aligned with national climate commitments. India's carbon market development focuses on improving energy efficiency, promoting renewable energy adoption, and enhancing corporate sustainability practices. However, challenges related to regulatory clarity, market liquidity, and institutional capacity remain significant(Aslam et al., 2023).

4.4.2. South Korea and Other Asian ETS Frameworks

South Korea launched its national emissions trading system in 2015, covering major industrial sectors and power generation facilities. The system has contributed to emission reductions and stimulated corporate investments in energy-efficient technologies. Other Asian economies, including Japan and Singapore, have introduced pilot carbon pricing initiatives and voluntary carbon trading mechanisms. These emerging markets highlight the growing regional commitment to market-based climate policies and sustainable economic development.

4.4.3. Latin American Carbon Trading Initiatives

Several Latin American countries, including Mexico, Chile, and Brazil, have initiated carbon pricing policies through pilot emissions trading systems and carbon tax frameworks. These initiatives aim to reduce greenhouse gas emissions while promoting sustainable industrial transformation. Latin American carbon markets are still in developmental stages, with policymakers focusing on building regulatory infrastructure, improving emissions monitoring systems, and attracting international climate finance investments.

5. RESEARCH METHODOLOGY

The study adopts a comparative case study methodology grounded in a mixed-methods research design. Institutionally, it undertakes a structured analysis of the regulatory architecture, sectoral coverage, and market evolution of the selected emissions trading systems. Empirically, the study integrates secondary data from carbon markets, equity and bond markets, sectoral investment reports, and climate finance databases. Quantitative analytical tools include event study analysis to capture market reactions to regulatory milestones, panel regression techniques to estimate carbon exposure effects on firm valuation, carbon-beta estimation to assess systematic climate risk, and sectoral capital flow analysis to trace investment shifts. Qualitative policy analysis complements the financial evidence by examining governance frameworks, disclosure regimes, and green finance ecosystems. This triangulated approach enhances analytical robustness and allows the study to capture both market behaviour and institutional drivers of capital reallocation.

5.1. Case analysis of global financial markets.

5.1.1. Case Analysis I: EU ETS and Financial Market Responses

The European Union Emissions Trading System (EU ETS) is the largest and most mature carbon market globally, covering an extensive array of industrial sectors including power generation, manufacturing, and aviation. Since its launch in 2005, the EU ETS has become the central compliance carbon pricing mechanism in Europe and a benchmark for designing emissions trading systems worldwide. Over time, the system has undergone successive reforms aimed at strengthening its environmental integrity and market performance, such as tighter emissions caps, centralized auctioning of allowances, and the introduction of the Market Stability Reserve (MSR) to address allowance oversupply. These reforms helped the benchmark EU carbon price escalate from under €25 per tonne of CO_2 in the early 2010s to more than €88 per tonne in January 2026, reaching an all-time peak above €105 per tonne in early 2023 before stabilizing at high levels in subsequent years . The evolution of carbon prices has had measurable impacts on European financial markets. Elevated and credible carbon prices increase compliance costs for high-emission firms, which are increasingly priced into equity valuations and reflected in sectoral risk premia.

Capital flows have shifted increasingly toward deployments in low-carbon infrastructure under the influence of EU ETS price signals. Investors and asset managers incorporate carbon price trajectories into long-term discount rates and cost of capital assumptions for energy projects. Rising EU carbon prices correlate with increased financing for renewable generation capacity, grid upgrades, energy storage systems, and low-carbon industrial conversions. These investment patterns reflect the financialization of carbon pricing: EUAs (European Union Allowances) are now treated as integral risk factors in project finance, corporate capital budgeting, and climate stress testing scenarios.

Investor behaviour within and beyond Europe has been reshaped by both carbon pricing and broader climate policy frameworks. Institutional investors increasingly embed EU ETS carbon prices into quantitative ESG screens, climate scenario analyses, and portfolio construction strategies. The proliferation of green bonds, sustainability-linked loans, and climate transition funds in Europe demonstrates the interplay between carbon pricing and investment products aimed at supporting the energy transition. In addition, climate disclosure mandates in the EU have enhanced transparency around carbon exposure, making carbon risk a more salient consideration for global investment decision-makers.

Taken together, the EU ETS underscores how a well-designed carbon market serves not only as a compliance tool but also as a financial signal that affects asset pricing, capital allocation, and investor choices — thus supporting a broader transition toward decarbonized economic pathways.

5.1.2. Case Analysis II: China ETS and Emerging Market Capital Dynamics

China's National Emissions Trading Scheme (ETS), formally launched in 2021, is currently the largest emissions trading system worldwide in terms of emissions coverage. It covers several thousand companies across key sectors, including power generation, steel, cement, and aluminium, reflecting China's significant contribution to global greenhouse gas emissions. According to institutional data, China's ETS encompasses an estimated 8 billion tonnes of CO_2 — accounting for more than 60% of the country's total emissions. Its allowance trading volumes and carbon prices, while rising from early low levels, have remained substantially below those in the EU ETS; recent price indices show Chinese carbon allowances around 66.86 yuan (~USD 9.40) per tonne in late 2025, indicating emerging but modest price discovery.

The institutional context of China's ETS reflects the country's hybrid governance model, where emissions trading mechanisms function alongside broader industrial and strategic planning. Carbon pricing in China operates in concert with five-year socio-economic plans, centrally managed climate targets, and industrial policies that seek to balance economic growth with environmental sustainability. This framework underpins the policy credibility of China's ETS even though carbon prices remain lower than in more mature markets. The ongoing expansion of sectoral coverage, from the power sector to industries such as petrochemicals and aviation, signals the state's intent to deepen market functionality and long-term emissions constraints. Market reactions and risk transmission under the China ETS exhibit distinct characteristics. Allowance prices, though low relative to EU levels, still influence investor expectations concerning future compliance costs, particularly in sectors with high carbon intensity.

Sectoral heterogeneity within China's ETS is significant. Renewable energy, electric vehicle manufacturing, battery technology, and related clean industries have witnessed accelerated capital inflows, driven by both carbon policy and explicit state incentives such as preferential financing and subsidised credit facilities. Conversely, traditional coal producers and energy-intensive manufacturing firms face tighter financing conditions and increased scrutiny from lenders due to heightened perceived transition risk. Moreover, China's major state-owned enterprises (SOEs) act as key intermediaries between climate policy and financial markets, often aligning corporate strategies with national decarbonization directives and influencing broader capital allocation trends.

Financial intermediation in China is evolving to support the carbon market's growth. Banks and state-affiliated financial institutions increasingly emphasise green finance instruments, such as green bonds and sustainability-linked loans, as vehicles for channelling investment to low-carbon sectors. These financial developments, combined with requirements for enhanced corporate climate disclosure, are gradually aligning investor behaviour with environmental policy signals. China's ETS thus represents an emerging model where regulated carbon markets interact with state-led financial mechanisms to guide capital toward strategic decarbonization objectives.

5.1.3. Case Analysis III: California Cap-and-Trade and North American Markets

The California Cap-and-Trade Program, implemented in 2013 and integral to the state's broader climate strategy, is one of the most comprehensive subnational carbon pricing systems in the world. Designed to cap greenhouse gas emissions across major economic sectors, the program functions as part of California's "Cap-and-Invest" framework, linking carbon pricing with complementary energy, transportation, and climate policies that reinforce decarbonization incentives. Carbon allowance prices in the California market have generally averaged around USD 30 per tonne, reflecting regulatory design choices and linkage with external markets such as Quebec's system.

A defining feature of the California market is its integration with energy and commodity markets. Carbon allowance costs influence electricity generation economics, fuel pricing decisions, and long-term investments in low-carbon energy sources. Utilities and industrial emitters incorporate cap-and-trade allowance prices into resource planning models and forward cost expectations, which in turn affect asset valuations, risk assessments, and financial disclosures. These dynamics reinforce the notion that carbon pricing extends beyond compliance costs to influence broader energy market behaviour.

Firm-level responses to California's carbon pricing regime demonstrate differentiated cost of capital effects. Companies with credible transition plans, investments in renewables, and operational strategies aligned with emissions reduction targets tend to experience more favourable financing conditions and investor sentiment. In contrast, firms heavily reliant on fossil fuel inputs or with limited decarbonization pathways face elevated compliance costs, investor scrutiny, and higher perceived risk premiums. This differentiation is reflected in corporate bond spreads, equity returns, and credit conditions, particularly for entities operating in emissions-intensive sectors.

Institutional investors play an outsized role in shaping the capital allocation effects of California's cap-and-trade program. Large pension funds, asset managers, and insurance entities with significant exposure to North American markets increasingly incorporate climate risk metrics, carbon price expectations, and regulatory scenarios into portfolio decisions. Regulatory requirements for enhanced climate risk disclosure in California have further heightened transparency around carbon exposure, enabling more granular risk assessment and adaptive investment strategies. These developments illustrate how carbon pricing, when embedded within robust governance and disclosure frameworks, can influence investor behaviour and foster climate–finance linkages even at a subnational level.

California's Cap-and-Trade Program thus underscores the importance of policy design and market integration in shaping the impacts of carbon prices. Its experience exhibits how allowance prices, even when lower than in major global markets like the EU ETS, can influence financial conditions, capital flows, and strategic investment decisions within a regionally significant economic system.

5.2.Cross-Case Comparative Discussion

5.2.1. Regulatory Credibility and Capital Responsiveness

Emissions trading system (ETS) design features influence financial markets through identifiable transmission mechanisms rather than operating as neutral regulatory details. Price floors and market stability mechanisms enhance carbon price predictability by limiting extreme volatility and allowance oversupply, thereby strengthening investor expectations about future regulatory stringency. Greater price stability allows financial markets to incorporate forward-looking carbon costs into discounted cash flow models, risk premia, and long-term valuation frameworks. Similarly, auction-based allocation increases direct compliance costs and accelerates cost-of-capital adjustments for carbon-intensive firms, while extensive sectoral coverage broadens systemic exposure to carbon risk across asset classes. In contrast, generous free allocation or narrow coverage can dampen immediate financial pressure and slow asset repricing. Thus, regulatory design choices shape not only environmental effectiveness but also the speed, magnitude, and breadth of capital reallocation across financial markets.

Across the three carbon pricing systems, regulatory credibility emerges as a decisive factor influencing financial market responsiveness and capital allocation behaviour. The European Union Emissions Trading System (EU ETS) demonstrates the highest degree of regulatory credibility due to its long operational history, progressively tightening emission caps, centralized auction mechanisms, and corrective instruments such as the Market Stability Reserve. These institutional safeguards have created predictable long-term carbon price signals, enabling investors to internalize transition risks and incorporate carbon costs into corporate valuation and capital budgeting decisions. As a result, European financial markets show strong responsiveness, with high-emission sectors facing valuation discounts and low-carbon sectors attracting sustained investment inflows.

China's ETS exhibits a different form of credibility rooted in policy consistency rather than market maturity. While price discovery remains relatively limited, China's carbon market benefits from strong state-backed climate commitments, centralized industrial planning, and integration with green credit policies. This governance structure fosters investor confidence in long-term emissions reduction trajectories, even though short-term carbon price signals remain weaker compared with the EU ETS. Capital responsiveness in China is therefore influenced by regulatory expectations and state incentives rather than purely market-driven price mechanisms.

In contrast, California's Cap-and-Trade Program illustrates credibility at a subnational level supported by regulatory transparency, strong enforcement mechanisms, and integration with broader climate and energy policies. Although its carbon price levels are lower than those of the EU ETS, the consistency of California's climate legislation and disclosure mandates has created a stable investment environment. Financial markets respond through differentiated financing conditions for firms depending on their carbon transition strategies, indicating that regulatory reliability, rather than price magnitude alone, shapes investor reactions.

5.2.2. Differences Between Developed and Emerging Carbon Markets

A clear distinction emerges between developed carbon markets such as the EU ETS and California Cap-and-Trade, and emerging markets like China's ETS in terms of institutional maturity, market efficiency, and investor integration. Developed carbon markets typically operate within advanced financial ecosystems characterized by sophisticated derivative instruments, active secondary trading, and extensive investor participation. The EU ETS exemplifies this maturity through deep liquidity, diverse carbon-linked financial products, and well-developed price discovery mechanisms.

Similarly, California's market benefits from strong institutional investor engagement and integration with regional energy and commodity markets.

Emerging markets, as illustrated by China's ETS, prioritize policy alignment and gradual institutional development over immediate financial market sophistication. China's market is characterized by strong administrative oversight, phased sectoral expansion, and limited speculative participation. Carbon price levels remain comparatively low, reflecting cautious regulatory calibration aimed at balancing environmental goals with economic growth. While financial depth remains limited, emerging carbon markets often demonstrate stronger policy-driven capital redirection through state-controlled financial institutions and targeted green financing incentives.

These structural differences suggest that developed markets rely primarily on decentralised market forces to transmit carbon price signals, whereas emerging markets rely more heavily on centralised policy coordination and directed capital flows to achieve decarbonization objectives (Balaji, K. 2025a).

5.2.3. Financial Depth, Volatility, and Transmission Mechanisms

Financial depth and volatility differ significantly across the three carbon pricing systems, influencing how carbon price signals are transmitted into financial markets. The EU ETS displays high financial depth characterised by robust allowance trading volumes, extensive derivative markets, and significant investor participation. This depth enhances price discovery but also introduces greater short-term volatility due to speculative trading and macroeconomic sensitivities. Carbon price fluctuations in the EU ETS rapidly transmit into equity markets, bond pricing, and corporate financing costs, reflecting strong integration between carbon and financial markets.

China's ETS demonstrates comparatively lower volatility and shallower financial depth. Limited derivative activity, restricted market participation, and strong regulatory control contribute to relatively stable but less informative carbon price signals. Transmission mechanisms in China operate primarily through policy expectations, green credit frameworks, and state-directed investment strategies rather than through purely market-based financial channels. Consequently, carbon pricing impacts firm valuations more indirectly through regulatory risk perception and long-term industrial transformation policies.

California's market occupies an intermediate position between the EU and China. While it exhibits moderate financial depth, its integration with electricity markets, fuel pricing, and regional energy planning creates strong cross-sector transmission mechanisms. Carbon price signals influence utility investment decisions, infrastructure financing, and corporate cost structures, demonstrating how sectoral integration can amplify financial transmission even in markets with moderate allowance price levels.

5.2.4. Carbon Pricing as a Catalyst for Sustainable Finance

Across all three case studies, carbon pricing functions as a powerful catalyst for the expansion of sustainable finance, albeit through different institutional pathways. The EU ETS has stimulated substantial growth in climate-aligned financial instruments, including green bonds, sustainability-linked loans, and transition funds. By providing a measurable and credible carbon cost benchmark, the EU ETS enables investors to quantify climate risks, incorporate carbon scenarios into financial modelling, and channel capital toward renewable energy, energy storage, and low-carbon industrial technologies.

China's ETS supports sustainable finance through state-led financial intermediation and policy-driven green investment frameworks. The integration of carbon pricing with green credit guidelines, preferential financing schemes, and state-supported infrastructure investment has accelerated capital flows toward renewable energy, electric mobility, and advanced battery technologies. In this model, carbon pricing complements broader industrial transformation strategies rather than functioning as the sole driver of sustainable finance.

California's Cap-and-Trade Program demonstrates how carbon pricing can catalyze sustainable finance within regional financial ecosystems. Strong climate disclosure requirements and institutional investor engagement have encouraged the incorporation of carbon metrics into portfolio management and corporate financing strategies. The Cap-and-Invest design further channels carbon revenues into clean energy and climate resilience projects, reinforcing the linkage between carbon pricing and sustainable infrastructure development.

5.2.5. Comparative Insights

The comparative analysis reveals that while carbon pricing mechanisms operate under diverse institutional arrangements, they consistently influence financial market behaviour, asset pricing, and capital allocation. Mature market-based systems such as the EU ETS emphasise strong price discovery and investor-driven capital flows. Hybrid governance models like China's ETS rely more on policy coordination and state-guided financial channels. Subnational systems such as California's Cap-and-Trade illustrate how regulatory integration and disclosure frameworks can generate significant financial impacts even with moderate carbon price levels.

Collectively, these cases demonstrate that carbon pricing has evolved beyond environmental regulation to become a central financial signal shaping sustainable investment strategies, corporate risk management practices, and global capital reallocation toward low-carbon economic pathways.

Table 1. Comparative Summary of ETS Design and Financial Outcomes

Dimension	EU ETS	China National ETS	California Cap-and-Trade
Launch Year	2005	2021 (national)	2013
Governance Model	Supranational market-based	Hybrid state-market model	Subnational regulatory model
Price Level	High (€80–100+ range in recent years)	Relatively low (~USD 9–10)	Moderate (~USD 30)
Price Stability Mechanism	Market Stability Reserve (MSR)	Administrative calibration & phased expansion	Price containment reserve & auction design
Sectoral Coverage	Power, heavy industry, aviation	Initially power; expanding to industry	Power, industry, transportation fuels
Allocation Method	Increasing auctioning; reduced free allocation	Predominantly free allocation (initial phase)	Mix of auctioning and free allocation
Financial Market Depth	Highly liquid; active derivatives	Limited derivatives; developing liquidity	Moderate liquidity; integrated with energy markets
Primary Transmission Channel	Market-driven asset repricing	Policy credibility & green credit guidance	Regulatory integration & investor disclosure
Impact on Carbon-Intensive Firms	Valuation discounts; higher risk premia	Gradual repricing; state-mediated adjustment	Higher compliance costs; credit differentiation

Source: Author's own compilation.

Table 1 presents a concise comparative overview of the selected emissions trading systems, highlighting key differences in institutional design, price levels, financial depth, and transmission mechanisms. The table synthesizes how variations in regulatory architecture shape financial market responses and capital reallocation dynamics across jurisdictions.

6. FINDINGS AND KEY INSIGHTS

6.1. Carbon Pricing and Asset Repricing Patterns

The findings demonstrate that carbon pricing has increasingly become a decisive factor influencing asset repricing across global financial markets. Evidence from major emissions trading systems indicates that rising and credible carbon prices systematically alter investor expectations regarding firm profitability, regulatory risk exposure, and long-term sustainability. In mature markets such as the EU ETS, persistent increases in carbon allowance prices have been closely associated with valuation discounts for carbon-intensive firms, particularly in sectors such as utilities, heavy manufacturing, and fossil fuel-based energy generation.

Conversely, carbon pricing has contributed to valuation premiums and enhanced investor sentiment for renewable energy companies, clean technology firms, and low-carbon infrastructure developers. Financial markets increasingly incorporate carbon risk into asset pricing frameworks, credit risk assessment, and portfolio construction strategies. Similar repricing dynamics are observed, though with varying intensity, in China's ETS and California's Cap-and-Trade Program. China's market exhibits gradual asset repricing influenced by regulatory expectations and state-led decarbonization strategies, while California's system demonstrates that even moderate carbon prices can influence equity performance, corporate bond spreads, and cost of capital differentiation. Overall, the findings confirm that carbon pricing acts as a powerful financial signal driving climate risk integration into asset valuation models.

6.2. Capital Reallocation Channels and Sectoral Shifts

The study identifies multiple transmission channels through which carbon pricing facilitates capital reallocation across economic sectors. First, cost of capital adjustments represent a primary mechanism. High-emission firms increasingly face higher borrowing costs, reduced investor confidence, and stricter credit conditions, prompting capital outflows from carbon-intensive industries. Second, portfolio rebalancing by institutional investors has emerged as a major driver of capital redirection. Asset managers and pension funds incorporate carbon exposure metrics, ESG frameworks, and climate scenario modelling into investment strategies, resulting in systematic reallocation toward low-carbon and transition-aligned sectors.

Sectoral investment patterns across case studies reveal consistent structural shifts. Renewable energy generation, electric mobility, battery technology, grid modernization, and energy storage infrastructure attract increasing financial inflows under rising carbon price regimes. The EU ETS demonstrates strong market-driven capital reallocation supported by advanced financial integration and deep carbon derivatives markets. In China, capital reallocation operates through a hybrid mechanism where carbon pricing interacts with green credit policies, subsidized financing, and state-directed industrial transformation strategies. California's cap-and-invest framework further reinforces sectoral shifts by recycling carbon revenues into climate infrastructure projects and clean energy development.

6.3. Implications for Stranded Assets and Systemic Risk

The expansion of carbon pricing mechanisms has significant implications for stranded asset risk and broader financial system stability. As carbon regulations tighten and decarbonization targets become more stringent, carbon-intensive infrastructure, fossil fuel reserves, and emission-heavy industrial assets face increasing risk of premature obsolescence. The findings indicate that financial markets are progressively recognising stranded asset exposure, leading to declining asset valuations, higher volatility, and rising risk premiums for firms with high carbon intensity.

From a systemic perspective, carbon pricing contributes to the emergence of climate-related financial risk transmission channels. These include potential revaluation shocks in energy and industrial sectors, credit risk concentration in carbon-intensive industries, and portfolio adjustment pressures for institutional investors heavily exposed to fossil fuel assets. While mature carbon markets such as the EU ETS provide clearer price signals that enable gradual risk adjustment, emerging markets may face transitional volatility due to evolving regulatory frameworks and uneven financial integration.

However, the study also highlights that credible carbon pricing can mitigate long-term systemic risk by promoting early capital reallocation, encouraging technological innovation, and strengthening financial resilience against climate transition shocks.

7. CHALLENGES AND LIMITATIONS OF CARBON PRICING SYSTEMS

7.1 Market Volatility and Price Uncertainty

One of the major limitations of carbon pricing systems is the presence of significant market volatility and price uncertainty. Carbon prices in emissions trading systems (ETS) are largely influenced by regulatory changes, macroeconomic fluctuations, technological developments, and energy market dynamics. Frequent variations in carbon prices create uncertainty for firms attempting to plan long-term investments in low-carbon technologies. When carbon prices are unstable or remain below expected thresholds, firms may delay or reduce investments in sustainable innovations due to unclear cost-benefit projections. Additionally, volatility can reduce the effectiveness of carbon pricing as a policy instrument because price signals may fail to provide consistent incentives for emission reduction. For financial markets, unpredictable carbon price movements can increase speculative trading and hinder the development of stable carbon derivatives markets, thereby limiting their risk-hedging potential.

7.2 Regulatory Fragmentation and Policy Inconsistency

Regulatory fragmentation across different jurisdictions poses a significant challenge to the effectiveness of carbon pricing mechanisms. Carbon markets often operate under diverse regulatory frameworks, coverage scopes, and pricing structures, leading to inconsistencies in policy implementation and enforcement. The absence of standardized global carbon pricing creates complexity for multinational corporations operating across multiple regulatory environments. Policy inconsistencies, such as sudden changes in emission caps, allowance allocation rules, or compliance requirements, can disrupt market stability and investor confidence. Furthermore, the lack of coordination among national and regional carbon markets limits opportunities for cross-border trading and reduces overall market efficiency. Fragmented regulatory systems also create administrative burdens and compliance challenges, which may discourage corporate participation and weaken the environmental effectiveness of carbon pricing policies.

7.3 Carbon Leakage and Competitiveness Concerns

Carbon leakage represents another critical limitation of carbon pricing systems, referring to the relocation of carbon-intensive production activities from jurisdictions with strict environmental regulations to regions with weaker or no carbon pricing policies. This shift can undermine the global objective of reducing greenhouse gas emissions while simultaneously affecting domestic industries subject to carbon costs. Firms operating in carbon-regulated markets may experience increased production costs, which can reduce their international competitiveness, particularly in energy-intensive industries such as steel, cement, and manufacturing. As a result, businesses may transfer operations to less-regulated regions to maintain profitability. Carbon leakage not only diminishes the environmental benefits of carbon pricing but also creates employment and economic stability concerns in regulated regions. Policymakers have attempted to address this issue through mechanisms such as carbon border adjustment taxes and free allowance allocations; however, these solutions introduce additional complexities in international trade relations.

7.4 Measurement and Verification Challenges

Accurate measurement, reporting, and verification (MRV) of emissions are fundamental to the success of carbon pricing systems. However, ensuring reliable emissions data remains a major challenge, particularly in developing economies and sectors with complex production processes. Inaccurate or inconsistent emissions reporting can lead to misallocation of allowances, manipulation of emission data, and reduced transparency in carbon markets. Monitoring difficulties arise from technological limitations, insufficient regulatory oversight, and variations in reporting standards across jurisdictions. Furthermore, certain industries, such as agriculture and small-scale manufacturing, face greater challenges in measuring emissions due to decentralized operations and a lack of standardized monitoring technologies. Weak MRV frameworks can undermine market credibility, reduce investor confidence, and create opportunities for fraudulent practices, ultimately limiting the effectiveness of carbon pricing in achieving emission reduction targets.

7.5 Equity and Distributional Impacts

Carbon pricing policies often raise concerns regarding their equity and distributional consequences, particularly for low-income households and vulnerable communities. By increasing the cost of fossil fuel consumption and energy-intensive goods, carbon pricing can lead to higher electricity, transportation, and production costs, which may disproportionately affect economically disadvantaged groups. Additionally, regions heavily dependent on carbon-intensive industries may experience employment losses and economic disruptions during the transition to low-carbon economies. Without adequate compensatory mechanisms, carbon pricing can exacerbate social inequalities and generate political resistance. To address these concerns, governments often implement revenue recycling strategies, such as providing tax rebates, subsidies for renewable energy adoption, or social welfare programs.

8. POLICY, MANAGERIAL, AND FINANCIAL IMPLICATIONS

8.1. Designing Carbon Markets for Financial Effectiveness

The findings suggest that the financial effectiveness of carbon markets depends largely on regulatory credibility, market transparency, and institutional stability. Well-designed carbon pricing systems should provide predictable and long-term policy signals that enable investors and corporations to incorporate carbon costs into strategic planning and capital allocation decisions. Gradual tightening of emissions caps, transparent allowance allocation mechanisms, and market stabilization instruments can improve price reliability and reduce excessive volatility. Stable and credible carbon prices enhance investor confidence and strengthen the role of emissions trading systems as financial signals guiding capital toward low-carbon technologies and infrastructure development.

Another critical policy design element is the integration of carbon markets with broader climate and energy policies. Complementary measures such as renewable energy incentives, climate disclosure mandates, and green finance taxonomies reinforce carbon price signals and strengthen capital reallocation mechanisms. Additionally, expanding sectoral coverage and improving cross-border carbon market linkages can enhance market liquidity and improve global investment efficiency.

Overall, effective carbon market design ensures that carbon pricing functions not only as an environmental compliance mechanism but also as a catalyst for sustainable financial transformation.

8.2. Implications for Regulators and Central Banks

For financial regulators and central banks, the growing financialization of carbon pricing highlights the need to integrate climate risk into financial supervision frameworks. Carbon markets increasingly influence asset valuations, credit risk assessments, and financial stability, making climate risk a macroprudential concern. Regulators should incorporate carbon exposure metrics into stress testing models, prudential regulation, and risk disclosure standards to improve the resilience of financial institutions against transition risks.

Central banks also play a vital role in promoting climate-aware monetary and financial policies. Incorporating climate risk considerations into asset purchase programs, collateral frameworks, and financial stability monitoring can support low-carbon investment and reduce systemic vulnerabilities. Furthermore, standardized climate disclosure requirements can improve market transparency and help investors assess carbon exposure more effectively. Strengthening coordination between environmental regulators, financial supervisors, and international policy institutions can further enhance regulatory effectiveness and ensure consistent climate–finance integration.

8.3. Strategic Responses for Corporations and Investors

Corporations operating in carbon-intensive industries must proactively integrate carbon pricing trajectories into corporate strategy, capital budgeting, and risk management frameworks. Firms should invest in emissions reduction technologies, renewable energy adoption, and operational efficiency improvements to mitigate compliance costs and maintain competitiveness. Developing credible decarbonization pathways, supported by transparent climate disclosures, can improve investor confidence and reduce financing costs.

Investors and asset managers are increasingly required to incorporate carbon risk into portfolio construction and investment valuation models. Climate scenario analysis, carbon intensity metrics, and ESG integration strategies enable investors to identify transition risks and capture emerging opportunities in sustainable industries. Institutional investors may also engage in active stewardship by encouraging corporate climate accountability and promoting long-term sustainability strategies. The growing availability of green bonds, sustainability-linked loans, and climate transition funds further supports investor participation in low-carbon economic development.

8.4. Strengthening the Climate–Finance Policy Interface

The interaction between climate policy and financial markets requires stronger institutional coordination to maximize policy effectiveness. Governments should promote policy coherence by aligning carbon pricing frameworks with sustainable finance regulations, industrial transition policies, and innovation strategies. Strengthening public–private partnerships can facilitate large-scale investments in renewable energy infrastructure, clean transportation systems, and climate-resilient technologies.

International collaboration is equally important for strengthening the climate–finance interface. Harmonizing carbon pricing standards, disclosure requirements, and sustainable finance taxonomies can reduce regulatory fragmentation and improve cross-border investment flows. Multilateral financial institutions and global regulatory bodies can support capacity building in emerging carbon markets, ensuring that developing economies effectively integrate climate policy into financial systems.

The combined policy, managerial, and financial implications demonstrate that carbon pricing has evolved into a central instrument linking environmental governance with global financial market transformation. Effective carbon market design, proactive corporate strategy, climate-aware investment practices, and strong regulatory coordination are essential for accelerating capital reallocation toward sustainable economic pathways and achieving long-term climate transition objectives..

9. ORIGINALITY, CONTRIBUTIONS, AND FUTURE RESEARCH DIRECTIONS

9.1. Theoretical and Empirical Contributions

This study contributes to the academic literature by integrating environmental economics, financial market theory, and climate finance into a unified analytical framework. The research extends traditional carbon pricing theory beyond its environmental compliance function by conceptualizing emissions trading systems as financial transmission mechanisms that influence asset pricing, investor behaviour, and capital reallocation. By linking carbon pricing with capital reallocation theory and climate-aware finance, the study offers a multidimensional perspective that explains how climate policy signals translate into financial market adjustments and sectoral investment transformations.

Empirically, the comparative case analysis across multiple emissions trading systems provides cross-jurisdictional evidence demonstrating that carbon pricing consistently triggers climate risk repricing and capital reallocation. The study highlights how differences in regulatory credibility, institutional design, and market maturity influence the strength and speed of financial market responses. It also contributes new insights into how carbon markets interact with ESG investing, sustainable finance instruments, and institutional investor behaviour. By examining developed, emerging, and subnational carbon markets simultaneously, the study broadens the empirical scope of climate finance research and enhances the global relevance of its findings.

9.2. Methodological Advancements

The research advances methodological approaches by adopting a mixed-methods comparative case study design that integrates quantitative financial analysis with institutional and policy evaluation. The study combines event study methodology, panel regression analysis, carbon-beta estimation, and sectoral capital flow analysis to capture both short-term market reactions and long-term investment shifts associated with carbon pricing dynamics. This multi-layered methodological framework enables a comprehensive assessment of how regulatory announcements, carbon price movements, and institutional reforms influence asset valuations and investment patterns.

Additionally, the research incorporates qualitative policy analysis to interpret financial market responses within their regulatory and governance contexts. This triangulated approach improves analytical robustness and allows the study to capture complex interactions between policy design, market maturity, and investor behaviour. By integrating financial econometric techniques with institutional analysis, the study provides a replicable research framework for analyzing climate-finance transmission mechanisms across different regulatory environments.

9.3. Future Research Avenues

a. AI-Based Carbon Risk Analytics

Future research can explore the application of artificial intelligence, machine learning, and big data analytics to improve carbon risk measurement and prediction. AI-driven models can analyze large volumes of emissions data, financial disclosures, satellite monitoring information, and policy announcements to generate real-time carbon risk indicators. These tools can enhance investor decision-making, improve carbon pricing forecasts, and strengthen corporate climate risk management systems. AI-based predictive analytics can also identify early warning signals of transition risk and stranded asset exposure across industries.

b. Climate Stress Testing and Financial Stability Assessment

Another promising research direction involves developing advanced climate stress testing models for financial institutions, corporations, and capital markets. Future studies could examine how carbon pricing shocks, policy tightening scenarios, and extreme climate transition pathways affect asset valuations, credit risk exposure, and systemic financial stability. Integrating climate scenarios into macroprudential regulation and financial risk modelling can improve understanding of how climate policies influence financial resilience and cross-sector risk transmission.

c. Transition Finance and Low-Carbon Investment Models

Further research is needed to develop robust transition finance models that support high-emission industries in shifting toward sustainable production systems. Investigating innovative financial instruments such as transition bonds, blended finance structures, sustainability-linked derivatives, and carbon-adjusted lending frameworks could provide practical solutions for balancing environmental targets with economic development objectives. Future research may also examine the role of public–private partnerships, green industrial policies, and international climate finance in accelerating capital reallocation toward decarbonization.

d. Cross-Border Carbon Market Integration and Emerging Economies

Additional research could focus on cross-border carbon pricing coordination, carbon market linkages, and their effects on global capital flows and regulatory harmonization. Expanding empirical analysis to include developing carbon markets in regions such as Southeast Asia, Latin America, and Africa would provide valuable insights into institutional capacity, financial integration, and policy transfer mechanisms. Such research would help identify strategies for strengthening climate-finance linkages in emerging economies and ensuring inclusive global decarbonization pathways.

10. CONCLUSION

This chapter shows that emissions trading systems influence financial markets not only through carbon price levels but through institutional design, regulatory credibility, and financial integration. By comparing the EU ETS, China's National ETS, and California's Cap-and-Trade Program, the analysis demonstrates that differences in price stability mechanisms, allocation rules, and market depth shape how strongly and how quickly capital shifts from carbon-intensive to low-carbon sectors. Importantly, the comparative perspective reveals insights that single-case studies cannot provide. While individual studies may identify asset repricing within one system, cross-case analysis shows that regulatory credibility and policy stability are decisive in determining the magnitude and durability of financial market responses. The findings, therefore, highlight that carbon pricing effectiveness depends not only on environmental ambition but on institutional architecture and financial transmission mechanisms.

REFERENCES

Aggarwal, S. K., Saini, L. M., & Kumar, A. (2009). Electricity price forecasting in deregulated markets: A review and evaluation. *International Journal of Electrical Power & Energy Systems*, *31*(1), 13–22. DOI: 10.1016/j.ijepes.2008.09.003

Aslam, F., Ali, I., Amjad, F., Ali, H., & Irfan, I. (2023). On the inner dynamics between Fossil fuels and the carbon market: A combination of seasonal-trend decomposition and multifractal cross-correlation analysis. *Environmental Science and Pollution Research International*, *30*(10), 25873–25891. DOI: 10.1007/s11356-022-23924-7

Balaji, K. (2023),"Exploring the Drivers and Effects on Supply Chain Resilience and Performance in an Emerging Market Using Artificial Intelligence," *2023 3rd International Conference on Smart Generation Computing, Communication and Networking (SMART GENCON)*, Bangalore, India, 2023, pp. 1-6, DOI: 10.1109/SMARTGENCON60755.2023.10442071

Balaji, K. (2025). Harnessing AI and Blockchain in Sustainability Assurance: Trends Shaping the Future of Verification. In Khatib, S., & Abbas, A. (Eds.), *Navigating Trust in Sustainability Reporting and Assurance* (pp. 215–242). IGI Global Scientific Publishing., DOI: 10.4018/979-8-3373-0117-4.ch007

Balaji, K. (2025). Revolutionizing High-Frequency Trading: The Impacts of Financial Technology and Data Science Innovations. In Chen, H. (Ed.), *Machine Learning and Modeling Techniques in Financial Data Science* (pp. 103–124). IGI Global Scientific Publishing., DOI: 10.4018/979-8-3693-8186-1.ch004

Balaji, K. (2025). Neuromarketing and Sustainable Finance: Real-World Case Studies of Green Investment Promotions. In Taneja, S., Chahal, B., Johri, A., Ozen, E., & Kumar, P. (Eds.), *Neuromarketing's Role in Sustainable Finance* (pp. 169–204). IGI Global Scientific Publishing., DOI: 10.4018/979-8-3693-9117-4.ch010

Balaji, K. (2025). AI as a Game Changer: How Digital Entrepreneurs Are Redefining Business Practices. In Tunio, M. (Ed.), *Improving Entrepreneurial Processes Through Advanced AI* (pp. 21–48). IGI Global Scientific Publishing., DOI: 10.4018/979-8-3693-1495-1.ch002

Balaji, K., & Rao, P. S. (2024), "Artificial Intelligence and Chatbots: Transforming User Experience in E-tailing," *2024 9th International Conference on Communication and Electronics Systems (ICCES)*, Coimbatore, India, 2024, pp. 1375-1379, DOI: 10.1109/ICCES63552.2024.10859474

Chai, S., Huo, W., Li, Q., Ji, Q., & Shi, X. (2025). Effects of carbon tax on energy transition, emissions and economy amid technological progress. *Applied Energy, 377*, 124578. DOI: 10.1016/j.apenergy.2024.124578

Deng, Z., Liu, C., & Zhu, Z. (2021). Inter-hours rolling scheduling of behind-the-meter storage operating systems using electricity price forecasting based on deep convolutional neural network. *International Journal of Electrical Power & Energy Systems, 125*, 106499. DOI: 10.1016/j.ijepes.2020.106499

Dutta, G., & Mitra, K. (2017). A literature review on dynamic pricing of electricity. *The Journal of the Operational Research Society, 68*(10), 1131–1145. DOI: 10.1057/s41274-016-0149-4

Foramitti, J., Savin, I., & van den Bergh, J. C. J. M. (2021). Emission tax vs. Permit trading under bounded rationality and dynamic markets. *Energy Policy, 148*, 112009. DOI: 10.1016/j.enpol.2020.112009

Gugler, K., Haxhimusa, A., & Liebensteiner, M. (2021). Effectiveness of climate policies: Carbon pricing vs. Subsidizing renewables. *Journal of Environmental Economics and Management, 106*, 102405. DOI: 10.1016/j.jeem.2020.102405

Hall, N. L., Jeanneret, T. D., & Rai, A. (2016). Cost-reflective electricity pricing: Consumer preferences and perceptions. *Energy Policy, 95*, 62–72. DOI: 10.1016/j.enpol.2016.04.042

He, J., & Ye, Z. (2019). Basic principles and equilibrium model of carbon cost pass-through in power industry. *Ecological Economics, 35*(7), 45–49.

Lee, D., Ooka, R., Ikeda, S., Choi, W., & Kwak, Y. (2020). Model predictive control of building energy systems with thermal energy storage in response to occupancy variations and time-variant electricity prices. *Energy and Building, 225*, 110291. DOI: 10.1016/j.enbuild.2020.110291

Leroutier, M. (2022). Carbon pricing and power sector decarbonisation: Evidence from the UK. *Journal of Environmental Economics and Management, 111*, 102580. DOI: 10.1016/j.jeem.2021.102580

Li, G., Zhang, R., & Masui, T. (2021). CGE modeling with disaggregated pollution treatment sectors for assessing China's environmental tax policies. *The Science of the Total Environment, 761*, 143264. DOI: 10.1016/j.scitotenv.2020.143264

Liu, D., Zeng, X., Su, B., Wang, W., Sun, K., & Sadia, U. H. (2020). A social network analysis regarding electricity consumption and economic growth in China. *Journal of Cleaner Production, 274*, 122973. DOI: 10.1016/j.jclepro.2020.122973

Mitridati, L., Kazempour, J., & Pinson, P. (2021). Design and game-Theoretic analysis of community-Based market mechanisms in heat and electricity systems. *Omega*, *99*, 102177. DOI: 10.1016/j.omega.2019.102177

Nelsons, T., Kelley, S., & Orton, F. (2012). A literature review of economic studies on carbon pricing and Australian wholesale electricity markets. *Energy Policy*, *49*, 217–224. DOI: 10.1016/j.enpol.2012.05.075

Ohler, A., Mohammadi, H., & Loomis, D. G. (2020). Electricity restructuring and the relationship between fuel costs and electricity prices for industrial and residential customers. *Energy Policy*, *142*, 111559. DOI: 10.1016/j.enpol.2020.111559

Qiang, M., Lai, H., & Lyu, Z. (2025). Carbon Emissions Trading and Employment: Evidence from China. *Sustainability (Basel)*, *17*(4), 1404. DOI: 10.3390/su17041404

Song, Y., Liu, T., Liang, D., Li, Y., & Song, X. (2019). A fuzzy stochastic model for carbon price prediction under the effect of demand-related policy in China's carbon market. *Ecological Economics*, *157*, 253–265. DOI: 10.1016/j.ecolecon.2018.10.001

Tost, M., Hitch, M., Lutter, S., Feiel, S., & Moser, P. (2020). Carbon prices for meeting the Paris Agreement and their impact on key metals. *The Extractive Industries and Society*, *7*(2), 593–599. DOI: 10.1016/j.exis.2020.01.012

Tu, Q., Betz, R., Mo, J., Fan, Y., & Liu, Y. (2019). Achieving grid parity of wind power in China—Present levelized cost of electricity and future evolution. *Applied Energy*, *250*, 1053–1064. DOI: 10.1016/j.apenergy.2019.05.039

Vrontisi, Z., Fragkiadakis, K., Kannavou, M., & Capros, P. (2020). Energy system transition and macroeconomic impacts of a European decarbonization action towards a below 2 °C climate stabilization. *Climatic Change*, *162*(4), 1857–1875. DOI: 10.1007/s10584-019-02440-7

Xu, H. T., Pan, X. F., Li, J. M., Feng, S. H., & Guo, S. C. (2023). Comparing the impacts of carbon tax and carbon emission trading, which regulation is more effective? *Journal of Environmental Management*, *330*, 117156. DOI: 10.1016/j.jenvman.2022.117156

Yuan, J., Na, C., Lei, Q., Xiong, M., Guo, J., & Hu, Z. (2018). Coal use for power generation in China. *Resources, Conservation and Recycling*, *129*, 443–453. DOI: 10.1016/j.resconrec.2016.03.021

Zhang, W., & Liu, L. (2019). Investment decisions of fired power plants on carbon utilization under the imperfect carbon emission trading schemes in China. *Processes (Basel, Switzerland)*, *7*(11), 828. DOI: 10.3390/pr7110828

Zhang, X., Loeschel, A., Lewis, J., Zhang, D., & Yan, J. (2020). Emissions trading systems for global low carbon energy and economic transformation. *Applied Energy*, *279*, 115858. DOI: 10.1016/j.apenergy.2020.115858

Chapter 4
Carbon Pricing, Capital Reallocation, and Financial Stability:
A Sustainability Accounting Perspective on Market Signals and Climate-Related Risks

Rismawati Rismawati
http://orcid.org/0000-0001-8046-6764
Universitas Muhammadiyah Palopo, Indonesia

Fibriyani Nur Khairin
Universitas Mulawarman, Indonesia

Monika Handayani
http://orcid.org/0000-0003-4186-9864
Politeknik Negeri Banjarmasin, Indonesia

ABSTRACT

This chapter analyzes the impact of carbon pricing on capital markets and financial stability through the lens of sustainable accounting. Carbon taxes and emissions trading systems alter cash flow, risk premium, and tail risk expectations, hence influencing stock valuation and credit pricing. The chapter subsequently correlates physical and transition risks with accounting materiality, illustrating the impact of climate on impairment, provisions, useful-life estimations, fair value inputs, and disclosures. It employs carbon price trajectories, emissions scopes, intensity metrics, internal carbon pricing, and result indicators such as cost of capital to assess policy stringency and business vulnerability and responsiveness, therefore

DOI: 10.4018/979-8-3373-8998-1.ch004

rendering policy signals decision-useful. It demonstrates how disclosure mandates and assurance mitigate information asymmetry, facilitating systematic repricing, capital reallocation, and macroprudential supervision of climate-related risks during the net zero transition.

INTRODUCTION

Carbon Pricing and Climate Risk as Economic–Accounting Problems

Carbon pricing serves not just as an environmental tool but also as a market indicator that alters expectations for companies' future cash flows, risk premiums, and capital distribution. When governments implement or intensify carbon taxes or emissions trading systems (ETS), they provide a clear or, at the very least, implicit shadow cost of carbon that financial markets can integrate into their valuations. In asset-pricing terms, carbon pricing modifies the anticipated profitability of carbon-intensive business models, increases uncertainty regarding transition paths, and adjusts the distribution of adverse outcomes (i.e., "tail risks") associated with policy tightening and technological substitution. Data from equity markets indicates that carbon exposure is factored into pricing: companies with higher emissions generally experience systematic return effects aligned with investors demanding compensation for assuming carbon-related risk (Bolton & Kacperczyk, 2021).

Carbon pricing serves as a signal that permeates lending markets. Lenders can incorporate emissions-related transition risk into loan spreads and contractual terms, so integrating climate risk into the cost of financing. Kleimeier and Viehs (2021) demonstrate that enterprises with higher emissions incur elevated loan spreads, aligning with the concept of an environmental risk premium. This is economically relevant as it illustrates that carbon price functions through a more extensive financial mechanism than mere stock repricing; it alters financing conditions, rather than solely influencing investor preferences.

The informational value of carbon pricing is fundamentally contingent upon legitimacy, stability, and supplementary disclosure frameworks. Volatile carbon pricing that are poorly implemented or subject to arbitrary reversals produce unreliable signals, diminishing their efficacy for capital planning and risk evaluation. In contrast, more transparent and predictable price signals enhance real-economy reactions, including green innovation and transition investment. Firm-level data indicates that carbon pricing signals can enhance green innovation, with the effect intensified by governance and ESG-related informational contexts (Feng et al., 2024). At the market level, carbon and stock markets may become intertwined through spillovers, suggesting that carbon-price dynamics can influence broader financial risk conditions (Dong et al., 2024).

The primary problem in sustainability accounting is converting policy signals into measurement and disclosure that are relevant for decision-making, enabling investors to differentiate between exposure (carbon intensity, regulation coverage) and management quality (governance, mitigation strategy). Regulatory measures in carbon reporting can enhance the prominence of carbon data and elicit varied market responses, particularly when institutional investors are vigilant and capable of responding to the signal (Florackis et al., 2025). Consequently, carbon pricing is most efficacious as a market signal when accompanied by robust carbon accounting, credible verification, and uniform climate-related disclosure standards that mitigate information asymmetry and facilitate efficient repricing instead of sudden, destabilizing adjustments.

This chapter enhances the research on carbon pricing and climate-related financial risk by framing sustainability accounting as the cohesive analytical framework that connects policy signals, company valuation, and financial stability. Initially, it defines carbon pricing via carbon taxes and emissions trading systems as a market signal that alters expectations for future cash flows, discount rates, and downside risk, consequently affecting equity value and credit pricing. Secondly, it clarifies how carbon-price trajectories and transition paths gain significance in financial reporting through accounting materiality assessments integrated into impairment testing, provisions, useful-life estimations, fair value inputs, and climate-related disclosures. The chapter broadens the analysis from firm-level valuation effects to macroprudential implications, illustrating how the quality, comparability, and assurance of sustainability-related information influence whether capital reallocation under carbon pricing transpires in an orderly fashion or exacerbates correlated losses and systemic risk. This chapter offers a cohesive framework for evaluating carbon-pricing signals across enterprises, markets, and regulatory environments by integrating policy design, accounting measurement, and financial stability considerations. Figure 1 summarizes the transmission mechanisms developed in this chapter, linking carbon pricing, accounting materiality, valuation effects, and financial stability.

Figure 1. Carbon Pricing–Accounting–Valuation–Stability Transmission Framework

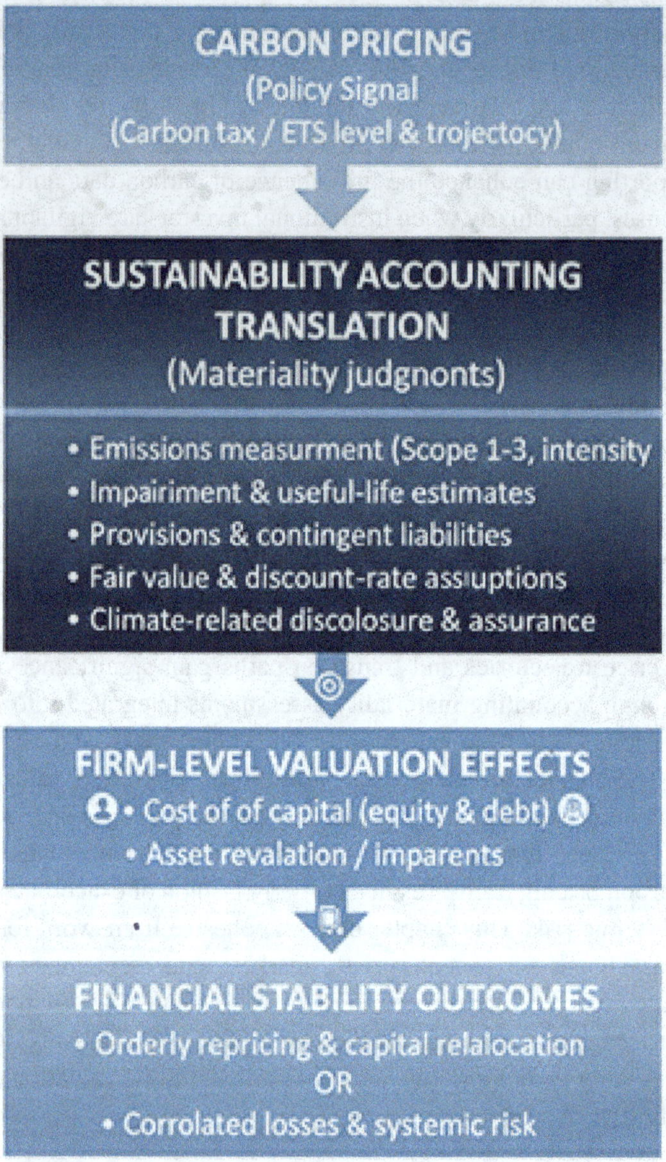

Figure 1 demonstrates the functioning of carbon pricing as a market signal, with its financial implications contingent upon its conversion into accounting metrics and disclosures. Sustainability accounting serves as the conduit through which carbon-price trajectories influence firm-level value and, when aggregated across enterprises and intermediaries, determine financial stability consequences. High-quality, comparable, and reliable accounting information enables systematic repricing and capital reallocation, while delayed or unclear recognition exacerbates systemic risk.

1. BACKGROUND

1.1 Carbon Pricing as a Market Signal

Carbon pricing is typically executed via two primary policy mechanisms: carbon taxes and emissions trading systems (ETS). A carbon tax establishes a definitive per-ton penalty for greenhouse gas emissions, transforming emissions into a foreseeable financial burden that companies can include into their budgeting and pricing strategies. In contrast, an ETS sets a total emissions limit and mandates that regulated entities submit allowances for confirmed emissions; allowance prices are established in the market based on supply and demand dynamics, making them more responsive to market conditions, regulatory frameworks, and anticipations. Notwithstanding their institutional disparities, both instruments operate as market indicators that influence business motivations and investor perceptions by imposing an explicit or implicit shadow cost on carbon.

The informative value of carbon pricing for companies and investors relies not only on the policy's presence but also on the elements that influence signal strength and trustworthiness. The price level denotes the current observed carbon price (tax rate or allowance price), which directly influences short-term compliance costs and operating profits, especially for carbon-intensive company models. The price trajectory pertains to predictions for the future evolution of carbon pricing, influenced by factors such as legislative tax escalators, anticipated emissions cap tightening, the establishment of price corridors, or political promises to net-zero paths. As several investment and valuation decisions are prospective, the anticipated trajectory frequently has equal significance to the present price. Third, volatility particularly prominent in ETS environments reflects uncertainty in the carbon price signal and may undermine long-term investment strategies by amplifying the variability of possible compliance expenses and transition results.

Fourth, coverage delineates the sectors, entities, and emissions sources that are controlled, thereby determining the extent of exposure throughout the economy and throughout value chains. Coverage parameters affect both direct compliance responsibilities (usually associated with Scope 1 and Scope 2 emissions) and indirect exposures conveyed through input costs, contractual agreements, and consumer demand. Fifth, free allocation (or alternative output-based rebates and exemptions) alters the effective carbon cost incurred by enterprises, especially in trade-exposed sectors, and can significantly influence short-term cash flow effects and competitive dynamics. The price level, trajectory, volatility, coverage, and free allocation collectively influence whether carbon pricing functions as a steady, decision-relevant signal or as an unpredictable, inconsistently conveyed policy shock.

The significance of these policy parameters transcends business strategy, impacting reporting and assurance, as capital markets increasingly evaluate carbon pricing based on profitability forecasts, risk premiums, and adverse scenarios. These criteria become pertinent to accounting when they alter estimates and materiality assessments.

1.2 Climate-Related Risks and Accounting Materiality

Climate-related risks attain economic significance for financial reporting when they are material, meaning they can feasibly influence users' judgments via recognized amounts, measurement uncertainty, or the sufficiency of disclosures. Materiality is influenced by two interrelated factors: physical risks, which include acute events and chronic changes impacting operations, asset condition, and insurability, and transition risks, encompassing policy tightening, carbon pricing, technological substitution, and demand shifts that alter the valuation of "high-carbon" cash flows. In sustainable accounting, a fundamental aspect is that carbon pricing transcends mere regulatory expense; it alters the foundational assumptions of cash-flow projections, asset longevity, discount rates, and liabilities thereby necessitating accounting determinations and disclosure duties.

Table 1. Summarizes how carbon-pricing signals translate into specific accounting judgments through materiality assessments

Carbon-Pricing Signal	Transmission to Accounting	Affected Accounting Judgments
Increase in carbon-price trajectory	Lower expected future cash flows for carbon-intensive assets	Impairment indicators; recoverable amount estimates
Expansion of regulatory coverage / higher compliance costs	Higher unavoidable costs of meeting obligations	Provisions; onerous contracts
Demand shift away from high-carbon products	Reduced revenue expectations and asset utilization	Revenue forecasts; useful-life reassessment
Higher transition-risk premium	Increased uncertainty and required returns	Discount rates; fair-value inputs in valuation models

continued on following page

Table 1. Continued

Carbon-Pricing Signal	Transmission to Accounting	Affected Accounting Judgments
Physical disruptions linked to climate risks	Higher operating and credit risk exposures	Insurance availability; provisions; expected credit losses (for lenders)
Mandatory climate-related disclosure requirements	Greater estimation uncertainty and need for connectivity	Note disclosures; estimation uncertainty; linkage between narrative and financial statements

Source: Author compilation, 2026

Evidence suggests that markets evaluate both exposure and the reliability of firms' materiality estimations. When climate risk is regarded as significant, non-disclosure might heighten perceived risk, while credible disclosure correlates with improved financing circumstances (Matsumura et al., 2024). Nonetheless, practice is inconsistent: climate-related data in audited financial statements has risen, yet frequently lacks uniform incorporation of forward-looking assumptions and quantitative impacts, particularly in carbon-intensive industries (Borghei et al., 2024). The existing gaps exacerbate estimation and comparability risks, underscoring the necessity for strong assurance capabilities and the shift from voluntary to mandatory climate reporting for effective decision-making and systematic repricing (Pham et al., 2024; Amel-Zadeh & Tang, 2025).

1.3 A Sustainability Accounting Lens on Policy Spillovers

Environmental policies rarely function independently. From a sustainability accounting standpoint, the primary concern is not solely the impact of carbon pricing on regulated entities, but also the manner in which it produces spillover effects that permeate many industries, information ecosystems, and financial markets. Carbon pricing methods and associated disclosure mandates convey signals beyond the formally included firms, whereas sustainability accounting serves as the interpretative framework that dictates whether these spillovers are managed in a systematic or disruptive fashion.

The initial spillover channel functions via the cost of capital and financing conditions. Improved carbon-related measurement and disclosure, frequently prompted by regulatory pressure, impact capital providers' evaluation of transition risk and risk management quality, thereby influencing enterprises' financing costs and capital allocation decisions (Long et al., 2023). The secondary channel pertains to information spillage and peer impacts. Standardized environmental reporting can transform the sectoral information landscape, promoting enhanced transparency among peer companies and broadening the policy's influence beyond directly regulated enterprises (Chen et al., 2025).

The third channel pertains to market and system-level spillovers. The mechanics of carbon pricing specifically price volatility and policy uncertainty can transmit risk across assets and markets, enhancing co-movement and the likelihood of linked losses, which may affect financial stability (Dong et al., 2024).

At the firm and industry levels, these spillovers predominantly affect capital allocation via financing conditions and disclosure-induced comparability. At the systemic level, they influence financial stability by impacting interconnection and the magnification of transition-related shocks. The spillover channels justify the chapter's transmission paradigm (Figure 1), which connects policy signals to accounting translation, valuation impacts, and macroprudential results.

2. MAIN FOCUS OF the CHAPTER

2.1. Metrics That Connect Policy to Performance

This section implements Figure 1 by delineating (i) the metrics that convert carbon-pricing signals into quantifiable exposure and responsiveness, (ii) the valuation and accounting mechanisms through which these signals influence recognized amounts and estimation uncertainty, and (iii) the disclosure–assurance conditions that ascertain whether repricing and capital reallocation are systematic or disruptive.

Table 2 categorizes the diverse measures linking policy signals to business performance outcomes, offering succinct definitions and representative key indicators for each category to facilitate navigation through this intricate measuring landscape.

Table 2. Classification and definition of Carbon Pricing Metrics

Metric Category	Focus & Definition	Operational Examples	Key Strategic Implications
Policy Metrics	Evaluates the stringency of carbon regulations. It distinguishes between **Price Stringency** (explicit costs via taxation or ETS) and **Shadow Pricing** (theoretical marginal abatement costs).	ETS Allowance Prices, Carbon Tax Rates, Implicit Subsidies.	Acts as a primary determinant of immediate regulatory expenditure and long-term policy risk exposure.
Exposure Metrics	Quantifies corporate vulnerability to transition risks. It focuses on **Carbon Intensity** (emissions relative to revenue/output) and the total scope of the carbon footprint.	Scope 1 & 2 Emissions, Carbon Intensity ($tCO_{2}e$ / $Revenue), Fossil Fuel Reserves.	Directly influences operational overheads and the risk of asset stranding under increasingly stringent climate mandates.
Internal Metrics	Strategic instruments utilized by firms to internalize climate externalities. Includes **Internal Carbon Pricing (ICP)** to inform capital budgeting and investment appraisal.	Internal Carbon Price (Shadow/Fee models), Science-Based Targets (SBTi), Decarbonization CAPEX.	Facilitates low-carbon capital reallocation and enhances long-term organizational resilience and strategic planning.
Outcome Metrics	Assesses the financial impact of carbon pricing on enterprise value and financing costs, linking regulatory exposure to **Financial Performance**.	Weighted Average Cost of Capital (WACC), ROIC, Tobin's Q, Credit Spreads.	Reflects capital market valuation of transition risks and dictates the firm's overall access to finance.

Source: Author's compilation based on Li et al. (2025) and industry standards.

Ultimately, outcome indicators must connect environmental and financial performance in a manner that is beneficial for decision-making by capital providers: cost of capital (WACC), credit spreads, and valuation impacts. The quality of carbon information disclosure serves as a critical parameter, influencing the pricing of policy risk by investors; for instance, disclosure may demonstrate nonlinear correlations with financing costs in the context of regulatory pressure (Long et al., 2023). Simultaneously, green investment functions as a response indicator linking policy incentives to long-term financial success and compliance results (Chen & Ma, 2021).

2.2. Valuation Channels and Accounting Treatments

Carbon pricing and climate policy modifications influence business value via two main channels: anticipated cash flows and the discount rate (risk premiums). Transition risk is included into pricing when investors foresee that stricter carbon pricing or an increased likelihood of rigorous regulatory scenarios will reduce margins in carbon-intensive sectors, elevate compliance and abatement expenses, and hasten the shift in demand toward low-carbon alternatives. Policy uncertainty may exacerbate necessary returns, resulting in a carbon-transition risk premium in addition to direct cash-flow impacts (Bolton & Kacperczyk, 2023).

From a sustainable accounting standpoint, the crucial concern is the timeliness and transparency with which these value effects are converted into accounting estimates and disclosures. Data from obligatory disclosures indicates that increased firm-specific climate risk exposure correlates with diminished market valuation (Berkman et al., 2024), whereas elevated emissions are associated with an increased cost of equity—aligning with the notion that information risk and cash-flow volatility exacerbate discount-rate impacts (Yan et al., 2025). Figure 2 illustrates the impact of carbon pricing on value via modifications in cash flows and alterations in discount rates.

Figure 2. Viluation Channels for Transition Risk

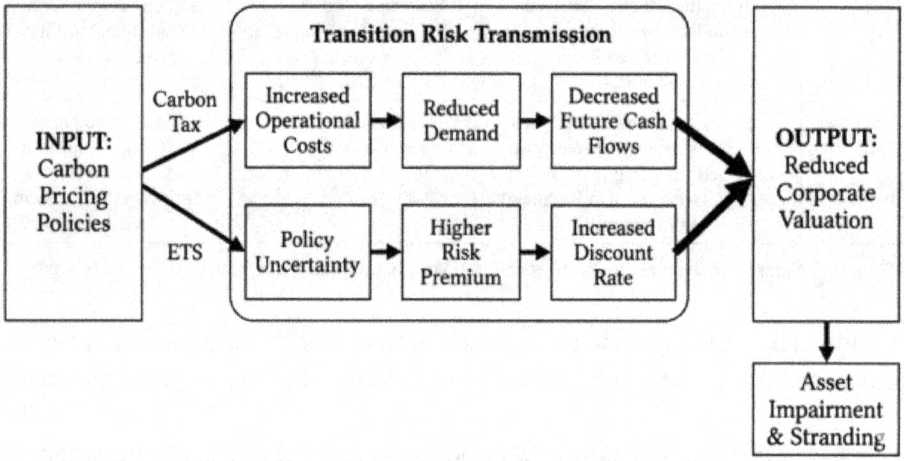

Source: Author's compilation, 2026.

In financial reporting, valuation methods correspond to particular accounting approaches. Carbon pricing and transition dynamics may serve as impairment indicators for long-lived assets when recoverable amounts decrease due to diminished cash-flow projections, increased operating costs, or reduced useful lives; empirical evidence associates firm-specific climate risk with both the probability and extent of tangible asset impairments (Ben-Amar et al., 2025). Secondly, transition and physical risks amplify measurement uncertainty in critical valuation assumptions such as discount rates, commodity and energy price trajectories, and carbon price paths, rendering the "connectivity" between these assumptions and financial statement line items vital to prevent delayed recognition and sudden repricing. In line with this worry, companies exhibit significant variation in the incorporation of climate risks within notes and accounting estimations, with data from the UK FTSE 100 demonstrating an increasing although inconsistent integration of climate factors into financial statements (Borghei et al., 2024).

2.3. Disclosure Standards and Assurance Implications

Disclosure standards dictate the extent to which carbon pricing and climate-related risks are converted into decision-useful information that is comparable across companies, verifiable, and timely for financial markets. Standards in measurement delineate (i) the disclosed elements (metrics, targets, governance, scenario assumptions), (ii) their structural organization (interconnectivity between narrative and numerical data), and (iii) the premise of decision usefulness (focused on enterprise value against a broader effect perspective). As carbon prices increase or regulatory frameworks get more stringent, investors must differentiate between firms' exposure (emissions profile, regulatory scope, cost pass-through potential) and capabilities (transition strategy, capital expenditure alignment, risk management). In the absence of standardization, disclosures are often fragmented, selective, and inadequately comparable, which might hinder repricing and elevate the likelihood of abrupt valuation declines.

An expanding body of empirical research indicates that standardized climate-related disclosures can significantly affect investor decision-making. Empirical findings from Australia demonstrate that investors direct greater capital towards firms offering climate-risk disclosures consistent with TCFD frameworks, with even higher allocations when disclosures encompass both risks and mitigation strategies, thereby supporting the assertion that structured disclosures enhance informativeness beyond generic statements (Hewa et al., 2025). This is significant in carbon pricing contexts as the policy signal is fundamentally anticipatory; hence, decision-useful reporting must explicitly articulate the assumptions connecting policy trajectories to financial results (e.g., margins, asset lifespans, and capital strategies).

Nonetheless, disclosure regulations are inadequate without credible assurance. Assurance mitigates information risk by enhancing the trustworthiness of emissions data, controls, and the foundational estimating procedures. Financial contracting evidence indicates that verified greenhouse gas disclosures and associated carbon-management information correlate with reduced debt costs, suggesting that assurance can transform climate reporting into concrete financing advantages, thus facilitating orderly capital reallocation (Mahmoudian et al., 2023). The efficacy of assurance concurrently relies on the competencies and motivations of the auditor. Empirical research at the firm level indicates that the probability and caliber of climate-risk reporting enhance when audit partners have climate-related expertise, particularly in sectors where climate risk is anticipated to be significant (Pham et al., 2024).

The consequences for assurance get increasingly intricate when governments adopt obligatory climate reporting. Mandatory carbon disclosure announcements can enhance the prominence of carbon information and elicit varied market reactions between high-carbon enterprises and those with concentrated institutional ownership (Florackis et al., 2025). Simultaneously, international evidence regarding sustainability reporting assurance underscores practical trade-offs concerning assurance timing (delays), assurance level (limited versus reasonable), and provider selection, emphasizing that "assurance design" functions as a governance mechanism influencing trust and comparability (Delgado Sánchez et al., 2026).

3. ANALYSIS AND RESPONSES

3.1. Corporate Responses: Investment, Innovation, and Financing

Carbon pricing transforms company strategy by translating emissions into a tangible financial expense and a proactive indication of shift. Companies generally react via three interconnected avenues: capital re-optimization, innovation, and finance, with their efficacy reliant on the quality of measurement, disclosure, and assurance that convert policy signals into pertinent decision-making information.

Capital expenditure and asset reallocation. Carbon pricing elevates anticipated operational expenses and amplifies uncertainties regarding future profit margins in emissions-intensive sectors, consequently modifying project NPVs and reallocating capital budgets towards lower-carbon assets and processes. Firms react not only to current prices but also to the credibility of policies and anticipated trends (e.g., price floors), which affect the timing and magnitude of low-carbon investments (Ohlendorf et al., 2022). Accounting implications: these changes directly influence useful-life assumptions, impairment indicators, and the clarity of capital expenditure plans and the foundational assumptions utilized in recoverable amount assessments and associated disclosures (Ben-Amar et al., 2025).

Innovation and operational efficacy. Carbon pricing enhances incentives for abatement technology, cleaner industrial techniques, and product redesign, particularly in contexts where governance and information frameworks facilitate credible transition implementation. Evidence suggests that carbon pricing signals can enhance green innovation outputs, with more pronounced benefits in environments characterized by high ESG-related information and oversight (Feng et al., 2024). Companies are progressively implementing internal carbon pricing (ICP) to incorporate policy risk into budgeting and management control, with ICP transparency correlated to performance outcomes (Veeravel et al., 2025). Effective accounting necessitates reliable innovation and operational responses, which depend on consistent emissions and intensity indicators, as well as a clear connection between targets and capital/operational expenditures, thereby mitigating "window-dressing" risks and enhancing decision-making utility.

Responses regarding financing and contracting. Carbon pricing influences corporate finance as lenders and investors integrate transition risk into pricing, covenants, and capital allocation. Data from bond markets indicates that carbon risk is incorporated into debt instruments, aligning with a transition-related risk premium (Wu & Tian, 2022). Companies may utilize labeled instruments like green bonds as a component of their financing strategy in response to climate exposure; nevertheless, pricing results may indicate residual risk instead of guaranteed cost reductions (Guesmi et al., 2025). Enhanced emissions declaration and verification can lead to more advantageous loan pricing, suggesting that credibility influences financing conditions (Mahmoudian et al., 2023). Accounting hook: reliable emissions data and credible transition disclosures mitigate information risk in debt pricing and contracting, facilitating more orderly capital reallocation.

Implementation limitations (practical obstacles). In actuality, response capacity is limited by measuring systems and assurance preparedness. Scope 3 data frequently exhibit incompleteness and heterogeneity, constraining comparability and the assessment of value-chain exposure (Amel-Zadeh & Tang, 2025). Incorporating carbon-price trajectories into budgeting and impairment models necessitates scenario capabilities and data governance that are inconsistent; companies also encounter organizational obstacles that undermine the use of internal carbon pricing as a capital-allocation mechanism (Riedel et al., 2021). Ultimately, the utility of disclosure is contingent upon the capacity for assurance: the quality of climate reporting is generally superior when auditors have experience in climate-related matters, highlighting the significance of controls, competence, and verification infrastructure (Pham et al., 2024).

3.2. Investor Behavior and Portfolio Reweighting

Carbon pricing alters investor behavior by transforming climate transition risk into a more measurable element of anticipated cash flows and requisite returns. For diversified investors, this generally leads to two synergistic actions: reallocating portfolios away from carbon-intensive assets and employing active ownership techniques to impact company transition outcomes. The dominant response is contingent upon mandate limits, the reliability of carbon-pricing signals, and, importantly, the availability of comparable, decision-relevant emissions statistics.

A fundamental mechanism is the creation of a carbon-transition risk premium. Global research indicates that companies with elevated (and increasing) emissions generally demonstrate higher projected returns, aligning with the notion that investors want compensation for assuming transition risk amid stricter policies and carbon pricing (Bolton & Kacperczyk, 2023). Investors may regard environmentally friendly assets as partial safeguards against negative climate-related developments; the observed return dynamics between green and brown assets seem to be associated with evolving climate worries rather than consistent return differentials (Pástor et al., 2022). Carbon risk include a tail component wherein policy or climatic shocks provide disproportionate negative risk, hence intensifying incentives to mitigate exposure to high-carbon enterprises amid increased transition uncertainty (Ilhan et al., 2021).

Institutional investors are progressively utilizing information demand and stewardship as strategic tools. Global evidence indicates that institutions exhibiting a heightened demand for climate information, as indicated by CDP signatory status, correlate with enhanced corporate climate disclosure and subsequent reductions in emissions, aligning with both engagement and selective divestment from significant emitters (Cohen et al., 2023). Simultaneously, claims of portfolio decarbonization may not consistently result in actual reductions: data suggests that voluntary commitments (e.g., PRI endorsement) may not reliably diminish portfolio carbon footprints without stringent measurement and measurable objectives (Allahdadi, 2025). In this context, carbon price is anticipated to promote systematic portfolio reallocation when combined with comprehensive carbon accounting, uniform disclosures, and reliable assurance that mitigate information risk, therefore minimizing postponed and destabilizing repricing.

3.3. Empirical Designs to Test Reallocation Effects

The empirical examination of capital reallocation under carbon pricing seeks to determine if policy-driven carbon costs and transparency mandates result in systematic changes in financing circumstances, investment behavior, and portfolio allocation, as opposed to gradual or sudden repricing. From a sustainability accounting viewpoint, identification relies on the capacity to correlate firm-level carbon exposure and disclosure quality with measurable financial results, including variations in the cost of capital, investment structure, and asset valuation, while differentiating policy impacts from simultaneous macroeconomic or sectoral disturbances.

Table 3 delineates the principal empirical methodologies employed in the literature to evaluate these reallocation effects, emphasizing their conceptual underpinnings and common outcomes rather than technical execution.

Table 3. Empirical Approaches to Carbon Pricing and Capital Reallocation

Empirical Design	What It Identifies	Typical Outcome
Quasi-natural experiments (e.g., ETS introductions or expansions)	Causal effects of carbon pricing on financing costs and investment behavior	Higher cost of capital and reallocation away from carbon-intensive activities
Event studies (policy or disclosure shocks)	Short-term market repricing and investor reactions	Negative abnormal returns for high-carbon firms following policy or disclosure announcements
Cross-sectional asset-pricing tests	Whether emissions and transition exposure are priced as risk factors	Evidence of a carbon-transition risk premium across firms and markets

The efficacy of these designs is fundamentally contingent upon the quality, comparability, and reliability of sustainability-related data. Validated emissions metrics, uniform definitions of carbon exposure, and reliable climate-related disclosures enhance traceability between policy signals and financial results, hence reinforcing causal interpretation. In contrast, poor data quality and insufficient assurance might mask reallocation effects, leading to mispricing and heightening the probability of sudden, chaotic repricing. Sustainability accounting supports both empirical identification and the comprehensive evaluation of whether carbon price promotes orderly capital reallocation in alignment with financial stability.

4. SOLUTIONS AND RECOMMENDATIONS

4.1 Transmission Mechanisms to Systemic Risk

Carbon pricing might enhance financial stability by facilitating progressive and anticipatory capital reallocation; yet, it may also induce systemic risk when markets rapidly and synchronously revalue carbon-intensive assets. This section elucidates the stability implications for an interdisciplinary audience by differentiating firm-level valuation effects from system-wide amplification and summarizing three fundamental transmission mechanisms.

Asset repricing mechanism (firm-specific → linked losses). Carbon pricing diminishes the anticipated profitability of carbon-intensive businesses by elevating operating expenses and amplifying uncertainty over future policy rigor. These consequences diminish anticipated cash flows and/or elevate risk premiums, resulting in valuation losses for carbon-exposed enterprises and assets. Systemic significance arises when exposures are concentrated among investors, banks, and industries, leading to correlated firm-level repricing across portfolios. The likelihood of sudden repricing escalates when transition effects are acknowledged belatedly—such as when significant carbon-cost assumptions are excluded from impairment tests, provisions, or valuation inputs until policy enforcement is inevitable.

Figure 3. Carbon Pricing, Accounting Recognition, and the Transmission of Systemic Risk

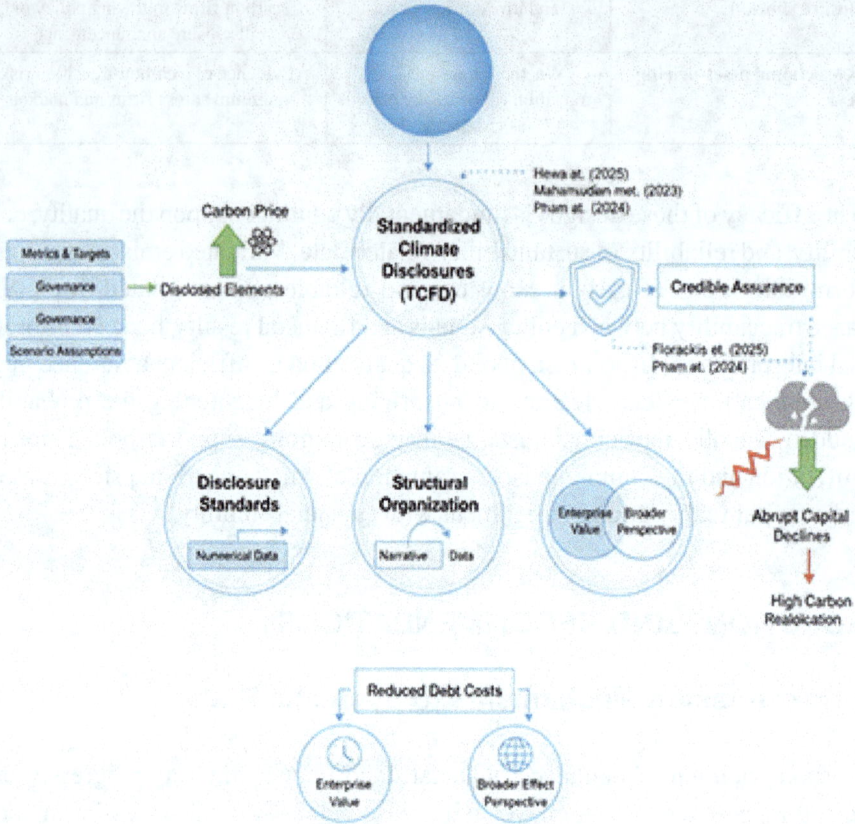

Author's compilation, 2026

Figure 3 depicts a chaotic transition scenario wherein a quick surge in carbon prices results in the swift repricing of carbon-intensive assets, balance-sheet magnification, and systemic instability. The image illustrates that these results are not predetermined: prompt, consistent, and reliable accounting acknowledgment of transition risk can mitigate repricing dynamics, diminish loss synchronization, and facilitate orderly adjustments within carbon-pricing frameworks.

Balance sheet amplification mechanism (intermediaries). Valuation losses may be exacerbated by leverage and liquidity factors. When assets exposed to carbon decrease in value, the quality of collateral diminishes, haircuts may increase, and margin requirements can become stricter, necessitating deleveraging and asset liquidation. These dynamics are especially pertinent for banks and leveraged investors with comparable exposures to energy, utilities, and heavy industries, because concurrent adjustments can constrict market liquidity and transmit stress beyond the originally impacted enterprises.

Systemic contagion channel. Systemic spillovers arise when correlated exposures interact with interrelated balance sheets and market structures. Co-movement among sectors, cross-holdings, and compelled divestitures can propagate shocks from carbon-intensive assets to wider markets, even when the initial policy shock is localized. In this context, the financial system's susceptibility is contingent not only on the magnitude of carbon-exposed losses but also on the synchronization of institutions adjusting their positions simultaneously under analogous constraints.

Implication in accounting. Timely, equivalent, and confident acknowledgment of transition risk mitigates the alignment of losses, thereby diminishing the likelihood that carbon-pricing shocks result in systemic instability. When carbon-price trajectories and transition assumptions are swiftly integrated into accounting estimates (such as impairment indicators, provisions, useful-life adjustments, and fair value inputs) and accompanied by consistent disclosures and assurance, markets can continually reprice exposures. In contrast, lack of transparency or delayed acknowledgment heightens information risk and the probability of abrupt, systemic changes transforming a policy signal into a destabilizing shock instead of a smooth transition mechanism.

4.2. Climate Stress Testing, Scenario Analysis, and Prudential Tools

Climate stress testing and scenario analysis have emerged as essential supervisory instruments for converting climate-transition pathways, typically represented by carbon pricing trajectories, into prospective evaluations of financial system resilience. This chapter emphasizes that the critical aspect is not the mechanics of any individual model, but rather the necessity of accounting-quality climatic knowledge to generate decision-useful prudential insights instead of simplistic outcomes.

Reasons for the divergence of climate stress testing from conventional stress tests. Climate stress testing diverge from traditional macro stress tests in three key aspects. Initially, they function over extended timeframes, since transition pathways develop over years instead of quarters. Secondly, climate shocks frequently exhibit non-linear characteristics and are contingent upon specific scenarios: the implementation of stricter policies, the substitution of technologies, and shifts in demand can induce threshold effects (e.g., sudden repricing of carbon-intensive assets). Third, outcomes are significantly influenced by assumptions especially the reliability and trajectory of carbon pricing, the capacity for sectoral pass-through, and the speed at which markets and enterprises adapt. These attributes render scenario design and parameter discipline more impactful than in conventional stress testing.

The significance of high-quality accounting data. The dependability of climatic stress testing fundamentally depends on the quality and comparability of the underlying firm-level data. Three data elements are particularly significant. Initially, emissions data (Scope 1–2 and, where pertinent to decision-making, Scope 3) are required to correlate carbon-pricing scenarios with firm-level cost exposure and transition susceptibility. Secondly, asset prices and valuation inputs dictate how transition pathways affect impairment risk, collateral quality, and market-value losses within portfolios. The timing of provisions and impairments is crucial, since deferred recognition can obscure underlying risks and exacerbate the scale and synchrony of losses when repricing ultimately takes place. In summary, stress testing necessitate ongoing measurement and disclosures that link scenario assumptions to acknowledged amounts and estimating uncertainty; otherwise, the results may represent data deficiencies rather than actual resilience.

Prudential ramifications. Supervisors are progressively regarding climate stress testing as instruments for learning and capacity enhancement, aimed at identifying concentrations, data inadequacies, and vulnerabilities in both orderly and disorderly transition scenarios. Significantly, the quality of disclosure and accounting can affect market responses to stress-testing exercises: when outcomes indicate deficiencies, investors may revise risk assessments and financing circumstances, thereby enhancing motivations for improved data governance and timely risk identification. Thus, prudential effectiveness relies not only on the complexity of scenarios but also on the architecture of analogous reporting, governance, and assurance that renders climate-related vulnerabilities visible and credible.

4.3 A Sustainability Accounting Contribution to Stability Monitoring

The assessment of financial stability increasingly relies on the transparency, comparability, and utility of decision-making about climate-transition risks intensified by carbon pricing among corporations and financial intermediaries. Sustainability accounting facilitates the conversion of diverse climatic exposures into organized, verifiable data that regulators and market actors can utilize for early-warning indicators, concentration analysis, and scenario-based resilience evaluations. Inadequate disclosure or delayed recognition can result in latent transition risk that may be abruptly repriced; conversely, prompt measurement and disclosure facilitate more continuous and predictable market adjustments.

A primary contribution resides in the field of materiality. Evidence suggests that markets deduce organizations' risk awareness and governance quality from materiality assessments inherent in disclosure choices, affecting perceived risk and financing circumstances (Matsumura et al., 2024). For stability monitoring, this indicates that supervisors may utilize sector-specific materiality benchmarks to detect disclosure deficiencies that could indicate inadequate acknowledgment of transition risk and an increased probability of postponed repricing.

Sustainability accounting enhances monitoring by augmenting the linkage between sustainability-related data and financial statements, together with capital market results. Integrated reporting that connects transition assumptions to impairments, provisions, and capital expenditure strategies correlates with enhanced liquidity, diminished capital costs, and increased accuracy in analyst forecasts results that align with decreased information risk and more seamless market adjustment (Wang et al., 2024). Connectivity indicators provide a pragmatic framework for identifying exposures that are susceptible to sudden valuation adjustments.

Third, assurance competence is fundamental to stability monitoring. Climate-risk disclosures are more common and of superior quality when audit partners have climate-related expertise, especially in high-risk industries (Pham et al., 2024). From a regulatory standpoint, the dependability of reported climatic data—and the proficiency supporting verification is significant, as mistakes in the exposures of banks and insurers can lead to systemic repercussions. Monitoring frameworks should evaluate not just the disclosure of climate information but also its credibility and assurance.

Ultimately, consistent sustainability disclosures facilitate system-wide measurement of climate risk. Firm-specific climate indicators obtained from obligatory filings enhance the explanatory capacity for market valuation and can be consolidated into metrics appropriate for monitoring and stress testing (Berkman et al., 2024). Integrating such data into comprehensive studies, encompassing tail-risk and network-based frameworks, modifies evaluations of interconnectedness and systemic vulnerability, illustrating the functional significance of sustainable accounting in the oversight of financial stability (Zhang et al., 2025).

Implications for policy. Sustainability accounting should be perceived by regulators and standard setters not just as a transparency obligation but also as a macroprudential information framework that influences the timing, stability, and credibility of market adjustments within carbon-pricing systems.

5. FUTURE RESEARCH DIRECTIONS

5.1. Designing Effective and Credible Carbon Pricing

Future research should progress beyond evaluating the significance of carbon pricing and focus on how carbon-pricing signals are interpreted in accounting decisions, capital reallocation, and systemic effects. A sustainability accounting viewpoint emphasizes three primary research avenues that are significantly pertinent to policy formulation and financial stability.

Initially, research ought to enhance the examination of accounting translation and value timing. Although evidence indicates that carbon-transition risk is reflected in expected returns, there is limited understanding of whether companies explicitly integrate carbon-price trajectories into impairment testing, provisions, useful-life estimates, and discount-rate assumptions, and whether prompt integration alleviates subsequent drastic repricing. Future research may investigate if the prompt identification of transition risk by accounting estimates results in more gradual value adjustments during restrictive regulatory environments.

Secondly, subsequent research should concentrate on the reliability of disclosures and assurance as moderating factors in capital reallocation. Current data suggests that transparency and verification might affect funding circumstances and market responses; nevertheless, the underlying mechanisms are insufficiently examined. Research may explore the impact of assurance quality, auditor skill, and disclosure comparability on investor reactions to carbon-pricing shocks, differentiating between systematic portfolio reallocation and postponed, destabilizing adjustments.

Third, enhanced integration of micro-level accounting data with macro-financial stability studies is essential. Studies on systemic risk increasingly depend on scenario analysis and stress testing, however frequently overlook firm-level recognition and disclosure policies. Future research may connect standardized climate disclosures and accounting estimates to network-based and tail-risk frameworks, therefore discovering early-warning signs of transition-related instability and enhancing the macroprudential use of sustainability information.

Methodologically, these agendas necessitate hybrid designs that integrate firm-level emissions and accounting data with policy scenarios and stress-testing methods. Incorporating accounting quality, recognition timing, and assurance into empirical and supervisory models will enable future research to elucidate the influence of sustainability accounting on market pricing and the robustness of the financial system amid the low-carbon transition.

5.2 Institutional Complements: Governance, Regulation, and Standards

Carbon pricing is most efficacious and least disruptive when integrated into an institutional framework that harmonizes governance, regulation, and reporting requirements. Robust governance facilitates credible transition implementation via board oversight, internal controls, and assurance capabilities; consistent evidence indicates that climate-risk disclosures are more probable and of superior quality when audit partners have climate expertise, especially in high-exposure sectors (Pham et al., 2024). Regulatory complements augment legitimacy and predictability: more robust climate-law enforcement correlates with enhanced financial stability outcomes, contingent upon enforcement capacity and institutional integrity (Alkatheeri et al., 2026), while prudential toolkits increasingly align with disclosure mandates and climate stress testing (Hidalgo-Oñate et al., 2023). Ultimately, reporting standards dictate the extent to which carbon-price signals convert into comparable, decision-relevant information. As governments transition from voluntary to mandatory climate reporting, fundamental difficulties such as border delineation, data integrity, recognition, and the integration of climate assumptions into financial statements emerge as important (Amel-Zadeh & Tang, 2025). Evidence indicates that enhanced connectedness between financial and non-financial information is esteemed by market participants and correlates with improved liquidity and capital cost outcomes (Wang et al., 2024)

5.3 Research Agenda at the Intersection of Carbon Pricing–Accounting–Stability

Future study should focus on three inquiries. How do enterprises convert carbon-price trajectories into accounting estimates (impairments, provisions, useful lives, discount-rate inputs), and does earlier recognition mitigate sudden repricing in response to stricter policy regimes (Bolton & Kacperczyk, 2023)? Secondly, in what manner can the credibility of disclosures and the capacity for assurance influence the velocity and organization of capital reallocation, considering evidence that transparency can reduce financing expenses and that auditor proficiency enhances the quality of climate reporting (Xu et al., 2024; Pham et al., 2024)? Third, how can micro-level accounting and transparency data be incorporated into macro-financial stability indicators and early-warning systems, considering evidence that disordered transition scenarios may exacerbate tail risk in financial institutions (Ojea-Ferreiro et al., 2024)? These goals necessitate hybrid methodologies that integrate emissions and accounting data with scenario analysis and stress-testing frameworks to predict dynamic policy routes and feedback loops (Acharya et al., 2023).

CONCLUSION

This chapter contends that carbon pricing transcends its role as an environmental policy tool; it functions as a market signal that alters expectations for future cash flows, risk premiums, and capital allocation, so directly affecting financial stability. When carbon pricing is credible, supported by predictable trajectories, consistent enforcement, and complementing regulations, markets can progressively internalize transition costs. Weak policy credibility and undeveloped information infrastructures can result in latent risks that may be rapidly repriced, exacerbating leverage and liquidity pressures while propagating shocks throughout interconnected financial institutions.

The chapter's primary contribution is to establish sustainability accounting as the interpretative framework that renders carbon-pricing signals meaningful for decision-making by enterprises, investors, and regulators. Converting policy into accounting-relevant information necessitates consistent emissions measurement (Scope 1–3 when pertinent), carbon intensity benchmarks, internal carbon pricing when applicable, and explicitly articulated assumptions. These inputs regulate essential financial reporting determinations such as impairment testing, provisions, useful-life estimates, and valuation inputs, thereby reducing the disparity between narrative transition commitments and recognized amounts that influence financing conditions and capital allocation.

Capital reallocation under carbon pricing is influenced by corporate actions (investment, innovation, and financing decisions) and investor conduct (portfolio adjustments and engagement). The efficiency and organization of reallocation are contingent upon the comparability and assurance of disclosures: high-quality, verifiable information mitigates information risk and facilitates ongoing repricing, while generic or delayed recognition heightens the probability of chaotic adjustments. At the macro-financial level, climate stress testing and scenario analysis are most insightful when based on high-quality accounting data that links carbon-price trajectories to asset values, provisions, and impairment timing, allowing supervisors to identify concentrations and evaluate amplification pathways.

The policy conclusion is unequivocal: carbon pricing must be assessed within the context of an institutional framework. Reliable price signals, consistent reporting standards, strong governance, and assurance capabilities are interconnected prerequisites for a systematic shift. Through the enhancement of measurement, recognition, and disclosure, sustainability accounting can serve as a macroprudential adjunct to carbon pricing facilitating prompt risk internalization, more efficient capital reallocation, and a reduced likelihood of transition dynamics escalating into systemic instability.

REFERENCES

Acharya, V. V., Berner, R., Engle, R., Jung, H., Stroebel, J., Zeng, X., & Zhao, Y. (2023). Climate stress testing. *Annual Review of Financial Economics, 15*(1), 291–326. DOI: 10.1146/annurev-financial-110921-101555

Alkatheeri, H., Mertzanis, C., & Kampouris, I. (2026). Climate laws and financial stability. *Research in International Business and Finance, 81*, 103151. DOI: 10.1016/j.ribaf.2025.103151

Allahdadi, M. R. (2025). Beyond green signaling: Are institutional investors decarbonizing their portfolios? *International Review of Economics & Finance, 104*, 104767. DOI: 10.1016/j.iref.2025.104767

Amel-Zadeh, A., & Tang, Q. (2025). Managing the shift from voluntary to mandatory climate disclosure: The role of carbon accounting. *The British Accounting Review, 57*(2), 101594. DOI: 10.1016/j.bar.2025.101594

Ben-Amar, W., Chourou, L., & Ding, X. (2025). Climate risk and long-lived tangible asset impairments. *Journal of Accounting and Public Policy, 54*, 107374. DOI: 10.1016/j.jaccpubpol.2025.107374

Berkman, H., Jona, J., & Soderstrom, N. (2024). Firm-specific climate risk and market valuation. *Accounting, Organizations and Society, 112*, 101547. DOI: 10.1016/j.aos.2024.101547

Bolton, P., & Kacperczyk, M. (2021). Do investors care about carbon risk? *Journal of Financial Economics, 142*(2), 517–549. DOI: 10.1016/j.jfineco.2021.05.008

Bolton, P., & Kacperczyk, M. (2023). Global pricing of carbon-transition risk. *The Journal of Finance, 78*(6), 3677–3754. DOI: 10.1111/jofi.13272

Borghei, Z., Linnenluecke, M., & Bui, B. (2024). The disclosure of climate-related risks and opportunities in financial statements: The UK's FTSE 100. *Meditari Accountancy Research, 32*(3), 1031–1063. DOI: 10.1108/MEDAR-05-2023-1998

Chen, S., Lin, W., Wang, M., & Zhang, Y. (2025). Spillover effects in mandatory environmental reporting. *Journal of Accounting and Public Policy, 54*, 107357. DOI: 10.1016/j.jaccpubpol.2025.107357

Chen, Y., & Ma, Y. (2021). Does green investment improve energy firm performance? *Energy Policy, 153*, 112252. DOI: 10.1016/j.enpol.2021.112252

Cohen, S., Kadach, I., & Ormazabal, G. (2023). Institutional investors, climate disclosure, and carbon emissions. *Journal of Accounting and Economics*, *76*(2–3), 101640. DOI: 10.1016/j.jacceco.2023.101640

Delgado Sánchez, V. P., Zorio-Grima, A., & Merello, P. (2026). Sustainability reporting assurance: Knowledge, lags, levels, and providers in leading global companies. *Journal of Innovation & Knowledge*, *12*, 100899. DOI: 10.1016/j.jik.2025.100899

Dong, Q., Zhao, Y., Ma, X., & Zhou, Y. (2024). Risk spillover between carbon markets and stock markets from a progressive perspective: Measurements, spillover networks, and driving factors. *Energy Economics*, *129*, 107228. DOI: 10.1016/j.eneco.2023.107228

Feng, T., Wang, X., Shi, Y., & Tu, Q. (2024). The role of carbon price signal in green innovation: Evidence from China. *Journal of Environmental Management*, *370*, 122787. DOI: 10.1016/j.jenvman.2024.122787 PMID: 39362165

Florackis, C., Muktadir-Al-Mukit, D., Sainani, S., & Zhang, Z. (2025). Stock market reaction to mandatory carbon disclosure announcements: The role of institutional investors. *Journal of International Financial Markets, Institutions and Money*, *99*, 102113. DOI: 10.1016/j.intfin.2025.102113

Guesmi, K., Makrychoriti, P., & Pyrgiotakis, E. G. (2025). Climate change exposure and green bonds issuance. *Journal of International Money and Finance*, *152*, 103281. DOI: 10.1016/j.jimonfin.2025.103281

Hewa, S. I., Mala, R., Chen, J., & Dumay, J. (2025). Climate related disclosures and investor behaviour: An Australian study. *Advances in Accounting*, *68*, 100809. DOI: 10.1016/j.adiac.2025.100809

Hidalgo-Oñate, D., Fuertes-Fuertes, I., & Cabedo, J. D. (2023). Climate-related prudential regulation tools in the context of sustainable and responsible investment: A systematic review. *Climate Policy*, *23*(6), 704–721. DOI: 10.1080/14693062.2023.2179587

Hidalgo-Oñate, D., Fuertes-Fuertes, I., & Cabedo, J. D. (2023). Climate-related prudential regulation tools in the context of sustainable and responsible investment: A systematic review. *Climate Policy*, *23*(6), 704–721. DOI: 10.1080/14693062.2023.2179587

Ilhan, E., Sautner, Z., & Vilkov, G. (2021). Carbon tail risk. *Review of Financial Studies*, *34*(3), 1540–1571. DOI: 10.1093/rfs/hhaa071

Kleimeier, S., & Viehs, M. (2021). Pricing carbon risk: Investor preferences or risk mitigation? *Economics Letters*, *205*, 109936. DOI: 10.1016/j.econlet.2021.109936

Li, D., Zhang, Z., & Gao, X. (2025). The impact of carbon emission trading system on the implied cost of equity capital. *International Review of Economics & Finance, 101*, 104157. Advance online publication. DOI: 10.1016/j.iref.2025.104157

Long, R., Wang, X., Wu, M., Chen, H., Li, Q., & Wang, Y. (2023). The impact of carbon information disclosure on the cost of capital: The moderating role of regulatory pressures. *Resources, Conservation and Recycling, 195*, 106970. DOI: 10.1016/j.resconrec.2023.106970

Mahmoudian, F., Yu, D., Lu, J., Nazari, J. A., & Herremans, I. M. (2023). Does cost of debt reflect the value of quality greenhouse gas emissions reduction efforts and disclosure? *International Journal of Accounting, Auditing and Performance Evaluation, 16*(?), 100563. https://doi.org/DOI: 10.1016/j.intaccaudtax.2023.100563

Matsumura, E. M., Prakash, R., & Vera-Muñoz, S. C. (2024). Climate-risk materiality and firm risk. *Review of Accounting Studies, 29*(1), 1–40. DOI: 10.1007/s11142-022-09718-9

Ohlendorf, N., Flachsland, C., Nemet, G. F., & Steckel, J. C. (2022). Carbon price floors and low-carbon investment: A survey of German firms. *Energy Policy, 169*, 113187. DOI: 10.1016/j.enpol.2022.113187

Ojea-Ferreiro, J., Reboredo, J. C., & Ugolini, A. (2024). Systemic risk effects of climate transition on financial stability. *International Review of Financial Analysis, 96*(Part B), 103722. https://doi.org/DOI: 10.1016/j.irfa.2024.103722

Pástor, Ľ., Stambaugh, R. F., & Taylor, L. A. (2022). Dissecting green returns. *Journal of Financial Economics, 146*(2), 403–424. DOI: 10.1016/j.jfineco.2022.07.007

Pham, L., Hay, D., Miihkinen, A., Myllymäki, E.-R., Niemi, L., & Sihvonen, J. (2024). Climate risk disclosures and auditor expertise. *The British Accounting Review, 101439*, 101439. Advance online publication. DOI: 10.1016/j.bar.2024.101439

Riedel, F., Gorbach, G., & Kost, C. (2021). Barriers to internal carbon pricing in German companies. *Energy Policy, 159*, 112654. DOI: 10.1016/j.enpol.2021.112654

Veeravel, V., Hiremath, R. B., & Panda, P. (2025). Does internal carbon pricing improve firm performance? Evidence from Indian listed companies. *Finance Research Letters, 86*, 108780. Advance online publication. DOI: 10.1016/j.frl.2025.108780

Wang, R., Chua, W. F., Simnett, R., & Zhou, S. (2024). Is greater connectivity of financial and non-financial information in annual reports valued by market participants? *The British Accounting Review, 56*(6), 101407. DOI: 10.1016/j.bar.2024.101407

Wu, Y., & Tian, Y. (2022). The price of carbon risk: Evidence from China's bond market. *China Journal of Accounting Research*, *15*(2), 100245. DOI: 10.1016/j.cjar.2022.100245

Xu, W., Sun, Z., & Ni, H. (2024). Transparency pays: How carbon emission disclosure lowers cost of capital. *Economic Analysis and Policy*, *83*, 165–177. DOI: 10.1016/j.eap.2024.05.020

Yan, J., Guo, Y., & Wen, F. (2025). Carbon risk and the cost of equity capital: Evidence from China. *International Review of Economics & Finance*, *99*, 103975. DOI: 10.1016/j.iref.2025.103975

Zhang, C., Li, Y., & Liang, S. (2025). Climate change attention and systemic financial risk: A TENET analysis. *Finance Research Letters*, *72*, 106555. DOI: 10.1016/j.frl.2024.106555

Chapter 5
Carbon, Clauses, and Chains: The New Architecture of Sustainable Global Trade

Bayu Tri Cahya
http://orcid.org/0000-0001-9277-5740
Universitas Islam Negeri Sunan Kudus, Indonesia

Muhammad Agus Irawan
http://orcid.org/0009-0002-4110-4538
Universitas Islam Negeri Sunan Kudus, Indonesia

Umi Hanifah
http://orcid.org/0009-0009-2062-6370
Universitas Duta Bangsa Surakarta, Indonesia

Muslim Marpaung
Politeknik Negeri Medan, Indonesia

Irma Suryani Lubis
Politeknik Negeri Medan, Indonesia

ABSTRACT

The international trade architecture is shifting from a focus on pure economic growth to global emissions mitigation, primarily to combat carbon leakage. By utilizing instruments like the Carbon Border Adjustment Mechanism (CBAM) and integrating environmental provisions into trade agreements, green production standards are harmonized to protect climate goals from policy asymmetries. This transition is systemically transmitted through Global Value Chains (GVCs), where multinational

DOI: 10.4018/979-8-3373-8998-1.ch005

transparency demands drive the adoption of environmental standards in developing nations. Ultimately, the synergy between carbon pricing, legal clauses, and GVC connectivity shifts the global paradigm from cost efficiency to sustainability, fostering transnational decarbonization and inclusive green growth.

INTRODUCTION

In the contemporary global market, integrating sustainability into trade practices has become urgent. The restructuring of global trade to incorporate sustainable practices is driven by the need to reduce environmental impacts, particularly carbon emissions, and promote long-term economic and social benefits (Chen & Zhang, 2025; Jayaswal et al., 2025; Sarkar et al., 2018). This shift is evident in the implementation of various carbon regulatory policies, such as carbon cap-and-trade systems, carbon taxes, and carbon offsets, which aim to reduce greenhouse gas emissions and encourage investment in carbon reduction technologies (Kang & Tan, 2023; Zarrinpoor & Khani, 2021).

However, this transformation effort directly confronts the realities of global trade. Global trade, encompassing production processes and cross-border transportation, is a major contributor to carbon emissions that drive climate change (IPCC, 2022). This dependency creates an economic dilemma: on the one hand, trade expansion stimulates economic growth through increased industrial activity and massive energy consumption, which linearly increases pollution (World Bank Group, 2020). On the other hand, the resulting economic growth serves as crucial capital to fund research on clean technologies and energy efficiency needed in the future (OECD, 2025). In this reciprocal relationship, the main challenge is achieving sustainability that balances economic ambitions with environmental protection (United Nations, 2019).

Here, the role of trade policy becomes vital (WTO, 2020). Trade liberalization, for example, is a double-edged sword: it can accelerate the spread of green technological innovation worldwide (UNCTAD, 2021), but without strict regulation, it also risks exacerbating environmental damage from surges in global production and transportation volumes (OECD, 2019). In particular, this study highlights the issue of carbon emissions, which has become a crucial part of international trade. Various approaches, ranging from carbon pricing regulations and carbon restrictions to integrating environmental provisions into agreements and efforts to transform industrial chains to move towards green production, have become an important part of efforts to create a sustainable trading system and to mitigate climate change. The literature shows that reducing carbon emissions in international trade can be achieved through various strategic measures, particularly carbon regulation and carbon restrictions, which drive change toward green trade through innovation and the use of environmentally friendly technologies. Awareness and shared commitment must continue to be built toward climate change mitigation and accelerating the transformation of a sustainable trade architecture.

THE IMPACTS OF CLIMATE CHANGE AND GLOBAL SUSTAINABLE DEVELOPMENT STRATEGIES

The issues of climate change and sustainable management are now serious concerns for scientists, industry, and governments worldwide. Various studies in the literature present different definitions of sustainability management and climate change, including explanations of operational procedures and their broad impacts on the world (Bick & Keele, 2022). Climate change is a significant long-term shift in global atmospheric conditions, such as changes in temperature and rainfall patterns, that have become increasingly noticeable since the mid-20th century and are a major factor in global warming and the greenhouse effect (NASA, n.d.). To understand this phenomenon, it is important to distinguish between weather and climate. Weather refers to short-term fluctuations in atmospheric conditions, such as temperature, rainfall, humidity, and wind, in a particular region, which can change drastically from hour to hour or day to day. In contrast, climate is defined as the average of these weather conditions measured over many years in a region or city. It is this difference in observation duration that separates daily weather dynamics from permanent, global-scale climate trends. The climate in a region generally changes very slowly and reflects long-term shifts in average weather, such as variations in annual rainfall. However, global climate change is not simply the average of local climates; it is the result of systemic connectivity that makes its effects felt worldwide. This phenomenon is driving global warming and extreme weather, affecting the lives of populations and the stability of cities worldwide.

Global warming is the increase in Earth's average temperature due to the greenhouse effect. This process occurs when greenhouse gases such as carbon dioxide and methane, produced by industrial and transportation activities, accumulate in the atmosphere. These emissions damage the ozone layer, which is supposed to absorb or re-emit heat radiation. Heat energy from the Sun and the Earth's surface is trapped in the atmosphere because it cannot dissipate into space quickly enough, ultimately triggering global warming (Filonchyk et al., 2024). However, it is currently a threat; the Earth's atmosphere has long acted as a giant greenhouse, trapping the sun's heat to create temperatures that support human life. Without this natural greenhouse effect, Earth's temperature would likely drop by more than 30°C, making it extremely cold and uninhabitable. However, the surge in greenhouse gas emissions that began with the Industrial Revolution has disrupted this natural balance, causing serious global warming and endangering the environment today. Climate change and greenhouse gas emissions have caused global temperatures to rise faster than at any other time in history, with greenhouse gases such as methane, carbon dioxide, and *chlorofluorocarbons* (CFCs) being the main contributors because they trap infrared radiation and heat. This phenomenon has made environmental management and sustainable development crucial for countries and global companies, and the issue has become an integral part of climate discussions since the Earth Summit in Rio in 1992. Although there was initially no universally agreed-upon definition, this concept continues to evolve as a key foundation for addressing the impacts of global climate change.

The most frequently cited definition of sustainable development comes from the UN Brundtland Commission, which states that "Sustainable development is development that meets the needs of the present without compromising the ability of future generations to meet their own needs" (United Nations, 1987). In addition, the World Commission on Environment and Development provides a complementary definition: sustainability is a process of change in which resource exploitation, investment direction, technology development orientation, and institutional change are harmonized and enhance the potential of the present and future to meet human needs and aspirations. Both definitions emphasize the importance of balancing human progress with nature conservation. In practice, leading international companies are now integrating environmental strategies into the core of their corporate strategies to support long-term global growth. This strategy aims to pursue the three pillars of sustainable development simultaneously, namely a healthy environment, economic prosperity, and social justice, to ensure cross-generational well-being. Global experience shows that integrating these three pillars is essential to the sustainability of business and society.

ENVIRONMENTAL POLICY AND EMISSIONS REGULATION

Environmental sustainability has gained increasing attention from governments and companies in recent decades. Governments worldwide have made reducing greenhouse gas emissions and addressing global warming among their highest priorities (Yilmaz, 2025), and business executives have placed environmental issues at the top of their agendas (Zhang et al., 2024). For example, the Chinese government is committed to achieving carbon neutrality by 2060. Apple Inc. has assumed a major responsibility for environmental protection and is working to achieve carbon neutrality for all its products by 2030. Environmental sustainability has become a major concern in business operations. In many countries, carbon taxes or emissions trading systems (ETS) have been implemented (He et al., 2015, 2017). Under climate regulations, companies have made environmentally friendly business operations a priority. (Yenipazarli, 2016). To meet government environmental standards, green technology has become a critical field because it can effectively reduce pollutant emissions.

In the operational sphere, environmental protection generally places government policy at the center of emissions regulation. An ideal climate policy is designed to maximize a region's social welfare, particularly when making optimal border-adjustment decisions. Production planning on the producer side is the focus of He et al. (2017), who analyze government emission limits and consider the difference between the purchase and sale prices of emission permits. Simultaneously, Hammami et al. (2018) link public environmental awareness, emission intensity, and product prices to design carbon tax levels that can maintain public welfare. Drake et al. (2016) Also describe the impact of carbon tax and cap-and-trade regulations on companies' technology choices and production capacity. The effectiveness of government subsidies for corporate green technology is also a crucial focus of Jung & Feng (2020). Their findings show that subsidies can be detrimental to the environment when the government focuses solely on the benefits of technology, failing to account for overall costs. Given that most previous thinking still focuses on regulatory strategies on the producer side, whether through permit allocation, taxes, or subsidies, the study aims to fill a gap that is rarely addressed. This approach not only reviews regulations for producers but also examines subsidy schemes for consumers related to carbon tax rates for more comprehensive environmental protection.

CARBON PRICING: MARKET DISCIPLINE ON EMISSIONS

The Paris Agreement marks the international community's official support for a transition towards more fragmented, domestically based climate cooperation. However, emission reduction commitments vary in timing, nature, and scope (MA et al., 2019). The Paris Agreement is a binding international legal instrument on climate change. The agreement was adopted by 195 Parties at the United Nations Climate Change Conference (COP21) in Paris, France, on December 12, 2015. The Paris Agreement entered into force on November 4, 2016. As of January 27, 2026, there were 194 Parties to the agreement (UNFCCC, 2026). Uneven climate change mitigation efforts can lead to environmental consequences, including shifts in production and investment from regions with strict carbon regulations to those with lower climate ambitions (Nielsen et al., 2021). This phenomenon, known as carbon leakage, has become an important issue in international climate policy, including in the European Union Emissions Trading System, the draft federal climate bill in the United States, and the national carbon market being developed in China.

Existing policy frameworks still largely rely on domestic measures to reduce the risk of leakage (MA et al., 2019). Implementing a cap-and-trade system can meet the needs of developing countries and efficiently control global emissions. Carbon tariffs can also reduce demand for carbon-intensive goods produced in countries with limited climate regulations. Carbon tariffs are imposed on both direct and indirect emissions from imported goods (Böhringer et al., 2016).

Carbon pricing is accepted as the most cost-effective approach to reducing emissions. The carbon pricing mechanism is flexible and can be implemented through fossil fuel taxes, cap-and-trade systems, hybrid schemes, or other national policies (MacKay et al., 2017). Carbon pricing is a climate policy instrument designed to align the cost of fossil fuel consumption or carbon-intensive processes with the social costs they generate. This means that market prices also reflect the external impacts on the environment and society. According to the State and Trends of Carbon Pricing 2025 report, 80 carbon pricing instruments, including 37 emissions trading systems (ETS) and 43 carbon taxes, have been implemented or are under development worldwide. This number has grown substantially from less than 10 instruments in 2005 to 80 instruments today. By 2025, approximately 28% of global emissions will be covered by carbon pricing, up from 5% in 2005. Revenue from carbon pricing mechanisms has exceeded US$ 100 billion annually for two consecutive years. The global average carbon price for emissions reached approximately US$19 per ton in 2025, nearly double the 2015 level of US$10 per ton. This increase was mainly driven by a significant increase in permit prices in the EU ETS over the past 10 years, while the contribution of carbon taxes has remained relatively stable. Countries such as Brazil, China, India, Indonesia, and Turkey are making significant progress in developing carbon pricing policies, including ETS and carbon taxes, while Zambia, Tanzania, Paraguay, and Vietnam are considering and preparing to participate in the international carbon market (The World Bank, 2025).

With increasing attention to carbon emissions, carbon taxes and emissions trading systems have become two key mechanisms for controlling them (Dou et al., 2023). The scope of carbon pricing policies has expanded globally, and empirical evidence of their effectiveness is growing. This underscores the importance of carbon pricing in the international climate policy mix. Carbon pricing is a crucial instrument that can strengthen jurisdictions' capacity to address broader economic and environmental challenges and facilitate the global transition to net-zero emissions (The World Bank, 2025). There are two types of carbon pricing (Pryor et al., 2023), namely:

1. Direct Carbon Pricing

Direct carbon pricing refers to a carbon pricing instrument that provides direct price incentives proportional to the greenhouse gas (GHG) emissions generated by a product or activity. This is achieved by applying the same price per metric ton of carbon dioxide equivalent (CO_2e) to various sources. This mechanism helps equalize the marginal cost of emission reductions, resulting in cost-effective climate change mitigation. Essentially, direct carbon pricing includes carbon taxes and emissions trading systems.

2. Indirect Carbon Pricing

Indirect carbon pricing refers to policy instruments that alter the price of carbon-intensive inputs in ways that are not always proportional to the emissions generated and vary between sources of greenhouse gas (GHG) emissions. These instruments provide carbon price signals even though they are often adopted for other socio-economic purposes, such as increasing government revenue or controlling air pollution. Prime examples of indirect carbon pricing are consumption taxes and fossil fuel subsidies.

CBAM: BALANCING CLIMATE POLICY AND GLOBAL TRADE

Carbon pricing policy designs differ across jurisdictions, making it difficult to compare and aggregate these efforts. One of the biggest challenges of emissions trading and carbon taxes is carbon leakage, as carbon pricing mechanisms only apply locally while production and trade are global. Companies may choose to move production to countries that do not impose carbon prices or import products from third countries, as long as it is more cost-effective. The implementation of explicit carbon pricing policies often sparks debate regarding differences in climate change mitigation commitments and efforts between jurisdictions. Industries in jurisdictions with strict carbon regulations and high carbon prices may experience a decline in competitiveness compared to industries in jurisdictions with more lenient carbon regulations (Zhong & Pei, 2024). These concerns reinforce the urgency of protecting equal opportunities for industrial sectors facing competitive pressures in the global market (MA et al., 2019). Border Carbon Adjustments (BCAs) are a strategy often proposed in policy and legislative proposals, but they have not yet led to significant-scale implementation (Kortum & Weisbach, 2017). Barriers related to legal uncertainty, implementation techniques, and political reactions hinder adoption, even though BCAs offer an architectural concept that enables equal treatment of domestic and foreign products.

However, calls for the adoption of BCAs are increasingly at a different level as policy heterogeneity increases, awareness of universal and strict climate policies grows, and countries become more willing and ready to implement protectionist trade policies. This trend signals a greater urgency for global climate action. Previous obstacles have changed, such as tariff conflicts and gridlock at the World Trade Organization (WTO), which could have led to a decline in trade-related environmental protection measures. However, international agreements on climate issues have been reached, reducing concerns about political conflicts in negotiations. Technological innovation has also become a crucial factor in the adoption of BCAs, alongside increased data availability, the quality of emissions data and measurement methodologies, and the administrative and technical capacity for implementation. These conditions strengthen both the readiness and opportunities for widespread implementation (MA et al., 2019).

The European Commission submitted a proposal for a Carbon Border Adjustment Mechanism (CBAM) on July 14, 2021. This proposal was first announced in 2019 as part of the European Green Deal, the European Union's policy to achieve carbon neutrality by 2050 and a 55% reduction in greenhouse gas emissions by 2030. CBAM is designed to comply with WTO rules and will be implemented gradually for certain products, so that the carbon price for imported and domestic products is equivalent (Erdoğan, 2024). The elimination of free emission allowances in the EU ETS (2026–2034) increases the risk of carbon leakage. CBAM aims to be a corrective instrument that ensures equal carbon pricing for imported and domestic products. CBAM currently covers more than 500 products, including iron, steel, aluminum, fertilizers, electricity, hydrogen, and cement, with a value of around EUR 89 billion or 4% of total EU imports in 2024. These products have been identified as the most significant sources of carbon leakage risk. However, CBAM does not currently cover downstream products, such as steel car parts, which creates a risk of carbon leakage through production relocation or import rerouting. The EU is considering expanding CBAM to cover downstream products and additional high-carbon-intensity sectors (Narloch, 2025).

CBAM gained legal legitimacy through Regulation (EU) 2023/956, which was adopted by the European Parliament and the Council on May 10, 2023. This legal basis outlines the stages of implementation of the CBAM mechanism. The definitive CBAM regime will come into force in early 2026. At this stage, importers of goods into the EU are required to pay a carbon price equal to the proportion of the products' emissions. Importers must register with the national authorities and submit CBAM certificates each year in an amount corresponding to their emissions liability. The price of the certificates is set based on the weekly average price of EU ETS emission allowance auctions in €/ton of CO_2. If importers can prove that a carbon price has been paid during production in the country of origin, the number of certificates to be submitted can be reduced. The implementation of CBAM is designed to gradually replace free allocation in the EU ETS during the 2026–2034 transition period. This transition is achieved through a progressive reduction in free emission allowances, starting at a low level at the beginning of the period and increasing significantly towards the end. The reduction scheme is set at 2.5% in 2026; 5% in 2027; 10% in 2028; 22.5% in 2029; 48.5% in 2030; 61% in 2031; 73.5% in 2032; 86% in 2033, and 100% in 2034 (Cammeo et al., 2025).

Many believe that implementing CBAM will face challenges because it could create trade barriers and trigger friction with World Trade Organization (WTO) rules. WTO trade rules aim to eliminate trade barriers because the more liberal a market is, the higher the overall economic potential. At the heart of these rules is the principle of non-discrimination, which ensures equal treatment for all parties in international trade. CBAM may violate the most-favored-nation (MFN) principle if it treats imports from WTO members differently based on their carbon content. Less developed countries have limited capacity to mitigate greenhouse gas emissions so that they will face higher carbon prices. Countries such as Russia, Turkey, the United Kingdom, China, and Ukraine are the largest exporters of products that CBAM will automatically cover. The United Kingdom, Serbia, and Mozambique are also exporters that depend on the EU, as 80% of their CBAM exports go to the European Union. These countries are potentially vulnerable to the impact of CBAM implementation. However, overall, the implementation of CBAM will not significantly affect exports from developed countries because they have the technological capacity to reduce the carbon intensity of their production. Developing countries are expected to experience only a 1.4–2.4 percent decline in CBAM product exports. This shows that the estimated consequences of CBAM for international trade are not as bad as some countries believe. (Blanc & Mendoza, 2023).

Unilateral carbon pricing risks partially offsetting domestic emission reductions by increasing emissions from overseas production. This risk of carbon leakage can be minimized by implementing Border Carbon Adjustments (BCAs). As the relative competitiveness and profitability of operations in countries that implement carbon pricing decline, the risk of carbon leakage increases. This type of leakage is most relevant to Energy-Intensive, Trade-Exposed (EITE) industries (Keen et al., 2021). CBAM has proven effective in reducing carbon leakage by imposing carbon costs on imported goods, thereby creating parity between domestic and imported products. This mechanism plays a crucial role in maintaining the competitiveness of EITE industries while preventing production relocation to countries with looser climate regulations. Empirical evidence shows that during 2015–2021, carbon leakage reduced the effectiveness of domestic emission reductions by 13% in carbon-intensive sectors such as aluminum, cement, and steel (Cammeo et al., 2025). The comparison of scenarios shows that without CBAM, carbon leakage is relatively high, ranging from 5% to 19% with an average of 12%. Conversely, implementing CBAM can reduce leakage to 2-12%, with an average of 6%. The implementation of CBAM can also balance trade competition by restoring some of the competitiveness losses caused by unilateral carbon policies (Zhong & Pei, 2024).

Beyond their direct effects, BCAs can also influence other countries to adopt carbon pricing through policy signals. The implementation of BCAs reinforces that carbon pricing is a key pillar of mitigation strategies, thereby encouraging other countries to consider similar instruments. Even if BCAs start unilaterally, countries could coordinate to form free trade zones with shared external levies, which could evolve into a more formal international framework for carbon price coordination. (Keen et al., 2021). CBAM provides a strong economic incentive for countries exporting to the EU to adopt or strengthen domestic carbon pricing policies. This step contributes to the global harmonization of carbon pricing policies and strengthens cross-border climate action. CBAM serves as a policy instrument that sends a strong economic signal to exporters to internalize carbon costs in production. Countries with an export orientation to the EU, such as Turkey and Brazil, face pressure to adjust their domestic policies to keep their industries competitive. In Turkey, the government is accelerating the establishment of a domestic emissions trading system in response to the implementation of CBAM. This is due to its close trade relations with the EU, particularly in carbon-intensive sectors such as steel, cement, and aluminum. Alignment with the EU carbon pricing mechanism is crucial to avoid competitive disadvantages. A similar situation is occurring in Brazil, where CBAM is accelerating the discourse on carbon market policies and the implementation of ETS. Malaysia has also initiated a domestic carbon market and drafted a climate bill that includes provisions on emissions trading. Meanwhile, countries such as Vietnam and Thailand are beginning to consider establishing their own carbon markets. (Cammeo et al., 2025).

Although the European Union is the pioneer, the United Kingdom and Norway are developing their own versions of carbon tariffs. Through the Ministry of Climate and Environment, Norway has affirmed its support for maintaining the integrity of CBAM during its consultation with the European Commission. Norway plans to introduce its version of CBAM in 2027, aligned with EU regulations. This harmonization effort aims to ensure that the Norwegian CBAM does not affect trade between the two parties, but rather extends the EU carbon regime to external trading partners, with the same reporting standards and compliance costs as the EU CBAM (Hermann et al., 2026). In addition, post-Brexit, the UK has established its own version of CBAM, which is scheduled to come into effect in 2027 (Dugast & Sanches, 2025). The UK government announced in its 2025 Budget that it will introduce its CBAM through the Finance Bill 2025-26. The UK CBAM will not adopt the EU (European Union) CBAM in its entirety, so there are differences in several aspects. First, the UK CBAM applies to iron, steel, aluminum, fertilizers, and cement, but not electricity. Second, this policy applies to direct and indirect emissions, although indirect emissions will not begin to be accounted for until 2029 at the earliest. Third, the method used to determine default emission values differs from the EU's. Finally, the UK CBAM payment system is a tax, with rates set by the government to match domestic carbon prices. There is no clear agreement yet between the UK and the EU regarding the treatment of UK exporters under the CBAM. However, a political declaration in May 2025 opens up the possibility of linking the EU and UK ETS. This step is reinforced by the Council's recommendation authorizing the European Commission to negotiate with the UK. If a binding agreement is reached, goods originating in the UK and exported to the EU could be exempt from CBAM, and conversely, goods originating in the EU and entering the UK could also be exempt (Hermann et al., 2026).

MEASURING EMISSIONS CONTENT IN TRADE

Emissions contained in trade refer to all greenhouse gas emissions, including carbon emissions, generated during the production process of internationally traded goods. The most commonly used approach in calculating greenhouse gas emissions is the production-based approach. These emissions calculations are based on actual greenhouse gas emissions within the country's territorial boundaries. The production-based approach considers only territorial emissions and does not account for trade-related emissions. Another approach is the consumption-based approach. This approach accounts for all greenhouse gas emissions from the production of goods, in accordance with a country's final consumption. The final consumption-based approach requires calculating all foreign emissions embedded in imported goods, as they are considered a consequence of domestic consumption patterns. This means that the final consumption-based approach accounts for carbon emissions associated with international trade (Dugast & Sanches, 2025).

It cannot be denied that accurately calculating a product's emission content is not easy. Limited data can influence this, so one step is to use default emission levels. I want to point out that default calculations require consideration regarding the determination of emission calculation system limits and alternative measures for calculating default rates (Zhong & Pei, 2024). The Greenhouse Gas Protocol classifies carbon emissions into three scopes. Scope 1 includes direct emissions from sources owned or controlled by the company (e.g., combustion of fossil fuels, company vehicles, and fugitive emissions). Scope 2 is indirect emissions from energy consumed in production (contained in electricity, heat, and steam). Scope 3 is indirect emissions from the supply chain, transportation, and waste (Michalek, 2016). The broader the system boundary, the greater the need for emissions data and the costs that must be borne. At the macro level, this can increase competitiveness and reduce carbon leakage; at the industry level, it can worsen competitiveness. Broader system boundaries contribute to cost savings in achieving climate targets. Defaults can be set at the product, company, sector, or economy-wide level, or a uniform default level can be set for all. More specific defaults provide greater incentives for companies to reduce emissions, although they also add complexity and implementation costs (Zhong & Pei, 2024). Despite the costs and complexity, setting defaults at the company level can maximize global welfare by encouraging companies to respond to various carbon restrictions in trade (Böhringer et al., 2017).

The World Economic Forum (WEF) provides several explanations for calculating emissions in trade. Emissions calculations in trade are usually conducted using a statistical approach, specifically a multi-regional input-output (MRIO) model. This model integrates input-output tables (IOTs), which describe the flow of economic transactions between countries (producers and consumers), with air emissions accounts (AEA), which record the greenhouse gas intensity of production activities in producer countries. Using MRIO to calculate trade emissions enables the estimation of emissions associated with internationally traded goods. The integration of IOT and AEA can produce a global database capable of tracking all emissions generated by sectors and subsectors in producer countries. The best-known environmental input-output model is the FIGARO dataset from Eurostat and the EXIOBASE database. The OECD also offers an Inter-Country Input-Output (ICIO) database that can be combined with air emissions accounts to provide data on emissions from imports and exports among the world's major economies, enabling analysis of emissions associated with international trade (Dugast & Sanches, 2025).

The application of embedded emissions calculations in the EU's CBAM covers greenhouse gas emissions inherent in imported goods, including direct emissions from production activities and indirect emissions from electricity use in production. Embedded emissions calculations for non-electrical goods are based on actual emissions measured using a measurement system. These emissions must be verified by an accredited verification body that prepares a report quantifying direct emissions from production facilities and embedded emissions from the materials used. The EU CBAM emissions calculation framework is designed to ensure that carbon costs are applied fairly, taking into account actual emissions. The use of default values applies only when actual emissions cannot be accurately calculated. Default values are determined by referring to the average emission intensity of the 10% of EU ETS installations with the worst performance in the relevant product category, particularly when the exporting country lacks reliable data. The EU CBAM sets default values for embedded emissions in electricity imports, unless the imports are made through a power purchase agreement with a foreign producer connected to the EU transmission network and with an emission intensity below 550 gCO_2/kWh. In addition, the EU CBAM does not ignore domestic climate regulations in trading partner countries. Regulations such as emission standards, energy-efficiency requirements in production, and bans on carbon-intensive technologies are still considered in the calculation of embedded emissions. As long as importers can provide evidence that the product complies with environmental regulations, this can reduce the number of CBAM certificates required and lower the CBAM burden on imported goods. The EU CBAM does not conflict with decarbonization efforts through domestic regulations in producer countries; rather, it allows the actual emissions data in a product to be used to obtain incentives (Boute, 2024).

GREEN TRADE ARCHITECTURE: PTAS AS A PILLAR OF SUSTAINABILITY

Trade rules are now seen as instruments of environmental protection. Trade and the environment are increasingly linked through bilateral and regional agreements that have proliferated in recent years. Preferential Trade Agreements (PTAs) increasingly feature environmental dimensions as an integral part of the international trade architecture. More than 700 PTAs include environmental provisions, signaling a trend toward the institutionalization of sustainability issues in trade agreements. Nearly all new PTAs consistently include environmental clauses. On average, each new PTA covers 48 environmental provisions, while some agreements exceed 100. American trade agreements include an average of 49 environmental provisions, while European PTAs include an average of only 26. This difference is mainly because many European PTAs were negotiated in the 1970s to 1990s, before environmental provisions in PTAs became a global trend. Recent trends show that environmental clauses are becoming increasingly prominent in PTAs. China leads the region with an average of 23 environmental provisions. PTAs involving African countries include an average of only 12 environmental provisions. The launch of the African Continental Free Trade Area (AfCFTA) marks an important milestone in African economic integration. This agreement still shows significant untapped potential, as it contains few environmental provisions, leaving room to strengthen the sustainability dimension in future trade negotiations (Brandi & Morin, 2023).

PTAs include many environmental provisions with a broader scope than those in the WTO. Some PTAs include environmental provisions that promote the harmonization, strengthening, and implementation of environmental policies. Environmental provisions in PTAs often require the spillover of environmentally friendly technology to developing countries and are accompanied by institutional capacity building. In addition, these provisions facilitate civil society engagement and cover a wide range of environmental issues, including restrictions on deforestation, protection of fish stocks, reduction of hazardous waste, and reduction of CO_2 emissions. The integration of environmental issues into PTAs now extends beyond trade. PTAs are evolving into instruments that integrate environmental obligations more broadly. The United States and the European Union have played a pioneering role in expanding environmental provisions and demonstrating that PTAs can serve as both an arena for experimentation and a means to drive innovation in the complexity of trade. Although environmental provisions are relatively rare in PTAs among developing countries, recent trends indicate that they are increasingly incorporating environmental clauses into their trade agreements (Brandi & Morin, 2023).

In-depth environmental provisions in regional trade agreements are an effective mechanism for reducing CO_2 leakage from developed to developing countries. This not only limits total CO_2 emission allocations but also encourages investment and innovation oriented towards low-carbon technologies. Deepening environmental provisions and fostering green technology cooperation help reduce CO_2 emissions by encouraging the green transformation of developing countries' economies through green technology spillovers. The inclusion of environmental protection clauses in PTAs and active participation in international environmental agreements have the potential to reduce both insourcing and outsourcing of cross-border pollution. South–North agreements have been shown to increase green energy efficiency. This shows that Southern countries need to actively engage in global environmental initiatives and adopt environmental provisions in PTAs to benefit from the spillover of environmental protection technologies from Northern countries (Gutsch et al., 2025).

SUSTAINABILITY CLAUSES: A NEW ERA IN WORLD TRADE ARCHITECTURE

The interaction between trade and the environment is not new. Since the Uruguay Round, sustainable development has been included in the Marrakesh Agreement (World Trade Law, n.d.). However, the relationship between trade and sustainability has not been central to trade governance. The WTO has begun to pay serious attention to this issue, as marked by the 2022 Agreement on Fisheries Subsidies, which focuses on sustainability. Member countries have also formed coalitions on climate issues, the circular economy, plastic pollution, and environmentally friendly trade (Aaken, 2024). The growth of international trade, the intensification of trade relations, and the level of trade openness are directly linked to environmental degradation, mainly due to the carbon emissions inherent in traded goods. The link between trade and the environment is reflected in international agreements through both the preamble and substantive provisions, including environmental obligations and trade-related environmental policies. More than 40% of the preambular sections of Free Trade Agreements (FTAs) contain declaratory language affirming the agreement's overall objectives, including commitments on environmental issues and sustainability. Substantive provisions cover domestic environmental legislation, the right to adopt regulations, and commitments to implement regulations. The history of the relationship between trade and the environment can be traced back to the 1947 GATT, through Article XX(g), which provides policy space for the conservation of limited natural resources. Further developments can be seen in the 1992 EEA Agreement, which adopted the precautionary principle, and NAFTA, which introduced the first supplementary agreement on trade and the environment. NAFTA was an important milestone because it set ambitious standards that later encouraged the integration of environmental issues into modern Free Trade Agreements (FTAs) (Panezi, 2024). Free Trade Agreements (FTAs) are a form of Preferential Trade Agreements (PTAs). FTAs provide preferential trade treatment among member countries by reducing or eliminating trade barriers.

As of January 2026, 138 countries, covering 74% of global emissions, have agreed to or are seriously considering net-zero CO_2 emission targets (Net Zero Tracker, n.d.). This reform includes a shift from high-carbon to low-carbon trade. A 2021 WTO study confirmed that integrating climate issues into FTAs remains limited. Only 18% explicitly refer to climate change or a low-emission economy. Climate-related provisions are also less detailed than those for other environmental issues, such as biodiversity or sustainable natural resource management. This indicates a gap between the international trade agenda and global commitments to climate mitigation. Major FTAs such as the Comprehensive and Progressive Agreement for Trans-Pacific Partnership (CPTPP), the United States-Mexico-Canada Agreement (USMCA), and the Regional Comprehensive Economic Partnership (RCEP) do not explicitly address climate change. This limits their role as strategic instruments for climate action, even though the CPTPP encourages cooperation towards a low-emission economy. The lack of integration of climate goals into FTAs indicates that the agreements were formulated before current global climate commitments (Lydgate, 2024). However, other studies show that FTAs can reduce companies' incentives to relocate production to jurisdictions with weak regulations. This makes FTAs a policy instrument that can suppress the emergence of pollution havens while promoting the harmonization of environmental standards across countries. Environmental provisions in FTAs not only raise environmental protection standards but also shift patterns of competitive specialization between countries. Companies are encouraged to invest in sustainable technologies to remain competitive, thereby enabling FTAs to serve as catalysts for industrial transformation towards sustainability (Gutsch et al., 2025).

The Agreement on Climate Change, Trade and Sustainability (ACCTS) marks a new evolution in the architecture of international trade agreements. Unlike traditional comprehensive FTAs, the ACCTS is designed to address specific climate and sustainability issues. This sectoral focus allows for more effective management of regulatory divergences while strengthening geopolitical relations between countries. ACCTS was initiated by New Zealand in September 2019 together with Fiji, Iceland, Norway, and Costa Rica with the main objectives of eliminating tariffs on more than 300 environmental goods (solar panels, wind and hydraulic turbines, electric vehicles, wool fiber, recycled paper, and wood products), commitments on environmental services (consulting on sustainable agriculture and forestry, professional engineering and architectural services), the elimination of harmful fossil fuel subsidies, and voluntary environmental labeling guidelines (New Zealand Foreign Affairs & Trade, n.d.). ACCTS is seen as a pathfinder and template for action on plurilateral agreements, demonstrating how trade rules can support broader climate and environmental goals (Lydgate, 2024).

In October 2021, the European Union and the United States announced an agreement to pursue a Global Arrangement on Sustainable Steel and Aluminium (GASSA) (Rimini et al., 2023). The main objective of GASSA is to restrict market access for non-participants that do not meet low-carbon intensity standards for steel and aluminium production. Restricting participation for high-carbon-intensity steel and aluminum producers confirms that GASSA marks a shift from a cooperative approach to an exclusive compliance-based mechanism. GASSA serves to control high carbon intensity in the steel and aluminum sectors. GASSA establishes a common minimum standard for embodied emissions that can be applied to countries with carbon pricing (the European Union) and performance standards (the United States). GASSA promotes the exchange of information and methodologies for calculating the carbon intensity of steel and aluminum to establish low-carbon intensity standards that exporters must comply with (Lydgate, 2024).

ENVIRONMENTAL ENFORCEMENT MECHANISMS IN GLOBAL TRADE ARCHITECTURE

The inclusion of environmental provisions in trade agreements helps achieve sustainability goals, particularly by reducing CO_2 emissions and air pollution (Brandi & Morin, 2023). The effectiveness of environmental provisions depends heavily on enforcement mechanisms. Trade agreements with effectively enforceable environmental clauses are reflected in reductions in CO_2 emissions in Asia. This shows that trade policy needs to be directed towards strengthening environmental provisions, establishing a transparent legal framework, and implementing consistent enforcement mechanisms. The EU–New Zealand trade agreement features important innovations, including stronger enforcement mechanisms for trade and sustainable development. One of its main breakthroughs is the possibility of imposing temporary trade sanctions in response to non-compliance with commitments under the Paris

Agreement (Gutsch et al., 2025). Non-compliance with environmental provisions in trade agreements is generally subject to Trade and Sustainable Development (TSD) mechanisms, which can ultimately lead to trade sanctions. However, the European Union initially relied solely on a cooperative policy dialogue approach to enforce environmental provisions (Brandi & Morin, 2023). In 2018, the EU, through Cecilia Malmström (EU Trade Commissioner), launched a 15-Point Action Plan to improve the effectiveness of TSD in EU trade agreements. Among the points are stricter law enforcement, expanding civil society's monitoring role, and EU resource support for sustainable development (Sofia, 2018).

The more in-depth the environmental provisions in trade agreements are, the greater their impact on reducing CO_2 emissions. This is achieved by facilitating cooperation on green technology, improving national environmental governance, and encouraging higher carbon productivity. The effectiveness of enforcing environmental provisions in trade agreements is strengthened by geographical proximity. This factor not only facilitates more intensive trade relations but also ensures that environmental protection provides mutual benefits for the countries involved. In addition, enforcement mechanisms that do not rely solely on sanctions can be implemented by integrating policy dialogue as a complementary instrument (Gutsch et al., 2025). Intergovernmental committees serve as institutional mechanisms to ensure compliance with environmental provisions. The 2011 trade agreement between the European Union and Korea established a Trade and Sustainable Development Committee that meets regularly to evaluate the implementation of environmental provisions and to formulate a priority agenda for cooperation. The approach of sanctions and cooperative dialogue has proven effective in enforcing environmental provisions (Brandi & Morin, 2023).

The effectiveness of environmental law enforcement at the micro level can be strengthened by involving civil society mechanisms. This participation legitimizes stakeholder demands, raises consumer awareness of environmental issues, and generates social pressure that encourages companies to be more responsible. Several jurisdictions, such as the EU, have imposed non-financial or sustainability disclosure requirements, particularly for large companies. The development of sustainability reporting standards indicates a global harmonization effort. Some of the key institutions involved in this process include the Global Reporting Initiative (GRI), the International Sustainability Standards Board (ISSB), the Sustainability Accounting Standards Board (SASB), and the European Financial Reporting Advisory Group (EFRAG) (Gutsch et al., 2025). Public reporting of non-compliance is a key element in enforcing environmental regulations (Brandi & Morin, 2023). On November 29, 2011, a local community organization in Mexico, Comité Pro-Mejoras de la Ribera Cahuaré, filed a complaint under the North American Agreement on Environmental Cooperation (NAAEC). The NAAEC is an environmental agreement that complements the North American Free Trade Agreement (NAFTA). This report, titled Sumidero Canyon II (SEM-11-002), highlights the Mexican government's failure to enforce environmental laws related to the mining operations of Cales y Morteros del Grijalva, S.A. de C.V., for limestone extraction in Sumidero Canyon National Park, which caused damage to the park. The Mexican government requested the termination of the submission process, citing three pending administrative procedures and asserting environmental law enforcement in accordance with Article 5(1)(b) of the NAAEC. However, the Secretariat of the Commission for Environmental Cooperation (CEC) identified several issues related to environmental compliance, prompting it to recommend that the CEC Council develop a factual record (CEC, 2013).

THE ROLE OF PTAS IN REDUCING GLOBAL VALUE CHAIN EMISSIONS

Preferential Trade Agreements (PTAs) have proven effective in promoting environmental regulations, particularly for global emissions issues (Brandi & Morin, 2023). The expansion of Global Value Chains (GVCs) is inextricably linked to PTAs that promote trade liberalization and reduce barriers. PTAs serve as catalysts for the cross-border movement of goods and services, particularly semi-finished goods, which are central to GVCs. The evolution of PTAs has shifted from a focus on market access and tariff reduction to sustainability integration. This is marked by the inclusion of environmental provisions to harmonize standards, maintain sustainability, and reduce negative externalities such as GVC pollution. PTAs play a dual role: they increase trade among members, which in turn increases emissions. However, environmental provisions in PTAs offset increased emissions by restructuring trade and spurring clean technology spillovers, thereby creating more environmentally friendly production processes and trade flows (Fairuz & Foster-McGregor, 2024). Porter's hypothesis has been shown to hold: well-designed environmental regulations can stimulate green innovation and corporate competitiveness (Zhang et al., 2024). The existence of environmental provisions is a win-win solution that can improve environmental quality and economic performance. Environmental provisions in PTAs reduce GVC emissions by around 72% of the additional emissions they generate (Fairuz & Foster-McGregor, 2024). This shows that although PTAs can increase emissions from GVC activities, the environmental provisions in the agreements serve as effective mitigation mechanisms, reducing negative environmental impacts.

The effectiveness of PTAs and their environmental provisions is more significant in low-income countries. PTAs expand export opportunities in GVCs, and environmental provisions play an important role in reducing emissions. Environmental provisions in GVCs integrated with PTAs can help offset the lack of domestic environmental regulations and encourage the adoption of cleaner technologies. In high- and upper-middle-income countries, the increase in GVC-related emissions is relatively small. This is in response to the environmental provisions in PTAs. The dynamics of GVC emissions are driven more by scale than by emission intensity. The diversification of GVC activities in high-income countries, ranging from upstream R&D to downstream high-tech manufacturing and financial services, may explain why the scale effect is more dominant than the emission-intensity factor. Exporters from high-income countries tend to focus on high-value-added services and activities in both the upstream and downstream sectors. This orientation results in lower emissions because the activities are not carbon-intensive (Fairuz & Foster-McGregor, 2024).

GVC TRANSFORMATION: GREEN TRADE INTEGRATION AND ENVIRONMENTAL INNOVATION

The main drivers of market greening in Global Value Chains (GVCs) are changing consumer and professional user preferences for green products and the shift towards stricter environmental regulations. GVC can play an important role in responding to stricter environmental regulations by encouraging innovation in renewable energy. Leading companies can promote the implementation of environmental standards at the supplier level (upstream supply chain). This is done by establishing strategic partnerships or by monitoring supplier compliance with established environmental standards. In 2007, Marks & Spencer (M&S) tested four green factories in Sri Lanka with environmentally friendly technologies such as rainwater harvesting, solar power, waste reduction, and energy-efficient cooling systems. This step was based on a 20-year relationship of trust with Sri Lankan suppliers and on efforts to strengthen the company's reputation for sustainable production practices. The application of technology in GVC greening efforts is also inseparable from helping efficiency and innovation to meet environmentally friendly production requirements. The adoption of robotics, 3D printing, wireless technology, and sensors plays a crucial role in increasing production efficiency and optimizing logistics, while significantly reducing carbon emissions (Gentile et al., 2023).

Smartphone manufacturers in China use robotics technology to improve production effectiveness. Environmental process innovations improve the efficiency of the value chain stage by reorganizing production and technology. Returpack, a Swedish recycling company, took an innovative step by installing bottle-compression equipment on its collection trucks to improve logistics efficiency in its recycling operations. This innovation reduces the number of trips, thereby lowering the carbon footprint. China's electronics industry has adopted Big Data Analytics (BDA) technology to enhance sustainable supply chain collaboration and industrial greening. BDA enables tracking of CO_2 emissions throughout the supply chain, predicting non-compliance risks, calculating carbon footprints, and monitoring logistics fleet routes. The Arzignano tanning district (Italy) has become a proactive GVC supplier in environmental innovation. Since the 1970s, this cluster has gradually and systematically improved the environment. Local government support has enabled the formation of a consortium that has built water treatment plants and waste disposal systems for the leather tanning industry. Other Italian companies, such as Aquafil, are also focusing on innovation in nylon yarn for floor carpets. The company has developed a new yarn called Econyl, which is made from recycled carpets, thereby reducing the use of raw materials and end-of-life waste. Vehicle manufacturers such as Piaggio, Aprilia, BMW, and Honda are committed to not using chemical products. These companies focus primarily on energy consumption, oil spills, and smoke and dust emissions during production (Gentile et al., 2023).

Major companies play a key role as actors in introducing environmental innovations in GVCs. Two mechanisms can be implemented in GVCs to apply environmental innovations (Gentile et al., 2023). The approaches that can be taken are as follows:

1. Standard-Based Approach

The standards-based approach emphasizes the company's primary role in establishing environmental regulations and codes of conduct that suppliers must comply with. These instruments can take the form of standards or certifications developed by independent institutions (third parties) or by the main company. In the case of IKEA, suppliers must hold ISO 4001 certification and Forest Stewardship Council (FSC) wood utilization certification, and comply with the IKEA IWAY supplier code of conduct. The standards-based approach can positively impact large companies by increasing production efficiency in line with environmental regulations and improving market cost efficiency.

2. Mentoring-Based Approach

A mentoring-focused approach is taken when certification is not yet available or when suppliers need additional support. The main company takes an active role by providing direct mentoring, transferring knowledge to suppliers, and ensuring the sustainability of the greening process. In China's electronics industry supply chain, strategic collaboration between buyers and suppliers plays a key role in accelerating digitalization and strengthening sustainability practices across the value chain. Another study of green textile manufacturers in Sri Lanka found that they often interact with international buyers to indirectly gain knowledge about environmental innovation in the production of complex products. Italian kitchen designer Valcucine also works closely with small suppliers to jointly commit to environmental goals and to develop standards that drive environmental innovation. A crucial factor in the mentoring-based approach is supplier competence and the strategic intent to engage in environmental improvement.

The carbon reduction effect of increased GVC is stronger in developing countries. This is because countries with weaker economic bases have greater potential to undergo green transformation by increasing their role in the global value chain, thereby facilitating technology and knowledge spillovers from developed countries. A country's increased participation in the GVC strengthens industrial system development, improves technology, and encourages movement from downstream to upstream. Technology is a significant factor in reducing carbon emissions, so that increased participation of a country or company as an upstream supplier in GVCs can lead to a deeper understanding of low-carbon technologies. Increased green innovation and the use of environmentally friendly technologies in global value chains have been shown to reduce carbon emissions across all industries, particularly in services, manufacturing, and primary industries (Yang et al., 2025).

CARBON REGULATION: DRIVING INNOVATION AND TECHNOLOGY SPILLOVER IN THE SUPPLY CHAIN

Carbon regulations can accelerate the green transition at the company level and significantly impact other companies across the supply chain. This strengthens cross-company cooperation and increases the impact of carbon-reduction efforts. Strict carbon regulations have been shown to correlate with increased green innovation, as reflected in rising green patent applications by companies. Carbon regulations are effective at stimulating green transformation by increasing the cost of emissions, thereby encouraging companies to adopt energy-efficient technologies, develop low-carbon technologies, reduce the carbon footprint of products, and implement comprehensive low-carbon management. Spillover effects in the supply chain from carbon regulations occur because they exert pressure on upstream companies but have little impact on downstream companies' green innovation capabilities. Carbon-reduction pressure on major (downstream) companies is transmitted to upstream suppliers, and the demand for emission reductions encourages them to innovate and develop green technologies (Qi et al., 2025).

Corporate carbon regulations generally influence upstream carbon regulations through three main mechanisms:

1. Demand Expansion

Strict carbon regulations encourage companies to improve their technology through the innovation compensation effect, which can also drive economic development (Welford & Starkey, 1996). These technological advances stimulate demand from downstream buyers and increase orders for supplier companies (Wei et al., 2024). Strict carbon regulations increase demand for low-carbon, green, and environmentally friendly intermediate inputs, particularly clean production technologies and products. This increase in demand motivates and creates positive pressure for upstream companies to innovate in low-carbon technologies (Qi et al., 2025).

2. Forced-Linkage

Forced linkage arises because downstream companies facing strict carbon regulations pass on the pressure to upstream suppliers (Godart & Görg, 2013). The dominance of downstream companies in the supply chain creates forced linkage with upstream suppliers. Strict carbon regulations encourage downstream companies to seek low-emission raw materials, so that pressure tends to be passed on to upstream companies (suppliers). Suppliers are both forced and encouraged to adopt green standards by proactively pursuing green innovation to remain competitive (Qi et al., 2025).

3. Knowledge Spillover

Knowledge spillover is an important mechanism for strengthening a company's innovation performance (Isaksson et al., 2016). Supply chain partnerships can provide companies with opportunities to continuously acquire innovative knowledge and experience. Strict carbon regulations accelerate the diffusion of green innovations from downstream to upstream companies, thereby enabling knowledge spillovers to play a significant role in strengthening cross-supply chain technological innovation (Qi et al., 2025).

Regulatory pressure on state-owned enterprises (SOEs) and large-scale companies can significantly stimulate green innovation among upstream suppliers. SOE suppliers contribute more significantly to improving green innovation capabilities. This is mainly due to the SOE's leading role in green development and its greater financial and technological resources to facilitate internal green transformation. This capacity makes SOE suppliers better able to meet downstream companies' demand for cleaner inputs (Qi et al., 2025).

IMPLICATIONS FOR DEVELOPING COUNTRIES AND INCLUSIVE GREEN GROWTH

The global crisis caused by the COVID-19 pandemic and the 2022 Ukraine–Russia conflict has reinforced the urgency of developing an inclusive green growth and sustainability model in response to economic uncertainty (Aslam & Ghouse, 2023). The World Bank introduced this model as a concept of sustainable growth oriented towards improving the welfare of the current generation (inclusive) and protecting the welfare of future generations (green) (The World Bank, 2012). Developing countries also face structural challenges in continuing to promote economic growth (green growth) without neglecting the risks of climate change and sustainability (Glavina et al., 2025). The Paris Agreement framework emphasizes that carbon pricing mechanisms play an important role for many countries in responding to the challenges of climate change (Li et al., 2026). Carbon pricing mechanisms, whether through carbon taxes or emissions trading schemes, are seen as the most effective instruments for steering the transition to a low-carbon economy (Verbruggen, 2021). The complex management of carbon pricing requires expertise and strategic planning to ensure compliance and to optimize environmental benefits and profits (Maqsoom et al., 2025).

Amid these global dynamics, developing countries have become highly vulnerable to policy decisions by developed countries (United Nations, 2023). One example is in May 2023, when the European Union officially passed the Carbon Border Adjustment Mechanism (CBAM), which will come into effect in 2026 and impose fees on imports of carbon-intensive products based on their carbon content and the difference in carbon prices between the exporting country and the European Union, which will put pressure on developing countries (Li et al., 2026). In line with the fact that regulatory frameworks adopted from European countries have become a source of pressure, resulting in high levels of non-compliance when applied in developing countries because they are incompatible with local contexts. Cases in South Africa and Indonesia show that businesses in the wine and forestry sectors face difficulties in meeting European standards that do not reflect the conditions of production and extraction in each country (Jia et al., 2018).

Limited knowledge, expertise, and funding make it difficult for developing countries to implement sustainable practices, and this is exacerbated by a lack of guidance on how to comply with sustainability standards (Jia et al., 2018). Developing countries are generally highly dependent on natural resource exploitation to drive economic growth, yet they also face structural problems, such as high levels of poverty and inequality. In addition, relatively limited governance capacity, weak institutional development, and limited science and technology programs often reduce the effectiveness of innovation systems (Arboleda-Munoz et al., 2026). These capacity constraints are particularly relevant in the context of developing countries' integration into global value chains (GVCs), where deeper participation not only opens up growth opportunities but also requires domestic capabilities to meet higher standards of production, innovation, and competitiveness (Rigo, 2021). Improved integration into GVCs has transformed international trade and global economic dynamics, with increasing implications for economic performance and employment, particularly in developing countries (Epede & Wang, 2022). GVCs can be drivers of growth, better job creation, and poverty reduction, as long as developing countries implement structural reforms and improve industries that maintain open and sustainable policies (World Bank Group, 2020).

Industrial upgrading now encompasses broader objectives, focusing not only on efficiency and value creation but also on improving energy efficiency and environmental sustainability, a process referred to as cleaner industrial upgrading (Xie & Teo, 2022). However, not all types of technological innovation can produce cleaner production or improve environmental performance; only green technological innovation can be considered a transformative process that drives holistic change from unsustainable development conditions (Marra et al., 2017). In line with this, developing countries are also striving to adopt green technologies to achieve carbon neutrality without sacrificing economic growth (Ling et al., 2024). The success of this sustainable transition is greatly influenced by proactive, targeted policies and government support that accelerate and capitalize on existing opportunities to apply green technology toward cleaner growth (Altenburg & Pegels, 2012).

CONCLUSION

Climate change has become a serious concern for scientists, industry, and governments worldwide. This condition has prompted discussions and actions on changes to the trading system and sustainable production management. Reducing carbon emissions in trade requires a global commitment through regulatory measures and carbon restrictions, as well as encouraging the development and adoption of environmentally friendly, low-carbon production technologies. Several strategic steps have been taken and must continue to be developed further for carbon-reduction efforts in trade, as follows:

First, the existence of carbon taxes and emissions trading systems, which are covered by carbon pricing regulations, has become an important tool for suppressing products with high carbon intensity. Carbon pricing is an economic discipline mechanism that assigns a value to the carbon emissions contained in a product. This mechanism aims to internalize the social and environmental costs of production and consumption activities. The scope of carbon pricing continues to expand globally because it is an effective regulatory tool for reducing carbon emissions and a tangible manifestation of the jurisdiction's commitment to the global transition to net-zero emissions.

Second, efforts to limit carbon in international trade are being spearheaded by the European Union with the implementation of a carbon border adjustment mechanism as a measure to balance the carbon pricing of each imported and domestic product, so that the nature of this regulation is intended as a corrective instrument for the heterogeneity of climate change policies between jurisdictions. It cannot be denied that the EU's move has sparked debate about the potential for product discrimination and its conflict with the most-favored-nation principle. However, in reality, awareness of the need for strict carbon regulations, coupled with advances in low-carbon technology and technical capacity, underpins their implementation. The consequences are not as severe as many countries predicted and can reduce carbon leakage and spur the transition to low-carbon production management, especially in the iron, steel, aluminum, fertilizer, electricity, hydrogen, and cement sectors. In addition, the domestic climate regulations of trading partners are also taken into account in carbon emission calculations, providing opportunities for incentives.

Third, the integration of environmental provisions into trade agreements has become a strategic pillar of sustainable trade architecture. This effort aims to align economic interests with environmental interests in line with global climate commitments. This mechanism is effective in reducing carbon leakage from developed to developing countries and in reducing the carbon footprint of trade. Investment in innovation and the adoption of low-carbon technologies are crucial priorities emphasized in preferential and free trade agreements to remain competitive, and green transformation efforts are carried out through cooperation that enables the spillover of green knowledge and technology. However, compliance with environmental commitments in agreements is a particular concern, so measures such as emphasizing commitments through dialogue, expanding monitoring, involving civil society, and trade sanctions are needed to support the effectiveness of environmental provisions in reducing carbon emissions.

Finally, the presence of environmental regulations, particularly those related to carbon in trade agreements, can help address the lack of climate regulations in developing countries and encourage the adoption of low-carbon technologies as part of global value chain transformation. In addition, applying environmental standards at the upstream supplier level is a key aspect of a sustainable global value chain. Downstream companies play a role in introducing global climate regulations and green innovation into the global value chain through both pressure and support.

REFERENCES

Altenburg, T., & Pegels, A. (2012). Sustainability-oriented innovation systems – managing the green transformation. *Innovation and Development*, *2*(1), 5–22. DOI: 10.1080/2157930X.2012.664037

Arboleda-Munoz, G. A., Chaparro-Banegas, N., & Roig-Tierno, N. (2026). Bridging the gap: Innovation systems and sustainable development in developing countries. *Journal of Open Innovation*, *12*(1), 1–13. DOI: 10.1016/j.joitmc.2025.100713

Aslam, A., & Ghouse, G. (2023). Targeting the new sustainable inclusive green growth: A review. *Cleaner and Responsible Consumption*, *11*, 1–13. DOI: 10.1016/j.clrc.2023.100140

Bick, N., & Keele, D. (2022). Sustainability and climate change: Understanding the political use of environmental terms in municipal governments. *Current Research in Environmental Sustainability*, *4*, 1–11. DOI: 10.1016/j.crsust.2022.100145

Böhringer, C., Bye, B., Fæhn, T., & Einar, K. (2017). Targeted carbon tariffs: Export response, leakage and welfare. *Resource and Energy Economics*, *50*, 51–73. DOI: 10.1016/j.reseneeco.2017.06.003

Böhringer, C., Carbone, J. C., & Rutherford, T. F. (2016). The Strategic Value of Carbon Tariffs. *American Economic Journal. Economic Policy*, *8*(1), 28–51. DOI: 10.1257/pol.20130327

Boute, A. (2024). Accounting for Carbon Pricing in Third Countries Under the EU Carbon Border Adjustment Mechanism. *World Trade Review*, *23*(2), 169–189. DOI: 10.1017/S1474745624000107

Brandi, C., & Morin, J. (2023). *Trade and the Environment*. Cambridge University Press., DOI: 10.1017/9781009461825

Cammeo, A., Ferrari, A., Borghesi, S., & Dokken, T. (2025). Understanding and assessing CBAM : vulnerability and impacts in the EU. In *SPES Working Paper* (7.2). https://www.sustainabilityperformances.eu/wp-content/uploads/2025/03/SPES-Deliverable-7.2_Understanding-and-assessing-CBAM_layout.pdf

CEC. (2013). *CEC recommends investigation of the Sumidero Canyon II submission and delivers a factual record for the Environmental Pollution in Hermosillo II submission*. Cec.Org. https://www.cec.org/news/cec-recommends-investigation-of-sumidero-canyon-ii-submission-and-delivers-factual-record-for-environmental-pollution-in-hermosillo-ii-submission/

Chen, W., & Zhang, Z. (2025). Decomposition of carbon emission chains in global value chains and its implications for bilateral trade between China and the United States. *Environmental Impact Assessment Review, 115*, 1–12. DOI: 10.1016/j.eiar.2025.108054

Dou, G., Ma, L., Wei, K., & Zhang, Q. (2023). *Operations Management Operational Measures, Sustainability for Environmental Regulations and Carbon Constrained Decisions*. Springer Nature Switzerland AG., DOI: 10.1007/978-3-031-37600-9

Drake, D. F., Kleindorfer, P. R., & Van Wassenhove, L. N. (2016). Technology Choice and Capacity Portfolios under Emissions Regulation Citation. *Production and Operations Management, 25*(6), 1006–1025. DOI: 10.1111/poms.12523

Dugast, C., & Sanches, A. L. (2025). *Emissions in trade: Where are they and how do we measure them?* World Economic Forum. https://www.weforum.org/stories/2025/03/emissions-in-trade-how-we-measure-them/

Epede, M. B., & Wang, D. (2022). Global value chain linkages: An integrative review of the opportunities and challenges for SMEs in developing countries. *International Business Review, 31*(5), 1–12. DOI: 10.1016/j.ibusrev.2022.101993

Fairuz, M., & Foster-McGregor, N. (2024). Do Environmental Emissions Traded In Trade Agreements Reduce Provisions In Preferential Global Value Chains? In *ADB Economics Working Paper Series* (755). DOI: 10.22617/WPS240541-2

Filonchyk, M., Peterson, M. P., Zhang, L., Hurynovich, V., & He, Y. (2024). Greenhouse gases emissions and global climate change: Examining the influence of CO2, CH4, and N2O. *The Science of the Total Environment, 935*, 1–7. DOI: 10.1016/j.scitotenv.2024.173359 PMID: 38768722

Gentile, E., Lema, R., Rabellotti, R., & Ribaudo, D. (2023). Greening Global Value Chains: A Conceptual Framework for Policy Action. In *Global Value Chain Development Report 2023: Resilient and Sustainable GVCs in Turbulent Times* (pp. 228–260). World Trade Organization. https://www.wto.org/english/res_e/booksp_e/gvc_dev_rep23_e.pdf

Glavina, A., Misic, K., Baleta, J., Wang, J., & Mikulci, H. (2025). Economic development and climate change : Achieving a sustainable balance. *Cleaner Engineering and Technology, 26*, 1–12. DOI: 10.1016/j.clet.2025.100939

Godart, O. N., & Görg, H. (2013). Suppliers of multinationals and the forced linkage effect: Evidence from firm level data. *Journal of Economic Behavior & Organization, 94*, 393–404. DOI: 10.1016/j.jebo.2013.01.007

Gutsch, M., Mai, J., Ukhova, N., & Dijkstra-silva, S. (2025). Effects of environmental provisions in international trade agreements on businesses and economies – a systematic review. *Sustainability Accounting. Management and Policy Journal, 16*(7), 1–27. DOI: 10.1108/SAMPJ-02-2024-0122

Hammami, R., Nouira, I., & Frein, Y. (2018). Effects of Customers' Environmental Awareness and Environmental Regulations on the Emission Intensity and Price of a Product. *Decision Sciences, 49*(6), 1116–1155. DOI: 10.1111/deci.12302

He, P., Dou, G., & Zhang, W. (2017). Optimal production planning and cap setting under cap-and-trade regulation. *The Journal of the Operational Research Society, 68*(9), 1094–1105. Advance online publication. DOI: 10.1057/s41274-016-0123-1

He, P., Zhang, W., Xu, X., & Bian, Y. (2015). Production lot-sizing and carbon emissions under cap-and-trade and carbon tax regulations. *Journal of Cleaner Production, 103*, 241–248. DOI: 10.1016/j.jclepro.2014.08.102

Hermann, T., Delille, T., & Giovannini, V. (2026). *Carbon border adjustment mechanisms – climate and trade policy issues*. Financier Worldwide. https://www.financierworldwide.com/carbon-border-adjustment-mechanisms-climate-and-trade-policy-issues

IPCC. (2022). *Climate Change 2022: Mitigation of Climate Change*. Intergovernmental Panel on Climate Change. https://www.ipcc.ch/report/ar6/wg3/

Isaksson, O. H. D., Simeth, M., & Seifert, R. W. (2016). Knowledge spillovers in the supply chain: Evidence from the high tech sectors. *Research Policy, 45*(3), 699–706. DOI: 10.1016/j.respol.2015.12.007

Jayaswal, M. K., Yadav, A. S., Mishra, A., & Seikh, M. R. (2025). Credit Financing Based Two-Level Green Supply Chain Model with Carbon Emissions for Eco-Friendly Demand Under a Fuzzy Environment. *Process Integration and Optimization for Sustainability*. DOI: 10.1007/s41660-025-00610-y

Jia, F., Zuluaga-Cardona, L., Bailey, A., & Rueda, X. (2018). Sustainable supply chain management in developing countries: An analysis of the literature. *Journal of Cleaner Production, 189*, 263–278. DOI: 10.1016/j.jclepro.2018.03.248

Jung, S. H., & Feng, T. (2020). Government subsidies for green technology development under uncertainty. *European Journal of Operational Research, 286*(2), 726–739. DOI: 10.1016/j.ejor.2020.03.047

Kang, K., & Tan, B. Q. (2023). Carbon emission reduction investment in sustainable supply chains under cap-and-trade. *Expert Systems with Applications, 227*, 1–16. DOI: 10.1016/j.eswa.2023.120335

Keen, M., Parry, I., & Roaf, J. (2021). Border Carbon Adjustments: Rationale, Design and Impact. In *IMF Working Paper* (239). https://www.imf.org/-/media/files/publications/wp/2021/english/wpiea2021239-print-pdf.pdf

Kortum, S., & Weisbach, D. (2017). The Design of Border Adjustments for Carbon Prices. *National Tax Journal, 70*(2), 421–446. DOI: 10.17310/ntj.2017.2.07

Le Blanc, B., & Mendoza, I. de L. (2023). *Potential conflicts between the European CBAM and the WTO rules*. Norton Rose Fulbright. https://www.nortonrosefulbright.com/en/knowledge/publications/9c5d9ec6/potential-conflicts-between-the-european-cbam-and-the-wto-rules

Li, M., Sun, Y., Xia, Y., Yang, Z., Chen, C., Yuan, Y., & Wang, P. (2026). The impacts of Carbon Border Adjustment Mechanism (CBAM) on international trade and policy responses: From an economic and environmental equity perspective. *Energy Policy, 210*, 1–13. DOI: 10.1016/j.enpol.2025.115014

Ling, S., Jin, S., Wang, H., Zhang, Z., & Feng, Y. (2024). Transportation infrastructure upgrading and green development efficiency: Empirical analysis with double machine learning method. *Journal of Environmental Management, 358*, 1–18. DOI: 10.1016/j.jenvman.2024.120922 PMID: 38657413

Lydgate, E. (2024). Integrating Climate Action into Free Trade Agreements. In *The Sustainability Revolution in International Trade Agreements* (pp. 181–198). Oxford University Press., DOI: 10.1093/9780191994470.003.0012

MacKay, D. J., Cramton, P., Ockenfels, A., & Stoft, S. (2017). Price Carbon—I Will If You Will. In *Global Carbon Pricing The Path to Climate Cooperation* (pp. 7–12). The MIT Press., DOI: 10.7551/mitpress/10914.003.0005

Maqsoom, A., Irfan, M., Basharat, M. U., Ali, U., & Ashraf, H. (2025). Carbon Markets and Carbon Pricing Mechanisms: How Developing Economies Can Benefit? *Procedia Computer Science, 256*, 1416–1426. DOI: 10.1016/j.procs.2025.02.274

Marra, A., Antonelli, P., & Pozzi, C. (2017). Emerging green-tech specializations and clusters – A network analysis on technological innovation at the metropolitan level. *Renewable & Sustainable Energy Reviews, 67*, 1037–1046. DOI: 10.1016/j.rser.2016.09.086

Michalek, G. (2016). Progressive Optimal Technology-based Border Carbon Adjustment (POT BCA) - A New Approach to an Old Carbon Problem. *Environmental Modeling and Assessment, 21*(3), 323–337. DOI: 10.1007/s10666-015-9484-0

Narloch, U. (2025). *CBAM 2.0 for carbon leakage protection*. CO2iq Solutions. https://co2-iq.com/en/cbam-for-carbon-leakage-protection

NASA. (n.d.). *What Is Climate Change?* Science.Nasa.Gov. Retrieved January 29, 2026, from https://science.nasa.gov/climate-change/what-is-climate-change/

Net Zero Tracker. (n.d.). *Net Zero Target Status*. Zerotracker.Net. Retrieved January 27, 2026, from https://zerotracker.net/

New Zealand Foreign Affairs & Trade. (n.d.). *Agreement on Climate Change, Trade and Sustainability (ACCTS)*. Mfat.Govt.Nz. Retrieved January 27, 2025, from https://www.mfat.govt.nz/en/trade/free-trade-agreements/free-trade-agreements-concluded-but-not-in-force/agreement-on-climate-change-trade-and-sustainability-accts

Nielsen, T., Baumert, N., Kander, A., Jiborn, M., & Kulionis, V. (2021). The risk of carbon leakage in global climate agreements. *International Environmental Agreement: Politics, Law and Economics, 21*(2), 147–163. DOI: 10.1007/s10784-020-09507-2

OECD. (2019). *Trade and the environment*. OECD Publishing., DOI: 10.1787/a83ce9d8-

OECD. (2025). *Investing in Climate for Growth and Development: The Case for Enhanced NDCs*. OECD Publishing., DOI: 10.1787/16b7cbc7-

Panezi, M. (2024). Exploring the Nexus of Environmental Sustainability and International Trade : The Significance of Self- Standing Obligations. In *The Sustainability Revolution in International Trade Agreements* (pp. 163–180). Oxford University Press. DOI: 10.1093/9780191994470.003.0011

Pryor, J., Agnolucci, P., Fischer, C., Heine, D., & Leon, M. M. de O. (2023). Carbon Pricing Around the World. In *Data for a Greener World: A Guide for Practitioners and Policymakers* (pp. 79–94). International Monetary Fund., DOI: 10.5089/9798400217296.071

Qi, Q., Lu, P., & Zhao, X. (2025). Corporate carbon regulation, green innovation and supply chain spillover. *Innovation and Green Development*, *4*(5), 1–12. DOI: 10.1016/j.igd.2025.100294

Rigo, D. (2021). Global value chains and technology transfer: New evidence from developing countries. *Review of World Economics*, *157*(2), 271–294. DOI: 10.1007/s10290-020-00398-8

Rimini, M., Peters, J., Vangenechten, D., & Lehne, J. (2023). The EU–US Global Arrangement On Sustainable Steel And Aluminium Resetting Negotiations For A Carbon-Based Sectoral Agreement. *E3G*, 1–14. https://www.e3g.org/wp-content/uploads/EU-US-global-arrangement-on-sustainable-steel-and-aluminium-briefing.pdf

Sarkar, B., Ahmed, W., & Kim, N. (2018). Joint effects of variable carbon emission cost and multi-delay-in- payments under single-setup-multiple-delivery policy in a global sustainable supply chain. *Journal of Cleaner Production, 185*, 421–445. DOI: 10.1016/j.jclepro.2018.02.215

Sofia. (2018). *Commissioner Malmström unveils 15-point plan to make EU trade and sustainable development chapters more effective*. Policy.Trade.Ec.Europa.Eu. https://policy.trade.ec.europa.eu/news/commissioner-malmstrom-unveils-15-point-plan-make-eu-trade-and-sustainable-development-chapters-more-2018-02-27_en

The World Bank. (2012). *Inclusive Green Growth: The Pathway to Sustainable Development*. The World Bank. https://documents1.worldbank.org/curated/en/368361468313515918/pdf/691250PUB0Publ067902B09780821395516.pdf

The World Bank. (2025). *State and Trends of Carbon Pricing 2025*. The World Bank. https://www.worldbank.org/en/publication/state-and-trends-of-carbon-pricing

UNCTAD. (2021). *Trade and development report 2021: From recovery to resilience. United Nations Conference on Trade and Development*. DOI: 10.18356/9789210010276

UNFCCC. (2026). *The Paris Agreement*. Unfccc.Int. https://unfccc.int/process-and-meetings/the-paris-agreement

United Nations. (1987). *Report of the World Commission on Environment and Development*. https://digitallibrary.un.org/record/139811?v=pdf

United Nations. (2019). *Global Sustainable Development Report 2019*. United Nations. https://www.un.org/en/desa/global-sustainable-development-report-2019

United Nations. (2023). *Trade and Development Report 2023 Growth, Debt and Climate: Realigning the Global Financial Architecture*. United Nations Publications. https://unctad.org/system/files/official-document/tdr2023_en.pdf

van Aaken, A. (2024). Making Trade Agreements Contribute to Sustainability The Potential of Behavioural Science. In *The Sustainability Revolution in International Trade Agreements* (pp. 23–38). Oxford University Press., DOI: 10.1093/9780191994470.003.0003

Verbruggen, A. (2021). *Pricing Carbon Emissions: Economic Reality and Utopia*. Routledge., DOI: 10.4324/9781003173816

Wei, J., Zhang, X., & Tamamine, T. (2024). Digital transformation in supply chains: Assessing the spillover effects on midstream firm innovation Jiangying. *Journal of Innovation & Knowledge*, *9*(2), 1–11. DOI: 10.1016/j.jik.2024.100483

Welford, R., & Starkey, R. (1996). *Business and the Environment: A Reader*. Taylor & Francis. https://books.google.co.id/books/about/Business_and_the_Environment.html?id=i7UDHlOGfPEC&redir_esc=y

World Bank Group. (2020). *World Development Report 2020: Trading For Development in The Age Of Global Value Chains*. The World Bank. https://www.worldbank.org/en/publication/wdr2020

World Trade Law. (n.d.). *Uruguay Round Agreements*. Worldtradelaw.Net. Retrieved January 27, 2026, from https://www.worldtradelaw.net/static.php?type=public&page=uragreements

WTO. (2020). *World trade report 2020: Government policies to promote innovation in the digital age* (`). World Trade Organization. https://digitallibrary.un.org/record/4038629?v=pdf

Xie, R., & Teo, T. S. H. (2022). Green technology innovation, environmental externality, and the cleaner upgrading of industrial structure in China — Considering the moderating effect of environmental regulation. *Technological Forecasting and Social Change*, *184*, 1–15. DOI: 10.1016/j.techfore.2022.122020

Yang, F., Li, T., & Qi, Y. (2025). The impact of upgrading in the global value chain on embodied carbon emissions: Does technological progress matter? *Finance Research Letters*, *84*, 1–12. DOI: 10.1016/j.frl.2025.107763

Yenipazarli, A. (2016). Managing new and remanufactured products to mitigate environmental damage under emissions regulation. *European Journal of Operational Research*, *249*(1), 117–130. DOI: 10.1016/j.ejor.2015.08.020

Yilmaz, S. (2025). The Impact of Environmental Protection Expenditures on Reducing Greenhouse Gas Emissions. *Sustainability (Basel)*, *17*(7), 1–17. DOI: 10.3390/su17073192

Zarrinpoor, N., & Khani, A. (2021). Designing a sustainable biofuel supply chain by considering carbon policies: A case study in Iran. *Energy, Sustainability and Society*, *11*(38), 1–22. DOI: 10.1186/s13705-021-00314-4

Zhang, W., Zhu, B., Li, Y., & Yan, D. (2024). Revisiting the Porter hypothesis: A multi-country meta-analysis of the relationship between environmental regulation and green innovation. *Humanities & Social Sciences Communications*, *11*(232), 1–15. DOI: 10.1057/s41599-024-02671-9

Zhong, J., & Pei, J. (2024). Carbon border adjustment mechanism : A systematic literature review of the latest developments. *Climate Policy*, *24*(2), 228–242. DOI: 10.1080/14693062.2023.2190074

Chapter 6

CBAM and the Western Balkans: Assessing Impacts on Production and Exports of 35 Carbon-Intensive Goods

Mikhail Lobanov
http://orcid.org/0000-0001-7122-1335
Institute of Economics of the Russian Academy of Sciences, Russia

Jelena Zvezdanović Lobanova
http://orcid.org/0000-0003-3159-3331
Institute of Social Sciences, Belgrade, Serbia

ABSTRACT

The chapter examines the effects of the EU's application of the Carbon Border Adjustment Mechanism (CBAM) on the Western Balkan countries, whose economies rely significantly on exports of goods produced with high levels of greenhouse gas emissions. The potential impact of CBAM on these countries is assessed across 35 product groups by comparing several indicators (absolute export volumes, the degree of dependence on the European market, significance for national exports, the existence of stable trade relationships, location and size of production facilities). The chapter also assesses national initiatives related to the implementation of the EU climate policy principles, in particular the establishment of carbon pricing instruments, which may be taken into account in the calculation of CBAM costs. In addition, indicative CBAM costs for ten carbon-intensive products from Serbia are estimated, taking into account embedded and direct emissions, exports to the EU, and projected CBAM certificate prices.

DOI: 10.4018/979-8-3373-8998-1.ch006

INTRODUCTION

The contemporary world is confronted with the urgent challenge of climate change, requiring comprehensive and immediate action from the international community. A substantial body of research attributes current climate change to the greenhouse effect, which arises predominantly from human economic activity. The efforts of numerous international organizations and states are focused on reducing the carbon footprint of key economic sectors such as energy, industry, and transportation. The European Commission explicitly recognized the "green transition" as one of six priorities for EU development in 2019-2024. Under the European Green Deal (European Commission, 2019), EU member states established the objective of creating a climate-neutral economy, defined as attaining net-zero human-induced greenhouse gas emissions by 2050. Achieving this objective is envisaged through a set of measures that includes the expansion of renewable energy sources, the diversification of the energy import structure, and the deployment of energy-efficient technologies. The "Fit for 55" package (European Commission, 2021a) establishes a goal of cutting net greenhouse gas emissions by a minimum of 55% by 2030 compared with 1990 levels, with the aim of attaining climate neutrality by the middle of the 21st century.

In an effort to contribute to global greenhouse gas (GHG) reduction, the EU has implemented the Carbon Border Adjustment Mechanism (CBAM). In July 2021, the European Commission unveiled the initial legislative proposals for CBAM as part of the "Fit for 55" package, which received formal adoption from the European Parliament and the Council of the EU (European Commission, 2021b). CBAM entered into force in May 2023.

Aligned with the policy goals of the EC, CBAM is designed to address the negative impacts resulting from the uneven application of climate policies and to encourage other countries to pursue development pathways consistent with the "green transition." The application of CBAM is expected to foster technological modernization in sectors producing carbon-intensive goods, notably aluminium, iron and steel, fertilizers, cement, electricity and hydrogen[1]. Moreover, it is intended to curb carbon leakage, whereby European companies transfer manufacturing activities to jurisdictions with lower environmental standards to reduce compliance costs associated with climate policies[2]. As a result, cheaper but more carbon-intensive products return to the EU market[3]. It is apparent that Brussels' intentions extend further than the development of a "green economy" and are also linked to enhancing industrial competitiveness and reducing the relocation of production outside the EU. In this regard, a number of experts consider CBAM as an instrument of protectionist policy, the application of which, inter alia, would enable member states to generate additional revenues to finance programmes related to the "green transition"[4]. In addition, the question arises regarding the compatibility of CBAM with World Trade Organisation (WTO) rules.

Introducing carbon tariffs involves substituting free allowances in various Emission Trading System (ETS) industries[5], aiming to enhance the EU carbon pricing mechanism and reduce potential carbon leakage (European Parliament & Council of the European Union, 2023a). CBAM establishes a specific carbon charge on imports, obliging importers to acquire certificates priced according to the CO_2 emissions embedded in the imported goods. The cost of these certificates will match that of allowances on the EU ETS market, thereby maintaining parity between domestic and foreign emitters. The cost of these certificates will be equivalent to the price of emission allowances on the EU ETS market, thereby ensuring a level playing field between domestic and foreign producers. CBAM helps to ensure fair competition by requiring foreign exporters to bear comparable carbon costs when accessing the European market, given that EU companies are already subject to charges under the ETS.

CBAM is scheduled for full implementation in 2026, following a transitional phase (2023-2025) with reporting obligations for embedded emissions but without charges. As for iron and steel and aluminium products, importers must purchase CBAM certificates, initially covering only direct emissions[6]. Indirect emissions are expected to be brought under CBAM in subsequent phases, which will enhance the system's effectiveness. The ultimate objective is for importers to bear the full CBAM charge by 2034, with free ETS allowances entirely phased out. The price of a CBAM certificate will correspond to the mean auction price of EU ETS allowances (in EUR/tonne of CO_2).

Annexes I and II of Regulation 2023/956 provide detailed information on goods for which only direct emissions are to be taken into account, as well as goods for which embedded emissions are considered. The choice of these commodities concentrated on primary products regulated under the EU ETS, with the objective of guaranteeing that emissions embedded in carbon-intensive imports are subject to a carbon price comparable to that applied to domestically produced goods, thereby reducing the potential for carbon leakage. The shortened list retained goods from sectors with traditionally high emissions potentially exposed to carbon leakage schemes, including aluminium, iron and steel, cement, refinery products, organic basic chemicals, fertilizers, and hydrogen. Organic chemicals were excluded from this Regulation because current technical limitations prevent a clear determination of their embedded emissions, and comparable constraints apply to refinery products, whose emissions cannot be unambiguously allocated to specific outputs. Certain products whose production generates negligible emissions were also not part of the Regulation (e.g. ferrous scrap, some ferro-alloys and fertilizers). In comparison, electricity is covered under the provisions of this Regulation owing to the carbon leakage risk arising from increased imports, a considerable share of which is generated by coal-burning power plants (European Parliament & Council of the European Union, 2023b).

Within Regulation 2025/2083, a new threshold based on the cumulative net mass of the imported goods per importer (except for electricity and hydrogen) was introduced and initially set at a level of 50 tonnes per year. If this 'single mass-based threshold' is not exceeded, the 'de minimis' exemption applies. Otherwise, the importer is obliged to submit a CBAM declaration for all emissions embedded in goods imported in the relevant calendar year, as well as to acquire and remit certificates in electronic format. Other important changes concerned the specifics of production processes. The embedded emissions of certain steel and aluminium goods are largely determined by the emissions of their constituent precursor materials. Since the finishing processes generate only a minor 'carbon footprint', the emissions from those production steps were excluded from the system (European Parliament & Council of the European Union, 2025).

To summarize, CBAM should not be viewed solely as a carbon regulation instrument whose implementation will entail narrowly sectoral consequences. This initiative is already exerting, and will continue to exert, an impact on a broad range of issues directly and indirectly linked to EU environmental policy, including international trade, technology and know-how transfer, transborder production relocation, institutional regulation, etc. Among its positive spillover effects are the reduction of carbon leakage, the stimulation of technological modernization, and the promotion of monitoring, reporting, and verification (MRV) systems for GHG emissions in third countries. Negative spillovers include a loss of price competitiveness (which may be particularly critical for less developed countries with low levels of export diversification), disruptions of local and regional value chains, pressure on labor markets, and additional adjustment costs arising from the need to adapt to externally imposed changes in international trade conditions (the so-called "Brussels Effect").

This chapter seeks to advance a more detailed understanding of the mechanisms through which CBAM affects the development of export-oriented industries in the Western Balkan countries whose production processes are associated with a high carbon footprint.

The Western Balkan countries have been selected as the object of this study, as they are characterized by small and vulnerable economic systems whose evolution largely depends on access to the sizeable EU market. The sectors encompassed by CBAM contribute substantially to the economic growth of these countries, and in some cases play a structurally pivotal role. In the event of a reduction in imports by EU-based companies, these economies would face considerable difficulties in redirecting exports to alternative large-scale markets. Moreover, the inertia inherent in their territorial and sectoral economic structures would prevent the rapid substitution of lost export volumes with new products. The transition to new technological standards is likewise constrained by deficits in innovation capacity and investment. In addition, the Western Balkan countries are at varying stages in their process of EU accession, which further affects the degrees of freedom available to them in pursuing independent industrial and foreign trade policies. The chapter also examines national legal initiatives developed within the framework of institutional harmonization with the EU, aimed at establishing carbon pricing instruments.

To address the research objective outlined above, it is necessary to analyze the potential consequences of the gradual implementation of CBAM for specific products and their groups covered by EU carbon regulation (electricity, iron and steel, aluminium, cement and fertilizers), in order to understand the differences in spillover effects. The advancement of a hydrogen-based economy in the region is still at the planning stage, with pilot projects under preparation; therefore, this sector is not covered in this chapter.

The scientific novelty of this study stems from the fact that we have conducted a detailed analysis of the export potential of the Western Balkan economies after the introduction of CBAM (based on more than 30 carbon-intensive products). It includes an assessment of technological constraints and risks, the degree of connectivity with key markets and dependence on them, geographical factors in production organization, and other relevant aspects. Furthermore, indicative CBAM costs have been calculated for ten carbon-intensive products from Serbia, taking into account both embedded and direct emissions, exports to the EU, and projected CBAM certificate prices. The results obtained enable more accurate forecasting of short- and medium-term risks to the region's economic development, while also increasing the practical relevance of recommendations for policymakers.

LITERATURE REVIEW

The literature often highlights the importance of implementing CBAM for improving environmental quality. However, there is considerable uncertainty and concern related to its economic and social effects on third countries. A number of studies show that the nature of CBAM's impact is shaped by multiple factors and is industry-dependent. The extent to which non-EU countries will be affected by the implementation of CBAM largely depends on the degree of their export integration with the EU, the proportion of these exports relative to their total production, and the economic importance of the impacted industries within their national economies (Erdogdu, 2025). Maliszewska et al. (2025) assert that, while high-emission sectors could experience a reduction in their share of the EU market, the aggregate level of economic vulnerability to CBAM-related costs is generally modest across most economies. Dechezleprêtre et al. (2025) find that CBAM, alongside higher

EU ETS carbon prices and phase-out of free allowances, produces only a limited impact on total value added in both EU and non-EU countries. While CBAM partly offsets losses for EU industries, reliance on CBAM-covered inputs limits this effect. Revenue redistribution could further reduce its impact.

The second group of studies examines the asymmetric impact of CBAM on countries at different levels of development, including potential changes in welfare indicators and national competitiveness. The literature suggests that CBAM's contribution to global emissions reduction is limited, and that it functions primarily as a foreign economic policy instrument rather than as a carbon regulation measure. It is expected that developing regions will encounter the most significant challenges following the implementation of CBAM. Perdana and Vielle (2022) assert that the implementation of this mechanism adversely affects least-developed countries (LDCs) by reducing energy-intensive industries (EIIs) and causing significant welfare losses. CBAM could undermine the exports and competitiveness of many trading partners, particularly the LDCs in Africa and Asia that export carbon-intensive goods to the EU. Granting exemptions to LDCs under the EU CBAM is less defensible, as it leads to greater carbon leakage than alternative policy options.

Zhong and Pei (2022) argue that CBAM is likely to influence national competitiveness, with the greatest burden falling on PRC, Russia, and India. Over the short term, production in the EU is forecast to increase by 0.38%, while output in other regions is anticipated to decrease by 0.1%. The authors emphasize that the contribution of CBAM to global emissions reduction is minimal, and it cannot be considered to be an efficient policy instrument to combat carbon leakage solely through its direct effects. However, it may function indirectly as a strategic lever: by imposing costs on countries without carbon pricing, CBAM creates an opportunity cost of inaction and strengthens its role as a policy threat.

Countries in Eastern and Southeastern Europe, some of which are selected as the focus of this study, are also examined in the literature with respect to the consequences of CBAM implementation. Amendola (2025) finds that while major economies, including China, the USA, and Japan, may even realize marginal net benefits, limited adverse effects are identified in India, Russia, and Turkey, with the substantial shifting of burdens concentrated primarily in Eastern European countries outside the EU. According to estimates, CBAM will reduce production in regulated sectors across non-adopting regions (cement, aluminium, and iron and steel sectors in the Rest of Europe region). Some Eastern European EU member states are expected to incur GDP losses of around 1% following the transition from free allowances to CBAM, with output in regulated sectors potentially declining by more than 20-30% due to intra-EU competitiveness imbalances. These effects may spill over into downstream industries, worsening macroeconomic outcomes and increasing carbon leakage risks. Consequently, resistance to CBAM may be strongest within the EU, highlighting the need for compensatory policies – such as technology transfer, innovation support, and targeted subsidies for high-emission sectors – financed through CBAM revenues.

Eicke et al. (2021) show that the impacts of CBAM are unevenly distributed, with South-Eastern European countries being exposed to especially elevated risks in both sector-specific and economy-wide scenarios. This vulnerability stems from carbon-intensive energy systems, limited export diversification, and strong reliance on EU markets for energy-intensive goods. The example of Bosnia and Herzegovina (BiH) illustrates that an export approach heavily focused on the EU can become problematic when it relies heavily on goods from EITE (emissions-intensive and trade-exposed) sectors. Similar patterns of vulnerability are observed in some other countries, including Albania, Montenegro, North Macedonia, Serbia, and Ukraine. Magacho et al. (2024) find that countries in the Western Balkans are among the most socio-economically exposed, with potential production reductions putting over 0.5% of both total wages and jobs at risk. According to Altaghlibi (2025), CBAM would further exacerbate inequalities among EU member states, as Central and Eastern European countries could bear the brunt of losses due to their economies' greater dependence on energy-intensive industries and fossil fuels. In contrast, more technologically advanced EU countries are likely to benefit, given their higher level of technological readiness and well-developed green industries (Petrović & Lobanov, 2022).

The third group includes studies that analyze the compatibility of CBAM with national carbon regulatory systems. Within CBAM framework, official Brussels intends to take into account national "carbon charges", but in practice, treatment of importers from third countries (especially those competing with the EU on global markets) may turn out to be entirely different. It should be noted that several countries outside the EU either have their own ETS linked to the European system (as in Switzerland) or participate directly in the EU ETS (other EFTA members). In the Western Balkan countries discussed in this article, the development of carbon pricing systems or the introduction of carbon taxes remains at an incipient stage. The introduction of carbon pricing in the United States could reduce CBAM costs by half or more, with US companies facing charges of only about 0.14% of the total value of exports directed to the EU in 2023 (Sandbag, 2025). The Chinese ETS, launched in 2021, does not comply with European principles of carbon regulation, and therefore, the corresponding payments are not currently taken into account. As for BRICS member countries such as Russia, India, and Brazil, they do not yet have a functioning ETS or carbon taxes in place. The 2022 sanctions on Russia, which have made exports of carbon-intensive products to the European Union uncertain, are likely to slow institutional changes in carbon regulation. Additionally, closer trade with Asian countries, most of which lack carbon governance, provides little incentive for Russia's decarbonization efforts. (Lobanov et al., 2024).

Among the important research topics are the potential conflicts of CBAM with WTO rules, in particular, concerning the Most Favored Nation and National Treatment principles (Ren & Du, 2025). Furthermore, many developing countries view CBAM as ignoring the spirit of the 1992 UNFCCC Common But Differentiated Responsibilities and Respective Capabilities principle and imposing implicit protectionist measures on cross-border trade. The introduction of CBAM will impact other countries, forcing them to adopt European standards that may conflict with their national capacities. CBAM imposes compulsory emission reductions, contradicting the Paris Agreement's principle of Nationally Determined Contributions, under which countries set their targets voluntarily (Cammeo et al., 2025). Thus, the introduction of CBAM raises both legal and economic questions, which may overlap but require distinct analytical approaches. While the economic implications include potential trade distortions, reduced export competitiveness, and implicit protectionist effects, the legal concerns relate to compliance with international trade rules and environmental obligations.

In Table 1, we highlight some pros and cons of CBAM across economic, environmental, political, and social dimensions[7].

Table 1. Pros and Cons of CBAM across key dimensions

Dimension	Pros	EU	Non-EU	Cons	EU	Non-EU
Economy	stimulates technological modernization		X	leads to high compliance costs		X
	promotes renewable energy consumption		X	reduces the competitiveness of exports		X
	generates funds for green development	X		triggers trade conflicts and protectionism	X	
	enhances energy efficiency and resource productivity		X	redistributive impacts, rising inequalities	X	
Environment	mitigates carbon leakage	X		production relocation to the new "pollution havens"	X	X
	encourages "green transition" in the energy sector and industry		X	risk of "greenwashing" in case of weak monitoring	X	
Internal and foreign policy	strengthens climate governance	X	X	possible political tensions	X	X
	promotes sustainable trade partnerships	X	X	disruption of traditional and profitable trade ties	X	X
	stimulates climate cooperation	X	X	potential disputes at the WTO	X	

continued on following page

Table 1. Continued

Dimension	Pros	EU	Non-EU	Cons	EU	Non-EU
Social sphere	supports just transition policies	X		deepens social inequalities		X
	creates green jobs		X	job losses in carbon-intensive industries		X
	raises public awareness about climate responsibility	X	X	risks of increasing public fatigue with green transition policies	X	X

Source: compiled by the authors.

INSTITUTIONAL HARMONIZATION IN THE SPHERE OF "GREEN TRANSITION"

The EU climate policy also extends to Balkan candidate countries. By signing the Sofia Declaration on the Green Agenda for the Western Balkans (2021-2030) under the Berlin Process framework in 2020, the countries of the region committed to follow the principles of EU climate policy with the aim of attaining climate neutrality (including harmonization with the EU Climate Law, setting 2030 energy and climate targets, introducing carbon pricing instruments, and continuing alignment with the EU ETS, among other measures). To strengthen long-term energy security, the Agenda calls for a reduction and progressive elimination of coal subsidies, which may affect the future prospects of coal-based power generation in the countries concerned. The Brdo Declaration, adopted at the EU-Western Balkans Summit in Slovenia in 2021, highlights the need to design carbon pricing policies within the framework of CBAM. The Action Plan presented at the same summit provides a strategy to support and track the implementation of the Agenda (it comprises 58 priority actions grouped into five pillars and seven roadmaps)[8]. The first Implementation Report of the Agenda, prepared by the Regional Cooperation Council (REC) (2022), indicated that five of the six Western Balkan countries had either adopted or were in the process of adopting climate-related legislation. Besides that, all had established energy and climate targets through their Nationally Determined Contributions or relevant governmental strategies[9].

The Western Balkan countries adopted the monitoring, reporting and verification (MRV) legislation targeting GHG emissions, which is an important prerequisite for the establishment of carbon pricing frameworks. According to the Energy Community Secretariat's Annual Implementation Reports (Energy Community Secretariat, 2024, 2025a), Serbia is denoted as the most advanced country in the Western Balkans in establishing ETS and implementing key components for monitoring, reporting, verification of emissions and the accreditation of verifiers (MRVA). Through the adoption of the Law on Climate Change, Serbia has largely transposed the key concepts of the EU ETS Directive, including permit and monitoring plan requirements, defined the scope of covered activities and greenhouse gases, and designated the competent authority for issuing GHG permits[10]. Montenegro has achieved solid progress in monitoring and reporting but continues to lag in verification and accreditation, while Albania shows partial progress in establishing the institutional framework; North Macedonia and BiH have yet to transpose elements of the EU ETS Directive into national law (Energy Community Secretariat, 2025a).

One way to address the loss of competitiveness of carbon-intensive commodities in EU markets is to develop domestic carbon pricing systems in the Western Balkans. Domestic taxation would ease the burden on CBAM-covered sectors by reducing the risk of double carbon pricing when exporting to the EU. Besides, it would increase budget revenues and encourage energy transition.

Montenegro launched a national ETS in 2020 – it remains the only Western Balkan country with an operational carbon pricing system, covering mainly power and industrial sectors (at a price lower than the EU ETS). Given the structure of Montenegro's exports to the EU, the practical benefits of this measure are largely limited to the electricity trade. Albania currently has a carbon tax and intends to establish a national ETS, North Macedonia is exploring the introduction of a carbon tax, and Serbia plans to implement a carbon tax that could eventually become a fixed-price ETS (see Table 2) (Energy Community Secretariat, 2025b).

Table 2. Plans for establishing carbon pricing instruments in the Western Balkans countries.

Country	Instrument	Starting year	Price	Sectors covered by regulation
Albania	Carbon tax -> ETS (planned)	2027/28	Coal: 6.5 cents per kg (2027); 15.3 (2030)	CBAM sectors
Bosnia and Herzegovina	ETS	2026/27	10-30 EUR/tCO2-eq (2026); 100-140 (2030)	Power sector -> all CBAM sectors
Montenegro	ETS	2020	24 EUR/tCO2-eq	Power and industry
North Macedonia	Carbon tax	2028	N/A	EU ETS scope
Serbia	Carbon tax -> fixed-price ETS (planned)	2026	4 EUR/tCO2-eq (2027); 40 (2030).	CBAM sectors

Source: compiled using data from Energy Community Secretariat (2025b) and Narodna skupština Republike Srbije (2025a). Note: sectors covered by regulation in the Western Balkan countries do not usually include hydrogen.

For example, in Serbia – the largest greenhouse gas emitter in the region – the Law on Greenhouse Gas Emissions Tax and the Law on Carbon-Intensive Product Imports Tax will come into effect since January 2026, covering all sectors included under CBAM, except hydrogen. The total tax obligation is set at EUR 4 per tCO_2-eq (Narodna skupština Republike Srbije, 2025a, 2025b). The first law envisages a tax credit available only to electricity producers, granting up to 20% of the financial resources invested in measures to reduce GHG emissions, on the condition that the total credit does not surpass 80% of the tax obligation. In contrast, the second law excludes electricity imports due to technical constraints. The tax obligation applies only to companies importing five or more tons of designated products per year into Serbia. Importers may use tax credits if an emissions levy has already been paid in the country of origin, in line with the EU system. The tax liability is imposed solely on companies importing five tons or more of specified products into Serbia annually. Importers are eligible to apply for tax credits if an emissions levy has previously been paid in the country of origin, consistent with the EU framework.

POTENTIAL IMPACTS OF CBAM ON INDUSTRIAL PRODUCTION AND EXPORT COMPETITIVENESS

The structure of the economy in the Western Balkans and leading EU economies exhibits a high degree of complementarity, thereby facilitating the expansion of bilateral trade. The dependence of the Western Balkans on exports to the European Union is higher than that of EU member states on imports from these candidate countries. Overall goods trade between the EU and the Western Balkan countries reached 83.6 billion EUR in 2024, remaining at approximately the same level over the past three years. The EU imports from the region declined by more than 5% between 2022 and 2024, amounting to 34.5 billion EUR. The European Union continues to be the main trading partner for the Western Balkans, representing approximately 62% of the region's total trade, while the Western Balkans account for just 1.7% of the EU's overall trade and 1.4% of imports (European Commission, 2025). Naturally, the substitution of imports from the Western Balkans in the event of a loss of price competitiveness does not appear to pose a major challenge at first glance; however, a detailed analysis by individual product groups is required for an accurate assessment. To develop practical proposals to mitigate the impacts of CBAM that can be used by policymakers, there is a need for a multi-level analysis, encompassing assessments of the potential benefits and risks linked to the production and export of particular product categories. Accordingly, this paper places additional emphasis on the modernization of technological processes that determine greenhouse gas emissions, the transformation of the export structure of carbon-intensive products, and the assessment of CBAM-related costs for EU importers from the Western Balkan countries. The main hypothesis is that CBAM has a selective impact, primarily on products that constitute the bulk of Western Balkan exports and for which alternative export markets are (so far) limited. For a number of goods not directly covered by CBAM, competitiveness may nevertheless be undermined indirectly by rising input and raw material costs.

Table 3 presents the main indicators related to exports from Albania, BiH, Montenegro, North Macedonia, and Serbia for 35 groups of goods covered by CBAM regulation. The primary sources were Eurostat, International Trade Centre, UNCTADstat, as well as United States Geological Survey (USGS) and Emerging Markets Information Service (EMIS).

The selection of indicators used to assess the state of exports of carbon-intensive products from the Western Balkan countries to the EU is driven by several considerations. The dispersion of EU companies' import volumes is important for understanding supply stability, namely, whether the provision of these products to the European market is based on one-off contractual arrangements or on established and sustained trade channels. In addition, this indicator reflects the level of specialization and the intensity of competition among countries for access to the EU market. The share of the EU in a product's exports helps to assess the extent to which Western Balkan countries depend on the European market and, consequently, how challenging a potential reorientation toward alternative export destinations might be. The scope of exposure to CBAM regulation is captured by the share of carbon-intensive products in a country's total exports. By identifying the main European importers of specific products, we assess the degree of export diversification and test for the presence of a "neighbourhood effect." Finally, the degree of localization of production of goods covered by CBAM in individual countries is evaluated by identifying the number of top production companies, as sectors dominated by small and medium-sized producers are potentially more vulnerable.

Greenhouse gases associated with CBAM-regulated goods include carbon dioxide, nitrous oxide, and perfluorocarbons (European Parliament & Council of the European Union, 2023b). It is important to emphasize that Serbia remains the largest GHG emitter in the Western Balkans (69 $MtCO_2e$ in 2022), significantly outperforming BiH (26 $MtCO_2e$) and North Macedonia (12 $MtCO_2e$). Within Southeast Europe, Bulgaria and Croatia lag behind Serbia by a factor of 3.5 in this indicator. Data for the economy's "climate footprint," measured as GHG emissions per unit of GDP, are comparable for Serbia and BiH (around 1300 tCO_2e per million USD of GDP in 2022), while the difference between these countries and, for example, Albania exceeds twofold (Climate Watch, 2025; Zvezdanovic Lobanova & Lobanov, 2023).

Table 3. Key indicators related to exports from the Western Balkan countries to the EU (products covered by CBAM regulation)

	EU import volume in 2022–24, range (thousand tonnes)					Share of the EU in the export of the product (%)	Share of product in the country's total exports in 2024, by value (%)	Main importers in the EU	Top production companies (USGS and EMIS data)
	AL	**BH**	**ME**	**MK**	**RS**				
Kaolinic clays	0-5,3	9,3-46,2			1-7,4	>70% (BH)	For CN codes 2507 and 2523: AL 1,9; BH 0,5; MK 0,3	Italy (BH)	Nemetali, Rudnik Kaolina Motajica (BH)
Cement clinkers		12,6-61,1		0-21,3	0-5	>95% (BH) c. 10% (RS)		Slovakia, Croatia (BH)	Fushe Kruje Cement Factory, Antea Cement, Colacem Albania (AL), Fabrika Cementa Lukavac, Heidelberg Materials (BH), Holcim Srbija, Moravacem (RS)
Portland cement (excl. white)	109,2-133,8	77,2-115,8		0,1-1	9,8-9,9			Italy (AL), Croatia (BH, RS)	
Cement (excl. portland cement and aluminous cement)		194,2-218,9						Croatia (BH)	
Electricity (in GW-h)	1278-1782	1353-1817	3603-4516	1916-2684	6119-11029	30% (AL), >40% (BH), >35% (ME), 55% (MK), 60% (RS)	For CN code 2716: AL 2,2; BH 4,2; ME 18,8; MK 2,4; RS 2,2	Greece (AL, MK), Croatia (BH), Slovenia, Italy (ME), Hungary, Romania (RS)	KESH (AL), Elektroprivreda BiH / HZ HB / RS (BH), EPCG (ME), ESM (MK), EPS (RS)
Nitrogenous fertilizers (excl. tablets and small packages)		4,6-6,2		0,3-2,9	37,3-96,9	40% (RS)	For CN codes 3102 and 3105: RS 0,6	Hungary, Romania (RS)	HIP-Azotara (potentially), Elixir Group (RS)
Fertilizers containing two or three elements (nitrogen, phosphorus, potassium)					143,3-206,9	55% (RS)		Croatia, Hungary, Romania (RS)	

continued on following page

Table 3. Continued

	EU import volume in 2022–24, range (thousand tonnes)					Share of the EU in the export of the product (%)	Share of product in the country's total exports in 2024, by value (%)	Main importers in the EU	Top production companies (USGS and EMIS data)
	AL	**BH**	**ME**	**MK**	**RS**				
Pig iron and spiegeleisen in primary forms					15,3-40,3	c. 100% (RS)	For CN codes 72 and 73: AL 11,0; BH 10,1; ME 2,1; MK 7,5; RS 4,5	Romania (RS)	HBIS Serbia (RS)
Ferro-chromium	21,0-44,4					c. 50% (AL)		Austria, Slovenia, the Netherlands (AL)	AlbChrome (AL)
Ferro-silicon		0,2-3,2				c. 100% (BH)		Italy (BH)	Steelmin BH (BH)
Ferro-nickel				0-18		>20% (MK)		Italy (MK)	Euronickel Industries (MK)
Granules and powders of pig iron, spiegeleisen, iron or steel		1-2		0,1-0,8	0-0,2	50% (BH)		Italy, Austria (BH)	ArcelorMittal Zenica (BH)
Semi-finished products of iron or non-alloy steel		0-4,8			0,2-0,6			Germany (BH)	Makstil (MK), HBIS Serbia (RS)
Flat-rolled products of iron or non-alloy steel	0-0,2	0,5-1,3		189,9-226,4	608,2-694,8	>60% (MK), >90% (RS)		Romania, Italy, Greece (MK), Poland, the Czech Republic, Austria, Bulgaria (RS)	
Flat-rolled products of alloy steel other than stainless				0-29,6	0,4-0,7			Romania, Italy (MK)	

continued on following page

Table 3. Continued

	EU import volume in 2022–24, range (thousand tonnes)					Share of the EU in the export of the product (%)	Share of product in the country's total exports in 2024, by value (%)	Main importers in the EU	Top production companies (USGS and EMIS data)
	AL	BH	ME	MK	RS				
Bars and rods of iron or non-alloy steel	6-33	48,5-153,4		46,8-62,9	7,0-63,8	c. 5% (AL), >30% (BH), 90% (MK), 20% (RS)		Croatia (AL, BH), Hungary (BH, RS), Greece, Romania (MK)	ArcelorMittal Zenica (BH), Metalfer (RS)
Angles, shapes and sections of iron or non-alloy steel	0-0,5	2,1-2,5		19,8-20,8	8,8-15,2	65% (MK), 75% (RS)		Bulgaria, Hungary (RS), Greece, Romania (MK)	
Wire of iron or non-alloy steel (excl. bars and rods)	15,3-18,6	2,4-5,2		1,5-4,5	1,1-1,4	70% (AL)		Italy, Greece (AL)	Çokyaşar, Kurum (AL)
Wire of alloy steel other than stainless (excl. bars and rods)	0-0,2			1-2,2	0,4-2,5				
Sheet piling, welded angles, shapes and sections of iron or steel				1,4-3,2	0,4-1,7				
Tubes, pipes and hollow profiles	2,6-4,8	6,9-8,3	0-0,1	85,7-128,8	29,0-33,8	75% (MK), 60% (RS)		the Czech Republic, Germany, Greece (MK), Italy, Croatia, Romania (RS)	IGM-Trade (MK), thyssenkrupp (RS)

continued on following page

Table 3. Continued

	EU import volume in 2022–24, range (thousand tonnes)					Share of the EU in the export of the product (%)	Share of product in the country's total exports in 2024, by value (%)	Main importers in the EU	Top production companies (USGS and EMIS data)
	AL	**BH**	**ME**	**MK**	**RS**				
Iron and steel structures and parts	12,2-16,3	59-67,6		5-8	56,7-63,9	>75% (AL), >85% (BH), 70% (RS)		Italy (AL, BH), Romania (AL, RS), Croatia (BH, RS), Austria (BH), Germany (RS)	
Reservoirs, tanks, vats		5,8-8,6			2,9-3,9	>75% (BH)		Germany, France (BH)	
Tanks, casks, drums, etc.	0,1-0,6	0,7-1,3		0,2-0,3	0,8-1,3				
Containers for compressed or liquefied gas	0,1-0,2	0,1-0,8			0,2-0,7				
Screws, bolts, nuts, etc.		13,7-16,2			10,1-11,4	>95% (BH), c. 65% (RS)		Italy, Austria, Germany (BH), Slovenia (RS)	
Articles of iron or steel, n.e.s. (excl. cast articles)	2,4-3,6	21,2-23,1	0-0,1	2,3-2,8	37,4-43,2	c. 95% (BH), 75% (RS)		Austria, Croatia (BH), Germany (BH, RS), Hungary, Italy (RS)	
Unwrought aluminium	14,7-16,6	46,7-117,9	19,7-32,1		4,6-6,4	c. 100% (AL), >95% (BH), >35% (ME)	For CN code 76: AL 3,3; BH 5,4; ME 7,3; MK 0,4; RS 2,1	Italy (AL, BH), Slovenia, Croatia (BH), Spain (ME)	Zodiac (AL), Aluminij Industries (BH), Uniprom (ME)*

continued on following page

Table 3. Continued

	EU import volume in 2022–24, range (thousand tonnes)					Share of the EU in the export of the product (%)	Share of product in the country's total exports in 2024, by value (%)	Main importers in the EU	Top production companies (USGS and EMIS data)
	AL	BH	ME	MK	RS				
Aluminium bars, rods and profiles	4,0-5,4	24,9-25,4		0,1-0,2	7,7-11,0	>95% (BH), c. 75% (RS)		Croatia, Austria (BH), Germany, (BH, RS), France (RS)	Zodiac, Alumil (AL), Aluminij Industries, Feal, Alpro (BH), Alumil, MTC Nissal (RS)
Aluminium plates, sheets and strips (> 0.2 mm)		0,1			34,3-45,9	>90% (RS)		Slovenia, Hungary, Germany (RS)	Impol (RS)
Aluminium foil (≤0.2 mm, excl. backing)	0-0,2				0,8-0,9				
Aluminium tubes and pipes	0,2-0,4	0,5			2,5-3,2				
Aluminium structures and parts; prepared plates, rods, profiles and tubes	2,0-2,8	12,1-12,9		0,4-1,3	3,4-4,0	>95% (BH)		Slovenia, Germany, Croatia (BH)	Feal, Alpro (BH)
Aluminium casks, drums, cans, etc. (≤300 l)					11,4-13,7	>70% (RS)		Croatia, Slovenia, Romania (RS)	Ball Packaging, Al Pack (RS)
Articles of aluminium, n.e.s.	0,2-0,3	1,7-2,3		0,5-1,0	2,7-5,6				

Note: the table shows products whose exports to the EU exceed 0.5 thousand tonnes for at least one of the Western Balkan countries. Our calculations are based on statistical data from Eurostat (2026), International Trade Centre (2026), UNCTADstat (2026). Information about the companies is sourced from USGS (2026) and EMIS (2026). C. – circa. * The production of primary aluminium at the Uniprom plant was discontinued in 2023.

Electricity stands out in the export structure of all countries in the region to the EU (see Table 3). In four out of five countries, electricity generation is associated with a significant carbon footprint, which, in the context of CBAM implementation, could seriously affect the export to the EU[11]. In Serbia, Montenegro and BiH, in addition to the extensive use of hydropower (classified as a renewable energy source), lignite and other low-calorific brown coal types are used as fuel for thermal power plants (TPPs). In the first half of the 2020s, the share of coal-fired TPPs in electricity generation reached 63%, 58%, 40%, and 38% in Serbia, BiH, North Macedonia, and Montenegro, respectively; in addition, natural gas accounts for 28% of electricity generation in North Macedonia. The share of hydropower is highest in Albania (up to 99%) and Montenegro (53%)[12].

The structure of electricity generation determines the carbon emissions intensity per unit of electricity generated. In Albania, the relative level of CO_2 emissions is exceptionally modest (24 gCO_2e per kWh in 2024), which is significantly below the EU average (212 gCO_2e per kWh). By contrast, the power sectors of the other Western Balkan countries continue to exhibit a much higher "carbon footprint" (667 and 639 gCO_2e per kWh in Serbia and BiH, respectively) (Ember, 2025; Zvezdanovic Lobanova & Lobanov, 2023). In 2021, Five Energy Community Contracting Parties, among them Albania, Montenegro, and North Macedonia, committed to coal phase-out timelines by joining the Powering Past Coal Alliance (PPCA).

According to Eurostat data, Serbia is the largest exporter of electricity to the EU, with exports directed primarily to Hungary and Romania (see Table 3). Only in Montenegro does electricity account for a substantial share of total exports, reaching 19%, while in the remaining countries it fluctuates within the range of 2-4%. A distinctive feature of the electricity market in the countries of the region is the monopolistic position of the state in the segments of electricity generation and export. Dependence on the European market is high, ranging from 30% of total electricity exports in Albania to 60% in Serbia, which is largely determined by geographical factors, as supplies are made to EU countries bordering the region and, via transit routes, to Switzerland. Intra-regional exchange of electricity surpluses is of comparable importance; however, such a reorientation following the implementation of CBAM will be challenging due to the lack of demand in the Western Balkan countries for significant additional volumes of electricity (see Table 3).

The main risk to electricity supplies to the EU following the implementation of CBAM is not merely the loss of price competitiveness of exports from the Western Balkans, but rather the additional administrative burden associated with carbon taxation borne by importers. Under these conditions, importers are likely to prefer sourcing electricity at comparable price levels but with lower bureaucratic complexity. Second, if CBAM certificates are priced on the basis of a weekly average of EU ETS prices, such volatility will generate uncertainty regarding the overall cost of electricity imports. Third, significant challenges arise from current EU practices for reporting electricity imports: the origin of electricity is typically attributed to the last non-EU country through which it transited, rather than to the country where it was actually generated (Energy Community Secretariat, 2025b). As a result, for instance, Hungarian companies importing electricity generated in Bulgaria but transiting through Serbia are likely to be subject to CBAM charges. The transit role of the Western Balkans is considerable. In 2024, only BiH maintained a meaningful net export position, while the large volumes scheduled from other Western Balkan countries into the EU largely reflected actual electricity trade between two member states, with the region functioning primarily as a transit territory. Serbia constitutes the most significant transit corridor, followed by North Macedonia and Montenegro (Energy Community Secretariat, 2025b).

The main requirement for exempting electricity exports from CBAM cross-border carbon tax is the official initiation of electricity market coupling with the EU, but none of the Western Balkan countries has met the necessary prerequisites (Energy Community Secretariat, 2024)[13]. According to the estimates for 2024, an average annual marginal CBAM price per MWh varied from 60 to 73 EUR, depending on the country[14]. Therefore, the total annual CBAM costs for EU importers from BiH, Montenegro, North Macedonia and Serbia would be 158, 190, 200 and 612 million EUR, respectively. Electricity exports routed via Albania, which are reported with a zero-emission factor, do not entail any CBAM exposure. CBAM-related import financial exposure is highest in Bulgaria, Croatia, and Hungary, while Greece faces much lower costs despite similar import volumes, due to a lower average CBAM price driven mainly by imports from Albania (see Table 3) (Energy Community Secretariat, 2025b).

Cement manufacturing is considered to be at risk of carbon leakage and was therefore included in CBAM regulation (Marcu et al., 2021). From the other side, Branger et al. (2016) report that carbon pricing does not significantly affect net imports of steel and cement, suggesting an absence of carbon leakage in these sectors over the short term. Cement partially competes with steel and relies on it for reinforcement, so if one of the materials falls under CBAM, the other should also be included to avoid substitution effects.

Cement is manufactured in various types, each characterized by a distinct clinker content and, consequently, different embodied GHG emissions. Producers from Europe have reduced their carbon intensity to below the worldwide mean by employing cleaner energy sources. However, process emissions from lime calcination (accounting for around 60% of emissions) are harder to abate and will require emerging technological solutions such as carbon capture and storage (Marcu et al., 2021; Lobanov et al. 2025)[15].

In contrast to the EU, GHG emission intensity in the Western Balkans remains elevated: Vidovic et al. (2023) show that among 17 countries studied, BiH and Serbia recorded the highest values for the production of grey clinker, aluminous cements, grey Portland, and hydraulic cement. To mitigate emissions originating from the cement industry, it is necessary to shift from the wet production process to the dry one. The wet process involves the initial treatment of cement clinker components (a mixture of limestone and clay) with water, grinding them into a slurry, followed by clinker burning and grinding. Carbon dioxide is released during the energy-intensive firing of the slurry. In the dry process, the clinker components are dried before grinding, and the resulting material is only slightly moistened prior to burning, which results in a twofold reduction in thermal energy consumption and a decrease in kiln gas emissions (Lobanov et al., 2024).

The leading exporters of cement products to the European Union are BiH (various types of cement, clinker, and kaolinic clays) and Albania (non-white Portland cement), both of which are among the top ten supplying countries with a share of 3-5%. For Albania, these products account for nearly 2% of total exports, which are primarily directed to Italy (see Table 3). Almost all exports from BiH are destined for the EU market (cement and clinker to Croatia, clays to Italy). Typically, 2-3 major producers operate in the national markets. The introduction of CBAM could have significant implications for cement plants in BiH, given the high level of GHG emission intensity and reliance on exports to the EU. One potential mitigation strategy is the use of low-carbon fuels in the production processes.

CBAM regulates the *fertilizer* market, in which carbon dioxide and nitrous oxide are emitted during production. Combining two or three of the main nutrients – nitrogen, phosphorus, and potassium – produces NPK fertilizers, with nitrogen being responsible for the most significant GHG emissions. The production of nitrogen-based fertilizers begins with the Haber-Bosch process, during which ammonia is synthesized through the reaction of atmospheric nitrogen with hydrogen under elevated temperature and pressure. Hydrogen is mainly produced from natural gas via methane steam reforming. Natural gas is also commonly used as a fuel to generate heat and pressure. These processes are among the most GHG-intensive due to both high energy requirements and the CO_2 released during conversion. Ammonia itself is a fertilizer but is often transformed further, for example, to nitric acid or urea (Vidovic et al., 2023; Marcu et al., 2021).

Nitric acid is manufactured by combining ammonia and oxygen (Ostwald process), while urea is made through the reaction of ammonia with carbon dioxide (Bosch-Meiser process). About 75-80% of ammonia and nitric acid output is used for further fertilizer production. Nitric acid, for instance, is used to produce the stable fertilizer ammonium nitrate, a process that releases significant amounts of the greenhouse gas nitrous oxide. The production processes for ammonia, nitric acid, urea, and ammonium nitrate are typically carried out in integrated facilities. Applying CBAM at the upstream level (ammonia or nitric acid) would reduce the majority of carbon leakage risks compared to targeting the downstream market (final fertilizers) (Vidovic et al., 2023; Marcu et al., 2021).

The only major fertilizer supplier from the region to the EU is Serbia (1.5% of EU imports; 0.6% of national exports), mainly to neighbouring Croatia, Hungary, and Romania (see Table 3). If NPK and nitrogen fertilizers lose competitiveness in the EU, their export could be redirected, for example, to the markets of the Western Balkans, Asia, and South America. GHG emission intensity is at an average level – for NPK and ammonium nitrate, it exceeds that of Algeria, Egypt, and Belarus, but is below that of Morocco and Russia; for ammonia, it surpasses levels in North African countries, but remains under those in Belarus and Russia (Vidovic et al., 2023). Options for low-carbon modernization in fertilizer production are difficult to achieve in Serbia, as they require significant investment (carbon capture and storage for the methane reforming process; renewable-energy-powered electrolysis as an alternative route for hydrogen production) (Zvezdanović Lobanova et al. 2018).

A considerable influence on the potential output and exports of the Western Balkan countries is exerted by CBAM regulation for the *iron and steel* sector (around 20 product groups are marketed in the EU; see Table 3). Inclusion in CBAM is driven by the sector's substantial environmental footprint and the high risks of carbon leakage for both upstream and downstream products. This sector produces a wide range of goods that fall under three primary categories: crude steel, semi-finished products, and finished products[16].

The ferrous metals value chain comprises coke ovens, sinter and pellet plants, blast furnaces, steelmaking furnaces, and rolling and finishing mills, with most steelmaking and related activities carried out on site[17]. Crude steel is produced through primary and secondary production routes. The most common primary production route (the BF-BOF route) involves a coke oven plant, sinter and/or pellet plants, a blast furnace (BF), and a basic oxygen furnace (BOF). The BF converts iron ore into pig iron, which is subsequently processed in the BOF to produce crude steel through the injection of high-purity oxygen into molten metal (in some cases, pig iron is combined with steel scrap). Another primary steelmaking process, which is considered promising but still scarcely used, is the fabrication of direct reduced iron (DRI), commonly referred to as sponge iron. DRI is manufactured through a smelt-reduction process (known as Corex and Finex), in which natural gas or coal serves as the reducing agent (natural gas accounts for around three-quarters of output). The secondary production route refers to steelmaking in an electric arc furnace (EAF), which melts steel scrap or, to a lesser extent, DRI[18]. Crude steel consists of ingots in conventional mills and semi-finished products (semis) in advanced mills using continuous casting. Semis are intermediate steel forms, including blooms, billets, slabs, ingots, and near net shapes. These semi-finished products are further hot-rolled or forged to produce finished steel, such as flat, long, and alloyed products (Vidovic et al., 2023; Marcu et al., 2021; Ecofys, Fraunhofer Institute for Systems and Innovative Research, Oko Institut, 2009).

Steel production via the primary route from iron ore exhibits higher energy and carbon intensity than the secondary route. CO2 emissions arise from fuel combustion in coking, sintering, and the blast furnace, as well as from the utilization of carbon as a reducing agent and limestone calcination. Within EAF steelmaking, direct emissions come from fuel used to melt scrap and carbon in electrodes, while indirect emissions are associated with electricity generation.

Countries of the region are significant exporters of ferrous metallurgical products to the EU. Large enterprises operate in Smederevo, Zenica, Skopje, and other cities (with the exception of Montenegro, where the plant in Nikšić was effectively shut down in 2021). For example, Serbia traditionally ranks among the ten largest exporting countries to the EU. In terms of absolute export volumes (in thousand tonnes), the following products stand out: pig iron (Serbia), ferro-chromium (Albania), flat-rolled products, tubes and pipes (Serbia, North Macedonia), bars and rods (BiH, North Macedonia, Serbia), as well structures and parts (BiH, Serbia) (see Table 3).

The share of ferrous metallurgy products in the export structure of the Western Balkan countries remains high, ranging from 2% in Montenegro to 10-11% in Albania and BiH. The degree of dependence on the EU market (Germany, Italy, Poland, the Czech Republic, Bulgaria, etc.) varies across the region, but for most key products it lies between 60% and 100%. The implementation of CBAM could significantly affect local producers, who are highly export-oriented; to avoid a sharp decline in production, they will have to redirect part of their output to the Balkan markets. The complementarity of exports and the intensity of intraregional flows should be regarded as high. Taking existing trends into account, alternative markets may include the following: for flat-rolled products from North Macedonia – Turkey and Serbia, from Serbia – BiH; for tubes and pipes from Serbia – BiH and Montenegro, from North Macedonia – Serbia and Montenegro; for bars and rods from Serbia – BiH, from North Macedonia – Serbia, from Albania – Serbia and North Macedonia, from BiH – Serbia and Montenegro. However, the limited capacity of neighboring markets will necessitate stimulating exports to more distant countries (for example, Albania supplies ferro-chromium to the United States) (see Table 3).

Under the introduction of CBAM, the ferrous metallurgy sector in the Western Balkan countries requires technological modernization[19]. Steel plants in Smederevo and Zenica rely on the primary steelmaking route (BF-BOF), which is significantly more emissions-intensive than the secondary route, applied in Skopje (scrap-based EAF). In particular, Serbia's GHG emissions intensity is among the highest compared to other major exporters of semi-finished products, hot-rolled flat products, and wire to the EU: it exceeds levels in China, Japan, Ukraine, and Turkey, though it remains below those of South Africa, Russia, and India (Vidovic et al., 2023). For five iron and steel products that are key to Serbian exports, direct emissions are, on average,

25% greater than those observed in the European Union, while indirect emissions surpass EU levels by over threefold (Vićentijević et al., 2024).

The first approach to modernization involves carbon capture and storage (CCS) and the use of lower-emission fuels, with renewable hydrogen considered a potential future source of process heat. Variability in emissions intensity among facilities utilizing an identical process is mainly driven by the type of fuel used for industrial heat and, for indirect emissions, by electricity purchased from outside the plant (although up to four-fifths of it is produced on-site using waste gas) (Ecofys, Fraunhofer Institute for Systems and Innovative Research, Oko Institut, 2009). Expanding secondary steel production via the EAF process represents another key direction for reducing the carbon intensity of steel, particularly when powered by renewable sources. Another key direction is the expansion of secondary steel production via the EAF process, which can reduce the carbon intensity of steel if powered by renewable electricity. This should be accompanied by increased recycling of steel scrap and by-products[20]. It is clear that the adoption of the DRI route in the Balkans is unlikely in the short term. Researchers are exploring the use of low-carbon hydrogen as a reducing agent instead of natural gas, which holds significant potential to lower the carbon footprint of steelmaking (EUROFER, 2019; Marcu et al., 2021; Lobanov et al., 2024).

The manufacturing of non-ferrous metals constitutes one of the most environmentally impactful industrial activities, with more than half of total GHG emissions attributable to *aluminium production*. To address carbon leakage, the scope of CBAM covers aluminium smelting (primary production), aluminium recycling (secondary production), fabrication (cast house), and manufacturing (rolling/sheet, cold rolling/foil, and extrusion). Key inputs to primary production – alumina and carbon anodes – are excluded from CBAM. Aluminium faces competition from substitute materials, including composites, magnesium, steel, and titanium in transport; glass, paper, plastics, and steel in packaging; and composites, steel, and vinyl in construction (Marcu, 2021). However, aluminium is increasingly substituting other materials. In particular, it is replacing steel in vehicles, where its lightweight properties enable significant emission reductions over the lifetime of cars.

Primary aluminium production begins with refining bauxite or other ores into aluminium oxide in alumina refineries (Bayer process). Alumina is then converted into aluminium metal in smelters or electrolysis plants via the Hall-Héroult process, operating at high temperatures and demanding large amounts of electricity . During the electrolytic process, carbon anodes are consumed. They are either produced in anode plants (pre-baked anodes) or manufactured in the smelter using Söderberg technology; European companies predominantly rely on pre-baked anodes. Secondary (recycled) aluminium is produced by refining or remelting scrap recovered from waste and recycling streams in high-temperature furnaces. Remelters mainly process new (pre-consumer) scrap, while refiners treat old (post-consumer) scrap. Refiners typically produce casting alloys, whereas remelters supply wrought alloys used for rolling, foil, and extrusion. Downstream, unwrought aluminium (produced as pure or alloyed ingots, blocks, billets, or slabs) is further processed into flat-rolled, extruded, and cast products. These include semi-finished bars, rods, profiles, sheets, plates, wire, and foil[21] (Vidovic et al., 2023; Marcu et al., 2021; Maratou & Marcu, 2021).

The primary route is highly electricity-intensive, with indirect emissions from power use exceeding direct emissions from alumina reduction and bauxite processing[22]. Direct emissions arise during smelting, where carbon anodes are immersed in an electrolytic cell containing aluminium oxide and fluorides. This produces CO_2 from fuel use (energy emissions) and CO_2, CO, and PFCs from anode consumption (process emissions). The process uses approximately 450 kg of anodes per tonne of aluminium[23]. Manufacturing secondary aluminium recovered from scrap and recycled materials uses just about 5% of the energy needed for primary production, and a 10% rise in recycling can cut sector GHG emissions by 15%.

EU countries meet about half of their aluminium demand through imports. Serbia, BiH, and Montenegro account for only marginal shares of it – 0.7%, 0.6%, and 0.4%, respectively. For the Western Balkans themselves, however, aluminium exports remain significant, reaching up to 5% of total exports in BiH and 7% in Montenegro (see Table 3). Key destination markets are Germany, Italy, Croatia, Slovenia, and the Czech Republic. In volume terms, exports are dominated by unwrought aluminium (from Mostar in BiH) and by bars, rods, structures, and parts (from Široki Brijeg and Vlasenica in BiH; Niš, Sevojno, and Nova Pazova in Serbia). Dependence on the EU market is very high, reaching 90-100% for core products, with few viable alternatives.

Several decarbonization options for the aluminium sector in the Western Balkans can draw on the experience of developed countries. The foremost is switching to renewable electricity. In the EU, carbon emissions per kg of aluminium are 60% below the global average (around four-fifths of electricity comes from renewables, including hydropower). In addition, a range of measures is needed to improve current manufacturing techniques (e.g., carbon capture and storage), adopt modern production technologies (inert instead of pre-baked anodes), and implement feedback innovations (alumina treatment). Recycling also offers strong potential, requiring just 5% of the energy necessary for primary production (Marcu, 2021; European Aluminium, 2025). Waste from aluminium refining (salt slag) can be used to recover recycled aluminium, which is returned to the metallurgical cycle, as well as aluminium oxide and fluxing salts, employed in construction materials (cement, refractories), insulating materials, and catalysts.

Table 4. Indicative CBAM costs for selected products from Serbia in 2026 and 2030

Product	Embedded emissions (t CO2e / t product), with direct emissions shown in parentheses	Benchmark / Default emissions (t CO2e / t product), with direct emissions shown in parentheses	Export to the EU (t), range	CBAM certificate price projection (EUR / t CO2e)	CBAM cost in 2026 (million EUR)	CBAM cost in 2030 (million EUR)
Pig iron and spiegeleisen in primary forms	2,63 (2,36)	2,07 (1,90)	15300-40300	85 (2026), 100 (2030)	0,66 – 1,74	2,39 – 6,30
Flat-rolled products of iron or non-alloy steel	2,93 (2,43)	2,28-2,39 (1,97-2,03)	608200-694800		23,30 – 30,08	103,34 – 121,99
Bars and rods of iron or non-alloy steel	2,93 (2,43)	2,21 (1,89)	7000-63800		0,35 – 3,18	1,25 – 11,43
Tubes, pipes and hollow profiles	2,96 (2,33)	2,56 (2,21)	29000-33800		0,43 – 0,50	4,76 – 5,55
Iron and steel structures and parts	5,72 (2,56)	5,01 (2,46)	56700-63900		0,78 – 0,88	17,80 – 20,06
Ammonium sulphate	0,75	0,94	22800-42500		–	0,61 – 1,13
Mixtures of urea and ammonium nitrate	1,60	1,34	0-42900		up to 1,07	up to 3,90
Fertilizers containing three elements (nitrogen, phosphorus, potassium)	1,08	1,35	96200-157800		–	3,70 – 6,07
Fertilizers containing two elements (nitrogen, phosphorus)	1,47	1,4	30400-38000		0,27 – 0,34	2,28 – 2,85
Portland cement (excl. white)	0,96	0,87	9800-9900		0,09	0,44

Own calculations. Data sources: Embedded emissions – from Vidovic et al. (2023); Benchmark / Default emissions – from European Commission (2023); Export to the EU – Eurostat (2026); CBAM certificate price – EEA (2026), Trading Economics (2026).

We estimated indicative CBAM costs for EU importers of selected Serbian products for 2026 and 2030 (see Table 4). The goods were selected based on their absolute export volumes to the EU in the first half of 2020s (Eurostat data) and corresponding embedded emissions calculated by the European Commission's Joint Research Centre (Vidovic et al., 2023). For iron and steel and aluminium, CBAM coverage from 2026 applies not to embedded emissions as a whole but only to direct ones, until the EU decides to extend the mechanism to include indirect emissions. CBAM cost was calculated on the basis of the formula presented by Fiskalni savet Republike Srbije (2025), with product-specific adaptations:

CBAM cost (2026) for iron and steel = [Direct emissions – (Benchmark direct emissions × 97,5%)] × Quantity imported × CBAM certificate price

CBAM cost (2026) for fertilizers, cement = [Embedded emissions – (Benchmark total emissions × 97,5%)] × Quantity imported × CBAM certificate price

CBAM cost (2030) for iron and steel, fertilizers, cement = [Embedded emissions – (Benchmark total emissions × 51,5%)] × Quantity imported × CBAM certificate price

It should be noted that in 2026-2033 only a portion of CBAM cost is payable, applying solely to emissions exceeding default (benchmark) levels and adjusted for the progressive removal of free allowances within the EU (e.g. 97.5% in 2026 and 51.5% in 2030). The formulas, therefore, reflect the pace of free allowance withdrawal for EU producers. The Fiscal Council of the Republic of Serbia carried out calculations for four aggregated sectors (iron and steel, aluminium, fertilizers, and cement), while this study seeks to provide indicative estimates for importers of ten specific products[24].

We acknowledge that our estimates for selected products may be overstated due to assumptions and data limitations. First, we do not account for the planned implementation of a carbon tax in Serbia, which could be offset against CBAM obligations. At the initial stage, the carbon cost in Serbia (around 4 EUR/tCO_2-eq in 2027) is expected to remain far below CBAM certificate price. Second, we assume that import volumes will remain broadly in line with those observed in the early 2020s and that carbon prices in 2026 and 2030 will reach 85 and 100 EUR/tCO_2e, respectively (they increased from 60 to 85 EUR/tCO_2e between April and December 2025). Third, it is difficult to estimate potential reductions in embedded emissions in the second half of the 2020s if Serbian companies undertake accelerated technological upgrades. Default emissions are taken from the European Commission (2023), while updated data are expected in 2026. Unlike in 2026, when only direct emissions were considered for iron and steel, in the calculations for 2030, we consider it appropriate to base the assessment on embedded emissions, given that the EU aims to reform CBAM along these lines. Fourth, further verification is needed for the specific embedded free allocation of complex goods, accounting for the production process (e.g., whether precursors were produced in the EU and already covered by ETS). Fifth, data on the size of Serbian product importers are unavailable, so the 'de minimis' exemption under Regulation 2025/2083 could not be applied in our calculations. Such small companies, which bring in fewer than 50 tonnes of CBAM goods annually, account for roughly 90% of all importers but only 1-2% of regulated emissions, leaving EU climate neutrality ambitions largely unaffected.

Thus, our indicative cost estimates for selected products from Serbia for 2030 may be considered overstated if the country not only introduces a carbon tax but also raises it to a level comparable to CBAM certificate price. A key factor in reducing embedded emissions may be the modernization of production processes, but the scale of this will vary across sectors. For certain products, a negative production trend is already observed, which, combined with declining price competitiveness, is likely to lead to lower export volumes and, consequently, to a reduction in aggregate CBAM costs. Throughout most of 2024 and 2025, carbon prices followed an upward trend; however, the wide range of short-term forecasts does not allow for a definitive assessment of whether their future dynamics will result in an increase or a decrease in the overall burden. Much will also depend on the policy trajectory chosen by European policymakers with respect to the development of CBAM – specifically, whether embedded emissions for iron and steel will be included in the calculations, default (benchmark) emission values lowered, the 'de minimis' exemption enforced more strictly, and precursors from the EU already covered by the ETS identified.

CONCLUSION

The stated objectives of CBAM include reducing greenhouse gas emissions in countries exporting carbon-intensive products to the EU by creating incentives for technological modernization or for the introduction of national carbon pricing systems. At the same time, the mechanism is intended to enhance the competitiveness of European producers, as well as to prevent carbon leakage and the emergence of "carbon havens" in countries with less developed climate policy frameworks. From the perspective of exporters of electricity, iron and steel, aluminium, fertilizers, and cement to the EU, CBAM is often viewed as a protectionist instrument aimed at raising additional revenues, which may adversely affect economic growth and worsen conditions in labour markets in developing countries while failing to reduce the global environmental burden. CBAM provisions are widely considered to be inconsistent with WTO rules and the principles of the UNFCCC. According to many expert assessments, countries of the Western Balkans are expected to face particularly significant impacts, as their development largely depends on exports of carbon-intensive products to European markets. In addressing these issues, the countries of the region have initiated a process of institutional harmonisation with the EU in the area of the "green transition" by signing multilateral agreements (Sofia Declaration on the Green Agenda for the Western Balkans, Brdo Declaration) and by developing low-carbon growth and/or climate change strategies. Montenegro remains the only Western Balkan country with an operational carbon pricing system, while the others either plan to introduce an ETS (e.g. BiH) or, as an initial step, intend to introduce a carbon tax from 2026 to 2028. According to the Energy Community Secretariat, Serbia is the most advanced country in the region in terms of establishing an ETS and implementing key components of MRVA.

In this article, we provide a detailed analysis of the impact of CBAM on the production capacity and exports of Western Balkan countries – not in a generalized manner across the five CBAM-covered sectors, as is common in many studies, but using 35 product groups and multiple indicators for assessment. We explain the characteristics of the technological processes and identify stages of production with high GHG emission intensity, as well as provide recommendations based on best existing practices while taking into account local specificities. Besides comparing countries by the volume of carbon-intensive goods exports (which largely determine the tax burden) we assess their share in national exports (ranging from 9-11% in Serbia and North Macedonia to 28% in Montenegro) and the degree of dependence on the European market (exceeding 90-95% for many products). For a substantial number of goods, we conclude that reorienting export flows would be difficult to achieve, taking into account the geographical structure of exports to the EU, influenced by the "neighbourhood effect", the level of intra-regional trade development, and the availability of alternative markets. Additionally, we calculate indicative CBAM costs for ten carbon-intensive products from Serbia, taking into account embedded and direct emissions, exports to the EU, and projected CBAM certificate prices. Among the selected products, flat-rolled products of iron or non-alloy steel stand out (CBAM costs may amount to EUR 23-30 million in 2026 and rise to EUR 103-122 million by 2030), as well as iron and steel structures and parts (EUR 1 million and 18-20 million, respectively). For comparison, for fertilizers containing three elements, these costs could reach EUR 4-6 million in 2030, while for Portland cement other than white, they would be less than half a million euros. The current situation requires swift action, including the further enhancement of the national carbon pricing system and the technological upgrading of export-oriented enterprises characterized by high greenhouse gas emissions.

Based on the results obtained, we identify a set of policy recommendations that may be applied by national and supranational regulatory authorities, as well as by the private sector. The governments of the Western Balkan countries should continue the process of institutional harmonisation with the EU in the field of greenhouse gas emission regulation, taking into account the strong dependence of their economic situation on exports to European markets. National low-carbon development strategies should balance economic and social policy objectives while creating financial incentives to support the implementation of structural reforms.

A key priority is the establishment of the core components of an MRVA system, along with the introduction of carbon pricing instruments, including a carbon tax and an ETS. Domestic taxation could help alleviate the burden on CBAM-covered sectors by reducing the risk of double carbon pricing on goods imported into the EU, while also increasing government revenues. A second, equally important task is the creation of favourable conditions for the technological modernization of power plants and enterprises producing carbon-intensive goods, aimed at reducing greenhouse gas emissions or enabling their capture. Support measures should cover both companies facing rising costs associated with upgrading and small and medium-sized businesses, which are expected to be especially vulnerable to the introduction of CBAM. Finally, accelerating export diversification should be recognized as an important factor in strengthening the economic resilience of the Western Balkan countries.

National exporters are advised to work closely with regulatory authorities to facilitate technological modernization, implement emissions accounting systems, undertake partial or full restructuring of production, and explore alternative export markets. European authorities should ensure transparency in the calculation of CBAM certificate costs and the effective application of the 'de minimis' exemption in order to reduce the burden on small and medium-sized enterprises in the developing market economies of the Western Balkans. CBAM electricity import reporting rules should be revised to attribute emissions to the country of generation, thereby avoiding charges on electricity flows transiting through non-EU countries. More broadly, the European Union should strengthen cooperation with the region to mitigate risks and address potential adverse effects of the "green transition" policies.

REFERENCES

Altaghlibi, M. (2025). *CBAM impact and opportunities*. https://assets.ctfassets.net/1u811bvgvthc/6bqifXzHR2Lxedk7NohOwE/aeea069da882395a5ff66782f82e188a/250520_CBAM_impacts_and_opportunities.pdf

Amendola, M. (2025). Winners and losers of the EU carbon border adjustment mechanism. An intra-EU issue? *Energy Economics*, *142*, 108139. DOI: 10.1016/j.eneco.2024.108139

Branger, F., Quirion, P., & Chevallier, J. (2016). Carbon leakage and competitiveness of cement and steel industries under the EU ETS: Much ado about nothing. *The Energy Journal (Cambridge, Mass.)*, *37*(3), 109–136. DOI: 10.5547/01956574.37.3.fbra

Cammeo, J., Ferrari, A., Borghesi, S., & Dokken, T. (2025). *Understanding and assessing CBAM: vulnerability and impacts in the EU*. SPES Working Paper no. 7.2, SPES project – Sustainability Performances, Evidence and Scenarios. Florence: University of Florence. https://www.sustainabilityperformances.eu/publications-deliverables

Climate Watch. (2025). *Historical GHG Emissions* [Data set]. https://www.climatewatchdata.org

Dechezleprêtre, A., Haramboure, A., Kögel, C., Lalanne, G., & Yamano, N. (2025). *Carbon Border Adjustments: The potential effects of the EU CBAM along the supply chain*. OECD Science, Technology and Industry Working Papers No. 2025/02. OECD Publishing, Paris. DOI: DOI: 10.1787/18151965

Ecofys, Fraunhofer Institute for Systems and Innovative Research, Oko Institut. (2009). *Methodology for the free allocation of emission allowances in the EU ETS post 2012. Sector report for the cement industry*. Technical Report. Retrieved from https://climate.ec.europa.eu/system/files/2016-11/bm_study-project_approach_and_general_issues_en.pdf

EEA. (2026). EU Emissions Trading System (ETS) data viewer [Data set]. https://www.eea.europa.eu/en/analysis/maps-and-charts/emissions-trading-viewer-1-dashboards

Eicke, L., Weko, S., Apergi, M., & Marian, A. (2021). Pulling Up the Carbon Ladder? Decarbonization, Dependence, and Third-Country Risks From the European Carbon Border Adjustment Mechanism. *Energy Research & Social Science*, *80*, 102240. DOI: 10.1016/j.erss.2021.102240

Ember. (2025). *Electricity Data Explorer* [Data set]. https://ember-energy.org/data/electricity-data-explorer

EMIS. (2026). *Company profiles – Emerging markets*. https://www.emis.com/php/company-profile/index/search

Energy Community Secretariat. (2024). *CBAM-Readiness Tracker 2024*. Vienna. https://www.energy-community.org/topics/CBAM/Tracker.html

Energy Community Secretariat. (2025a). *Annual Implementation Report 2025*. Vienna. https://www.energy-community.org/publications/flagships/IRs.html

Energy Community Secretariat. (2025b). *CBAM-Readiness Tracker 2025*. Vienna. https://www.energy-community.org/topics/CBAM/Tracker.html

Erdogdu, E. (2025). The Carbon Border Adjustment Mechanism: Opportunities and Challenges for Non-EU Countries. *Wiley Interdisciplinary Reviews. Energy and Environment*, *14*(1), e70000. DOI: 10.1002/wene.70000

EUROFER. (2019). *Low Carbon Roadmap: Pathways to a CO2-neutral European steel industry*. https://www.eurofer.eu/assets/Uploads/EUROFER-Low-Carbon-Roadmap-Pathways-to-a-CO2-neutral-European-Steel-Industry.pdf

EUROFER. (2020). *European Steel in Figures 2020*. https://www.eurofer.eu/assets/Uploads/European-Steel-in-Figures-2020.pdf

European Aluminium. (2025). *Environmental Profile Report 2024. V.2.0*. https://european-aluminium.eu/wp-content/uploads/2025/07/Environmental-Profile-Report_2024-V20.pdf

European Commission. (2019). *The European Green Deal*. COM(2019) 640 final. https://ec.europa.eu/info/sites/default/files/european-green-deal-communication_en.pdf

European Commission. (2021a). *"Fit for 55": Delivering the EU's 2030 climate target on the way to climate neutrality*. COM(2021)550 final, Brussels.

European Commission. (2021b). *Proposal for a regulation of the European Parliament and of the Council establishing a carbon border adjustment mechanism*. COM (2021) 564 final, 2021/0214 COD. Brussels.

European Commission. (2023). *Default values for the transitional period of the CBAM between 1 October 2023 and 31 December 2025*. Brussels. https://taxation-customs.ec.europa.eu/system/files/202312/Default%20values%20transitional%20period.pdf

European Commission. (2025). *EU trade relations with the Western Balkans. Facts, figures and latest developments*. https://policy.trade.ec.europa.eu/eu-trade-relationships-country-and-region/countries-and-regions/western-balkans_en

European Parliament & Council of the European Union. (2023a). Directive (EU) 2023/959 of the European Parliament and of the Council of 10 May 2023 amending Directive 2003/87/EC establishing a system for greenhouse gas emission allowance trading within the Union and Decision (EU) 2015/1814 concerning the establishment and operation of a market stability reserve for the Union greenhouse gas emission trading system. *Official Journal of the European Union* (L 130/134). https://data.europa.eu/eli/dir/2023/959/oj

European Parliament & Council of the European Union. (2023b). Regulation (EU) 2023/956 of the European Parliament and of the Council of 10 May 2023 establishing a carbon border adjustment mechanism. *Official Journal of the European Union* (L 130/52). https://data.europa.eu/eli/reg/2023/956/oj

European Parliament & Council of the European Union. (2025). Regulation (EU) 2025/2083 of the European Parliament and of the Council of 8 October 2025 amending Regulation (EU) 2023/956 as regards simplifying and strengthening the carbon border adjustment mechanism. *Official Journal of the European Union* (L series). https://data.europa.eu/eli/reg/2025/2083/oj

Eurostat. (2026). EU trade since 1988 by HS2-4-6 and CN8 [Data set]. https://ec.europa.eu/eurostat

Fiskalni savet Republike Srbije (2025). *Klimatsko-energetska tranzicija Srbije i javne finansije: hoće li CBAM biti okidač promena?* Fiskalni savet Republike Srbije.

Gérardin, M., & Ferrière, S. (2025). *Décarbonation de l'acier et des métaux de base: envoyons les bons signaux*. La note d'analyse, No. 149. France Stratégie. https://www.strategie-plan.gouv.fr/publications/decarbonation-de-lacier-metaux-de-base-envoyons-bons-signaux

International Trade Centre. (2026). Trade Map [Data set]. https://www.trademap.org

Lobanov, M., Zvezdanović Lobanova, J., & Zvezdanović, M. (2024). Climate Discourse in Russia: From the Dichotomy of Climate Consciousness to Four Forms of Climate Policy. *Mir Rossii*, *33*(3), 141–169. DOI: 10.17323/1811-038X-2024-33-3-141-169

Lobanov, M. M., Zvezdanović Lobanova, J., Milinčić, M., & Zvezdanović, M. (2025). Impact Of Coal-Based Electricity Generation, Land Use Change, Steel And Cement Production On CO2 Emissions: Evidence From Eastern European And Central Asian Countries. *Geography, Environment, Sustainability*, *18*(1), 139–151. DOI: 10.24057/2071-9388-2025-3754

Magacho, G., Espagne, E., & Godin, A. (2024). Impacts of the CBAM on EU trade partners: Consequences for developing countries. *Climate Policy, 24*(2), 243–259. DOI: 10.1080/14693062.2023.2200758

Maliszewska, M., Chepeliev, M., Fischer, C., & Jung, E. (2025). *How developing countries can measure exposure to the EU's carbon border adjustment mechanism* [Online forum post]. World Bank Blogs. https://blogs.worldbank.org/en/trade/how-developing-countries-can-measure-exposure-eus-carbon-border-adjustment-mechanism

Maratou, A., & Marcu, A. (2021). *The Aluminium Value Chain and Implications for CBAM Design.* ERCST. https://ercst.org/wp-content/uploads/2021/08/The-aluminium-value-chain-and-implications-for-CBAM-design.pdf

Marcu, A., Mehling, M., & Cosbey, A. (2021). *Border Carbon Adjustments in the EU: Sectoral Deep Dive.* ERCST. https://ercst.org/wp-content/uploads/2021/08/20210317-CBAM-II_Report-I-Sectors.pdf

Narodna skupština Republike Srbije. (2025a). *Zakon o porezu na emisije gasova sa efektom staklene baste* („Službeni glasnik RS", br. 109/2025).

Narodna skupština Republike Srbije. (2025b). *Zakon o porezu na uvoz ugljenično intenzivnih proizvoda* („Službeni glasnik RS", br. 109/2025).

Pavlović, B., & Trtica, N. (2024). Projecting short to medium-term effects of carbon emissions trading on Serbia's GDP. *Utilities Policy, 91*, 101855. DOI: 10.1016/j.jup.2024.101855

Perdana, S., & Vielle, M. (2022). Making the EU Carbon Border Adjustment Mechanism acceptable and climate friendly for least developed countries. *Energy Policy, 170*, 113245. DOI: 10.1016/j.enpol.2022.113245

Petrović, P., & Lobanov, M. M. (2022). Energy intensity and foreign direct investment nexus: Advanced panel data analysis. *Applied Energy, 311*, 118669. DOI: 10.1016/j.apenergy.2022.118669

Porfiriev, B. N., Shirov, A. A., & Kolpakov, A. Yu. (2021). An Integrated Approach to the Strategy of Low-carbon Socio-economic Development of Russia. *Georesursy, 23*(3), 3–7. DOI: 10.18599/grs.2021.3.1

Regional Cooperation Council. (2022). *Green Agenda for the Western Balkans Action Plan - Implementation Report 2022*. Sarajevo. https://www.rcc.int/pubs/162/green-agenda-for-the-western-balkans-action-plan--implementation-report-2022

Ren, Q., & Du, J. (2025). The EU's carbon border adjustment mechanism: Theoretical dimensions, implementation challenges and WTO compliance. *Journal of International Trade Law & Policy*, *24*(3), 228–249. DOI: 10.1108/JITLP-12-2024-0081

Sandbag. (2025). *CBAM impact on US trade: an analysis.* https://sandbag.be/wp-content/uploads/CBAM-impact-on-US-trade.pdf

Trading Economics. (2026). *EU Carbon Permits.* https://tradingeconomics.com/commodity/carbon

UNCTADstat. (2026). UNCTADstat Data centre [Data set]. https://unctadstat.unctad.org

USGS. (2026). International Minerals Statistics and Information [Data set]. https://www.usgs.gov/centers/national-minerals-information-center/international-minerals-statistics-and-information

Vićentijević, A., Parežanin, M., & Jednak, S. (2024). Assessing Serbian Iron and Steel Exports to the EU under CBAM. In *Proceedings of 19th International Symposium Unlocking the Hidden Potentials of Organization Through Merging of Humans and Digitals*. University of Belgrade – Faculty of Organizational Sciences.

Vidovic, D., Marmier, A., Zore, L. & Moya, J. A. (2023). *Greenhouse gas emission intensities of the steel, fertilisers, aluminium and cement industries in the EU and its main trading partners*. JRC Technical Report, Luxembourg. DOI: .DOI: 10.2760/359533

Zhong, J., & Pei, J. (2022). Beggar thy neighbor? On the competitiveness and welfare impacts of the EU's proposed carbon border adjustment mechanism. *Energy Policy*, *162*, 112802. DOI: 10.1016/j.enpol.2022.112802

Živanović, Z., Popović, V., Djordjević, A., Protić, B., Šećerov, V., & Jeftić, M. (2026). "Signs by the Roadside": On the Road to Just Green Transitions in Serbia. In Berisha, E., Moodie, J., Allkja, L., & Jeftić, M. (Eds.), *The Palgrave Handbook of Just Green Transitions in the Western Balkans and Beyond* (pp. 265–282). Palgrave Macmillan. DOI: 10.1007/978-3-031-95075-9_15

Zvezdanović Lobanova, J., Kračun, D., & Kavkler, A. (2018). Effects of cross-border mergers and acquisitions on GDP per capita and domestic investment in transition countries. *Journal of Business Economics and Management*, *19*(1), 124–137. DOI: 10.3846/16111699.2017.1408677

Zvezdanović Lobanova, J., & Lobanov, M. (2023). Problems and perspectives of the European Green Deal with the focus on the SEE countries and Serbia. *The Review of International Affairs*, *LXXIV*(1188), 51–77. DOI: 10.18485/iipe_ria.2023.74.1188.3

KEY TERMS AND DEFINITIONS

Carbon Border Adjustment Mechanism (CBAM): A policy instrument that imposes a carbon cost on imported goods originating from countries with less stringent climate regulations.

Carbon Leakage: The phenomenon in which emission reductions in one country result in increased emissions in another, typically due to the relocation of production to regions with less rigorous environmental standards.

Carbon Pricing: An approach that assigns a monetary value to carbon emissions in order to incentivize companies and individuals to decrease their environmental impact.

Decarbonization: The process of reducing or eliminating carbon emissions from energy production and industrial activities, typically through the adoption of cleaner energy sources and advanced technologies.

Embedded Emissions: The aggregate greenhouse gas emissions generated throughout the entire life cycle of a product, from production through to end use, reflecting its comprehensive carbon footprint.

Emissions Trading System (ETS): A regulatory framework that establishes a cap on total emissions and permits the trading of emission allowances, thereby incentivizing companies to achieve emission reductions more efficiently.

Western Balkans: A region in Southeast Europe comprising Albania, Bosnia and Herzegovina, Montenegro, North Macedonia, and Serbia, frequently examined in the context of European Union integration.

ENDNOTES

1 It's noteworthy, that the greenhouse gases covered by CBAM regulation include not only carbon dioxide, but also nitrous oxide and perfluorocarbons.

2 According to one study, CBAM is expected to reduce carbon leakage from 17% to 12.6% by 2040 (Perdana & Vielle, 2022).

3 This process is associated with the "pollution haven hypothesis," whereby developed countries seek to relocate environmentally harmful industries to developing countries (characterized by abundant natural resources, low labor costs, and less stringent environmental regulations) which ultimately results in significant environmental consequences for the recipients of FDI. Countries that attract foreign investment due to lax regulation of GHG emissions are referred to as "carbon havens".

4 Maximizing revenues from CBAM will help cover expenditures under the European Green Deal and support funding for climate change mitigation initiatives that prioritize social justice (Porfiriev et al., 2021).

5 The ETS was set up in 2005 with an ambition to reduce emissions from energy-intensive industries. It actually represents a market for carbon permits that determines the allowable emissions for power plants, industrial facilities, and airlines to release into the atmosphere.

6 Direct emissions are «from the production processes of goods, including emissions from the production of heating and cooling», while indirect emissions are «from the production of electricity that is consumed during the production processes». Embedded emissions consist of both direct and indirect emissions. CBAM certificate is defined as an electronic certificate corresponding to one tonne of CO_2e of embedded emissions in goods (European Parliament & Council of the European Union, 2023b).

7 The societal and economic impacts of CBAM need to be evaluated within the wider framework of the EGD strategy's effects across countries at different development levels (the so-called just green transition) (Živanović et al., 2026).

8 The first revision of the of the Action Plan for the implementation of the Sofia Declaration by the RCC was launched in 2025, and the next one is planned for 2027.

9 The countries of the region have issued several strategic documents in the field of climate policy, including – depending on the country – low-carbon or low-emission development strategies, energy development strategies, as well as national climate change strategies and climate resilience action plans.

10 Pavlovic and Trtica (2024) find that the introduction of carbon pricing could result in a deceleration of Serbia's GDP growth during the initial years following the implementation of the ETS.

11 It is notable that the energy sector accounts for 25% of global GHG emissions, whereas in the EU this share reaches 75%.

12 The dependence on hydroelectric facilities results in highly volatile electricity generation in Albania, with year-on-year variations of 30-40%. Similar challenges have affected Serbia, Montenegro, and BiH, which have relied on hydropower since the mid-20th century.

13 In the case of Serbia, the market coupling process with Hungary and Bulgaria needs to be completed by the end of 2026, and a carbon trading system should

be launched from 2030. However, this would subject the entire country's energy sector to carbon regulation, which may be a less advantageous option compared to maintaining the status quo – where only exported volumes are burdened by CBAM cross-border carbon tax (Fiskalni savet Republike Srbije, 2025).

14 CBAM calculation for electricity should be based on the country's average emissions over a five-year period.

15 Apart from clinker-related emissions from limestone decomposition, the remaining one-third arise from burning carbon-based fuels to achieve the elevated temperatures needed for calcination and clinker sintering (Vidovic et al., 2023).

16 In Europe, construction and automotive manufacturing are the largest end users of steel, where substitution is possible – by aluminium, cement, and wood in the first case, and by aluminium, fibreglass, or other plastics in the second.

17 Preparatory stages include coke production in the coke oven and the agglomeration of iron ore in sinter and pellet plants. Coke-making emissions are not covered by CBAM regulation when calculating the embedded emissions of iron and steel products.

18 In 2019, primary production using the BOF method accounted for 59% of crude steel in the EU, with secondary production via the EAF method representing the remaining 41% (EUROFER, 2020).

19 In the EU, two main pathways for reducing CO2 in steel sector are Smart Carbon Usage (SCU) and Carbon Direct Avoidance (CDA). Adoption of these technologies could cut emissions by 80-95% by 2050 compared to 1990, but production costs may rise by 35-100% per tonne of steel (EUROFER, 2019).

20 Rising costs of steel production via the BF-BOF route due to carbon pricing may lead to higher demand and growing scrap prices in Europe, which is used in EAF and exempt from CBAM. As a result, it may be more profitable for non-EU countries to export scrap rather than develop their own secondary steel production based on it (Gérardin & Ferrière, 2025).

21 The EU aluminium value chain includes about 600 plants, from raw materials to semi-fabricated products and recycling. In 2019, 13 smelters operated across nine countries (Maratou & Marcu, 2021). Smelters and rolling mills are mainly controlled by multinationals, while extrusion and recycling are dominated by SMEs.

22 In the EU, electricity accounts for roughly 37% of total production costs.

23 Aluminium production emits around 7 tCO_2e per tonne in the EU countries, compared with 16.5 tCO_2e globally, up to 20 tCO_2e in China, and at a minimum of 1.5 tCO_2e in regions with abundant hydroelectric power (Marcu et al., 2021).

24 The Council's report estimates that in 2026 the total cost across all sectors would amount to around 46 million EUR (with iron and steel accounting for about 75%), while by 2030 it could rise to 150-200 million EUR, depending on export volumes to the EU and carbon prices (Fiskalni savet Republike Srbije, 2025).

Chapter 7
The Ripple and Spillover Effects of Environmental Policy Stringency on Environmental Degradation in EU-14 Countries

Çağla Bucak
http://orcid.org/0000-0003-3169-110X
Ege University, Turkey

ABSTRACT

This study examines the spatial spillover effects of environmental policy stringency, GDP per capita, and fossil energy consumption on the ecological footprint in EU–14 countries over the period 1990–2020 using spatial econometric techniques. The results reveal strong and positive spatial dependence in the ecological footprint, indicating significant cross-country spillovers. Environmental policy stringency is found to reduce the ecological footprint both directly and indirectly, while fossil energy consumption and GDP per capita increase environmental pressure through significant domestic and spillover effects. Notably, indirect effects dominate direct effects, highlighting the critical role of regional interdependence in shaping environmental outcomes. These findings demonstrate that environmental policies generate ripple effects beyond national borders and emphasize the necessity of coordinated environmental and energy policies, increased investment in renewable energy, and strategies to decouple economic growth from fossil fuel dependence across the EU–14 region.

DOI: 10.4018/979-8-3373-8998-1.ch007

1. INTRODUCTION

Environmental pollution is among the most pressing and complex challenges facing countries worldwide. The accelerating pace of climate change has triggered profound and unprecedented environmental transformations. Greenhouse gas concentrations have reached historic highs, pushing global near-surface temperatures beyond pre-industrial levels. Simultaneously, ocean heat content has risen to record levels, sea levels have continued to increase, and glaciers have undergone rapid and widespread melting. These developments have intensified the frequency and severity of weather- and climate-related extreme events, generating severe consequences for ecosystems, human livelihoods, and economic systems across the globe (WMO, 2025).

Beyond their environmental implications, these adverse trends pose substantial risks to economic stability and sustainable development. Climate change and environmental degradation affect productivity, investment decisions, public finances, and long-term growth prospects, making them central concerns for economic analysis. Consequently, economists have increasingly sought to quantify the economic costs of climate change, as well as its broader macroeconomic implications (Stern, 2006). In addition to estimating these costs, environmental economists employ econometric methods to examine how environmental degradation is affected by key economic factors such as growth and energy consumption, with the aim of informing effective policy design.

Within the environmental economics literature, environmental degradation has traditionally been measured using proxies such as carbon dioxide (CO_2) emissions. Although these metrics capture important dimensions of environmental pressure, they offer a partial view by overlooking other critical aspects of ecological stress, including land use, resource extraction, and ecosystem capacity. This limitation has motivated the development of more comprehensive indicators, most notably the ecological footprint (EF) (Wackernagel & Rees, 1997). By accounting for both resource consumption and the regenerative capacity of ecosystems, it provides a more comprehensive assessment of humanity's environmental impact and offers a broader perspective on environmental sustainability.

Given the multidimensional nature of degradation, evaluating environmental outcomes also requires indicators that reflect the effectiveness of environmental policy interventions. In response to growing climate risks and the need to promote sustainability, governments have adopted a wide range of policy measures to mitigate climate-related challenges, most notably through international frameworks such as the Kyoto Protocol, and the Paris Agreement (UN, 2026). These initiatives underscore the growing recognition that effective climate action requires international cooperation and that sustainable development depends on integrated policy approaches linking economic, social, and environmental dimensions (Kozal, 2025). Alongside these global initiatives, countries have progressively increased the stringency of their environmental policies in an effort to limit degradation (Sohag et al., 2024). As environmental science and economics have advanced through the development of more extensive indicators, there has emerged a corresponding need for systematic measures that capture the environmental policy stringency. To address this need, OECD (2022) introduced the environmental policy stringency index (EPSI), which quantifies the extent to which environmental regulations constrain environmentally harmful activities. The EPSI has since become a widely used indicator for assessing regulatory effort and policy commitment in empirical environmental economics.

Although studies have explored the nexus between EPSI and degradation (e.g., Balsalobre-Lorente et al., 2023; Luo et al., 2024; Kartal et al., 2025), to the best of the author's knowledge, no study has yet simultaneously examined the indirect and direct impacts of EPSI on ecological footprints while explicitly accounting for spill-over impacts and associated ripple effects. To address this research gap, the present study examines EU–14 countries, the older member states of the European Union, which have been extensively examined in the empirical literature, particularly within econometric and environmental economics research (e.g., Janicka & Sajnóg, 2022; Çoban et al., 2025; Biekša et al., 2022). Accordingly, EU–14 countries are adopted as the sample of analysis. By employing a Spatial Durbin Model for the period 1990–2020, this study decomposes the indirect and direct impacts of environmental policy stringency, fossil energy usage, and economic growth on ecological footprints, while simultaneously capturing spatial spillovers and feedback mechanisms across neighboring countries. This framework not only provides a more comprehensive understanding of the transboundary impacts of environmental policies but also offers valuable insights for designing coordinated and effective regional strategies to mitigate environmental degradation.

The European Union (EU) provides a particularly suitable context for analyzing such ripple and spillover effects. Its high degree of economic integration, open internal markets, and coordinated environmental policy frameworks suggest that environmental actions undertaken in one member state may influence environmental outcomes in others. Moreover, the EU has asserted its role as a global leader in climate governance. To support this ambition, EU member states have implemented comprehensive policy initiatives (European Council, 2025). The European Green Deal represents a transformative strategy to shift the European Union toward a clean and circular economy. The initiative prioritizes investment in innovation, clean technologies, and green infrastructure, while also emphasizing a just transition that supports communities and regions most affected by the green transformation (European Commission, 2026).

The Fit for 55 package represents a comprehensive policy framework designed to reduce the European Union's emissions by at least 55 percent for 2030. Central to this objective is the strengthening of the EU Emissions Trading System, which aims not only to enhance emissions reductions but also to generate increased financial resources. Moreover, the package introduces the Social Climate Fund to provide targeted support and investment for vulnerable households and regions. To ensure fair competition, the framework also incorporates the Carbon Border Adjustment Mechanism. The Fit for 55 initiative also includes binding commitments that aim to enhance carbon removals in the land use and forestry sectors. Furthermore, the package places specific emphasis on reducing methane emissions in the energy sector (European Council, 2026).

In this regard, this chapter advances the existing literature by providing a more differentiated spatial analysis of the link between EPSI and ecological footprint. Rather than treating countries as isolated units, the analysis explicitly accounts for ripple and spillover effects by examining the mechanisms through which environmental regulations in the domestic country and its neighboring countries jointly influence domestic environmental outcomes. Employing a Spatial Durbin Model, the study advances existing research by decomposing policy impacts into direct and indirect effects, thereby providing clearer insights into the cross-border transmission of EPSI. This approach enables a systematic consideration of spatial interdependencies and highlights the role of neighboring countries in shaping local environmental quality.

2. ECOLOGICAL FOOTPRINT AND ENVIRONMENTAL POLICY STRINGENCY: DESCRIPTIVE EVIDENCE AND SPATIAL PATTERNS

Figure 1 illustrates global trends in ecological footprint and biocapacity. The figure reveals that the majority of countries operate under an ecological deficit, where ecological footprint exceeds available biocapacity, as indicated by the areas highlighted in red. These deficit countries tend to cluster geographically, suggesting that environmental pressure is not randomly distributed but exhibits clear spatial patterns. The European region is also predominantly shown in red, indicating that European countries experience a persistent ecological deficit. Although some countries are depicted in green, indicating that their biocapacity surpasses their ecological footprint, many of them share close borders with ecologically deficit countries. This geographic proximity exposes them to the risk of ecological overshoot through transboundary environmental pressures, trade linkages, and shared ecosystems, increasing the likelihood that they may also transition into ecological deficit over time.

Figure 1. Spatial Patterns of Ecological Footprint and Biocapacity Worldwide

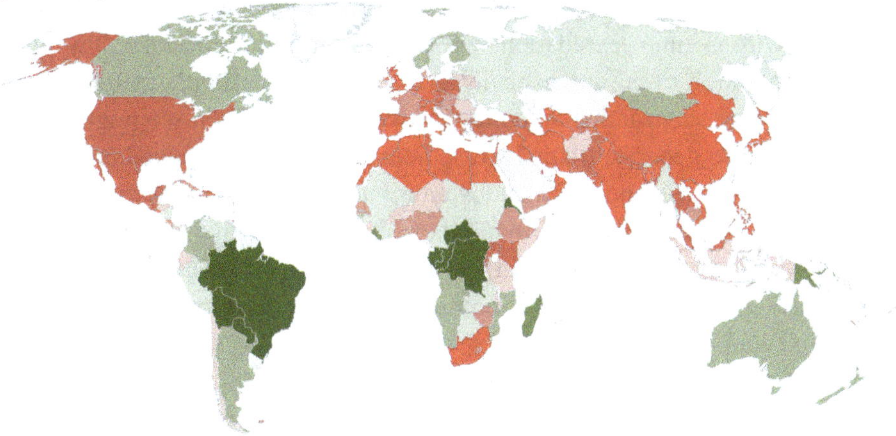

Source: *Global Footprint Network (2026).*

Note: Countries shown in red indicate an ecological deficit (ecological footprint exceeds biocapacity), while countries shown in green indicate an ecological surplus (biocapacity exceeds ecological footprint). The geographical clustering of these patterns suggests that environmental pressures are spatially dependent and exhibit transboundary characteristics.

Figure 2 illustrates the main components of EPSI. As illustrated, the EPSI consists of three main components. Market-based instruments capture the extent to which countries rely on mechanisms such as CO_2 emissions trading schemes and energy taxes to strengthen environmental regulation. Non-market-based instruments focus on regulatory measures, particularly emission limit values imposed on polluting activities. The third component, technology support policies, reflects public support for environmental innovation through research and development expenditures and incentives for renewable energy sources, especially solar and wind power. The index is scaled from zero, indicating the absence of environmental policy stringency, to six, representing the highest level of policy strictness (OECD, 2022). This increasing ability to measure and compare policy stringency reflects the growing importance of environmental regulation, which has evolved from a peripheral policy issue into a central pillar of modern economic governance.

While environmental policies are primarily designed to alleviate environmental pressures, their indirect effects and cross-border spillover implications remain relatively underexplored in the academic literature. In particular, the broader economic and environmental consequences of stricter environmental policies, as well as the spatial diffusion of environmental degradation, call for more systematic and rigorous investigation. Understanding the spatial diffusion and spillover transmission of environmental outcomes is also essential for capturing the broader ripple effects generated by environmental policies. Changes in economic growth structures may intensify environmental degradation, whereas stricter environmental policy regimes can mitigate pollution both domestically and beyond national borders (Ronaghi et al., 2020). Moreover, environmental policy instruments not only discourage polluting activities but also generate financial resources that can be redirected toward clean energy investments, technological innovation, and sustainable production structures (Ali et al., 2023; EEA, 2022). Through these channels, environmental policies initiate ripple effects that extend across sectors, regions, and countries, influencing environmental performance and economic dynamics well beyond their initial point of implementation. Consequently, a spatial perspective is indispensable for fully understanding the interconnected and multi-layered impacts of EPSI.

Figure 2. The main components of EPSI

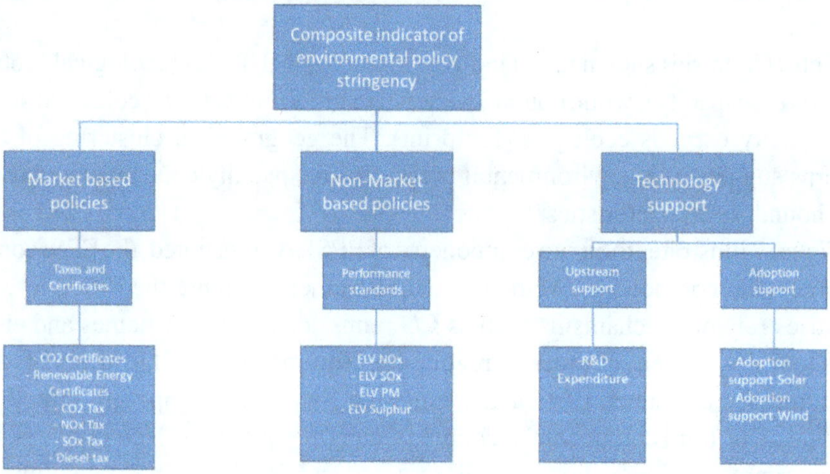

Source: *OECD (2022).*

Note: The index quantifies regulatory effort across three primary dimensions: market-based instruments (e.g., taxes and trading schemes), non-market-based instruments (e.g., emission limits), and technology support (e.g., research and development incentives). It is scored on a 0–6 scale, where higher values reflect stronger policy measures targeting the reduction of environmental degradation.

Figure 3 denotes the trends in environmental policy stringency index for these countries. As shown, all EU–14 nations exhibit a clear and substantial increase in policy stringency over the past three decades, reflecting a broader regional and global shift toward more rigorous environmental regulation. This upward trajectory underscores the increasing commitment of EU–14 countries to mitigate environmental degradation. However, the mere rise in policy stringency does not automatically guarantee environmental protection, warranting a more nuanced understanding of policy effectiveness. A holistic framework, such as the one employed in this study, provides an empirical basis to evaluate both the direct and spillover effects of stringent environmental policies across these countries.

Figure 3. Trends in Environmental Policy Stringency (EPSI) for EU–14 Countries, 1990–2020

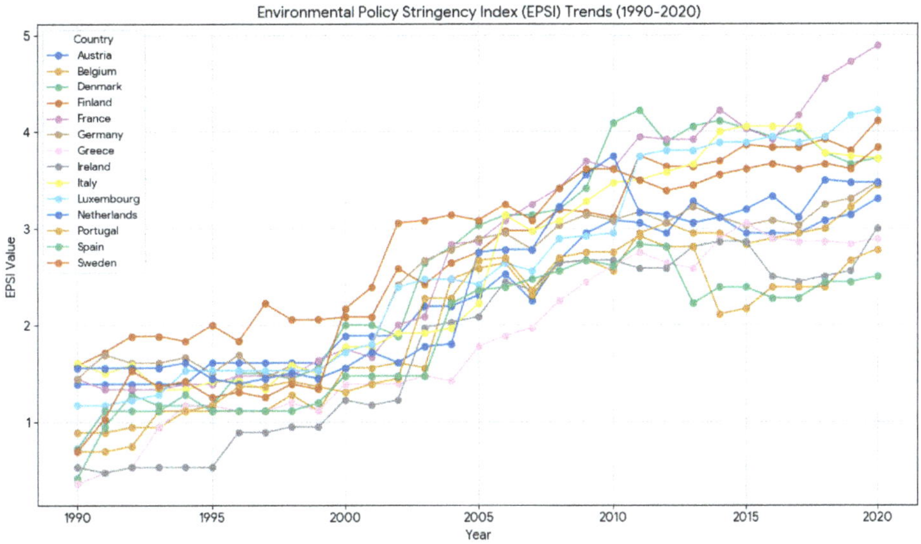

Source: *Author's own elaboration based on OECD (2026) data.*

Figure 4 presents the trends in ecological footprints for the EU–14 countries. The results indicate that ecological footprints peaked in the mid-2000s and declined noticeably thereafter. When considered together with Figure 3, which shows a steady increase in environmental policy stringency over the same period, these trends may suggest a potential negative link between EPSI and ecological footprint. However, simple visual inspection of time trends is insufficient to draw robust conclusions regarding causality, magnitude, or the presence of spillover and indirect effects across countries. Therefore, moving beyond descriptive graphical analysis, a spatial econometric framework is required to rigorously examine both direct and cross-border impacts of environmental policies on ecological footprint.

Figure 4. Trends in Ecological Footprint (EF) for EU–14 Countries, 1990–2020

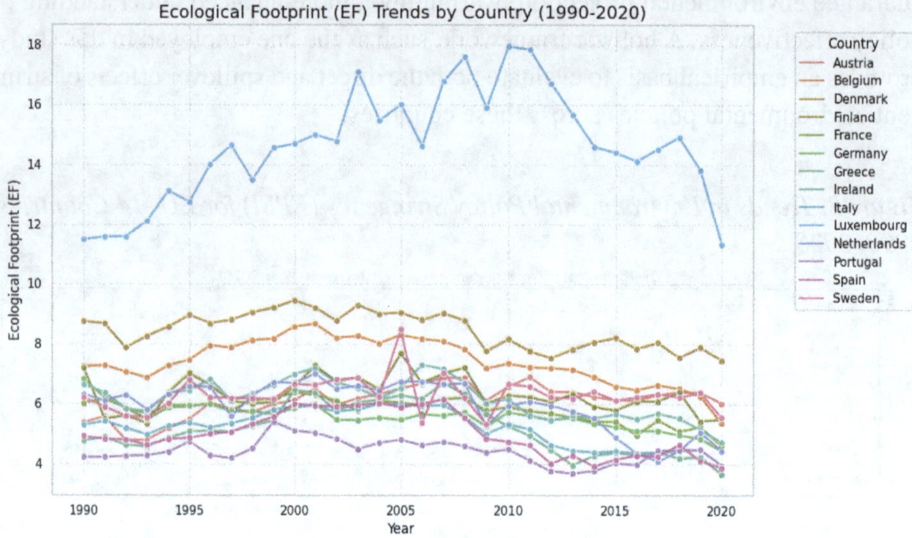

Source: *Author's own elaboration based on York University (2026) data.*

3. LITERATURE REVIEW

3.1. The Nexus Between Environmental Policies and Degradation

Extensive scholarly work has explored the determinants of environmental degradation, placing particular emphasis on the rigor of environmental regulations. In response to growing environmental degradation and climate change, countries have adopted a diverse array of policy instruments. Understanding these policies, particularly through measures of their stringency, is therefore essential. Given the close linkage between environmental policy stringency and degradation, numerous papers have examined the effects of such policies on air pollution indicators. Early studies primarily focused on air pollution and consistently demonstrated that higher regulatory stringency significantly mitigates CO_2 and greenhouse gas emissions across different economies (Yirong, 2022; Wolde-Rufael & Mulat-Weldemeskel, 2021; Albulescu et al., 2022; Wang et al., 2020). Within the European context, recent evidence confirms that such policies are particularly effective in reducing air pollution (Dmytrenk et al., 2024; Kartal et al., 2024).

Although these studies provide important empirical evidence, they primarily focus on a single dimension of environmental degradation—air pollution. Environmental degradation, however, is a multidimensional concept encompassing impacts on air, water, and soil. To address this limitation, an increasing number of studies employ the EF as a more multidimensional indicator to assess degradation. For example, Balsalobre-Lorente et al. (2023) show that stricter environmental policies reduce ecological footprint in APEC countries. Similarly, Sohag et al. (2024) find that EPSI curbs EF in OECD countries from 1990 to 2018. Focusing on BRICS economies, Kartal et al. (2025) report that market-based environmental policies reduce EF in Brazil, India, and Russia, increase them in China, and have no significant effect in South Africa, while non-market-based instruments appear largely ineffective. Luo et al. (2024) demonstrate that EPSI enhances beneficial effect of macroprudential policies on ecological footprints. In addition, Dai and Du (2023) find that environmental policy stringency reduces ecological footprints across conditional quantiles in BRICST countries from 1995 to 2021, while Kongbuamai et al. (2021) document a negative link between policy stringency and ecological footprints in BRICS countries over the period 1995–2016. Chu and Tran (2022) further show that environmental policy stringency consistently mitigates production-based ecological footprints in seven OECD countries during 1990–2015.

Despite the expanding literature on environmental policy stringency and ecological footprint, most existing studies rely on non-spatial econometric frameworks and therefore overlook potential cross-country interactions. As far as the author is aware, no empirical study has yet employed spatial econometric methodologies to explicitly capture the spillover and indirect transmission effects of environmental policy stringency. Given the inherently transboundary nature of environmental degradation, neglecting spatial linkages may result in incomplete or biased inferences. While a limited number of studies examine spillover effects in ecological footprints, they do not explicitly incorporate environmental policy stringency into their analytical frameworks. For instance, Guliyev (2024), using data for 40 European countries over the period 1992–2020, identifies significant positive spillover effects in ecological footprints. Similarly, Bucak et al. (2024), analyzing 26 EU countries, report positive cross-country spillovers. On a global scale, Zambrano-Monserrate et al. (2020), who studied 158 countries from 2007 to 2016, also provide evidence of positive ecological footprint spillover effects. In addition, Radmehr et al. (2024) document positive spillovers among selected EU countries over the period 1995–2018. However, none of these studies explicitly consider the key role of EPSI when analyzing ecological footprint spillovers.

3.2. The Nexus Between Energy Consumption, Growth, and Degradation

In this chapter, fossil energy consumption and GDP per capita are incorporated as control variables to strengthen the robustness of the econometric framework. Both variables are widely acknowledged as fundamental drivers of environmental degradation in the empirical literature. A large body of existing studies has relied on conventional econometric techniques to examine the relationships between energy usage and degradation, as well as between economic progress and natural resource depletion, for individual countries or panel data sets. These studies have consistently shown that energy use and output growth exacerbate environmental pressure across various country samples (Nathaniel, 2021; Öncel et al., 2024; Radmehr et al., 2022). While some studies emphasize the mitigating role of renewable or nuclear energy, they generally confirm that economic expansion intensifies ecological footprints (Alola et al., 2019). Notwithstanding these contributions, the existing literature largely overlooks the spatial dimension of these relationships and fails to account for spillover and indirect effects. Yet, energy structure and growth are not only key determinants of domestic environmental outcomes but also central channels through which environmental impacts may diffuse across borders, underscoring the need for a spatial econometric perspective.

In this regard, fossil energy consumption is generally found to exacerbate environmental degradation, with both its direct and indirect effects typically exerting a positive influence on pollution indicators (Bucak et al., 2024; Lawson, 2020; Abbdo et al., 2022). In contrast, the environmental impact of growth remains inconclusive. Some authors state that growth—fueled by energy-intensive industrialization and reliance on fossil fuels—intensifies pollution through positive spillover effects (Arogundade et al., 2022; Ronaghi et al., 2020). Others, however, report negative indirect effects of growth on contamination, attributing these outcomes to technological progress, efficiency improvements, and structural transformation associated with higher income levels (Tran and Ngoc, 2025; Miao et al., 2025).

Against this backdrop, this chapter employs spatial econometric techniques to systematically examine the direct, indirect, and spillover impacts of fossil energy usage and growth on EF, thereby contributing to a more integrated understanding of their function in shaping cross-border dynamics.

3.3. Literature Gap and Research Questions

Despite the growing body of literature on EPSI and deterioration, important gaps remain. Existing studies do not adequately account for spatial interdependencies across countries. Moreover, based on a comprehensive review of the literature, this study appears to be the first to specifically focus on the EU–14 countries, while explicitly incorporating environmental policy stringency within a spatial econometric framework that allows for the decomposition of direct and indirect effects.

By addressing this gap, this chapter seeks to advance the existing body of research by providing a more comprehensive understanding of how environmental policies, economic factors and energy structure interact across borders. Accordingly, the inquiry centers on the following research questions: (i) Does ecological footprint exhibit spillover effects among EU–14 countries? (ii) Does environmental policy stringency exert positive or negative direct and indirect effects on EF? (iii) How do fossil energy and growth influence EF through direct and spillover channels?

4. DATA AND METHODOLOGY

4.1. Data

To test the research questions set forth in the prior section, this study focuses on EU–14 countries (Austria, Belgium, Denmark, Finland, France, Germany, Greece, Ireland, Italy, Luxembourg, the Netherlands, Portugal, Spain, and Sweden), which provide a unique context for examining cross-border environmental dynamics over the period 1990–2020. The analysis is confined to the period for which data are available. The analysis employs the EF as the dependent variable, obtained from York University (2026). This indicator offers a holistic assessment of environmental pressure by capturing human demand on natural ecosystems. The key explanatory variable is EPSI, developed by the OECD (2026), which reflects the overall strictness of environmental policies implemented across countries. To control for additional factors influencing environmental pressure, the empirical model includes several variables. Economic development is proxied by GDP per capita, sourced from the World Bank (2026), while energy-related factors are represented by fossil energy consumption, obtained from Our World in Data (2026). The variables are log-transformed, allowing coefficients to be interpreted as percentage changes. Table 1 provides a summary of the variables used in this chapter, including their definitions and data sources.

Table 1. Variable Descriptions and Data Sources

Dependent Variable	Description	Source
Ecological Footprint (EF)	Measured in global hectares (gha) per capita; higher values indicate greater environmental degradation.	York University (2026)
Independent Variables	**Description**	**Source**
Environmental Policy Stringency Index (EPSI)	Index ranging from 0 to 6, where higher values represent more stringent environmental policies.	OECD (2026)
Fossil Energy Consumption (FOS)	Fossil energy consumption per capita, measured in kilowatt-hour (kWh) equivalents.	Our World in Data (2026)
GDP per capita (GDPPC)	Gross domestic product per capita, measured in constant 2015 US dollars.	World Bank (2026)

Source: Author's own elaboration.

4.2. Methodology

Tobler's (1970) First Law of Geography posits that all phenomena are spatially interrelated, but the strength of their relationship diminishes with distance. Building on this principle, econometric theory has increasingly incorporated spatial interactions into empirical analysis. Anselin (1988) emphasizes that ignoring such spatial dependence may lead to biased and inconsistent estimates. Therefore, this chapter employs a spatial econometric methodology to explicitly capture and distinguish both direct and indirect effects. This approach enables the analysis of not only the impact of a country's own explanatory variables but also the influence of adjacent countries on the focal country's dependent variable, namely the ecological footprint.

Despite the importance of these spatial dynamics, contemporary environmental economics often relies on techniques such as MMQR (method of moments quantile regression), PLFC (partial linear functional-coefficient model), or AMG (augmented mean group estimator). While robust in other dimensions, these methods typically fail to account for spatial dependence and the associated spillover effects of both dependent and explanatory variables (Bucak & Çatık, 2025). In contrast, spatial econometric methodologies are specifically designed to address this limitation by incorporating information from neighboring units via spatial weight matrices. By accounting for spillovers through the model structure or error terms (Elhorst, 2014), this study identifies the most appropriate spatial specification to rigorously examine how policy drivers influence ecological footprints across national borders.

To identify the most appropriate model, a systematic selection process is followed:

1. Diagnostic Tests for Spatial Dependence: The analysis begins with the Lagrange Multiplier (LM) test (Anselin, 1988) and the robust LM test (Anselin et al., 1996) to detect the presence of spatial dependence. Support for the alternative

hypothesis implies that traditional econometric methods are inadequate and that a spatial framework is required (Elhorst, 2014). When a spatial framework is required, these tests statistically confirm that the environmental outcomes of one country are significantly influenced by those of its neighbors.

2. Model Selection: If spatial correlation is confirmed, likelihood ratio (LR) tests are used to determine whether the Spatial Durbin Model (SDM) can be simplified into more restricted specifications, such as the Spatial Lag Model or the Spatial Error Model (LeSage & Pace, 2009). If the model cannot be simplified, the SDM is retained. This model is particularly robust, as it captures spillover effects arising from both the dependent variable and the explanatory variables. The SDM is uniquely designed to capture how both a country's own policies and the actions of its neighbors jointly shape environmental quality.

If the SDM is identified as the appropriate specification, the econometric model employed in this study is defined as follows:

$$\ln EF_{it} = \alpha_i + \rho \sum_{j=1}^{N} w_{ij} \ln EF_{jt} + \beta_1 \ln EPSI_{it} + \beta_2 \ln FOS_{it} + \beta_3 \ln GDPPC_{it} + \sum_{j=1}^{N} w_{ij} x_{jt} \gamma + \varepsilon_{it} \tag{1}$$

In this model, EF_{it} denotes the environmental deterioration of member i at time t; α_i represents country-specific fixed effects; ρ shows the spatial autocorrelation coefficient; w_{ij} refers to the ij-th element of the spatial weight matrix. The spatially lagged dependent variable is expressed as $\sum_{j=1}^{N} w_{ij} \ln EF_{jt}$. The parameter vector γ captures the coefficients associated with spatially lagged explanatory variables. Finally, ε_{it} denotes the error term.

Unlike traditional econometric techniques, spatial econometrics methods incorporate information from neighboring units by employing a spatial weight matrix based on Euclidean distance, which is constructed using latitude and longitude coordinates, as specified below:

$$w_{ij} = \frac{1}{d_{ij}} \tag{2}$$

where d_{ij} denotes the proximity between member countries i and j. To assess robustness, a different spatial weight matrix is constructed based on the 5-nearest-neighbors criterion following Lin and Lin (2025).

5. ECONOMETRIC RESULTS

5.1. Spatial Findings From the Spatial Durbin Model

Identifying the presence of spatial dependence through the LM and robust LM tests is a crucial step in spatial econometric analysis. The results are presented in Table 2. The null hypothesis is rejected for both the LMρ and LMλ statistics. Consequently, the robust versions of the LM tests are conducted. The robust test results reject the null hypothesis, indicating the presence of spatial dependence. Moreover, the LR tests are statistically significant, demonstrating that the SDM cannot be reduced to either the SAR or SEM. These findings confirm that the SDM is the most appropriate specification for this chapter and provide strong justification for the use of a spatial econometric framework. Given that the EU–14 countries are not randomly chosen, this study uses a fixed-effects model, following Elhorst (2014). This method controls for country-specific factors that may influence both ecological footprint and the explanatory variables, thereby reducing omitted variable bias, whereas a random-effects specification would rely on the unlikely assumption that country-specific characteristics are uncorrelated with the regressors.

Table 2 displays the estimated results of the SDM, revealing several key patterns:

1. The regulatory power of environmental policy stringency: EPSI has a negative and statistically significant direct impact on the ecological footprint. Specifically, a 1% rise in the EPSI leads to a 0.04% reduction in the ecological footprint, suggesting that stricter environmental policies significantly reduce domestic environmental degradation, demonstrating their effectiveness in curbing local ecological pressures. This finding aligns with the results reported by Dmytrenk et al. (2024) and Kartal et al. (2024).
2. The impact of fossil energy consumption: Fossil energy use exhibits a positive and statistically significant effect on the EF. A 1% rise in fossil energy consumption raises the EF by 0.14%, indicating that greater reliance on fossil fuels intensifies environmental pressure. This finding is in line with Lawson (2020) and Abbdo et al. (2022).
3. The effect of economic growth: GDP per capita shows a positive and statistically significant effect on the ecological footprint. A 1% increase in GDP per capita results in a 0.21% increase in the ecological footprint, implying that growth contributes to higher environmental pressure. This result is consistent with the evidence reported by Arogundade et al. (2022) and Ronaghi et al. (2020).
4. The effects of neighbors: The coefficients on the spatially lagged explanatory variables further reinforce these findings:

4a. The negative and statistically significant coefficient on W × EPSI denotes that stricter environmental policies in neighboring countries contribute to reductions in the domestic ecological footprint. Specifically, a 1% increase in EPSI in neighboring countries leads to a 0.06% decrease in the ecological footprint of the focal country.

4b. The positive and statistically significant coefficients on W × FOS and W × GDPPC suggest that higher fossil energy use and growth in neighboring countries exacerbate environmental pressure in the focal country. In particular, a 1% increase in fossil energy use and GDP per capita in neighboring countries raises the domestic ecological footprint by 0.30% and 0.23%, respectively. These results are consistent with the findings of Bucak et al. (2024) and Ronaghi et al. (2020).

5. The spatial autocorrelation coefficient: The central result of this study is the statistically significant and positive spatial autocorrelation coefficient (ρ) obtained from the SDM. This indicates that a 1% increase in a country's ecological footprint is associated with a 0.28% increase in the ecological footprints of its neighboring countries, and vice versa. This finding is consistent with the results of Guliyev (2024) and Zambrano-Monserrate et al. (2020), providing further evidence of environmental degradation spillover effects within the sample.

5.2. SDM Effect Decomposition: Direct, Indirect, and Total Effects

Although the spatial autocorrelation coefficient (ρ) and the spatially lagged explanatory variables (W × EPSI, W × FOS and W × GDPPC) provide clear evidence of spatial interactions, they cannot be interpreted as standard marginal effects due to spatial feedback mechanisms. In a spatial setting, a change in an explanatory variable in one country affects not only its own ecological footprint but also that of neighboring countries, whose responses subsequently feed back to the originating country. These feedback effects arise from both the spatially lagged dependent variable and the spatial lags of the explanatory variables. Consequently, the direct, indirect, and total effects derived from the SDM are employed to properly decompose and quantify these impacts (Elhorst, 2014).

Table 2 presents the SDM estimation results, highlighting several important findings:

1. The direct effects (how a country's own actions affect its environment): The direct effect of EPSI is -0.05, indicating that stricter domestic environmental policies reduce ecological footprints. The use of fossil fuels has a positive direct effect of 0.15, while GDP per capita shows a positive direct effect of 0.22.

These direct effects capture the impact of domestic conditions on a country's ecological footprint.

2. The indirect effects (how the actions of neighboring countries affect the local environment): Indirect effects reflect the spillover impact from neighboring countries. EPSI exhibits an indirect effect of -0.10, demonstrating that environmental policies in neighboring countries also reduce domestic ecological footprints. FOS and GDPPC show positive indirect effects of 0.46 and 0.40, respectively, indicating that fossil energy use and economic growth in neighboring countries increase domestic environmental pressure.
3. The total effects, comprising both direct and indirect impacts: These effects combine direct and indirect effects, yielding -0.15 for EPSI, 0.61 for FOS, and 0.62 for GDPPC.

Overall, the indirect effects are consistently larger than the direct effects. This indicates that neighboring countries' environmental policies, fossil energy consumption, and levels of economic growth exert a stronger influence on a country's ecological footprint than its own domestic factors. These findings underscore the importance of spatial econometric methods, as they effectively capture indirect effects and cross-country spillover dynamics.

Table 2. Econometric Results Based on Euclidean Distance

	SDM	**Direct Effect**	**Indirect Effect**	**Total Effect**
EPSI	-0.04** (-2.18)	-0.05** (-2.35)	-0.10* (-2.09)	-0.15*** (-3.36)
FOS	0.14*** (3.15)	0.15*** (3.50)	0.46*** (6.27)	0.61*** (10.18)
GDPPC	0.21*** (4.65)	0.22*** (5.00)	0.40*** (2.98)	0.62*** (4.69)
W*EPSI	-0.06 (-1.59)			
W*FOS	0.30*** (3.92)			
W*GDPPC	0.23** (2.10)			
ρ	0.28*** (3.63)			
R^2	0.93			
LMρ	118.67***			
LMλ	43.89***			

continued on following page

Table 2. Continued

	SDM	Direct Effect	Indirect Effect	Total Effect
Robust LMρ	82.71***			
Robust LMλ	7.93***			
LRρ	20.49***			
LRλ	52.21***			
# of obs.	434			

Source: Author's own elaboration.
Note: *** $p < 0.01$, ** $p < 0.05$, and * $p < 0.10$ indicate significance at the 1%, 5%, and 10% levels, respectively. t-statistics are in parentheses.

5.3. Robustness Check

As a robustness check, this chapter employs an alternative spatial weight matrix constructed using the 5-nearest-neighbors criterion, where the spatial weight element w_{ij} equals 1 if country *j* is among the five geographically closest neighbors of country *i* in the sample and 0 otherwise. The results presented in Table 3 confirm the robustness of the baseline findings. Both the LM and robust LM test statistics remain statistically significant, providing strong evidence of spatial dependence and further supporting the suitability of the Spatial Durbin Model under this alternative spatial matrix structure. Moreover, the LR tests, which are significant at the 1% level, rule out the possibility of reducing the model to either a SAR or SEM. The estimated effects are robust, maintaining consistent direction and statistical significance.

Environmental policy stringency continues to exert a negative effect on environmental deterioration. Specifically, a 1% increase in EPSI leads to a 0.04% reduction in the domestic EF, while a 1% increase in EPSI in neighboring countries reduces the local EF by 0.14%. When both channels are combined, the total effect indicates that a 1% increase in EPSI results in a 0.18% decline in EF. The fact that the indirect effect exceeds the direct effect once again highlights the importance of spatial spillovers and cross-country policy interactions. In contrast, consumption of fossil fuels exhibits positive and statistically significant effects. A 1% increase in domestic FOS raises the EF by 0.23%, while a 1% increase in FOS in neighboring countries increases the domestic EF by 0.32%. The total effect suggests that a 1% rise in FOS leads to an overall increase of 0.55% in ecological footprint. Similarly, GDP per capita maintains a positive and significant impact. A 1% increase in domestic GDP per capita raises the EF by 0.26%, whereas a 1% increase in GDP per capita in neighboring countries raises the domestic EF by 0.40%. The corresponding total effect implies that a 1% increase in GDP per capita results in a 0.66% increase in ecological footprint.

Overall, these results demonstrate that indirect effects are consistently larger than direct effects, confirming that environmental policies, fossil energy consumption, and economic growth in neighboring countries exert stronger influences on a country's ecological footprint than domestic factors alone. The consistency of these findings under an alternative spatial weight matrix provides strong evidence that the main conclusions of this study are robust to changes in the definition of spatial proximity.

Table 3. Robustness Check–Econometric Results Based on 5-Nearest Neighbors

	Direct Effect	Indirect Effect	Total Effect
EPSI	-0.04* (-1.96)	-0.14** (-2.95)	-0.18*** (-4.00)
FOS	0.23*** (5.68)	0.32*** (4.57)	0.55*** (8.91)
GDPPC	0.26*** (5.76)	0.40*** (3.03)	0.66*** (4.96)
LMρ	77.48***		
LMλ	31.68***		
Robust LMρ	51.84***		
Robust LMλ	6.04**		
LRρ	14.37***		
LRλ	47.96***		
# of obs.	434		

Source: Author's own elaboration.

Note: Table 3 presents the findings of the spatial panel estimations based on the 5-nearest-neighbors criterion, where the spatial weight element w_{ij} equals 1 if country j is among the five closest neighbors of country i in the sample, and 0 otherwise. *** $p < 0.01$, ** $p < 0.05$, and * $p < 0.10$ indicate significance at the 1%, 5%, and 10% levels, respectively. t-statistics are in parentheses.

6. CONCLUSION

The link between environmental policy stringency and environmental degradation has been widely investigated in the existing literature. However, the role of spatial spillover dynamics in this relationship—particularly within the EU–14 context—has largely been overlooked. To address this gap, this chapter examines the spillover effects of ecological footprints and the direct and indirect impacts of environmental policy stringency, GDP per capita, and fossil energy consumption. Using spatial econometric techniques, the analysis focuses on EU–14 countries over the period 1990–2020, subject to data availability.

The results reveal strong spatial interdependence in ecological footprints, emphasizing the importance of accounting for cross-country interactions when analyzing environmental degradation. These findings indicate that environmental degradation in one country cannot be examined independently of developments in neighboring countries.

Empirical findings from the SDM show that EPSI has a statistically significant and negative direct effect on ecological footprints, suggesting that stricter environmental policies effectively reduce domestic environmental pressure. Moreover, the negative coefficient of the spatially lagged EPSI variable shows that stricter policies implemented in neighboring countries also contribute to lowering domestic ecological footprints. This finding highlights the presence of beneficial policy spillovers and underscores the transboundary nature of environmental regulation outcomes within the EU–14 region.

In contrast, fossil energy consumption and economic development are found to increase EF both directly and indirectly. The positive coefficients of fossil energy consumption and GDP per capita imply that greater reliance on fossil fuels and growth patterns driven by energy-intensive production structures exacerbate environmental pressure in EU–14 countries. Furthermore, the positive coefficients of the spatially lagged fossil energy consumption and GDP per capita variables indicate that increases in these factors in neighboring countries also raise domestic ecological footprints, reinforcing the existence of adverse spillover effects.

The ρ is positive and statistically significant, providing further evidence of ecological footprint spillovers among EU–14 countries. This result indicates that increases in environmental degradation in one country are associated with corresponding increases in neighboring countries, highlighting the interconnected nature of environmental challenges across national borders.

Importantly, the decomposition of impacts into direct, indirect, and total effects reveals that indirect effects consistently exceed direct effects for all explanatory variables. This suggests that cross-country spillovers play a more dominant role than domestic factors in shaping ecological footprints within the EU–14 region. While environmental policy stringency in both domestic and neighboring countries contributes to reductions in ecological footprints, fossil energy use and growth exert positive spillover effects that intensify environmental degradation. These findings demonstrate that neighboring countries' policies and economic activities have a stronger influence on a country's ecological footprint than its own domestic characteristics alone. Consequently, ignoring spatial interactions may lead to underestimation of the true environmental impacts of economic activity and policy interventions.

Finally, the robustness check confirms the stability of the results. The direct and indirect effects of EPSI remain negative and statistically significant, while fossil energy consumption and GDP per capita continue to exhibit positive direct and spillover effects. Overall, these findings underscore the importance of spatial econometric approaches and highlight the need for coordinated environmental and energy policies to effectively address environmental degradation in an increasingly interconnected European context.

7. POLICY IMPLICATIONS

The empirical findings of this study provide a comprehensive guide for environmental policies. Considering the prominence of indirect effects and the spatial characteristics of ecological footprints, the policy implications are organized into two categories: national strategies for domestic policymakers and cooperative frameworks for international coordination.

7.1. Implications for National Policymakers

Stringent environmental policies are crucial in reducing environmental pollution. Both market-based instruments and non-market-based instruments are crucial policy tools for EU-14 countries. Market-based instruments not only provide incentives to reduce emissions but also generate financial resources that can be strategically allocated to technology-support policies. In particular, revenues from environmental taxes and emissions trading schemes can be used to finance government R&D expenditures on low-carbon energy technologies and to support the expansion of renewable energy sources, especially solar and wind power. At the same time, non-market-based instruments, such as emission limit standards, remain essential for directly constraining environmentally harmful activities and safeguarding environmental and climate quality.

Given the detrimental environmental impacts of fossil energy consumption, increasing public and private investment in R&D aimed at clean and energy-efficient technologies is of paramount importance. In this regard, environmental tax revenues represent a critical funding mechanism for advancing the shift to renewable energy systems.

The positive association between GDP per capita and ecological footprint suggests that economic growth in the EU–14 countries remains coupled with environmental degradation, indicating limited progress toward decoupling. This highlights the need for a structural transformation of growth models toward cleaner production processes, sustainable consumption patterns, and environmentally friendly export structures. Policies that seek to decouple growth from fossil fuel dependence by fostering innovation, improving energy efficiency, and advancing green industrial strategies are therefore crucial for achieving long-term ecological resilience.

7.2. Implications for International Coordination

From a policy standpoint, the results highlight the critical need for coordinated and harmonized environmental strategies among EU–14 countries. While national environmental regulations effectively mitigate domestic ecological pressures, the presence of significant spillover effects indicates that unilateral policy actions are insufficient to address regional environmental challenges. Given the strong cross-country interdependence identified in this study, isolated national efforts may yield limited effectiveness unless supported by broader regional cooperation. The dominance of indirect effects highlights the need for coordinated, cross-border policy approaches that recognize shared environmental responsibilities.

Coordinated environmental policies that target fossil energy consumption and promote sustainable growth trajectories are essential for achieving substantial and lasting reductions in ecological footprints across the EU–14 region. These findings suggest that environmental policy effectiveness can be significantly enhanced when countries align their regulatory approaches and jointly address shared environmental pressures.

However, implementing such policies in isolation is unlikely to deliver meaningful outcomes, as national efforts can be weakened by the lack of commitment from neighboring countries. Accordingly, EU–14 countries should establish a common supranational authority to monitor policy implementation, ensure consistent compliance across member states, and introduce effective incentive mechanisms, including rewards for compliance and sanctions for non-compliance, to enhance collective responsibility and policy effectiveness.

As highlighted by the policy implications, the key variables examined in this chapter are deeply interconnected and jointly generate ripple effects across countries. Increased environmental policy stringency not only directly reduces ecological footprints but also mobilizes financial resources through environmental taxes and emissions trading schemes. These revenues can be redirected toward renewable energy investments and technology-support policies, thereby supporting the separation of economic growth from environmental harm. When such funds are allocated to research and development in clean energy technologies, they further reinforce spillover effects by accelerating technological diffusion and reducing fossil fuel dependence across neighboring countries. In this sense, the chapter identifies the core economic and institutional mechanisms through which environmental policies generate both spillover and ripple effects in an integrated regional context.

8. RECOMMENDATIONS FOR FUTURE STUDIES

Overall, this chapter extends the existing literature by integrating environmental policy stringency into a spatial econometric framework and by presenting new empirical evidence on both the direct and cross-country spillover effects of environmental policies on EF in EU–14 members. The results highlight the relevance of spatial econometric approaches in environmental research and provide important policy insights for the design of effective and coordinated environmental strategies within an increasingly interconnected regional setting.

This chapter has certain limitations that point to promising directions for future research. First, the country sample could be expanded to include a larger and diverse set of nations, allowing for broader generalization of the findings. Second, alternative dependent variables could be explored, such as the load capacity factor. Third, as environmental policy stringency indicators are continuously updated, future studies could extend the analysis beyond 2020 to incorporate more recent developments and policy changes. Finally, additional control variables may be introduced to enrich the econometric framework, such as institutional quality, democratic governance, energy security, or risk indicators, and globalization, which may further shape environmental outcomes and spillover dynamics.

REFERENCES

Abbdo, A. B., Li, B., Qahtan, A. S. A., & Elshennawy, A. (2022). The influence of FDI on GHG emissions in BRI countries using spatial econometric analysis strategy: The significance of biomass energy consumption. *Environmental Science and Pollution Research International*, *29*(36), 54571–54595. DOI: 10.1007/s11356-022-19384-8 PMID: 35304721

Albulescu, C. T., Boatca-Barabas, M.-E., & Diaconescu, A. (2022). The asymmetric effect of environmental policy stringency on CO_2 emissions in OECD countries. *Environmental Science and Pollution Research International*, *29*(18), 27311–27327. DOI: 10.1007/s11356-021-18267-8 PMID: 34981390

Ali, K., Jianguo, D., Kirikkaleli, D., Oláh, J., & Bakhsh, S. (2023). Do environmental taxes, environmental innovation, and energy resources matter for environmental sustainability: Evidence of five sustainable economies. *Heliyon*, *9*(11), e21577. DOI: 10.1016/j.heliyon.2023.e21577 PMID: 38034728

Alola, A. A., Bekun, F. V., & Sarkodie, S. A. (2019). Dynamic impact of trade policy, economic growth, fertility rate, renewable and non-renewable energy consumption on ecological footprint in Europe. *The Science of the Total Environment*, *685*, 702–709. DOI: 10.1016/j.scitotenv.2019.05.139 PMID: 31203164

Anselin, L. (1988). *Spatial Econometrics: Methods and Models*. Springer Netherlands. DOI: 10.1007/978-94-015-7799-1

Anselin, L., Bera, A. K., Florax, R., & Yoon, M. J. (1996). Simple diagnostic tests for spatial dependence. *Regional Science and Urban Economics*, *26*(1), 77–104. DOI: 10.1016/0166-0462(95)02111-6

Arogundade, S., Mduduzi, B., & Hassan, A. S. (2022). Spatial impact of foreign direct investment on ecological footprint in Africa. *Environmental Science and Pollution Research International*, *29*(34), 51589–51608. DOI: 10.1007/s11356-022-18831-w PMID: 35247175

Balsalobre-Lorente, D., Topaloglu, E. E., Nur, T., & Evcimen, C. (2023). Exploring the linkage between financial development and ecological footprint in APEC countries: A novel view under corruption perception and environmental policy stringency. *Journal of Cleaner Production*, *414*(137686), 137686. Advance online publication. DOI: 10.1016/j.jclepro.2023.137686

Biekša, K., Valiulė, V., Šimanskienė, L., & Silvestri, R. (2022). Assessment of sustainable economic development in the EU countries with reference to the SDGs and environmental footprint indices. *Sustainability (Basel)*, *14*(18), 11265. DOI: 10.3390/su141811265

Bucak, Ç., & Çatık, A. N. (2025). Spillover effects of economic complexity on load capacity factor in the EU: A spatial econometrics perspective. *Journal of Environmental Planning and Management*, 1–34. Advance online publication. DOI: 10.1080/09640568.2025.2462229

Bucak, Ç., Önder, A. Ö., & Çatık, A. N. (2024). Spatial effects of renewable and fossil energy consumption on the ecological footprint for the EU countries. *Environmental Science and Pollution Research International*, *31*(39), 55204–55221. DOI: 10.1007/s11356-024-34803-8 PMID: 39225931

Chu, L. K., & Tran, T. H. (2022). The nexus between environmental regulation and ecological footprint in OECD countries: Empirical evidence using panel quantile regression. *Environmental Science and Pollution Research International*, *29*(33), 49700–49723. DOI: 10.1007/s11356-022-19221-y PMID: 35220531

Çoban, M. N., Biçen, Ö. F., Nassani, A. A., & Anser, M. K. (2025). Exploring the effects of global value chain participation, technological eco-innovation and natural resource rents on environmental quality in the EU–14. *Scientific Reports*, *15*(17572), 17572. Advance online publication. DOI: 10.1038/s41598-025-01569-z PMID: 40399380

Dai, S., & Du, X. (2023). Discovering the role of trade diversification, natural resources, and environmental policy stringency on ecological sustainability in the BRICST region. *Resources Policy*, *85*(103868), 103868. Advance online publication. DOI: 10.1016/j.resourpol.2023.103868

EEA. (2022). *The role of (environmental) taxation in supporting sustainability transitions*. https://www.eea.europa.eu/en/analysis/publications/the-role-of-environmental-taxation-in-supporting-sustainability-transitions

Elhorst, J. P. (2014). *Spatial Econometrics from Cross-Sectional Data to Spatial Panels*. Springer. DOI: 10.1007/978-3-642-40340-8

European Commission. (2026). *The European Green Deal*. https://commission.europa.eu/strategy-and-policy/priorities-2019-2024/story-von-der-leyen-commission/european-green-deal_en

European Council. (2025). *Taking the lead on climate change*. https://www.consilium.europa.eu/en/eu-climate-change/

European Council. (2026). *Fit for 55*. https://www.consilium.europa.eu/en/policies/fit-for-55/

Global Footprint Network. (2026). https://data.footprintnetwork.org/#/

Guliyev, H. (2024). Ecological footprint spillover effects in Europe: New insights from dynamic spatial panel data model with common shocks. *Journal of Environmental Management*, *368*(122194), 122194. Advance online publication. DOI: 10.1016/j.jenvman.2024.122194 PMID: 39168005

Janicka, M., & Sajnóg, A. (2022). The ESG reporting of EU public companies—Does the company's capitalisation matter? *Sustainability (Basel)*, *14*(7), 4279. DOI: 10.3390/su14074279

Kartal, M. T., Kirikkaleli, D., & Pata, U. K. (2024). Role of environmental policy stringency on sectoral CO2 emissions in EU–5 countries: Disaggregated level evidence by novel quantile-based approaches. *Energy & Environment*, •••, 1–26. DOI: 10.1177/0958305X241241026

Kartal, M. T., Sharif, A., Magazzino, C., Mukhtarov, S., & Kirikkaleli, D. (2025). The effects of energy transition and environmental policy stringency subtypes on ecological footprint: Evidence from BRICS countries via a KRLS approach. *Engineering (Beijing)*. Advance online publication. DOI: 10.1016/j.eng.2025.02.007

Kongbuamai, N., Bui, Q., & Nimsai, S. (2021). The effects of renewable and nonrenewable energy consumption on the ecological footprint: The role of environmental policy in BRICS countries. *Environmental Science and Pollution Research International*, *28*(22), 27885–27899. DOI: 10.1007/s11356-021-12551-3 PMID: 33517549

Kozal, Ö. (2025). Uneven human development: Revisiting economic, environmental, and political determinants in OECD. In Meçik, O. (Ed.), *Macroeconomic challenges to structural reform and industrial development* (pp. 361–3186). IGI Global.

Lawson, L. A. (2020). GHG emissions and fossil energy use as consequences of efforts of improving human well-being in Africa. *Journal of Environmental Management*, *273*(111136), 111136. Advance online publication. DOI: 10.1016/j.jenvman.2020.111136 PMID: 32768760

LeSage, J., & Pace, R. K. (2009). *Introduction to spatial econometrics*. Chapman and Hall/CRC. DOI: 10.1201/9781420064254

Lin, M., & Lin, H. (2025). Asymmetric spatial effects of unemployment on health outcomes. *Spatial Economic Analysis*, 1–23. Advance online publication. DOI: 10.1080/17421772.2025.2492212

Luo, H., Sun, Y., & Zhang, L. (2024). Effects of macroprudential policies on ecological footprint: The moderating role of environmental policy stringency in the top 11 largest countries. *Scientific Reports*, *14*(7423), 7423. Advance online publication. DOI: 10.1038/s41598-024-58015-9 PMID: 38548882

Miao, Y., Bukhari, A. A. A., Bukhari, W. A. A., Ahmad, S., & Hayat, N. (2025). Why fossil fuels stifle green economic growth? An environmental management perspective in assessing the spatial spillover impact of energy consumption in South Asia. *Journal of Environmental Management*, *373*(123471), 123471. Advance online publication. DOI: 10.1016/j.jenvman.2024.123471 PMID: 39642839

Nathaniel, S. P. (2021). Ecological footprint, energy use, trade, and urbanization linkage in Indonesia. *GeoJournal*, *86*(5), 2057–2070. DOI: 10.1007/s10708-020-10175-7

OECD. (2022). *Measuring environmental policy stringency in OECD countries: An update of the OECD composite EPS indicator*. https://www.oecd.org/content/dam/oecd/en/publications/reports/2022/03/measuring-environmental-policy-stringency-in-oecd-countries_5655fe2c/90ab82e8-en.pdf

OECD. (2026). *Data explorer.* https://data-explorer.oecd.org/?lc=en

Öncel, A., Kabasakal, A., Kutlar, A., & Acar, S. (2024). Energy consumption, economic growth and ecological footprint relationship in the top Russian energy importers: A panel data analysis. *Environment, Development and Sustainability*, *26*(8), 21019–21052. DOI: 10.1007/s10668-023-03517-1

Our World in Data. (2026). *Energy mix.* https://ourworldindata.org/energy-mix#fossil-fuels-what-share-of-energy-comes-from-fossil-fuels

Radmehr, R., Shayanmehr, S., Ali, E. B., Ofori, E. K., Jasińska, E., & Jasiński, M. (2022). Exploring the nexus of renewable energy, ecological footprint, and economic growth through globalization and human capital in G7 economics. *Sustainability (Basel)*, *14*(12227), 12227. Advance online publication. DOI: 10.3390/su141912227

Radmehr, R., Shayanmehr, S., Baba, E. A., Samour, A., & Adebayo, T. S. (2024). Spatial spillover effects of green technology innovation and renewable energy on ecological sustainability: New evidence and analysis. *Sustainable Development (Bradford)*, *32*(3), 1743–1761. DOI: 10.1002/sd.2738

Ronaghi, M., Reed, M., & Saghaian, S. (2020). The impact of economic factors and governance on greenhouse gas emission. *Environmental Economics and Policy Studies*, *22*(2), 153–172. DOI: 10.1007/s10018-019-00250-w

Sohag, K., Husain, S., & Soytas, U. (2024). Environmental policy stringency and ecological footprint linkage: Mitigation measures of renewable energy and innovation. *Energy Economics, 136*(107721), 107721. Advance online publication. DOI: 10.1016/j.eneco.2024.107721

Stern, N. (2006). *The economics of climate change: The Stern review*. Cambridge University Press., DOI: 10.1017/CBO9780511817434

Tobler, W. R. (1970). A computer movie simulating urban growth in the Detroit region. *Economic Geography, 46*(2), 234–240. DOI: 10.2307/143141

UN. (2026). *United Nations Framework Convention on Climate Change (UNFCCC) and Climate, Peace and Security*. https://www.un.org/climatesecuritymechanism/en/united-nations-framework-convention-climate-change-unfccc-and-climate-peace-and-security

Wackernagel, M., & Rees, W. E. (1997). Perceptual and structural barriers to investing in natural capital: Economics from an ecological footprint perspective. *Ecological Economics, 20*(1), 3–24. DOI: 10.1016/S0921-8009(96)00077-8

Wang, K., Yan, M., Wang, Y., & Chang, C.-P. (2020). The impact of environmental policy stringency on air quality. *Atmospheric Environment, 231*(117522), 117522. Advance online publication. DOI: 10.1016/j.atmosenv.2020.117522

WMO. (2025). *State of the climate update for COP30*. https://library.wmo.int/records/item/69674-state-of-the-climate-update-for-cop30

Wolde-Rufael, Y., & Mulat-Weldemeskel, E. (2021). Do environmental taxes and environmental stringency policies reduce CO_2 emissions? Evidence from 7 emerging economies. *Environmental Science and Pollution Research International, 28*(18), 22392–22408. DOI: 10.1007/s11356-020-11475-8 PMID: 33417133

World Bank. (2026). *World Development Indicators*. https://databank.worldbank.org/source/world-development-indicators

Yirong, Q. (2022). Does environmental policy stringency reduce CO_2 emissions? Evidence from high-polluted economies. *Journal of Cleaner Production, 341*(130648), 130648. Advance online publication. DOI: 10.1016/j.jclepro.2022.130648

York University. (2026). *Data*. https://footprint.info.yorku.ca/data/

Zambrano-Monserrate, M. A., Ruano, M. A., Ormeño-Candelario, V., & Sanchez-Loor, D. A. (2020). Global ecological footprint and spatial dependence between countries. *Journal of Environmental Management, 272*(111069), 111069. Advance online publication. DOI: 10.1016/j.jenvman.2020.111069 PMID: 32854881

Chapter 8

Fiscal Trade-Offs of Green Public Expenditure: Crowding-Out, Healthcare Financing, and Welfare Effects

P. Praveen Kumar
http://orcid.org/0000-0002-0707-039X
SRM Institute of Science and Technology, Vadapalani, India

K. C. Raja Shree
http://orcid.org/0009-0009-1029-910X
Saveetha School of Management, Saveetha Institute of Medical and Technical Sciences, India

ABSTRACT

The examination of green public expenditure is highly important and this cannot be studied as an individual factor where in healthcare financing and welfare measures also should be embedded to understand this interdependent concept which will provide details about current budgetary pressures and also futuristic fiscal capacity. By exploring about the fiscal transmission channels through short, medium and long-term aspects, this chapter would study the static budgetary analysis by capturing the dynamic interactions throughout the environmental spending and reduced health care costs. This chapter also integrates the welfare economics towards the fiscal analysis by examining the green public expenditure and its contribution towards resilience, equity and well-being through generations globally. The linkage between the green spending and population health will help in supporting the fiscal sustainability. Therefore, this chapter purely studies about the sustainable healthcare financing in long-term welfare outcomes and the green expenditure can be considered as a strategic tool.

DOI: 10.4018/979-8-3373-8998-1.ch008

1. INTRODUCTION

The fastened pace of climatic change along with increase the president challenge and pressure on governments across the globe, reaching about the developmental strategies towards public expenditures (Fonjong et al., 2024). The rising temperatures, over water and air quality along with loss of biodiversity has increased the climatic events in an unexpected way which is creating a need for standard national as well as international policies (Izah et al., 2023; Shivanna, 2022). The government has to invest in renewable energy and mitigate the climate deterioration factors and adopt sustainable infrastructure and environmental protection mechanisms for enhanced living standards (Batra, 2023). In the larger scale, renewable energy is utilized in urban sustainability initiatives and climate resilient infrastructure where public budgets are provided to mobilize the environmental transitions (Yatzkan et al., 2025; Saleh & Hassan, 2024). However, the extension of the green public expenditure occurs and elevates the financial stress aspects (Peng et al., 2023).

The governments face fiscal constraints and also increased public debt, demographic pressures and economic consequences through global shocks, especially during COVID-19 pandemic (Reznikova et al., 2022). Health systems have experienced budgetary pressure compelled by aging population and increased likelihood of non-communicable diseases and also elevated demand towards public health preparedness (Goswami, 2024). The policymakers are usually confronted with challenging fiscal choices with respect to allocation of scarce public resources (Wenjuan & Zhao, 2023). Therefore, green public expenditure is usually framed as a competitor to healthcare and also social spending in increasing the concerns about fiscal crowding-out along with welfare trade-offs. On considering all these, the current chapter would focus on examining the fiscal trade-offs that are associated with the green public expenditure by providing emphasis on the interactions with financing towards healthcare and social welfare measures. By combining the insights from the economics of environment, health, and public finance, this chapter would develop a holistic financial sustainability framework, which will be useful in the green transition.

The global extension in the green public expenditure shows the growing concern towards environmental sustainability and also economic development (Liu et al., 2022). Governments based on income levels have implemented policies and employed public resources to the climatic change along with environmental degradation by creating sustainable development goals (Mpofu, 2022). Public spending towards renewable energy infrastructures. energy efficient systems. reduced carbon transportation, climatic adaptation measures and restoration of ecosystems have enhanced the commitments of governments towards environmental protection activities (Batra, 2023). This transformation has recognized the substantial economic as social costs.

Therefore, environmental health risks highly translate into healthcare expenditures leading to productivity, loss and failure in vulnerable populations.

Many countries have entered into increasing the public spending, thereby reducing the challenges in health of populations (Kentikelenis & Stubbs, 2022). Health budgets have become a pressure for people due to unavailability of proper resources during emergency (Gooding et al., 2022). Even social protection systems also failed to address the unemployment, equality and economic and security aspects (Razavi, 2022). The policymakers also face increased scrutiny with respect to public fund allocation, thereby opportunity cost always get challenges due to public spending initiatives (Ardiputra et al., 2025). The physical pressures lead to prioritizing the green public expenditure and large scale investments are required to provide adequate resources towards environmental protection and therefore public spending is essential which lead to sustainable growth (Mpofu, 2022). The findings suggest that the green spending and green public investments should be strengthened to create trust among the people in the nation and also to meet up emergencies in future (Abdelfattah et al., 2025).

Significance of This Chapter

The most important fiscal trade-off question is that do this increased green public expenditure, help crowding out the healthcare and also social spending or just accolade or does it ultimately intensify the welfare systems. The traditional theories on public finance shows that government budgets become zero-sum allocations when the spending increases from one sector to another and within this framework, the public expenditure towards green spending compete with other budgets also. The concept of fiscal crowding out is utilized to examine the effects of public spending on the private investment and public expenditures. However, contemporary measures are taken towards sustainability initiatives by interpreting the fiscal trade-offs. From this aspect green public expenditure, functions as an important factor for elevating the fiscal pressures on the health systems (Peng et al., 2023). Despite the increased importance for economic as well as environmental impacts towards green public expenditure, still studies are rare which incorporates environmental policy towards health outcomes and the healthcare costs (Zhang, 2024). Therefore, this chapter would address this gap by adopting an integral system which provides welfare measures for environmental, economic and health aspects through green public expenditure. The primary objective of the current chapter is to develop comprehensive framework for analyzing the fiscal trade off related with green public expenditure with focus on the healthcare financing, and also welfare measures. The examination of green public expenditure is highly important and this cannot be studied as an individual factor where in healthcare financing and welfare measures also should be embedded to understand this interdependent concept which will provide details about current budgetary pressures and also futuristic fiscal capacity. By exploring about the fiscal transmission channels through short, medium and long-term aspects, this chapter would study the static budgetary analysis by capturing the dynamic interactions throughout the environmental spending and reduced health care costs. This challenges the traditional view and inevitability leads to contemporary aspect of green public expenditure through proper institutional design and financing mechanisms. This chapter also integrates the welfare economics towards the fiscal analysis by examining the green public expenditure and its contribution towards resilience, equity and well-being through generations globally. The linkage between the green spending and population health will help in supporting the fiscal sustainability. Therefore, this chapter purely studies about the sustainable healthcare financing in long-term welfare outcomes and the green expenditure function as strategic fiscal mechanism under specified settings.

Research Questions

Does the green public expenditure multitude out the healthcare supporting under fiscal restraints, or does it produce intertemporal crowding-in consequences through abridged disease burden and efficiency benefits? The hypotheses addressed in this chapter are mentioned below.

Green public expenditure may create short-term budgetary dislocation under fixed fiscal ceilings.

Green expenditure decreases environmentally mediated disease burden in the medium term.

Reduced disease burden progresses fiscal sustainability through productivity and revenue effects.

Institutional quality and financing mechanisms influences the net fiscal outcome.

2. THEORETICAL PERSPECTIVES

a) Green Public Expenditure in Public Finance Theory

Green public expenditure demonstrates the government spending on environmental protection, mitigation strategies for climatic changes, pollution control aspects, and biodiversity conservation along with promoting low carbon and resource efficient pathways for developmental dimensions. This is explored using public finance theory propounded by Musgrave and Peacock in 1958, where expenditure is considered as a core component for modern fiscal policy, which aims to correct the market failures and safeguard the long-term societal interest and welfare. Therefore, the scope of this green public is done through diversified setting such as renewable energy, investments, waste management systems, urban green spaces, sustainable healthcare, infrastructure. Spending on green resources helps in bridging the governance with public health objectives (Johnson, 2025). The traditional spending in public finance focus on economic growth acceleration whereas the green public expenditure, overlaps with these capital investments and differ in temporal orientation using fossil fuel-based infrastructures and immediate economic returns. The green spending internalises the environmental externalities and prioritise investments and focus on value for money by extending the fiscal valuation beyond the GDP centric metrics by including environmental integrity along with population health outcomes. Environmental dimensions like clean air, safe water, stable climate and prosperous biodiversity are notable examples for public goods that are characterised by public expenditure spending. The Environmental healing health strategies like preventive health care, sanitation systems and pollution control helps in generating social benefits exceeding the private benefits through public provision and standardisation (Khanam et al., 2023). Public spending collectively enhances human capital and the welfare by strengthening the physical legitimacy of green spending in public finance frameworks (Morales et al., 2025).

b) Fiscal Crowding-Out

Crowding out is an economic phenomenon where elevation in government spending and deterioration in borrowing reduces the private sector investment and also consumption leading to increase in the interest rates by absorbing the available resources resulting in expensive or difficulty for businesses and individuals to borrow and spend.

Fiscal crowding-out signifies the decrease in government spending in one segment due to augmented disbursement in additional division under fixed income and scrounging constraints. Under these abridged government budget restraints: $G = T + \Delta B$;

where G = total expenditure, T = tax revenue, and ΔB = borrowing.

If green expenditure (Ge) upsurges while income and borrowing capability endure fixed:

$\Delta Ge > 0 \rightarrow \Delta Gh < 0$; where Gh = healthcare expenditure.

This characterises intra-governmental crowding-out, discrete from conventional monetary crowding-out distressing private venture.

The neo classical theory with respect to fiscal crowding out explains that increase in government spending especially related to borrowing, higher interest rates reduces the private investment (Alymkulova et al., 2023). This framework of public expenditure competes with the private demand using scarce financial resources, leading to neutral and negative impact on economic growth. Therefore, large scale public investments are often considered as fiscal deficits leading to inefficiencies. Also neo classical theory raises concerns with respect to green public expenditure which may displace the private investment regarding the productive sectors, but interpretation shows that full employment leads to efficient capital markets due to absence of externalities in contemporary economic realities.

Keynesian economics shows idle capacity and demand deficiency might stimulate the public expenditure through economic activity without using private investment (Seccareccia, 1995). Governments spending in infrastructure, health along with environmental protection will generate multiplier effects that increases income, employment and also private sector confidence. This framework uses green public expenditure as an expansionary and also contemporary aspect during economic downturns which moves towards sustainability.

Endogenous growth theory proposed by Meng and Ye, 2009 also show that usage of public investment helps in improving the human capital, innovation and also knowledge spillovers. Green investments using clean technologies, preventive health and sustainable systems will elevate the long-term productivity by deteriorating environmental and health related risk and productivity losses. Therefore, crowding out the expenditure can create new markets and reduce uncertainty in long-term growth (Ngo & Stanfield, 2022).

c) Healthcare financing and Welfare Economics

Healthcare financing remains in an important position where it directly influences the population, well-being, social equity and productivity of labour within the welfare economics. The welfare economics increasingly conceptualises the healthcare expenditure through government spending which is considered as an important social investment. This investment makes the evaluation shift from the short-term aspect to long-term welfare and productivity measure. The improved population health reduces the absenteeism and extend the working lives of labour community. The investments would reduce the fiscal pressure that are associated with chronic diseases and disability. Green public expenditure gets embedded with the healthcare financing as an investment logic. The disease burden is considered as an environmental mediator, which is linked directly to air pollution, water contamination, poor sanitation, and climate variability. Therefore, investments in clean water systems, waste management and climate resilient societies would remain as a crucial determinant of government spending for green systems. Environmental spending can also be considered as a preventive healthcare aspect. The welfare theory strengthens this by positioning the health care as an important public responsibility which is essential for social protection and equity. Healthy individuals of societies will improve the fiscal sustainability and will integrate environmental impacts towards sustainability. The green public expenditure would support the health outcomes by sustaining in the welfare systems globally (Yang et al., 2022).

Integration of Environmental, Health and Welfare Economics

The integration of environmental, health and welfare economics is usually done using the concept of externalities (Eaton et al., 2023). The environmental degradation would generate negative externalities by increasing the health care costs and reducing the quality of life. Green public expenditure would use corrective by internalising the externalities and aligning the behaviour of individuals along with welfare objectives. The significant co-benefits across the globe could be interconnected for outcome basis. For instance, clean energy investments reduce the emissions and improve the air quality by lowering the respiratory as well as cardiovascular diseases. Likewise, green spaces enhance the mental health and physical activity leading to reduced stress disorders. The intertemporal welfare analysis also explains the same through immediate physical balance and long term impacts. The life-cycle accounting helps in providing a comprehensive framework for evaluating the long term fiscal benefits through public expenditure decisions (Shaviro, 2025). The fiscal implications through the public expenditure decisions that are made beyond the short term by usage of public investments and also unexposed future physical benefits. These costs and savings should be accounted throughout the life cycle of a policy to make policymakers to understand about the importance of preventive investment through public spending. Therefore, by integrating these aspects long-term wealth, gains and physical resilience can be obtained in modernised settings (Vallee-Dubois, 2023).

Table 1. Integrated Theoretical Perspectives

S.No	*Theory*	*Core Idea*	*Implications related to Green Public Expenditure*
1	Public Finance Theory	Government spending for market failures and assists in promoting social welfare	Environmental spending, Long term welfare and sustainability
2	Environmental Public Goods	Clean air, water, stable climate	Renewable energy, Waste management, Proper sanitation
3	Fiscal Crowding-Out (Neoclassical View)	Increased government borrowing intensifies interest rates and diminishes private investment	Displace private investment for immediate effects
4	Keynesian Perspective	Public spending inspires demand during ineffective competence	Employment, Income, and Economic recovery
5	Endogenous Growth Theory	Public investment augments human capital and improvement	Long-term productivity
6	Welfare Economics	Healthcare spending is considered as social investment cultivating equity and productivity	Reduced disease burden and decreased healthcare costs
7	Environmental–Health Link	Environmental deprivation upsurges health costs	Preventive environmental spending
8	Intertemporal Fiscal Analysis	Long-term assessment of costs and benefits	Fiscal sustainability and resilience

Source: (Derived from Various Literatures as mentioned in above table)

3. CONCEPTUAL MODEL

The conceptual model proposed in this chapter implements, a system oriented approach for examining the fiscal interactions between the healthcare financing, green public expenditure and welfare outcomes. The traditional approaches focus on government budgets as a county exercises and the public expenditures generate feedback across times. In contrast, this integrated approach would enable us to understand the fiscal ecosystem through interlinked components such as green spending, population, health, health, care, costs, employee, productivity and welfare of society.

The framework shifts towards analytical focus using annual budget allocations in multi period evaluation mechanisms. This incorporates strategic investment choices in short, medium and long-term aspects which provides reduce health care cost by enhancing the welfare outcomes. Therefore, the policymakers can have a holistic view to understand the implications by adopting green public expenditure.

This framework lies in the foundation of green public expenditure, which is described as a government spending for environmental protection through sustainable infrastructure development by managing the natural resources in such a way to promote long-term ecological balance, providing human well-being. This includes investments in renewable energy, water facilities, urban development, pollution, control dimensions, environmental health aspects, and waste management. These expenditures are usually classified under environment at global levels and This mainly targets the health and welfare of the community for economic resilience.

The next component in this framework is physical transmission channels and it explains the effects of the green public spending across the finance systems. This channel operates in short, medium and long-term basis. The budgetary allocation which is short-term targets the budget constraints that are shaped by the availability of revenue and policies that are framed. During this stage, the green spending appears to be a crowd out financing policy during large spending. The health co-benefit pathway is a medium-term aspect where in the actual transmission is translated into sustainable benefits, where in the conditions of environment are improved through pollution control, urban design and climatic adaptation programmes to reduce the health risk exposure of the community. The lower disease burden then gets translated into health utilisation reduction and decreased cost pressure towards public health systems. The macroeconomic and welfare pathway, functions as a long-term dimension which improves the population health by enhancing the labour productivity and increased workforce participation towards social protection programmes. The fiscal trade-offs arise here and results in improved welfare as well as fiscal sustainability. Thus, these transmission channels demonstrate the way green public expenditure transformed the welfare gains over a period of time.

The mediating factors in this framework include the strength and direction of fiscal interactions. These mediators will determine the impact of green public expenditure that generates crowding in for the purpose of health care, financing, or it might remain as crowding out. Institutional quality plays a major role as Effective coordination is a sensual between environment, finance and health ministries for enabling the co-benefits preventing the budgeting aspects. The fragmented governance structures, obscure fiscal linkages and assist in reinforcing the sectoral competence. The time horizon helps in allocating the budget systems effectively and evaluating the annual performance metrics for investments by gaining long-term savings. The institutional capacity measures the environmental health linkages and shapes the overall outcomes with respect to green investments.

The final output of this conceptual framework explores the welfare as well as sustainability outcomes, emerging from the interaction among green public expenditure, healthcare, financing, and the fiscal dynamics. The benefits of the framework include enhanced population health, decreased healthcare costs and improved labour productivity along with reduction in poverty and sustainability in fiscal resources leading to protection in the environment resulting in intergenerational welfare. Healthier populations expect lesser medical interventions, thereby decrease the public expenditure on healthcare. The savings help in chronic diseases and impose long-term benefits for the welfare. Also, the healthier individuals are more productive and has longer working lives, they strengthen the economic output by contributing towards higher productivity. The environmental degradation and investment in preventive health measures will reduce the long-term cost for future generation towards disease burdens and reduce economic constraints with respect to public finances. The green public expenditure would create healthier environment and also resilient fiscal systems.

Figure 1. Conceptual Model

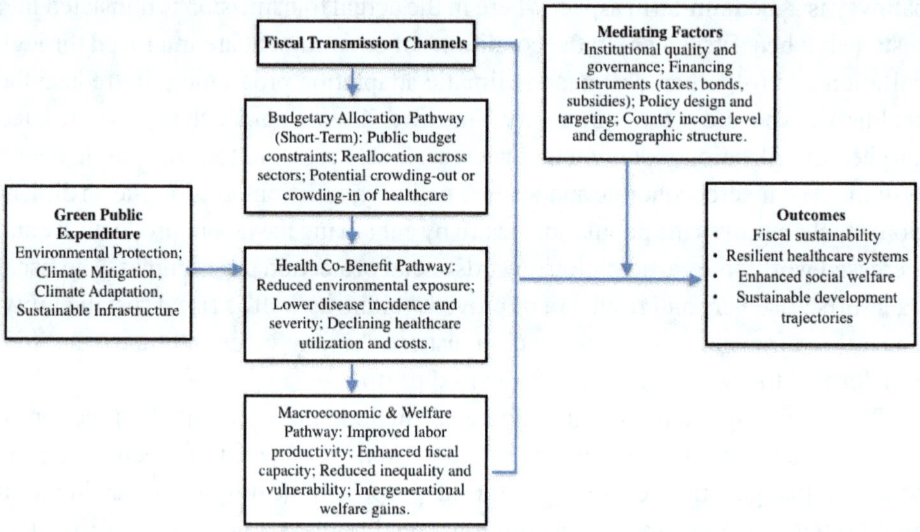

Source: *(Primary)*

This integrative framework would help in designing fiscal sustainable green investments, which are healthier, and this will also highlight the core value of green public expenditure towards strengthening the environmental protection, healthcare systems, and welfare outcomes.

4. FINANCING & INSTITUTIONAL CONDITIONS

Green Public Expenditure Through Fiscal Transmission Channels

The public expenditure shifts through the fiscal system and influences the healthcare financing for welfare outcomes. The transmission is linear and not instantaneous and occurs in three interlinked pathways such as short term allocation of budget; medium to long term co-benefits of health and macroeconomic as well as welfare gains reshaping the fiscal capacity.

Budgetary Allocation Pathway (Short term fiscal effects): The fixed budget constraints and budgeting cycles usually function under hard physical ceilings, and shaped by revenue forecast and deficit targets. These ceilings usually compete for allocations. While the green priorities increases like renewables, pollution control, urban green, infrastructure, and climate resilience, more funds are required. In short run, this will generate zero-sum game between the spending for environmental and social impacts for welfare outcomes. This dynamic shift is highly visible in developing countries where there are fiscal constraints. Under these constraints, green allocations get diffused and long term healthcare demands become visible (Cherniaieva et al., 2025). Short term reallocation for resources are challenging and capital budgets gets reshuffled towards green infrastructure which is used for mass transit, proper wastage systems, clean energy resources for public facilities to cope up with budget constraints and increased service demand. The healthcare required continuous funding and becomes politically sensitive. The reallocation can help in economic sustainability which will indirectly support health outcomes. Consequently, policymakers face challenge in larger immediate allocations justifying the green spending that saves cost over time. Empirical observations show that green transitions prioritise the growth of health budget by materialising the health savings by reducing the disease burden. The budgetary pathway in short term will include subsequent pathways in the temporal framework (Abbasov, 2025).

Health Co-Benefit Pathway (Medium to Long term effect): The global disease burden considers environmental risk factors such as air pollution, water contamination, poor sanitation, exposure to chemical agents along with climate hazards. All these exposures enhance the respiratory diseases along with cardiovascular problems, inflections leading to severe illness. Therefore, health systems generate recurring cost that originates in the medical field. The public expenditure targets the determinants and investments through emission and reduces the air pollution, water contamination, green space planning, climate adaptability and waste treatment by decreasing the population exposure towards health risks (Sampedro et al., 2023). Public expenditure reduces the incidence rate prevailing as part of environmentally linked diseases. The air quality should be improved through cleaner energy and policies should be implemented to reduce the pollution aspects, this will lead to enhanced pulmonary and heart health of population. Also, investments in drinking water will decrease the diarrhoea related diseases and infections leading to child mortality. Green investments are therefore considered as a prevention aspect and environmental causes can be reduced through proper government spending on various sectors and this will reduce the expensive clinical interventions in long-term and contribute towards healthier lifestyle. This second transmission channel thus demonstrates the short-term crowding out towards medium-term crowding in, where environmental spending impacts the health care sustainability by avoiding cost indirectly (Sicilliani & Cylus, 2025).

Macroeconomic and Welfare Pathway (Long Term Effects): The macroeconomic and welfare pathway denotes to the transmission link through which the public expenditure usually the green public expenditure is spent and impacts the broader economy along with the social well-being. This transmission pathway assists in understanding the enhancements in environmental quality and also population health translation into improved labour productivity and enhanced economic output. This is contributed towards the macroeconomic performance. Healthier communities tend to produce more towards economic growth and strengthened social systems. This also reduces the poverty and disease incidence in the populations. Healthier populations become productive and the morbidity level gets reduced which leads to increased labour productivity and enhanced cognitive performance. This elevates the quality of human capacity across the globe. The productive labour force helps in increased tax collection, tax consumption and the economic dynamism. Similarly, the healthy population showcase the reduced disease burden that lowers social welfare and payments for disabled individuals. This dual effects usually improves the fiscal balance over a period of time enabling the government to obtain more resources without increased tax rates. The green public expenditure thereby improves the living conditions of these vulnerable populations by enhancing the financial protection and also social equity. The poverty reduction can be done through green spending for welfare objectives globally. The green public expenditure results in better outcomes for generations across the globe (Liu et al., 2022). The preservation of environmental quality would reduce the long term health risk of population and thereby prevent the transmission of ecological burdens towards future generations. The children grow in cleaner environment by experiencing prosperous health benefits leading to economic resilience. Intergenerational assistance investigation displays that green expenditure currently diminishes both healthcare expenses and environmental obligations tomorrow. This elongated prospect influence accomplishes the fiscal transmission practice from a short-term economic pressure to long-term prosperity and financial reinforcement. Thus, the macroeconomic and welfare path expounds in what way green public expenditure adds to sustainable progression, fiscal resilience, and enduring social welfare effects (Dafermos et al., 2022).

The three above mentioned fiscal transmission paths expose an unblemished progressive outcomes of green public expenditure towards healthcare financing as well as welfare outcomes. The green spending operates in fixed budget constraints and expenditures compete in limited fiscal setup. These pressures are financial challenges due to policy choices in short term whereas health co-benefit pathway materialises in medium term and investments are made for environmental protection and lower disease incidence rates. The long term can contribute towards healthier communities through extended fiscal capacity by obtaining health outcomes and extended economic capacity with long term social welfare.

Figure 2. Fiscal Transmission Channels for Green Public Expenditure

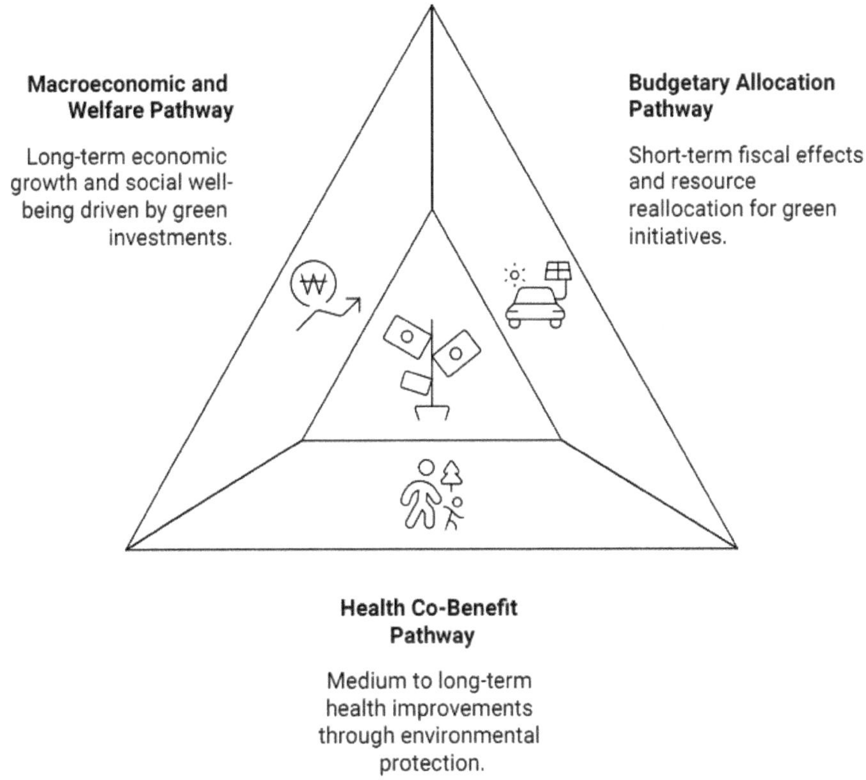

Source: *(Primary)*

Financing Mechanisms and Institutional Mediation

Green public expenditure operates through interactions among various sectors, particularly with respect to financing instruments that are spent on public budgets for creating new spaces (Li et al., 2023). The institution quality determines the effect of environmental and health objectives, whether they are coordinated or not. The countries income also shapes, the degree of green investments that are made. There are different ways through which green public expenditure financing has been done in a country.

Environmental taxes play the primary role as they take care of pollution, alleviations, carbon taxes, and congestion charges which serve as an important component towards public finance. Environmental taxes are financial mechanisms enforced on undertakings or merchandises that produce ecological destruction, such as carbon emissions, pollution, etc. These excises reduce the environmentally detrimental conduct while creating public income and the obtained revenues can be utilised to financing green as well as health-related communal spending. They also generate revenue streams for financing green expenditures for health support. These revenues are utilised for environmental protection activities and them occurs proper fiscal trade of between the green expenditure and the healthcare spending. These environmental taxes can create new pathway for citizens to accept the taxation and contribute towards public expenditure (Athari et al., 2025).

Green bonds have arrived as financing mechanism that allows government to raise capital for environmental sustainability without burdening, the annual budgets. Green bonds are liability mechanisms dispensed by governments and institutions to fund assignments, schemes and projects that provide environmental benefits. The earnings are allocated completely for green reserves like renewable energy, clean transportation, and climate acclimatization. Green bonds empower long-term funding without instantaneous economic tension. They support capital markets through sustainability purposes. On issuance of green bonds, government can spread the cost incurred in green infrastructure over a period of time by aligning with long-term investments (Lin & Hong, 2022).

Blended finance plays an important role as private investment and also multilateral support for reducing the physical stress. Blended finance insinuates to the premeditated use of public and concessional resources to activate private security for sustainable development ventures. Public funds are disbursed to condense risk and recuperate project practicality. This methodology draws private investment into green infrastructure and climate schemes. It develops fiscal capability without accumulative public debt encumbrances. The public funds are used for de-risking the projects and attract private investors to use the renewable energy sources and sustainable water systems along with building green infrastructure. These approaches reduce the need for budgetary reallocations towards healthcare and welfare program programs (Onabowale, 2024).

Market-Based Instruments can pressure the fiscal resources that are designed. Some of these instruments include emissions trading arrangements, pollution assessing, and pay-as-you-pollute schemes modify the financing encumbrance toward contaminators and polluters rather than these taxpayers. Market-based instruments utilise price indications to impact environmental consequences. Examples incorporate emissions trading schemes, pollution accountabilities, and tradable licences. They enable firms and also individuals to diminish eco-friendly destruction in cost-effective methods. These mechanisms condense the requirement for large public subventions. Market-based mechanisms decrease the fiscal expenditure of green transitions leading to progression in environmental objectives (Baker & Nenonen, 2025).

Environmental subsidies are monetary incentives postulated to authorize environmentally constructive accomplishments and technologies. They depress the expense of renewable energy, clean technologies, and sustainable practices. Although effectual in hastening modifications, poorly proposed subsidies might strain public finances. Targeted subsidisations augment competence and fairness.

Budget Rules shape the green spending interaction with the healthcare budgets. Traditional budgeting systems are often fixed and may not be sufficient throughout the year, whereas flexible multi-year budgeting mechanisms allow the governments to plan for green investments along with healthcare savings. Budget rules are legitimately or institutionally described restraints on government expenditure, discrepancies, or liability. They are calculated to stimulate fiscal regulation and macroeconomic firmness. Examples comprise deficit ceilings insufficiencies and expenditure restrictions. Flexible budget instructions permit area for long-term savings in green and also health sectors (Huang & Lu, 2025).

Fiscal federalism helps in correcting the misalignments between various levels of governments that create coordination failures during green investments, which doesn't translate towards savings. When the fiscal federal structures are properly translated and coordinated, these spending reduces the healthcare burdens and also create fiscal benefits. Fiscal federalism denotes the apportionment of revenue-raising besides expenditure accountabilities across diverse levels of administration. It regulates how fundamental, public, and confined administrations segment fiscal influence. Efficient fiscal federalism funds synchronised ecological and healthcare strategies. Deprived organization can generate fiscal inadequacies (Singh, 2025).

Transparency in the public spending demonstrates that green investments contribute towords health as well as welfare outcomes and without also reporting systems, it might fail. Transparent mechanisms are essential to reinforce assistance for policymakers. It signifies about honesty and simplicity of government budget developments and expenditure reportage. It empowers stakeholders to recognise how public resources are distributed and recycled. Transparent reporting progresses trust and policy reliability. It is indispensable for estimating green and health expenditure consequences (Steuer & Troger, 2022).

Accountability mechanisms include green budgetary allocations, sustainability audits and environmental performance metrics tracking the environmental health indicators enabling the policymakers to be fiscally responsible for environmental luxury. It indicates to contrivances that safeguard public administrators are accountable for fiscal resolutions and after-effects. It encompasses supervising, assessment, and implementation through examinations and functioning taxations. Accountability confirms competent and principled usage of public resources. It toughens assurance in green and healthcare savings (Sun et al., 2024).

Using these instruments, green expenditure remains as a capital market and helps in crowding out pressures.

Income Level Heterogeneity: The interaction among green public expenditure and the healthcare financing remains significantly diversified with respect to income levels due to the disparities in the fiscal capacity, resilience and institutional maturity. These structural diversifications create fiscal trade of with respect to green investments and can generate complimentary health as well as welfare outcomes. In low and middle income countries, the authorities operate under budget constraints and create stressed atmosphere while allocation of resources for green initiatives, which can intensify the short budgetary pressure on the policy makers. Public health systems in these countries are limited and creates infrastructure deficiencies, personnel insufficiencies and lack of essential supplies. Consequently, re-allocations with respect to expenditure might generate better healthcare service delivery. Therefore, they experience crowding out in short run during green transitions, especially in environmental investments. Additionally, healthcare systems in these countries create burden due to environmental pollution and climate related shocks and develop health risk in larger aspects (Iordachi & Ciobu, 2024). When the systems are supported by proper financing, green public expenditure will reduce the healthcare demand and also strengthen the welfare outcomes in the community. The high income countries are usually positioned with life-cycle fiscal planning, and they have prevented budgeting approaches for disease burden. These long-term servings helped them to have proper health investments and integrate green spending for welfare strategies. They also facilitate green bonds along with innovative financing instruments for spreading cost over time and reduce the budget tensions. The financing mechanisms and institutional quality will determine the green spending as a fiscal opportunity and strong governance is essential for countries to have health co-benefits. Ultimately financing structures properly aligned with institution capacities play a vital role in strengthening the healthcare system and welfare outcomes globally (Chen & Zhang, 2025).

Figure 3. Financing Mechanisms

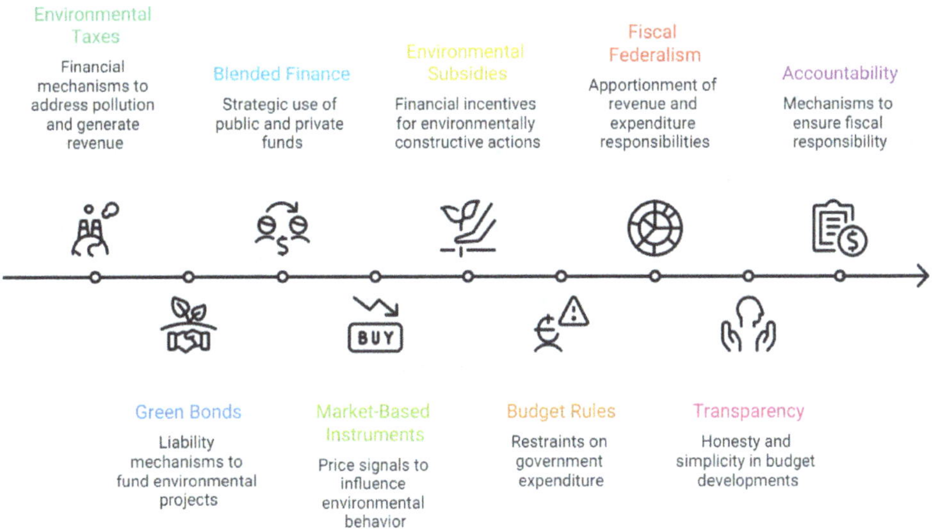

Source: *(Primary)*

5. EMPIRICAL EVIDENCES

Throughout the globe, different income levels along with institutional capacities have observed fiscal effects and measure improvement in the public health, particularly resulting in better healthcare recovery in long-term and improved welfare outcomes. Some of the notable cases are explained below.

Air Quality and Healthcare Costs

Air pollution demonstrates the destruction of air quality through various substances such as fine particulate matter, sulphur dioxide, nitrogen oxides, etc which result in respiratory diseases, cardiovascular problems, cancerous outcomes, etc. The health impacts because of air pollution are more crucial in industrial areas due to the increase exposure levels which amplifies as a result of population density. The epidemiological literature mentions about the reduction of pollution aspects and sustained enhancements in the health outcomes (Sharma et al., 2024). The World health organisation suggest that modest reduction in the substances will reduce the pollution level in the air and improve the air-quality which is translated to healthcare outcomes and also reduction in chronic diseases. Cities like Beijing have come up with emission control policies for migrating air pollution. They have strict industrial emission standards, restrictions for vehicle emissions, including gas transitions and also they invest heavily in public transport. Within few years of implementing these policies, the pollution level has decreased and subsequent health data also have shown that hospital admissions related to chronic respiratory and heart diseases have been reduced. Similar patterns were seen in London where they implemented clean transport policies and measured the air-quality improvement. The documentation showcased that respiratory hospitalisation have diminished and there was reduction in public healthcare expenditure for emergency healthcare services. The fiscal costs implemented for air pollution mitigation measures like upgrading the vehicle standards, implementing industrial filters, transitioning of cleaner fuels, often considered as expensive, but still it leads to better outcomes. Cost benefit analysis shows that the regulatory compliance costs gets translated into reduced disease burden, which lowers the healthcare expenditure and improve the productivity. This together reinforces that green public expenditure towards pollution control should be properly evaluated and considered as an environmental intervention for welfare policy measures globally (Fazakas et al., 2024).

Climate Adaptation Investments and Resilient Healthcare Systems

The climate adaptation strategies have increased the green public expenditure by reducing the healthcare pressures and improving the fiscal resilience. The climate catastrophes like heat waves, cyclones, floods, droughts, increased precipitation are usually linked with increased healthcare demand. These happenings amplify the stress, dehydration and also disease outbreak leading to mental health trauma. Without proper measures, this leads to stress in public budgets. Adaptation oriented expenditure towards green characteristics are vulnerable during these circumstances. Investments related to early warning systems, urban cooling, disaster preparedness, flood control enables to mitigate the climate events from mounting into public health challenges. Once such example can be seen in the heat action plan employed by Ahmedabad. They have implemented coordinated strategy for heat response through enabling early warning systems and public awareness campaigns where they have implemented, hydration initiatives, protocols for hospital emergencies. Measurements conducted following the implementation have shown substantial deterioration in the heat related mortality, particularly in outdoor workers and also elderly population. The fiscal perspective in this scenario shows that the plan created have reduced emergency healthcare responses and have dwindled the healthcare cost and expenditure towards these emergencies. Similarly, flood control plan implemented by Rotterdam remains as significant example for long-term investments with respect to drainage systems. The contagion has been reduced because of the implementation and extreme weather events are completely controlled, which condensed the water borne diseases also. The spending for climate change adaptation support in stabilising the healthcare expenditure and avoidance of physical spikes associated towards major disasters. Climate resilience investments are mandatory for governments to prevent shock observers and protect population health and similarly public finances because of climate induced volatility (DOrazio, 2025).

Sustainable Cities and Disease Prevention

The urban design creates individual behaviours, exposure patterns, and decide the psychosocial environments, making an important determinant for non-communicable diseases along with mental health outcomes. Car-dependent cities experience poor house quality, inadequate public transport, which are associated with increased obesity, diabetes, anxiety, hypertension, cardiovascular diseases, stress, etc. These conditions expose long-term and also burdens the public healthcare systems. Therefore, cities should be promoted with proper urban planning where physical activity, environmental quality and social interaction are higher contributing towards healthier community (Dehkordi et al., 2022). Cities like Copenhagen have implemented in cycling infrastructure, integrated public transport, pedestrian friendly roads as an important feature in daily life mobility. Consequently, they have reported reduced obesity rates and improved cardiovascular health, which abridged the lifestyle related disorders while compared to cities where car plays a major role for transportation. Likewise, Singapore have implemented green spaces and public housing as urban development strategy with urban greenery, where park access is provided. This have resulted in enhancement of health and elevated cognitive functioning for individuals by drop in their stress levels. The benefits are significant in urban environments where mental health is becoming a major concern. The green public expenditure towards housing quality also provides health dividends. The investments with respect to ventilation, sanitation and also safe building materials have reduced the outbreak of infectious diseases, respiratory conditions and mortality rates. These improvements have reduced healthcare utilisation and chronic conditions. The implications of sustainable urban design have boosted the long-term benefits and quality of life (Firooz & Firoozi, 2025).

Figure 4. Effects of Green Public Expenditure towards Efficient Outcomes

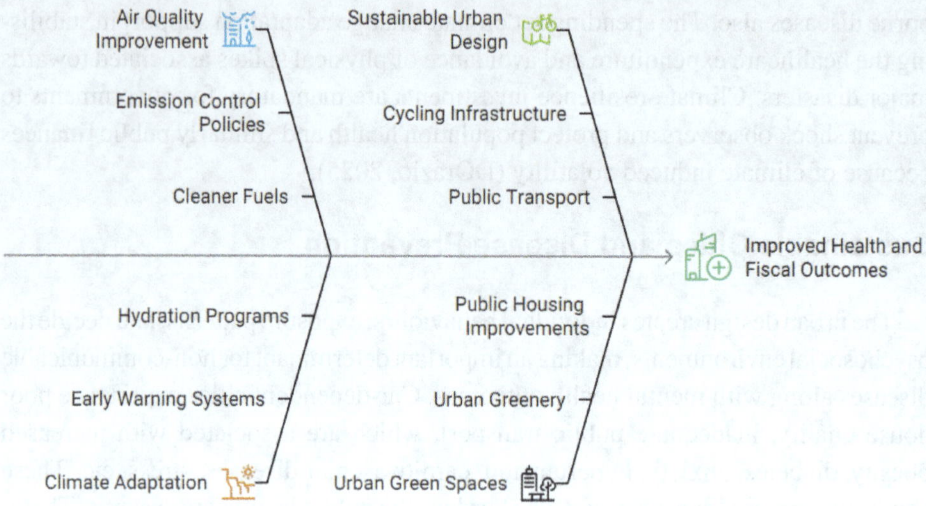

Source: *(Primary)*

The health benefits generated by the green public expenditure gets deciphered into fiscal returns. These recompenses discern towards reduced health and improved productivity resulting in welfare outcomes. The evaluation through integrative framework suggested by this chapter would intensify the healthcare financing along with long-term welfare for communities (Domapielle et al., 2022). Therefore, public expenditure can be contemplated as strategic investment by governments in order to improve the health and welfare pathways. This assist in prevention of diseases, and enrichment in the urban living circumstances through instigation of environmental policies for ecological welfares. Cities that are ranked in the top with respect to cleaner aspects, show the prominence of green public expenditure. The cities have invested in sustainable energies, transportation facilities, air quality regulations, waste management and extended urban green spaces. Consequently, their record shows less particulate matter and have reduction in disease prevalence. The trajectories explain that green public expenditure gets translated into environmental improvement and result in long-term outcomes which are measured in monetary aspects and preventive health (Zhang & Wang, 2023).

Analytical Comprehensions into Fiscal Dynamics of Green Public Expenditure

The examination of fiscal trade-offs explain that the green public expenditure would significantly give better outcomes rather than traditional budgetary analysis. When examined the system oriented approach would emerge and green public expenditure will be considered as a strategic investment that reshapes, the healthcare demand and fiscal sustainability in dynamic environments. The analysis also shows that short-term budgetary constraints increase the budgetary tensions and lead to higher spending from individual in an economy. When environmental investments are done, it indirectly contributes towards better health and sustainable lifestyle. Medium term results show that health benefits also become inevitable. The environmental interventions through pollution control measures, climate adaptation policies along with sustainable urban designs would reduce the disease incidents and create a holistic environment where expenditure for healthcare become reduced and standard of living of the people improves through green investments. The analysis also highlights that chronic diseases gets reduced through the green investments indirectly and it becomes a competing policy domain for governments. The long-term analysis explores that green public expenditure impacts the macroeconomic outcomes wherein healthier population contributes towards higher productivity and prolonged working lives. These welfare measures would increase economic output and extend the tax base by refining the economic standards. The poverty levels and illness related issues also become abridged in vulnerable populations. Therefore, the green public expenditure can be considered as a strategic investment choice by government for disease prevalence, disaster response and also social protection. Therefore, appropriate policy framework should be implemented, and this can be considered as a crucial mediator to get better outcomes. The analysis also explains about the crowding out through green expenditure and how it helps governments to reduce the burden in financial terminology. Income level heterogeneity is also explained with respect to short term pressures in monetary aspects. The financial instruments facilitate the green investments to function for better outcomes. The analysis also explains about the intergenerational considerations where in green public expenditure would progress the population health and endorse better future for upcoming generations through ecological resilience. This perspective reinforces more justification with respect to green spending in terms of welfare economics. Together, these analyses confirm that the perceived trade off among the relationships mentioned shows that green public expenditure directly influences the environmental spending and environmental sustainability, leading to better health outcomes of the population. The analytical findings show that green public expenditure should be considered as an imperative component by the government to reshape the health outcomes and productivity of a community. Therefore, it will result in integrated fiscal sustainability.

6. POLITICAL ECONOMY & EQUITY

Political Frugality of Fiscal Trade-Offs

The fiscal trade-offs demonstrate about the choices that government make when they have limited public resources towards competing policies. The public budget become constrained due to resource availability and deficit limitations which increases the borrowing level. In economic analysis, this trade off utilises the opportunity cost and provide benefit for public spending. While considering green public expenditure, this trade off occurs when there is balance between the environmental investments and healthcare spending leading to welfare outcomes. The political economy also influences the public expenditure contributed for green initiatives. This is examined through political values and strategies are provided to overcome the political constraints. The political dynamics is more crucial for understanding the environmental investments that remain underfunded for preventive healthcare spending and also long-term welfare outcomes (Wenjuan & Zhao, 2023).

The public expenditure is highly influenced by political visibility and healthcare occupies an important role in determining this. This is directly experienced by citizens in daily basis. The hospital overcrowding and shortage of medicines, ambulance turnover time and disaster preparedness are considered as major examples. The healthcare delivery often fails due to various reasons and this becomes public dissatisfaction and publicized in media also. This results in increased healthcare budgets, but then occurs negotiations. The degree of visibility becomes a significant political factor in order to prioritise the healthcare spending, when this becomes short-term aspect. The political salience will result in public backlash and shortfall. When this is properly capitalised, environmental initiatives like improving the water quality, air quality and green spaces (Liu et al., 2022). The well-being of individuals in that political rule will progress and citizens get enhanced health resulting in better living. Therefore, political decision makers should have a proper incentive structure for procurement and preventive health crisis. The electoral cycle intensifies this by and ranges from every period. The time frame makes the green investments highly partial, whoever is materialising the investments would get more benefits. The short-term concept should be emanated and green public expenditure should be a continuous concept to evade these kind of disproportions (Nylund, 2025).

The political salience also incorporates institutional fragmentation as there ascends difference of opinions from different levels of governments and institutions when policies been implemented. For instance, investments related to air pollution mitigation will diminish the respiratory diseases in the community which are rarely reflected in the budgets of health ministry. The costs towards environmental and transport ministries which indirectly benefits the healthcare systems but misalignment occurs due to incentive structure and reinforcement at different levels and institutions (Maedgen & Wlezian, 2024). Therefore, evaluation framework should be properly developed and performance metrics should be created to understand the entire system, how it works. This visibility will improve the benefits and outcomes in an enhanced level. Perceptual barriers also arise with respect to environment taxation, where the taxation will reduce the financial burden and improve the health aspects, but the taxation policies are largely understood by the citizens and its difficult for government to mobilise the green revenues. The amalgamation of health impact assessments reduces the futuristic healthcare demands which will be visible and constitutionally legible (Shen, 2026).

Equity Considerations and Social Welfare

Negotiations on fiscal aspects of green public expenditure explains that there occur unequal social realities. Environmental risk sand health outcomes are not accessible to everyone in the country. Therefore, fiscal decisions related with green public expenditure should be propounded with equity along with social welfare (Dridi et al., 2025). Understanding of environmental risk will benefit about public spending towards green impact over a period of time. Environment exposure should be shaped through socio economic status. The informal workers and the urban poor population should have awareness about the environmentally degraded areas and understand about the regions to have better health. They should be educated with housing facilities, sanitation, clean energy resources, and better living spaces to reduce environmental hazards and improve the health outcomes of vulnerable populations. The environmental health risk interacts with the economic vulnerability and these households are prone to more disease incidence. The environmental degradation would also affect their physical health, reinforcing existing inequalities. The green public expedition intervenes with this concept and intersects with environment, health and the vulnerable populations. Therefore, investments made with respect to green public expenditure should be equally distributed among all the population and should promote better outcomes for the poor communities. Also, the policymakers should construct proper strategy for addressing the disparity that occur in the population globally. The equity implications are more complex when fiscal trade off occur, therefore green spending should be consciously done during budget constraints. The distributional paradox should be used to understand the short run and longer aspects of investments that generate unequal distribution. When a city spends for pollution mitigation measures like clean transport systems and strict penalties for emission standards, the fiscal policies might limit the progression of healthcare budgets. This will affect the low income group who depend on public hospitals and the policy will be harmful for them, but over time the improvements in air quality will significantly reduce the disease prevalence which will benefit the low income community regarding their health. Therefore, this policy will provide long term benefit although at the initial stages it might look as harmful. This is a critical exemplar for distributional paradox. The equity considerations should extend towards future generations also and avoid environmental debt. Future generation should inherit the implications of present choices made for green investments. The environment should have better living standards. On balancing environmental along with healthcare spending today will improve the living of people tomorrow. Green public expenditure will internalise the health outcomes and welfare consultations of populations. Ultimately, equity should be implemented to strengthen the green public expenditure for sustainable welfare policies (Li et al., 2023).

7. POLICY IMPLICATIONS AND RECOMMENDATIONS

The analysis explained in this chapter shows that public policy on fiscal governance should be shaped in such a way that green public expenditure is evaluated for welfare spending. When the environmental investments are efficiently scrutinised, the preventive healthcare measures arise. This leads to sustainable development objectives. The conventional policies consider public budgets as zero sum allocations and static exercise can be seen. Whereas, this chapter strongly argues that dynamic fiscal analysis is essential to build proper decisions on public spending. The environmental investments will reduce to health risk and helps in long term betterment. Integration of preventive mechanisms along with resilient fiscal structure will enable the policymakers to reconceptualise the green spending as strategic funding and choice. Also, health sensitive green budgeting can be designed to reallocate the fiscal processes for recognizing the health impacts leading to long term monetary benefits through environmental investments using instruments like health impact assessments, cross sectoral coordination and co-benefit evaluation. By embedding into these mechanisms, authorities move towards budget comparisons that are implemented in short-term and capture the avoidance of healthcare costs, productivity gains and welfare enhancements. This sustainable development framework enables the embedding of environmental, social along with health objectives in a unified framework. The integrated planning boosts public acceptance enhancing policy coherence building long term resilience and sustainability.

CONCLUSION

This chapter demonstrates that fiscal crowding-out amid green public expenditure and healthcare financing is principally a short-term budgeting occurrence. When assessed intertemporally, the green spending may decrease disease burden, progress productivity, and augment fiscal sustainability. The net fiscal effect differs on institutional strategy, financing instruments, and time perspective. Static budget assessments therefore miscalculate the long-term fiscal and welfare assistances of environmental investment.

REFERENCES

Abbasov, R. (2025). Government Budgeting and Expenditure: A Multifaceted Analysis of Economic Growth, Fiscal Sustainability, and Social Impact. *Fiscal Sustainability, and Social Impact (December 20, 2024). iBusiness, 17*(01), 10-4236. DOI: 10.4236/ib.2025.171002

Abdelfattah, F., Salah, M., Dahleez, K., Darwazeh, R., & Al Halbusi, H. (2025). Public policy and sustainability: How green core competence, government trust, and policy satisfaction influence green R&D investments in the private sector. *Sustainable Futures : An Applied Journal of Technology, Environment and Society, 9*, 100461. DOI: 10.1016/j.sftr.2025.100461

Alonso-Morales, N., Sáez-Martín, A., & Haro-de-Rosario, A. (2025). The role of local public spending in the achievement of the social dimension of sustainable development: An empirical analysis. *Sustainable Futures : An Applied Journal of Technology, Environment and Society, 9*, 100475. DOI: 10.1016/j.sftr.2025.100475

Alymkulova, N., Iorember, P. T., & Omotesho, O. (2023). Public spending and private sector investment in Nigeria: an investigation of the crowding-in (or crowding-out) effect amidst deteriorating fiscal balance. In *Post-Independence Development in Africa: Decolonisation and Transformation Prospects* (pp. 263–278). Springer International Publishing., DOI: 10.1007/978-3-031-30541-2_15

Ardiputra, S., Milyan, M., Akhmad, Z., Sulthan, M., & Ardiputra, M. A. (2025). Optimizing budget policy in village fund allocation (ADD): A governance and public administration perspective on rural development. *Frontiers in Political Science, 7*, 1581806. DOI: 10.3389/fpos.2025.1581806

Athari, S. A., Addia, K., Kirikkaleli, D., Al Geitany, S. H., Al Fadhel, L., & Saliba, C. (2025). Do environmental taxes and green electricity matter for environmental quality? Fresh evidence in France based on Fourier methods. *Energies, 18*(19), 5046. DOI: 10.3390/en18195046

Baker, J. J., & Nenonen, S. (2025). Shaping Markets, Shifting Burdens: Collective Opportunism and Asymmetrical Market-Shaping. *Journal of Macromarketing, 02761467251388876*. Advance online publication. DOI: 10.1177/02761467251388876

Batra, G. A. U. R. E. S. H. (2023). Renewable energy economics: achieving harmony between environmental protection and economic goals. *Social science chronicle,* 2(2), 1-32. DOI: 10.56106/ssc.2023.009

Chen, E., & Zhang, H. (2025). The relationship between public health expenditure and urban economic resilience. *Frontiers in Public Health*, *13*, 1550528. DOI: 10.3389/fpubh.2025.1550528 PMID: 40027499

Cherniaieva, O., Mykhalchenko, H., Ataieva, O., Marshalok, T., & Petrukha, S. (2025). Optimizing Budgeting and Financial Management for Sustainable Economic Growth and Fiscal Resilience. *European Journal of Sustainable Development*, *14*(2), 430–430. DOI: 10.14207/ejsd.2025.v14n2p430

D'Orazio, P. (2025). Addressing climate risks through fiscal policy in emerging and developing economies: What do we know and what lies ahead? *Energy Research & Social Science*, *119*, 103852. DOI: 10.1016/j.erss.2024.103852

Dafermos, Y., Monserand, A., & Nikolaidi, M. (2022). Green public investment, consumption patterns and the ecological transition: a macroeconomic analysis. *Available at SSRN* 4097746. DOI: 10.2139/ssrn.4097746

Domapielle, M. K., Sumankuuro, J., & Bebelleh, F. D. (2022). Revisiting the debate on health financing in Low and Middle-income countries: An integrative review of selected models. *The International Journal of Health Planning and Management*, *37*(6), 3061–3074. DOI: 10.1002/hpm.3566 PMID: 36030531

Dridi, D., Hasni, R., & Kahia, M. (2025). Environmental degradation and financial development nexus in BRICS plus countries: Do financial development drivers make a difference? *Journal of the Knowledge Economy*, *16*(2), 10222–10254. DOI: 10.1007/s13132-024-02266-4

Eaton, E., Hunt, A., & Black, D. (2023). Developing and testing an environmental economics approach to the valuation and application of urban health externalities. *Frontiers in Public Health*, *11*, 1070200. DOI: 10.3389/fpubh.2023.1070200 PMID: 36875392

Fazakas, E., Neamtiu, I. A., & Gurzau, E. S. (2024). Health effects of air pollutant mixtures (volatile organic compounds, particulate matter, sulfur and nitrogen oxides)–a review of the literature. *Reviews on Environmental Health*, *39*(3), 459–478. DOI: 10.1515/reveh-2022-0252 PMID: 36932657

Fazeli Dehkordi, Z. S., Khatami, S. M., & Ranjbar, E. (2022). The associations between urban form and major non-communicable diseases: A systematic review. *Journal of Urban Health*, *99*(5), 941–958. DOI: 10.1007/s11524-022-00652-4 PMID: 35776285

Firoozi, A. A., & Firoozi, A. A. (2025). Architectural Innovations for Infection Control in Healthcare Environments: Spatial Strategies, Material Selection, and Ventilation Systems. In *Transformative Design in Healthcare: Infection Control and Patient Well-being through Architectural Innovation* (pp. 47-79). Cham: Springer Nature Switzerland. DOI: 10.1007/978-3-032-08019-6_3

Fonjong, L., Matose, F., & Sonnenfeld, D. A. (2024). Climate change in Africa: Impacts, adaptation, and policy responses. *Global Environmental Change*, *89*, 102912. DOI: 10.1016/j.gloenvcha.2024.102912

Gooding, K., Bertone, M. P., Loffreda, G., & Witter, S. (2022). How can we strengthen partnership and coordination for health system emergency preparedness and response? Findings from a synthesis of experience across countries facing shocks. *BMC Health Services Research*, *22*(1), 1441. DOI: 10.1186/s12913-022-08859-6 PMID: 36447261

Goswami, N. (2024). A dual burden dilemma: Navigating the global impact of communicable and non-communicable diseases and the way forward. *International Journal of Medical Research*, *12*(3), 65–77. DOI: 10.55489/ijmr.11202412

Huang, W. H., & Lu, C. T. (2025). The effect of hospital budgeting system on physician-executives' budget cognitive consciousness and medical decision making. *Cost Effectiveness and Resource Allocation : C/E*, *23*(1), 22. DOI: 10.1186/s12962-025-00629-5 PMID: 40400001

Iordachi, V., & Ciobu, S. (2024). Sustainable financing for the health sector: building a resilient healthcare system. In *Creşterea economica in condiţiile globalizarii* (pp. 95-112). DOI: 10.36004/nier.cecg.III.2024.18.10

Izah, S. C., Iyiola, A. O., Yarkwan, B., & Richard, G. (2023). Impact of air quality as a component of climate change on biodiversity-based ecosystem services. In *Visualization techniques for climate change with machine learning and artificial intelligence* (pp. 123–148). Elsevier., DOI: 10.1016/B978-0-323-99714-0.00005-4

Johnson, M. (2025). Lessons from a History of Histories of Public Finance. *Available at SSRN* 5615620. DOI: 10.2139/ssrn.5615620

Kentikelenis, A., & Stubbs, T. (2022). Austerity redux: The post-pandemic wave of budget cuts and the future of global public health. *Global Policy*, *13*(1), 5–17. DOI: 10.1111/1758-5899.13028

Khanam, Z., Sultana, F. M., & Mushtaq, F. (2023). Environmental pollution control measures and strategies: an overview of recent developments. *Geospatial Analytics for Environmental Pollution Modeling: Analysis, Control and Management*, 385-414. DOI: 10.1007/978-3-031-45300-7_15

Li, L., Shen, Z., Song, M., & Vardanyan, M. (2023). Public expenditure, green finance, and environmental governance: Evidence from China. *Environmental Modeling and Assessment*, *28*(5), 859–873. DOI: 10.1007/s10666-023-09899-w

Lin, L., & Hong, Y. (2022). Developing a green bonds market: Lessons from China. *European Business Organization Law Review*, *23*(1), 143–185. DOI: 10.1007/s40804-021-00231-1

Liu, Z., Yin, T., Surya Putra, A. R., & Sadiq, M. (2022). Public spending as a new determinate of sustainable development goal and green economic recovery: Policy perspective analysis in the Post-Covid ERA. *Climate Change Economics (Singapore)*, *13*(03), 2240007. DOI: 10.1142/S2010007822400073

Maedgen, J., & Wlezien, C. (2024). Institutional friction and policy responsiveness: The puzzle of coalitional fragmentation and executive-legislative balance. *Political Research Quarterly*, *77*(4), 1262–1278. DOI: 10.1177/10659129241263481

Mpofu, F. Y. (2022). Green Taxes in Africa: Opportunities and challenges for environmental protection, sustainability, and the attainment of sustainable development goals. *Sustainability (Basel)*, *14*(16), 10239. DOI: 10.3390/su141610239

Ngo, P. T., & Stanfield, J. (2022). Does government spending crowd out R&D investment? Evidence from government-dependent firms and their peers. *Journal of Financial and Quantitative Analysis*, *57*(3), 888–922. DOI: 10.1017/S0022109020000927

Nylund, A. (2025). Alternative dispute resolution and the judiciary. In *Research Handbook on Judging and the Judiciary* (pp. 13–34). Edward Elgar Publishing., DOI: 10.4337/9781788978743.00007

Onabowale, O. (2024). Blended finance partnerships combining public funds, private investments, and philanthropic contributions to expand essential healthcare infrastructure sustainably. *Int J Finance Manag Econ*, 7(2), 787–798. DOI: 10.33545/26179210.2024.v7.i2.626

Peng, F., Zhou, S., Ding, T., & Wu, H. (2023). Impact of fiscal expenditure stress on green transformation risk: Evidence from China education authority reform. *Economic Change and Restructuring*, *56*(6), 4565–4601. DOI: 10.1007/s10644-023-09567-9

Razavi, S. (2022). Making the right to social security a reality for all workers. *The Indian Journal of Labour Economics : the Quarterly Journal of the Indian Society of Labour Economics*, *65*(2), 269–294. DOI: 10.1007/s41027-022-00378-6 PMID: 35911186

Reznikova, N., Bulatova, O., Yatsenko, O., & Ivashchenko, O. (2022). Fiscal instruments of regulatory competition in the face of challenges to macroeconomic stability during a pandemic. *COVID*, *19*(2). Advance online publication. DOI: 10.57111/econ.21(2).2022.35-41

Saleh, H. M., & Hassan, A. I. (2024). The challenges of sustainable energy transition: A focus on renewable energy. *Applied Chemical Engineering*, *7*(2), 2084. DOI: 10.59429/ace.v7i2.2084

Sampedro, J., Markandya, A., Rodés-Bachs, C., & Van de Ven, D. J. (2023). Short-term health co-benefits of existing climate policies: The need for more ambitious and integrated policy action. *The Lancet. Planetary Health*, *7*(7), e540–e541. DOI: 10.1016/S2542-5196(23)00126-2 PMID: 37437994

Seccareccia, M. (1995). Keynesianism and public investment: A left-Keynesian perspective on the role of government expenditures and Debt. *Studies in Political Economy*, *46*(1), 43–78. DOI: 10.1080/19187033.1995.11675366

Sharma, R., Kurmi, O. P., Hariprasad, P., & Tyagi, S. K. (2024). Health implications due to exposure to fine and ultra-fine particulate matters: A short review. *International Journal of Ambient Energy*, *45*(1), 2314256. DOI: 10.1080/01430750.2024.2314256

Shaviro, D. (2025). Time is, time was: evaluating the use of the life cycle model as a fiscal policy tool. In *Research Handbook on Law and Time* (pp. 232–252). Edward Elgar Publishing., DOI: 10.4337/9781035316762.00019

Shen, J. (2026). State Capacity, Social Fragmentation, and Public Goods Provision: A Cross-National Comparative Analysis. *Governance: An International Journal of Policy, Administration and Institutions*, *39*(1), e70088. DOI: 10.1111/gove.70088

Shivanna, K. R. (2022). Climate change and its impact on biodiversity and human welfare. *Proceedings of the Indian National Science Academy. Part A, Physical Sciences*, *88*(2), 160–171. DOI: 10.1007/s43538-022-00073-6

Singh, A. (2025). Fiscal Federalism and Climate Change: Building the Institutional Framework in India. *Indian Public Policy Review*, *6*(1), 78–122. DOI: 10.55763/ippr.2025.06.01.003

Steuer, S., & Troger, T. H. (2022). The role of disclosure in green finance. *Journal of Financial Regulation*, *8*(1), 1–50. DOI: 10.1093/jfr/fjac001

Sun, J., Li, P., & Wang, Y. (2024). Policy tools for sustainability: Evaluating the effectiveness of fiscal measures in natural resource efficiency. *Resources Policy*, *89*, 104575. DOI: 10.1016/j.resourpol.2023.104575

Vallee-Dubois, F. (2023). Government spending preferences over the life cycle. *Journal of Public Policy*, *43*(3), 468–489. DOI: 10.1017/S0143814X23000065

Wenjuan, S., & Zhao, K. (2023). Balancing fiscal expenditure competition and long-term innovation investment: Exploring trade-offs and policy implications for local governments. *PLoS One*, *18*(11), e0293158. DOI: 10.1371/journal.pone.0293158 PMID: 38032928

Yang, X., Li, N., Mu, H., Ahmad, M., & Meng, X. (2022). Population aging, renewable energy budgets and environmental sustainability: Does health expenditures matter? *Gondwana Research*, *106*, 303–314. DOI: 10.1016/j.gr.2022.02.003

Yatzkan, O., Cohen, R., Yaniv, E., & Rotem-Mindali, O. (2025). Urban Energy Transitions: A Systematic Review. *Land (Basel)*, *14*(3), 566. DOI: 10.3390/land14030566

Zhang, D. (2024). Eco-friendly revenues for healthcare: Assessing the relationship between green taxation, public health expenditures, and life expectancy in China. *Frontiers in Public Health*, *12*, 1358730. DOI: 10.3389/fpubh.2024.1358730 PMID: 38841673

Zhang, Z., Ma, C., & Wang, A. (2023). Environmental governance, public health expenditure, and economic growth: Analysis in an OLG model. *International Journal of Environmental Research and Public Health*, *20*(4), 3033. DOI: 10.3390/ijerph20043033 PMID: 36833725

KEY TERMS AND DEFINITIONS

Climate Adaptation Investments: refer to public or private expenditures aimed at reducing vulnerability to the adverse impacts of climate change.

Fiscal Crowding-Out: occurs when increased government expenditure in one sector reduces available budgetary resources for other sectors under fixed revenue and borrowing constraints. In this context, it refers to potential displacement of healthcare financing due to increased environmental spending.

Fiscal Sustainability: refers to the government's ability to maintain stable public finances over time without excessive debt accumulation or compromising future fiscal capacity.

Fiscal Trade-Offs: refer to the allocation decisions governments must make when limited public resources are distributed across competing sectors.

Green Public Expenditure: refers to government spending directed toward environmental protection, climate mitigation and adaptation, renewable energy, pollution control, biodiversity conservation, and sustainable infrastructure aimed at promoting ecological sustainability and long-term societal welfare.

Healthcare Costs: refer to the total financial resources required to provide medical services, preventive care, treatment, rehabilitation, and public health interventions.

Healthcare Financing: refers to the mechanisms through which funds are mobilized, allocated, and utilized to provide health services, including public budget allocations, taxation, insurance systems, and external funding sources.

Intertemporal Effects: describe the consequences of policy decisions across different time horizons, distinguishing between short-term budget impacts and long-term economic and welfare outcomes.

Welfare Effects: denote the impact of public policies on overall societal well-being, including health outcomes, income levels, productivity, equity, and intergenerational sustainability.

Chapter 9
Strengthening Green Sukuk Policy as a Strategy for Sustainable Investment Transformation in Indonesia

Susenohaji Susenohaji
http://orcid.org/0009-0002-0363-4124
Universitas Brawijaya, Indonesia

Fitriana Rakhma Dhanias
Universitas Brawijaya, Indonesia

Rifki Muhammad Bintang
http://orcid.org/0009-0002-4601-5390
Universitas Brawijaya, Indonesia

Ali Roziqin
http://orcid.org/0000-0001-8336-3103
Universitas Muhammadiyah Malang, Indonesia

ABSTRACT

Since its first sovereign issuance in 2018, green sukuk has become a central component of Indonesia's sustainable finance strategy. While Indonesia has achieved global recognition as the largest sovereign green sukuk issuer, limited research

DOI: 10.4018/979-8-3373-8998-1.ch009

evaluates whether this growth translates into structural investment transformation and measurable environmental outcomes. This chapter examines how Indonesia's green sukuk policy framework can be strengthened to enhance corporate participation, optimize fiscal incentives, and improve inter-institutional coordination while maintaining public finance sustainability. Using a qualitative document analysis of regulatory frameworks, fiscal policies, impact reports, and sustainable finance roadmaps (2018–2025), the study identifies structural constraints including regulatory complexity, tax neutrality, fragmented institutional coordination, and limited corporate uptake.

1. INTRODUCTION

Green sukuk has emerged as a significant climate finance instrument that integrates Islamic financial principles with global sustainable investment frameworks (Abdullah & Keshminder, 2022; Faisal et al., 2023). As a Sharia-compliant adaptation of green bonds, green sukuk channels capital toward environmentally sustainable projects while adhering to ethical and asset-backed financing structures (Musari & Hidayat, 2023).The first corporate green sukuk was issued in Malaysia in 2017 to finance a solar energy project, marking a turning point in the institutionalization of Islamic climate finance (Keshminder et al., 2022). Indonesia followed shortly thereafter by issuing the world's first sovereign green sukuk in the international market in March 2018 (Mujizat, 2021). Since then, green sukuk has evolved from an experimental financial innovation into a strategic component of Indonesia's sustainable financing architecture. This rapid development positions Indonesia as a leading laboratory for examining the policy effectiveness of Islamic sustainable finance instruments.

Indonesia's performance in the green sukuk market has been particularly remarkable. By 2025, Indonesia had become the largest sovereign green sukuk issuer globally, with cumulative issuance reaching approximately US$11.75 billion (Kamalina, 2024). The sovereign issuances have consistently been oversubscribed, indicating strong international investor confidence and credibility in Indonesia's climate financing commitment. In addition to global issuance, Indonesia pioneered retail green sukuk targeting domestic investors with a minimum investment of IDR 1,000,000 per unit. This dual strategy, global institutional issuance and domestic retail mobilization has expanded both foreign capital inflows and local investor participation in sustainable finance. However, while issuance volume signals market acceptance, it does not automatically indicate structural investment transformation or effective climate impact.

Figure 1. Data Sale of Green Sukuk (2018–2025)

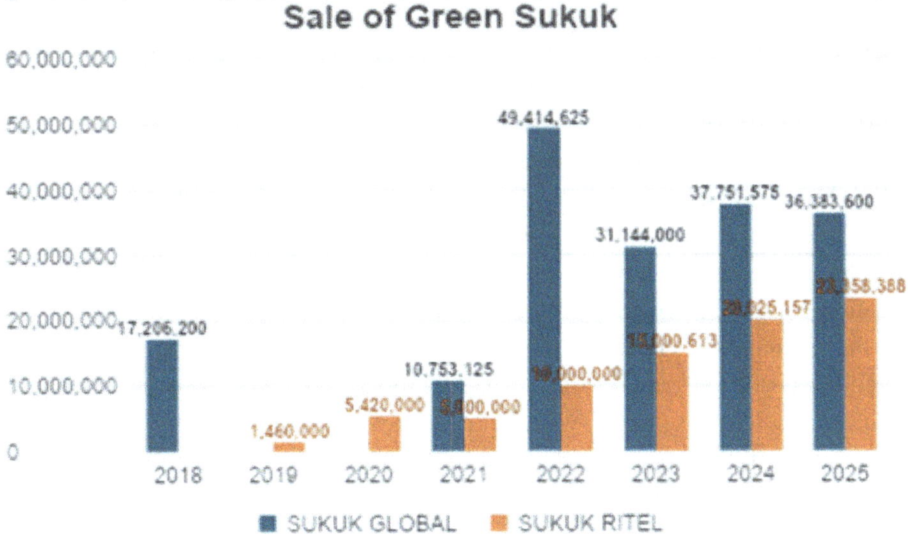

Source: Ministry of Finance 2025 (processed)

The development of green sukuk in Indonesia can be divided into two primary categories: global green sukuk and retail green sukuk (Khalilurrahman & Mubarrak, 2022). Global green sukuk are issued in foreign currency through international bookbuilding mechanisms and primarily target institutional investors. Retail green sukuk, by contrast, are denominated in rupiah and distributed domestically through financial intermediaries, offering accessible entry points for individual investors. Since its first issuance in 2018, global green sukuk has grown substantially, reaching more than IDR 182 trillion by 2025. Retail green sukuk has also expanded rapidly, accumulating approximately IDR 80 trillion with a significant increase in retail investor numbers (Ministry of Finance Republic Indonesia, 2023). Notably, while global sukuk dominates in nominal value due to institutional investor participation, retail sukuk demonstrates higher percentage growth and broader financial inclusion impact. This distinction is analytically important when assessing policy roles and investment mobilization strategies.

The increasing number of retail investors, reaching more than 238,000 by 2025—suggests rising environmental awareness among Indonesian citizens. Investment decisions are no longer driven solely by financial return considerations, but increasingly incorporate sustainability motivations (Syafari, 2022). The broader green bond movement, initiated by multilateral institutions such as the World Bank, has reinforced the linkage between capital markets and climate objectives (Tolliver et al., 2019; Pereira, 2021). Islamic finance subsequently adapted this framework to align environmental objectives with maqasid al-shariah principles emphasizing public welfare and intergenerational responsibility (Ulfah et al., 2024). Green sukuk therefore operates at the intersection of financial innovation, religious ethics, and climate governance. This multidimensional character requires analytical evaluation beyond descriptive issuance statistics.

Despite its rapid expansion, several structural challenges remain. Sovereign green sukuk has grown consistently under strong government leadership, yet corporate green sukuk issuance remains limited (Hania et al., 2022). Regulatory complexity, high transaction costs, limited fiscal incentives, and fragmented institutional coordination continue to constrain broader private-sector participation. Moreover, the causal relationship between green sukuk issuance and measurable environmental outcomes is often assumed rather than critically examined. Without evaluating how regulatory design, fiscal policy, and institutional mechanisms interact, green sukuk risks functioning primarily as a symbolic climate finance instrument rather than a transformative investment tool.

Indonesia's broader sustainable finance framework—including the Sustainable Finance Roadmap (2021–2025) and the Indonesian Sustainable Finance Taxonomy (TKBI 2) seeks to align financial flows with national climate commitments and Sustainable Development Goals (SDGs). The Financial Services Authority (OJK), Bank Indonesia, the Ministry of Finance, and technical ministries collectively shape this architecture. However, effective implementation depends on coordination efficiency, regulatory clarity, and incentive compatibility. The existence of regulatory frameworks alone does not guarantee effective capital reallocation toward low-carbon sectors. Policy effectiveness must therefore be assessed in terms of investment mobilization capacity and environmental impact accountability.

This chapter addresses a critical gap in the literature. While prior studies predominantly document green sukuk growth trends and institutional frameworks, limited research evaluates its policy effectiveness in driving sustainable investment transformation. Accordingly, this study asks how can green sukuk policy in Indonesia be strengthened to enhance corporate participation, optimize fiscal incentives, and improve institutional coordination while safeguarding public finance sustainability? By shifting focus from descriptive development to structural evaluation, this chapter contributes to Islamic sustainable finance scholarship through a policy-oriented analytical lens. Ultimately, green sukuk holds significant potential for Indonesia, given its large Muslim population, expanding investor base, and substantial infrastructure financing needs. However, realizing this potential requires more than continued sovereign issuance. It requires calibrated fiscal design, streamlined regulatory processes, strengthened inter-agency coordination, and mechanisms that translate financing flows into measurable environmental outcomes. Only through such integration can green sukuk evolve from a successful issuance instrument into a strategic driver of sustainable investment transformation.

2. LITERATURE REVIEW

2.1 Concept and Development of Green Sukuk

Green sukuk is commonly defined as a Sharia-compliant financing instrument whose proceeds are specifically allocated to environmentally sustainable projects (Fitrah & Soemitra, 2022). Unlike conventional green bonds, green sukuk must comply not only with environmental eligibility criteria but also with Islamic contractual structures and asset-backing requirements (Karina, 2019). This dual compliance structure positions green sukuk at the intersection of Islamic finance principles and global ESG standards, creating both opportunities and regulatory complexities. Scholars argue that green sukuk serves as a bridge between maqasid al-shariah objectives—such as public welfare and environmental stewardship, and international sustainable finance frameworks (Masood, Rahim, & Lee, 2024 ; Wan Zahari, 2025). The first issuance in Malaysia in 2017 demonstrated the feasibility of integrating Sharia governance with green certification mechanisms (Keshminder et al., 2022). Subsequent issuances across various jurisdictions indicate that green sukuk has moved from conceptual innovation toward institutional consolidation. However, the extent to which these instruments generate measurable environmental transformation remains debated.

Indonesian case has received significant scholarly attention due to its pioneering sovereign issuance in 2018 (Mujizat, 2021). Early studies primarily emphasize issuance size, oversubscription rates, and investor composition as indicators of success (Kahina & Lamya, 2025). By 2025, Indonesia had become the world's largest sovereign green sukuk issuer (Laila, 2025). reinforcing the perception that Islamic capital markets can effectively mobilize climate finance. Nevertheless, much of this literature remains performance-oriented, focusing on growth metrics rather than evaluating policy effectiveness or private-sector spillover effects. Limited research investigates whether sovereign leadership translates into corporate issuance expansion, reduced financing costs, or improved environmental performance indicators (Hania et al., 2022). Moreover, the interaction between global institutional markets and domestic retail participation remains underexplored. This gap is analytically important, as the dynamics of sovereign credibility, retail inclusion, and corporate uptake differ significantly in terms of incentives and risk structures.

Existing scholarship also highlights governance challenges. Integration of Sharia compliance, green taxonomy standards, and impact reporting requirements increases transaction complexity compared to conventional instruments (Ulfah et al., 2024). While proponents argue that such rigor enhances credibility and investor trust, critics suggest that excessive procedural requirements may deter corporate participation. The literature therefore presents a tension between regulatory robustness and market accessibility. This tension is particularly relevant in emerging markets, where institutional capacity and administrative coordination influence implementation outcomes. Consequently, green sukuk development must be examined not only as a financial innovation but also as an institutional policy process.

2.2 Green Finance Policy Framework in Indonesia

Indonesia's green finance architecture is shaped by interactions among monetary authorities, financial regulators, and fiscal institutions (Guild, 2020). Bank Indonesia (BI) incorporates climate considerations into macroprudential frameworks, while the Financial Services Authority (OJK) develops sustainable finance regulations and taxonomies (Setyowati, 2023). The Sustainable Finance Roadmap (2021–2025) and POJK No. 18/2023 formally integrate green and social instruments into Indonesia's capital market regulations (Ali et al., 2025). These regulatory developments reflect a transition from voluntary sustainability initiatives toward a more institutionalized sustainable finance regime. However, institutional presence alone does not guarantee effective capital allocation.

From a monetary perspective, Bank Indonesia employs macroprudential incentives such as relaxed Loan-to-Value ratios for green properties and liquidity facilities that encourage environmentally aligned lending (Juhro et al., 2024). These policies illustrate how central banking tools are increasingly linked to climate objectives. Yet empirical evidence on whether such measures significantly redirect credit toward low-carbon sectors remains limited. The literature suggests that macroprudential green policies can reduce systemic climate risk, but their impact depends on coordination with fiscal and regulatory instruments.

Fiscal policy plays an equally central role. The Ministry of Finance integrates climate objectives into budget planning through mechanisms such as climate budget tagging and green bond/sukuk frameworks (Wang et al., 2022). Tax incentives for renewable energy sectors and reduced import duties for clean technologies are intended to stimulate private investment (Abolhosseini & Heshmati, 2014). However, the effectiveness of fiscal incentives depends on calibration: poorly targeted subsidies may create fiscal burdens without generating additional green investment. Scholars therefore emphasize the importance of evaluating fiscal trade-offs and long-term sustainability of green financing incentives. Despite this multi-layered framework, coordination challenges persist. Indonesia's green finance governance involves multiple ministries and regulatory bodies whose mandates intersect but are not always fully harmonized. Fragmented implementation, procedural duplication, and varying interpretation of taxonomy standards may increase transaction costs and delay project realization. Existing studies acknowledge these coordination issues but often stop short of analyzing their implications for green sukuk expansion and corporate participation. Therefore, a policy-oriented evaluation of institutional alignment becomes essential for assessing green sukuk's transformative potential.

3. METHODS

This chapter employs a qualitative document analysis approach to examine the development and policy framework of green sukuk in Indonesia. Qualitative document analysis is appropriate for this study because green sukuk operates primarily within a regulatory, fiscal, and institutional policy environment, where official documents, regulatory frameworks, and public reports constitute primary sources of evidence. Rather than measuring quantitative financial performance alone, this research seeks to interpret policy design, institutional coordination mechanisms, and fiscal strategies shaping green sukuk development.

The analysis draws upon three categories of documents: (1) official government publications, including Ministry of Finance reports, Climate Budget Tagging documents, and Sustainable Finance Roadmaps; (2) regulatory texts issued by the Financial Services Authority (OJK) and Bank Indonesia; and (3) academic and policy literature related to green sukuk and sustainable finance in Indonesia. Document selection was based on relevance to green sukuk governance, fiscal policy instruments, regulatory implementation, and environmental impact reporting. Priority was given to documents issued between 2018 and 2025, corresponding to the period of sovereign and retail green sukuk expansion.

The analytical procedure involved systematic reading, coding, and thematic categorization of policy objectives, institutional roles, fiscal instruments, and reported outcomes. Key themes were identified, including regulatory complexity, fiscal incentives, investor participation, environmental accountability, and inter-agency coordination. These themes were then interpreted using a policy-effectiveness perspective, linking regulatory design to investment mobilization and sustainable development objectives. This qualitative approach enables a contextual and institutional understanding of green sukuk beyond descriptive issuance statistics, focusing instead on structural mechanisms that influence its effectiveness as a sustainable investment instrument.

4. RESULT

4.1 Opportunities and Challenges for the Development of Green Sukuk in Indonesia

The Ministry of Finance positions green sukuk as a central instrument within Indonesia's climate-oriented fiscal strategy. Beyond functioning as a debt instrument, sovereign green sukuk integrates climate mitigation and adaptation objectives into the state budget framework through earmarked allocation and climate budget tagging mechanisms. This integration represents a shift in fiscal philosophy, environmental sustainability is no longer treated as a supplementary policy objective, but as an embedded component of public financing architecture. By issuing both global and retail green sukuk, the government combines international capital mobilization with domestic financial inclusion. This dual approach enhances credibility in global markets while strengthening citizen participation in climate financing. However, the transformative capacity of this instrument depends not only on issuance volume but on the alignment between financing flows, project implementation, and measurable environmental outcomes.

Several structural opportunities support further expansion of green sukuk the following reasons (Dwi Irianti Hadiningdyah, Director of Sharia Financing, Directorate General of Financing and Risk Management, Ministry of Finance). First, rising environmental awareness—particularly among younger investors has increased demand for sustainable financial products. Second, Indonesia's early-mover advantage as a sovereign issuer enhances reputational capital and investor trust. Third, explicit government commitment to climate mitigation provides policy stability signals to the market. Fourth, the existence of a green project pipeline, including renewable energy and sustainable transportation initiatives, ensures allocation feasibility. These factors collectively reduce market uncertainty and strengthen demand-side and supply-side conditions for green sukuk expansion. Nevertheless, opportunity conditions do not automatically translate into corporate participation or systemic investment transformation.

Retail green sukuk provides a useful illustration of impact transmission mechanisms. A retail investment of IDR 1,000,000 in instruments such as ST007 indirectly finances infrastructure projects including railway development and renewable energy facilities. According to impact reporting data, funded projects have contributed to measurable emission reductions, such as an estimated 213,000 tons of carbon mitigation in certain project cycles. This linkage between capital mobilization and environmental impact reporting strengthens transparency and investor confidence. However, the scale of emission reduction must be evaluated relative to Indonesia's overall national emission targets. Without proportional scaling of green project pipelines, retail participation alone cannot significantly alter aggregate emission trajectories. Therefore, environmental impact must be assessed in terms of systemic contribution rather than symbolic illustration.

Despite favorable demand conditions, several structural constraints limit further development. Public literacy regarding green sukuk remains uneven, particularly outside urban financial centers. While retail instruments lower entry barriers, informational asymmetry and limited financial education constrain broader participation. From a market perspective, this represents a financial inclusion challenge rather than a demand deficiency. Moreover, corporate issuers face higher transaction costs due to Sharia compliance procedures, green certification requirements, and reporting obligations. These procedural complexities may increase credibility but simultaneously raise issuance costs, creating a regulatory–accessibility trade-off.

Institutional coordination also presents implementation challenges. Effective green sukuk execution requires alignment between the Ministry of Finance, sectoral ministries, project implementing agencies, and independent verifiers such as CICERO. Delays in project reporting, inconsistent environmental metrics, and fragmented data systems can weaken accountability mechanisms. Where monitoring frameworks lack harmonization, environmental claims risk being perceived as procedural compliance rather than measurable climate contribution. Strengthening standardized impact indicators and cross-ministerial reporting protocols becomes essential for sustaining investor trust.

From a macro-fiscal perspective, green sukuk must also be evaluated within long-term public finance sustainability. While earmarked financing enhances transparency, excessive reliance on sovereign issuance without expanding corporate participation may concentrate fiscal burden on the state. Indonesia's development agenda guided by National Development Planning Agency (BAPPENAS) through green economy initiatives—requires substantial private-sector capital mobilization. If corporate green sukuk issuance remains limited, sovereign dominance may inadvertently crowd out private innovation in sustainable financing markets. Encouraging SOEs and private corporations to participate therefore becomes a structural necessity rather than a supplementary objective.

Ultimately, green sukuk development in Indonesia reflects a dynamic interaction between opportunity structures and institutional constraints. Strong political commitment, investor demand, and international credibility provide a favorable foundation. Yet regulatory complexity, literacy gaps, reporting capacity limitations, and limited corporate uptake constrain systemic transformation. The central challenge is therefore not whether green sukuk can be issued successfully, but whether it can catalyze sustained capital reallocation toward low-carbon sectors at scale. Addressing this challenge requires coordinated regulatory refinement, calibrated fiscal incentives, and strengthened institutional accountability mechanisms.

4.2 Strengthening Regulations and Policies in the Development of Green Sukuk

1. Regulatory Simplification and Institutional Streamlining

The expansion of corporate green sukuk in Indonesia is constrained less by the absence of regulation than by the complexity of its implementation. While sovereign green sukuk has benefited from centralized state coordination since 2018, corporate issuers face multilayered compliance requirements involving OJK capital market regulations, National Sharia Board (MUI) fatwas, and green taxonomy eligibility standards. This multi-stage verification process enhances credibility but increases transaction costs, documentation burdens, and time uncertainty for issuers. For corporations—particularly first-time issuers, these additional layers create cost differentials relative to conventional bonds or alternative financing instruments. From an institutional perspective, this reflects a regulatory–accessibility trade-off: stricter standards improve legitimacy but may discourage private-sector participation.

Indonesia has already developed a robust sustainable finance architecture through the Sustainable Finance Roadmap and the Indonesian Sustainable Finance Taxonomy (TKBI). The challenge therefore lies not in regulatory absence but in regulatory fragmentation and procedural duplication across institutions. Parallel approval processes, inconsistent interpretation of taxonomy classifications, and coordination delays extend issuance timelines and increase implicit costs. For state-owned enterprises and publicly listed firms operating under strict financial schedules, administrative delays may alter financing strategies or shift capital toward simpler instruments. A streamlined issuance framework—potentially through a coordinated fast-track mechanism for certified green projects, could reduce procedural inefficiencies without compromising prudential standards. Regulatory reform in this context should aim to optimize institutional efficiency rather than dilute environmental safeguards.

Time certainty is particularly important in capital markets where interest rate volatility and market conditions affect borrowing costs. Delays in issuance approval may expose corporations to unfavorable pricing environments, thereby weakening the competitiveness of green sukuk. From a market design perspective, predictability and procedural transparency are as important as regulatory stringency. Indonesia's success in sovereign issuance demonstrates that when regulatory coordination is centralized and predictable, investor confidence remains strong. Replicating this coordination model for corporate issuers could reduce entry barriers and expand market depth. Without such adjustments, sovereign dominance may persist while corporate participation remains structurally limited.

2. Tax Incentives and Fiscal Trade-Offs

The main driver of fiscal policy in Indonesia is taxation of income from investments, which also plays a major role in the development of green sukuk. The return to investors in green sukuk is taxed in the same way as other conventional and sharia government securities (SBN). This means there has been no specific fiscal treatment for green sukuk that would recognize its attributes as a sustainable finance mechanism. In fact, with public benefits far beyond private investor interests provided by green sukuk, this lack-of-tax-incentives policy area remains unaddressed effectively so far. Taxation on yields greatly influences investment decisions made by retail investors within the domestic market.

Green sukuk instruments, particularly the retail series, are in direct competition with other products of retail SBN like non-green SR and ST as well as all other low-risk financial market instruments. In the absence of differential tax treatment, benefits from green sukuk depend more on sustainability aspects than any real economic incentive. For some investors-mostly new investors into investment-the consideration of net returns after tax is a very important factor; thus, tax incentives could be an important differentiator. Offering first time domestic investors in green sukuk a tax incentive can be used consciously to increase the base among domestic investors .It's exclusive and temporary hence does not create any long term fiscal liability.It aims at creating initial curiosity among public while encouraging them to explore & engage with green investment solutions. This approach tallies with the overall national policy on Islamic finance to foster greater albeit comparatively lower inclusion of the Islamic capital market. In this case, tax incentives work as an initial bridge and not a substitute for market attractiveness.

Do not merely count tax incentives for green sukuk as a short-term loss of government revenue. Green sukuk capital is the redirection of capital toward the government's priority programs that support facilitation in climate change mitigation and adaptation, as per Indonesia's Climate Budget Tagging and Green Bond/Sukuk Framework. The economic resilience impacts environmental hazard risks and long-lasting social benefits. Therefore, tax incentives can be construed as part and parcel of proactive fiscal policy in reducing future economic costs, which falls very much in line with how Indonesia has construed its sustainable fiscal policies.

On the other hand, meanwhile, tax incentives clearly show and acknowledge investors as partners or collaborators in the funding of sustainable development. Green sukuk investors are sharing with the government the risk of financing public projects that have positive environmental externalities. Recognition through a more accommodative tax policy for this contribution as well as an indication by the government to support green investment can be strategically important in developing healthy financial markets where transparency on fiscal policy increases investor confidence leading to market stability hence should be systematically articulated based on evidence within national fiscal policy framework accompanied probably targeted specific segments such beginner retail investors first issuance phase evaluated periodically maintain fiscal discipline. If articulated transparently and clearly, this could add to the attractiveness of green sukuk without causing major distortions in the market. In the development process of sustainable financing in Indonesia, tax incentives are not only supplementary but relevant and strategic policy tools as well.

3. Socialisation of Green Sukuk to the Public through Religious Institutions

Strengthening the socialisation of green sukuk in Indonesia cannot be separated from the religious nature of society, which makes religious institutions the main reference in sharia economic decision-making. Although retail green sukuk has shown significant investor growth, the level of public understanding of policy objectives, financing mechanisms, and environmental impacts is still uneven. So far, socialisation has mostly been carried out through formal financial market channels and digital platforms, which have not fully reached all levels of society. This condition has created a gap between the large market potential and the actual level of literacy.

In the Indonesian context, religious institutions such as mosques, Islamic boarding schools, *majelis taklim* (Islamic study groups), and Islamic community organisations have a very strong position in shaping public opinion. Public's economic decisions about sharia are frequently shaped by moral and religious legitimacy rather than merely financial factors. Green sukuk as a Sharia-compliant sustainable financial instrument fits perfectly within the objectives of these religious groups. The involvement of religious organizations in the dissemination of green sukuk will provide sharia and moral legitimacy to this financial instrument and encourage the public's participation in sustainable financing.

Participation of religious institutions supports the objective related to structuring the national Islamic economic framework. Indonesian government through Ministry of Finance, Financial Services Authority, and National Committee for Islamic Economics and Finance (KNEKS), is actively promoting the improvement of Islamic financial literacy and inclusion. In this context, the socialisation of green sukuk through religious institutions can be an effective complement to formal education programmes. This approach does not require the establishment of new institutions, but rather utilises existing social networks that have a high level of trust in the community. So that policies can reach community groups that have not been reached by official socialisation channels.

In essence, green sukuk can be understood as the embodiment of Islamic values in preserving sustainability and public welfare. Financing renewable energy projects, sustainable transportation, and climate resilience is in line with the principle of trust in resource management and responsibility towards future generations. Policies that emphasise the compatibility between sustainable development goals and sharia values will be more easily accepted by the community. In this case, scholars and religious leaders play an important role as liaisons between public policy and the community's understanding of religious values.

The approach of socialisation through religious institutions is also relevant to expanding sharia financial inclusion, especially for communities that are not yet familiar with capital market instruments. Even though retail green sukuk has a modest minimum investment, a lack of information is still a big problem. Regular and contextual learning on green sukuk can be done through religious activities on a regular basis and in a thorough way. This will let people see that capital market investments are not just for certain groups of people. The incorporation of green sukuk into religious institutions ought to be prioritized as a fundamental component of national policy development. Working together with the government, financial institutions, and religious groups will make this strategy more legitimate and help it work better in communities. Consistent and systematic implementation will cultivate investors' belief that green investment constitutes a social and religious obligation, thus enhancing the role of green sukuk as both a fiscal and Islamic finance policy instrument in Indonesia.

4.3 Institutional and Interagency Coordination in the Implementation of Green Sukuk

Institutional arrangements in implementing green sukuk in Indonesia are inherently multisectoral and cross-institutional. The Ministry of Finance, particularly through the Directorate General of Financing and Risk Management (DJPPR), plays a central role in designing, issuing, and allocating green sukuk proceeds toward environmentally sustainable projects. At the same time, the Financial Services Authority (OJK) regulates sustainable financial instruments, including enforcement of POJK No. 18 of 2023 and the operationalisation of the Indonesian Sustainable Finance Taxonomy (TKBI). Bank Indonesia supports the ecosystem through macroprudential incentives, including liquidity facilities, relaxed Loan-to-Value ratios for green properties, and adjustments to the Macroprudential Inclusive Financing Ratio. This multi-layered institutional structure reflects a comprehensive governance framework; however, its effectiveness depends on the degree of operational alignment among these actors rather than on the existence of formal mandates alone. In practice, coordination challenges arise when regulatory objectives, fiscal priorities, and sectoral implementation timelines are not synchronised. Thus, institutional complexity becomes both a strength and a potential bottleneck in green sukuk implementation.

Beyond financial authorities, technical ministries play a decisive role in determining project eligibility and environmental compliance. The Ministry of Environment and Forestry establishes environmental standards and sustainability criteria, while the Ministry of Energy and Mineral Resources identifies renewable energy projects aligned with national climate commitments. Bappenas integrates green financing into national development planning and monitors progress using SDG and climate indicators. This distribution of responsibilities ensures sectoral expertise but also introduces coordination risks, particularly in harmonising project selection criteria and reporting standards. Differences in interpretation of environmental metrics or delays in inter-ministerial data exchange may slow project certification and fund disbursement. Although collaboration platforms exist, including sustainable finance working groups, their authority is often consultative rather than binding. Without clear procedural hierarchies or standardized cross-agency protocols, institutional fragmentation may reduce implementation efficiency.

Inter-agency coordination remains one of the primary structural constraints in the development of green sukuk. Policy inconsistencies between central and local governments, as well as complex licensing procedures for green infrastructure projects, have slowed the realisation of investment even under an established regulatory framework. Additionally, domestic financial institutions often perceive green projects as high-risk and long-term, which affects credit appetite despite macroprudential support. These challenges indicate that the core issue is not the availability of instruments or legislation, but the effectiveness of cross-sectoral execution mechanisms. Coordination gaps may generate uncertainty for investors and project developers, weakening the catalytic potential of green sukuk. Therefore, improving coordination is not merely administrative reform but a prerequisite for scaling sustainable investment.

Strengthening coordination requires more than informal cooperation; it demands a clearer national framework with defined accountability mechanisms. A cross-ministerial green finance coordination body with operational authority, standardized environmental performance indicators, and integrated digital reporting systems could reduce duplication and enhance transparency. Establishing unified impact measurement standards would also strengthen credibility with international investors and external reviewers such as CICERO. Furthermore, aligning fiscal incentives, monetary policies, and sectoral project pipelines within a single strategic roadmap would reduce policy fragmentation. Regional governments should also be integrated into this framework to support the potential development of regional green sukuk instruments. Through improved institutional coherence, Indonesia can transform green sukuk from a well-regulated instrument into a fully coordinated national sustainable finance ecosystem.

4.4 Impact of Retail Green Sukuk Issuance on Sustainable Development in Indonesia

Even if corporate issuers have not yet fully embraced green sukuk, the existence of retail green sukuk has generated multiple positive impacts for sustainable development in Indonesia. The principles of Islamic economics and finance are inherently aligned with sustainable development, particularly through commitments to ethics, justice, fairness, and social welfare. Islamic financial instruments, including retail green sukuk, facilitate productive economic activities while enabling broader wealth participation among society, thereby contributing to the achievement of the Sustainable Development Goals (SDGs) (Riana et al., 2020). Retail green sukuk simultaneously functions as a fiscal instrument for revenue mobilization and as an environmental instrument for carbon emission mitigation. Its allocation toward renewable energy, sustainable infrastructure, and climate-related projects demonstrates Indonesia's seriousness in advancing SDGs such as affordable clean energy, decent work and economic growth, industry innovation, infrastructure development, and climate action. As a Sharia-compliant instrument, retail green sukuk also reflects the government's commitment to strengthening domestic financing sources. Investment in retail green sukuk therefore represents both a financial decision and a form of civic participation in national development financing.

Secondly, one of the structural advantages of retail green sukuk is its denomination in rupiah, which avoids exchange rate risk. Unlike global green sukuk issued in US dollars, retail green sukuk is financed through domestic currency and domestic investors. After the 1998 economic crisis, Indonesia adopted a strategy of prioritizing domestic financing to reduce vulnerability to currency fluctuations. Borrowing from domestic investors through retail green sukuk reduces exposure to external shocks and exchange rate volatility, particularly against the US dollar. This feature strengthens fiscal resilience and contributes to the stability of the domestic financial system. In addition, retail green sukuk plays an important benchmarking role in the capital market. The yield curve formed by retail sukuk provides pricing references for other green-oriented sukuk or bonds, thereby supporting market transparency and valuation accuracy for investors and issuers.

Third, the government's initiative in issuing retail green sukuk creates a demonstration and signaling effect for the private sector. By establishing standards for transparency, environmental reporting, and fund allocation, the government sets a precedent for sustainable financing practices. The issuance of corporate green bonds by PT Sarana Multi Infrastruktur (PT SMI) illustrates how sovereign leadership can encourage similar initiatives in the private sector. This catalytic function reduces informational uncertainty and builds confidence among potential corporate issuers. Although private sector participation remains limited, retail green sukuk establishes institutional credibility that may gradually stimulate broader market adoption. In this way, the instrument contributes indirectly to expanding Indonesia's sustainable finance ecosystem.

Fourth, retail green sukuk has implications for literacy and inclusion within Indonesia's Islamic capital market, where participation rates remain relatively low. Based on OJK data, financial literacy and capital market inclusion levels, particularly within the Islamic segment, have historically been minimal. These conditions have encouraged the government to expand Sharia-based investment instruments and increase awareness campaigns. Retail green sukuk, with its relatively low minimum investment requirement, lowers entry barriers for first-time investors and environmentally conscious citizens. By combining Sharia compliance with environmental objectives, the instrument appeals to both religious and sustainability motivations. This dual appeal supports efforts to expand domestic investor bases while enhancing Islamic capital market inclusion.

The socialisation of retail green sukuk also contributes to strengthening environmental culture in society. Investment culture can be synergised with environmental awareness, integrating sustainability into daily economic decisions. Environmental responsibility can extend beyond consumption patterns to include green-based investment choices. When green investment becomes socially normalized, it reinforces demand for environmentally sustainable infrastructure and supports long-term climate resilience. Retail green sukuk thus operates not only as a financing tool but also as a medium for cultivating environmental consciousness. This cultural dimension complements fiscal and regulatory strategies in achieving national climate commitments.

Based on Riana et al. (2020), the positive impacts of retail green sukuk can be summarized into several interrelated dimensions. First, it enables community contribution to national development and supports Indonesia's commitments to the Paris Agreement and SDGs. Second, it contributes to greenhouse gas emission reduction through financing environmentally oriented projects. Third, it increases fiscal revenue and strengthens independence in development financing. Fourth, it provides a benchmark and reference model for subsequent green issuances by corporations or regional governments. Fifth, it reaches new investor segments, particularly green and Sharia-oriented investors, thereby broadening financial inclusion. Sixth, it promotes environmental culture by enhancing public understanding of sustainable investment practices. These impacts collectively illustrate that retail green sukuk contributes simultaneously to environmental, fiscal, financial, and socio-cultural dimensions of sustainable development.

5. DISCUSSION

The purpose of this chapter is to formulate policy ideas that facilitate the optimal use of green sukuk as a financing instrument for sustainable development in Indonesia. The findings indicate that although issuance volume and market acceptance of green sukuk have increased significantly, structural constraints continue to limit its transformative impact. One of the central issues is the absence of differentiated fiscal incentives that clearly distinguish green sukuk from other government securities. Because green sukuk yields are taxed similarly to conventional instruments, their environmental attributes are not reflected in post-tax return comparisons. This situation creates a neutrality effect in the market, where environmental value does not automatically translate into economic advantage for investors. As a result, green sukuk may compete primarily on financial performance rather than sustainability differentiation. This finding supports earlier studies emphasizing the importance of targeted fiscal instruments in strengthening green finance demand.

Another important constraint lies in regulatory and bureaucratic complexity. Renewable energy and environmentally oriented infrastructure projects often require multiple approvals across central and local government levels. The cross-sectoral nature of green projects results in overlapping administrative procedures, which may delay fund disbursement and reduce investor confidence. Although Indonesia has established a comprehensive sustainable finance framework, implementation gaps remain due to coordination inefficiencies rather than regulatory absence. This suggests that policy effectiveness depends less on introducing new rules and more on improving harmonization among institutions. In practice, streamlining licensing processes and aligning sectoral project pipelines with green sukuk allocation mechanisms would significantly improve execution efficiency.

From a policy perspective, the government has demonstrated commitment through regulatory reforms, sustainable finance roadmaps, and the expansion of green taxonomy classifications. The Job Creation Law and renewable energy tax relaxations indicate movement toward a more supportive fiscal environment. However, these policies remain general and are not specifically tailored to enhance the competitiveness of green sukuk relative to other financing instruments. The absence of targeted measures may limit the instrument's capacity to attract broader corporate participation. Moreover, the effectiveness of financial regulations such as POJK No. 18 of 2023 depends heavily on coordinated implementation between OJK, Bank Indonesia, the Ministry of Finance, and technical ministries. Without synchronized execution, regulatory legitimacy may not translate into market expansion.

Investor participation remains a determining factor in the long-term sustainability of green sukuk. International investors have responded positively to Indonesia's sovereign green sukuk, indicating that credibility and transparency are recognized in global markets. Domestically, however, participation levels are influenced not only by financial returns but also by literacy, awareness, and perceived alignment with Sharia principles. This highlights the importance of combining fiscal and regulatory measures with structured public communication strategies. Engagement of religious leaders and institutions, when supported by measurable literacy programs, can strengthen trust and expand the domestic investor base. Therefore, demand-side reinforcement complements supply-side reforms.

Overall, the findings demonstrate that green sukuk in Indonesia possesses a strong institutional and market foundation. Nevertheless, achieving transformative investment impact requires coordinated policy alignment across fiscal, monetary, regulatory, and sectoral dimensions. The key issue is not the viability of the instrument itself, but the coherence of the ecosystem supporting its expansion. Strengthened regulatory harmonization, calibrated fiscal incentives, and improved inter-agency coordination would allow green sukuk to function not only as a financing tool but as a strategic driver of sustainable investment transformation. Consistency across sectors remains essential to ensure that green sukuk evolves into a long-term alternative to conventional financing for climate-related development.

6. CONCLUSION

This chapter set out to evaluate how green sukuk policy in Indonesia can be strengthened to support sustainable investment transformation rather than merely increase issuance volume. The findings demonstrate that Indonesia has successfully institutionalized sovereign green sukuk within its fiscal architecture, combining global capital mobilization with domestic retail participation. However, structural transformation requires more than continued sovereign issuance. Regulatory complexity, limited fiscal differentiation, fragmented institutional coordination, and uneven corporate participation constrain broader ecosystem development. The absence of targeted tax incentives creates neutrality in post-tax returns, limiting green sukuk's competitive differentiation in domestic markets. Moreover, bureaucratic layering increases transaction costs for corporate issuers despite the existence of a comprehensive regulatory framework. Therefore, the central policy challenge lies not in expanding issuance, but in strengthening institutional coherence and incentive compatibility.

The results indicate that green sukuk contributes positively to sustainable development through fiscal revenue mobilization, emission reduction financing, Islamic capital market inclusion, and environmental culture formation. Retail green sukuk, in particular, enhances domestic financial resilience by avoiding exchange rate exposure and broadening investor participation. Nevertheless, the link between financing flows and measurable environmental outcomes must be strengthened through standardized impact reporting and cross-ministerial data harmonization. Fiscal incentives, while potentially beneficial, must be carefully calibrated to avoid long-term revenue distortion or market substitution effects. Institutional coordination mechanisms require operational clarity rather than additional formal mandates. Without synchronized execution among the Ministry of Finance, OJK, Bank Indonesia, and sectoral ministries, policy credibility may not translate into sustainable capital reallocation. Thus, effectiveness depends on systemic integration rather than isolated policy initiatives.

Beyond Indonesia, this study offers broader implications for emerging and Islamic finance markets. Sovereign leadership can establish credibility and market depth, but private-sector expansion requires regulatory streamlining and targeted incentives. Islamic finance instruments such as green sukuk possess strong normative legitimacy grounded in maqasid al-shariah principles; however, normative alignment alone does not guarantee structural investment transformation. Indonesian experience demonstrates that climate-oriented Islamic finance must operate within a coordinated fiscal–monetary–regulatory ecosystem to achieve measurable impact. Future policy design should therefore prioritize institutional alignment, transparent impact measurement, and calibrated fiscal support. By integrating these elements, green sukuk can evolve from a successful financing instrument into a strategic driver of low-carbon development and sustainable investment transformation.

REFERENCES

Abdullah, M. S., & Keshminder, J. S. (2022). What drives green sukuk? A leader's perspective. *Journal of Sustainable Finance & Investment*, *12*(3), 985–1005. DOI: 10.1080/20430795.2020.1821339

Abolhosseini, S., & Heshmati, A. (2014). The main support mechanisms to finance renewable energy development. *Renewable & Sustainable Energy Reviews*, *40*, 876–885. DOI: 10.1016/j.rser.2014.08.013

Ali, M., Wahjuni, E., Wardhana, R. W., Haryani, I., & Prakoso, B. (2025). Protection Policy Strategy for Green Bond Investors Against the Risk of Greenwashing Practices in the Capital Market. *International Journal of Advanced Multidiciplinary Research and Studies*, *5*(5), 854–862.

Faisal, Y. A., Gunawan, I., Cupian, , Hayati, A., Apriliadi, A., & Fajri, M. (2023). Examining the purchase intentions of Indonesian investors for green sukuk. *Sustainability (Basel)*, *15*(9), 7430. DOI: 10.3390/su15097430

Fitrah, R., & Soemitra, A. (2022). Green Sukuk for sustainable development goals in Indonesia: A literature study. *Jurnal Ilmiah Ekonomi Islam*, *8*(1), 231–240. DOI: 10.29040/jiei.v8i1.4591

Guild, J. (2020). The political and institutional constraints on green finance in Indonesia. *Journal of Sustainable Finance & Investment*, *10*(2), 157–170. DOI: 10.1080/20430795.2019.1706312

Hania, B. T., Endri, E., & Indra, I. (2022). Identify the issuance problem of corporate green sukuk in Indonesia. *Islamic Economics Journal*, *8*(2), 187–204. DOI: 10.21111/iej.v8i2.8404

Juhro, S. M., Robinson, I., Rahadyan, H., & Rishanty, A. (2024). Climate Risks, Just Transition, and Central Bank Policy for Sustainable Economic Growth. *Jurnal Ekonomi Indonesia*, *13*(3), 215–248. DOI: 10.52813/jei.v13i3.587

Kahina, H., & Lamya, B. (2025). The Role of Green Islamic Sukuk in Achieving Environmental Sustainability in Indonesia: Reality, Challenges, and Future Prospects. *Science. Education and Innovations in the Context of Modern Problems*, *8*(3), 734–751.

Kamalina, A. R. (2024). *RI Jadi Penerbit Sukuk Terbesar di Dunia, Kalahkan IsDB*. Bisnis.Com. https://finansial.bisnis.com/read/20241031/231/1812126/ri-jadi-penerbit-sukuk-terbesar-di-dunia-kalahkan-isdb#goog_rewarded)

Karina, L. A. (2019). Peluang dan tantangan perkembangan green sukuk di Indonesia. *Proceeding of Conference on Islamic Management, Accounting, and Economics*, 259–265.

Keshminder, J. S., Abdullah, M. S., & Mardi, M. (2022). Green sukuk–Malaysia surviving the bumpy road: Performance, challenges and reconciled issuance framework. *Qualitative Research in Financial Markets*, *14*(1), 76–94. DOI: 10.1108/QRFM-04-2021-0049

Khalilurrahman, K., & Mubarrak, H. (2022). Retail green sukuk in Indonesia: Toward a maqashid approach. *Share: Jurnal Ekonomi Dan Keuangan Islam*, *11*(1), 208–228. DOI: 10.22373/share.v11i1.12460

Laila, N. (2025). *Green Sovereign Sukuk: Indonesia's Sustainable Financial Innovation in the Global Market*. Unair.Ac.Id. https://unair.ac.id/green-sovereign-sukuk-inovasi-keuangan-berkelanjutan-indonesia-di-pasar-global/

Masood, A., Rahim, N., & Lee, U. H. M. S. (2024). Driving Green Sukuk Development to Meet ESGs and Society 5.0 Aspirations Through Innovative Technology. In *Strategic Islamic Business and Management: Solutions for Sustainability* (pp. 1–18). Springer.

Ministry of Finance Republic Indonesia. (2023). *Early Redemption of Sukuk Tabungan (ST) Series ST009*. Http://Www.Djppr.Kemenkeu.Go.Id/. https://www.djppr.kemenkeu.go.id/kperst009

Mujizat, D. A. (2021). *The sovereign green Sukuk: an analysis of its process and barriers to funding renewable energy projects in Indonesia*.

Musari, K., & Hidayat, S. E. (2023). The role of green sukuk in maqasid al-shariah and SDGs: Evidence from Indonesia. In *Islamic finance, fintech, and the road to sustainability: Reframing the approach in the post-pandemic era* (pp. 181–203). Springer. DOI: 10.1007/978-3-031-13302-2_9

Pereira, M. Y. B. (2021). Green bonds in the emerging multilateral development banks: A (sufficient) alternative to catalysing private capital? *Asia Pacific Viewpoint*, *62*(1), 116–130. DOI: 10.1111/apv.12297

Riana, N., Sadono, M. D., Septianto, M. R., Hardiana, M. D., Nathalia, D., Sukmajaya, M., & Aini, A. N. (2020). Studi mengenai green sukuk ritel di indonesia. *UNDP Kementerian Keuangan RI. Direktorat Jenderal Pengelolaan Pembiayaan Dan Risiko, Kementerian Keuangan*. Https://Www. Google. Com/Search

Setyowati, A. B. (2023). Governing sustainable finance: Insights from Indonesia. *Climate Policy*, *23*(1), 108–121. DOI: 10.1080/14693062.2020.1858741

Tolliver, C., Keeley, A. R., & Managi, S. (2019). Green bonds for the Paris agreement and sustainable development goals. *Environmental Research Letters*, *14*(6), 64009. DOI: 10.1088/1748-9326/ab1118

Ulfah, I. F., Sukmana, R., Laila, N., & Sulaeman, S. (2024). A structured literature review on green sukuk (Islamic bonds): Implications for government policy and future studies. *Journal of Islamic Accounting and Business Research*, *15*(7), 1118–1133. DOI: 10.1108/JIABR-10-2022-0255

Wan Zahari, W. M. Z. (2025). Operationalising Green Sukuk within the World Bank environmental and social framework. *Discover Environment*, *3*(1), 288. DOI: 10.1007/s44274-025-00490-6

Wang, S., Sun, L., & Iqbal, S. (2022). Green financing role on renewable energy dependence and energy transition in E7 economies. *Renewable Energy*, *200*, 1561–1572. DOI: 10.1016/j.renene.2022.10.067

Chapter 10
Sustainable Investments for a Greener Future-Exploring the Impact of SRI Funds

Ambati Suvarna
http://orcid.org/0009-0007-1715-6713
SR University, Warangal, India

Md Kafila
http://orcid.org/0009-0006-9443-6412
SR University, Warangal, India

ABSTRACT

Socially Responsible Investment (SRI) funds have achieved financial legitimacy and often match or outperform conventional funds. The proof of their environmental and social effects in actual situations remains uncertain. The paper defines the SRI Performance Impact Paradox as a situation that shows strong financial results but produces minor sustainability results. The study uses a structured narrative review to analyze literature from 2000 to 2024 while combining stakeholder theory with legitimacy theory and behavioral finance into a single analytical framework. The analysis reveals that ESG metrics, which are often disconnected, along with companies that only meet basic requirements and have little involvement from shareholders, as well as gaps in regulations, prevent capital from making a real difference. The paper presents a causal framework that explains how SRI capital starts to generate actual impact while it identifies policy changes that will enhance organizational responsibility and operational efficiency.

DOI: 10.4018/979-8-3373-8998-1.ch010

INTRODUCTION

The mounting concern of climate change, social inequality, and corporate responsibility has changed the way investments are done in the world today, with Socially Responsible Investment (SRI) funds rapidly increasing. Compared to traditional investment strategies where long-term returns on investment are given less priority, SRI incorporates the three components of environmental, social, and governance, namely ESG, in the process of selecting a portfolio and capital allocation. Consequently, SRI funds are being considered as the tool that can be used to balance financial results with the overall societal and environmental goals. In the last twenty years SRI has developed from an extension of niche screening of ethics to now become a mainstream section of the world.

The existing tension continues to exist because nobody has solved this main problem, which remains. The studies show that SRI funds achieve risk-adjusted returns that match the performance of traditional funds, yet their capacity to produce consistent environmental and social results remains uncertain. The chapter presents this SRI Performance–Impact Paradox as a fundamental conflict that shows how financial performance competes with actual sustainability effects that remain uncertain. The paradox raises a fundamental research question: Why do SRI funds often succeed as financial products yet fall short as mechanisms for transforming corporate environmental and social behavior? The resolution of this question impacts our assessment of SRI as either a genuine advancement in sustainable finance or an instrument for reputation management within capital markets.

The chapter presents two separate dimensions that measure SRI effectiveness to answer this question. Financial performance refers to traditional investment outcomes such as returns, risk mitigation, and resilience during market downturns, whereas real-world impact concerns observable changes in corporate environmental practices, social responsibility, and governance quality. The assumption that capital reallocation toward high-ESG firms will produce beneficial behavior changes does not hold because current research shows this process operates through weak channels that exist in disconnected parts or depend on disclosure methods instead of actual business advancements.

This chapter uses an analytical framework composed of three different theories, Stakeholder Theory, Legitimacy Theory, and Behavioural Finance, to develop its centralized argument. Stakeholder Theory provides a foundation for explaining how Socially Responsible Investing (SRI) would impact firms through aligning corporate strategies with the objectives of multiple stakeholder groups, whereas Legitimacy Theory describes the risks associated with firms' responses to SRI pressures via symbolic compliance as opposed to real change (with regard to enhanced ESG reporting). Whereas behavioral finance creates a mechanism for understanding the continued inflow of capital into SRI funds, in light of the fact that the investment decisions made by investors are driven by their values, identity, and moral satisfaction (even when there is no scientific evidence to provide validation of SRI performance metrics). The framework provided by all three perspectives provides researchers with an organized framework within which to study the mechanisms behind the SRI Performance-Impact Paradox.

This chapter utilises an empirical/theoretical narrative review to gather and assess all of the key arguments regarding the performance, impact, strategy (screening/ engagement), and regulatory effectiveness of SRI (Sustainable Responsible Investment) based on research that has been conducted from 2000 to 2024. This chapter also develops a new avenue of research within the sustainable finance literature by demonstrating the relationship between company behaviour and financial results as it relates to existing policy frameworks. The analysis should provide significant advantages to both policymakers/regulators and investors looking to enhance the credibility, accountability and actual results of SRI funds.

REVIEW METHODOLOGY

The study adopts a qualitative research design that combines systematic literature review and comparative case analysis to investigate the SRI performance-impact paradox. Secondary data were collected using peer-reviewed journals and acquired from the Google Scholar database based on relevance and analytical rigor. The study selected case studies representing different types of governance and varying levels of regulatory oversight and public involvement. Thematic synthesis was used in conjunction with stakeholder theory, legitimacy theory, and behavioral finance to investigate how SRI strategies impact both financial performance and environmental and social impacts while acknowledging the problems associated with measuring and disclosing ESG. This methodology is appropriate because the purpose of this research is to provide a theoretical and analytical explanation of the SRI Performance-Impact Paradox rather than to test specific quantitative hypotheses.

Methodological Limitations

This chapter has been developed based almost exclusively on secondary academic literature, policy documents, and institutional publications; empirical data collection has not been undertaken as a precursor to this chapter being created.

- Quantitative or longitudinal data are unavailable and therefore restrict the ability to correlate the impacts of SRI investment with social and environmental reality.
- There is little consistency or comparability of ESG ratings and disclosure frameworks across most providers, making it very difficult to assess the impact of SRI investment.
- The theoretical nature of the proposed framework limits the extent of application until a significant quantity of fund-level capital empirical data has been collected.

LITERATURE REVIEW: PERFORMANCE, IMPACT, AND THE CENTRAL DEBATE IN SRI

Although there are numerous publications associated with Socially Responsible Investment (SRI), little coherence exists across this body of literature as it needs several different approaches to be examined. The majority of current SRI research is focused on answering two major questions in relation to SRI.

- Do SRI funds tend to be economically superior compared with more conventional funds?
- Do SRI funds create large-scale social and/or environmental returns?

The extensive literature on the first question provides a strong basis for comparison, while there has been a lack of literature supporting a specific theory and/or methodology to comprehensively address the second question; therefore, there continues to be some ambiguity surrounding the relative success of SRI in creating social benefits.

Research on financial performance indicates that SRI (Socially Responsible Investing) investments produce comparable risk-adjusted returns as traditional portfolios of investments, particularly when measured over long-term time frames and periods of significant market downturns. This evidence has demonstrated that SRI has become an acceptable form of investment by the investing community. The connection of SRI fund increases in capital with a corresponding change in corporate behavior is still inconclusive. Studies also show that companies cannot achieve environmental improvement, improved labor conditions, and effective governance systems solely from capital allocation systems due to the requirement of both shareholder involvement and legal enforcement.

In ongoing debates surrounding the relative effectiveness of different screening and engagement methods, scholars agree that two types of screening methods—

negative exclusion screening and best-in-class screening—will improve the ESG performance of portfolios but do nothing for previously invested companies in existing SRI portfolios. Theoretical studies provide evidence supporting the argument that corporate behavior can be changed through engagement-based strategies, but empirical research suggests that engagement tends to yield only marginal results as it is generally poorly measured. Further, the SRI Performance-Impact Paradox exemplifies this mechanism, as financial performance is trackable, whereas actual impacts cannot be tracked as they diffuse through the system.

A separate literature stream exists on the importance of measurement/disclosure of ESG impacts. The difficulty of assessing impacts occurs due to the fact that there are many different ESG rating systems, the manner in which companies report information is inconsistent, and most reporting is self-reported by companies. Consequently, investors will assume that companies with good disclosure practices have not changed their operations, leading to heightened concerns over greenwashing and symbolic compliance.

In Table 1, previous research is categorized according to SRI evolution, technological influences, sustainability challenges, and methodological gaps. By categorizing the prior research in this manner, it is clear that there is an existing structural imbalance in the literature, as there is strong evidence of financial performance but very weak and inconsistent evidence of environmental and social impacts. This existing imbalance will be the basis of the analytical framework presented in the following section.

Table 1. Thematic Synthesis of Prior Research on Socially Responsible Investment

Category	Proposed by	Key Findings	Estimated Impact
SRI Evolution	(Beisenbina et al., 2022)	SRI strategies have evolved from simple screening to more sophisticated approaches like best-in-class and ESG integration.	The evolving strategies suggest a growing sophistication in sustainable investing, potentially increasing investor engagement with sustainability goals.
Technological Innovation	(Brahmi et al., 2023)	Technological innovations are facilitating financial inclusion for carbon neutrality, with a favorable regulatory environment potentially generating positive environmental and economic effects.	This approach could significantly accelerate the transition to a more sustainable economic model by leveraging technological advancements.
Private Equity Sustainability	(Crifo & Forget, 2013)	Private Equity is emerging as a powerful channel for fostering sustainable practices in unlisted companies, driven by new value creation and risk management needs.	The approach may transform how private companies approach sustainability, creating new economic opportunities and environmental benefits.
Research Challenges	(Beloskar et al., 2023)	The field of sustainable investments remains undertheorized, with fragmented research and a lack of academic collaboration.	These challenges could hinder the development of comprehensive sustainable investment strategies and theoretical frameworks.
Green Washing	(Beloskar et al., 2023)	Greenwashing poses a significant challenge, emphasizing the need for measures to ensure the authenticity of sustainable investments.	The prevalence of greenwashing could undermine investor trust and the credibility of sustainable investment approaches.
Corporate Behavior and Real Impact	(Heath et al. 2023; Peng et al. 2023)	Evidence shows that SRI funds have limited or conditional influence on corporate environmental and social behavior, with impact depending on governance quality and engagement intensity.	Explains the gap between financial success and measurable sustainability outcomes, reinforcing the SRI Performance–Impact Paradox.

Table 1 shows that SRI literature has a structural imbalance. The research documents the development of SRI strategies together with their financial outcomes, yet there exists only minimal proof about their capacity to create lasting environmental and social benefits. Most studies concentrate on strategy development and ESG integration, yet their research findings produce weaker evidence about corporate behavior changes. The SRI Performance–Impact Paradox shows an imbalance because researchers have dedicated more effort to studying financial results than they have spent on understanding actual sustainability impacts.

CONCEPTUAL FRAMEWORK: EXPLAINING THE SRI PERFORMANCE–IMPACT PARADOX

The quick increase of Socially Responsible Investment (SRI) funds, together with their ability to generate competitive, risk-wise financial returns, creates a direct contradiction with the restricted and inconsistent environmental and social results that companies display at their operational level. This chapter presents the SRI Performance–Impact Paradox as a conceptual framework that shows how companies achieve successful financial results yet fail to achieve their sustainability goals, which create actual environmental effects. The framework investigates SRI funds by examining why their rising market share fails to produce significant changes in corporate environmental and social practices instead of questioning their financial performance.

The framework combines stakeholder theory with legitimacy theory and behavioral finance to show how the paradoxical situation functions. The stakeholder theory perspective of SRI indicates that the investment practice will change corporate practices because it directs funds toward companies that fulfill the needs of all their stakeholders, which include employees and communities and environmental requirements. Companies should use capital reallocation to enhance their ESG practices because this approach helps them secure investor backing while decreasing their capital expenses. The research findings show that the incentive system achieves minimal effect because ESG results do not establish a direct connection to executive pay or funding arrangements.

Legitimacy theory explains the gap between financial results and their actual effects because it shows how companies use strategic responses to SRI pressures. As companies face growing demands for ESG disclosure, their response will focus on meeting reporting requirements instead of making real changes to their operations. The behavior enables companies to sustain their capital market legitimacy while they maintain existing environmental and social practices, which results in greenwashing that strengthens the performance–impact paradox.

Behavioral finance enables better understanding of investor behavior by studying their reasons for making investment choices. SRI fund investors want their financial choices to reflect their personal beliefs according to their moral values and public image requirements. The reasons that drive investors to purchase SRI products help sustain product demand and maintain SRI financial success. SRI funds keep attracting capital because companies show minimal proof of their environmental effects.

Figure 1. Conceptual Framework Explaining the SRI Performance – Impact Paradox

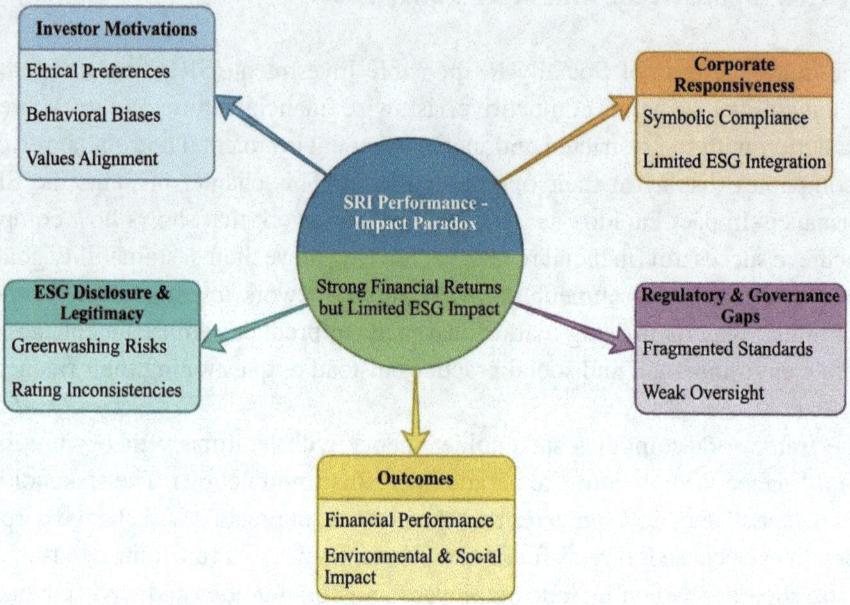

(Author's own creation)

Figure 1 shows the SRI frameworks display two separate paths that lead to different financial results and sustainable performance outcomes. SRI funds receive capital from investors who want to invest in sustainable companies, whereas ESG disclosure quality determines which companies investors will choose. The legitimacy concerns drive corporate responses, which result in companies following minimal legal requirements instead of making actual improvements. The existing regulatory and governance mechanisms establish rules that determine whether SRI investments create genuine environmental and social benefits. The figure explains how companies with good financial results can produce minimal results because it shows the fundamental reasoning behind the SRI Performance–Impact Paradox.

Causal Interpretation of the Conceptual Framework

The effectiveness of SRI funds depends on the interaction between four mechanisms, which are connected to each other through three core elements: investor motivation, EGS information quality, corporate behavior, and regulatory supervision. Investor demand initiates capital allocation toward SRI products, while ESG disclosure quality determines firm eligibility and portfolio composition. Corporate responses may be substantive or symbolic, depending on governance incentives and monitoring intensity. The dynamic system depends on regulatory and institutional frameworks because they determine the level of transparency and accountability and stakeholder involvement. The SRI Performance–Impact Paradox exists because any of these mechanisms become weak, which allows financial performance to continue yet sustainability results to remain absent.

Behavioral Finance and the Persistence of the SRI Performance–Impact Paradox

The SRI Performance-Impact Paradox maintains its existence because behavioral finance shows how investor values and identity and moral satisfaction drive investors to make investment choices. SRI fund investors choose ethical alignment together with reputational signaling as their primary investment criteria, which they consider more important than environmental and social results that can be measured. The value-driven motivation that drives capital investment into SRI products continues to function because companies demonstrate only limited or unclear evidence of their actual corporate impact.

Fund managers do not face strong requirements to show actual sustainable results that exceed their environmental, social, and governance ESG assessments and their sustainability reports. The behavioral pattern decreases the effectiveness of capital distribution to drive corporate transformations because it lets businesses maintain their financial success while environmental and social results fall behind actual progress. Investor actions in the SRI Performance–Impact Paradox function as an additional force that strengthens the existing relationship between the two elements.

Mechanisms of Impact Transmission in SRI

The global capital market is valuing socially responsible investment (SRI) funds as a very powerful tool, which balances morale and monetary interests. Such funds analyze businesses according to the standards of environmental, social, and governance (ESG), like pollution control, board diversity, workplace safety, and worker welfare. Research shows that even passively managed SRI funds are still very important contributions to the field of sustainable finance and the shift to a green economy (Chen & Scholtens, 2018).

The main factors constituting the aspect of sustainable investments are

ESG Screening: It is selecting investments based on environmental, social, and governance criteria to avoid unethical or harmful companies.

Shareholder Engagement: It is using investor influence to push companies toward more responsible practices through voting and dialogue.

Impact Measurement: It is tracking and reporting the real-world social and environmental outcomes of investments.

Transparency and Disclosure: It is emphasizing open reporting and clear sustainability goals to build investor trust and accountability.

As a combination, these parts are part of sustainable financial behavior that encourages long-term environmental and social health.

Figure 2. Additional Key Elements of Sustainable Investments

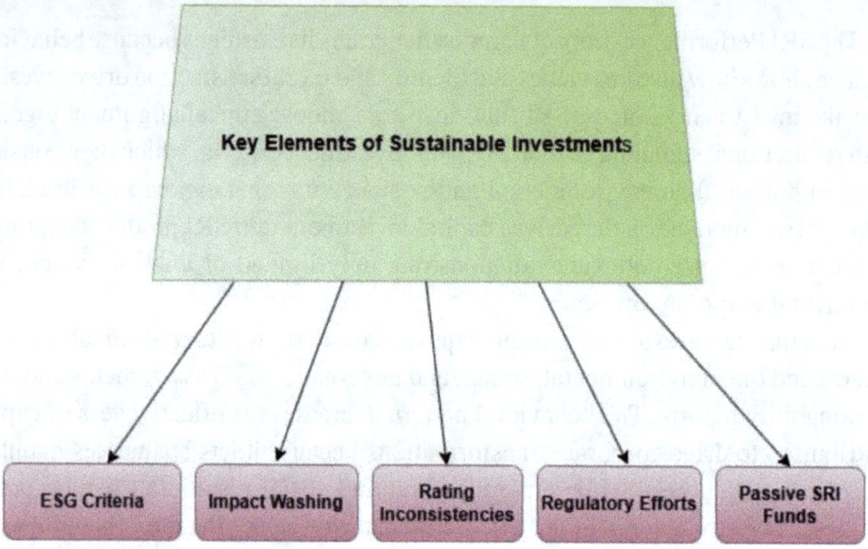

(Author's own creation by using App Diagram)

Figure 2 shows that sustainable investment success depends on ESG screening and shareholder engagement and impact measurement and transparency working together. The screening process helps portfolios achieve better sustainability outcomes, but organizations need strong engagement practices and trustworthy impact assessment methods to achieve their goals. The interaction between these elements shows that SRI funds that design their operations to be sustainable will not achieve equal environmental and social outcomes, which leads to the performance–impact paradox.

Foundations of Sustainable and Responsible Investing

Sustainable and Responsible Investing (SRI) is an idea that is based on the premise that financial markets are able to internalize environmental and social externalities by making informed capital allocation and governance decisions. With an aim to facilitate the creation of long-term values and reduce non-financial risks that might impact the performance of firms, SRI attempts to incorporate the environmental, social, and governance (ESG) aspects into the conventional financial analysis (Gupta et al., 2021; Palma-Ruiz et al., 2020).

The SRI intellectual foundations are largely based on the stakeholder theory and the legitimacy theory. The stakeholder theory assumes that companies will create sustainable value by considering the interests of various stakeholders, as opposed to focusing on the interests of shareholders; hence, the need to integrate ESG considerations in investment decision-making. Legitimacy theory also justifies the behavior of firms that react to the SRI-related pressures by increasing their sustainability disclosures and their governance procedures, especially when the availability of capital is dependent on the perceived social approval.

SRI is also conceptually similar to other traditions of ethical finance, especially Islamic finance, in its focus on responsible economic practices, avoidance of destructive activities, and the long-term well-being of society. Nonetheless, Islamic finance is based on the religious ideals, whereas SRI is based on the secular principles of sustainability and governance systems, and therefore their intersection is philosophical as opposed to institutional.

As much as these foundations offer normative legitimacy of the growth of SRI, they also demonstrate some structural constraints that assist in explaining the lack of proportional environmental or social consequences of ethical intent and financial achievement.

SRI STRATEGIES AND INNOVATIONS

Socially Responsible Investing (SRI) strategies have evolved from basic negative screening to more sophisticated approaches such as best-in-class selection, ESG integration, and thematic investing (Revelli, 2017; Tripathi & Kaur, 2022). This evolution reflects an attempt to align ethical considerations with financial performance while responding to increasing investor demand for sustainability-oriented products. However, empirical evidence suggests that greater strategic sophistication does not automatically translate into proportional environmental or social outcomes.

The ESG integration practices of asset management companies show diverse levels of implementation, which result from their different sustainability commitments and their various regulatory obligations (Lestari & Frömmel, 2024). The development of better disclosure practices together with ESG analytics has improved the sustainability alignment of portfolios, but these improvements mainly help companies build their reputational standing instead of bringing actual changes to their operations (Martini, 2021). The SRI Performance-Impact Paradox demonstrates its main operational principle through the fact that new SRI strategies need to build financial credibility, which then results in better investor trust without bettering their impact capabilities.

People who invest their money publicly demand environmental social governance standards and sustainable investment methods to be fully assessed according to their performance (Camilleri, 2021), yet existing methods to engage investors and track results through standardized metrics do not help organizations to achieve their objectives for sustainable development (Palma Ruiz et al., 2020; Tripathi Kaur, 2022). The ongoing development of socially responsible investment strategies has helped companies to expand their market presence while reducing their financial risks, yet this approach fails to solve the existing problem regarding performance and impact assessment.

Sectoral Analysis of ESG Integration in SRI Funds

SRI funds use different ESG criteria for their investment evaluation process because each industry has different levels of regulatory compliance requirements and available data resources and different ways to motivate their managers. The different approaches that each industry sector uses to handle SRI capital distribution explain why their environmental and social results show such inconsistent patterns, which support the SRI Performance-Impact Paradox.

Asset management companies and fund managers implement ESG criteria in different ways across various sectors according to existing evidence because their ESG implementation shows greater success in regulated industries and high-risk industries such as energy and finance, and their ESG application diminishes in sectors that require minimal disclosure (Sciarelli et al., 2021). The main focus of ESG integration in those situations centers on improving disclosure standards together with managing risks instead of bringing about complete business process changes.

The intensity of disclosure requirements essential to particular sectors determines their environmental, social, and governance outcomes. In jurisdictions with less stringent sustainability disclosure standards, firms with strong reporting capabilities can improve ESG ratings without corresponding improvements in underlying practices, enhancing portfolio-level ESG scores while limiting real-world impact (D Apice et al., 2021). The current situation results in organizations increasing their legitimacy-based actions, which decrease the connection between socially responsible investment capital and organizational transformation.

Research from emerging markets, especially India, shows that ESG mutual funds provide better risk-adjusted returns compared to traditional funds according to sector-based evidence, which supports this finding (Vishali & Shafi M. K., 2024). The financial stability of this situation does not lead to better environmental or social results because the sector lacks effective methods for engagement and enforcement. The transition away from exclusion-based screening toward best-in-class and integrated ESG strategies has improved portfolio sustainability alignment, but sector-specific impact gaps remain unresolved (Roselle, 2016).

Evidence from different institutional contexts shows that pension funds in multiple countries use different methods to operate their funds. U.S. pension funds that use ESG integration frameworks between their existing regulatory systems and their available technological resources show better performance than countries that lack institutional strength to implement similar approaches (Ikwue et al., 2023). The results show that the effectiveness of sectoral ESG programs depends on two factors, which are governance quality and regulatory enforcement, more than it depends on strategic design.

The sectoral analysis shows that ESG integration improves the financial legitimacy and stability of SRI funds across all industries, but its effects depend on specific circumstances. The SRI Performance-Impact Paradox continues to exist because of this imbalance, which shows the necessity for different industry regulations and more effective methods to connect SRI investments with actual sustainability results.

ENVIRONMENTAL AND SOCIAL IMPACT OF SRI FUNDS

The primary determinant of success of the socially responsible investment (SRI) funds is the investors' aptitude in detecting and backing firms observing high standards of environmental, social, and governance (ESG) practices, i.e., reduced pollution, leadership with diversity, employee satisfaction, and safety at the workplace. It is true that SRI funds can weed out the firms based on ESG compliance; however, their input in driving more corporate changes through shareholder engagement and activism is still very limited (Heath et al., 2023). This limitation is the same as the corporate responsiveness gap shown in Figure 1, where the firms' response to ESG pressures is mainly through symbolic compliance instead of real operational transformation. However, recent research revealed that SRI mutual funds could negatively impact ESG outcomes in portfolio companies but only under unfavorable conditions such as a lack of diverse boards, non-transparent ownership structures, and ceased investor engagement, among others (Peng et al., 2023). This teaches us when, where, and how to properly create funds and apply long-term engagement strategies to maximize the environmental and social impact of SRI funds.

Case Study 1: Institutional Success — Norway's Government Pension Fund Global (GPFG)

Norway's Government Pension Fund Global (GPFG) serves as a common example for demonstrating successful implementation of institutional socially responsible investment practices. The fund, which manages excess funds from Norway's oil industry, operates its long-term investment approach by using environmental, social, and governance factors as fundamental elements. The GPFG fund establishes strict rules that prohibit investments based on environmental destruction, human rights violations, corrupt practices, and major governance breakdowns while it conducts active ownership through its voting rights and communication efforts.

The essential characteristic of GPFG extends beyond its ESG screening because its institutional framework functions as its primary distinctive element. The combination of strong regulatory support and transparency demands, together with specific ethical standards, guarantees that ESG factors affect both investment distribution and business interactions. The fund has maintained its financial success through this system, which also enforces responsibility by using exclusion methods and shareholder activism. The SRI Performance–Impact Paradox receives partial resolution through the combination of strong governance and regulatory oversight, which strengthens SRI capital transmission into actual changes in corporate behavior.

CHALLENGES AND LIMITATIONS OF SRI FUNDS

Socially responsible investment funds encounter different hurdles to their growth notwithstanding their rising market success. The key difficulty with socially responsible investment rests in the absence of established guidelines for assessing environmental, social, and governance factors. The financial loss may pose a problem for investors who choose SRI fund options. Ethical funds operating within Australia between 1986 and 2005 delivered an average annual underperformance of 1.52% to investors based on research of 89 such funds by (Jones et al., 2008). The performance results between SRI funds and conventional funds remain comparable, according to multiple previous research papers. The review of (Heath et al., 2023) indicates that SRI funds choose sustainable firms. SRI funds face three major issues: conflicting ESG rating systems together with performance problems and suspicion regarding their capability to change corporate conduct. Standardization with better transparency and engagement methods must be implemented in SRI to match investors' expectations alongside social goals. As shown in Figure 1, fragmented ESG metrics and weak regulatory oversight amplify legitimacy-driven behavior.

SRI Fund Performance During Market Crises

Evidence from multiple financial crises suggests that SRI funds provide better protection against losses during market downturns than conventional funds because the SRI funds show greater resilience during times of market uncertainty. Studies that analyze the global financial crisis and the COVID-19 pandemic and geopolitical shocks show that SRI portfolios maintain their value better and achieve faster recovery because they prioritize governance standards and risk management practices and long-term investment strategies (Schröder, 2004; Mill, 2006; Paul, 2017; Wu et al., 2017; Arefeen & Shimada, 2020; Cosma et al., 2024).

The financial performance benefits of this crisis resilience demonstrate its value according to your assessment, which shows no existing environmental or social impacts. The evidence shows that SRI funds perform better than traditional funds during market declines, yet this evidence fails to show that these periods lead to better corporate performance in environmental protection and employee rights and business governance practices. The financial sustainability of SRI funds shows strong ties to crisis performance because it establishes their financial credibility and institutional trustworthiness, although it does not enhance their capacity to create positive effects.

The case study demonstrates that institutional stability together with portfolio resilience does not guarantee better sustainability results. The findings demonstrate that SRI funds operate as effective risk-reduction financial instruments during market crises but fail to produce measurable environmental and social progress.

Case Study 2: Impact Failure — The Abraaj Group

The Abraaj Group failure demonstrates that impact-driven investments will not succeed when investors trust sustainability claims. Abraaj, which once led the world in impact investing, managed more than USD 14 billion in assets through its investments in healthcare and infrastructure and renewable energy initiatives across developing countries. The investigation discovered multiple governance problems, which included both financial misconduct and the organization's failure to disclose its actual environmental impacts.

The Abraaj case shows that insufficient regulatory control together with insufficient company transparency and weak enforcement of regulations enable legitimate operation between companies to replace actual performance assessment. The firm succeeded in securing funding through its advertising of social and environmental goals because the organization lacked proper methods to track progress. Financial resources advanced their path but failed to deliver any environmental sustainability results. The case demonstrates that ethical behavior together with reputation protection does not produce actual results according to the SRI Performance–Impact Paradox.

Table 2. Key Aspects of SRI Funds for Sustainable Development

Category	Description	Examples/Applications	Challenges/barriers	Impacts
SRI Investment Screening	Investment selection based on ESG criteria	Renewable energy firms	Difficulty in standardizing screening criteria	Portfolio diversification impact, alignment with values
Institutional Sri funds	Pension funds and large institutional investors adopting SRI	Public pension funds ESG integration, University endowments	Fiduciary duty constraints, regulatory complexity	Scale of sustainable investment growth
SRI Index Funds	Passive investment vehicles tracking SRI indices	ESG-focused ETFs, sustainable index mutual funds	Cost considerations, index methodology debates l	Lower-cost access to sustainable investing
Shareholder Engagement	Active ownership and voting rights exercise	Shareholder resolutions, corporate dialogue	Limited evidence of behavior change	Corporate governance influence
ESG Integration	Incorporating ESG factors into investment analysis	ESG ratings, sustainability metrics	Data gaps, lack of standardization	Mainstreaming of sustainable investing practices
Impact Measurement	Assessment of social and environmental outcomes	Social impact metrics, environmental key performance indicators	Difficulty in quantifying impact	Accountability and performance tracking

Table 2 demonstrates that SRI funds use multiple operational methods, which include ESG screening, institutional adoption, and shareholder engagement, but all three methods face implementation challenges that decrease their effectiveness. The table demonstrates that SRI strategies face three main operational obstacles, which include data deficiencies and standardization problems and insufficient proof of contact outcomes. The financial growth of SRI funds depends on these restrictions, which produce inconsistent results for their sustainability performance.

Table 3. Challenges, Opportunities, and Solutions in SRI Investments

Category	Challenges	Opportunities	Proposed solutions
Regulatory frameworks	Inconsistent ESG reporting requirements across regions; Varying fiduciary duty interpretations	Growing regulatory support for ESG integration; Standardization initiatives	Develop uniform global ESG reporting standards and clear guidelines on fiduciary responsibility
Financial Performance	Perception of lower returns; Portfolio diversification constraints	Growing evidence of competitive returns; New SRI investment products	Enhanced research on SRI performance; Development of sophisticated screening tools
Data and Metrics	Limited ESG data quality; Inconsistent measurement methodologies	Improved data analytics capabilities; Standardized ESG metrics	Implement universal ESG measurement frameworks; Enhance data verification systems
Investment Screening	Complex screening criteria; Difficulty in measuring social impact	Growing demand for values-based investing; Better screening technologies	Develop standardized screening methodologies; Create impact measurement frameworks
Institutional Adoption	Fiduciary duty concerns; Implementation costs	Rising institutional interest; Pressure from stakeholders	Create institutional-grade SRI products; Develop clear implementation guidelines
Market Integration	Limited market depth; Lack of specialized expertise	Expanding SRI market opportunities; Growing professional expertise	Enhance market infrastructure; Develop professional certification programs

Table 3 shows that three major obstacles need to be resolved before organizations can effectively implement sustainable and responsible investment practices. The market contains possibilities for growth and innovative solutions but lacks standardized regulations that would establish accountability through enforcement mechanisms. The table shows that institutional and regulatory changes need to take place before organizations can solve the SRI Performance-Impact Paradox that exists between their current two SRI products.

Future Trends in Sustainable Investments

Future developments in sustainable investments will become subject to three main factors, which include regulatory consolidation, technological innovation, and changing investor expectations. The ongoing growth of ESG-linked financial instruments, which include green bonds and sustainability-linked loans and climate-focused ETFs and impact-oriented funds, demonstrates that sustainable finance has become a permanent part of international capital markets. The expansion of SRI financial instruments creates stronger financial legitimacy for SRI, but it remains uncertain whether these developments will produce actual environmental and social improvements.

The upcoming stage of SRI development will depend on regulatory harmonization as its main driving force. The existing initiatives that aim to create standardized ESG disclosure systems and connect reporting requirements with international sustainability standards and enhance taxonomy classification systems will decrease existing jurisdictional fragmentation. The success of these reforms will depend on regulatory systems establishing enforceable outcome-based accountability systems that extend beyond basic disclosure compliance.

Artificial intelligence, big data analytics, and real-time ESG monitoring tools create technological progress that enhances sustainability information quality, comparability, and accessibility. The new technologies that protect investors' information will create equal access to data while making investment choices more transparent. Technology exists as an asset that supports governance reform efforts rather than providing a complete solution. Advanced data capabilities need to become part of strong shareholder engagement methods and regulatory enforcement practices because they will not bring about real corporate change by themselves.

The growth of sustainable investment will be influenced by developing markets throughout the world. The ESG principles, which now operate as fundamental components of worldwide capital markets, will require developing countries to establish their institutional frameworks and regulatory systems before they can achieve sustainable responsible investment (SRI) benefits, which extend beyond basic portfolio tracking.

Figure 3 shows that three main forces drive future development of socially responsible investing (SRI), which include stronger regulations, better technological progress, and more available environmental, social, and governance (ESG) financial products.

Figure 3. Future Trends in SRI Funds

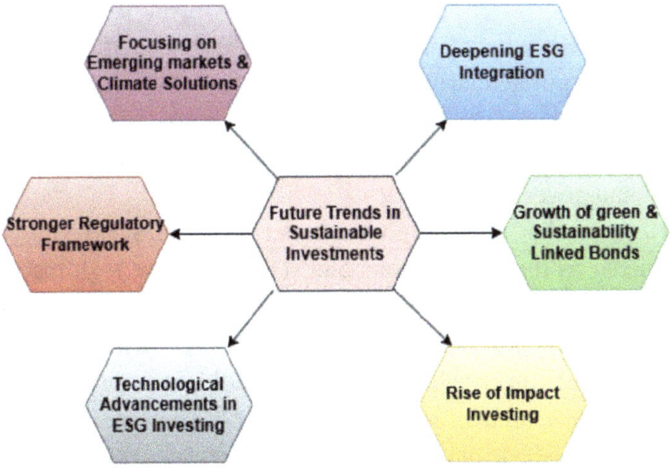

(Author's own creation using App Diagram Net)

The figure shows that sustainable investment growth does not provide a solution to the SRI performance-impact paradox. The existing gap requires a shift from input-based ESG integration to systems that validate results through testing and to systems that need strict monitoring and to systems that use active involvement as their primary investment approach. The long-term credibility of SRI will therefore depend not only on capital expansion but also on its capacity to generate demonstrable environmental and social progress.

Technology as a Supporting Mechanism in the SRI Performance–Impact Paradox

Emerging technologies, which include artificial intelligence and big data analytics, will improve ESG data quality and decrease information asymmetry, which will make it harder for organizations to practice greenwashing. The SRI Performance–Impact Paradox requires more solutions than what technology can provide. The improved data systems will only create legitimacy through disclosure processes without generating actual environmental and social impacts until standardized impact metrics and regulatory enforcement and active shareholder engagement develop. Technology serves as a mechanism that supports institutional accountability because it does not replace institutional accountability.

Comparative Analysis of ESG Disclosure Frameworks

Environmental, Social, and Governance (ESG) disclosure frameworks are an essential part of corporate clarity and sustainability. The comparative analysis of the two frameworks shows that there are different approaches and theoretical bases that guide companies in their reporting on environmental sustainability, social responsibilities, and governance.

The first one is that many theories underpin the ESG disclosure, with the stakeholder theory as the most famous one. The others are legitimacy, institutional, agency, and signaling theories. Such theories tend to converge into composite theories, which provide new insight on ESG disclosure, including, amongst others, cognitions within the upper echelons and stakeholder importance (Del Gesso & Lodhi, 2025). Such theoretical variety highlights the complexity and multiplicity of motives to make ESG disclosures.

The role of ESG disclosure in the performance of corporate sustainability demonstrated in different studies is considerable. Economic, environmental, and social sustainability performance is better with ESG disclosures, especially in association with sound corporate governance institutions. Such a positive correlation is stressed using shared value and stakeholder theories, which propose that the comprehensive ESG disclosure introduces a competitive advantage and leads to the development of long-term value (Alsayegh et al., 2020).

One systematic review done in the SCM settings identifies some of the driving forces behind the practice of ESG disclosure. The specified beliefs, behaviors, and results imply the need for firms to invest considerable effort in developing SCM-linked ESG programs. This holistic framework reveals certain practices and performances related to ESG disclosure, and even though there is more and deeper research that can be done, it offers a map to be navigated in research that is studied within SCM (Yan et al., 2024).

Moreover, such universal frameworks as Refinitiv and industry-specific ESG indicators contribute to the better comprehension of ESG performance, especially in the context of emerging economies, such as Indonesia. In this case, cluster analyses show that sectors are more or less transparent with strengths and weaknesses, and the global measures must require the ESG reporting (Saraswati et al., 2024).

ESG disclosures are tied to investor involvement and corporate governance. Firms that adopt a fully fledged ESG approach increase their Sustainability Performance Transformation Index (SPTI), implying that disclosures perform better when combined with effective management practices and shareholder engagement (Ray & Hardi, 2024).

Religion and social traditions also play an important role in determining the ESG disclosure. According to the empirical finding, there is a U-shaped relationship between religiosity and ESG disclosure, which indicates that the corporate non-financial disclosures are highly influenced by the religious environment, observed through the perspective of social norms (Terzani & Turzo, 2021).

Both the issue of financial performance and that of ESG disclosure are interesting to note as well. They also find that the ESG disclosure is linked positively to the financial and market performance, particularly that ESG integration can increase the overall financial health of companies, although it depends on regions and industries (Sharma et al., 2020).

On the whole, disclosure frameworks of ESG and theories that they are based on are becoming extremely influential in increasingly thrusting transparency and sustainability on companies. Indications are that the ESG reporting practices can not only enhance corporate governance and competitive strength but also play a major role in the long-term economic and social objectives. Reflective reports and sound models are still under development, helping companies around the world improve their ESG outcomes in various markets and conditions.

Companies share information on their ESG activities quite diversely, though three frameworks are most commonly applied globally.

They are

Global Reporting Initiative (GRI)
Sustainability Accounting Standards Board (SASB)
Task Force on Climate-related Financial Disclosures (TCFD)

Each one has a different focus. GRI looks at overall sustainability. SASB focuses on what's financially important for investors, and TCFD deals mainly with climate-related financial risks. The table below gives a comparative overview of these three ESG disclosure frameworks.

Table 4. Comparative Overview of Major ESG Disclosure Frameworks (GRI, SASB, and TCFD)

Frame Work	Focus Area	Target audience	Key Components	Strengths	Challenges
GRI(Global Reporting Initiative)	Environmental, Social, Economic (Triple Bottom Line: people, Planet, & Profit)	All stakeholders (investors, regulators, civil society)	Universal standards, sector-wide sustainability disclosures	Broad applicability, promotes transparency and accountability (Truant et al., 2017)	Variable quality and depth of reports may lead to confusion (Pizzi et al., 2024)
SASB (Sustainability Accounting Standards Board)	Industry-specific financial materiality	Investors	ESG metrics aligned with financial reporting, industry-specific standards	Enhances comparability, integrates ESG into financial disclosures, supports long-term value (Jebe, 2019)	Adoption varies across sectors; some industries face integration challenges (Busco et al., 2020)
TCFD (Task Force on Climate related Financial Disclosures	Climate-related financial risk and opportunity	Investors, regulators, financial institutions	Governance, strategy, risk management, metrics, and targets	Widely adopted, improves climate risk transparency in financial markets (Dye et al., 2021; Dilling et al., 2024)	Limited compliance; weak strategic alignment in certain sectors (e.g., air transport) (David & Giordano-Spring, 2022)

Table 4 shows how international ESG disclosure standards have developed into multiple distinct frameworks. GRI emphasizes broad stakeholder sustainability, SASB focuses on financially material information for investors, and TCFD concentrates on climate-related financial risk. The different goals of these organizations create difficulties for comparing their results because they permit organizations to choose which information they will disclose. The enhanced disclosure standards will boost financial trustworthiness yet will not lead to actual improvements in environmental and social performance, according to the SRI Performance-Impact Paradox.

Case Study 3: ESG Controversy and Greenwashing — Tesla Inc.

Tesla has gained recognition as an environmentally innovative company because it leads the electric vehicle market. The company needs to be evaluated through multiple sustainability standards because it does not qualify for major environmental, social, and governance indices. Tesla demonstrates excellent environmental innovation capabilities, but its overall ESG performance suffers because of its labor practices and governance systems and supply chain disclosure shortcomings.

The case demonstrates that companies will hide their social and governance deficiencies when they focus only on showing their environmental performance. Investors who focused on environmental, social, and governance matters were first attracted to the company because of its strong disclosure practices and its positive market image, but they later became disappointed because the company had not yet solved its governance and labor problems. Tesla participates in ESG activities to create a brand image of sustainability while the company fails to fulfill complete ESG requirements. The case shows that the SRI performance-impact paradox remains active because organizations achieve financial success while showing incomplete social and governance results.

Expansion of ESG-Driven Financial Products

The rapid growth of sustainable investing has led to a global expansion of environmental, social, and governance (ESG) investment products, reflected in the increasing number of ESG exchange-traded funds (ETFs) and the rising demand for sustainable and social investments in the mutual funds industry (Pacelli et al., 2023; Xu et al., 2024). As ESG investment gains prominence among ethical and sustainable investors, particularly salaried employees seeking socially responsible asset preservation and expansion, the financial landscape continues to evolve (Misra et al., 2024). While ESG adoption is becoming more sophisticated in large and developed economies, developing markets are gradually improving their non-financial information disclosure practices. In the Baltic countries, for instance, around 81% of financial market players incorporate ESG data in investment evaluations, assigning an average weight of 0.39 to sustainability factors, a trend largely driven by regulatory influences, especially among private equity and venture funds managing local and international public funding (Zumente & Bistrova, 2021). Ultimately, the expansion of ESG-driven financial products is a global phenomenon shaped by investor demand, regulatory pressures, and the strategic recognition of ESG principles in financial decision-making. As concepts such as green investing, the circular economy, and RE100 gain traction, continued growth and innovation in ESG-driven financial products can be expected (Senadheera et al., 2022).

Global Growth of Green Bonds and Impact Investing

Green bonds are mushrooming due to a paradigm shift of investors towards the protection of the environment to have sustainable and balanced economic growth. The companies aiming for such growth have shifted their focus to greener environments to promote greener financing options. The advent of green bonds by the European Investment Bank in the year 2007 has significantly motivated other countries, thus showing a greater growth in SRI funds. China has witnessed a commendable growth in such funds since 2016. (Chen & Zhao, 2021) have written regarding the need for reporting standards for improving the ethical and legal constraints required for the success of green bonds. Research on these bonds has raised an alarming concern about firms adopting ESG as their goal but sometimes unknowingly contributing to CO_2 emissions (Sethi et al., 2024). Their prime concern was on the companies operating in developing countries, which cannot give their hundred percent to the attainment of environmental goals.

Advancing SRI Practices in Emerging Markets

(Yen et al., 2019) have published an article highlighting the opportunities and challenges caused by a paradigm shift in investments toward green bonds in the developing markets. Asian markets witness a huge change in terms of SRI portfolios outperforming the conventional portfolios. The governments in these countries should realize the need for rewarding the industries promoting ESG and sustainable growth. According to (Zou et al., 2020), companies operating in emerging markets of Brazil, China, and South Africa that have adopted the SRI funds have been performing abnormally in the stock market, thus contributing to economic growth. (Lestari & Frömmel, 2024) have identified an opposite trend in the performance of equity funds operational in developing countries in comparison to developed countries. SRI funds in wealthier nations follow more ethical guidelines in comparison to developing nations.

Policy and Regulatory Roadmap for Strengthening SRI

To strengthen Sustainable and Responsible Investment (SRI) through policy and regulatory frameworks, several critical aspects and proposals have emerged from the literature.

The development of ESG standards suggests there is an opportunity to identify and unify globally through international/global frameworks and global commitments, such as the Sustainable Development Goals (SDGs) and the Paris climate agreement/accord. The U.S. Securities and Exchange Commission (SEC) ESG disclosure regulations and the European Commission's Sustainable Finance Disclosure Regulation are examples of regulatory measures now being implemented to improve the efficiency of ESG reporting and eliminate greenwashing. However, inconsistent reporting standards for ESG remain an obstacle to developing broader acceptance of ESG standards. Therefore, there is strong interest in the global harmonization of standards for ESG to improve transparency and build investor confidence (Sinha, 2025).

As socially responsible investing (SRI) combines economic prosperity with sustainable advancement, it's essential that unlimited access to diversification provided by SRI doesn't come at the expense of investing, particularly between developed & developing nations. The creation of guides for both socially responsible index investing and 'conventional'/traditional investing could provide a suitable pathway for maintaining this harmony. Additionally, both types of instruments could deliver positive social outcomes while producing good returns to investors in situations of economic distress (Tripathi & Kaur, 2022).

One major strategy for making responsible investing easier for first-time responsible investors is to help them lower their costs of information by using sustainability or transparency labels. By having certification that demonstrates adherence to sustainability standards, these labels can assist an investor as they attempt to overcome barriers, such as lack of trust in the provider of a socially responsible investment product (Gutsche & Zwergel, 2020).

As companies implement their social responsibility practices into the normal course of business, SRI strategies will increase the importance of Environmental, Social, and Governance (ESG) integration through the broad scope of both conventional (micro) and macro SRI strategies. Successful ESG integration into both micro SRI strategies will play an integral role in the transition to a more sustainable financial system (Sciarelli et al., 2021).

A successful transition to green energy will depend on sustained collaboration between stakeholders to also support sustainable finance mechanisms, such as green bonds and investment vehicles. In order to mobilize capital for sustainable projects, there must be significant regulatory support and regulatory certainty through the establishment of standardised ESG criteria (Ikevuje et al., 2024).

Finally, regulatory mandates that enhance transparency and encourage stakeholder involvement are essential for creating a well-developed SRI landscape, especially in widely varied geographic areas such as Asia and Africa. These geographic areas demonstrate that for global sustainable finance initiatives to become a reality, it is critical to have defined regulations in place and that financial institutions significantly increase the integration of sustainability within their operations (Muhammad et al., 2023). To close the SRI Performance–Impact Paradox shown in Figure 1, it is necessary to strengthen the harmonization of regulations, establish ESG disclosure standards, and develop stronger governance systems.

To address the SRI Performance–Impact Paradox, SRI regulatory enforcement mechanisms must become more robust; ESG disclosure standards must be harmonized; and SRI shareholder engagement requirements must be enhanced. To do this, SRI regulatory institutions need to move from an emphasis on meeting disclosures toward achieving sustainable outcomes. More robust enforcement mechanisms, standardized reporting frameworks, and greater accountabilities on the part of SRI institutions will ensure that SRI capital provides for real environmental and social change, rather than serving as a symbolic mark of compliance.

Theoretical Implications and Directions for Future Research

The paradox of SRI performance versus impact that is part of the topic addressed in this chapter adds a new component to the study of sustainable finance because of the way that the results are evaluated. Researchers will need to evaluate their results in terms of the effects rather than to verify the financial aspects only. In addition, the results also demonstrate that evaluating the financial legitimacy of an investment does not provide evidence of the effectiveness of the investment regarding sustainability; however, the majority of prior studies have examined the financial performance based on how well the investments perform after adjusting for risk and how resilient their portfolios are to market volatility.

The use of the paradox framework provides a new way to understand why the systems that allocate capital have been unsuccessful in creating environmental and social improvements by giving further attention to determining what the causal pathways are, through additional studies. Research on how the relative importance of each stakeholder impacts SRI methods through engagement-based practices will be a major focus of future studies. This chapter shows that legitimacy pressures function differently depending on the institutional context, and as a result, cross-national comparisons should be conducted to assess if countries with greater levels of regulatory requirements also have reduced levels of symbolic compliance. The field of behavioral finance allows researchers to test the extent to which investors motivated by moral values require greater reporting of impact to be demonstrated by companies over time.

One of the valuable research opportunities lies in developing standardized impact measurement methodologies. The inability to develop standard ESG metrics presents barriers to testing real-world outcomes empirically. Future research should look at whether the level of interaction with companies is demonstrating an improvement in environmental and social performance when compared to passive screening methods.

Emerging market countries represent an important area of research that requires study. Various jurisdictions show differing levels of institutional quality and enforcement capacity as well as differing levels of disclosure standards, which can have an effect on performance outcomes. Through comparative institutional analysis, researchers will be able to determine the circumstances under which SRI capital creates transformational performance instead of merely providing symbolic performance. The development of sustainable finance needs to progress from its current state because organizations need to adopt outcome-based accountability systems instead of their existing input-based ESG integration methods. Future scholarship should prioritize measurable impact indicators, engagement intensity metrics, and regulatory enforcement effectiveness to empirically validate or refine the SRI Performance–Impact Paradox framework.

CONCLUSION

This chapter details the financial legitimacy of socially responsible investment (SRI) funds by showing they are able to deliver competitive financial returns but not consistently deliver on their stated goals and objectives in terms of producing sustainable environmental and social performance. The authors establish what they have termed the SRI Performance-Impact Paradox, which stipulates that both ESG integration and capital reallocation will contribute positively toward financial performance; however, they will not systematically lead to an increase in sustainability performance. The text suggests that disjointed ESG metrics, ineffective interactions between shareholders and corporate management, and token regulatory compliance controls contribute to the impediment of capital investment in making fundamental changes in the behaviors of corporations. The chapter incorporates stakeholder theory, legitimacy theory, and behavioral finance to illustrate how institutional-level incentives, investor preference, and regulatory frameworks affect both financial performance and sustainability results.

Results suggest the following methods for reconciling the paradox: improved enforcement of regulations; standardised systems of ESG measurement; timely, accurate, and complete disclosure of relevant information from issuers; and ownership engagement. To address sustainability regulatory issues, regulators must move to a model of sustainability regulation based on outcomes. Investors who use engagement-based approaches to SRI must do so without regard to financial return. The chapter's primary contribution to the field is that it presents an integrated analytical framework that illustrates the interaction of financial performance with sustainability impacts when applied to SRI systems. The success of SRI in the future will depend on two factors: (1) growth of SRI in the financial sector and (2) how SRI converts investment capital into realised environmental and social progress.

REFERENCES

Alsayegh, M. F., Abdul Rahman, R., & Homayoun, S. (2020). Corporate economic, environmental, and social sustainability performance transformation through ESG disclosure. *Sustainability (Basel)*, *12*(9), 3910. DOI: 10.3390/su12093910

Arefeen, S., & Shimada, K. (2020). Performance and resilience of socially responsible investing (SRI) and conventional funds during different shocks in 2016: Evidence from Japan. *Sustainability (Basel)*, *12*(2), 540. DOI: 10.3390/su12020540

Beisenbina, M., Fabregat-Aibar, L., Barberà-Mariné, M.-G., & Sorrosal-Forradellas, M.-T. (2022). The burgeoning field of sustainable investment: Past, present and future. *Sustainable Development*. Advance online publication. DOI: 10.1002/sd.2422

Beloskar, V. D., Haldar, A., & Rao, S. V. D. N. (2023). Socially responsible investments: A retrospective review and future research agenda. *Business Strategy and the Environment*, *32*(7), 4841–4860. DOI: 10.1002/bse.3396

Brahmi, M., Esposito, L., Parziale, A., Dhayal, K. S., Agrawal, S., Giri, A. K., & Loan, N. T. (2023). The role of greener innovations in promoting financial inclusion to achieve carbon neutrality: An integrative review. *Economies*, *11*(7), 194. DOI: 10.3390/economies11070194

Busco, C., Consolandi, C., Eccles, R. G., & Sofra, E. (2020). A preliminary analysis of SASB reporting: Disclosure topics, financial relevance, and the financial intensity of ESG materiality. *The Bank of America Journal of Applied Corporate Finance*, *32*(2), 117–125. DOI: 10.1111/jacf.12411

Camilleri, M. A. (2021). The market for socially responsible investing: A review of the developments. *Social Responsibility Journal*, *17*(3), 412–428. DOI: 10.1108/SRJ-06-2019-0194

Chen, X., & Scholtens, B. (2018). The urge to act: A comparison of active and passive socially responsible investment funds in the United States. *Corporate Social Responsibility and Environmental Management*, *25*(6), 1154–1173. DOI: 10.1002/csr.1529

Chen, Y., & Zhao, Z. J. (2021). The rise of green bonds for sustainable finance: Global standards and issues with the expanding Chinese market. *Current Opinion in Environmental Sustainability*, *52*, 54–57. DOI: 10.1016/j.cosust.2021.06.013

Cosma, S., Cucurachi, P., Gentile, V., & Rimo, G. (2024). Sustainable finance disclosure regulation insights: Unveiling socially responsible funds performance during COVID-19 pandemic and Russia–Ukraine war. *Business Strategy and the Environment*, *33*(4), 3242–3257. DOI: 10.1002/bse.3650

Crifo, P., & Forget, V. D. (2013). Think global, invest responsible: Why the private equity industry goes green. *Journal of Business Ethics*, *116*(1), 21–48. DOI: 10.1007/s10551-012-1443-y

D'Apice, V., Ferri, G., & Intonti, M. (2021). Sustainable disclosure versus ESG intensity: Is there a cross effect between holding and SRI funds? *Corporate Social Responsibility and Environmental Management*, *28*(5), 1496–1510. DOI: 10.1002/csr.2178

David, B., & Giordano-Spring, S. (2022). Climate reporting related to the TCFD framework: An exploration of the air transport sector. *Social and Environmental Accountability Journal*, *42*(1–2), 18–37. DOI: 10.1080/0969160X.2021.2007784

Del Gesso, C., & Lodhi, R. N. (2025). Theories underlying environmental, social and governance (ESG) disclosure: A systematic review of accounting studies. *Journal of Accounting Literature*, *47*(2), 433–461. DOI: 10.1108/JAL-08-2023-0143

Dilling, P. F. A., Harris, P., & Caykoylu, S. (2024). The impact of corporate characteristics on climate governance disclosure. *Sustainability (Basel)*, *16*(5), 1962. DOI: 10.3390/su16051962

Dye, J., Mckinnon, M., & Byl, C. (2021). Green Gaps: Firm ESG Disclosure and Financial Institutions' Reporting Requirements. *Journal of Sustainability Research*, *3*(1). Advance online publication. DOI: 10.20900/jsr20210006

Gupta, A., Sharma, U., & Gupta, S. K. (2021). The role of ESG in sustainable development: An analysis through the lens of machine learning. *2021 IEEE International Humanitarian Technology Conference (IHTC)*, 1–5. IEEE. http://doi.org/ DOI: 10.1109/IHTC53077.2021.9698939

Gutsche, G., & Zwergel, B. (2020). Investment barriers and labeling schemes for socially responsible investments. *Schmalenbach Business Review*, *72*(2), 111–157. DOI: 10.1007/s41464-020-00085-z

Heath, D., Macciocchi, D., Michaely, R., & Ringgenberg, C., M. (. (2023). Does socially responsible investing change firm behavior? *Review of Finance*, *27*(6), 2057–2083. DOI: 10.1093/rof/rfad002

Ikevuje, A. H., Anaba, D. C., & Iheanyichukwu, U. T. (2024). Exploring sustainable finance mechanisms for green energy transition: A comprehensive review and analysis. *Finance & Accounting Research Journal*, *6*(7), 1224–1247. DOI: 10.51594/farj.v6i7.1314

Ikwue, U., Ekwezia, A. V., Oguejiofor, B. B., Agho, M. O., & Daraojimba, C. (2023). Sustainable Investment strategies in Pension Fund Management: A comparative review of esg principles adoption in the u.S. And Nigeria. *International Journal of Management & Entrepreneurship Research*, *5*(9), 652–673. DOI: 10.51594/ijmer.v5i9.547

Jebe, R. (2019). The convergence of financial and ESG materiality: Taking sustainability mainstream. *American Business Law Journal*, *56*(3), 645–702. DOI: 10.1111/ablj.12148

Jones, S., van der Laan, S., Frost, G., & Loftus, J. (2008). The investment performance of socially responsible investment funds in Australia. *Journal of Business Ethics*, *80*(2), 181–203. DOI: 10.1007/s10551-007-9412-6

Lestari, J. S., & Frömmel, M. (2024). Socially responsible investments: Doing good while doing well in developed versus emerging markets? *Research in International Business and Finance*, *69*(102229), 102229. DOI: 10.1016/j.ribaf.2024.102229

Martini, A. (2021). Socially responsible investing: From the ethical origins to the sustainable development framework of the European Union. *Environment, Development and Sustainability*, *23*(11), 16874–16890. DOI: 10.1007/s10668-021-01375-3

Mill, G. A. (2006). The financial performance of a socially responsible investment over time and a possible link with corporate social responsibility. *Journal of Business Ethics*, *63*(2), 131–148. DOI: 10.1007/s10551-005-2410-7

Misra, A., Bohra, N. S., & Sharma, M. (2024). Impact of financial literacy towards ESG investing among salaried employees: A mediating effect of perceived usefulness of Robo-advisors. In *Advances in Logistics, Operations, and Management Science* (pp. 274–284). IGI Global. http://doi.org/DOI: 10.4018/979-8-3693-2849-1.ch018

Muhammad, A., Ibitomi, T., Durotimi Amos, D., Idris, M. B., & Ishaq, A. A. (2023). Comparative analysis of sustainable finance initiatives in Asia and Africa: A path towards global sustainability. *Global Sustainability Research*, *2*(3), 33–51. DOI: 10.56556/gssr.v2i3.559

Pacelli, V., Pampurini, F., & Quaranta, A. G. (2023). Environmental, Social and Governance investing: Does rating matter? *Business Strategy and the Environment*, *32*(1), 30–41. DOI: 10.1002/bse.3116

Palma-Ruiz, J. M., Castillo-Apraiz, J., & Gómez-Martínez, R. (2020). Socially responsible investing as a competitive strategy for trading companies in times of upheaval amid COVID-19: Evidence from Spain. *International Journal of Financial Studies*, *8*(3), 41. DOI: 10.3390/ijfs8030041

Paul, K. (2017). The effect of business cycle, market return and momentum on financial performance of socially responsible investing mutual funds. *Social Responsibility Journal*, *13*(3), 513–528. DOI: 10.1108/SRJ-09-2016-0154

Peng, H., Zhang, Z., Goodell, J. W., & Li, M. (2023). Socially responsible investing: Is it for real or just for show? *International Review of Financial Analysis*, *86*(102553), 102553. DOI: 10.1016/j.irfa.2023.102553

Pizzi, S., Caputo, F., & de Nuccio, E. (2024). Do sustainability reporting standards affect analysts' forecast accuracy? *Sustainability Accounting Management and Policy Journal*, *15*(2), 330–354. DOI: 10.1108/SAMPJ-04-2023-0227

Ray, S., & Hardi, I. (2024). Refining ESG disclosure's role in corporate economic, environmental, and social sustainability performance. *Indatu Journal of Management and Accounting*, *2*(1), 1–8. DOI: 10.60084/ijma.v2i1.144

Revelli, C. (2017). Socially responsible investing (SRI): From mainstream to margin? *Research in International Business and Finance*, *39*, 711–717. DOI: 10.1016/j.ribaf.2015.11.003

Roselle, P. (2016). The evolution of integrating ESG analysis into wealth management decisions. *The Bank of America Journal of Applied Corporate Finance*, *28*(2), 75–79. DOI: 10.1111/jacf.12178

Saraswati, E., Ghofar, A., Atmini, S., & Dewi, A. A. (2024). Clustering of companies based on sustainability performance using ESG materiality approach: Evidence from Indonesia. *International Journal of Energy Economics and Policy*, *14*(2), 112–125. DOI: 10.32479/ijeep.15393

Schröder, M. (2004). The performance of socially responsible investments: Investment funds and indices. *Financial Markets and Portfolio Management*, *18*(2), 122–142. DOI: 10.1007/s11408-004-0202-1

Sciarelli, M., Cosimato, S., Landi, G., & Iandolo, F. (2021). Socially responsible investment strategies for the transition towards sustainable development: The importance of integrating and communicating ESG. *The TQM Journal*, *33*(7), 39–56. DOI: 10.1108/TQM-08-2020-0180

Senadheera, S. S., Gregory, R., Rinklebe, J., Farrukh, M., Rhee, J. H., & Ok, Y. S. (2022). The development of research on environmental, social, and governance (ESG): A bibliometric analysis. *Sustainable Environment*, *8*(1), 2125869. Advance online publication. DOI: 10.1080/27658511.2022.2125869

Sethi, L., Behera, B., & Sethi, N. (2024). Do green finance, green technology innovation, and institutional quality help achieve environmental sustainability? Evidence from the developineconomies. *Sustainable Development (Bradford)*, *32*(3), 2709–2723. DOI: 10.1002/sd.2811

Sharma, P., Panday, P., & Dangwal, R. C. (2020). Determinants of environmental, social and corporate governance (ESG) disclosure: A study of Indian companies. *International Journal of Disclosure and Governance*, *17*(4), 208–217. DOI: 10.1057/s41310-020-00085-y

Sinha, M.Janki Devi Memorial College. (2025). Responsible capital: The evolution and performance of ESG investing. *Exploresearch*, *01*(03), 1–18. DOI: 10.62823/ExRe//01/03.10

Terzani, S., & Turzo, T. (2021). Religious social norms and corporate sustainability: The effect of religiosity on environmental, social, and governance disclosure. *Corporate Social Responsibility and Environmental Management*, *28*(1), 485–496. DOI: 10.1002/csr.2063

Tripathi, V., & Kaur, A. (2022). Does socially responsible investing pay in developing countries? A comparative study across select developed and developing markets. *FIIB Business Review*, *11*(2), 189–205. DOI: 10.1177/2319714520980288

Truant, E., Corazza, L., & Scagnelli, S. D. (2017). Sustainability & risk disclosure: An exploratory study on sustainability reports. In *Preprints*. https://doi.org/DOI: 10.20944/preprints201704.0021.v1

Vishali, M., & Shafi, M. K. M. (2024). Emerging paradigms in socially responsible investment (SRI)—A study with focus on ESG mutual funds in India. *Environment and Social Psychology*, *9*(4). Advance online publication. DOI: 10.54517/esp.v9i4.2006

Wu, J., Lodorfos, G., Dean, A., & Gioulmpaxiotis, G. (2017). The market performance of socially responsible investment during periods of the economic cycle – illustrated using the case of FTSE: Investment performance of SRI in an economic cycle. *MDE. Managerial and Decision Economics*, *38*(2), 238–251. DOI: 10.1002/mde.2772

Xu, D., Corbet, S., Lang, C., & Hu, Y. (2024). Understanding dynamic return connectedness and portfolio strategies among international sustainable exchange-traded funds. *Economic Modelling*, *141*(106864), 106864. DOI: 10.1016/j.econmod.2024.106864

Yan, F., Chen, L., & Jia, F. (2024). Environmental, social, and governance disclosure in supply chains: A systematic literature review. *Production Planning and Control*, ●●●, 1–22. DOI: 10.1080/09537287.2024.2434147

Yen, M.-F., Shiu, Y.-M., & Wang, C.-F. (2019). Socially responsible investment returns and news: Evidence from Asia. *Corporate Social Responsibility and Environmental Management*, *26*(6), 1565–1578. DOI: 10.1002/csr.1833

Zou, P., Wang, Q., Xie, J., & Zhou, C. (2020). Does doing good lead to doing better in emerging markets? Stock market responses to the SRI index announcements in Brazil, China, and South Africa. *Journal of the Academy of Marketing Science*, *48*(5), 966–986. DOI: 10.1007/s11747-019-00651-z

Zumente, I., & Bistrova, J. (2021). Do Baltic investors care about environmental, social and governance (ESG)? *Journal of Entrepreneurship and Sustainability Issues*, *8*(4), 349–362. DOI: 10.9770/jesi.2021.8.4(20)

Chapter 11
Institutional Factors and Green Economic Growth in China:
Traversing the Path of Sustainability

Rochna Arora
http://orcid.org/0000-0002-2399-2538
Amity University, Noida, India

Baljit Kaur
http://orcid.org/0000-0002-3606-8053
Guru Nanak Dev University, India

ABSTRACT

The work tries to investigate the role of institutions for achieving green economic growth for the Chinese economy by considering the period from 1996- 2021. Besides institutional factors, foreign direct investment, renewable energy consumption, and expenditure on research and development also are considered. The results from the Bounds test show a high degree of long-term relationship. The research investigates the overall impact of governance on green growth and the individual impact of each of the governance indicators. For institutional quality, a positive impact on green economic growth is observed. Within institutional quality it is seen that barring rule of law and control of corruption, all other variables show a positive impact on our dependent variable. With respect to Foreign direct investment it is seen that the impact is negative which means the Pollution haven hypothesis is upheld for Chinese economy. For renewable energy consumption and expenditure incurred on research and development the impact yet again is positive.

DOI: 10.4018/979-8-3373-8998-1.ch011

1 INTRODUCTION

The world is witnessing trailblazing revolutions in the form of artificial intelligence, the internet of things (IoT), and Blockchain technology, among many others but what remains old and still relevant is the environment within which the world is shaping their own growth trajectories. The environment, the emissions, the climate change still is placed at the central stage that attracts major attention. Among all the threats that the world faces, global warming and climate change still loom badly in the 21st century. Different intergovernmental agreements have shaped the global landscape but all with very little success. What inroads the success of these is the institutional and governance quality of the countries that are party to the movement. Within the institutions, there are legal, political, and economic factors that can help cut down the emissions of carbon dioxide (Sarkodie and Adams 2018). With a stringent institutional environment being put in place, the path to sustainability will be much easier and more gradual (Ibrahim and Law 2016). According to Greenidge *et al.,* (2016) political stability, corruption, rule of law are effective pillars of governance. A stringent institutional set up can provide double benefit firstly to the domestic economy and as well as generate a positive spillover to neighbouring country via a spatial effect. The earlier works have tried to assess the correlation between institutional quality and level of carbon emissions (Galinato and Galinato, 2012; Purcel, 2019; Cole, 2007; Chen *et al.,* 2018 and Hassan *et al.,*2020). The research hitherto has not talked about how institutional quality can affect green economic growth. The only paper to address the same was Tawiah et al (2021) wherein the authors tried to look at the major determinants of green growth for both developed as well as developing countries. As China looks to strike a balance between long-term development and environmental sustainability, green economic growth has emerged as a key governmental goal. The majority of research on China that has already been done looks at green growth through the prisms of sectoral transitions, energy structure, technical innovation, and environmental regulation. Institutions are frequently treated as background circumstances rather than as active drivers.

The contribution of the chapter is meaningful. This work is certainly an innovative contribution by studying the role of institutional quality for green economic growth. Majority or rather all the earlier works have investigated the causes of increased carbon emissions at large. Secondly, the present work is first to be based on Chinese economy while the same has been done for India, Romania (single country cases) and Organisation for Economic Co-operation and Development (OECD) and set of developed as well as developing countries. Lastly, we have adopted ARDL methodology which distinguishes between short run and long run effects unlike the other works that work on estimating only long run coefficients. This chapter's contribution is to empirically show how various aspects of institutional quality produce diverse knock-on consequences on China's green economic growth, differentiating between short-term fixes and long-term structural implications. The main contribution of this chapter is to demonstrate that institutional characteristics are important conduits via which environmental regulations result in green economic growth, rather than only contextual elements. In particular, it looks at how investment-related institutions, regulatory efficacy, and governance quality influence the immediate and long-term effects of environmental policy on China's sustainable growth. This puts the chapter ahead of the current literature on China, which usually assesses policy results without taking institutional variation into systematic consideration. Given this background, the two major research questions that the present study will attempt to answer are given below.

> **RQ1:** What is the relationship between institutional factors and green economic growth?
> **RQ2:** Do the separate institutional factors affect green growth promise uniformly or differently in China?

In order to situate the chapter's contribution within the current discussions on institutions and green growth, the following section expands on this approach by reviewing the body of existing literature.

2 REVIEW OF EARLIER WORKS

The idea of economic growth was postulated by Malthus (1798) who posited that the production depends on natural resources as well as environmental quality. Green economic growth was modelled in works of Smulders (1994) and Bovenberg and Smulders (1995, 1996). The green economic growth fosters development alongside sustainably using natural resources to not deprive future generations from experiencing the bounties of nature in its purest form. The concept of Green growth found its empirical testament with works of Lin and Benjamin (2017), Bagheri *et al.* (2018), Li *et al.,* (2018), Dai *et al.* (2016), Sohag *et al.* (2019), Wu *et al.* (2019) and Wang and Shao (2019). The factor that single handedly contributed towards helping the economy transit towards sustainable growth is renewable energy usage. The largest dependence for fuel is on coal but an attempt to switch to non-conventional sources of energy can aid in moving the economy up the ladder of green growth. The dependence on renewable energy has become the need of the hour for majority of reasons. Firstly, non-renewable energy generates implicit costs by lowering the global GDP by 25% (Stern, 2007). Second, with volatile political conditions especially now circling around Russia Ukraine war, oil imports involve price instability leading to another form of risk which can be overcome by increasing the reliance on renewable energy (Shahbaz et al., 2016). Since the dependence of renewable energy will increase, it will tend to cut down the non-eco-friendly sources of energy Zaman et al. (2016); Pahle et al. (2016); Dai et al. (2016); Sohag et al. (2019); Wu et al. (2019) and Sadiq et al. (2024).

The conceptual framework linking Institutions, Environmental Policy and Green Growth can be explained through the works of Gagliardi (2008); Abid (2017); Bhattacharya et al. (2017); Lee & ozturk (2020); Muhammad and long (2021). Because they influence the incentives and capacities that control how economies react to environmental concerns, institutions are a key factor in determining the emergence of the green economy. By coordinating market incentives with environmental goals, high-quality institutions allow for resource-efficient and environmentally sustainable economic growth. Weak institutions, on the other hand, frequently fail to separate sustainability from growth, allowing environmental deterioration to continue alongside economic progress. There exist multiple channels through which institutions exert a favourable influence on environment viz; Policy effectiveness wherein the effectiveness of environmental policies is decided by institutions. By ensuring consistent enforcement, lowering regulatory ambiguity, and improving compliance, strong institutional capacity enables environmental regulation to foster efficiency and innovation rather than just raise costs (Cole, (2007); Tamazian and Rao, 2010 and Sarkodie and Adams, 2018); technology diffusion through which institutions encourage research and development, speed up the use of clean technologies, and facilitate the diffusion of new technologies (Hosseini and Kaneko, (2013); Cao et al., 2021). Lastly through reallocating Investment and capital between polluting and green sectors. In order to promote green growth, transparent governance and reliable regulatory frameworks lower investment risk and draw long-term capital into energy efficiency, renewable energy, and green infrastructure (Arminen and Menegaki, (2019); Lau et al. 2014). Stricter institutional norms would make it difficult for firms and organisations to survive without addressing the environmental concerns and the result will be a transition toward sustainable growth Damania et al (2003); Welsch, (2004); Aisen and Veiga (2013); Lau et al., (2014); Slesman et al., (2015); ; Purcel, (2019); Tawiah et al. (2021); Muhammad and Long, (2021); Zhao et al (2022) and Behera et al., (2024). For voice and accountability, Manu et al.,2024; Liu et al., 2022; Liu, 2022 concluded that it is important for controlling the adverse impact on environment. For political stability, Behera et al (2024); Al Zubairi et al (2024); Abid (2017); Purcel (2019); Adebayo (2022); Ayhan (2023) and Han et al (2024) verified the positive impact of same on sustainable growth. Chen et al (2022) and Chin. et al. (2023) suggested how effective government can act to curtail the emissions intensity in the economy. Hasni (2023); Karim et al (2022);

Kwakwa (2024) suggested that regulatory quality, control of corruption and rule of law correct the adverse environmental impact.

With respect of impact of Foreign Direct Investment on environment two competing hypothesis exist: Pollution Haven Hypothesis and Pollution Halo Hypothesis. With regard to former FDI directs the pollution-intensive production activities into those countries where the environmental regulations are bit more relaxed leading to a detrimental impact on green growth prospects of the economy. Pollution-intensive FDI is drawn to nations with weak institutions and inadequate environmental regulations (Grossman and Krueger, 1991; Zhang and Zhou, 2016). The quality of institutions has a significant impact on the Pollution Haven Hypothesis' applicability. Pollution-intensive activities may continue even in the presence of official environmental restrictions due to a lack of effective governance, regulatory capture, and enforcement capacity. On the other hand, strong institutions make it more expensive for polluting companies to comply with regulations and make nations less desirable as havens for pollution (Lee, 2013; Kivyiro and Arminen, 2014; Lau *et al.,* 2014; Seker *et al.* 2015; Solarin *et al.* 2017). The Pollution Haven Hypothesis emphasizes that the ability of institutions to control and direct capital inflows is just as important to the results of green growth as capital inflows themselves (Sun *et al.*, 2017; Rana and Sharma, 2019; Caglar, 2020). On the other hand, FDI when comes from the developed countries actually benefit the host country by reducing their emissions resulting from green technology which is the product of the developed countries' sincere efforts in the direction of technological richness thereby upholding Pollution Halo hypothesis (Tang and Tan, 2015; Mert and Boluk 2016; Rafindadi et al. 2018).

Lastly, Research and development exerts influence on green growth as the investment in R and D will facilitate the country to develop alternatives to using better energy sources than those in existence (Zeng et al., (2013); Song et al (2019); Fang et al (2022); Lin and Zhou (2022); Mohsin et al (2022) and Kwilinski et al (2023)

3 DATABASE AND ECONOMETRIC MODEL SPECIFICATION

3.1 Database Description

This section explains the data, variables, and empirical technique used to investigate the institutional determinants of green economic growth in China, guided by the conceptual framework previously mentioned. The present chapter investigates the major factors of green economic growth for chinese economy. For this, secondary data have been extracted from major international sources for a period starting from 1996-2021. The rationale for starting and terminal points of the study have been dictated majorly by the availability of data especially with respect to Worldwide

Governance Indicators (WGI) by Kaufmann and Kraay (2018). Since the data for Institutional quality starts from 1996 and hence all the variables are taken from that year. Table 1 provides the data specifications.

Table 1. List of variables and data source

Variables	Symbol
Dependent Variable Green economic growth[1]	GG
Independent variable • Index of Governance A composite index of the six Worldwide Governance Indicators[2] 1. Voice and Accountability (VA) 2. Political Stability and Absence of Violence/Terrorism (PS) 3. Government Effectiveness (GE) 4. Regulatory Quality (RQ) 5. Rule of Law (RL) 6. Control of Corruption (CC)	INDX
• Research and development expenditure (% of GDP)	RD
• Foreign direct investment, net inflows (% of GDP)	FDI
• Renewable energy consumption (% of total final energy consumption)	REN

Source: World Development Indicators

Natural logarithms are used, barring only index variable which is constructed using Principal Component Analysis (PCA) (Refer to appendix).

3.2 Model Specification

The literature reviewed provides the foundations that provides the basic regression model which takes the following form:

GG = f (INDX, RD, FDI, REN)

All the variables used in the analysis are converted into natural logarithmic (barring index) to address the issue of heteroscedasticity, multicollinearity and volatility which tend to crop up especially when dealing with an annual time series data. This logarithmic transformation helps to improve the fitness of the regression model (Murray, 2021). The empirical representation of the model:

MODEL 1 (M1): $GG = \alpha + \beta 1FDI_t + \beta 2REN + \beta 3RD_t + \beta 4INDX + \mu_t$

The α represents the intercept term while the different beta coefficients of $\beta 1$,$\beta 2, \beta 3$ *and*$\beta 4$ are all slope coefficient of different explanatory variables and μ_t is residual term which is normally distributed, and t is the time which in present case is (1996–2021).

Since the institutional quality indicator comprises of 6 variables as delineated above, so an attempt is made alongside to examine the impact of each of these governance variables on green economic growth. The inclusion of each of these explanatory variables separately into our regression model will take the forms as expressed in the appendix (A2) (Model 2 to model 7).

3.3 Methodological Procedure

The analysis is based on the infamous ARDL modelling as developed by Pesaran et al. (2001). In the presence of serial correlation found between the error terms and also with the variables attaining stationarity at I (0) or I (1), the ARDL model seems to be the best fit. It enables to also ascertain the long run relationship, which in economic terms is called cointegration (Nkoro and Uko, 2016). Because we attempt to estimate long run as well as sort run impact instead of only long run impact, the study considers the popular ARDL model proposed by Pesaran et al. (2001). The separation of effect into long run and short run makes sense only if the variables show long run relationship. In the absence of long run relationship or cointegration the results would be spurious. To establish meaningful long run results, Pesaran et al. (2001) proposed bounds F-test and Error Correction Model (ECM) test which developed critical values for these tests. Significance of any of these tests would confirm the presence of cointegration. Having established cointegration the ARDL results then separate out the long run and short run effects. The short run effects are depicted by ECM estimates.

But before commencing with the application of ARDL testing, a major litmus test of stationarity needs to be carried out. For the application of ARDL, it needs to be ensured that none of our variable is integrated of order 2. In the event of stationarity being achieved at second order, ARDL cannot be applied.

4 RESULTS AND DISCUSSION

Table 2 reports the results of unit root tests. From the results it is seen that our variables display a mixed order of integration. The variables of green economic growth, index of governance, renewable energy consumption and regulatory quality are stationary at level. All other variables are stationery after first difference. Hence our data meets the basic requirement of adopting ARDL because none of our variable is integrated of second order i.e., I (2).

Table 2. Unit root tests with breaks

	At level		At First Difference		Conclusion
	t-Statistics	Break Point	Statistics	Break Point	
GG	-6.743***	2004			I(0)
INDX	-5.39***	2016			I(0)
RD	-3.580	2019	-5.349***	2000	I(1)
FDI	-3.552	2014	-6.09***	2009	I(1)
REN	-5.449***	2002			I(0)
VA	-3.22	2005	-7.07***	2009	I(1)
PS	-3.226	2016	-6.68***	2003	I(1)
GE	-3.56	2013	-5.2655***	2014	I(1)
RQ	-4.22*	2002			I(0)
RL	-2.09	2013	-4.70**	2008	I(1)
CC	-2.71	2019	-6.71***	2002	I(1)

***,**,* imply 1 percent, 5 percent and 10 percent level of significance NR= Not Required

The long run relationship is tested under each of the model. The results for bounds test are presented in the following table i.e., Table 3.

Table 3. ARDL bounds test

Test Statistic	M1	M2	M3	M4	M5	M6	M7
F statistic	13.22***	13.90***	96.38***	105.69***	87.11***	4.27	104.73***
Lag length	(2, 0, 2, 2, 2)	(2, 2, 0, 2, 2)	(1, 0, 1, 0, 0)	(1, 0, 1, 0, 0)	(1, 2, 2, 2, 2)	(2, 2, 0, 2, 1)	(1, 0, 1, 0, 0)
Result	Present	Present	Present	Present	Present	Inconclusive	Present
Critical bounds	10%	5%	2.5%	1%			
I (0)	2.2	2.56	2.88	3.29			
I (1)	3.09	3.49	3.87	4.37			

Source: Calculated by authors. *** signify 1 percent level of significance.

Under each of the models it is seen that the f statistics is above the upper critical bound. In each of these cases we can reject the null hypothesis of no cointegration. It is only in case of Model 6 in which the estimated F statistics is 4.27 which lies between the lower and upper bound. Hence in this case we cannot conclude anything about long run relationship.

Table 4. Long run results from ARDL

VAR	M1	M2	M3	M4	M5	M6[3]	M7
FDI	-0.08** 0.03	-0.58*** 0.04	0.02 0.15	-0.07 0.10	-0.25*** 0.06	-0.96** 0.31	-0.11 0.24
REN	-0.37 0.05	0.32*** 0.08	0.76*** 0.20	0.56*** 0.16	0.88*** 0.11	0.10 0.34	0.51 0.43
RD	0.93*** 0.05	-0.98 0.07	-0.71 0.20	-0.61 0.14	-0.34 0.10	-1.04 0.27	-0.68 0.37
INDX	0.07*** 0.00	-	-	-	-	-	-
VA	-	0.17** 0.07	-	-	-	-	-
PS	-	-	0.80* 0.45	-	-	-	-
GE	-	-	-	0.83** 0.31	-	-	-
RQ	-	-	-	-	1.14*** 0.20	-	-
RL	-	-	-	-	-	-1.89 1.20	-
CC	-	-	-	-	-	-	-1.70 1.59
Constant	30.49*** 0.20	32.80*** 0.30	31.49***0.69	30.97***0.58	30.08***0.43	34.30***1.78	33.51***2.20

***,**,* imply 1 percent, 5 percent and 10 percent level of significance

Moving from establishing long run relationship, we now proceed to distinguish between long run effects[4] and the short run effects of variables on green economic growth. The long run effects of each of the models is presented in the table 4.

With respect to the overall index of governance, it is seen that better quality of institutions further improve the green growth prospects of the economy (Ganaie et al (2024), Jaishree and Tejwani (2024) and Mehmood et al, (2021). The results hold true in both long as well as short run. Salman et al. (2019) also stated how a well-established institutional set up tends to reduce carbon emissions together with economic activities. Abid (2017) studied individual components of governance index and concluded that only regulatory quality and the rule of law promote sustainability. Muhammad and long (2021) found that political stability, corruption control and rule of law can reduce carbon emissions and thereby improve environment quality.

With overall impact of index being positive, it is even more interesting to separate the individual impact of each of the constituted variables. With respect to Voice and Accountability, it is seen that the impact is yet again positive but only in the long run. The short run impact of voice and accountability is though positive but insignificant. One percent improvement in voice and accountability will promote economic growth by 0.17 points keeping other factors constant. As more stakeholders take part in decision-making, increased voice and accountability may sometimes lead to more debate, contestation, and policy uncertainty. Measurable growth effects may be momentarily diluted by these adjustment expenses. The advantages of increased accountability, such decreased corruption and better service delivery, are limited in their potential to grow right away since they require institutional learning and enforcement power (Manu et al.,2024; Liu et al., 2022; Liu, 2022)

With respect to political stability yet again the impact is positive and significant but only in the long run; the point estimate being 0.80. it means that a percent improvement of political stability in the country will better the chances of green economic growth in the Chinese economy. Since many green investments—like clean technology adoption, renewable energy infrastructure, or long-term environmental projects—require long-horizon capital commitments, political stability fosters a predictable and consistent legislative climate, which is crucial for green growth. If investors anticipate stable policy regimes that won't change suddenly owing to political unrest or changes in governmental direction, they are more willing to invest in projects with long payoff periods. Long-term green economic growth is positively impacted by this dynamic since it encourages consistent investment in green industries (Qamruzzaman and Karim, 2024). Over time, complicated environmental legislation, and enforcement procedures can be more effectively implemented under stable political contexts (Socol et al.,2025).

Similarly, for government effectiveness as an indicator we again find that the impact is positive as well as significant in the long run with estimate being at 0.83. This implies that a percent improvement in government effectiveness will better the chances of green economic growth. How well public institutions create and carry out policies that accomplish their goals—including growth and environmental goals—is a measure of government performance. Successful governments are able to convert green growth ideas into practical initiatives. This ability helps incorporate environmental objectives into more comprehensive economic planning and enhances resource allocation toward sustainable sectors (Qi, 2024). Transparency, rule of law, and decreased corruption are all associated with increased government efficacy and boost investor trust. When investors, both local and foreign, have confidence that rules won't be badly enforced or quickly altered, they are more likely to invest in long-term green initiatives. Long-term green growth can be facilitated by this, as it can boost the spread of sustainable technologies and speed up innovation in green industries.

Lastly regulatory quality influences green economic growth positively both in the short run as well as long run. The long run estimate is 1.14 and the short run estimate is 0.09. This implies that a percent improvement in regulatory quality improves green economic growth by 1.14 percent in the long run and 0.09 percent in the short run respectively keeping other factors constant. The findings show that regulatory quality has a favorable and noteworthy impact on green economic growth over the long term, with the latter effect being noticeably stronger. Short-term gains in regulatory quality promote compliance and efficiency-boosting firm adjustments, which have modest growth implications, by clarifying policies and lowering ambiguity. However, over time, strong regulatory quality has a transformative effect by bolstering the legitimacy of policies, promoting sustained investment in clean technology, and enabling structural changes toward environmentally sustainable industries. The greater long-term elasticity can be explained by these cumulative effects, which emphasize the importance of regulatory quality as a crucial institutional factor in long-term green economic growth (Costantiello & Leogrande (2024) and Dechezleprêtre & Sato (2017).

For Rule of Law and control of corruption it is seen that the impact is insignificant in the long run. Environmental courts, pollution fines, and sectoral standards are examples of environmental-specific legal enforcement that may not be reflected in indicators of the rule of law, which measure general legal enforcement and judicial quality. Although the formal legal structure is robust in many rising economies, including China, the implementation of environmental laws is primarily dependent on administrative regulation rather than judicial procedures. The impact of the rule of law on green growth may become less measurable as a result. Environmental governance in China has traditionally placed more emphasis on administrative and regulatory mechanisms (such as five-year plans and command-and-control measures) than on court enforcement. As a result, unless environment-specific enforcement institutions are matched, gains in the general rule of law may not result in increased green growth.

Moving to other control variables, it is seen that FDI exerts a negative and significant in almost all models. This means that increase in FDI will adversely affect green growth in the long run keeping all other factors constant. A percent increase in FDI will lead to detrimental impact on growth to the magnitude of 0.96 (in case of model 6) to 0.08 (in case of model 1). This reiterates the findings of Shahbaz et al., 2015; Rana and Sharma, 2019; Anastacio, 2020; Caglar, 2020; Halliru et al., 2020. The common link through which the FDI deteriorates the magnitude of green growth is understood in terms of increased carbon emissions which is a result of increased economic activity fuelled with the influx of foreign capital. There are three ways that FDI might impact green growth: technique, mix, and size. China's potential technique effect (diffusion of cleaner technologies) has frequently been overshadowed by the scale effect (larger total production resulting in higher energy use and emissions) and the composition effect (larger weight of pollution-intensive industries), particularly over long time horizons. Research shows that even when certain technology spillovers take place, the expansion of production that results from FDI entering high-emission industries without strict control can exacerbate environmental burdens (Jun et al.,2018). According to research on China's regional environmental effects, local investment incentives might occasionally weaken environmental regulations, which raises emissions in the areas where foreign investment is made.

For renewable energy, it is seen that a percent increase in renewable energy consumption will lead to 0.32 to 0.88 percent increase in green economic growth from Model 2 to model 5. In the short run we see that the renewable energy consumption generates positive impact with a lag. The findings endorse the works of Wei et al. (2023); Li et al. (2019c) and Saidi and Omri (2020).

Table 5. ECM Short-run elasticities

Variable	Coefficient	Std. error	Variable	Coefficient	Std. error
Model 1				**Model 2**	
D(GG (-1))	0.20**	0.07	D(GG (-1))	1.11***	0.03
D(REN)	-0.11**	0.04	D(FDI)	-0.06***	0.01
D(REN(-1))	0.24***	0.04	D(FDI(-1))	0.05***	0.01
D(RD)	-0.05*	0.02	D(REN)	-0.16***	0.03
D(RD(-1))	-0.21***	0.04	D(REN(-1))	0.17***	0.04
D(INDX)	0.01***	0.00	D(VA)	0.00	0.01
D(INDX(-1))	-0.01	0.00	D(VA (-1))	-0.06***	0.01
ECT	-0.01***	0.00	ECT	-0.28***	0.02
Variable	**Coefficient**	**Std.error**	**Variable**	**Coefficient**	**Std.error**
Model 3				**Model 4**	
D(RD)	-0.08*	0.04	D(RD)	-0.02	0.03
ECT	-0.12***	0.00	ECT	-0.14***	0.01
Variable	**Coefficient**	**Std. error**	**Variable**	**Coefficient**	**Std.error**
Model 5				**Model 6**	
D(FDI)	-0.03***	0.01	D(GG(-1))	0.85***	0.04
D(FDI(-1))	0.03	0.01	D(FDI)	-0.03**	0.01
D(RD)	-0.04	0.03	D(FDI(-1))	0.05	0.01
D(RD(-1))	-0.20	0.04	D(REN)	-0.10**	0.04
D(REN)	-0.16***	0.04	D(REN(-1))	0.20***	0.05
D(REN(-1))	0.15**	0.05	D(RL)	-0.16	0.04

continued on following page

Table 5. Continued

Variable	Coefficient	Std. error	Variable	Coefficient	Std. error
D(RQ)	0.09***	0.03	**ECT**	-0.13***	0.02
D(RQ(-1))	-0.16	0.03			
ECT	-0.29***	0.01			
Variable	**Coefficient**	**Std. error**			
Model 7					
D(RD)	-0.06	0.04			
ECT	-0.05***	0.00			

Source: Calculated by authors. *, ** and *** represent 10%, 5% and 1% significance levels respectively

With respect to short run estimates, the first thing to be studied is the level of error correction term (ECT). It is seen that the adjustment term is negative and significant in all the models thereby stating that there is long run cointegration among all the variables in each of the case. This suggests that the economy will restore back to equilibrium in the event of disequilibrium.

Table 6 details robustness tests of heteroscedasticity, autocorrelation and normality are conducted. The non rejection of the test statistics for all the models reinstate the validity of our results. The stability tests of indicate a fair degree of stability in our regression model.

Table 6. Diagnostic tests

F statistics	M1	M2	M3	M4	M5	M6	M7
Breusch–Pagan- Godfrey	2.3274 (0.0951)	1.0897 (0.4522)	1.5365 (0.2259)	4.7947 (0.2049)	1.4945 (0.2765)	1.9836 (0.1357)	0.8626 (0.5413)
Breusch-Godfrey LM Test	3.6002 (0.0767)	2.0969 (0.1853)	0.2907 (0.5972)	0.1339 (0.7191)	5.2242 (0.1409)	1.5853 (0.2571)	1.9599 (0.1753)
Jarque-Bera	0.0915 (0.9535)	1.1138 (0.5729)	0.6119 (0.7363)	0.6742 (0.7138)	0.7385 (0.6912)	0.3953 (0.8206)	2.3771 (0.3046)
Ramsey reset test	0.1362 (0.7206)	0.9380 (0.3581)	1.3332 (0.2652)	0.1027 (0.7527)	0.0571 (0.8171)	3.6624 (0.1847)	0.1363 (0.7167)
CUSUM test	S	S	S	S	S	S	S
CUSUM Squares Test	S	S	S	S	S	S	S

Source: Calculated by authors. The figure in parenthesis indicates the p-values

5 CONCLUSION

This chapter takes a "policy ripple effects" stance, contending that institutional quality shapes long-term economic incentives, and the efficacy of environmental policies, hence influencing green economic growth both directly and indirectly. Improvements in governance—such as regulatory quality, political stability, and government effectiveness—generate cascading effects by enhancing policy credibility, strengthening enforcement, guiding foreign and domestic investment toward cleaner sectors, and reducing uncertainty surrounding green transitions. On the other hand, institutional flaws can increase environmental externalities and reduce the impact of environmental regulations that are otherwise well-thought-out. The technique of Autoregressive distributed lag model is used to distinguish between short run as well as long run effects. The major findings of the work state that strong institutions promote green growth. By influencing investing behavior, influencing businesses' environmental performance, and bolstering the legitimacy of sustainability-focused legislation, these institutional advancements have a cascading effect. The importance of regulatory quality, indicates that policy design and implementation are more important for green growth than the creation of formal legal frameworks alone. Reducing regulatory overlap, enhancing agency coordination, and guaranteeing consistent application of green policies should be prioritized. Transforming the goals of green policies into long-term economic results requires efficient public service delivery, monitoring, and enforcement systems. For investment in clean technologies, green infrastructure, and renewable energy, a stable political climate lowers uncertainty and encourages long-term planning. To maintain investor confidence and innovation, policymakers should make sure that environmental and climate strategies remain consistent over planning cycles. Thus, political stability improves the legitimacy and sustainability of green growth initiatives. The fact that corruption control and the rule of law are insignificant in China does not mean that they are irrelevant; rather, it indicates that their effects can be situation-specific or indirect. Rather than being viewed as stand-alone institutional reforms, initiatives to improve anti-corruption and rule of law should be better integrated with sector-specific environmental governance. Instead of functioning independently, these organizations may interact with government efficacy and regulatory quality to produce benefits for green growth.

In addition, it is seen that China seems to verify the Pollution haven hypothesis with point estimate being negative and significant. Renewable energy consumption will aid in promoting green economic growth as is evident from the point estimate which ranges from 0.32 to 0.88 in different models. What is suggestive from the perspective of policy recommendation is that governance needs to be taken seriously and stringent enforcement of laws need to be put in place to curtail emissions and achieve the objective of green growth. Also, the Chinese economy needs to take into consideration the possible impact of increased foreign investment on the green economic growth perspective and hence needs to closely monitor this aspect because there exists a trade-off between the two hence the policy prerogative for the government should be aligned with the changing role of foreign direct investment. China has over 4 million jobs being created in renewable energy sector alone and the country has declared its commitment towards sustainability by abandoning the building of any new coal-fired power plants abroad rather will ramp up the global efforts directed towards developing green and low-carbon energy. With a huge surge in clean energy investments in three main sectors of solar power, electric vehicles (EVs) and batteries, China has emerged as an energy innovator.

Limitations of the Work

The study despite its approach to idea and methodological rigour is not free from limitations. The data on the Chinese economy in respect of limitations of the data especially with regard to Governance indicator wherein the data starts only from 1996. Additionally, the research can be extended by taking up a comprehensive global panel to see if the effectiveness of institutions in supporting green growth holds true or not. Also, the study may also reflect biasedness with regard to alternate application of methodology or to alternative specifications of our dependent variable.

REFERENCES

Abid, M. (2017). Does economic, financial and institutional developments matter for environmental quality? A comparative analysis of EU and MEA countries. *Journal of Environmental Management, 188*, 183–194. DOI: 10.1016/j.jenvman.2016.12.007

Aisen, A., & Veiga, F. J. (2013). How does political instability affect economic growth? *European Journal of Political Economy, 29*, 151–167. DOI: 10.1016/j.ejpoleco.2012.11.001

Arminen, H., & Menegaki, A. N. (2019). Corruption, climate and the energy-environment-growth nexus. *Energy Economics, 80*, 621–634. DOI: 10.1016/j.eneco.2019.02.009

Bagheri, M., Guevara, Z., Alikarami, M., Kennedy, C. A., & Doluweera, G. (2018). Green growth planning: A multi-factor energy input-output analysis of the Canadian economy. *Energy Economics, 74*, 708–720. DOI: 10.1016/j.eneco.2018.07.015

Behera, B., Behera, P., Sucharita, S., & Sethi, N. (2024). Mitigating ecological footprint in BRICS countries: Unveiling the role of disaggregated clean energy, green technology innovation and political stability. *Discover Sustainability, 5*(1), 165. DOI: 10.1007/s43621-024-00378-0

Behera, P., Behera, B., Sethi, N., & Handoyo, R. D. (2024). What drives environmental sustainability? The role of renewable energy, green innovation, and political stability in OECD economies. *International Journal of Sustainable Development and World Ecology, 31*(7), 1–15. DOI: 10.1080/13504509.2024.2333812

Bovenberg, A. L., & Smulders, S. (1995). Environmental quality and pollution-augmenting technological change in a two-sector endogenous growth model. *Journal of Public Economics, 57*(3), 369–391. DOI: 10.1016/0047-2727(95)80002-Q

Bovenberg, A. L., & Smulders, S. (1996). Transitional impacts of environmental policy in an endogenous growth model. *International Economic Review, 37*(4), 861–895. DOI: 10.2307/2527315

Caglar, A. E. (2020). The importance of renewable energy consumption and FDI inflows in reducing environmental degradation: Bootstrap ARDL bound test in selected 9 countries. *Journal of Cleaner Production, 264*, 121663. DOI: 10.1016/j.jclepro.2020.121663

Chen, H., Hao, Y., Li, J., & Song, X. (2018). The impact of environmental regulation, shadow economy, and corruption on environmental quality: Theory and empirical evidence from China. *Journal of Cleaner Production, 195*, 200–214. DOI: 10.1016/j.jclepro.2018.05.206

Cole, M. A. (2007). Corruption, income and the environment: An empirical analysis. *Ecological Economics, 62*(3-4), 637–647. DOI: 10.1016/j.ecolecon.2006.08.003

Costantiello, A., & Leogrande, A. (2024). The regulatory quality in the light of environmental, social and governance framework at world level. *Discover Global Society, 2*(1), 1. DOI: 10.1007/s44282-023-00024-6

Dai, H., Xie, X., Xie, Y., Liu, J., & Masui, T. (2016). Green growth: The economic impacts of large-scale renewable energy development in China. *Applied Energy, 162*, 435–449. DOI: 10.1016/j.apenergy.2015.10.049

Dechezleprêtre, A., & Sato, M. (2017). The impacts of environmental regulations on competitiveness. *Review of Environmental Economics and Policy, 11*(2), 183–206. DOI: 10.1093/reep/rex013

Fang, W., Liu, Z., & Putra, A. R. S. (2022). Role of research and development in green economic growth through renewable energy development: Empirical evidence from South Asia. *Renewable Energy, 194*, 1142–1152. DOI: 10.1016/j.renene.2022.04.125

Galinato, G. I., & Galinato, S. P. (2012). The effects of corruption control, political stability and economic growth on deforestation-induced carbon dioxide emissions. *Environment and Development Economics, 17*(1), 67–90. DOI: 10.1017/S1355770X11000222

Greenidge, K., McIntyre, M., & Yun, H. (2016). *Structural reform and growth: what really matters? Evidence from the caribbean.* IMF Work., DOI: 10.5089/9781484321812.001

Grossman GM, Krueger AB (1991) Environmental impacts of a North American free trade agreement (No. w3914). National Bureau of Economic ResearchDOI: 10.1504/IJGE.2020.112576

Halliru, A.M., Loganathan, N., Sethi, N; Hassan, A.A. G. (2020). FDI inflows, energy consumption and sustainable economic growth for ECOWAS countries: The pollution haven hypothesis approach. *International Journal of Green Economics, 14*(4), 327-348. DOI: 10.1504/IJGE.2020.112576

Hassan, S. T., Khan, S. U. D., Xia, E., & Fatima, H. (2020). Role of institutions in correcting environmental pollution: An empirical investigation. *Sustainable Cities and Society, 53*, 101901. DOI: 10.1016/j.scs.2019.101901

Hosseini, H. M., & Kaneko, S. (2013). Can environmental quality spread through institutions? *Energy Policy*, *56*, 312–321. DOI: 10.1016/j.enpol.2012.12.067

Ibrahim, M. H., & Law, S. H. (2016). Institutional quality and CO2 emission–trade relations: Evidence from Sub-Saharan Africa. *The South African Journal of Economics*, *84*(2), 323–340. DOI: 10.1111/saje.12095

Jun, W., Zakaria, M., Shahzad, S. J. H., & Mahmood, H. (2018). Effect of FDI on pollution in China: New insights based on wavelet approach. *Sustainability (Basel)*, *10*(11), 3859. DOI: 10.3390/su10113859

Kaufmann, D., & Kraay, A. (2018). The worldwide governance indicators. The World Bank. https://info.worldbank.org/governance/wgi/

Kivyiro, P., & Arminen, H. (2014). Carbon dioxide emissions, energy consumption, economic growth, and foreign direct investment: Causality analysis for sub-Saharan Africa. *Energy*, *74*, 595–606. DOI: 10.1016/j.energy.2014.07.025

Kwilinski, A., Lyulyov, O., & Pimonenko, T. (2023). Greenfield investment as a catalyst of green economic growth. *Energies*, *16*(5), 2372. DOI: 10.3390/en16052372

Lau, L. S., Choong, C. K., & Eng, Y. K. (2014). Investigation of the environmental Kuznets curve for carbon emissions in Malaysia: Do foreign direct investment and trade matter? *Energy Policy*, *68*, 490–497. DOI: 10.1016/j.enpol.2014.01.002

Lau, L.S., Choong, C.K., Eng, Y.K., 2014. Carbon dioxide emission, institutional quality, and economic growth: empirical evidence in Malaysia. Renew. *Energy* 68, 276e281. .DOI: 10.1016/j.renene.2014.02.013

Lee, J. W. (2013). The contribution of foreign direct investment to clean energy use, carbon emissions and economic growth. *Energy Policy*, *55*, 483–489. DOI: 10.1016/j.enpol.2012.12.039

Li, X., Du, J., & Long, H. (2018). A comparative study of Chinese and foreign green development from the perspective of mapping knowledge domains. *Sustainability (Basel)*, *10*(12), 43–57. DOI: 10.3390/su10124357

Li, X., Du, J., & Long, H. (2019c). Green development behavior and performance of industrial enterprises based on grounded theory study: Evidence from China. *Sustainability (Basel)*, *11*(15), 4133. DOI: 10.3390/su11154133

Lin, B., & Benjamin, N. I. (2017). Green development determinants in China: A non-radial quantile outlook. *Journal of Cleaner Production*, *162*, 764–775. DOI: 10.1016/j.jclepro.2017.06.062

Lin, B., & Zhou, Y. (2022). Measuring the green economic growth in China: Influencing factors and policy perspectives. *Energy, 241*, 122518. DOI: 10.1016/j.energy.2021.122518

Malthus, T. R. (1798). *First Essay on Population*. University of MI Press.

Mehmood, U., Tariq, S., Ul-Haq, Z., & Meo, M. S. (2021). Does the modifying role of institutional quality remains homogeneous in GDP-CO2 emission nexus? New evidence from ARDL approach. *Environmental Science and Pollution Research International, 28*(8), 10167–10174. DOI: 10.1007/s11356-020-11293-y

Mert, M., & Bölük, G. (2016). Do foreign direct investment and renewable energy consumption affect the CO 2 emissions? New evidence from a panel ARDL approach to Kyoto Annex countries. *Environmental Science and Pollution Research International, 23*(21), 21669–21681. DOI: 10.1007/s11356-016-7413-7

Mohsin, M., Taghizadeh-Hesary, F., Iqbal, N., & Saydaliev, H. B. (2022). The role of technological progress and renewable energy deployment in green economic growth. *Renewable Energy, 190*, 777–787. DOI: 10.1016/j.renene.2022.03.076

Muhammad, S., & Long, X. (2021). Rule of law and CO2 emissions: A comparative analysis across 65 belt and road initiative (BRI) countries. *Journal of Cleaner Production, 279*, 123539. DOI: 10.1016/j.jclepro.2020.123539

Murray, J. S. (2021). Log-linear Bayesian additive regression trees for multinomial logistic and count regression models. *Journal of the American Statistical Association, 116*(534), 756–769. DOI: 10.1080/01621459.2020.1813587

Nkoro, E., & Uko, A. K. (2016). Autoregressive Distributed Lag (ARDL) cointegration technique: Application and interpretation. *Journal of Statistical and Econometric Methods, 5*(4), 63–91.

Pahle, M., Pachauri, S., & Steinbacher, K. (2016). Can the green economy deliver it all? Experiences of renewable energy policies with socio-economic objectives. *Applied Energy, 179*, 1331–1341. DOI: 10.1016/j.apenergy.2016.06.073

Pesaran, M. H., Shin, Y., & Smith, R. J. (2001). Bounds testing approaches to the analysis of level relationships. *Journal of Applied Econometrics, 16*(3), 289–326. DOI: 10.1002/jae.616

Purcel, A. A. (2019). Does political stability hinder pollution? Evidence from developing states. *Economic Research Guardian, 9*(2), 75–98.

Qamruzzaman, M., & Karim, S. (2024). Green energy, green innovation, and political stability led to green growth in OECD nations. *Energy Strategy Reviews*, *55*, 101519. DOI: 10.1016/j.esr.2024.101519

Qi, J. (2024). Greening economic sectors through trade liberalization and efficient governance. *Humanities & Social Sciences Communications*, *11*(1), 1–8. DOI: 10.1057/s41599-024-04214-8

Rafindadi, A. A., Muye, I. M., & Kaita, R. A. (2018). The effects of FDI and energy consumption on environmental pollution in predominantly resource-based economies of the GCC. *Sustainable Energy Technologies and Assessments*, *25*, 126–137. DOI: 10.1016/j.seta.2017.12.008

Rana, R., & Sharma, M. (2019). Dynamic causality testing for EKC hypothesis, pollution haven hypothesis and international trade in India. *The Journal of International Trade & Economic Development*, *28*(3), 348–364. DOI: 10.1080/09638199.2018.1542451

Sadiq, M., Chau, K. Y., Ha, N. T. T., Phan, T. T. H., Ngo, T. Q., & Huy, P. Q. (2024). The impact of green finance, eco-innovation, renewable energy and carbon taxes on CO2 emissions in BRICS countries: Evidence from CS ARDL estimation. *Geoscience Frontiers*, *15*(4), 101689. DOI: 10.1016/j.gsf.2023.101689

Salman, M., Long, X., Dauda, L., & Mensah, C. N. (2019). The impact of institutional quality on economic growth and carbon emissions: Evidence from Indonesia, South Korea and Thailand. *Journal of Cleaner Production*, *241*, 118331. DOI: 10.1016/j.jclepro.2019.118331

Sarkodie, S. A., & Adams, S. (2018). Renewable energy, nuclear energy, and environmental pollution: Accounting for political, institutional quality in South Africa. *The Science of the Total Environment*, *643*, 1590–1601. DOI: 10.1016/j.scitotenv.2018.06.320

Seker, F., Ertugrul, H. M., & Cetin, M. (2015). The impact of foreign direct investment on environmental quality: A bounds testing and causality analysis for Turkey. *Renewable & Sustainable Energy Reviews*, *52*, 347–356. DOI: 10.1016/j.rser.2015.07.118

Shahbaz, M., Nasreen, S., Abbas, F., & Anis, O. (2015). Does foreign direct investment impede environmental quality in high-, middle-, and low-income countries? *Energy Economics*, *51*, 275–287. DOI: 10.1016/j.eneco.2015.06.014

Shahbaz, M., Rasool, G., Ahmed, K., & Mahalik, M. K. (2016). Considering the effectof biomass energy consumption on economic growth: Fresh evidence from BRICS region. *Renewable & Sustainable Energy Reviews*, *60*, 1442–1450. DOI: 10.1016/j.rser.2016.03.037

Slesman, L., Baharumshah, A.Z., Ra'ees, W., 2015. Institutional infrastructure and economic growth in member countries of the Organization of Islamic Cooperation (OIC). *Economic Modelling*. 51, 214e226. .DOI: 10.1016/j.econmod.2015.08.008

Smulders, J. (1994). *Growth Market Structure and the Environment: Essays on the Theory of Endogenous Economic Growth*. Tilburg University.

Socol, A., Ivan, O. R., Danuletiu, A. E., Cioca, I. C., Botar, C. F., & Virdea, D. E. (2025). The moderating role of governmental artificial intelligence in shaping green growth dynamics in the European Union. *Sustainability (Basel)*, *17*(22), 10329. DOI: 10.3390/su172210329

Sohag, K., Taskın, F. D., & Malik, M. N. (2019). Green economic growth, cleaner energy and militarization: Evidence from Turkey. *Resources Policy*, *63*, 101407. DOI: 10.1016/j.resourpol.2019.101407

Solarin, S. A., Al-Mulali, U., Musah, I., & Ozturk, I. (2017). Investigating the pollution haven hypothesis in Ghana: An empirical investigation. *Energy*, *124*, 706–719. DOI: 10.1016/j.energy.2017.02.089

Stern, N. (2007), "Stern review on the economics of climate change", available at: https://webarchive. nationalarchives.gov.uk/20100407172811/http://www.hm-treasury.gov.uk/stern_review_report.htm

Sun, C., Zhang, F., & Xu, M. (2017). Investigation of pollution haven hypothesis for China: An ARDL approach with breakpoint unit root tests. *Journal of Cleaner Production*, *161*, 153–164. DOI: 10.1016/j.jclepro.2017.05.119

Tang, C. F., & Tan, B. W. (2015). The impact of energy consumption, income and foreign direct investment on carbon dioxide emissions in Vietnam. *Energy*, *79*, 447–454. DOI: 10.1016/j.energy.2014.11.033

Tawiah, V., Zakari, A., & Adedoyin, F. F. (2021). Determinants of green growth in developed and developing countries. *Environmental Science and Pollution Research International*, *28*(29), 39227–39242. DOI: 10.1007/s11356-021-13429-0

Wang, X., & Shao, Q. (2019). Non-linear effects of heterogeneous environmental regulations on green growth in G20 countries: Evidence from panel threshold regression. *The Science of the Total Environment*, *660*, 1346–1354. DOI: 10.1016/j.scitotenv.2019.01.094

Wei, S., Jiandong, W., & Saleem, H. (2023). The impact of renewable energy transition, green growth, green trade and green innovation on environmental quality: Evidence from top 10 green future countries. *Frontiers in Environmental Science*, *10*, 1076859. DOI: 10.3389/fenvs.2022.1076859

Welsch, H., 2004. Corruption, growth, and the environment: a cross-country analysis. Environ. Dev. Econ. 9 (5), 663e693. .DOI: 10.1017/S1355770X04001500

Wu, W., Cheng, Y., Lin, X., & Yao, X. (2019). How does the implementation of the policy of electricity substitution influence green economic growth in China? *Energy Policy*, *131*, 251–261. DOI: 10.1016/j.enpol.2019.04.043

Zaman, K., Abdullah, A., Khan, A., Nasir, M. R. M., Hamzah, T. A. A. T., & Hussain, S. (2016). Dynamic linkages among energy consumption, environment, health and wealth in BRICS countries: Green growth key to sustainable development. *Renewable & Sustainable Energy Reviews*, *56*, 1263–1271. DOI: 10.1016/j.rser.2015.12.010

ENDNOTES

1 Green growth is calculated by the sum of particulate emission damage, carbon dioxide damage and natural resource depletion times GDP per capita

2 Refer Appendix A1

3 It's interesting to see that because the results for bounds test showed that there is no long run relationship among the variables and the same is seen with respect to insignificance of Rule of law as a determinant of green economic growth.

4 The distinction between short run and long run effect stems from the methodology adopted in the form of ARDL

APPENDIX

A1: Institutional Index

In most of the cases, first principal component or sum of the first two to three principal components is normally used for constructing the index. For the construction of index, 2 components are extracted. In this case, if first principal component is sufficient enough to explain 50 percent variation then the index would be based on that very component but in the event when this condition is not met then combined component scores are used. The number of variables that make upto 65 to 73 percent of the variation will be eventually used. The construction of combined component scores is given as:

Combined component scores (CCS) = $W_1S_1+W_2S_2$

Where $W_1 = \frac{V1}{V1 + V2}$; $W_2 = \frac{V2}{V1 + V2}$

W_1 is the proportion of variance explained by the first component; W_2 is the proportion of variance explained by the second principal component and S_1 and S_2 are the first and second component scores respectively.

Figure 1. KMO Measure of Sampling Adequacy and Bartlett's Test of Sphericity

KMO and Bartlett's Test

Kaiser-Meyer-Olkin Measure of Sampling Adequacy.		.587
Bartlett's Test of Sphericity	Approx. Chi-Square	100.773
	df	15
	Sig.	.000

Source: *Own calculations.*

Figure 2. Eigenvalues and variance explained by the selected components after PCA

Total Variance Explained

Component	Initial Eigenvalues			Extraction Sums of Squared Loadings			Rotation Sums of Squared Loadings		
	Total	% of Variance	Cumulative %	Total	% of Variance	Cumulative %	Total	% of Variance	Cumulative %
1	2.589	43.144	43.144	2.589	43.144	43.144	2.585	43.080	43.080
2	1.972	32.873	76.017	1.972	32.873	76.017	1.976	32.937	76.017
3	.915	15.257	91.274						
4	.319	5.320	96.594						
5	.160	2.665	99.259						
6	.044	.741	100.000						

Extraction Method: Principal Component Analysis.

Source: *Own calculations.*

Figure 3. Component Matrix

Component Matrix[a]

	Component	
	1	2
Zscore(VAR00002)	-.122	.933
Zscore(VAR00003)	.176	.886
Zscore(VAR00004)	.891	-.389
Zscore(VAR00005)	.371	-.084
Zscore(VAR00006)	.963	.009
Zscore(VAR00007)	.827	.397

Extraction Method: Principal Component Analysis.

a. 2 components extracted.

A2: Equations Used for Regression

Given that the institutional quality indicator is composed of the six elements listed above, an effort is made to investigate the effects of each of these governance characteristics on the growth of the green economy.The forms shown in the appendix (Model 2 to Model 7) will be used to incorporate each of these explanatory variables independently into our regression model.

MODEL 2 (M2): $GG = \alpha + \gamma FDI_t + \delta REN_t + \o RD_t + \beta VA \mu_t$

MODEL 3 (M3): $GG = \alpha + \gamma FDI_t + \delta REN_t + \o RD_t + \beta PS + \mu_t$

MODEL 4 (M4): $GG = \alpha + \gamma FDI + \delta REN_t + \phi RD_t + \beta GE + \mu_t$

MODEL 5 (M5): $GG = \alpha + \gamma FDI + \delta REN_t + \phi RD_t + \beta RQ + \mu_t$

MODEL 6 (M6): $GG = \alpha + \gamma FDI + \delta REN_t + \phi RD_t + \beta RL + \mu_t$

MODEL 7 (M7): $GG = \alpha + \gamma FDI + \delta REN_t + \phi RD_t + \beta CC + \mu_t$

Chapter 12
The Governance Ripple: How Environmental Policies Reshape Natural Resource Institutions and Socioeconomic Equity in Resource-Dependent Economies

Lawal Olamilekan Abdulwahab
http://orcid.org/0000-0003-4955-244X
School of Business and Economics, Universiti Brunei Darussalam, Brunei

Pang Wei Loon
School of Business and Economics, Universiti Brunei Darussalam, Brunei

Roslee bin Hj Baha
School of Business and Economics, Universiti Brunei Darussalam, Brunei

Ahmed M. Khalid
Lahore University of Management Sciences, Lahore, Pakistan

ABSTRACT

Environmental policies have evolved from narrow regulatory tools to key instruments of economic governance, affecting resource-dependent economies by influencing extractive sectors, revenue systems, and governance. This chapter introduces the Governance Ripple Framework, viewing environmental policies as institutional shocks that cause sequential fiscal, institutional, and equity effects. Using a qualitative–comparative approach, it analyzes Nigeria, Indonesia, and Chile, illustrating that governance capacity is essential for policy success and inclusive development, highlighting the responsibility of researchers and policymakers. The chapter integrates

DOI: 10.4018/979-8-3373-8998-1.ch012

environmental policy, governance, and equity, emphasizing governance capacity as crucial to policy success and offering insights for designing sustainable, inclusive policies in resource-dependent economies.

1. INTRODUCTION

Environmental policy has increasingly evolved from a peripheral regulatory concern into a central instrument of economic governance, fiscal restructuring, and institutional transformation. Governments across both developed and developing economies are adopting environmental fiscal tools such as carbon pricing, green taxation, subsidy reforms, and regulatory standards not only to address climate change and environmental degradation but also to realign economic incentives and public finance systems toward sustainability objectives. Recent evidence indicates that these policies exert effects well beyond environmental outcomes, shaping fiscal capacity, institutional behavior, and long-term development trajectories (Ezquerro et al., 2024; Shahzad et al., 2024).

These governance implications are particularly pronounced in resource-dependent economies, where natural resource rents remain a dominant source of public revenue and political power. In such contexts, environmental policies interact directly with extractive industries, rent distribution mechanisms, and fiscal structures, thereby influencing institutional accountability, decentralization, and social cohesion. Studies demonstrate that natural resource dependence, when coupled with weak governance, amplifies inequality, environmental degradation, and institutional fragility. In contrast, strong institutional quality can mitigate these adverse effects and transform resource wealth into sustainable development gains (Abdulahi et al., 2025; Bambi et al., 2024). This transformation reflects broader structural shifts in global economic governance. As climate risks intensify and traditional extractive growth models face fiscal and ecological constraints, governments, particularly in resource-dependent economies, have increasingly turned to environmental policy to manage revenue volatility, strengthen institutional accountability, and maintain social stability.

Environmental instruments such as carbon pricing, subsidy reform, and green taxation have thus moved beyond environmental regulation to become integral components of fiscal and governance reform agendas. Despite growing attention to environmental fiscal reform, much of the existing literature continues to treat environmental performance, governance quality, and socioeconomic equity as analytically separate domains. Recent studies emphasize that fiscal and environmental policies produce policy feedback effects, whereby institutional quality conditions whether reforms enhance transparency and inclusiveness or exacerbate rent-seeking and distributional inequities (Barra & Falcone, 2025; Bosomtwe, 2025). This disconnect is especially problematic in resource-dependent economies, where poorly designed environmental interventions may unintentionally destabilize fiscal systems, weaken public trust, or deepen regional disparities.

Emerging studies increasingly highlight governance as the critical mediating factor in determining whether environmental policies yield inclusive and resilient outcomes. Strong institutions characterized by transparency, accountability, and administrative capacity enable governments to recycle green revenues productively, support innovation, and cushion vulnerable populations during structural transitions (Li & Zhang, 2025). Conversely, weak institutional environments may experience policy resistance, elite capture, and uneven socioeconomic impacts, undermining both environmental and developmental objectives (Abdulwahab & Bubari Umar, 2025; Powell, 2024).

Against this backdrop, this chapter advances the central argument that environmental policies generate governance and equity ripple effects that are especially consequential in resource-dependent economies. Rather than viewing environmental reforms solely through an ecological lens, the chapter conceptualizes them as institutional shocks that reshape fiscal incentives, governance arrangements, and distributive outcomes. By integrating insights from political economy, environmental fiscal reform, and institutional governance, the chapter develops a structured framework for understanding these multidimensional effects.

The chapter pursues three core objectives. First, it examines how environmental fiscal policies and regulatory interventions reshape governance incentives and institutional structures in resource-dependent contexts. Second, it analyzes the channels through which these policies influence socioeconomic equity, including income distribution, employment, and regional development. Third, it identifies the institutional conditions under which environmental interventions can strengthen governance and foster inclusive sustainability. To achieve these aims, the chapter employs a comparative analytical approach, drawing on evidence from Nigeria, Indonesia, and Chile, which exhibit varying degrees of resource dependence and institutional capacity.

In doing so, this chapter contributes directly to the objectives of the edited volume, The Ripple Effects of Environmental Policies: Economic, Financial, and Institutional Perspectives, by offering an integrated, governance-centered analysis of environmental policy impacts. It bridges critical gaps in the literature by demonstrating that environmental ambition, fiscal stability, and social equity are not independent policy goals but interconnected outcomes shaped by institutional quality. The insights developed herein aim to inform policymakers, scholars, and development practitioners seeking to design environmentally practical, fiscally sound, and socially just policy frameworks in resource-dependent economies. While other contributions to this volume examine the economic, financial, or institutional consequences of environmental policies in isolation, this chapter complements them by offering an integrated governance-centered framework. In doing so, it provides a connective analytical lens that helps situate diverse empirical findings within a coherent political economy perspective, thereby enhancing the volume's cumulative explanatory power.

The chapter is organized from context to analysis to application. Section 2 establishes the background and context for environmental policy in resource-dependent economies. Section 3 synthesizes the relevant literature and identifies unresolved analytical gaps. Section 4 develops the Governance Ripple Framework that guides the analysis. Sections 5 and 6 operationalize the framework through a comparative research design and case analysis of Nigeria, Indonesia, and Chile. Sections 7 to 9 discuss analytical insights, policy, and managerial implications, followed by future research directions and conclusions.

2. BACKGROUND AND CONCEPTUAL FRAMEWORK

2.1 Environmental Policy Evolution in Resource-Dependent Economies

Resource-dependent economies face a distinct policy environment shaped by heavy reliance on extractive industries for public revenue, employment, and political bargaining. In these contexts, environmental degradation is not merely an ecological concern but a fiscal and governance challenge, as environmental damage directly affects revenue sustainability, public expenditure needs, and institutional legitimacy. Understanding this background is essential for interpreting why environmental policy reforms often trigger far-reaching economic and governance consequences in such economies.

Over the past two decades, environmental policy has undergone a fundamental transformation from a narrowly defined regulatory tool into a broader mechanism of fiscal, economic, and institutional governance. Rather than focusing solely on pollution control or conservation, contemporary environmental policies increasingly incorporate fiscal instruments such as environmental taxation, carbon pricing, and green public expenditure to influence production structures, investment behavior, and long-term development pathways. This evolution reflects growing recognition that environmental degradation and climate risks are deeply intertwined with macroeconomic management and public finance systems (Qi et al., 2025; Selvakumar et al., 2024).

Figure 1 shows the evolution of environmental policy in resource-dependent economies, from narrow regulation to integrated fiscal and governance frameworks. Initially, policies are command-and-control, with pollution limits and permits, operating separately from fiscal and governance systems, resulting in weak integration. The second phase sees the adoption of market instruments, such as taxes and subsidies, with partial fiscal integration and limited governance influence, and relies on institutional capacity. The third phase advances to environmental fiscal reform, including carbon pricing, green budgeting, and integrated fiscal-environmental strategies. Policies embed environmental goals into public finance and governance, making environmental policy a key economic governance tool. This evolution highlights how environmental policy shifts from regulation to institutional and fiscal interventions in resource-dependent economies.

Figure 1. Evolution of Environmental Policy in Resource-Dependent Economies

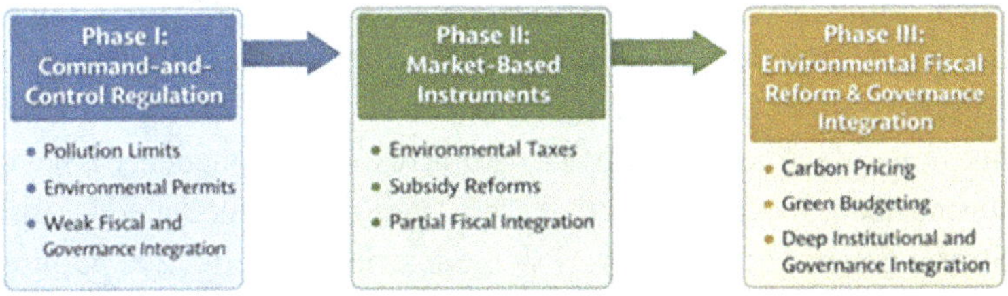

Source: *Author's concept based on the environmental policy and governance studies.*

The figure illustrates the progression of environmental policy in resource-dependent economies from narrow command-and-control regulation toward integrated fiscal and governance frameworks, highlighting how environmental policy increasingly functions as an instrument of economic and institutional governance. In resource-dependent economies, this policy shift carries heightened significance. Governments whose fiscal systems rely heavily on extractive revenues face unique trade-offs when introducing environmental regulations or green fiscal reforms. Environmental policies can directly constrain extractive activities, alter rent flows, and reshape state–business relations. Recent empirical work demonstrates that environmental fiscal reforms often interact with existing revenue structures in complex ways, sometimes reinforcing fiscal sustainability but, in other cases, intensifying revenue volatility and political resistance when institutional safeguards are weak (Abdulwahab, 2026; Ameer & Ahmad, 2024).

Moreover, environmental policies increasingly serve as instruments for advancing international commitments related to sustainable development and climate governance. Evidence from emerging and developing economies suggests that environmental policy effectiveness depends not only on technical design but also on the broader governance environment within which such policies are embedded. Countries with stronger institutional quality are better able to integrate environmental objectives into fiscal systems without undermining growth or social stability (Akhundov et al., 2025; Lucy, 2025).

2.2 Natural Resource Dependence and Institutional Structures

Historically, the institutional structures of resource-dependent economies have evolved alongside extractive revenue systems, shaping fiscal governance, political incentives, and state–society relations. Natural resource dependence profoundly shapes institutional arrangements, fiscal incentives, and political economy dynamics. In economies where natural resource rents constitute a substantial share of government revenue, public finance systems often become vulnerable to rent-seeking behavior, weakened tax effort, and procyclical spending patterns. These structural characteristics influence how governments respond to environmental policy interventions, particularly when such policies threaten established revenue streams (Asiamah et al., 2022; Peres-Cajías et al., 2022).

Recent empirical studies reaffirm that natural resource dependence is not inherently detrimental; instead, its developmental consequences are mediated by institutional quality. Strong governance frameworks characterized by effective public financial management, accountability mechanisms, and regulatory capacity can transform resource rents into productive investments and social welfare gains. Conversely, weak institutions tend to magnify the adverse effects of resource dependence, leading to fiscal fragility, inequality, and environmental degradation (Abdulwahab et al., 2026; Mollick & Sui, 2024).

Institutional arrangements also shape the degree of fiscal centralization and decentralization in resource-dependent economies. Studies indicate that centralized control over resource revenues may undermine local accountability and exacerbate regional inequalities, particularly when environmental policies impose uneven costs across regions. Conversely, well-designed decentralization frameworks can enhance institutional responsiveness and align environmental objectives with local development needs (Arroyave et al., 2025).

2.3 Linking Environmental Policy, Governance, and Socioeconomic Equity

The interaction between environmental policy and governance has increasingly been conceptualized through the lens of policy feedback and institutional adaptation. Environmental fiscal reforms not only influence prices and incentives but also reshape governance practices by altering revenue allocation, administrative responsibilities, and stakeholder engagement. These institutional shifts, in turn, have significant implications for socioeconomic equity, particularly in resource-dependent economies where livelihoods and public services are closely tied to extractive sectors (Cao et al., 2022; Xu et al., 2024).

Empirical evidence suggests that environmental policies can either exacerbate or mitigate inequality depending on how revenues are managed and redistributed. Studies show that green fiscal measures, when accompanied by strong institutional quality and targeted public spending, can reduce income inequality and support inclusive development. In contrast, poorly governed reforms may intensify social disparities by disproportionately imposing adjustment costs on vulnerable populations (Abdulwahab, 2024; Zhao et al., 2025).

Furthermore, the governance context determines whether environmental policies foster institutional learning or reinforce existing power asymmetries. Research highlights that transparency, participatory governance, and accountability mechanisms are critical for ensuring that environmental interventions generate positive distributive outcomes rather than elite capture. Where governance is robust, environmental policies can strengthen public trust and social cohesion; where it is weak, they risk provoking resistance and undermining policy credibility (Borozan & Borozan, 2025; Handoyo, 2024). These dynamics underscore the need for an integrated conceptual approach that treats environmental policy, governance quality, and socioeconomic equity as mutually reinforcing components of sustainable development. This perspective provides the foundation for the analytical framework developed in the subsequent section.

To ensure conceptual clarity and analytical consistency, Table 1 summarizes the core concepts employed throughout the chapter and provides their operational definitions. By explicitly defining key terms such as environmental policy, environmental fiscal reform, institutional quality, governance ripple effects, and socioeconomic equity, the table establishes a common analytical language that underpins the theoretical framework and comparative analysis. This clarification is significant given the interdisciplinary nature of the literature spanning environmental economics, political economy, and governance studies. The definitions presented in Table 1 guide the interpretation of empirical evidence and ensure coherence between the conceptual discussion, literature review, and case analysis.

Table 1. Core Concepts and Operational Definitions Used in the Chapter

Concept	Operational Definition in This Chapter	Role in the Analysis
Environmental Policy	A set of regulatory, fiscal, and market-based instruments (including environmental taxes, carbon pricing, subsidy reforms, and regulatory standards) designed to internalize environmental externalities and influence economic behavior.	Serves as the primary policy intervention generating governance and equity ripple effects in resource-dependent economies.
Environmental Fiscal Reform (EFR)	The integration of environmental objectives into fiscal policy through taxation, public expenditure, and subsidy restructuring to promote sustainability while maintaining fiscal stability.	Acts as a key transmission channel through which environmental policies affect fiscal incentives, institutional behavior, and redistribution.
Natural Resource Dependence	A structural condition in which a significant share of government revenue, exports, or economic activity is derived from extractive natural resources such as oil, gas, or minerals.	Conditions include fiscal vulnerability, governance incentives, and the sensitivity of institutions to environmental policy interventions.
Institutional Quality	The effectiveness of governance structures, including transparency, accountability, administrative capacity, and rule enforcement, in managing public resources and implementing policy.	Functions as the central moderating variable shaping the direction and magnitude of governance ripple effects.
Governance Ripple Effects	Sequential and interconnected institutional, fiscal, and socioeconomic effects triggered by environmental policy interventions over time.	Provides the chapter's core analytical lens, linking environmental policy design to governance transformation and equity outcomes.
Fiscal Governance	The rules, institutions, and practices governing revenue collection, expenditure allocation, and fiscal accountability within the public sector.	Mediates how environmental revenues are managed, recycled, and translated into institutional and equity outcomes.
Socioeconomic Equity	The distribution of economic opportunities, income, public services, and adjustment costs across individuals, regions, and social groups.	Serves as a key outcome variable for assessing the inclusiveness of environmental policy reforms.
Policy Feedback	The process through which policy outcomes influence future political support, institutional capacity, and policy credibility.	Explains dynamic interactions between environmental policies, governance adaptation, and long-term sustainability.
Governance Capacity	The ability of public institutions to design, implement, coordinate, and enforce policies effectively across levels of government.	Determines whether environmental policies generate virtuous cycles of institutional strengthening or adverse outcomes.

Source: Designed by the Author, 2025.

3. REVIEW OF RELATED LITERATURE

The literature relevant to this chapter can be organized into three interrelated strands. The first examines natural resource dependence, institutional quality, and development outcomes. The second focuses on environmental fiscal reform and the feedback effects on governance. The third analyzes the distributional and equity implications of environmental policies. While each strand offers important insights, they are rarely integrated into a unified analytical framework, particularly in resource-dependent economies.

3.1 Resource Dependence, Institutions, and Development Outcomes

The relationship between natural resource dependence and development outcomes has long been debated, with contemporary studies emphasizing institutional quality as the decisive mediating factor. Recent empirical evidence confirms that economies heavily reliant on natural resources often experience distorted fiscal incentives, reduced tax effort, and weakened institutional accountability, particularly when governance frameworks are fragile. However, this relationship is not deterministic; somewhat, it is shaped by the interaction between resource rents and institutional capacity (Adeniyi et al., 2022; Khezri, 2024).

Studies focusing on emerging and resource-intensive economies highlight that governance structures determine whether resource wealth supports long-term development or entrenches structural vulnerabilities. Weak institutions tend to channel resource rents toward consumption and politically motivated spending, while strong institutions facilitate productive investment and fiscal discipline. This institutional mediation perspective has gained renewed relevance in the context of environmental policy reforms, which increasingly target extractive sectors and resource rents directly (Abdulwahab et al., 2024; Mahmood, 2025). Significantly, recent literature moves beyond aggregate growth outcomes to examine multidimensional development indicators, including environmental sustainability, inequality, and fiscal resilience. This shift underscores the need to integrate environmental governance into the broader resource-dependence debate, particularly as environmental policies impose new constraints and opportunities on resource-based fiscal systems (Lozhkina et al., 2021).

3.2 Environmental Fiscal Reform and Governance Feedback Effects

Environmental fiscal reform (EFR) has emerged as a central policy instrument for aligning environmental objectives with fiscal sustainability. Contemporary studies emphasize that EFR generates both direct price effects and indirect governance feedback effects, influencing institutional behavior, administrative capacity, and public trust. Evidence from recent cross-country and subnational analyses suggests that green fiscal policies can improve environmental efficiency and innovation outcomes when embedded in coherent governance frameworks (Mehta & Derbeneva, 2024; Zhang et al., 2025).

However, the literature also cautions that the governance effects of environmental fiscal reforms are highly context-dependent. In economies with limited institutional capacity, environmental taxes and expenditure programs may suffer from implementation gaps, misallocation of funds, and weak monitoring mechanisms. Studies on fiscal environmental protection expenditures indicate that efficiency gains depend critically on transparent budgeting processes and institutional coordination across levels of government (Zatti, 2020).

Further studies highlight the role of fiscal decentralization and financial governance in shaping environmental outcomes. While decentralization can enhance local responsiveness, it may also dilute accountability if institutional oversight is weak. Empirical findings from highly populated and rapidly industrializing economies demonstrate that the interaction between fiscal structures and governance quality determines whether environmental fiscal reforms translate into sustained environmental and economic benefits (Lobonț et al., 2025).

3.3 Environmental Policy, Socioeconomic Equity, and Distributional Effects

A growing body of literature examines the distributional consequences of environmental policies, with particular attention to income inequality, employment, and regional disparities. Recent studies emphasize that environmental policies are inherently redistributive, as they alter relative prices, employment structures, and access to public resources. The equity outcomes of such policies depend mainly on how revenues are recycled and how adjustment costs are managed (García-Muros et al., 2022).

Evidence from developing and resource-dependent economies suggests that environmental fiscal measures can exacerbate inequality when institutional mechanisms for redistribution are weak. Conversely, when green revenues are reinvested in education, social protection, and infrastructure, environmental policies can improve equity outcomes. Institutional adaptation and policy design flexibility are therefore critical for ensuring that environmental reforms support inclusive development rather than social fragmentation (Escuela, 2025).

Studies also highlight the role of digital governance and financial innovation in enhancing equity outcomes. Fintech-driven fiscal transparency and financial inclusion mechanisms have been shown to strengthen the distributive impact of environmental and fiscal policies, particularly in developing economies with high resource dependence. These findings suggest that technological and institutional innovations can complement environmental policy in addressing socioeconomic disparities (Carè et al., 2025; Sharma et al., 2025).

3.4 Governance, Innovation, and Sustainable Transitions

The literature increasingly recognizes that environmental sustainability cannot be achieved solely through technological innovation. Recent empirical studies demonstrate that green innovation contributes to environmental improvement only when supported by strong governance and regulatory frameworks. Without effective institutions, innovation may fail to offset the environmental pressures associated with resource dependence and fiscal expansion (Bhutta et al., 2022). This perspective aligns with broader institutional governance studies emphasizing feedback effects, policy learning, and institutional adaptation.

Scholars also emphasize the importance of integrating ethical governance and long-term fiscal discipline into sustainability strategies. Comparative analyses of fiscal systems highlight that governance models prioritizing transparency, accountability, and social justice are better equipped to manage the trade-offs inherent in environmental transitions. These insights reinforce the argument that governance reform is a necessary complement to environmental and fiscal policy interventions (Abdulwahab, 2023; Le Billon et al., 2021).

Despite these advances, three limitations persist in the existing literature. First, environmental policy, governance quality, and socioeconomic equity are often analyzed in isolation, limiting understanding of their interactive and feedback-driven dynamics. Second, empirical studies explicitly focused on resource-dependent economies remain fragmented, with limited comparative analysis across different institutional contexts. Third, there is a lack of integrative frameworks that systematically trace how environmental policies reshape fiscal incentives, institutional behavior, and equity outcomes over time. As a result, the governance consequences of environmental policy interventions remain under-theorized and empirically under-integrated.

Table 2 synthesizes the core empirical findings from the literature reviewed in this section, highlighting consistent patterns in how environmental policies interact with governance structures and socioeconomic equity. Across diverse country contexts and methodological approaches, the evidence indicates that institutional quality is the decisive factor shaping whether environmental policy interventions produce inclusive and sustainable outcomes or exacerbate inequality and fiscal fragility. The studies summarized in Table 2 collectively demonstrate that environmental fiscal reforms, green taxation, and regulatory interventions tend to yield positive governance and equity effects only when supported by transparency, accountability, and administrative capacity. This synthesis directly informs the development of the Governance Ripple Framework introduced in the subsequent section.

Table 2. Summary of Empirical Evidence on Environmental Policy, Governance, and Socioeconomic Equity

Author(s) & Year	Country/Context	Methodology	Key Empirical Finding Relevant to This Chapter
Adeniyi et al. (2022).	Resource-dependent economies	Panel econometric analysis	Natural resource dependence undermines development outcomes when institutional quality is weak, but not under strong governance.
Asiamah et al. (2022).	Developing economies	Cross-country regression	Resource rents weaken fiscal discipline and tax effort in the absence of effective institutions.
Mollick & Sui (2024).	Global sample	Dynamic panel analysis	Institutional quality moderates the relationship between resource dependence and inequality.
Ameer & Ahmad (2024).	Emerging economies	Panel data analysis	Environmental fiscal reforms improve sustainability outcomes only when embedded in strong governance frameworks.
Mehta & Derbeneva (2024).	Multi-country	Comparative empirical analysis	Environmental fiscal reforms generate governance feedback effects through institutional learning and administrative adaptation.
García-Muros et al. (2022).	Developing economies	Policy simulation and empirical review	Environmental policies are redistributive and can exacerbate inequality without compensatory fiscal mechanisms.
Zhao et al. (2025).	Emerging markets	Panel threshold analysis	Green fiscal measures reduce inequality when revenue recycling and institutional quality exceed critical thresholds.
Borozan & Borozan (2025).	European and emerging economies	Institutional analysis	Transparency and accountability determine whether environmental policies foster social cohesion or elite capture.
Lobon et al. (2025)	Industrializing economies	Panel regression	Fiscal decentralization improves environmental outcomes only when supported by strong institutional oversight.
Bhutta et al. (2022).	Resource-intensive economies	Empirical innovation analysis	Green innovation improves environmental performance only under strong governance conditions.
Carè et al. (2025).	Developing economies	Fintech-based empirical study	Digital governance enhances fiscal transparency and strengthens equity outcomes of environmental policies.
Abdulkareem et al. (2025).	Resource-dependent economies	Panel econometric analysis	Weak governance amplifies the inequality effects of environmental policy interventions.

Source: Designed by the Author, selected from the empirical studies reviewed.

Responding to these gaps, the next section develops the Governance Ripple Framework, which integrates insights from political economy, environmental fiscal reform, and institutional governance. The framework explicitly links environmental policy interventions to sequential fiscal, institutional, and equity effects, providing a structured lens for analytically unifying the fragmented literature.

4. THEORETICAL FRAMEWORK (THE GOVERNANCE RIPPLE MODEL)

4.1 Political Economy of Environmental Governance

The political economy of environmental governance provides a foundational lens for understanding how environmental policies function as instruments of institutional change rather than merely regulatory controls. Contemporary studies emphasizes that environmental policies intervene directly in distributional structures, revenue allocation, and power relations, particularly in economies where natural resource rents dominate fiscal systems. These interventions alter incentives for political actors, bureaucracies, and private stakeholders, thereby reshaping governance dynamics (Eitan, 2025).

Recent studies highlight that environmental governance outcomes depend critically on the interaction between fiscal policy design and institutional quality. Environmental regulations and fiscal instruments, such as green taxes or subsidy removals, reconfigure state–market relations and expose governance weaknesses that may have remained latent under extractive growth models. Where institutional checks and balances are weak, environmental policies can intensify rent-seeking behavior and policy resistance. Conversely, strong governance frameworks enable environmental interventions to reinforce accountability and policy credibility (Akpan & Kama, 2024; Nasution et al., 2025). This political economy perspective underscores that environmental policy effectiveness cannot be evaluated independently of governance structures. Instead, environmental reforms act as institutional stress tests, revealing the capacity of governance systems to manage trade-offs between ecological objectives, fiscal stability, and social equity.

4.2 Conceptualizing the Governance Ripple Framework

This subsection explains the internal logic of the Governance Ripple Framework and how environmental policies generate sequential institutional effects. Figure 2 depicts the Governance Ripple Framework, viewing environmental policy interventions as dynamic institutional shocks that produce sequential effects across fiscal, governance, and socioeconomic systems. Policies like taxes, carbon pricing, and standards generate first-order fiscal and regulatory effects, such as revenue shifts, cost internalization, and changes in production incentives, which affect resource-dependent economies and public finance. These effects lead to second-order institutional adaptations, where governments modify capacity, transparency, and coordination based on existing governance quality, fiscal capacity, and administrative competence. These adaptations influence policy credibility, public trust, and socioeconomic equity, thereby generating third-order feedback effects, particularly when revenues are transparently managed.

The framework also highlights a feedback loop: governance and equity outcomes shape future policy credibility and institutional learning, emphasizing that policy effectiveness depends not only on immediate environmental results but also on long-term governance and distributive impacts. Analytically, the framework emphasizes causal mechanisms rather than correlations. Environmental policies affect fiscal incentives by altering revenue composition and cost structures; these fiscal shifts then reshape institutional behavior through changes in administrative priorities, accountability pressures, and intergovernmental coordination. The resulting governance adjustments influence socioeconomic equity by determining how costs and benefits are distributed, thereby generating feedback effects that either reinforce or undermine policy credibility over time.

Figure 2. The Governance Ripple Framework: Sequential and Feedback Effects of Environmental Policy Interventions

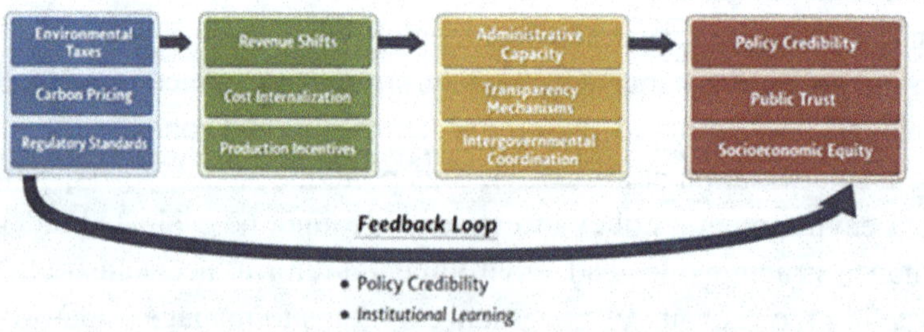

Source: Author's conceptual framework, developed from the reviewed studies.

The figure visually clarifies how environmental policy interventions initiate sequential fiscal, institutional, and equity effects, highlighting the feedback loops central to the chapter's analytical argument. Building on this perspective, the Governance Ripple Framework conceptualizes environmental policies as catalysts that generate sequential and interconnected effects across fiscal systems, institutions, and socioeconomic outcomes. The framework posits that environmental interventions produce direct, indirect, and feedback effects, collectively referred to as governance ripples. First-order (direct) effects arise from changes in fiscal incentives and regulatory constraints. Environmental taxes, pricing mechanisms, and regulatory standards directly affect extractive activities, public revenues, and production structures. In resource-dependent economies, these direct effects often involve shifts in resource rent allocation and public expenditure priorities (Bambi & Pea-Assounga, 2025; Zhang & Zhou, 2025).

Second-order (indirect) effects emerge as institutions adapt to these fiscal and regulatory changes. These include adjustments in administrative capacity, transparency mechanisms, intergovernmental fiscal relations, and monitoring systems. Empirical evidence suggests that institutional adaptation varies significantly across countries, depending on governance quality and fiscal decentralization structures (Dinh Thanh et al., 2023). Third-order (feedback) effects occur when institutional changes influence future policy credibility, public trust, and socioeconomic equity. These feedback loops determine whether environmental policies reinforce inclusive governance or generate social and political backlash. Studies indicate that positive feedback effects are more likely when environmental revenues are visibly reinvested in public goods and social protection, thereby strengthening state–society relations (Ibrahim, 2023).

4.3 Institutional Conditions Shaping Ripple Effects

This subsection identifies the institutional conditions that determine whether governance ripple effects are positive or adverse. A central proposition of the Governance Ripple Framework is that institutional quality conditions the magnitude and direction of environmental policy ripple effects. Institutions determine whether environmental interventions trigger virtuous cycles of governance improvement or vicious cycles of instability and inequality. Key institutional conditions include transparency in revenue management, accountability mechanisms, administrative competence, and coordination across government levels. Studies demonstrate that strong institutions mitigate the adverse fiscal and distributional effects associated with environmental and resource-related reforms, enabling governments to sustain policy momentum and social legitimacy (Adhikari et al., 2023; Sun & Stephen, 2025). Moreover, fiscal decentralization plays a dual role within the framework. While decentralization can enhance local responsiveness and policy tailoring, it may also complicate environmental governance if institutional oversight is fragmented. Empirical studies show that decentralization enhances environmental efficiency only when accompanied by clear accountability structures and institutional capacity at subnational levels (Li et al., 2025).

Figure 3 shows how institutional quality influences environmental policy outcomes. Weak institutions, with limited capacity, transparency, and accountability, lead to rent-seeking, policy resistance, inequality, and fiscal fragility, undermining environmental and social goals. Strong institutions, on the other hand, foster positive outcomes such as credibility, revenue recycling, inclusive growth, and stronger governance. The figure emphasizes that institutional quality shapes whether policies yield good or poor governance and equity results. Overall, it illustrates that governance quality is a key factor in the effectiveness of environmental policies, acting as a stress test that reveals existing governance conditions and explains varying outcomes across resource-dependent economies.

Figure 3. Institutional Quality as a Moderator of Environmental Policy Governance and Equity Outcomes

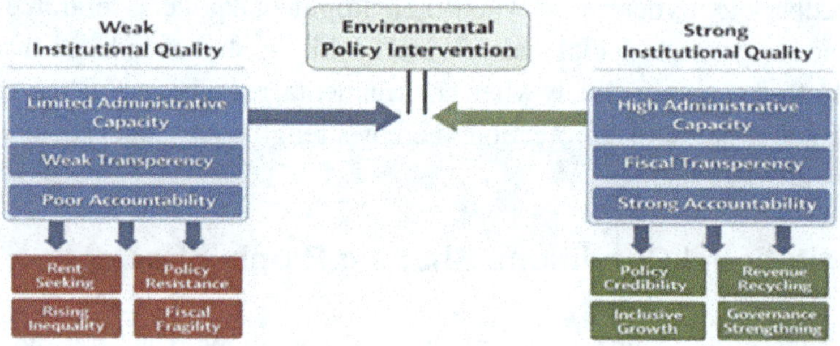

Source: *Designed by the Author from the institutional governance and environmental policy studies.*

The figure demonstrates how differences in institutional quality condition the direction and magnitude of governance and equity outcomes, contrasting virtuous cycles of institutional strengthening with adverse dynamics such as rent-seeking, policy resistance, and inequality.

4.4 Governance, Innovation, and Equity Pathways

This subsection integrates innovation and equity considerations into the Governance Ripple Framework. The Governance Ripple Framework also integrates innovation and equity considerations as endogenous components of environmental policy outcomes. Recent evidence indicates that green innovation contributes to environmental sustainability only when embedded within strong governance systems. In weak institutional contexts, innovation may fail to offset the environmental and social pressures generated by resource dependence and fiscal expansion (Wang & Yuan, 2026).

Equity pathways are similarly mediated by governance. Environmental policies redistribute costs and benefits across sectors, regions, and income groups. Where institutions support revenue recycling, participatory decision-making, and targeted social spending, environmental reforms can promote inclusive transitions. Conversely, weak governance increases the risk that environmental policies exacerbate inequality and social exclusion (Abdulkareem et al., 2025). By integrating these pathways, the Governance Ripple Framework provides a multidimensional analytical structure that links environmental policy design to institutional transformation and socioeconomic outcomes in resource-dependent economies.

4.5 Analytical Implications of the Framework

The Governance Ripple Framework offers several analytical advantages. First, it moves beyond static evaluations of environmental policy effectiveness by emphasizing dynamic institutional feedback processes. Second, it highlights governance quality as a central explanatory variable rather than a background condition. Third, it provides a flexible structure for comparative analysis across countries with differing resource profiles and institutional capacities. These features make the framework particularly suitable for examining the heterogeneous experiences of resource-dependent economies undergoing environmental transitions. The framework also informs policy design by identifying leverage points where institutional strengthening can amplify positive ripple effects and mitigate adverse outcomes. Having established the conceptual logic and analytical propositions of the Governance Ripple Framework, the chapter now turns to empirical application. The next section outlines the methodological approach used to operationalize the framework in a comparative analysis of resource-dependent economies.

5. METHODOLOGY

5.1 Research Design

This chapter adopts a mixed qualitative–comparative research design to examine how environmental policies generate governance and socioeconomic equity ripple effects in resource-dependent economies. This approach is particularly suited to the study's objectives, as it allows for the systematic exploration of institutional processes, policy feedback mechanisms, and contextual heterogeneity that cannot be fully captured through single-method or purely quantitative analyses. Recent methodological studies emphasize that governance and institutional change are best analyzed through designs that combine conceptual modeling with comparative empirical evidence. Such approaches enable researchers to trace causal mechanisms, identify contextual moderators, and account for path dependency in policy outcomes (Bergougui & Satrovic, 2025; Cai et al., 2024). In the context of environmental governance, where policy effects unfold through complex institutional channels, a mixed qualitative–comparative design provides the analytical flexibility needed to capture dynamic, non-linear relationships.

5.2 Case Selection and Comparative Logic

The empirical analysis focuses on Nigeria, Indonesia, and Chile, selected through a purposive comparative logic. These countries share a high degree of natural resource dependence but differ markedly in institutional quality, governance capacity, and experience with environmental policy. This variation enables the chapter to examine how similar environmental policy interventions produce divergent governance and equity outcomes under different institutional conditions. Comparative case study research is particularly valuable for disentangling the role of institutions in shaping policy outcomes. By examining countries with contrasting governance trajectories, the analysis isolates institutional quality as a key explanatory factor in determining the direction and magnitude of governance ripple effects. This logic aligns with recent comparative governance studies emphasizing cross-contextual learning and theory refinement rather than statistical generalization (de Abreu et al., 2023; Dokuzoğlu & Güzel, 2024).

Table 3 presents the key comparative characteristics of Nigeria, Indonesia, and Chile, illustrating structured variation in natural resource dependence, institutional quality, and environmental policy orientation. This comparison clarifies the purposive logic underlying case selection and demonstrates how the three countries represent distinct governance contexts within resource-dependent economies. Nigeria exemplifies high resource dependence combined with weak institutional capacity; Indonesia reflects intermediate outcomes shaped by decentralization and uneven governance capacity. At the same time, Chile serves as a benchmark case of strong institutions and effective environmental fiscal integration. The variation summarized in Table 3 provides the empirical foundation for examining how environmental policies generate divergent governance and equity ripple effects across institutional settings.

Table 3. Comparative Characteristics of Nigeria, Indonesia, and Chile

Country	Degree of Natural Resource Dependence	Institutional Quality Profile	Key Environmental Policy Focus	Analytical Relevance to the Chapter
Nigeria	Very high dependence on oil and gas revenues, which dominate public finance and export earnings.	Poor institutional quality is characterized by limited transparency, fiscal fragility, and constraints on accountability.	Environmental taxation, pollution control, and early-stage fiscal–environmental reforms targeting oil-related degradation.	Illustrates how environmental policies generate limited positive governance ripple effects under weak institutional conditions.
Indonesia	High dependence on natural resources, including mining, forestry, and energy, with significant regional variation.	Mixed institutional quality is shaped by decentralization, uneven administrative capacity, and variable enforcement across regions.	Deforestation control, mining regulation, subnational environmental fiscal instruments, and decentralization-linked reforms.	Demonstrates conditional governance ripple effects under intermediate institutional capacity and decentralized governance.
Chile	Resource-dependent economy heavily reliant on mining revenues, particularly copper.	Strong institutional quality marked by fiscal discipline, transparency, and effective public financial management.	Environmental taxation, regulatory standards, and integration of environmental policy within fiscal sustainability frameworks.	Serves as a benchmark case demonstrating virtuous governance and equity-ripple effects under strong institutional conditions.

Source: Author's comparative synthesis based on case evidence and governance indicators discussed.

5.3 Analytical Methods

Three complementary analytical methods are employed. First, comparative institutional analysis is used to assess how environmental policies interact with fiscal systems, regulatory frameworks, and governance structures across cases. This method focuses on institutional arrangements, incentive structures, and accountability mechanisms that mediate the effects of policy. Second, process tracing is applied to identify causal pathways linking environmental policy interventions to governance transformation and socioeconomic outcomes. Process tracing enables the examination of intermediate steps such as changes in revenue allocation, administrative practices, and stakeholder responses that generate observable ripple effects over time. This method is widely recognized as essential for unpacking policy feedback and institutional adaptation processes in governance studies (Meyer et al., 2018; Vanhala, 2017). Third, conceptual modeling operationalizes the Governance Ripple Framework developed in Section 4. The model maps relationships between environmental policy instruments, institutional conditions, and equity outcomes, providing a structured lens through which empirical evidence is interpreted.

5.4 Data Sources

The analysis draws on multiple secondary data sources to enhance validity and triangulation. These include national environmental policy documents, fiscal and budgetary reports, governance indicators, and peer-reviewed empirical studies. Particular attention is given to data on environmental fiscal measures, public revenue composition, and social expenditure patterns, which are critical for assessing governance and equity effects. Studies underscore the importance of combining fiscal, institutional, and social data when evaluating environmental policy outcomes, especially in resource-dependent contexts where data fragmentation is common. Multi-source triangulation strengthens analytical robustness and reduces the risk of single-source bias (Marlina et al., 2024; Meydan & Akkaş, 2024).

6. COMPARATIVE CASE ANALYSIS

This section applies the Governance Ripple Framework to three resource-dependent economies, Nigeria, Indonesia, and Chile, to illustrate how environmental policies interact with governance structures and socioeconomic conditions in distinct institutional contexts. The comparative analysis highlights how differences in institutional quality shape the direction and magnitude of governance and equity ripple effects.

6.1 Environmental Policy, Fiscal Fragility, and Institutional Constraints in Nigeria

This subsection examines how environmental policies interact with fiscal systems, institutional capacity, and equity outcomes in Nigeria. Nigeria represents a paradigmatic case of high resource dependence combined with persistent institutional challenges. Oil revenues dominate public finance, rendering fiscal systems susceptible to environmental policy interventions that affect extractive activities. Recent empirical evidence indicates that Nigeria's fiscal framework remains structurally weak, with limited sustainability and strong dependence on volatile revenue sources (Samuel & Kouhy, 2025; Sanusi et al., 2025). Environmental and fiscal policy reforms in Nigeria have begun to address ecological degradation, yet their governance-related ripple effects have yielded mixed outcomes. Studies examining fiscal policy and ecological footprints show that tax mechanisms can reduce environmental pressure, whereas poorly governed public expenditure may exacerbate environmental degradation. This asymmetry underscores the role of institutional effectiveness in translating environmental policies into sustainable outcomes (Omodero et al., 2022).

From a governance perspective, environmental policy reforms have exposed coordination failures between fiscal authorities and environmental institutions. Weak accountability mechanisms and limited transparency in revenue allocation have constrained the redistributive potential of environmental revenues. Evidence suggests that without institutional reforms targeting expenditure efficiency and fiscal responsibility, environmental policies risk reinforcing existing inequalities rather than promoting inclusive transitions (Nwozor et al., 2021). Nigeria's experience illustrates a fragile governance ripple, where environmental policies generate limited positive institutional feedback due to entrenched fiscal and governance constraints. Analytically, Nigeria's experience demonstrates that when environmental policies are introduced into fiscally fragile and weakly accountable systems, they amplify existing governance failures rather than correcting them, turning environmental reform into a stress multiplier rather than a governance catalyst.

6.2 Decentralization, Environmental Regulation, and Institutional Adaptation in Indonesia

This subsection examines how environmental policies interact with fiscal systems, institutional capacity, and equity outcomes in Indonesia, with particular attention to decentralization and regional variation. Indonesia offers a contrasting case characterized by substantial natural resource dependence alongside a more advanced, though complex, decentralization framework. Environmental policies in Indonesia increasingly target deforestation, mining, and energy use, with fiscal instruments deployed at both national and subnational levels. Comparative governance research highlights that Indonesia's institutional architecture enables greater policy experimentation and local adaptation, though with uneven outcomes across regions (Widjanarko & Gultom, 2024). Environmental policy reforms in Indonesia have produced notable second-order governance ripple effects, particularly in the strengthening of administrative capacity and intergovernmental coordination.

Fiscal decentralization has enabled subnational governments to tailor environmental measures to local contexts, enhancing policy responsiveness. However, empirical evidence also points to disparities in institutional capacity across regions, which influence the effectiveness of environmental enforcement and revenue recycling (Zahroh & Najicha, 2022). From an equity perspective, Indonesia's environmental policies demonstrate conditional success. Where institutional capacity is strong, environmental revenues support social and infrastructure investments that mitigate adjustment costs. Conversely, weaker regions experience uneven distributional outcomes, reinforcing regional inequality. These findings underscore the framework's emphasis on institutional quality as the key moderator of governance ripple effects. The Indonesian case illustrates that decentralization transforms environmental policy outcomes into a function of subnational institutional capacity, producing heterogeneous governance ripple effects that depend less on policy design than on local administrative competence.

6.3 Institutional Strength, Environmental Fiscal Reform, and Inclusive Outcomes in Chile

This subsection examines how environmental policies interact with fiscal systems, institutional capacity, and equity outcomes in Chile, highlighting the role of strong institutions and fiscal discipline. Chile represents a case of relatively strong institutional quality within a resource-dependent economy, particularly in the mining sector. Environmental policies in Chile have increasingly incorporated fiscal instruments, including environmental taxation and regulatory standards, to internalize ecological costs while maintaining fiscal discipline. Empirical study on resource-dependent economies indicate that Chile's governance framework enables effective management of resource revenues and environmental reforms (Bergamini et al., 2025). Environmental fiscal reforms in Chile have generated positive governance ripple effects by enhancing transparency, policy credibility, and institutional coordination.

Strong public financial management systems facilitate the productive recycling of environmental revenues into social and environmental programs, reinforcing public trust. This institutional strength has mitigated the risk of policy backlash and supported long-term sustainability goals (Hernández-Luis & Fontaine, 2025). Equity outcomes in Chile further illustrate the benefits of governance capacity. Environmental policies are embedded within broader social protection and development strategies, reducing the distributive burden on vulnerable groups. As a result, Chile demonstrates a virtuous governance ripple effect, in which environmental interventions strengthen institutions and promote inclusive development. Chile's experience confirms that strong institutional quality converts environmental policy into a governance-enhancing instrument by stabilizing fiscal expectations, reinforcing transparency, and enabling equitable revenue recycling.

6.4 Cross-Case Comparison and Synthesis

This subsection synthesizes the comparative evidence from Nigeria, Indonesia, and Chile to explain how differences in institutional quality shape governance and equity ripple effects of environmental policies. Comparing the three cases reveals clear patterns consistent with the Governance Ripple Framework. Nigeria exhibits weak institutional mediation, resulting in limited positive feedback and heightened equity risks. Indonesia demonstrates intermediate outcomes, where decentralization enables adaptation but also introduces variability. Chile exemplifies intense institutional mediation, producing positive governance and equity ripple effects. These contrasts highlight that environmental policy outcomes are not determined solely by policy ambition, but by the institutional environments within which policies operate. Strong governance transforms environmental interventions into opportunities for institutional strengthening and inclusive development, while weak governance constrains their effectiveness.

The cross-case comparison also reveals key trade-offs inherent in environmental policy reform. In weak institutional settings, environmental ambition can undermine fiscal stability and provoke social resistance, while in decentralized systems, it may increase regional inequality if capacity is uneven. Strong institutions mitigate these trade-offs by aligning fiscal discipline with redistribution mechanisms, but even in such contexts, environmental reforms require sustained administrative coordination to avoid policy fatigue and political backlash.

Figure 4 compares how environmental policy interventions create governance ripple effects in Nigeria, Indonesia, and Chile, reflecting differences in institutional quality and governance capacity in resource-dependent economies. Despite high resource dependence, each country exhibits distinct institutional contexts that shape governance and equity outcomes. Nigeria, with high dependence and weak institutions, faces adverse effects like policy resistance and increased inequality due to ineffective governance structures. Indonesia, with decentralized governance and mixed capacity, yields uneven outcomes that depend on regional administrative strength. Chile, with strong institutions, experiences positive ripple effects, including policy credibility and inclusive outcomes, where reforms reinforce governance. The figure underscores that institutional quality determines whether environmental policies yield positive or negative governance impacts, thereby linking the framework to broader policy insights.

Figure 4. Comparative Governance Ripple Effects of Environmental Policies in Nigeria, Indonesia, and Chile

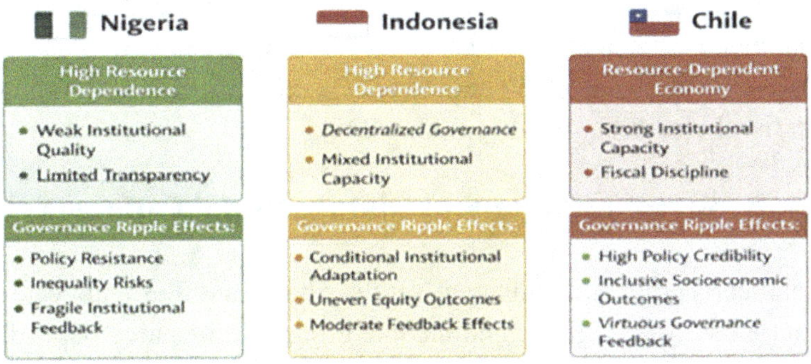

Source: *Author's comparative synthesis based on the Governance Ripple Framework and the case evidence reviewed.*

The figure synthesizes the comparative case analysis by showing how similar environmental policy interventions generate divergent governance and equity ripple effects across Nigeria, Indonesia, and Chile, driven by differing institutional capacities.

7. ENVIRONMENTAL POLICY, GOVERNANCE TRANSFORMATION, AND EQUITY OUTCOMES

7.1 Institutional Transformation Effects of Environmental Policies

Environmental policies increasingly function as catalysts for institutional transformation, particularly in resource-dependent economies where fiscal systems and governance structures are closely tied to extractive activities. Evidence from recent studies demonstrates that environmental fiscal instruments, such as green taxes, subsidy reforms, and environmentally targeted public expenditures, reshape institutional incentives by altering revenue sources, administrative responsibilities, and regulatory priorities (Sun et al., 2024). These institutional effects manifest through changes in fiscal governance, including improved budget transparency, strengthened monitoring mechanisms, and enhanced inter-agency coordination.

However, the extent of such transformation depends critically on pre-existing institutional capacity. Empirical studies show that where institutions are weak, environmental policies may increase administrative complexity without improving governance outcomes, thereby reinforcing inefficiencies and policy fragmentation (Lima et al., 2020). Conversely, economies with stronger institutional foundations are better positioned to leverage environmental reforms as opportunities for governance upgrading. Institutionalized fiscal rules, transparent revenue management, and accountability mechanisms enable governments to integrate environmental objectives into broader development strategies, reinforcing policy coherence and long-term fiscal credibility (Chong et al., 2026).

7.2 Socioeconomic Equity and Distributional Outcomes

Environmental policies are inherently redistributive, as they reallocate costs and benefits across sectors, regions, and income groups. In resource-dependent economies, these distributional effects are particularly salient because environmental interventions often target industries that provide employment, fiscal revenue, and regional economic stability. Recent empirical studies demonstrate that environmental fiscal policies can either mitigate or exacerbate inequality, depending on governance-mediated revenue use (Anjarwi, 2025; Noubissi Domguia, 2023). Where environmental revenues are recycled into social protection, education, and infrastructure, environmental policies contribute to inclusive growth and poverty reduction.

Studies examining fiscal policy and poverty dynamics reveal that targeted public spending plays a crucial role in translating fiscal reforms into tangible welfare gains, especially in contexts marked by high inequality and resource dependence (Lustig, 2023). In contrast, poorly governed environmental reforms risk imposing disproportionate adjustment costs on vulnerable populations. Evidence suggests that when environmental taxes are introduced without compensatory mechanisms, they may exacerbate unemployment, regional disparities, and social exclusion. These findings highlight the centrality of institutional design in shaping the equity ripple effects of environmental policies (Liu et al., 2023).

7.3 Policy Trade-Offs and Governance Synergies

The interaction between environmental ambition, fiscal stability, and social equity generates unavoidable policy trade-offs. Environmental policies that constrain extractive activities may reduce short-term fiscal revenues, thereby increasing pressure on public spending and social programs. However, studies suggest that these trade-offs can be managed through governance-sensitive policy design that emphasizes long-term sustainability over short-term fiscal gains (Ding et al., 2025). Governance synergies emerge when environmental policies are aligned with fiscal discipline and institutional reform. Studies show that integrating environmental objectives with fiscal sustainability frameworks enhances policy credibility and reduces macroeconomic instability.

Coordinated fiscal and environmental strategies enable governments to manage revenue volatility while supporting ecological transition and social inclusion (Lu et al., 2023). Institutional learning plays a key role in transforming trade-offs into synergies. As governments gain experience with environmental policy implementation, administrative capacity improves, and policy instruments become more refined. This adaptive process reinforces positive governance ripple effects, enabling environmental policies to evolve from isolated interventions into core components of sustainable development strategies (Dressel et al., 2021). These findings show governance is key to whether environmental policies improve or harm socioeconomic equity. Strong institutions boost positive effects through transparency, redistribution, and engagement, while weak ones reduce benefits and increase risks. The Governance Ripple Framework emphasizes that policy success depends on how effectively governance systems are reshaped to support equitable development. Policies should be judged not just on environmental outcomes but also on their ability to manage fiscal and social trade-offs without harming institutions' legitimacy.

8. POLICY IMPLICATIONS AND PRACTICAL RECOMMENDATIONS

Building on the empirical findings and the Governance Ripple Framework, Table 4 translates the chapter's analytical insights into concrete policy design considerations. The table outlines key environmental policy instruments and identifies the governance conditions required for these instruments to generate positive institutional and socioeconomic equity outcomes. By explicitly linking policy design levers to governance capacity and redistribution mechanisms, Table 4 shows how environmental ambition, fiscal stability, and social inclusion can be pursued jointly. This framework highlights that environmental policies are most effective when embedded within transparent fiscal systems, strong accountability structures, and adaptive institutional arrangements.

Table 4. Environmental Policy Design Levers and Expected Governance and Socioeconomic Equity Outcomes

Policy Design Lever	Governance Condition Required	Expected Governance Effects	Expected Socioeconomic Equity Outcomes
Environmental Taxes and Carbon Pricing	Transparent tax administration, strong enforcement capacity, and fiscal accountability mechanisms.	Enhances revenue credibility, strengthens fiscal governance, and improves policy predictability.	Reduces inequality by recycling revenues into social protection, education, and employment-support programs.
Environmental Fiscal Reform (EFR)	Integrated fiscal–environmental institutions and coordinated public financial management systems.	Aligns environmental objectives with fiscal sustainability and improves inter-agency coordination.	Supports inclusive growth by reallocating public spending toward long-term social and environmental investments.
Revenue Recycling Mechanisms	Rule-based allocation frameworks, budget transparency, and independent oversight institutions.	Builds public trust, reduces rent-seeking, and strengthens state–society relations.	Mitigates the regressive impacts of environmental policies and protects vulnerable populations.
Subsidy Reform and Fossil Fuel Phase-Out	Strong political commitment, stakeholder engagement, and compensatory policy design.	Reduces fiscal leakage, improves expenditure efficiency, and enhances policy credibility.	Prevents social backlash when accompanied by targeted transfers and regional development programs.
Fiscal Decentralization of Environmental Policies	Clear accountability structures and sufficient subnational administrative capacity.	Improves local responsiveness while maintaining national policy coherence.	Reduces regional disparities by allowing local governments to tailor policies to community needs.

continued on following page

Table 4. Continued

Policy Design Lever	Governance Condition Required	Expected Governance Effects	Expected Socioeconomic Equity Outcomes
Green Public Investment	Transparent project selection, performance monitoring, and long-term fiscal planning.	Strengthens institutional capacity and supports sustainable development strategies.	Generates employment opportunities and promotes equitable access to infrastructure and services.
Digital Governance and Fintech Integration	Digital infrastructure, data transparency, and regulatory oversight.	Enhances monitoring of environmental revenues and expenditures, reducing corruption risks.	Improves financial inclusion and enables targeted redistribution during environmental transitions.

Source: Designed by the Author, derived from the Governance Ripple Framework and policy literature reviewed.

8.1 Designing Governance-Sensitive Environmental Policies

A central policy implication emerging from this analysis is that environmental policies in resource-dependent economies must be explicitly designed with governance capacity in mind. Uniform environmental policy instruments, such as carbon taxes or subsidy removals, are unlikely to yield consistent outcomes across institutional contexts. Recent evidence indicates that governance quality determines whether environmental reforms enhance fiscal credibility and institutional accountability or generate resistance and implementation failure (Q. J. Wang et al., 2024). Policymakers should therefore adopt context-sensitive policy sequencing, prioritizing institutional strengthening alongside environmental ambition. This includes investing in administrative capacity, regulatory oversight, and inter-agency coordination before or concurrently with the introduction of complex environmental fiscal instruments. Governance-sensitive design increases the likelihood that environmental policies will produce positive ripple effects across fiscal and institutional systems.

8.2 Revenue Recycling and Equity-Oriented Policy Design

Effective revenue recycling is essential for mitigating the distributional impacts of environmental policies. Empirical studies consistently show that environmental fiscal measures gain political and social legitimacy when revenues are transparently reinvested in social protection, education, infrastructure, and employment-support programs. In resource-dependent economies, such recycling mechanisms are particularly important for cushioning regions and populations affected by reduced extractive activity (Waris, 2024). Policy frameworks should institutionalize earmarking mechanisms or rule-based allocation systems that link environmental revenues to equity-enhancing expenditures. Evidence suggests that such arrangements reduce inequality and strengthen public trust, provided they are supported by robust monitoring and accountability structures (Ravaioli et al., 2025). Revenue recycling should be adaptive, allowing governments to respond to evolving socioeconomic conditions during environmental transitions.

8.3 Strengthening Fiscal and Institutional Accountability

Environmental policies increase the complexity of fiscal systems, creating new revenue streams, expenditure categories, and regulatory responsibilities. Without strong accountability mechanisms, this complexity can exacerbate governance weaknesses. Recent studies highlight that transparent public financial management, independent oversight institutions, and performance-based budgeting are critical for ensuring that environmental policies translate into improved governance outcomes (Y. Wang et al., 2024). Governments should prioritize reforms that enhance fiscal transparency, including digital reporting systems, open-budget initiatives, and independent audits of environmental revenues and expenditures. Such measures reduce the risk of elite capture and improve the effectiveness of environmental spending, thereby reinforcing positive governance ripple effects.

8.4 Leveraging Green Finance and Digital Innovation

Green finance and digital innovation offer important complementary tools for strengthening environmental governance in resource-dependent economies. Research indicates that fintech-enabled financial inclusion and digital fiscal systems can enhance the transparency, efficiency, and equity of environmental policy implementation. These tools facilitate real-time monitoring of revenue flows, improve access to green investment opportunities, and support targeted social transfers (Singh et al., 2025). Policymakers should integrate green bonds, sustainable finance instruments, and digital payment platforms into environmental policy frameworks. When embedded within strong governance systems, these innovations can amplify the institutional and equity benefits of environmental reforms while reducing administrative burdens and implementation costs.

8.5 Managing Trade-Offs and Ensuring Policy Resilience

Finally, environmental policies inevitably involve trade-offs between ecological objectives, fiscal stability, and short-term economic performance. The findings of this chapter suggest that these trade-offs are manageable when policies are anchored in long-term institutional reform strategies. Evidence from recent fiscal policy studies underscores the importance of policy coherence, inter-temporal fiscal planning, and coordination between fiscal and environmental authorities (Chen et al., 2026). Governments should adopt adaptive policy frameworks that allow for iterative learning, stakeholder feedback, and policy adjustment. Such flexibility enhances resilience and enables environmental policies to evolve in response to economic shocks, political constraints, and institutional learning processes.

Beyond national policy design, these recommendations carry direct managerial relevance for public-sector executives responsible for budgeting, environmental regulation, and fiscal coordination. Senior managers in ministries of finance, environment, and planning play a critical role in operationalizing environmental policies through budget execution, inter-agency coordination, and performance monitoring. The effectiveness of environmental reforms, therefore, depends not only on political commitment but also on managerial capacity to translate policy mandates into enforceable rules, transparent financial practices, and equitable service delivery.

9. MANAGERIAL AND STAKEHOLDER IMPLICATIONS

Environmental policies in resource-dependent economies do not operate in isolation; they affect and are shaped by the actions of multiple stakeholders, including policymakers, public-sector managers, development institutions, private-sector actors, and civil society. Understanding the governance and equity ripple effects of environmental policies, therefore, has critical managerial and stakeholder implications.

9.1 Implications for Policymakers and Public Sector Managers

For policymakers and senior public sector managers, the findings underscore the need to treat environmental policy as a governance reform agenda rather than merely an environmental intervention. Environmental fiscal measures introduce new revenue streams, regulatory responsibilities, and coordination demands that require enhanced managerial capacity. Recent governance research emphasizes that public sector effectiveness depends on the alignment between policy ambition and administrative capability, particularly in complex reform areas such as environmental governance (Kaplaner et al., 2025). Public managers must therefore prioritize institutional coordination across ministries of finance, environment, energy, and planning. The absence of such coordination has been shown to undermine environmental policy implementation and weaken fiscal accountability. Strengthening performance management systems, inter-ministerial task forces, and data-sharing platforms can improve policy coherence and reduce implementation bottlenecks.

9.2 Implications for Subnational Governments

Subnational governments play a critical role in implementing environmental policies, especially in decentralized and resource-dependent economies. Evidence suggests that environmental outcomes and equity effects vary significantly across regions, driven by differences in local governance capacity and fiscal autonomy. Strengthening subnational institutional capacity is therefore essential for ensuring consistent policy outcomes (Li & Li, 2024; Sagita & Budi, 2024). For subnational managers, the findings imply a need to move beyond compliance-focused implementation toward adaptive environmental management. Local public managers should develop region-specific environmental fiscal plans, strengthen administrative capacity for monitoring and enforcement, and actively engage communities to manage adjustment costs and prevent policy resistance. Local governments require technical expertise, fiscal resources, and decision-making autonomy to adapt environmental policies to local conditions. At the same time, central governments must establish clear accountability frameworks to prevent policy fragmentation and uneven enforcement. Capacity-building programs and conditional fiscal transfers linked to environmental performance can enhance subnational effectiveness while maintaining national policy coherence.

9.3 Implications for Development Institutions and International Partners

International development institutions and donors increasingly support environmental and climate-related reforms in resource-dependent economies. The findings of this chapter suggest that such support should move beyond financing environmental projects to strengthening governance systems that sustain policy effectiveness. Recent studies indicate that development assistance is most effective when it reinforces institutional capacity, transparency, and policy learning rather than substituting for domestic governance functions (Dzinamarira & Moyo, 2024). Development partners should therefore integrate governance diagnostics into environmental program design, ensuring that financial and technical assistance aligns with institutional realities. Supporting peer learning, policy experimentation, and monitoring systems can help governments manage the governance ripple effects of environmental reforms more effectively.

9.4 Implications for the Private Sector

The private sector, particularly firms operating in extractive and resource-intensive industries, is directly affected by environmental policy reforms. Environmental regulations and fiscal measures reshape investment incentives, cost structures, and risk profiles. Evidence suggests that policy predictability and institutional credibility are key determinants of private sector response to environmental reforms (Lobon et al., 2025). Managers in the private sector benefit from engaging proactively with policymakers to support transparent and stable regulatory frameworks. Firms that align investment strategies with environmental and governance reforms are better positioned to manage transition risks and capitalize on emerging green opportunities. Public–private dialogue mechanisms can facilitate this alignment and reduce policy uncertainty. From a managerial perspective, firms operating in resource-dependent sectors should incorporate environmental policy scenarios into risk management and capital allocation decisions, ensuring alignment with evolving regulatory and governance expectations.

9.5 Implications for Civil Society and Local Communities

Civil society organizations and local communities are central to ensuring the social legitimacy of environmental policies. Research indicates that participatory governance mechanisms enhance transparency, accountability, and equity outcomes by giving affected communities a voice in policy design and implementation (Fontaine et al., 2022). Empowering civil society through access to information, consultation processes, and monitoring roles strengthens downward accountability and reduces the risk of elite capture. Community engagement is critical in resource-dependent regions where environmental policies directly affect livelihoods and regional development prospects.

These implications highlight that effective environmental governance requires coordinated action across stakeholder groups. Policymakers set strategic direction, public managers operationalize reforms, development partners support institutional strengthening, private actors adapt investment behavior, and civil society ensures accountability. The success of environmental policies in resource-dependent economies, therefore, hinges on aligning stakeholder incentives within robust governance frameworks.

10. FUTURE RESEARCH DIRECTIONS

This chapter outlines future research directions on environmental policy governance and equity in resource-dependent economies. A key gap is the focus on short- to medium-term analyses, while ignoring long-term effects such as institutional learning, political adaptation, and fiscal restructuring. Future studies should adopt longitudinal, long-horizon approaches to differentiate between temporary costs and lasting transformations, and to assess policy resilience and fiscal sustainability. Expanding geographic scope to regions such as the Middle East, Central Asia, and fragile states would improve cross-contextual understanding and test governance frameworks. Subnational research, crucial for understanding decentralization and local capacity, remains underdeveloped. Methodologically, combining econometrics with qualitative methods, such as process tracing, enhances insight into institutional mechanisms. Incorporating environmental policy variables and institutional indicators into fiscal models increases rigor and relevance. Greater focus on labor and employment effects in extractive regions undergoing environmental change can inform just transition strategies. The rise of digital governance and fintech offers new research avenues; however, careful analysis is needed to determine if digital innovation reduces or deepens existing governance and digital divides.

11. CONCLUSION

This chapter examines how environmental policies extend far beyond ecological objectives to reshape governance structures and socioeconomic equity in resource-dependent economies. Drawing on the Governance Ripple Framework, the analysis demonstrates that environmental policies function as institutional interventions that reconfigure fiscal incentives, administrative practices, and distributional outcomes. The chapter's central contribution lies in conceptualizing these effects as dynamic and interlinked ripples rather than isolated policy outcomes.

The comparative evidence from Nigeria, Indonesia, and Chile underscores a consistent pattern: governance quality is the decisive factor that determines whether environmental policies generate virtuous or adverse ripple effects. In contexts of weak institutional capacity, environmental reforms tend to expose fiscal fragility, intensify inequality, and provoke policy resistance. Conversely, strong institutions enable environmental policies to reinforce transparency, fiscal discipline, and inclusive development. The chapter also highlights that environmental policies are inherently redistributive. Their equity outcomes depend on how revenues are managed, how adjustment costs are distributed, and whether affected communities are meaningfully engaged. The evidence reviewed in this chapter shows that governance-sensitive revenue recycling, particularly toward education, social protection, and regional development, can transform environmental reforms into tools for reducing inequality and strengthening social cohesion.

The analysis challenges technocratic approaches that treat environmental policy design as purely economic or regulatory exercises. Instead, it demonstrates that environmental ambition, fiscal sustainability, and social equity are inseparable policy objectives, jointly shaped by institutional arrangements. The Governance Ripple

Framework offers a structured lens through which policymakers and scholars can anticipate policy feedback effects, manage trade-offs, and design reforms that are both environmentally effective and socially legitimate. The chapter contributes to the edited volume's overarching goal by advancing a governance-centered understanding of the ripple effects of environmental policies. It provides theoretical, empirical, and practical insights for resource-dependent economies navigating the complex transition toward sustainable development. Ultimately, the findings affirm that environmental policies can serve as powerful catalysts for institutional reform and inclusive growth, but only when embedded within robust, accountable, and adaptive governance systems.

Within the broader context of this volume, the Governance Ripple Framework helps unify diverse insights on environmental policy impacts by demonstrating how economic, financial, and institutional effects are dynamically interconnected. The chapter thus reinforces the book's central message: that environmental policies should be understood not as sector-specific tools, but as systemic interventions with far-reaching governance and equity implications. By foregrounding institutional quality as the key mediator of these ripple effects, the chapter strengthens the volume's analytical coherence and practical relevance.

CONFLICT OF INTEREST DECLARATION

The authors declare that they have no conflicts of interest regarding the publication of this chapter.

AI USE DECLARATION

The authors acknowledge that artificial intelligence tools were used solely to improve language clarity and readability. The authors reviewed and approved all content and are fully responsible for the final version of this chapter.

REFERENCES

Abdulahi, M. E., Shu, Y., & Khan, M. A. (2025). Impact of natural resource management on entrepreneurial activity and SME growth in emerging economies: Does the rule of law matter? *Resources Policy*, *108*, 105674. DOI: 10.1016/j.resourpol.2025.105674

Abdulkareem, S. A., Mohammed, A. H., Hassan, S. N. S., Fahmi, A. M., & Saeed, M. N.Sarah Ali AbdulkareemAws Hamid MohammedShahd Nasser Saadi HassanAhmed Mohammed FahmiMatai Nagi Saeed. (2025). Decision-making in environmental risk management: Case study on adaptive strategies in U.S. cities under uncertainty. *Environment and Social Psychology*, *10*(9). Advance online publication. DOI: 10.59429/esp.v10i9.3968

Abdulwahab, L. O. (2023). The role of Institutional quality, human capital development on economic growth in Sub-Saharan Africa. [IJBE]. *International Journal of Business Economics*, *5*(1), 92–115. DOI: 10.30596/ijbe.v5i1.16161

Abdulwahab, L. O. (2024). Assessing the Resource Curse Hypothesis across the ECOWAS Region: A Systematic Review of Socioeconomic and Political Impacts. *Proceeding Medan International Conference on Economic and Business*, *2*(0), 490–499. https://doi.org/DOI: 10.30596/MICEB.V2I0.795

Abdulwahab, L. O. (2026). Healthy Aging and Resource Sustainability. *Economic Transformations in Population Aging*, 313–348. DOI: 10.4018/979-8-3373-6117-8.ch010

Abdulwahab, L. O., & Azam, H. (2026). Platform Work in Europe's Green and Care Economies: Regulatory Pathways for Sustainability, Social Protection, and Fair Work. In *Regulating the Gig Economy in the European Union: Challenges, Innovations, and Global Impacts* (pp. 99-124). IGI Global Scientific Publishing.

Abdulwahab, L. O., & Bubari Umar, H. (2025). *Can a Blessing Become a Peril? Exploring Resource Abundant, Economic Growth, and Conflict in the Economic Community of West African States (ECOWAS)*. DOI: 10.20944/preprints202504.2139.v1

Abdulwahab, L. O., & Firmansyah, E. A. (2024). Are abundant natural resources in the Democratic Republic of the Congo a blessing or curse? *Journal of Innovation in Business and Economics*, *8*(01), 47–60.

Adeniyi, O., Kumeka, T. T., & Alagbada, O. (2022). NATURAL RESOURCE DEPENDENCE AND TAX EFFORT IN SUB-SAHARAN AFRICA. *Journal of Economic Development*, *47*(1), 29–64. DOI: 10.35866/caujed.2022.47.1.002

Adhikari, B., King, J., Vadlamannati, K. C., & Chachu, D. O. (2023). Why do some natural resource-rich countries adopt prudent fiscal rules? An empirical analysis. *The Extractive Industries and Society*, *14*, 101234. Advance online publication. DOI: 10.1016/j.exis.2023.101234

Akhundov, R., Tangirov, A., & Sultonov, A. (2025). Political Dimensions of Global Ecological Governance Frameworks. *BIO Web of Conferences, 151*. DOI: 10.1051/bioconf/202515102008

Akpan, U., & Kama, U. (2024a). Does institutional quality really matter for environmental quality? *Energy & Environment*, *35*(8), 4361–4385. DOI: 10.1177/0958305X231180702

Akpan, U., & Kama, U. (2024b). Does institutional quality really matter for environmental quality? *Energy & Environment*, *35*(8), 4361–4385. DOI: 10.1177/0958305X231180702

Ameer, W., & Ahmad, K. (2024). How wealthy in natural resource leads environmental sustainability in developing economies? An empirical investigation. *Journal of Environmental Management*, *370*, 122496. Advance online publication. DOI: 10.1016/j.jenvman.2024.122496

Anjarwi, A. W. (2025). Tax burden and poverty in lower-middle-income countries: The moderating role of fiscal freedom. *Development Studies Research*, *12*(1), 2466511. Advance online publication. DOI: 10.1080/21665095.2025.2466511

Arroyave, L. O., Lopes, R., & Santos, R. (2025). Leveraging local environmental management in the scope of an administrative decentralization process: The case of Portuguese coastal municipalities. *Journal of Environmental Management*, *394*, 127052. Advance online publication. DOI: 10.1016/j.jenvman.2025.127052

Asiamah, O., Agyei, S. K., Bossman, A., Agyei, E. A., Asucam, J., & Arku-Asare, M. (2022). Natural resource dependence and institutional quality: Evidence from Sub-Saharan Africa. *Resources Policy*, *79*, 102967. Advance online publication. DOI: 10.1016/j.resourpol.2022.102967

Bambi, P. D. R., Batatana, M. L. D., Appiah, M., & Tetteh, D. (2024). Governance, institutions, and climate change resilience in Sub-Saharan Africa: Assessing the threshold effects. *Frontiers in Environmental Science*, *12*, 1352344. Advance online publication. DOI: 10.3389/fenvs.2024.1352344

Bambi, P. D. R., & Pea-Assounga, J. B. B. (2025). Impact of gold price, financial development, renewable energy, economic growth, urbanization, and environmental tax on environmental degradation. *Frontiers in Environmental Science*, *13*, 1631189. Advance online publication. DOI: 10.3389/fenvs.2025.1631189

Barra, C., & Falcone, P. M. (2025). Institutional factors and environmental performance: Insights from global economies. *Economic Systems*, 101364. Advance online publication. DOI: 10.1016/j.ecosys.2025.101364

Bergamini, K., Rugiero, V., Ángel, P., Mollenhauer, K., Alarcón, A., & Manríquez, G. (2025). Global Challenges and National Responses: Indicators to Evaluate Public Policies for Mining Development in Chile in the Context of the Global Energy Transition. *Sustainability (Basel)*, *17*(17), 7814. Advance online publication. DOI: 10.3390/su17177814

Bergougui, B., & Satrovic, E. (2025). Towards eco-efficiency of OECD countries: How does environmental governance restrain the destructive ecological effect of the excess use of natural resources? *Ecological Informatics*, *87*, 103093. Advance online publication. DOI: 10.1016/j.ecoinf.2025.103093

Bhutta, A. I., Ullah, M. R., Sultan, J., Riaz, A., & Sheikh, M. F. (2022). Impact of Green Energy Production, Green Innovation, Financial Development on Environment Quality: A Role of Country Governance in Pakistan. *International Journal of Energy Economics and Policy*, *12*(1), 316–326. DOI: 10.32479/ijeep.11986

Borozan, D., & Borozan, L. (2025). Estimating the Governance Effect on Carbon Dioxide Emissions in Croatia. *Natural Resources Forum*. DOI: 10.1111/1477-8947.70025

Bosomtwe, E. (2025). Fiscal Policy, Institutional Quality, and Sustainable Development Goals: A Perspective of Anglophone Countries in West Africa. *Circular Economy and Sustainability*, *5*(1), 347–366. DOI: 10.1007/s43615-024-00422-1

Cai, H. H., Lee, H. F., Khan, N. U., & Yuan, Q. (2024). Are natural resources a curse, a blessing, or a double-edged sword? Implications for environmental sustainability. *Journal of Environmental Management*, *367*, 122008. Advance online publication. DOI: 10.1016/j.jenvman.2024.122008

Cao, H., Zhang, L., Qi, Y., Yang, Z., & Li, X. (2022). Government auditing and environmental governance: Evidence from China's auditing system reform. *Environmental Impact Assessment Review*, *93*, 106705. Advance online publication. DOI: 10.1016/j.eiar.2021.106705

Carè, R., Boitan, I. A., Stoian, A. M., & Fatima, R. (2025). Exploring the landscape of financial inclusion through the lens of financial technologies: A review. *Finance Research Letters*, *72*, 106500. Advance online publication. DOI: 10.1016/j.frl.2024.106500

Chen, G., Rjoub, H., & Shao, X. (2026). The Expository Role of Fiscal Policy in Achieving Environmental Sustainability: Evidence Based on Positive and Negative Fluctuations. *Fluctuation and Noise Letters*, 2650022. Advance online publication. DOI: 10.1142/S0219477526500227

Chong, Z., Chen, G., Lu, H., & Li, Z. (2026). Environmental Judicial Reform and Corporate Sustainable Development: A Quasi-Natural Experiment in China. *Sustainability (Basel)*, *18*(1), 15. Advance online publication. DOI: 10.3390/su18010015

de Abreu, M. C. S., Soares, R. A., Daniel-Vasconcelos, V., & Crisóstomo, V. L. (2023). Does board diversity encourage an environmental policy focused on resource use, emission reduction and innovation? The case of companies in Latin America. *Corporate Social Responsibility and Environmental Management*, *30*(3), 1161–1176. DOI: 10.1002/csr.2411

Ding, R., Dai, J., Zhang, Y., Tan, T., & Chou, L. C. (2025). Dynamics in green governance in China: Exploring the relationship between carbon emissions, water consumption and economic planning. *Desalination and Water Treatment*, *322*, 101120. Advance online publication. DOI: 10.1016/j.dwt.2025.101120

Dinh Thanh, S., Nguyen, C. P., Duy-Tung, B., Binh, N. Q., & Van, D. T. B. (2023). Spatial spillover effects of fiscal decentralization on governance and public administration quality. *Regional Studies*, *57*(3), 478–496. DOI: 10.1080/00343404.2022.2078801

Dokuzoğlu, S., & Güzel, A. E. (2024). Democracy, governance, and environmental policy effectiveness: A cross-country analysis with Sustainable Governance Indicators. *European Journal of Government and Economics*, *13*(1), 103–119. DOI: 10.17979/ejge.2024.13.1.9902

Dressel, S., Sjölander-Lindqvist, A., Johansson, M., Ericsson, G., & Sandström, C. (2021). Achieving social and ecological outcomes in collaborative environmental governance: Good examples from swedish moose management. *Sustainability (Basel)*, *13*(4), 1–21. DOI: 10.3390/su13042329

Dzinamarira, T., & Moyo, E. (2024). Expanding technical assistance: A call for a more nuanced approach for sustainable HIV programs in Sub-Saharan Africa. *International Journal of Infectious Diseases*, *146*, 107135. Advance online publication. DOI: 10.1016/j.ijid.2024.107135

Eitan, A. (2025). Privatizing environmental governance: The evolving relationship between regulators and private entities. *Journal of Environmental Policy and Planning*, 1–27. Advance online publication. DOI: 10.1080/1523908X.2025.2576781

Escuela, M. B. (2025). Inclusive institutions and policies: stakeholders in the promotion of sustainable practices[Instituciones y políticas inclusivas: stakeholders en la promoción de prácticas sostenibles (1)]. *Trabajo y Derecho, 2025-June*(21). DOI: 10.32029/2386-8112.10.21.2025

Ezquerro, L., Coimbra, R., Bauluz, B., Núñez-Lahuerta, C., Román-Berdiel, T., & Moreno-Azanza, M. (2024). Large dinosaur egg accumulations and their significance for understanding nesting behaviour. *Geoscience Frontiers*, *15*(5), 101872. Advance online publication. DOI: 10.1016/j.gsf.2024.101872

Fontaine, G., Carrasco, C., & Rodrigues, C. (2022). How transparency enhances public accountability: The case of environmental governance in Chile. *The Extractive Industries and Society*, *9*, 101040. Advance online publication. DOI: 10.1016/j.exis.2021.101040

García-Muros, X., Morris, J., & Paltsev, S. (2022). Toward a just energy transition: A distributional analysis of low-carbon policies in the USA. *Energy Economics*, *105*, 105769. Advance online publication. DOI: 10.1016/j.eneco.2021.105769

Handoyo, S. (2024). Public governance and national environmental performance nexus: Evidence from cross-country studies. *Heliyon*, *10*(23), e40637. Advance online publication. DOI: 10.1016/j.heliyon.2024.e40637

Hernández-Luis, A., & Fontaine, G. (2025). Transparency and Corruption Control in Latin America: Lessons from Chile. In *International Series on Public Policy: Part F4940* (pp. 251–273). Palgrave Macmillan. DOI: 10.1007/978-3-031-90649-7_12

Ibrahim, M. (2023). From policy to politics? Exploring feedback effects of social protection on state-citizen relations in Ghana. *Social Policy and Administration*, *57*(6), 902–918. DOI: 10.1111/spol.12938

Kaplaner, C., Knill, C., & Steinebach, Y. (2025). Administrative overload and policy triage: Causal evidence from the introduction of the Acid Rain Program in the United States. *Journal of Public Administration: Research and Theory*, *35*(4), 422–433. DOI: 10.1093/jopart/muaf020

Khezri, M. (2024). The Interplay Between Resource Wealth and Tax Revenue: Implications for Fiscal Policy and Institutional Development in the Kurdistan Region. In *Perspectives on Development in the Middle East and North Africa (MENA) Region: Part F3979* (pp. 63–74). Springer. DOI: 10.1007/978-981-97-7725-9_4

Le Billon, P., Lujala, P., & Rustad, S. A. (2021). Transparency in environmental and resource governance: Theories of change for the eiti. *Global Environmental Politics, 21*(3), 124–146. DOI: 10.1162/glep_a_00610

Li, G., Zong, Q., Chen, X., & Song, M. (2025). Intergovernmental environmental affairs division and environmental public services supply: Evidence from 289 cities in China. *Energy & Environment, 36*(4), 1929–1948. DOI: 10.1177/0958305X231201974

Li, Q., & Zhang, S. (2025). Impact of globalization and industrialization on ecological footprint: Do institutional quality and renewable energy matter? *Frontiers in Environmental Science, 13*, 1535638. Advance online publication. DOI: 10.3389/fenvs.2025.1535638

Li, Z., & Li, Y. (2024). The Impact of Intergovernmental Cooperation and Local Fiscal Autonomy on Environmental Regional Governance: Evidence From China Yangtze River Delta Urban Agglomeration. *SAGE Open, 14*(2), 21582440241252253. Advance online publication. DOI: 10.1177/21582440241252253

Lima, A. T., Bastos, F. A., Teubner, F. J.Jr, Neto, R. R., Cooper, A., & Barroso, G. F. (2020). Strengths and Weaknesses of a Hybrid Post-disaster Management Approach: The Doce River (Brazil) Mine-Tailing Dam Burst. *Environmental Management, 65*(6), 711–724. DOI: 10.1007/s00267-020-01279-4

Liu, Y., Zhang, Y., Yang, Y., & Chen, X. (2023). Dark side of environmental regulation: Wage inequality cost. *Journal of Comparative Economics, 51*(2), 524–544. DOI: 10.1016/j.jce.2022.11.004

Lobonț, O. R., Varadi, A. E., Vătavu, S., & Doran, N. M. (2025). Bridges or Barriers? Unpacking the Institutional Drivers of Business Climate Adaptation in the EU. *Sustainability (Basel), 17*(11), 4865. Advance online publication. DOI: 10.3390/su17114865

Lozhkina, S. L., Gusarova, O. M., Mamrukova, O. I., Sivakova, S. Y., & Lozhkin, V. A. (2021). Forecasting the environmental and economic indicators of the enterprise, taking into account their mutual proportionality in dynamics for the purposes of sustainable development. *Rivista di Studi sulla Sostenibilità*, (2), 319–332. DOI: 10.3280/RISS2021-002021

Lu, J., Wang, T., & Liu, X. (2023). Can environmental governance policy synergy reduce carbon emissions? *Economic Analysis and Policy, 80*, 570–585. DOI: 10.1016/j.eap.2023.09.003

Lucy. (2025). Climate Action and Resilience for a Sustainable Future: The Roles of the UN, WTO, and IMF. In *Approaches to Global Sustainability, Markets, and Governance: Part F745* (pp. 177–198). Springer. DOI: 10.1007/978-981-96-7181-6_10

Lustig, N. (2023). Fiscal policy, income redistribution, and poverty reduction in low-and middle-income countries. In *Commitment to Equity Handbook* (2nd ed.). Estimating the Impact of Fiscal Policy on Inequality and Poverty., https://www.scopus.com/pages/publications/105014232554?origin=scopusAI

Mahmood, H. (2025). An Empirical Assessment of Oil, Natural Gas, Mineral, and Forest Rents on CO2 Emissions in Saudi Arabia. *Challenges in Sustainability*, *13*(3), 366–376. DOI: 10.56578/cis130304

Marlina, E., Purwaningsih, M., Siagian, A. H. A. M., Al Hakim, S., & Maryati, I. (2024). Ensuring Trustworthiness in Qualitative Research: The Role of Triangulation Techniques. In *Qualitative Research Methods for Dissertation Research* (pp. 347–375). IGI Global. DOI: 10.4018/979-8-3693-3069-2.ch012

Mehta, D., & Derbeneva, V. (2024). Impact of environmental fiscal reforms on carbon emissions of EURO-4 countries: CS-NARDL approach. *International Journal of Thermofluids*, *21*, 100550. Advance online publication. DOI: 10.1016/j.ijft.2023.100550

Meydan, C. H., & Akkaş, H. (2024). The role of triangulation in qualitative research: Converging perspectives. In *Principles of Conducting Qualitative Research in Multicultural Settings* (pp. 98–129). IGI Global., DOI: 10.4018/979-8-3693-3306-8.ch006

Meyer, C., Chen, C., & Matzdorf, B. (2018). Qualitative comparative institutional analysis of environmental governance: Implications from research on payments for ecosystem services. *Ecosystem Services*, *34*, 169–180. DOI: 10.1016/j.ecoser.2018.07.008

Mollick, A., & Sui, L. (2024). Entrepreneurship, Resource Rents and Institutions. *Entrepreneurship Research Journal*, *14*(4), 1669–1699. DOI: 10.1515/erj-2023-0028

Nasution, M. S., Rusli, Z., Heriyanto, M., Zulkarnaini, , Syahza, A., Adianto, , Mayarni, , & Ismandianto, . (2025). Green governance and institutional resilience: Strengthening environmental policies for a low-carbon economy in mangrove ecosystems. *Frontiers in Political Science*, *7*, 1631249. Advance online publication. DOI: 10.3389/fpos.2025.1631249

Noubissi Domguia, E. (2023). Taxing for a better life? The impact of environmental taxes on income distribution and inclusive education. *Heliyon*, *9*(11), e21443. Advance online publication. DOI: 10.1016/j.heliyon.2023.e21443

Nwozor, A., Oshewolo, S., Owoeye, G., & Okidu, O. (2021). Nigeria's quest for alternative clean energy development: A cobweb of opportunities, pitfalls and multiple dilemmas. *Energy Policy*, *149*, 112070. Advance online publication. DOI: 10.1016/j.enpol.2020.112070

Omodero, C. O., Okafor, M. C., Nmesirionye, J. A., & Abaa, E. O. (2022). Environmental Taxation and CO2 Emission Management. *Environment and Ecology Research*, *10*(1), 1–10. DOI: 10.13189/eer.2022.100101

Peres-Cajías, J., Torregrosa-Hetland, S., & Ducoing, C. (2022). Resource abundance and public finances in five peripheral economies, 1850s–1930s. *Resources Policy*, *76*, 102539. Advance online publication. DOI: 10.1016/j.resourpol.2021.102539

Powell, R. (2024). Power sharing with weak institutions*. *Journal of Theoretical Politics*, *36*(2), 186–211. DOI: 10.1177/09516298241232655

Qi, Y., Shi, W., & Xu, Y. (2025). Evolutionary logic and development trends of China's ecological and environmental fiscal polocies—Quantitative analysis based on policy texts [中国生态环境财政政策演进逻辑与发展趋势——基于政策文本的量化分析]. *Bulletin of Chinese Academy of Sciences*, *40*(11), 2034–2048. DOI: 10.3724/j.issn.1000-3045.20240521002

Ravaioli, G., Lamperti, F., Roventini, A., & Domingos, T. (2025). Tackling emissions and inequality: Policy insights from an agent-based model. *Journal of Economic Behavior & Organization*, *237*, 107188. Advance online publication. DOI: 10.1016/j.jebo.2025.107188

Sagita, G. D., & Budi, E. R. (2024). Regional rights, environmental wrongs: Unpacking the paradox of autonomy in indonesia's environmental governance. *Indonesian Journal of Environmental Law and Sustainable Development*, *3*(1), 191–228. DOI: 10.15294/ijel.v3i1.78890

Samuel, S. E., & Kouhy, R. (2025). Paradox of oil revenue allocation and utilisation in resource-rich countries: The case of Nigeria. *Resources Policy*, *111*, 105782. Advance online publication. DOI: 10.1016/j.resourpol.2025.105782

Sanusi, A. R., Ul Hassan, M., & Iliyasu, J. (2025). Towards the creation of an independent fiscal council for growth sustainability and development in oil-exporting small-open economy. *Policy Studies*, 1–24. Advance online publication. DOI: 10.1080/01442872.2025.2482047

Selvakumar, P., Seenivasan, S., Deshmukh, S. M., Ponnapalli, H., & Das, A. (2024). Environmental protection and policies. In *Renewable Energy and the Economic Welfare of Society* (pp. 71–101). IGI Global., DOI: 10.4018/979-8-3693-7580-8.ch004

Shahzad, M. F., Xu, S., Lim, W. M., Yang, X., & Khan, Q. R. (2024). Artificial intelligence and social media on academic performance and mental well-being: Student perceptions of positive impact in the age of smart learning. *Heliyon*, *10*(8), e29523. Advance online publication. DOI: 10.1016/j.heliyon.2024.e29523

Sharma, V., Gupta, M., Arora, N., & Shaikh, A. A. (2025). FinTech and Financial Inclusion: Leveraging Digital Finance for Economic Empowerment and Sustainable Growth. In *FinTech and Financial Inclusion: Leveraging Digital Finance for Economic Empowerment and Sustainable Growth*. Taylor and Francis., DOI: 10.4324/9781003514114

Singh, S., Singh, P., Pandey, S., & Yadav, S. (2025). Harnessing Digital Finance for Sustainability and Equity in Marine and Seaside Economies. In *World Sustainability Series: Part F794* (pp. 107–125). Springer Science and Business Media Deutschland GmbH. DOI: 10.1007/978-3-031-92390-6_6

Sun, J., Li, P., & Wang, Y. (2024). Policy tools for sustainability: Evaluating the effectiveness of fiscal measures in natural resource efficiency. *Resources Policy*, *89*, 104575. Advance online publication. DOI: 10.1016/j.resourpol.2023.104575

Sun, Y., & Stephen, E. (2025). Sustainable Development Pathways: How Fiscal Policy, Green Innovation, and Environmental Governance Shape Ecological Footprints in G-20 Economies? *Sustainable Development*. Advance online publication. DOI: 10.1002/sd.70310

Vanhala, L. (2017). Process tracing in the study of environmental politics. *Global Environmental Politics*, *17*(4), 88–105. DOI: 10.1162/GLEP_a_00434

Wang, Q. J., Sharma, S. S., Ni, G. H., & Chang, C. P. (2024). Governance, energy utilization and environmental protection: Role of extreme events. *Energy Economics*, *136*, 107765. Advance online publication. DOI: 10.1016/j.eneco.2024.107765

Wang, Y., Han, L., Sun, J., & Sun, Z. (2024). Financing the green transition: Mobilizing resources for efficient natural resource management. *Resources Policy*, *89*, 104522. Advance online publication. DOI: 10.1016/j.resourpol.2023.104522

Wang, Y., & Yuan, G. (2026). Natural resource exploitation and productive capacity as drivers of ecological footprint: The roles of technology and economic policy uncertainty. *Geoscience Frontiers*, *17*(2), 102247. DOI: 10.1016/j.gsf.2026.102247

Waris, A. (2024). A Principled Approach to Financial Resource Collection and Allocation for the Realization of Human Rights in Creating a Global Fiscal Institution. *Bulletin for International Taxation*, *78*(9–10), 388–393. DOI: 10.59403/36t1v90

Widjanarko, A. P., & Gultom, Y. M. L. (2024). A Changing Landscape: Exploring the Relationship between Clean and Clear Status Policy, Coal Mining, and Deforestation. *Jurnal Manajemen Hutan Tropika*, *30*(1), 94–106. DOI: 10.7226/jtfm.30.1.97

Xu, H., Li, Y., Lin, W., & Li, Y. (2024). Government fiscal decentralization and haze and carbon reduction: Evidence from the fiscal Province-Managing-County reform. *Environmental Research*, *252*, 119020. Advance online publication. DOI: 10.1016/j.envres.2024.119020

Zahroh, U. A., & Najicha, F. U. (2022). Problems and Challenges on Environmental Law Enforcement in Indonesia: AMDAL in the Context of Administrative Law. *Indonesian State Law Review*, *5*(2), 53–66. DOI: 10.15294/islrev.v5i2.46511

Zatti, A. (2020). Environmental taxes and subsidies: Some insights from the Italian experience. *Environment and Ecology*, *11*(1), 39–53. DOI: 10.21511/ee.11(1).2020.04

Zhang, Y., Shi, X., Wu, H., & Wu, Y. (2025). The synergetic effects of government concerns and public awareness on environmental protection. *Applied Economics*, 1–20. Advance online publication. DOI: 10.1080/00036846.2025.2606187

Zhang, Z., & Zhou, Y. (2025). Economic growth vs environmental sustainability: Examining resource extraction in the World's largest economies. *Frontiers in Environmental Science*, *13*, 1586619. Advance online publication. DOI: 10.3389/fenvs.2025.1586619

Zhao, Y., Dou, S., Li, J., Cheng, J., & Xu, D. (2025). The economic inequality effect of environmental policies—A case from China's "authoritarian environmentalism" actions. *Journal of Environmental Management*, *374*, 123926. Advance online publication. DOI: 10.1016/j.jenvman.2024.123926

Compilation of References

Aarthi, S., Ravikumar, R. N., Sobirova, K., & Mamadiyarov, Z. (2025). Empowering a sustainable future through digital learning and the SDGs. In *Harnessing E-Learning to Create a Sustainable Future* (pp. 145–172). IGI Global Scientific Publishing., DOI: 10.4018/979-8-3373-0112-9.ch006

Abbasov, R. (2025). Government Budgeting and Expenditure: A Multifaceted Analysis of Economic Growth, Fiscal Sustainability, and Social Impact. *Fiscal Sustainability, and Social Impact (December 20, 2024). iBusiness, 17*(01), 10-4236. DOI: 10.4236/ib.2025.171002

Abbdo, A. B., Li, B., Qahtan, A. S. A., & Elshennawy, A. (2022). The influence of FDI on GHG emissions in BRI countries using spatial econometric analysis strategy: The significance of biomass energy consumption. *Environmental Science and Pollution Research International, 29*(36), 54571–54595. DOI: 10.1007/s11356-022-19384-8 PMID: 35304721

Abdelfattah, F., Salah, M., Dahleez, K., Darwazeh, R., & Al Halbusi, H. (2025). Public policy and sustainability: How green core competence, government trust, and policy satisfaction influence green R&D investments in the private sector. *Sustainable Futures : An Applied Journal of Technology, Environment and Society, 9*, 100461. DOI: 10.1016/j.sftr.2025.100461

Abdulahi, M. E., Shu, Y., & Khan, M. A. (2025). Impact of natural resource management on entrepreneurial activity and SME growth in emerging economies: Does the rule of law matter? *Resources Policy, 108*, 105674. DOI: 10.1016/j.resourpol.2025.105674

Abdulkareem, S. A., Mohammed, A. H., Hassan, S. N. S., Fahmi, A. M., & Saeed, M. N.Sarah Ali AbdulkareemAws Hamid MohammedShahd Nasser Saadi HassanAhmed Mohammed FahmiMatai Nagi Saeed. (2025). Decision-making in environmental risk management: Case study on adaptive strategies in U.S. cities under uncertainty. *Environment and Social Psychology*, *10*(9). Advance online publication. DOI: 10.59429/esp.v10i9.3968

Abdullah, M. S., & Keshminder, J. S. (2022). What drives green sukuk? A leader's perspective. *Journal of Sustainable Finance & Investment*, *12*(3), 985–1005. DOI: 10.1080/20430795.2020.1821339

Abdulwahab, L. O. (2026). Healthy Aging and Resource Sustainability. *Economic Transformations in Population Aging*, 313–348. DOI: 10.4018/979-8-3373-6117-8.ch010

Abdulwahab, L. O., & Azam, H. (2026). Platform Work in Europe's Green and Care Economies: Regulatory Pathways for Sustainability, Social Protection, and Fair Work. In *Regulating the Gig Economy in the European Union: Challenges, Innovations, and Global Impacts* (pp. 99-124). IGI Global Scientific Publishing.

Abdulwahab, L. O. (2023). The role of Institutional quality, human capital development on economic growth in Sub-Saharan Africa. [IJBE]. *International Journal of Business Economics*, *5*(1), 92–115. DOI: 10.30596/ijbe.v5i1.16161

Abdulwahab, L. O. (2024). Assessing the Resource Curse Hypothesis across the ECOWAS Region: A Systematic Review of Socioeconomic and Political Impacts. *Proceeding Medan International Conference on Economic and Business, 2*(0), 490–499. https://doi.org/DOI: 10.30596/MICEB.V2I0.795

Abdulwahab, L. O., & Bubari Umar, H. (2025). *Can a Blessing Become a Peril? Exploring Resource Abundant, Economic Growth, and Conflict in the Economic Community of West African States (ECOWAS)*. DOI: 10.20944/preprints202504.2139.v1

Abdulwahab, L. O., & Firmansyah, E. A. (2024). Are abundant natural resources in the Democratic Republic of the Congo a blessing or curse? *Journal of Innovation in Business and Economics*, *8*(01), 47–60.

Abid, M. (2017). Does economic, financial and institutional developments matter for environmental quality? A comparative analysis of EU and MEA countries. *Journal of Environmental Management*, *188*, 183–194. DOI: 10.1016/j.jenvman.2016.12.007

Abolhosseini, S., & Heshmati, A. (2014). The main support mechanisms to finance renewable energy development. *Renewable & Sustainable Energy Reviews*, *40*, 876–885. DOI: 10.1016/j.rser.2014.08.013

Acemoglu, D., Aghion, P., Bursztyn, L., & Hemous, D. (2010). The environment and directed technical change. SSRN *Electronic Journal*. DOI: 10.2139/ssrn.1668575

Acemoglu, D., Aghion, P., Bursztyn, L., & Hemous, D. (2012). The environment and directed technical change. *The American Economic Review*, *102*(1), 131–166. DOI: 10.1257/aer.102.1.131 PMID: 26719595

Acharya, V. V., Berner, R., Engle, R., Jung, H., Stroebel, J., Zeng, X., & Zhao, Y. (2023). Climate stress testing. *Annual Review of Financial Economics*, *15*(1), 291–326. DOI: 10.1146/annurev-financial-110921-101555

Adelekan, O. A., Ilugbusi, B. S., Adisa, O., Obi, O. C., Awonuga, K. F., Asuzu, O. F., & Ndubuisi, N. L. (2024). Energy Transition Policies: A global review of shifts towards renewable sources. *Engineering Science & Technology Journal*, *5*(2), 272–287. DOI: 10.51594/estj.v5i2.752

Adeneye, Y. (2023). Climate finance research: A thematic review and directions for the future. Social and Environmental Accountability Journal, 1–4.

Adeniyi, O., Kumeka, T. T., & Alagbada, O. (2022). NATURAL RESOURCE DEPENDENCE AND TAX EFFORT IN SUB-SAHARAN AFRICA. *Journal of Economic Development*, *47*(1), 29–64. DOI: 10.35866/caujed.2022.47.1.002

Adeyemi, F., Jempeji, A.-B., Olaniran, A., Taliat, M., & Adeleke, A. (2025). Climate risks and financial stability: A global evidence. *Finance Research Open*, *1*(3), 100032. DOI: 10.1016/j.finr.2025.100032

Adhikari, B., King, J., Vadlamannati, K. C., & Chachu, D. O. (2023). Why do some natural resource-rich countries adopt prudent fiscal rules? An empirical analysis. *The Extractive Industries and Society*, *14*, 101234. Advance online publication. DOI: 10.1016/j.exis.2023.101234

Aggarwal, S. K., Saini, L. M., & Kumar, A. (2009). Electricity price forecasting in deregulated markets: A review and evaluation. *International Journal of Electrical Power & Energy Systems*, *31*(1), 13–22. DOI: 10.1016/j.ijepes.2008.09.003

Aghion, P., Dechezleprêtre, A., Hemous, D., Martin, R., & Van Reenen, J. (2012). Carbon taxes, path dependency and directed technical change: Evidence from the auto industry. *Journal of Political Economy*, *124*(1), 1–35. DOI: 10.1086/684581

Aisen, A., & Veiga, F. J. (2013). How does political instability affect economic growth? *European Journal of Political Economy*, *29*, 151–167. DOI: 10.1016/j.ejpoleco.2012.11.001

Akhundov, R., Tangirov, A., & Sultonov, A. (2025). Political Dimensions of Global Ecological Governance Frameworks. *BIO Web of Conferences, 151*. DOI: 10.1051/bioconf/202515102008

Akpan, U., & Kama, U. (2024a). Does institutional quality really matter for environmental quality? *Energy & Environment*, *35*(8), 4361–4385. DOI: 10.1177/0958305X231180702

Albulescu, C. T., Boatca-Barabas, M.-E., & Diaconescu, A. (2022). The asymmetric effect of environmental policy stringency on CO_2 emissions in OECD countries. *Environmental Science and Pollution Research International*, *29*(18), 27311–27327. DOI: 10.1007/s11356-021-18267-8 PMID: 34981390

Aldy, J. E., & Pizer, W. A. (2011). The competitiveness impacts of climate change mitigation policies. *Journal of the Association of Environmental and Resource Economists*, *2*(4), 1–29. DOI: 10.1086/683305

Alexandra-Gabriela, M. (2022). General requirements exposure draft: Comments about responsible reporting. *Revista Economica (Sibiu)*, *74*(2), 22–29. DOI: 10.56043/reveco-2022-0013

Ali, K., Jianguo, D., Kirikkaleli, D., Oláh, J., & Bakhsh, S. (2023). Do environmental taxes, environmental innovation, and energy resources matter for environmental sustainability: Evidence of five sustainable economies. *Heliyon*, *9*(11), e21577. DOI: 10.1016/j.heliyon.2023.e21577 PMID: 38034728

Ali, M., Wahjuni, E., Wardhana, R. W., Haryani, I., & Prakoso, B. (2025). Protection Policy Strategy for Green Bond Investors Against the Risk of Greenwashing Practices in the Capital Market. *International Journal of Advanced Multidiciplinary Research and Studies*, *5*(5), 854–862.

Alkatheeri, H., Mertzanis, C., & Kampouris, I. (2026). Climate laws and financial stability. *Research in International Business and Finance*, *81*, 103151. DOI: 10.1016/j.ribaf.2025.103151

Allahdadi, M. R. (2025). Beyond green signaling: Are institutional investors decarbonizing their portfolios? *International Review of Economics & Finance*, *104*, 104767. DOI: 10.1016/j.iref.2025.104767

Alola, A. A., Bekun, F. V., & Sarkodie, S. A. (2019). Dynamic impact of trade policy, economic growth, fertility rate, renewable and non-renewable energy consumption on ecological footprint in Europe. *The Science of the Total Environment*, *685*, 702–709. DOI: 10.1016/j.scitotenv.2019.05.139 PMID: 31203164

Alonso-Morales, N., Sáez-Martín, A., & Haro-de-Rosario, A. (2025). The role of local public spending in the achievement of the social dimension of sustainable development: An empirical analysis. *Sustainable Futures : An Applied Journal of Technology, Environment and Society*, *9*, 100475. DOI: 10.1016/j.sftr.2025.100475

Alsayegh, M. F., Abdul Rahman, R., & Homayoun, S. (2020). Corporate economic, environmental, and social sustainability performance transformation through ESG disclosure. *Sustainability (Basel)*, *12*(9), 3910. DOI: 10.3390/su12093910

Altaghlibi, M. (2025). *CBAM impact and opportunities*. https://assets.ctfassets.net/1u811bvgvthc/6bqifXzHR2Lxedk7NohOwE/aeea069da882395a5ff66782f82e188a/250520_CBAM_impacts_and_opportunities.pdf

Altenburg, T., & Pegels, A. (2012). Sustainability-oriented innovation systems – managing the green transformation. *Innovation and Development*, *2*(1), 5–22. DOI: 10.1080/2157930X.2012.664037

Alymkulova, N., Iorember, P. T., & Omotesho, O. (2023). Public spending and private sector investment in Nigeria: an investigation of the crowding-in (or crowding-out) effect amidst deteriorating fiscal balance. In *Post-Independence Development in Africa: Decolonisation and Transformation Prospects* (pp. 263–278). Springer International Publishing., DOI: 10.1007/978-3-031-30541-2_15

Ambec, S., Cohen, M., Elgie, S., & Lanoie, P. (2010). The Porter hypothesis at 20: Can environmental regulation enhance innovation and competitiveness? CIRANO Working Papers, 7. DOI: 10.2139/ssrn.1682001

Ameer, W., & Ahmad, K. (2024). How wealthy in natural resource leads environmental sustainability in developing economies? An empirical investigation. *Journal of Environmental Management*, *370*, 122496. Advance online publication. DOI: 10.1016/j.jenvman.2024.122496

Amel-Zadeh, A., & Tang, Q. (2025). Managing the shift from voluntary to mandatory climate disclosure: The role of carbon accounting. *The British Accounting Review*, *57*(2), 101594. DOI: 10.1016/j.bar.2025.101594

Amendola, M. (2025). Winners and losers of the EU carbon border adjustment mechanism. An intra-EU issue? *Energy Economics*, *142*, 108139. DOI: 10.1016/j.eneco.2024.108139

Anderson, S. T., Kellogg, R., & Salant, S. W. (2014). Hotelling under pressure. SSRN Electronic Journal. DOI: 10.2139/ssrn.2537827

Anjarwi, A. W. (2025). Tax burden and poverty in lower-middle-income countries: The moderating role of fiscal freedom. *Development Studies Research, 12*(1), 2466511. Advance online publication. DOI: 10.1080/21665095.2025.2466511

Anselin, L. (1988). *Spatial Econometrics: Methods and Models.* Springer Netherlands. DOI: 10.1007/978-94-015-7799-1

Anselin, L., Bera, A. K., Florax, R., & Yoon, M. J. (1996). Simple diagnostic tests for spatial dependence. *Regional Science and Urban Economics, 26*(1), 77–104. DOI: 10.1016/0166-0462(95)02111-6

Anwar, S., Maulidiyah, D. R., Rusanti, E., & Mochlasin, M. (2024). Book review: Sustainable finance and ESG; risk, management, regulations and implications for financial institutions. *Rajagiri Management Journal, 18*(1), 99–103. DOI: 10.1108/RAMJ-01-2024-246

Arboleda-Munoz, G. A., Chaparro-Banegas, N., & Roig-Tierno, N. (2026). Bridging the gap: Innovation systems and sustainable development in developing countries. *Journal of Open Innovation, 12*(1), 1–13. DOI: 10.1016/j.joitmc.2025.100713

Ardiputra, S., Milyan, M., Akhmad, Z., Sulthan, M., & Ardiputra, M. A. (2025). Optimizing budget policy in village fund allocation (ADD): A governance and public administration perspective on rural development. *Frontiers in Political Science, 7*, 1581806. DOI: 10.3389/fpos.2025.1581806

Arefeen, S., & Shimada, K. (2020). Performance and resilience of socially responsible investing (SRI) and conventional funds during different shocks in 2016: Evidence from Japan. *Sustainability (Basel), 12*(2), 540. DOI: 10.3390/su12020540

Armiento, M., & Villa, A. (2025). 7. Energy transition and industrial competitiveness in the EU. In *Open Reports Series* (pp. 115–124). Open Book Publishers., DOI: 10.11647/obp.0499.07

Arminen, H., & Menegaki, A. N. (2019). Corruption, climate and the energy-environment-growth nexus. *Energy Economics, 80*, 621–634. DOI: 10.1016/j.eneco.2019.02.009

Arogundade, S., Mduduzi, B., & Hassan, A. S. (2022). Spatial impact of foreign direct investment on ecological footprint in Africa. *Environmental Science and Pollution Research International, 29*(34), 51589–51608. DOI: 10.1007/s11356-022-18831-w PMID: 35247175

Arroyave, L. O., Lopes, R., & Santos, R. (2025). Leveraging local environmental management in the scope of an administrative decentralization process: The case of Portuguese coastal municipalities. *Journal of Environmental Management*, *394*, 127052. Advance online publication. DOI: 10.1016/j.jenvman.2025.127052

Asiamah, O., Agyei, S. K., Bossman, A., Agyei, E. A., Asucam, J., & Arku-Asare, M. (2022). Natural resource dependence and institutional quality: Evidence from Sub-Saharan Africa. *Resources Policy*, *79*, 102967. Advance online publication. DOI: 10.1016/j.resourpol.2022.102967

Aslam, A., & Ghouse, G. (2023). Targeting the new sustainable inclusive green growth: A review. *Cleaner and Responsible Consumption*, *11*, 1–13. DOI: 10.1016/j.clrc.2023.100140

Aslam, F., Ali, I., Amjad, F., Ali, H., & Irfan, I. (2023). On the inner dynamics between Fossil fuels and the carbon market: A combination of seasonal-trend decomposition and multifractal cross-correlation analysis. *Environmental Science and Pollution Research International*, *30*(10), 25873–25891. DOI: 10.1007/s11356-022-23924-7

Athari, S. A., Addia, K., Kirikkaleli, D., Al Geitany, S. H., Al Fadhel, L., & Saliba, C. (2025). Do environmental taxes and green electricity matter for environmental quality? Fresh evidence in France based on Fourier methods. *Energies*, *18*(19), 5046. DOI: 10.3390/en18195046

Bagheri, M., Guevara, Z., Alikarami, M., Kennedy, C. A., & Doluweera, G. (2018). Green growth planning: A multi-factor energy input-output analysis of the Canadian economy. *Energy Economics*, *74*, 708–720. DOI: 10.1016/j.eneco.2018.07.015

Bai, Y., & Yang, X. (2016). The research on the economic effect of market-based environmental policy instruments. *Open Journal of Social Sciences*, *04*(04), 38–47. DOI: 10.4236/jss.2016.44006

Baker, J. J., & Nenonen, S. (2025). Shaping Markets, Shifting Burdens: Collective Opportunism and Asymmetrical Market-Shaping. *Journal of Macromarketing*, *02761467251388876*. Advance online publication. DOI: 10.1177/02761467251388876

Balaji, K. (2023),"Exploring the Drivers and Effects on Supply Chain Resilience and Performance in an Emerging Market Using Artificial Intelligence," *2023 3rd International Conference on Smart Generation Computing, Communication and Networking (SMART GENCON)*, Bangalore, India, 2023, pp. 1-6, DOI: 10.1109/SMARTGENCON60755.2023.10442071

Balaji, K., & Rao, P. S. (2024), "Artificial Intelligence and Chatbots: Transforming User Experience in E-tailing," *2024 9th International Conference on Communication and Electronics Systems (ICCES)*, Coimbatore, India, 2024, pp. 1375-1379, DOI: 10.1109/ICCES63552.2024.10859474

Balaji, K. (2025). AI as a Game Changer: How Digital Entrepreneurs Are Redefining Business Practices. In Tunio, M. (Ed.), *Improving Entrepreneurial Processes Through Advanced AI* (pp. 21–48). IGI Global Scientific Publishing., DOI: 10.4018/979-8-3693-1495-1.ch002

Balaji, K. (2025). Harnessing AI and Blockchain in Sustainability Assurance: Trends Shaping the Future of Verification. In Khatib, S., & Abbas, A. (Eds.), *Navigating Trust in Sustainability Reporting and Assurance* (pp. 215–242). IGI Global Scientific Publishing., DOI: 10.4018/979-8-3373-0117-4.ch007

Balaji, K. (2025). Neuromarketing and Sustainable Finance: Real-World Case Studies of Green Investment Promotions. In Taneja, S., Chahal, B., Johri, A., Ozen, E., & Kumar, P. (Eds.), *Neuromarketing's Role in Sustainable Finance* (pp. 169–204). IGI Global Scientific Publishing., DOI: 10.4018/979-8-3693-9117-4.ch010

Balaji, K. (2025). Revolutionizing High-Frequency Trading: The Impacts of Financial Technology and Data Science Innovations. In Chen, H. (Ed.), *Machine Learning and Modeling Techniques in Financial Data Science* (pp. 103–124). IGI Global Scientific Publishing., DOI: 10.4018/979-8-3693-8186-1.ch004

Balsalobre-Lorente, D., Topaloglu, E. E., Nur, T., & Evcimen, C. (2023). Exploring the linkage between financial development and ecological footprint in APEC countries: A novel view under corruption perception and environmental policy stringency. *Journal of Cleaner Production*, *414*(137686), 137686. Advance online publication. DOI: 10.1016/j.jclepro.2023.137686

Bambi, P. D. R., Batatana, M. L. D., Appiah, M., & Tetteh, D. (2024). Governance, institutions, and climate change resilience in Sub-Saharan Africa: Assessing the threshold effects. *Frontiers in Environmental Science*, *12*, 1352344. Advance online publication. DOI: 10.3389/fenvs.2024.1352344

Bambi, P. D. R., & Pea-Assounga, J. B. B. (2025). Impact of gold price, financial development, renewable energy, economic growth, urbanization, and environmental tax on environmental degradation. *Frontiers in Environmental Science*, *13*, 1631189. Advance online publication. DOI: 10.3389/fenvs.2025.1631189

Bárcena-Ruiz, J. C., & Garzón, M. B. (2022). Environmental policy instruments and ownership of firms. *Manchester School*, *90*(4), 385–408. DOI: 10.1111/manc.12412

Barra, C., & Falcone, P. M. (2025). Institutional factors and environmental performance: Insights from global economies. *Economic Systems*, 101364. Advance online publication. DOI: 10.1016/j.ecosys.2025.101364

Batra, G. A. U. R. E. S. H. (2023). Renewable energy economics: achieving harmony between environmental protection and economic goals. *Social science chronicle, 2*(2), 1-32. DOI: 10.56106/ssc.2023.009

Battiston, S., Mandel, A., Schuetze, F., & Visentin, G. (2017). A climate stress-test of the financial system. *Nature Climate Change*, *7*(4), 283–288. DOI: 10.1038/nclimate3255

Behera, B., Behera, P., Sucharita, S., & Sethi, N. (2024). Mitigating ecological footprint in BRICS countries: Unveiling the role of disaggregated clean energy, green technology innovation and political stability. *Discover Sustainability*, *5*(1), 165. DOI: 10.1007/s43621-024-00378-0

Behera, P., Behera, B., Sethi, N., & Handoyo, R. D. (2024). What drives environmental sustainability? The role of renewable energy, green innovation, and political stability in OECD economies. *International Journal of Sustainable Development and World Ecology*, *31*(7), 1–15. DOI: 10.1080/13504509.2024.2333812

Beisenbina, M., Fabregat-Aibar, L., Barberà-Mariné, M.-G., & Sorrosal-Forradellas, M.-T. (2022). The burgeoning field of sustainable investment: Past, present and future. *Sustainable Development*. Advance online publication. DOI: 10.1002/sd.2422

Beloskar, V. D., Haldar, A., & Rao, S. V. D. N. (2023). Socially responsible investments: A retrospective review and future research agenda. *Business Strategy and the Environment*, *32*(7), 4841–4860. DOI: 10.1002/bse.3396

Ben-Amar, W., Chourou, L., & Ding, X. (2025). Climate risk and long-lived tangible asset impairments. *Journal of Accounting and Public Policy*, *54*, 107374. DOI: 10.1016/j.jaccpubpol.2025.107374

Bergamini, K., Rugiero, V., Ángel, P., Mollenhauer, K., Alarcón, A., & Manríquez, G. (2025). Global Challenges and National Responses: Indicators to Evaluate Public Policies for Mining Development in Chile in the Context of the Global Energy Transition. *Sustainability (Basel)*, *17*(17), 7814. Advance online publication. DOI: 10.3390/su17177814

Bergougui, B., & Satrovic, E. (2025). Towards eco-efficiency of OECD countries: How does environmental governance restrain the destructive ecological effect of the excess use of natural resources? *Ecological Informatics*, *87*, 103093. Advance online publication. DOI: 10.1016/j.ecoinf.2025.103093

Berkman, H., Jona, J., & Soderstrom, N. (2024). Firm-specific climate risk and market valuation. *Accounting, Organizations and Society*, *112*, 101547. DOI: 10.1016/j.aos.2024.101547

Bhutta, A. I., Ullah, M. R., Sultan, J., Riaz, A., & Sheikh, M. F. (2022). Impact of Green Energy Production, Green Innovation, Financial Development on Environment Quality: A Role of Country Governance in Pakistan. *International Journal of Energy Economics and Policy*, *12*(1), 316–326. DOI: 10.32479/ijeep.11986

Bianco, D. (2018). Environmental policy in an endogenous growth model with expanding variety. *Revue d'Économie Politique*, *127*(6), 1013–1028. DOI: 10.3917/redp.276.1013

Bick, N., & Keele, D. (2022). Sustainability and climate change: Understanding the political use of environmental terms in municipal governments. *Current Research in Environmental Sustainability*, *4*, 1–11. DOI: 10.1016/j.crsust.2022.100145

Biekša, K., Valiulė, V., Šimanskienė, L., & Silvestri, R. (2022). Assessment of sustainable economic development in the EU countries with reference to the SDGs and environmental footprint indices. *Sustainability (Basel)*, *14*(18), 11265. DOI: 10.3390/su141811265

Bohringer, C., & Lange, A. (2003). Economic implications of alternative allocation schemes for emission allowances. SSRN *Electronic Journal*. DOI: 10.2139/ssrn.423401

Böhringer, C., Bye, B., Fæhn, T., & Einar, K. (2017). Targeted carbon tariffs: Export response, leakage and welfare. *Resource and Energy Economics*, *50*, 51–73. DOI: 10.1016/j.reseneeco.2017.06.003

Böhringer, C., Carbone, J. C., & Rutherford, T. F. (2016). The Strategic Value of Carbon Tariffs. *American Economic Journal. Economic Policy*, *8*(1), 28–51. DOI: 10.1257/pol.20130327

Bolton, P., & Kacperczyk, M. (2019). Do investors care about carbon risk? SSRN Electronic Journal. DOI: 10.2139/ssrn.3398441

Bolton, P., & Kacperczyk, M. (2021). Do investors care about carbon risk? *Journal of Financial Economics*, *142*(2), 517–549. DOI: 10.1016/j.jfineco.2021.05.008

Bolton, P., & Kacperczyk, M. (2023). Global pricing of carbon-transition risk. *The Journal of Finance*, *78*(6), 3677–3754. DOI: 10.1111/jofi.13272

Borck, J., & Coglianese, C. (2009). Voluntary environmental programs: Assessing their effectiveness. *Annual Review of Environment and Resources*, *34*(1), 305–324. DOI: 10.1146/annurev.environ.032908.091450

Borghei, Z., Linnenluecke, M., & Bui, B. (2024). The disclosure of climate-related risks and opportunities in financial statements: The UK's FTSE 100. *Meditari Accountancy Research*, *32*(3), 1031–1063. DOI: 10.1108/MEDAR-05-2023-1998

Borozan, D., & Borozan, L. (2025). Estimating the Governance Effect on Carbon Dioxide Emissions in Croatia. *Natural Resources Forum*. DOI: 10.1111/1477-8947.70025

Bosomtwe, E. (2025). Fiscal Policy, Institutional Quality, and Sustainable Development Goals: A Perspective of Anglophone Countries in West Africa. *Circular Economy and Sustainability*, *5*(1), 347–366. DOI: 10.1007/s43615-024-00422-1

Boute, A. (2024). Accounting for Carbon Pricing in Third Countries Under the EU Carbon Border Adjustment Mechanism. *World Trade Review*, *23*(2), 169–189. DOI: 10.1017/S1474745624000107

Bovenberg, A. L., & Smulders, S. (1995). Environmental quality and pollution-augmenting technological change in a two-sector endogenous growth model. *Journal of Public Economics*, *57*(3), 369–391. DOI: 10.1016/0047-2727(95)80002-Q

Bovenberg, A. L., & Smulders, S. (1996). Transitional impacts of environmental policy in an endogenous growth model. *International Economic Review*, *37*(4), 861–895. DOI: 10.2307/2527315

Brahmi, M., Esposito, L., Parziale, A., Dhayal, K. S., Agrawal, S., Giri, A. K., & Loan, N. T. (2023). The role of greener innovations in promoting financial inclusion to achieve carbon neutrality: An integrative review. *Economies*, *11*(7), 194. DOI: 10.3390/economies11070194

Brandi, C., & Morin, J. (2023). *Trade and the Environment*. Cambridge University Press., DOI: 10.1017/9781009461825

Branger, F., Quirion, P., & Chevallier, J. (2016). Carbon leakage and competitiveness of cement and steel industries under the EU ETS: Much ado about nothing. *The Energy Journal (Cambridge, Mass.)*, *37*(3), 109–136. DOI: 10.5547/01956574.37.3.fbra

Bretschger, L. (2019). Malthus in the light of climate change. SSRN *Electronic Journal*. DOI: 10.2139/ssrn.3377220

Bucak, Ç., & Çatık, A. N. (2025). Spillover effects of economic complexity on load capacity factor in the EU: A spatial econometrics perspective. *Journal of Environmental Planning and Management*, 1–34. Advance online publication. DOI: 10.1080/09640568.2025.2462229

Bucak, Ç., Önder, A. Ö., & Çatık, A. N. (2024). Spatial effects of renewable and fossil energy consumption on the ecological footprint for the EU countries. *Environmental Science and Pollution Research International*, *31*(39), 55204–55221. DOI: 10.1007/s11356-024-34803-8 PMID: 39225931

Busco, C., Consolandi, C., Eccles, R. G., & Sofra, E. (2020). A preliminary analysis of SASB reporting: Disclosure topics, financial relevance, and the financial intensity of ESG materiality. *The Bank of America Journal of Applied Corporate Finance*, *32*(2), 117–125. DOI: 10.1111/jacf.12411

Caglar, A. E. (2020). The importance of renewable energy consumption and FDI inflows in reducing environmental degradation: Bootstrap ARDL bound test in selected 9 countries. *Journal of Cleaner Production*, *264*, 121663. DOI: 10.1016/j.jclepro.2020.121663

Cai, H. H., Lee, H. F., Khan, N. U., & Yuan, Q. (2024). Are natural resources a curse, a blessing, or a double-edged sword? Implications for environmental sustainability. *Journal of Environmental Management*, *367*, 122008. Advance online publication. DOI: 10.1016/j.jenvman.2024.122008

Calel, R., & Dechezleprêtre, A. (2016). Environmental policy and directed technological change: Evidence from the European carbon market. *The Review of Economics and Statistics*, *98*(1), 173–191. DOI: 10.1162/REST_a_00470

Camilleri, M. A. (2021). The market for socially responsible investing: A review of the developments. *Social Responsibility Journal*, *17*(3), 412–428. DOI: 10.1108/SRJ-06-2019-0194

Cammeo, A., Ferrari, A., Borghesi, S., & Dokken, T. (2025). Understanding and assessing CBAM : vulnerability and impacts in the EU. In *SPES Working Paper* (7.2). https://www.sustainabilityperformances.eu/wp-content/uploads/2025/03/SPES-Deliverable-7.2_Understanding-and-assessing-CBAM_layout.pdf

Cammeo, J., Ferrari, A., Borghesi, S., & Dokken, T. (2025). *Understanding and assessing CBAM: vulnerability and impacts in the EU*. SPES Working Paper no. 7.2, SPES project – Sustainability Performances, Evidence and Scenarios. Florence: University of Florence. https://www.sustainabilityperformances.eu/publications-deliverables

Cao, H., Zhang, L., Qi, Y., Yang, Z., & Li, X. (2022). Government auditing and environmental governance: Evidence from China's auditing system reform. *Environmental Impact Assessment Review*, *93*, 106705. Advance online publication. DOI: 10.1016/j.eiar.2021.106705

Carbon pricing and emissions trading systems: Legal mechanisms for reducing greenhouse gas emissions. (2025). [Source details not provided].

Carè, R., Boitan, I. A., Stoian, A. M., & Fatima, R. (2025). Exploring the landscape of financial inclusion through the lens of financial technologies: A review. *Finance Research Letters*, *72*, 106500. Advance online publication. DOI: 10.1016/j.frl.2024.106500

CEC. (2013). *CEC recommends investigation of the Sumidero Canyon II submission and delivers a factual record for the Environmental Pollution in Hermosillo II submission*. Cec.Org. https://www.cec.org/news/cec-recommends-investigation-of-sumidero-canyon-ii-submission-and-delivers-factual-record-for-environmental-pollution-in-hermosillo-ii-submission/

Chai, S., Huo, W., Li, Q., Ji, Q., & Shi, X. (2025). Effects of carbon tax on energy transition, emissions and economy amid technological progress. *Applied Energy*, *377*, 124578. DOI: 10.1016/j.apenergy.2024.124578

Chen, E., & Zhang, H. (2025). The relationship between public health expenditure and urban economic resilience. *Frontiers in Public Health*, *13*, 1550528. DOI: 10.3389/fpubh.2025.1550528 PMID: 40027499

Chen, G., Rjoub, H., & Shao, X. (2026). The Expository Role of Fiscal Policy in Achieving Environmental Sustainability: Evidence Based on Positive and Negative Fluctuations. *Fluctuation and Noise Letters*, 2650022. Advance online publication. DOI: 10.1142/S0219477526500227

Cheng, J. (2025). Climate change: Impacts on the global economy. Highlights in Business. *Economics and Management*, *64*, 116–123. DOI: 10.54097/x97r9877

Chen, H., Hao, Y., Li, J., & Song, X. (2018). The impact of environmental regulation, shadow economy, and corruption on environmental quality: Theory and empirical evidence from China. *Journal of Cleaner Production*, *195*, 200–214. DOI: 10.1016/j.jclepro.2018.05.206

Chen, S., Lin, W., Wang, M., & Zhang, Y. (2025). Spillover effects in mandatory environmental reporting. *Journal of Accounting and Public Policy*, *54*, 107357. DOI: 10.1016/j.jaccpubpol.2025.107357

Chen, W., & Zhang, Z. (2025). Decomposition of carbon emission chains in global value chains and its implications for bilateral trade between China and the United States. *Environmental Impact Assessment Review*, *115*, 1–12. DOI: 10.1016/j.eiar.2025.108054

Chen, X., & Scholtens, B. (2018). The urge to act: A comparison of active and passive socially responsible investment funds in the United States. *Corporate Social Responsibility and Environmental Management*, *25*(6), 1154–1173. DOI: 10.1002/csr.1529

Chen, Y., & Ma, Y. (2021). Does green investment improve energy firm performance? *Energy Policy*, *153*, 112252. DOI: 10.1016/j.enpol.2021.112252

Chen, Y., & Zhao, Z. J. (2021). The rise of green bonds for sustainable finance: Global standards and issues with the expanding Chinese market. *Current Opinion in Environmental Sustainability*, *52*, 54–57. DOI: 10.1016/j.cosust.2021.06.013

Cherniaieva, O., Mykhalchenko, H., Ataieva, O., Marshalok, T., & Petrukha, S. (2025). Optimizing Budgeting and Financial Management for Sustainable Economic Growth and Fiscal Resilience. *European Journal of Sustainable Development*, *14*(2), 430–430. DOI: 10.14207/ejsd.2025.v14n2p430

Chong, Z., Chen, G., Lu, H., & Li, Z. (2026). Environmental Judicial Reform and Corporate Sustainable Development: A Quasi-Natural Experiment in China. *Sustainability (Basel)*, *18*(1), 15. Advance online publication. DOI: 10.3390/su18010015

Chu, L. K., & Tran, T. H. (2022). The nexus between environmental regulation and ecological footprint in OECD countries: Empirical evidence using panel quantile regression. *Environmental Science and Pollution Research International*, *29*(33), 49700–49723. DOI: 10.1007/s11356-022-19221-y PMID: 35220531

Climate Watch. (2025). *Historical GHG Emissions* [Data set]. https://www.climatewatchdata.org

Çoban, M. N., Biçen, Ö. F., Nassani, A. A., & Anser, M. K. (2025). Exploring the effects of global value chain participation, technological eco-innovation and natural resource rents on environmental quality in the EU–14. *Scientific Reports*, *15*(17572), 17572. Advance online publication. DOI: 10.1038/s41598-025-01569-z PMID: 40399380

Cohen, M., & Tubb, A. (2015). The impact of environmental regulation on firm and country competitiveness: A meta-analysis of the Porter hypothesis. SSRN Electronic Journal. DOI: 10.2139/ssrn.2692919

Cohen, S., Kadach, I., & Ormazabal, G. (2023). Institutional investors, climate disclosure, and carbon emissions. *Journal of Accounting and Economics*, *76*(2–3), 101640. DOI: 10.1016/j.jacceco.2023.101640

Cole, M. A. (2007). Corruption, income and the environment: An empirical analysis. *Ecological Economics*, *62*(3-4), 637–647. DOI: 10.1016/j.ecolecon.2006.08.003

Cosma, S., Cucurachi, P., Gentile, V., & Rimo, G. (2024). Sustainable finance disclosure regulation insights: Unveiling socially responsible funds performance during COVID-19 pandemic and Russia–Ukraine war. *Business Strategy and the Environment*, *33*(4), 3242–3257. DOI: 10.1002/bse.3650

Costantiello, A., & Leogrande, A. (2024). The regulatory quality in the light of environmental, social and governance framework at world level. *Discover Global Society*, *2*(1), 1. DOI: 10.1007/s44282-023-00024-6

Crifo, P., & Forget, V. D. (2013). Think global, invest responsible: Why the private equity industry goes green. *Journal of Business Ethics*, *116*(1), 21–48. DOI: 10.1007/s10551-012-1443-y

Cui, B., Shui, Z., Yang, S., & Lei, T. (2022). Evolutionary game analysis of green technology innovation under the carbon emission trading mechanism. *Frontiers in Environmental Science*, *10*, 997724. Advance online publication. DOI: 10.3389/fenvs.2022.997724

D'Apice, V., Ferri, G., & Intonti, M. (2021). Sustainable disclosure versus ESG intensity: Is there a cross effect between holding and SRI funds? *Corporate Social Responsibility and Environmental Management*, *28*(5), 1496–1510. DOI: 10.1002/csr.2178

D'Orazio, P. (2025). Addressing climate risks through fiscal policy in emerging and developing economies: What do we know and what lies ahead? *Energy Research & Social Science*, *119*, 103852. DOI: 10.1016/j.erss.2024.103852

Dafermos, Y., Monserand, A., & Nikolaidi, M. (2022). Green public investment, consumption patterns and the ecological transition: a macroeconomic analysis. *Available at SSRN* 4097746. DOI: 10.2139/ssrn.4097746

Dai, H., Xie, X., Xie, Y., Liu, J., & Masui, T. (2016). Green growth: The economic impacts of large-scale renewable energy development in China. *Applied Energy*, *162*, 435–449. DOI: 10.1016/j.apenergy.2015.10.049

Dai, S., & Du, X. (2023). Discovering the role of trade diversification, natural resources, and environmental policy stringency on ecological sustainability in the BRICST region. *Resources Policy*, *85*(103868), 103868. Advance online publication. DOI: 10.1016/j.resourpol.2023.103868

David, B., & Giordano-Spring, S. (2022). Climate reporting related to the TCFD framework: An exploration of the air transport sector. *Social and Environmental Accountability Journal*, *42*(1–2), 18–37. DOI: 10.1080/0969160X.2021.2007784

de Abreu, M. C. S., Soares, R. A., Daniel-Vasconcelos, V., & Crisóstomo, V. L. (2023). Does board diversity encourage an environmental policy focused on resource use, emission reduction and innovation? The case of companies in Latin America. *Corporate Social Responsibility and Environmental Management*, *30*(3), 1161–1176. DOI: 10.1002/csr.2411

Dechezleprêtre, A., Haramboure, A., Kögel, C., Lalanne, G., & Yamano, N. (2025). *Carbon Border Adjustments: The potential effects of the EU CBAM along the supply chain*. OECD Science, Technology and Industry Working Papers No. 2025/02. OECD Publishing, Paris. DOI: DOI: 10.1787/18151965

Dechezleprêtre, A., & Sato, M. (2017). The impacts of environmental regulations on competitiveness. *Review of Environmental Economics and Policy*, *11*(2), 183–206. DOI: 10.1093/reep/rex013

Del Gesso, C., & Lodhi, R. N. (2025). Theories underlying environmental, social and governance (ESG) disclosure: A systematic review of accounting studies. *Journal of Accounting Literature*, *47*(2), 433–461. DOI: 10.1108/JAL-08-2023-0143

Delgado Sánchez, V. P., Zorio-Grima, A., & Merello, P. (2026). Sustainability reporting assurance: Knowledge, lags, levels, and providers in leading global companies. *Journal of Innovation & Knowledge*, *12*, 100899. DOI: 10.1016/j.jik.2025.100899

Delvaux, B., & Leuven, K. (2005). The EU greenhouse gas emission allowance trading directive. *Environmental Law Review*, *7*(1), 63–68. DOI: 10.1177/146145290500700104

Deng, H., Li, C., & Wang, L. (2022). The impact of corporate innovation on environmental performance: The moderating effect of financing constraints and government subsidies. *Sustainability (Basel)*, *14*(18), 11530. DOI: 10.3390/su141811530

Deng, Z., Liu, C., & Zhu, Z. (2021). Inter-hours rolling scheduling of behind-the-meter storage operating systems using electricity price forecasting based on deep convolutional neural network. *International Journal of Electrical Power & Energy Systems*, *125*, 106499. DOI: 10.1016/j.ijepes.2020.106499

Deschênes, O. (2018). Environmental regulations and labor markets. *IZA World of Labor: Evidence-Based Policy Making*. Advance online publication. DOI: 10.15185/izawol.22.v2

Dilling, P. F. A., Harris, P., & Caykoylu, S. (2024). The impact of corporate characteristics on climate governance disclosure. *Sustainability (Basel), 16*(5), 1962. DOI: 10.3390/su16051962

Ding, R., Dai, J., Zhang, Y., Tan, T., & Chou, L. C. (2025). Dynamics in green governance in China: Exploring the relationship between carbon emissions, water consumption and economic planning. *Desalination and Water Treatment, 322*, 101120. Advance online publication. DOI: 10.1016/j.dwt.2025.101120

Dinh Thanh, S., Nguyen, C. P., Duy-Tung, B., Binh, N. Q., & Van, D. T. B. (2023). Spatial spillover effects of fiscal decentralization on governance and public administration quality. *Regional Studies, 57*(3), 478–496. DOI: 10.1080/00343404.2022.2078801

Dokuzoğlu, S., & Güzel, A. E. (2024). Democracy, governance, and environmental policy effectiveness: A cross-country analysis with Sustainable Governance Indicators. *European Journal of Government and Economics, 13*(1), 103–119. DOI: 10.17979/ejge.2024.13.1.9902

Domapielle, M. K., Sumankuuro, J., & Bebelleh, F. D. (2022). Revisiting the debate on health financing in Low and Middle-income countries: An integrative review of selected models. *The International Journal of Health Planning and Management, 37*(6), 3061–3074. DOI: 10.1002/hpm.3566 PMID: 36030531

Dong, Q., Zhao, Y., Ma, X., & Zhou, Y. (2024). Risk spillover between carbon markets and stock markets from a progressive perspective: Measurements, spillover networks, and driving factors. *Energy Economics, 129*, 107228. DOI: 10.1016/j.eneco.2023.107228

Dou, G., Ma, L., Wei, K., & Zhang, Q. (2023). *Operations Management Operational Measures, Sustainability for Environmental Regulations and Carbon Constrained Decisions*. Springer Nature Switzerland AG., DOI: 10.1007/978-3-031-37600-9

Drake, D. F., Kleindorfer, P. R., & Van Wassenhove, L. N. (2016). Technology Choice and Capacity Portfolios under Emissions Regulation Citation. *Production and Operations Management, 25*(6), 1006–1025. DOI: 10.1111/poms.12523

Dressel, S., Sjölander-Lindqvist, A., Johansson, M., Ericsson, G., & Sandström, C. (2021). Achieving social and ecological outcomes in collaborative environmental governance: Good examples from swedish moose management. *Sustainability (Basel), 13*(4), 1–21. DOI: 10.3390/su13042329

Dridi, D., Hasni, R., & Kahia, M. (2025). Environmental degradation and financial development nexus in BRICS plus countries: Do financial development drivers make a difference? *Journal of the Knowledge Economy*, *16*(2), 10222–10254. DOI: 10.1007/s13132-024-02266-4

Dugast, C., & Sanches, A. L. (2025). *Emissions in trade: Where are they and how do we measure them?* World Economic Forum. https://www.weforum.org/stories/2025/03/emissions-in-trade-how-we-measure-them/

Dutta, G., & Mitra, K. (2017). A literature review on dynamic pricing of electricity. *The Journal of the Operational Research Society*, *68*(10), 1131–1145. DOI: 10.1057/s41274-016-0149-4

Dye, J., Mckinnon, M., & Byl, C. (2021). Green Gaps: Firm ESG Disclosure and Financial Institutions' Reporting Requirements. *Journal of Sustainability Research*, *3*(1). Advance online publication. DOI: 10.20900/jsr20210006

Dzinamarira, T., & Moyo, E. (2024). Expanding technical assistance: A call for a more nuanced approach for sustainable HIV programs in Sub-Saharan Africa. *International Journal of Infectious Diseases*, *146*, 107135. Advance online publication. DOI: 10.1016/j.ijid.2024.107135

Eaton, E., Hunt, A., & Black, D. (2023). Developing and testing an environmental economics approach to the valuation and application of urban health externalities. *Frontiers in Public Health*, *11*, 1070200. DOI: 10.3389/fpubh.2023.1070200 PMID: 36875392

Ecofys, Fraunhofer Institute for Systems and Innovative Research, Oko Institut. (2009). *Methodology for the free allocation of emission allowances in the EU ETS post 2012. Sector report for the cement industry*. Technical Report. Retrieved from https://climate.ec.europa.eu/system/files/2016-11/bm_study-project_approach_and_general_issues_en.pdf

EEA. (2022). *The role of (environmental) taxation in supporting sustainability transitions*. https://www.eea.europa.eu/en/analysis/publications/the-role-of-environmental-taxation-in-supporting-sustainability-transitions

EEA. (2026). EU Emissions Trading System (ETS) data viewer [Data set]. https://www.eea.europa.eu/en/analysis/maps-and-charts/emissions-trading-viewer-1-dashboards

Eicke, L., Weko, S., Apergi, M., & Marian, A. (2021). Pulling Up the Carbon Ladder? Decarbonization, Dependence, and Third-Country Risks From the European Carbon Border Adjustment Mechanism. *Energy Research & Social Science*, *80*, 102240. DOI: 10.1016/j.erss.2021.102240

Eissa, Y., & Zaki, C. (2023). On GVC and innovation: The moderating role of policy. *Economia e Politica Industriale, 50*(1), 49–71. Advance online publication. DOI: 10.1007/s40812-022-00255-9

Eitan, A. (2025). Privatizing environmental governance: The evolving relationship between regulators and private entities. *Journal of Environmental Policy and Planning*, 1–27. Advance online publication. DOI: 10.1080/1523908X.2025.2576781

Elhorst, J. P. (2014). *Spatial Econometrics from Cross-Sectional Data to Spatial Panels*. Springer. DOI: 10.1007/978-3-642-40340-8

Ells, K. (2018). The tragedy of the commons. In [Book/source details not provided]. DOI: 10.4324/9781315640051-24

Ember. (2025). *Electricity Data Explorer* [Data set]. https://ember-energy.org/data/electricity-data-explorer

EMIS. (2026). *Company profiles – Emerging markets*. https://www.emis.com/php/company-profile/index/search

Energy Community Secretariat. (2024). *CBAM-Readiness Tracker 2024*. Vienna. https://www.energy-community.org/topics/CBAM/Tracker.html

Energy Community Secretariat. (2025a). *Annual Implementation Report 2025*. Vienna. https://www.energy-community.org/publications/flagships/IRs.html

Energy Community Secretariat. (2025b). *CBAM-Readiness Tracker 2025*. Vienna. https://www.energy-community.org/topics/CBAM/Tracker.html

Engle, R. F., Giglio, S., Lee, H., Kelly, B., & Stroebel, J. (2019). Hedging climate change news. SSRN Electronic Journal. DOI: 10.2139/ssrn.3422236

Epede, M. B., & Wang, D. (2022). Global value chain linkages: An integrative review of the opportunities and challenges for SMEs in developing countries. *International Business Review, 31*(5), 1–12. DOI: 10.1016/j.ibusrev.2022.101993

Erdogdu, E. (2025). The Carbon Border Adjustment Mechanism: Opportunities and Challenges for Non-EU Countries. *Wiley Interdisciplinary Reviews. Energy and Environment, 14*(1), e70000. DOI: 10.1002/wene.70000

Ererdi, E., & Güneren Genç, E. (2025). Short-term costs and long-term benefits of environmental, Social, and governance performance on corporate credit ratings. *International Journal of Finance & Banking Studies (2147-4486), 14*(1), 90–97. DOI: 10.20525/ijfbs.v14i1.4014

Escuela, M. B. (2025). Inclusive institutions and policies: stakeholders in the promotion of sustainable practices[Instituciones y políticas inclusivas: stakeholders en la promoción de prácticas sostenibles (1)]. *Trabajo y Derecho, 2025-June*(21). DOI: 10.32029/2386-8112.10.21.2025

EUROFER. (2019). *Low Carbon Roadmap: Pathways to a CO2-neutral European steel industry*. https://www.eurofer.eu/assets/Uploads/EUROFER-Low-Carbon-Roadmap-Pathways-to-a-CO2-neutral-European-Steel-Industry.pdf

EUROFER. (2020). *European Steel in Figures 2020*. https://www.eurofer.eu/assets/Uploads/European-Steel-in-Figures-2020.pdf

European Aluminium. (2025). *Environmental Profile Report 2024. V.2.0*. https://european-aluminium.eu/wp-content/uploads/2025/07/Environmental-Profile-Report_2024-V20.pdf

European Commission. (2019). *The European Green Deal*. COM(2019) 640 final. https://ec.europa.eu/info/sites/default/files/european-green-deal-communication_en.pdf

European Commission. (2021a). *"Fit for 55": Delivering the EU's 2030 climate target on the way to climate neutrality*. COM(2021)550 final, Brussels.

European Commission. (2021b). *Proposal for a regulation of the European Parliament and of the Council establishing a carbon border adjustment mechanism*. COM (2021) 564 final, 2021/0214 COD. Brussels.

European Commission. (2023). *Default values for the transitional period of the CBAM between 1 October 2023 and 31 December 2025*. Brussels. https://taxation-customs.ec.europa.eu/system/files/202312/Default%20values%20transitional%20period.pdf

European Commission. (2025). *EU trade relations with the Western Balkans. Facts, figures and latest developments*. https://policy.trade.ec.europa.eu/eu-trade-relationships-country-and-region/countries-and-regions/western-balkans_en

European Commission. (2026). *The European Green Deal*. https://commission.europa.eu/strategy-and-policy/priorities-2019-2024/story-von-der-leyen-commission/european-green-deal_en

European Council. (2025). *Taking the lead on climate change*. https://www.consilium.europa.eu/en/eu-climate-change/

European Council. (2026). *Fit for 55*. https://www.consilium.europa.eu/en/policies/fit-for-55/

European Parliament & Council of the European Union. (2023a). Directive (EU) 2023/959 of the European Parliament and of the Council of 10 May 2023 amending Directive 2003/87/EC establishing a system for greenhouse gas emission allowance trading within the Union and Decision (EU) 2015/1814 concerning the establishment and operation of a market stability reserve for the Union greenhouse gas emission trading system. *Official Journal of the European Union* (L 130/134). https://data.europa.eu/eli/dir/2023/959/oj

European Parliament & Council of the European Union. (2023b). Regulation (EU) 2023/956 of the European Parliament and of the Council of 10 May 2023 establishing a carbon border adjustment mechanism. *Official Journal of the European Union* (L 130/52). https://data.europa.eu/eli/reg/2023/956/oj

European Parliament & Council of the European Union. (2025). Regulation (EU) 2025/2083 of the European Parliament and of the Council of 8 October 2025 amending Regulation (EU) 2023/956 as regards simplifying and strengthening the carbon border adjustment mechanism. *Official Journal of the European Union* (L series). https://data.europa.eu/eli/reg/2025/2083/oj

Eurostat. (2026). EU trade since 1988 by HS2-4-6 and CN8 [Data set]. https://ec.europa.eu/eurostat

Ezquerro, L., Coimbra, R., Bauluz, B., Núñez-Lahuerta, C., Román-Berdiel, T., & Moreno-Azanza, M. (2024). Large dinosaur egg accumulations and their significance for understanding nesting behaviour. *Geoscience Frontiers, 15*(5), 101872. Advance online publication. DOI: 10.1016/j.gsf.2024.101872

Fairuz, M., & Foster-McGregor, N. (2024). Do Environmental Emissions Traded In Trade Agreements Reduce Provisions In Preferential Global Value Chains? In *ADB Economics Working Paper Series* (755). DOI: 10.22617/WPS240541-2

Faisal, Y. A., Gunawan, I., Cupian, , Hayati, A., Apriliadi, A., & Fajri, M. (2023). Examining the purchase intentions of Indonesian investors for green sukuk. *Sustainability (Basel), 15*(9), 7430. DOI: 10.3390/su15097430

Fang, W., Liu, Z., & Putra, A. R. S. (2022). Role of research and development in green economic growth through renewable energy development: Empirical evidence from South Asia. *Renewable Energy, 194*, 1142–1152. DOI: 10.1016/j.renene.2022.04.125

Fan, H., & Liang, C. (2025). Effective government and regional technological innovation: Evidence from 284 cities in China. *Regulation & Governance, 19*(4), 1101–1121. DOI: 10.1111/rego.12649

Farooq, R. L., & Khoshnaw, A. Q. H. (2025). *The impact of financial independence on strategic decision- making: An analytical study of leaders' perspectives in public polytechnic universities of the Kurdistan Region*. Academic Journal of International University of Erbil., DOI: 10.63841/iue24550

Fazakas, E., Neamtiu, I. A., & Gurzau, E. S. (2024). Health effects of air pollutant mixtures (volatile organic compounds, particulate matter, sulfur and nitrogen oxides)–a review of the literature. *Reviews on Environmental Health, 39*(3), 459–478. DOI: 10.1515/reveh-2022-0252 PMID: 36932657

Fazeli Dehkordi, Z. S., Khatami, S. M., & Ranjbar, E. (2022). The associations between urban form and major non-communicable diseases: A systematic review. *Journal of Urban Health, 99*(5), 941–958. DOI: 10.1007/s11524-022-00652-4 PMID: 35776285

Febriyanti, D. (2025). Green jobs and employment growth: Global analysis of policy impacts and investment trends. In [Proceedings/source details not provided]. DOI: 10.2991/978-94-6463-758-8_164

Feng, T., Wang, X., Shi, Y., & Tu, Q. (2024). The role of carbon price signal in green innovation: Evidence from China. *Journal of Environmental Management, 370*, 122787. DOI: 10.1016/j.jenvman.2024.122787 PMID: 39362165

Filonchyk, M., Peterson, M. P., Zhang, L., Hurynovich, V., & He, Y. (2024). Greenhouse gases emissions and global climate change: Examining the influence of CO2, CH4, and N2O. *The Science of the Total Environment, 935*, 1–7. DOI: 10.1016/j.scitotenv.2024.173359 PMID: 38768722

Firoozi, A. A., & Firoozi, A. A. (2025). Architectural Innovations for Infection Control in Healthcare Environments: Spatial Strategies, Material Selection, and Ventilation Systems. In *Transformative Design in Healthcare: Infection Control and Patient Well-being through Architectural Innovation* (pp. 47-79). Cham: Springer Nature Switzerland. DOI: 10.1007/978-3-032-08019-6_3

Fiskalni savet Republike Srbije (2025). *Klimatsko-energetska tranzicija Srbije i javne finansije: hoće li CBAM biti okidač promena?* Fiskalni savet Republike Srbije.

Fitrah, R., & Soemitra, A. (2022). Green Sukuk for sustainable development goals in Indonesia: A literature study. *Jurnal Ilmiah Ekonomi Islam, 8*(1), 231–240. DOI: 10.29040/jiei.v8i1.4591

Florackis, C., Muktadir-Al-Mukit, D., Sainani, S., & Zhang, Z. (2025). Stock market reaction to mandatory carbon disclosure announcements: The role of institutional investors. *Journal of International Financial Markets, Institutions and Money*, *99*, 102113. DOI: 10.1016/j.intfin.2025.102113

Fonjong, L., Matose, F., & Sonnenfeld, D. A. (2024). Climate change in Africa: Impacts, adaptation, and policy responses. *Global Environmental Change*, *89*, 102912. DOI: 10.1016/j.gloenvcha.2024.102912

Fontaine, G., Carrasco, C., & Rodrigues, C. (2022). How transparency enhances public accountability: The case of environmental governance in Chile. *The Extractive Industries and Society*, *9*, 101040. Advance online publication. DOI: 10.1016/j.exis.2021.101040

Foramitti, J., Savin, I., & van den Bergh, J. C. J. M. (2021). Emission tax vs. Permit trading under bounded rationality and dynamic markets. *Energy Policy*, *148*, 112009. DOI: 10.1016/j.enpol.2020.112009

Galinato, G. I., & Galinato, S. P. (2012). The effects of corruption control, political stability and economic growth on deforestation-induced carbon dioxide emissions. *Environment and Development Economics*, *17*(1), 67–90. DOI: 10.1017/S1355770X11000222

García-Muros, X., Morris, J., & Paltsev, S. (2022). Toward a just energy transition: A distributional analysis of low-carbon policies in the USA. *Energy Economics*, *105*, 105769. Advance online publication. DOI: 10.1016/j.eneco.2021.105769

Genc, T., & Kosempel, S. (2023). Energy transition and the economy: A review article. *Energies*, *16*(7), 2965. DOI: 10.3390/en16072965

Gentile, E., Lema, R., Rabellotti, R., & Ribaudo, D. (2023). Greening Global Value Chains: A Conceptual Framework for Policy Action. In *Global Value Chain Development Report 2023: Resilient and Sustainable GVCs in Turbulent Times* (pp. 228–260). World Trade Organization. https://www.wto.org/english/res_e/booksp_e/gvc_dev_rep23_e.pdf

Gérardin, M., & Ferrière, S. (2025). *Décarbonation de l'acier et des métaux de base: envoyons les bons signaux*. La note d'analyse, No. 149. France Stratégie. https://www.strategie-plan.gouv.fr/publications/decarbonation-de-lacier-metaux-de-base-envoyons-bons-signaux

Glavina, A., Misic, K., Baleta, J., Wang, J., & Mikulci, H. (2025). Economic development and climate change : Achieving a sustainable balance. *Cleaner Engineering and Technology*, *26*, 1–12. DOI: 10.1016/j.clet.2025.100939

Global Footprint Network. (2026). https://data.footprintnetwork.org/#/

Godart, O. N., & Görg, H. (2013). Suppliers of multinationals and the forced linkage effect: Evidence from firm level data. *Journal of Economic Behavior & Organization, 94*, 393–404. DOI: 10.1016/j.jebo.2013.01.007

Gooding, K., Bertone, M. P., Loffreda, G., & Witter, S. (2022). How can we strengthen partnership and coordination for health system emergency preparedness and response? Findings from a synthesis of experience across countries facing shocks. *BMC Health Services Research, 22*(1), 1441. DOI: 10.1186/s12913-022-08859-6 PMID: 36447261

Goswami, N. (2024). A dual burden dilemma: Navigating the global impact of communicable and non-communicable diseases and the way forward. *International Journal of Medical Research, 12*(3), 65–77. DOI: 10.55489/ijmr.11202412

Goulder, L. H., & Schein, A. R. (2013). Carbon taxes versus cap and trade: A critical review. *Climate Change Economics (Singapore), 4*(3), 1350010. Advance online publication. DOI: 10.1142/S2010007813500103

Greenidge, K., McIntyre, M., & Yun, H. (2016). *Structural reform and growth: what really matters? Evidence from the caribbean*. IMF Work., DOI: 10.5089/9781484321812.001

Green, J. E., & Koebele, E. A. (2025). Coordinating school improvement: Understanding the impact of state implementation approach on coordination in multilevel governance systems. *The Review of Policy Research, 42*(2), 188–211. DOI: 10.1111/ropr.12612

Griggs, D., Stafford Smith, M., Gaffney, O., Rockström, J., Öhman, M., Shyamsundar, P., Steffen, W., Glaser, G., Kanie, N., & Noble, I. (2013). Sustainable development goals for people and planet. *Nature, 495*(7441), 305–307. DOI: 10.1038/495305a PMID: 23518546

Grossman GM, Krueger AB (1991) Environmental impacts of a North American free trade agreement (No. w3914). National Bureau of Economic ResearchDOI: 10.1504/IJGE.2020.112576

Guesmi, K., Makrychoriti, P., & Pyrgiotakis, E. G. (2025). Climate change exposure and green bonds issuance. *Journal of International Money and Finance, 152*, 103281. DOI: 10.1016/j.jimonfin.2025.103281

Gugler, K., Haxhimusa, A., & Liebensteiner, M. (2021). Effectiveness of climate policies: Carbon pricing vs. Subsidizing renewables. *Journal of Environmental Economics and Management, 106*, 102405. DOI: 10.1016/j.jeem.2020.102405

Guild, J. (2020). The political and institutional constraints on green finance in Indonesia. *Journal of Sustainable Finance & Investment, 10*(2), 157–170. DOI: 10.1080/20430795.2019.1706312

Guliyev, H. (2024). Ecological footprint spillover effects in Europe: New insights from dynamic spatial panel data model with common shocks. *Journal of Environmental Management, 368*(122194), 122194. Advance online publication. DOI: 10.1016/j.jenvman.2024.122194 PMID: 39168005

Gupta, A., Sharma, U., & Gupta, S. K. (2021). The role of ESG in sustainable development: An analysis through the lens of machine learning. *2021 IEEE International Humanitarian Technology Conference (IHTC)*, 1–5. IEEE. http://doi.org/ DOI: 10.1109/IHTC53077.2021.9698939

Gutsche, G., & Zwergel, B. (2020). Investment barriers and labeling schemes for socially responsible investments. *Schmalenbach Business Review, 72*(2), 111–157. DOI: 10.1007/s41464-020-00085-z

Gutsch, M., Mai, J., Ukhova, N., & Dijkstra-silva, S. (2025). Effects of environmental provisions in international trade agreements on businesses and economies – a systematic review. *Sustainability Accounting. Management and Policy Journal, 16*(7), 1–27. DOI: 10.1108/SAMPJ-02-2024-0122

Hale, T. (2020). Catalytic cooperation. *Global Environmental Politics, 20*(4), 73–98. DOI: 10.1162/glep_a_00561

Hall, N. L., Jeanneret, T. D., & Rai, A. (2016). Cost-reflective electricity pricing: Consumer preferences and perceptions. *Energy Policy, 95*, 62–72. DOI: 10.1016/j.enpol.2016.04.042

Hammami, R., Nouira, I., & Frein, Y. (2018). Effects of Customers' Environmental Awareness and Environmental Regulations on the Emission Intensity and Price of a Product. *Decision Sciences, 49*(6), 1116–1155. DOI: 10.1111/deci.12302

Handoyo, S. (2024). Public governance and national environmental performance nexus: Evidence from cross-country studies. *Heliyon, 10*(23), e40637. Advance online publication. DOI: 10.1016/j.heliyon.2024.e40637

Hania, B. T., Endri, E., & Indra, I. (2022). Identify the issuance problem of corporate green sukuk in Indonesia. *Islamic Economics Journal, 8*(2), 187–204. DOI: 10.21111/iej.v8i2.8404

Haščič, I., de Vries, F., Johnstone, N., & Medhi, N. (2010). Effects of environmental policy on the type of innovation. OECD Journal: Economic Studies, 1–18. DOI: 10.1787/eco_studies-v2009-art2-en

Hassan, S. T., Khan, S. U. D., Xia, E., & Fatima, H. (2020). Role of institutions in correcting environmental pollution: An empirical investigation. *Sustainable Cities and Society*, *53*, 101901. DOI: 10.1016/j.scs.2019.101901

Heath, D., Macciocchi, D., Michaely, R., & Ringgenberg, C., M. (. (2023). Does socially responsible investing change firm behavior? *Review of Finance*, *27*(6), 2057–2083. DOI: 10.1093/rof/rfad002

He, J., & Ye, Z. (2019). Basic principles and equilibrium model of carbon cost pass-through in power industry. *Ecological Economics*, *35*(7), 45–49.

Helleiner, E., DiLeo, M., & Klooster, J. (2024). Financial technocrats as competitive regime creators: The founding and design of the Network for Greening the Financial System. *Regulation & Governance*, *19*(3), 901–916. Advance online publication. DOI: 10.1111/rego.12629

He, P., Dou, G., & Zhang, W. (2017). Optimal production planning and cap setting under cap-and-trade regulation. *The Journal of the Operational Research Society*, *68*(9), 1094–1105. Advance online publication. DOI: 10.1057/s41274-016-0123-1

He, P., Zhang, W., Xu, X., & Bian, Y. (2015). Production lot-sizing and carbon emissions under cap-and-trade and carbon tax regulations. *Journal of Cleaner Production*, *103*, 241–248. DOI: 10.1016/j.jclepro.2014.08.102

Hermann, T., Delille, T., & Giovannini, V. (2026). *Carbon border adjustment mechanisms – climate and trade policy issues*. Financier Worldwide. https://www.financierworldwide.com/carbon-border-adjustment-mechanisms-climate-and-trade-policy-issues

Hernández-Luis, A., & Fontaine, G. (2025). Transparency and Corruption Control in Latin America: Lessons from Chile. In *International Series on Public Policy: Part F4940* (pp. 251–273). Palgrave Macmillan. DOI: 10.1007/978-3-031-90649-7_12

Hewa, S. I., Mala, R., Chen, J., & Dumay, J. (2025). Climate related disclosures and investor behaviour: An Australian study. *Advances in Accounting*, *68*, 100809. DOI: 10.1016/j.adiac.2025.100809

Hidalgo-Oñate, D., Fuertes-Fuertes, I., & Cabedo, J. D. (2023). Climate-related prudential regulation tools in the context of sustainable and responsible investment: A systematic review. *Climate Policy*, *23*(6), 704–721. DOI: 10.1080/14693062.2023.2179587

Hosseini, H. M., & Kaneko, S. (2013). Can environmental quality spread through institutions? *Energy Policy*, *56*, 312–321. DOI: 10.1016/j.enpol.2012.12.067

Hourcade, J.-C., Pottier, A., & Etienne, E. (2012). The environment and directed technical change: Comment. SSRN *Electronic Journal*. DOI: 10.2139/ssrn.1991109

Huang, W. H., & Lu, C. T. (2025). The effect of hospital budgeting system on physician-executives' budget cognitive consciousness and medical decision making. *Cost Effectiveness and Resource Allocation : C/E, 23*(1), 22. DOI: 10.1186/s12962-025-00629-5 PMID: 40400001

Huliselan, M. (2025). Environmental accounting and financial management: A strategic approach to corporate sustainability. *Journal of Economics and Management Scienties*, 164–170. DOI: 10.37034/jems.v7i3.106

Ibrahim, M. (2023). From policy to politics? Exploring feedback effects of social protection on state-citizen relations in Ghana. *Social Policy and Administration, 57*(6), 902–918. DOI: 10.1111/spol.12938

Ibrahim, M. H., & Law, S. H. (2016). Institutional quality and CO2 emission–trade relations: Evidence from Sub-Saharan Africa. *The South African Journal of Economics, 84*(2), 323–340. DOI: 10.1111/saje.12095

Ikevuje, A. H., Anaba, D. C., & Iheanyichukwu, U. T. (2024). Exploring sustainable finance mechanisms for green energy transition: A comprehensive review and analysis. *Finance & Accounting Research Journal, 6*(7), 1224–1247. DOI: 10.51594/farj.v6i7.1314

Ikwue, U., Ekwezia, A. V., Oguejiofor, B. B., Agho, M. O., & Daraojimba, C. (2023). Sustainable Investment strategies in Pension Fund Management: A comparative review of esg principles adoption in the u.S. And Nigeria. *International Journal of Management & Entrepreneurship Research, 5*(9), 652–673. DOI: 10.51594/ijmer.v5i9.547

Ilhan, E., Sautner, Z., & Vilkov, G. (2020). Carbon tail risk. *Review of Financial Studies, 34*(3), 1540–1571. DOI: 10.1093/rfs/hhaa071

International Trade Centre. (2026). Trade Map [Data set]. https://www.trademap.org

Iordachi, V., & Ciobu, S. (2024). Sustainable financing for the health sector: building a resilient healthcare system. In *Creşterea economica in condiţiile globalizarii* (pp. 95-112). DOI: 10.36004/nier.cecg.III.2024.18.10

IPCC. (2022). *Climate Change 2022: Mitigation of Climate Change*. Intergovernmental Panel on Climate Change. https://www.ipcc.ch/report/ar6/wg3/

Isaksson, O. H. D., Simeth, M., & Seifert, R. W. (2016). Knowledge spillovers in the supply chain: Evidence from the high tech sectors. *Research Policy*, *45*(3), 699–706. DOI: 10.1016/j.respol.2015.12.007

Ivahnenko, I. S., Molodko, O. V., Shepeta, M. O., Pylypchuk, V. V., & Borodynia, V. V. (2025). The essence and evolution of organizational and managerial decisions in construction. *Building Production*, (80), 43–52. DOI: 10.36750/2524-2555.80.43-52

Izah, S. C., Iyiola, A. O., Yarkwan, B., & Richard, G. (2023). Impact of air quality as a component of climate change on biodiversity-based ecosystem services. In *Visualization techniques for climate change with machine learning and artificial intelligence* (pp. 123–148). Elsevier., DOI: 10.1016/B978-0-323-99714-0.00005-4

Jaffe, A. B., & Palmer, K. (1997). Environmental regulation and innovation: A panel data study. *The Review of Economics and Statistics*, *79*(4), 610–619. DOI: 10.1162/003465397557196

Janicka, M., & Sajnóg, A. (2022). The ESG reporting of EU public companies—Does the company's capitalisation matter? *Sustainability (Basel)*, *14*(7), 4279. DOI: 10.3390/su14074279

Jayaswal, M. K., Yadav, A. S., Mishra, A., & Seikh, M. R. (2025). Credit Financing Based Two-Level Green Supply Chain Model with Carbon Emissions for Eco-Friendly Demand Under a Fuzzy Environment. *Process Integration and Optimization for Sustainability*. DOI: 10.1007/s41660-025-00610-y

Jebe, R. (2019). The convergence of financial and ESG materiality: Taking sustainability mainstream. *American Business Law Journal*, *56*(3), 645–702. DOI: 10.1111/ablj.12148

Jia, F., Zuluaga-Cardona, L., Bailey, A., & Rueda, X. (2018). Sustainable supply chain management in developing countries: An analysis of the literature. *Journal of Cleaner Production*, *189*, 263–278. DOI: 10.1016/j.jclepro.2018.03.248

Johnson, M. (2025). Lessons from a History of Histories of Public Finance. *Available at SSRN* 5615620. DOI: 10.2139/ssrn.5615620

Johnstone, N., Haščič, I., & Popp, D. (2009). Renewable energy policies and technological innovation: Evidence based on patent counts. *Environmental and Resource Economics*, *45*(1), 133–155. DOI: 10.1007/s10640-009-9309-1

Jones, S., van der Laan, S., Frost, G., & Loftus, J. (2008). The investment performance of socially responsible investment funds in Australia. *Journal of Business Ethics*, *80*(2), 181–203. DOI: 10.1007/s10551-007-9412-6

Juhro, S. M., Robinson, I., Rahadyan, H., & Rishanty, A. (2024). Climate Risks, Just Transition, and Central Bank Policy for Sustainable Economic Growth. *Jurnal Ekonomi Indonesia, 13*(3), 215–248. DOI: 10.52813/jei.v13i3.587

Jung, S. H., & Feng, T. (2020). Government subsidies for green technology development under uncertainty. *European Journal of Operational Research, 286*(2), 726–739. DOI: 10.1016/j.ejor.2020.03.047

Jun, W., Zakaria, M., Shahzad, S. J. H., & Mahmood, H. (2018). Effect of FDI on pollution in China: New insights based on wavelet approach. *Sustainability (Basel), 10*(11), 3859. DOI: 10.3390/su10113859

Kahina, H., & Lamya, B. (2025). The Role of Green Islamic Sukuk in Achieving Environmental Sustainability in Indonesia: Reality, Challenges, and Future Prospects. *Science. Education and Innovations in the Context of Modern Problems, 8*(3), 734–751.

Kahn, M. E., Mohaddes, K., Ng, R., Pesaran, M. H., Raissi, M., & Yang, J.-C. (2019). Long-term macroeconomic effects of climate change: A cross-country analysis. IMF Working Papers. DOI: 10.5089/9781513514598.001

Kamalina, A. R. (2024). *RI Jadi Penerbit Sukuk Terbesar di Dunia, Kalahkan IsDB.* Bisnis.Com. https://finansial.bisnis.com/read/20241031/231/1812126/ri-jadi-penerbit-sukuk-terbesar-di-dunia-kalahkan-isdb#goog_rewarded)

Kang, K., & Tan, B. Q. (2023). Carbon emission reduction investment in sustainable supply chains under cap-and-trade. *Expert Systems with Applications, 227*, 1–16. DOI: 10.1016/j.eswa.2023.120335

Kaplaner, C., Knill, C., & Steinebach, Y. (2025). Administrative overload and policy triage: Causal evidence from the introduction of the Acid Rain Program in the United States. *Journal of Public Administration: Research and Theory, 35*(4), 422–433. DOI: 10.1093/jopart/muaf020

Karina, L. A. (2019). Peluang dan tantangan perkembangan green sukuk di Indonesia. *Proceeding of Conference on Islamic Management, Accounting, and Economics*, 259–265.

Kartal, M. T., Kirikkaleli, D., & Pata, U. K. (2024). Role of environmental policy stringency on sectoral CO2 emissions in EU–5 countries: Disaggregated level evidence by novel quantile-based approaches. *Energy & Environment*, •••, 1–26. DOI: 10.1177/0958305X241241026

Kartal, M. T., Sharif, A., Magazzino, C., Mukhtarov, S., & Kirikkaleli, D. (2025). The effects of energy transition and environmental policy stringency subtypes on ecological footprint: Evidence from BRICS countries via a KRLS approach. *Engineering (Beijing)*. Advance online publication. DOI: 10.1016/j.eng.2025.02.007

Kaufmann, D., & Kraay, A. (2018). The worldwide governance indicators. The World Bank. https://info.worldbank.org/governance/wgi/

Kaushiva, A. (2025). Green economic transition and green skills: A pathway for sustainable development. *Shanlax International Journal of Economics*, *13*(3), 71–78. DOI: 10.34293/economics.v13i3.8611

Keen, M., Parry, I., & Roaf, J. (2021). Border Carbon Adjustments: Rationale, Design and Impact. In *IMF Working Paper* (239). https://www.imf.org/-/media/files/publications/wp/2021/english/wpiea2021239-print-pdf.pdf

Kentikelenis, A., & Stubbs, T. (2022). Austerity redux: The post-pandemic wave of budget cuts and the future of global public health. *Global Policy*, *13*(1), 5–17. DOI: 10.1111/1758-5899.13028

Keshminder, J. S., Abdullah, M. S., & Mardi, M. (2022). Green sukuk–Malaysia surviving the bumpy road: Performance, challenges and reconciled issuance framework. *Qualitative Research in Financial Markets*, *14*(1), 76–94. DOI: 10.1108/QRFM-04-2021-0049

Khalilurrahman, K., & Mubarrak, H. (2022). Retail green sukuk in Indonesia: Toward a maqashid approach. *Share: Jurnal Ekonomi Dan Keuangan Islam*, *11*(1), 208–228. DOI: 10.22373/share.v11i1.12460

Khanam, Z., Sultana, F. M., & Mushtaq, F. (2023). Environmental pollution control measures and strategies: an overview of recent developments. *Geospatial Analytics for Environmental Pollution Modeling: Analysis, Control and Management*, 385-414. DOI: 10.1007/978-3-031-45300-7_15

Khezri, M. (2024). The Interplay Between Resource Wealth and Tax Revenue: Implications for Fiscal Policy and Institutional Development in the Kurdistan Region. In *Perspectives on Development in the Middle East and North Africa (MENA) Region: Part F3979* (pp. 63–74). Springer. DOI: 10.1007/978-981-97-7725-9_4

Kivyiro, P., & Arminen, H. (2014). Carbon dioxide emissions, energy consumption, economic growth, and foreign direct investment: Causality analysis for sub-Saharan Africa. *Energy*, *74*, 595–606. DOI: 10.1016/j.energy.2014.07.025

Kleimeier, S., & Viehs, M. (2021). Pricing carbon risk: Investor preferences or risk mitigation? *Economics Letters*, *205*, 109936. DOI: 10.1016/j.econlet.2021.109936

Kongbuamai, N., Bui, Q., & Nimsai, S. (2021). The effects of renewable and nonrenewable energy consumption on the ecological footprint: The role of environmental policy in BRICS countries. *Environmental Science and Pollution Research International, 28*(22), 27885–27899. DOI: 10.1007/s11356-021-12551-3 PMID: 33517549

Kortum, S., & Weisbach, D. (2017). The Design of Border Adjustments for Carbon Prices. *National Tax Journal, 70*(2), 421–446. DOI: 10.17310/ntj.2017.2.07

Kozal, Ö. (2025). Uneven human development: Revisiting economic, environmental, and political determinants in OECD. In Meçik, O. (Ed.), *Macroeconomic challenges to structural reform and industrial development* (pp. 361–3186). IGI Global.

Krueger, P., Sautner, Z., & Starks, L. T. (2020). The importance of climate risks for institutional investors. *Review of Financial Studies, 33*(3), 1067–1111. DOI: 10.1093/rfs/hhz137

Kwilinski, A., Lyulyov, O., & Pimonenko, T. (2023). Greenfield investment as a catalyst of green economic growth. *Energies, 16*(5), 2372. DOI: 10.3390/en16052372

Laila, N. (2025). *Green Sovereign Sukuk: Indonesia's Sustainable Financial Innovation in the Global Market.* Unair.Ac.Id. https://unair.ac.id/green-sovereign-sukuk-inovasi-keuangan-berkelanjutan-indonesia-di-pasar-global/

Lau, L.S., Choong, C.K., Eng, Y.K., 2014. Carbon dioxide emission, institutional quality, and economic growth: empirical evidence in Malaysia. Renew. *Energy* 68, 276e281. .DOI: 10.1016/j.renene.2014.02.013

Lau, L. S., Choong, C. K., & Eng, Y. K. (2014). Investigation of the environmental Kuznets curve for carbon emissions in Malaysia: Do foreign direct investment and trade matter? *Energy Policy, 68*, 490–497. DOI: 10.1016/j.enpol.2014.01.002

Lawson, L. A. (2020). GHG emissions and fossil energy use as consequences of efforts of improving human well-being in Africa. *Journal of Environmental Management, 273*(111136), 111136. Advance online publication. DOI: 10.1016/j.jenvman.2020.111136 PMID: 32768760

Le Billon, P., Lujala, P., & Rustad, S. A. (2021). Transparency in environmental and resource governance: Theories of change for the eiti. *Global Environmental Politics, 21*(3), 124–146. DOI: 10.1162/glep_a_00610

Le Blanc, B., & Mendoza, I. de L. (2023). *Potential conflicts between the European CBAM and the WTO rules.* Norton Rose Fulbright. https://www.nortonrosefulbright.com/en/knowledge/publications/9c5d9ec6/potential-conflicts-between-the-european-cbam-and-the-wto-rules

Lee, D., Ooka, R., Ikeda, S., Choi, W., & Kwak, Y. (2020). Model predictive control of building energy systems with thermal energy storage in response to occupancy variations and time-variant electricity prices. *Energy and Building*, *225*, 110291. DOI: 10.1016/j.enbuild.2020.110291

Lee, J. W. (2013). The contribution of foreign direct investment to clean energy use, carbon emissions and economic growth. *Energy Policy*, *55*, 483–489. DOI: 10.1016/j.enpol.2012.12.039

Leroutier, M. (2022). Carbon pricing and power sector decarbonisation: Evidence from the UK. *Journal of Environmental Economics and Management*, *111*, 102580. DOI: 10.1016/j.jeem.2021.102580

LeSage, J., & Pace, R. K. (2009). *Introduction to spatial econometrics*. Chapman and Hall/CRC. DOI: 10.1201/9781420064254

Lestari, J. S., & Frömmel, M. (2024). Socially responsible investments: Doing good while doing well in developed versus emerging markets? *Research in International Business and Finance*, *69*(102229), 102229. DOI: 10.1016/j.ribaf.2024.102229

Li, D., Zhang, Z., & Gao, X. (2025). The impact of carbon emission trading system on the implied cost of equity capital. *International Review of Economics & Finance*, *101*, 104157. Advance online publication. DOI: 10.1016/j.iref.2025.104157

Li, G., Zhang, R., & Masui, T. (2021). CGE modeling with disaggregated pollution treatment sectors for assessing China's environmental tax policies. *The Science of the Total Environment*, *761*, 143264. DOI: 10.1016/j.scitotenv.2020.143264

Li, G., Zong, Q., Chen, X., & Song, M. (2025). Intergovernmental environmental affairs division and environmental public services supply: Evidence from 289 cities in China. *Energy & Environment*, *36*(4), 1929–1948. DOI: 10.1177/0958305X231201974

Li, L., Shen, Z., Song, M., & Vardanyan, M. (2023). Public expenditure, green finance, and environmental governance: Evidence from China. *Environmental Modeling and Assessment*, *28*(5), 859–873. DOI: 10.1007/s10666-023-09899-w

Li, M., Sun, Y., Xia, Y., Yang, Z., Chen, C., Yuan, Y., & Wang, P. (2026). The impacts of Carbon Border Adjustment Mechanism (CBAM) on international trade and policy responses: From an economic and environmental equity perspective. *Energy Policy*, *210*, 1–13. DOI: 10.1016/j.enpol.2025.115014

Lima, A. T., Bastos, F. A., Teubner, F. J.Jr, Neto, R. R., Cooper, A., & Barroso, G. F. (2020). Strengths and Weaknesses of a Hybrid Post-disaster Management Approach: The Doce River (Brazil) Mine-Tailing Dam Burst. *Environmental Management*, *65*(6), 711–724. DOI: 10.1007/s00267-020-01279-4

Lin, B., & Benjamin, N. I. (2017). Green development determinants in China: A non-radial quantile outlook. *Journal of Cleaner Production, 162*, 764–775. DOI: 10.1016/j.jclepro.2017.06.062

Lin, B., & Zhou, Y. (2022). Measuring the green economic growth in China: Influencing factors and policy perspectives. *Energy, 241*, 122518. DOI: 10.1016/j.energy.2021.122518

Linden, J., O'Donoghue, C., & Sologon, D. (2026). Modelling distributional impacts of carbon taxation: A systematic review and meta-analysis. arXiv. https://doi.org//arXiv.2601.07713DOI: 10.48550

Ling, S., Jin, S., Wang, H., Zhang, Z., & Feng, Y. (2024). Transportation infrastructure upgrading and green development efficiency: Empirical analysis with double machine learning method. *Journal of Environmental Management, 358*, 1–18. DOI: 10.1016/j.jenvman.2024.120922 PMID: 38657413

Lin, L., & Hong, Y. (2022). Developing a green bonds market: Lessons from China. *European Business Organization Law Review, 23*(1), 143–185. DOI: 10.1007/s40804-021-00231-1

Lin, M., & Lin, H. (2025). Asymmetric spatial effects of unemployment on health outcomes. *Spatial Economic Analysis*, 1–23. Advance online publication. DOI: 10.1080/17421772.2025.2492212

Li, Q., & Zhang, S. (2025). Impact of globalization and industrialization on ecological footprint: Do institutional quality and renewable energy matter? *Frontiers in Environmental Science, 13*, 1535638. Advance online publication. DOI: 10.3389/fenvs.2025.1535638

Listyarini, S., & Warlina, L. (2017). The development model of the policy alternatives in controlling air pollution in the Jakarta province, Indonesia. *International Journal of Environmental Sciences and Development, 8*(7), 496–500. DOI: 10.18178/ijesd.2017.8.7.1003

Liu, D., Zeng, X., Su, B., Wang, W., Sun, K., & Sadia, U. H. (2020). A social network analysis regarding electricity consumption and economic growth in China. *Journal of Cleaner Production, 274*, 122973. DOI: 10.1016/j.jclepro.2020.122973

Liu, Y., Zhang, Y., Yang, Y., & Chen, X. (2023). Dark side of environmental regulation: Wage inequality cost. *Journal of Comparative Economics, 51*(2), 524–544. DOI: 10.1016/j.jce.2022.11.004

Liu, Z., Yin, T., Surya Putra, A. R., & Sadiq, M. (2022). Public spending as a new determinate of sustainable development goal and green economic recovery: Policy perspective analysis in the Post-Covid ERA. *Climate Change Economics (Singapore), 13*(03), 2240007. DOI: 10.1142/S2010007822400073

Li, X., Du, J., & Long, H. (2018). A comparative study of Chinese and foreign green development from the perspective of mapping knowledge domains. *Sustainability (Basel), 10*(12), 43–57. DOI: 10.3390/su10124357

Li, X., Du, J., & Long, H. (2019c). Green development behavior and performance of industrial enterprises based on grounded theory study: Evidence from China. *Sustainability (Basel), 11*(15), 4133. DOI: 10.3390/su11154133

Li, Z., & Li, Y. (2024). The Impact of Intergovernmental Cooperation and Local Fiscal Autonomy on Environmental Regional Governance: Evidence From China Yangtze River Delta Urban Agglomeration. *SAGE Open, 14*(2), 21582440241252253. Advance online publication. DOI: 10.1177/21582440241252253

Lobanov, M. M., Zvezdanović Lobanova, J., Milinčić, M., & Zvezdanović, M. (2025). Impact Of Coal-Based Electricity Generation, Land Use Change, Steel And Cement Production On CO2 Emissions: Evidence From Eastern European And Central Asian Countries. *Geography, Environment, Sustainability, 18*(1), 139–151. DOI: 10.24057/2071-9388-2025-3754

Lobanov, M., Zvezdanović Lobanova, J., & Zvezdanović, M. (2024). Climate Discourse in Russia: From the Dichotomy of Climate Consciousness to Four Forms of Climate Policy. *Mir Rossii, 33*(3), 141–169. DOI: 10.17323/1811-038X-2024-33-3-141-169

Lobon , O. R., Varadi, A. E., Vătavu, S., & Doran, N. M. (2025). Bridges or Barriers? Unpacking the Institutional Drivers of Business Climate Adaptation in the EU. *Sustainability (Basel), 17*(11), 4865. Advance online publication. DOI: 10.3390/su17114865

Long, R., Wang, X., Wu, M., Chen, H., Li, Q., & Wang, Y. (2023). The impact of carbon information disclosure on the cost of capital: The moderating role of regulatory pressures. *Resources, Conservation and Recycling, 195*, 106970. DOI: 10.1016/j.resconrec.2023.106970

Lozhkina, S. L., Gusarova, O. M., Mamrukova, O. I., Sivakova, S. Y., & Lozhkin, V. A. (2021). Forecasting the environmental and economic indicators of the enterprise, taking into account their mutual proportionality in dynamics for the purposes of sustainable development. *Rivista di Studi sulla Sostenibilità*, (2), 319–332. DOI: 10.3280/RISS2021-002021

Lucy. (2025). Climate Action and Resilience for a Sustainable Future: The Roles of the UN, WTO, and IMF. In *Approaches to Global Sustainability, Markets, and Governance: Part F745* (pp. 177–198). Springer. DOI: 10.1007/978-981-96-7181-6_10

Lu, J., Wang, T., & Liu, X. (2023). Can environmental governance policy synergy reduce carbon emissions? *Economic Analysis and Policy*, *80*, 570–585. DOI: 10.1016/j.eap.2023.09.003

Luo, H., Sun, Y., & Zhang, L. (2024). Effects of macroprudential policies on ecological footprint: The moderating role of environmental policy stringency in the top 11 largest countries. *Scientific Reports*, *14*(7423), 7423. Advance online publication. DOI: 10.1038/s41598-024-58015-9 PMID: 38548882

Lustig, N. (2023). Fiscal policy, income redistribution, and poverty reduction in low-and middle-income countries. In *Commitment to Equity Handbook* (2nd ed.). Estimating the Impact of Fiscal Policy on Inequality and Poverty., https://www.scopus.com/pages/publications/105014232554?origin=scopusAI

Lydgate, E. (2024). Integrating Climate Action into Free Trade Agreements. In *The Sustainability Revolution in International Trade Agreements* (pp. 181–198). Oxford University Press., DOI: 10.1093/9780191994470.003.0012

MacKay, D. J., Cramton, P., Ockenfels, A., & Stoft, S. (2017). Price Carbon—I Will If You Will. In *Global Carbon Pricing The Path to Climate Cooperation* (pp. 7–12). The MIT Press., DOI: 10.7551/mitpress/10914.003.0005

Maedgen, J., & Wlezien, C. (2024). Institutional friction and policy responsiveness: The puzzle of coalitional fragmentation and executive-legislative balance. *Political Research Quarterly*, *77*(4), 1262–1278. DOI: 10.1177/10659129241263481

Magacho, G., Espagne, E., & Godin, A. (2024). Impacts of the CBAM on EU trade partners: Consequences for developing countries. *Climate Policy*, *24*(2), 243–259. DOI: 10.1080/14693062.2023.2200758

Mahmood, H. (2025). An Empirical Assessment of Oil, Natural Gas, Mineral, and Forest Rents on CO2 Emissions in Saudi Arabia. *Challenges in Sustainability*, *13*(3), 366–376. DOI: 10.56578/cis130304

Mahmoudian, F., Yu, D., Lu, J., Nazari, J. A., & Herremans, I. M. (2023). Does cost of debt reflect the value of quality greenhouse gas emissions reduction efforts and disclosure? *International Journal of Accounting, Auditing and Performance Evaluation, 16*(?), 100563. https://doi.org/DOI: 10.1016/j.intaccaudtax.2023.100563

Maliszewska, M., Chepeliev, M., Fischer, C., & Jung, E. (2025). *How developing countries can measure exposure to the EU's carbon border adjustment mechanism* [Online forum post]. World Bank Blogs. https://blogs.worldbank.org/en/trade/how-developing-countries-can-measure-exposure-eus-carbon-border-adjustment-mechanism

Malthus, T. R. (1798). *First Essay on Population*. University of MI Press.

Maqsoom, A., Irfan, M., Basharat, M. U., Ali, U., & Ashraf, H. (2025). Carbon Markets and Carbon Pricing Mechanisms: How Developing Economies Can Benefit? *Procedia Computer Science*, *256*, 1416–1426. DOI: 10.1016/j.procs.2025.02.274

Maratou, A., & Marcu, A. (2021). *The Aluminium Value Chain and Implications for CBAM Design*. ERCST. https://ercst.org/wp-content/uploads/2021/08/The-aluminium-value-chain-and-implications-for-CBAM-design.pdf

Marcu, A., Mehling, M., & Cosbey, A. (2021). *Border Carbon Adjustments in the EU: Sectoral Deep Dive*. ERCST. https://ercst.org/wp-content/uploads/2021/08/20210317-CBAM-II_Report-I-Sectors.pdf

Markkanen, S., & Anger, A. (2019). Social impacts of climate change mitigation policies and their implications for inequality. *Climate Policy*, *19*(7), 1–18. DOI: 10.1080/14693062.2019.1596873

Marlina, E., Purwaningsih, M., Siagian, A. H. A. M., Al Hakim, S., & Maryati, I. (2024). Ensuring Trustworthiness in Qualitative Research: The Role of Triangulation Techniques. In *Qualitative Research Methods for Dissertation Research* (pp. 347–375). IGI Global. DOI: 10.4018/979-8-3693-3069-2.ch012

Marra, A., Antonelli, P., & Pozzi, C. (2017). Emerging green-tech specializations and clusters – A network analysis on technological innovation at the metropolitan level. *Renewable & Sustainable Energy Reviews*, *67*, 1037–1046. DOI: 10.1016/j.rser.2016.09.086

Martini, A. (2021). Socially responsible investing: From the ethical origins to the sustainable development framework of the European Union. *Environment, Development and Sustainability*, *23*(11), 16874–16890. DOI: 10.1007/s10668-021-01375-3

Martin, R., de Preux, L. B., & Wagner, U. J. (2012). The impact of a carbon tax on manufacturing: Evidence from microdata. *Journal of Public Economics*, *117*. Advance online publication. DOI: 10.2139/ssrn.1367149

Masood, A., Rahim, N., & Lee, U. H. M. S. (2024). Driving Green Sukuk Development to Meet ESGs and Society 5.0 Aspirations Through Innovative Technology. In *Strategic Islamic Business and Management: Solutions for Sustainability* (pp. 1–18). Springer.

Mathieu, E. (2023). Policy coherence versus regulatory governance. Electricity reforms in Algeria and Morocco. *Regulation & Governance*, *17*(3), 694–708. DOI: 10.1111/rego.12488

Matsumura, E. M., Prakash, R., & Vera-Muñoz, S. C. (2024). Climate-risk materiality and firm risk. *Review of Accounting Studies*, *29*(1), 1–40. DOI: 10.1007/s11142-022-09718-9

Maund, K., Gajendran, T., & Brewer, G. (2018). Key issues for implementation of environmental planning policy: Construction management practice. *Sustainability (Basel)*, *10*(7), 2156. DOI: 10.3390/su10072156

Mehmood, U., Tariq, S., Ul-Haq, Z., & Meo, M. S. (2021). Does the modifying role of institutional quality remains homogeneous in GDP-CO2 emission nexus? New evidence from ARDL approach. *Environmental Science and Pollution Research International*, *28*(8), 10167–10174. DOI: 10.1007/s11356-020-11293-y

Mehta, D., & Derbeneva, V. (2024). Impact of environmental fiscal reforms on carbon emissions of EURO-4 countries: CS-NARDL approach. *International Journal of Thermofluids*, *21*, 100550. Advance online publication. DOI: 10.1016/j.ijft.2023.100550

Mert, M., & Bölük, G. (2016). Do foreign direct investment and renewable energy consumption affect the CO 2 emissions? New evidence from a panel ARDL approach to Kyoto Annex countries. *Environmental Science and Pollution Research International*, *23*(21), 21669–21681. DOI: 10.1007/s11356-016-7413-7

Meydan, C. H., & Akkaş, H. (2024). The role of triangulation in qualitative research: Converging perspectives. In *Principles of Conducting Qualitative Research in Multicultural Settings* (pp. 98–129). IGI Global., DOI: 10.4018/979-8-3693-3306-8.ch006

Meyer, C., Chen, C., & Matzdorf, B. (2018). Qualitative comparative institutional analysis of environmental governance: Implications from research on payments for ecosystem services. *Ecosystem Services*, *34*, 169–180. DOI: 10.1016/j.ecoser.2018.07.008

Miao, Y., Bukhari, A. A. A., Bukhari, W. A. A., Ahmad, S., & Hayat, N. (2025). Why fossil fuels stifle green economic growth? An environmental management perspective in assessing the spatial spillover impact of energy consumption in South Asia. *Journal of Environmental Management*, *373*(123471), 123471. Advance online publication. DOI: 10.1016/j.jenvman.2024.123471 PMID: 39642839

Michalek, G. (2016). Progressive Optimal Technology-based Border Carbon Adjustment (POT BCA) - A New Approach to an Old Carbon Problem. *Environmental Modeling and Assessment*, *21*(3), 323–337. DOI: 10.1007/s10666-015-9484-0

Mill, G. A. (2006). The financial performance of a socially responsible investment over time and a possible link with corporate social responsibility. *Journal of Business Ethics*, *63*(2), 131–148. DOI: 10.1007/s10551-005-2410-7

Ministry of Finance Republic Indonesia. (2023). *Early Redemption of Sukuk Tabungan (ST) Series ST009*. Http://Www.Djppr.Kemenkeu.Go.Id/. https://www.djppr.kemenkeu.go.id/kperst009

Misra, A., Bohra, N. S., & Sharma, M. (2024). Impact of financial literacy towards ESG investing among salaried employees: A mediating effect of perceived usefulness of Robo-advisors. In *Advances in Logistics, Operations, and Management Science* (pp. 274–284). IGI Global. http://doi.org/DOI: 10.4018/979-8-3693-2849-1.ch018

Mitridati, L., Kazempour, J., & Pinson, P. (2021). Design and game-Theoretic analysis of community-Based market mechanisms in heat and electricity systems. *Omega*, *99*, 102177. DOI: 10.1016/j.omega.2019.102177

Mohsin, M., Taghizadeh-Hesary, F., Iqbal, N., & Saydaliev, H. B. (2022). The role of technological progress and renewable energy deployment in green economic growth. *Renewable Energy*, *190*, 777–787. DOI: 10.1016/j.renene.2022.03.076

Mollick, A., & Sui, L. (2024). Entrepreneurship, Resource Rents and Institutions. *Entrepreneurship Research Journal*, *14*(4), 1669–1699. DOI: 10.1515/erj-2023-0028

Mpofu, F. Y. (2022). Green Taxes in Africa: Opportunities and challenges for environmental protection, sustainability, and the attainment of sustainable development goals. *Sustainability (Basel)*, *14*(16), 10239. DOI: 10.3390/su141610239

Mu, D., Ren, H., & Wang, C. (2021). A literature review of taxes in cross-border supply chain modeling: Themes, tax types and new trade-offs. *Journal of Theoretical and Applied Electronic Commerce Research*, *17*(1), 20–46. DOI: 10.3390/jtaer17010002

Muhammad, A., Ibitomi, T., Durotimi Amos, D., Idris, M. B., & Ishaq, A. A. (2023). Comparative analysis of sustainable finance initiatives in Asia and Africa: A path towards global sustainability. *Global Sustainability Research*, *2*(3), 33–51. DOI: 10.56556/gssr.v2i3.559

Muhammad, S., & Long, X. (2021). Rule of law and CO2 emissions: A comparative analysis across 65 belt and road initiative (BRI) countries. *Journal of Cleaner Production*, *279*, 123539. DOI: 10.1016/j.jclepro.2020.123539

Mujizat, D. A. (2021). *The sovereign green Sukuk: an analysis of its process and barriers to funding renewable energy projects in Indonesia.*

Murray, J. S. (2021). Log-linear Bayesian additive regression trees for multinomial logistic and count regression models. *Journal of the American Statistical Association*, *116*(534), 756–769. DOI: 10.1080/01621459.2020.1813587

Musari, K., & Hidayat, S. E. (2023). The role of green sukuk in maqasid al-shariah and SDGs: Evidence from Indonesia. In *Islamic finance, fintech, and the road to sustainability: Reframing the approach in the post-pandemic era* (pp. 181–203). Springer. DOI: 10.1007/978-3-031-13302-2_9

Narloch, U. (2025). *CBAM 2.0 for carbon leakage protection.* CO2iq Solutions. https://co2-iq.com/en/cbam-for-carbon-leakage-protection

Narodna skupština Republike Srbije. (2025a). *Zakon o porezu na emisije gasova sa efektom staklene baste* („Službeni glasnik RS", br. 109/2025).

Narodna skupština Republike Srbije. (2025b). *Zakon o porezu na uvoz ugljenično intenzivnih proizvoda* („Službeni glasnik RS", br. 109/2025).

NASA. (n.d.). *What Is Climate Change?* Science.Nasa.Gov. Retrieved January 29, 2026, from https://science.nasa.gov/climate-change/what-is-climate-change/

Nasution, M. S., Rusli, Z., Heriyanto, M., Zulkarnaini, , Syahza, A., Adianto, , Mayarni, , & Ismandianto, . (2025). Green governance and institutional resilience: Strengthening environmental policies for a low-carbon economy in mangrove ecosystems. *Frontiers in Political Science*, *7*, 1631249. Advance online publication. DOI: 10.3389/fpos.2025.1631249

Nathaniel, S. P. (2021). Ecological footprint, energy use, trade, and urbanization linkage in Indonesia. *GeoJournal*, *86*(5), 2057–2070. DOI: 10.1007/s10708-020-10175-7

Nawn, N. (2025). Addressing climate-related financial risks. In [Book/source details not provided]. DOI: 10.4324/9781003589709-10

Nelsons, T., Kelley, S., & Orton, F. (2012). A literature review of economic studies on carbon pricing and Australian wholesale electricity markets. *Energy Policy*, *49*, 217–224. DOI: 10.1016/j.enpol.2012.05.075

Net Zero Tracker. (n.d.). *Net Zero Target Status*. Zerotracker.Net. Retrieved January 27, 2026, from https://zerotracker.net/

New Zealand Foreign Affairs & Trade. (n.d.). *Agreement on Climate Change, Trade and Sustainability (ACCTS)*. Mfat.Govt.Nz. Retrieved January 27, 2025, from https://www.mfat.govt.nz/en/trade/free-trade-agreements/free-trade-agreements-concluded-but-not-in-force/agreement-on-climate-change-trade-and-sustainability-accts

Ngo, P. T., & Stanfield, J. (2022). Does government spending crowd out R&D investment? Evidence from government-dependent firms and their peers. *Journal of Financial and Quantitative Analysis*, *57*(3), 888–922. DOI: 10.1017/S0022109020000927

Nielsen, T., Baumert, N., Kander, A., Jiborn, M., & Kulionis, V. (2021). The risk of carbon leakage in global climate agreements. *International Environmental Agreement: Politics, Law and Economics*, *21*(2), 147–163. DOI: 10.1007/s10784-020-09507-2

Nkoro, E., & Uko, A. K. (2016). Autoregressive Distributed Lag (ARDL) cointegration technique: Application and interpretation. *Journal of Statistical and Econometric Methods*, *5*(4), 63–91.

Noubissi Domguia, E. (2023). Taxing for a better life? The impact of environmental taxes on income distribution and inclusive education. *Heliyon*, *9*(11), e21443. Advance online publication. DOI: 10.1016/j.heliyon.2023.e21443

Nwozor, A., Oshewolo, S., Owoeye, G., & Okidu, O. (2021). Nigeria's quest for alternative clean energy development: A cobweb of opportunities, pitfalls and multiple dilemmas. *Energy Policy*, *149*, 112070. Advance online publication. DOI: 10.1016/j.enpol.2020.112070

Nylund, A. (2025). Alternative dispute resolution and the judiciary. In *Research Handbook on Judging and the Judiciary* (pp. 13–34). Edward Elgar Publishing., DOI: 10.4337/9781788978743.00007

OECD. (2019). *Trade and the environment*. OECD Publishing., DOI: 10.1787/a83ce9d8-

OECD. (2022). *Measuring environmental policy stringency in OECD countries: An update of the OECD composite EPS indicator*. https://www.oecd.org/content/dam/oecd/en/publications/reports/2022/03/measuring-environmental-policy-stringency-in-oecd-countries_5655fe2c/90ab82e8-en.pdf

OECD. (2025). *Investing in Climate for Growth and Development: The Case for Enhanced NDCs*. OECD Publishing., DOI: 10.1787/16b7cbc7-

OECD. (2026). *Data explorer.* https://data-explorer.oecd.org/?lc=en

Ohlendorf, N., Flachsland, C., Nemet, G. F., & Steckel, J. C. (2022). Carbon price floors and low-carbon investment: A survey of German firms. *Energy Policy*, *169*, 113187. DOI: 10.1016/j.enpol.2022.113187

Ohler, A., Mohammadi, H., & Loomis, D. G. (2020). Electricity restructuring and the relationship between fuel costs and electricity prices for industrial and residential customers. *Energy Policy*, *142*, 111559. DOI: 10.1016/j.enpol.2020.111559

Ojea-Ferreiro, J., Reboredo, J. C., & Ugolini, A. (2024). Systemic risk effects of climate transition on financial stability. *International Review of Financial Analysis, 96*(Part B), 103722. https://doi.org/DOI: 10.1016/j.irfa.2024.103722

Ojo, D. D., & Delaney, M. (2021). Regulating climate risks and liability risks: Breaking the tragedy of the horizon, climate change and financial stability. [Source details not provided].

Omodero, C. O., Okafor, M. C., Nmesirionye, J. A., & Abaa, E. O. (2022). Environmental Taxation and CO2 Emission Management. *Environment and Ecology Research*, *10*(1), 1–10. DOI: 10.13189/eer.2022.100101

Onabowale, O. (2024). Blended finance partnerships combining public funds, private investments, and philanthropic contributions to expand essential healthcare infrastructure sustainably. *Int J Finance Manag Econ*, *7*(2), 787–798. DOI: 10.33545/26179210.2024.v7.i2.626

Öncel, A., Kabasakal, A., Kutlar, A., & Acar, S. (2024). Energy consumption, economic growth and ecological footprint relationship in the top Russian energy importers: A panel data analysis. *Environment, Development and Sustainability*, *26*(8), 21019–21052. DOI: 10.1007/s10668-023-03517-1

Our World in Data. (2026). *Energy mix.* https://ourworldindata.org/energy-mix #fossil-fuels-what-share-of-energy-comes-from-fossil-fuels

Pacelli, V., Pampurini, F., & Quaranta, A. G. (2023). Environmental, Social and Governance investing: Does rating matter? *Business Strategy and the Environment*, *32*(1), 30–41. DOI: 10.1002/bse.3116

Pahle, M., Pachauri, S., & Steinbacher, K. (2016). Can the green economy deliver it all? Experiences of renewable energy policies with socio-economic objectives. *Applied Energy*, *179*, 1331–1341. DOI: 10.1016/j.apenergy.2016.06.073

Palma-Ruiz, J. M., Castillo-Apraiz, J., & Gómez-Martínez, R. (2020). Socially responsible investing as a competitive strategy for trading companies in times of upheaval amid COVID-19: Evidence from Spain. *International Journal of Financial Studies*, *8*(3), 41. DOI: 10.3390/ijfs8030041

Panezi, M. (2024). Exploring the Nexus of Environmental Sustainability and International Trade : The Significance of Self- Standing Obligations. In *The Sustainability Revolution in International Trade Agreements* (pp. 163–180). Oxford University Press. DOI: 10.1093/9780191994470.003.0011

Parry, I. W. H., Black, S., & Roaf, J. (2021). Proposal for an international carbon price floor among large emitters. *Staff Climate Notes*, *001*(1), 1. Advance online publication. DOI: 10.5089/9781513583204.066

Pástor, Ľ., Stambaugh, R. F., & Taylor, L. A. (2022). Dissecting green returns. *Journal of Financial Economics*, *146*(2), 403–424. DOI: 10.1016/j.jfineco.2022.07.007

Patil, A., & Vonk, W. A. (2025). Stakeholder perspectives on EU regulatory frameworks: Navigating critical raw materials, battery innovation, and recycling challenges. *Open Research Europe*, *5*, 104. DOI: 10.12688/openreseurope.19634.1

Pattillo, C., Mauro, P., Parry, I., Baunsgaard, T., Gbohoui, W., Lam, R., Mylonas, V., Raissi, M., Shah, A., & Shang, B. (2019). *IMF fiscal monitor: How to mitigate climate change (October 2019)*. International Monetary Fund.

Paul, K. (2017). The effect of business cycle, market return and momentum on financial performance of socially responsible investing mutual funds. *Social Responsibility Journal*, *13*(3), 513–528. DOI: 10.1108/SRJ-09-2016-0154

Pavlović, B., & Trtica, N. (2024). Projecting short to medium-term effects of carbon emissions trading on Serbia's GDP. *Utilities Policy*, *91*, 101855. DOI: 10.1016/j.jup.2024.101855

Peng, F., Zhou, S., Ding, T., & Wu, H. (2023). Impact of fiscal expenditure stress on green transformation risk: Evidence from China education authority reform. *Economic Change and Restructuring*, *56*(6), 4565–4601. DOI: 10.1007/s10644-023-09567-9

Peng, H., Zhang, Z., Goodell, J. W., & Li, M. (2023). Socially responsible investing: Is it for real or just for show? *International Review of Financial Analysis*, *86*(102553), 102553. DOI: 10.1016/j.irfa.2023.102553

Perdana, S., & Vielle, M. (2022). Making the EU Carbon Border Adjustment Mechanism acceptable and climate friendly for least developed countries. *Energy Policy*, *170*, 113245. DOI: 10.1016/j.enpol.2022.113245

Pereira, M. Y. B. (2021). Green bonds in the emerging multilateral development banks: A (sufficient) alternative to catalysing private capital? *Asia Pacific Viewpoint*, *62*(1), 116–130. DOI: 10.1111/apv.12297

Peres-Cajías, J., Torregrosa-Hetland, S., & Ducoing, C. (2022). Resource abundance and public finances in five peripheral economies, 1850s–1930s. *Resources Policy*, *76*, 102539. Advance online publication. DOI: 10.1016/j.resourpol.2021.102539

Perman, R. (1994). The economics of the greenhouse effect. *Journal of Economic Surveys*, *8*(2), 99–132. DOI: 10.1111/j.1467-6419.1994.tb00096.x

Pesaran, M. H., Shin, Y., & Smith, R. J. (2001). Bounds testing approaches to the analysis of level relationships. *Journal of Applied Econometrics*, *16*(3), 289–326. DOI: 10.1002/jae.616

Petrović, P., & Lobanov, M. M. (2022). Energy intensity and foreign direct investment nexus: Advanced panel data analysis. *Applied Energy*, *311*, 118669. DOI: 10.1016/j.apenergy.2022.118669

Pham, L., Hay, D., Miihkinen, A., Myllymäki, E.-R., Niemi, L., & Sihvonen, J. (2024). Climate risk disclosures and auditor expertise. *The British Accounting Review*, *101439*, 101439. Advance online publication. DOI: 10.1016/j.bar.2024.101439

Pindyck, R. S. (2012). The climate policy dilemma. *Review of Environmental Economics and Policy*, *7*(2), 219–237. Advance online publication. DOI: 10.1093/reep/ret007

Pizer, W. A. (2002). Combining price and quantity controls to mitigate global climate change. *Journal of Public Economics*, *85*(3), 409–434. DOI: 10.1016/S0047-2727(01)00118-9

Pizzi, S., Caputo, F., & de Nuccio, E. (2024). Do sustainability reporting standards affect analysts' forecast accuracy? *Sustainability Accounting Management and Policy Journal*, *15*(2), 330–354. DOI: 10.1108/SAMPJ-04-2023-0227

Popp, D. (1997). Induced innovation, energy prices, and the environment. [Source details not provided].

Porfiriev, B. N., Shirov, A. A., & Kolpakov, A. Yu. (2021). An Integrated Approach to the Strategy of Low-carbon Socio-economic Development of Russia. *Georesursy*, *23*(3), 3–7. DOI: 10.18599/grs.2021.3.1

Porter, M. E., & van der Linde, C. (1995). Toward a new conception of the environment-competitiveness relationship. *The Journal of Economic Perspectives*, *9*(4), 97–118. DOI: 10.1257/jep.9.4.97

Powell, R. (2024). Power sharing with weak institutions*. *Journal of Theoretical Politics*, *36*(2), 186–211. DOI: 10.1177/09516298241232655

Pryor, J., Agnolucci, P., Fischer, C., Heine, D., & Leon, M. M. de O. (2023). Carbon Pricing Around the World. In *Data for a Greener World: A Guide for Practitioners and Policymakers* (pp. 79–94). International Monetary Fund., DOI: 10.5089/9798400217296.071

Purcel, A. A. (2019). Does political stability hinder pollution? Evidence from developing states. *Economic Research Guardian*, *9*(2), 75–98.

Qamruzzaman, M., & Karim, S. (2024). Green energy, green innovation, and political stability led to green growth in OECD nations. *Energy Strategy Reviews*, *55*, 101519. DOI: 10.1016/j.esr.2024.101519

Qiang, M., Lai, H., & Lyu, Z. (2025). Carbon Emissions Trading and Employment: Evidence from China. *Sustainability (Basel)*, *17*(4), 1404. DOI: 10.3390/su17041404

Qi, J. (2024). Greening economic sectors through trade liberalization and efficient governance. *Humanities & Social Sciences Communications*, *11*(1), 1–8. DOI: 10.1057/s41599-024-04214-8

Qi, Q., Lu, P., & Zhao, X. (2025). Corporate carbon regulation, green innovation and supply chain spillover. *Innovation and Green Development*, *4*(5), 1–12. DOI: 10.1016/j.igd.2025.100294

Qi, Y., Shi, W., & Xu, Y. (2025). Evolutionary logic and development trends of China's ecological and environmental fiscal polocies—Quantitative analysis based on policy texts [——]. *Bulletin of Chinese Academy of Sciences*, *40*(11), 2034–2048. DOI: 10.3724/j.issn.1000-3045.20240521002

Radmehr, R., Shayanmehr, S., Ali, E. B., Ofori, E. K., Jasińska, E., & Jasiński, M. (2022). Exploring the nexus of renewable energy, ecological footprint, and economic growth through globalization and human capital in G7 economics. *Sustainability (Basel)*, *14*(12227), 12227. Advance online publication. DOI: 10.3390/su141912227

Radmehr, R., Shayanmehr, S., Baba, E. A., Samour, A., & Adebayo, T. S. (2024). Spatial spillover effects of green technology innovation and renewable energy on ecological sustainability: New evidence and analysis. *Sustainable Development (Bradford)*, *32*(3), 1743–1761. DOI: 10.1002/sd.2738

Rafindadi, A. A., Muye, I. M., & Kaita, R. A. (2018). The effects of FDI and energy consumption on environmental pollution in predominantly resource-based economies of the GCC. *Sustainable Energy Technologies and Assessments*, *25*, 126–137. DOI: 10.1016/j.seta.2017.12.008

Rana, R., & Sharma, M. (2019). Dynamic causality testing for EKC hypothesis, pollution haven hypothesis and international trade in India. *The Journal of International Trade & Economic Development, 28*(3), 348–364. DOI: 10.1080/09638199.2018.1542451

Ranasinghaarachchi, N. (2024). IFRS S2: Climate-related disclosures—Governance & strategy [Report].

Rausch, S., Metcalf, G. E., & Reilly, J. M. (2011). Distributional impacts of carbon pricing: A general equilibrium approach with micro-data for households. *Energy Economics, 33*, S20–S33. DOI: 10.1016/j.eneco.2011.07.023

Ravaioli, G., Lamperti, F., Roventini, A., & Domingos, T. (2025). Tackling emissions and inequality: Policy insights from an agent-based model. *Journal of Economic Behavior & Organization, 237*, 107188. Advance online publication. DOI: 10.1016/j.jebo.2025.107188

Ravikumar, & Aarthi, S. (2025). AI-driven climate resilience. In *Advances in Computational Intelligence and Robotics* (pp. 207–238). IGI Global Scientific Publishing. DOI: 10.4018/979-8-3373-5540-5.ch007

Ravikumar, A. S., Kalandarov, A., Djumaniyazova, M., & Habib, M. (2025). A roadmap to a sustainable future. In *Advances in Computational Intelligence and Robotics* (pp. 267–302). IGI Global Scientific Publishing. DOI: 10.4018/979-8-3373-3017-4.ch010

Ravikumar, R. N., & Aarthi, S. (2025a). Climate data without borders. In *Cross-Border Cooperation in the Age of Climate Change* (pp. 61–90). IGI Global Scientific Publishing., DOI: 10.4018/979-8-3373-3972-6.ch003

Ravikumar, R. N., & Aarthi, S. (2025b). Green retrofitting of warehouses. In *Innovations in Green and Energy-Efficient Warehousing* (pp. 309–338). IGI Global Scientific Publishing., DOI: 10.4018/979-8-3373-3176-8.ch012

Ravikumar, R. N., Aarthi, S., Pardaev, J., & Shukla, P. (2025). Quantum computing for financial modelling. In *Quantum-Driven Financial Intelligence* (pp. 221–252). IGI Global Scientific Publishing., DOI: 10.4018/979-8-3373-2893-5.ch010

Ray, S., & Hardi, I. (2024). Refining ESG disclosure's role in corporate economic, environmental, and social sustainability performance. *Indatu Journal of Management and Accounting, 2*(1), 1–8. DOI: 10.60084/ijma.v2i1.144

Razavi, S. (2022). Making the right to social security a reality for all workers. *The Indian Journal of Labour Economics : the Quarterly Journal of the Indian Society of Labour Economics*, *65*(2), 269–294. DOI: 10.1007/s41027-022-00378-6 PMID: 35911186

Regional Cooperation Council. (2022). *Green Agenda for the Western Balkans Action Plan - Implementation Report 2022*. Sarajevo. https://www.rcc.int/pubs/162/green-agenda-for-the-western-balkans-action-plan--implementation-report-2022

Ren, Q., & Du, J. (2025). The EU's carbon border adjustment mechanism: Theoretical dimensions, implementation challenges and WTO compliance. *Journal of International Trade Law & Policy*, *24*(3), 228–249. DOI: 10.1108/JITLP-12-2024-0081

Ren, S., Yang, X., Hu, Y., & Chevallier, J. (2022). Emission trading, induced innovation and firm performance. *Energy Economics*, *112*, 106157. DOI: 10.1016/j.eneco.2022.106157

Revelli, C. (2017). Socially responsible investing (SRI): From mainstream to margin? *Research in International Business and Finance*, *39*, 711–717. DOI: 10.1016/j.ribaf.2015.11.003

Reznikova, N., Bulatova, O., Yatsenko, O., & Ivashchenko, O. (2022). Fiscal instruments of regulatory competition in the face of challenges to macroeconomic stability during a pandemic. *COVID*, *19*(2). Advance online publication. DOI: 10.57111/econ.21(2).2022.35-41

Riana, N., Sadono, M. D., Septianto, M. R., Hardiana, M. D., Nathalia, D., Sukmajaya, M., & Aini, A. N. (2020). Studi mengenai green sukuk ritel di indonesia. *UNDP Kementerian Keuangan RI. Direktorat Jenderal Pengelolaan Pembiayaan Dan Risiko, Kementerian Keuangan.* Https://Www. Google. Com/Search

Riedel, F., Gorbach, G., & Kost, C. (2021). Barriers to internal carbon pricing in German companies. *Energy Policy*, *159*, 112654. DOI: 10.1016/j.enpol.2021.112654

Rigo, D. (2021). Global value chains and technology transfer: New evidence from developing countries. *Review of World Economics*, *157*(2), 271–294. DOI: 10.1007/s10290-020-00398-8

Rimini, M., Peters, J., Vangenechten, D., & Lehne, J. (2023). The EU–US Global Arrangement On Sustainable Steel And Aluminium Resetting Negotiations For A Carbon-Based Sectoral Agreement. *E3G*, 1–14. https://www.e3g.org/wp-content/uploads/EU-US-global-arrangement-on-sustainable-steel-and-aluminium-briefing.pdf

Ronaghi, M., Reed, M., & Saghaian, S. (2020). The impact of economic factors and governance on greenhouse gas emission. *Environmental Economics and Policy Studies*, *22*(2), 153–172. DOI: 10.1007/s10018-019-00250-w

Roselle, P. (2016). The evolution of integrating ESG analysis into wealth management decisions. *The Bank of America Journal of Applied Corporate Finance*, *28*(2), 75–79. DOI: 10.1111/jacf.12178

Sadiq, M., Chau, K. Y., Ha, N. T. T., Phan, T. T. H., Ngo, T. Q., & Huy, P. Q. (2024). The impact of green finance, eco-innovation, renewable energy and carbon taxes on CO2 emissions in BRICS countries: Evidence from CS ARDL estimation. *Geoscience Frontiers*, *15*(4), 101689. DOI: 10.1016/j.gsf.2023.101689

Sagita, G. D., & Budi, E. R. (2024). Regional rights, environmental wrongs: Unpacking the paradox of autonomy in indonesia's environmental governance. *Indonesian Journal of Environmental Law and Sustainable Development*, *3*(1), 191–228. DOI: 10.15294/ijel.v3i1.78890

Saleh, H. M., & Hassan, A. I. (2024). The challenges of sustainable energy transition: A focus on renewable energy. *Applied Chemical Engineering*, *7*(2), 2084. DOI: 10.59429/ace.v7i2.2084

Salman, M., Long, X., Dauda, L., & Mensah, C. N. (2019). The impact of institutional quality on economic growth and carbon emissions: Evidence from Indonesia, South Korea and Thailand. *Journal of Cleaner Production*, *241*, 118331. DOI: 10.1016/j.jclepro.2019.118331

Sampedro, J., Markandya, A., Rodés-Bachs, C., & Van de Ven, D. J. (2023). Short-term health co-benefits of existing climate policies: The need for more ambitious and integrated policy action. *The Lancet. Planetary Health*, *7*(7), e540–e541. DOI: 10.1016/S2542-5196(23)00126-2 PMID: 37437994

Samuel, S. E., & Kouhy, R. (2025). Paradox of oil revenue allocation and utilisation in resource-rich countries: The case of Nigeria. *Resources Policy*, *111*, 105782. Advance online publication. DOI: 10.1016/j.resourpol.2025.105782

Sandbag. (2025). *CBAM impact on US trade: an analysis.* https://sandbag.be/wp-content/uploads/CBAM-impact-on-US-trade.pdf

Sang, L. T., Ravikumar, R. N., Aarthi, S., & Ben, T. L. (2025). Optimizing sales and inventory performance using AI and business intelligence in POS environments. In *Advances in Computational Intelligence and Robotics* (pp. 259–290). IGI Global Scientific Publishing. DOI: 10.4018/979-8-3373-4392-1.ch011

Sanusi, A. R., Ul Hassan, M., & Iliyasu, J. (2025). Towards the creation of an independent fiscal council for growth sustainability and development in oil-exporting small-open economy. *Policy Studies*, 1–24. Advance online publication. DOI: 10.1080/01442872.2025.2482047

Saraswati, E., Ghofar, A., Atmini, S., & Dewi, A. A. (2024). Clustering of companies based on sustainability performance using ESG materiality approach: Evidence from Indonesia. *International Journal of Energy Economics and Policy*, *14*(2), 112–125. DOI: 10.32479/ijeep.15393

Sarkar, B., Ahmed, W., & Kim, N. (2018). Joint effects of variable carbon emission cost and multi-delay-in- payments under single-setup-multiple-delivery policy in a global sustainable supply chain. *Journal of Cleaner Production*, *185*, 421–445. DOI: 10.1016/j.jclepro.2018.02.215

Sarkodie, S. A., & Adams, S. (2018). Renewable energy, nuclear energy, and environmental pollution: Accounting for political, institutional quality in South Africa. *The Science of the Total Environment*, *643*, 1590–1601. DOI: 10.1016/j.scitotenv.2018.06.320

Schröder, M. (2004). The performance of socially responsible investments: Investment funds and indices. *Financial Markets and Portfolio Management*, *18*(2), 122–142. DOI: 10.1007/s11408-004-0202-1

Sciarelli, M., Cosimato, S., Landi, G., & Iandolo, F. (2021). Socially responsible investment strategies for the transition towards sustainable development: The importance of integrating and communicating ESG. *The TQM Journal*, *33*(7), 39–56. DOI: 10.1108/TQM-08-2020-0180

Sciuchina, N. (2026). Legal aspects of sustainable employment in the green transition of the labor market. Revista Moldovenească de Drept Internaţional şi Relaţii Internaţionale, 21, 47–56. DOI: 10.61753/1857-1999/2345-1963/2026.21-1.04

Seccareccia, M. (1995). Keynesianism and public investment: A left-Keynesian perspective on the role of government expenditures and Debt. *Studies in Political Economy*, *46*(1), 43–78. DOI: 10.1080/19187033.1995.11675366

Seck, G., Parajuli, B., & Casals, X. (2023). IRENA world energy transitions outlook 2023 (Vol. 2). DOI: 10.13140/RG.2.2.10445.65768

Seker, F., Ertugrul, H. M., & Cetin, M. (2015). The impact of foreign direct investment on environmental quality: A bounds testing and causality analysis for Turkey. *Renewable & Sustainable Energy Reviews*, *52*, 347–356. DOI: 10.1016/j.rser.2015.07.118

Selvakumar, P., Seenivasan, S., Deshmukh, S. M., Ponnapalli, H., & Das, A. (2024). Environmental protection and policies. In *Renewable Energy and the Economic Welfare of Society* (pp. 71–101). IGI Global., DOI: 10.4018/979-8-3693-7580-8.ch004

Senadheera, S. S., Gregory, R., Rinklebe, J., Farrukh, M., Rhee, J. H., & Ok, Y. S. (2022). The development of research on environmental, social, and governance (ESG): A bibliometric analysis. *Sustainable Environment*, *8*(1), 2125869. Advance online publication. DOI: 10.1080/27658511.2022.2125869

Sethi, L., Behera, B., & Sethi, N. (2024). Do green finance, green technology innovation, and institutional quality help achieve environmental sustainability? Evidence from the developineconomies. *Sustainable Development (Bradford)*, *32*(3), 2709–2723. DOI: 10.1002/sd.2811

Setyowati, A. B. (2023). Governing sustainable finance: Insights from Indonesia. *Climate Policy*, *23*(1), 108–121. DOI: 10.1080/14693062.2020.1858741

Shafizadeh, H. (2024). Decision-making under uncertainty: How organizations adapt to environmental changes? *Journal of Resource Management and Decision Engineering*, *3*(1), 4–10. DOI: 10.61838/kman.jrmde.3.1.2

Shahbaz, M., Nasreen, S., Abbas, F., & Anis, O. (2015). Does foreign direct investment impede environmental quality in high-, middle-, and low-income countries? *Energy Economics*, *51*, 275–287. DOI: 10.1016/j.eneco.2015.06.014

Shahbaz, M., Rasool, G., Ahmed, K., & Mahalik, M. K. (2016). Considering the effectof biomass energy consumption on economic growth: Fresh evidence from BRICS region. *Renewable & Sustainable Energy Reviews*, *60*, 1442–1450. DOI: 10.1016/j.rser.2016.03.037

Shahzad, M. F., Xu, S., Lim, W. M., Yang, X., & Khan, Q. R. (2024). Artificial intelligence and social media on academic performance and mental well-being: Student perceptions of positive impact in the age of smart learning. *Heliyon*, *10*(8), e29523. Advance online publication. DOI: 10.1016/j.heliyon.2024.e29523

Sharma, P., Panday, P., & Dangwal, R. C. (2020). Determinants of environmental, social and corporate governance (ESG) disclosure: A study of Indian companies. *International Journal of Disclosure and Governance*, *17*(4), 208–217. DOI: 10.1057/s41310-020-00085-y

Sharma, R., Kurmi, O. P., Hariprasad, P., & Tyagi, S. K. (2024). Health implications due to exposure to fine and ultra-fine particulate matters: A short review. *International Journal of Ambient Energy*, *45*(1), 2314256. DOI: 10.1080/01430750.2024.2314256

Sharma, V., Gupta, M., Arora, N., & Shaikh, A. A. (2025). FinTech and Financial Inclusion: Leveraging Digital Finance for Economic Empowerment and Sustainable Growth. In *FinTech and Financial Inclusion: Leveraging Digital Finance for Economic Empowerment and Sustainable Growth*. Taylor and Francis., DOI: 10.4324/9781003514114

Shaviro, D. (2025). Time is, time was: evaluating the use of the life cycle model as a fiscal policy tool. In *Research Handbook on Law and Time* (pp. 232–252). Edward Elgar Publishing., DOI: 10.4337/9781035316762.00019

Shen, C. (2024). The impact of carbon emission trading system on ESG of agricultural enterprises: Evidence from 24 listed agricultural companies in China. *Transactions on Economics. Business and Management Research*, *5*, 46–58. DOI: 10.62051/ca4vcy22

Shen, J. (2026). State Capacity, Social Fragmentation, and Public Goods Provision: A Cross-National Comparative Analysis. *Governance: An International Journal of Policy, Administration and Institutions*, *39*(1), e70088. DOI: 10.1111/gove.70088

Shivanna, K. R. (2022). Climate change and its impact on biodiversity and human welfare. *Proceedings of the Indian National Science Academy. Part A, Physical Sciences*, *88*(2), 160–171. DOI: 10.1007/s43538-022-00073-6

Simpa, P., Solomon, N. O., Adenekan, O. A., & Obasi, S. C. (2024). Strategic implications of carbon pricing on global environmental sustainability and economic development: A conceptual framework. *International Journal of Advanced Economics*, *6*(5), 139–172. DOI: 10.51594/ijae.v6i5.1134

Singh, S., Singh, P., Pandey, S., & Yadav, S. (2025). Harnessing Digital Finance for Sustainability and Equity in Marine and Seaside Economies. In *World Sustainability Series: Part F794* (pp. 107–125). Springer Science and Business Media Deutschland GmbH. DOI: 10.1007/978-3-031-92390-6_6

Singh, A. (2025). Fiscal Federalism and Climate Change: Building the Institutional Framework in India. *Indian Public Policy Review*, *6*(1), 78–122. DOI: 10.55763/ippr.2025.06.01.003

Sinha, M.Janki Devi Memorial College. (2025). Responsible capital: The evolution and performance of ESG investing. *Exploresearch*, *01*(03), 1–18. DOI: 10.62823/ExRe//01/03.10

Sinn, H.-W. (2015). The green paradox: A supply-side view of the climate problem. SSRN Electronic Journal. DOI: 10.2139/ssrn.2621998

Skea, J., Shukla, P. R., Reisinger, A., Slade, R., Pathak, M., Al Khourdajie, A., van Diemen, R., Abdulla, A., Akimoto, K., Babiker, M., Bai, Q., Bashmakov, I., Bataille, C., Berndes, G., Blanco, G., Blok, K., Bustamante, M., Byers, E., Cabeza, L., & Winkler, H. (2022). Summary for policymakers. In *Climate change 2022: Mitigation of climate change. Contribution of Working Group III to the Sixth Assessment Report of the Intergovernmental Panel on Climate Change*. Cambridge University Press., DOI: 10.1017/9781009157926.001

Slesman, L., Baharumshah, A.Z., Ra'ees, W., 2015. Institutional infrastructure and economic growth in member countries of the Organization of Islamic Cooperation (OIC). *Economic Modelling*. 51, 214e226. .DOI: 10.1016/j.econmod.2015.08.008

Smulders, J. (1994). *Growth Market Structure and the Environment: Essays on the Theory of Endogenous Economic Growth*. Tilburg University.

Sneeringer, S. (2009). A question of balance: Weighing the options on global warming policies. *Global Environmental Politics*, *9*(1), 146–147. DOI: 10.1162/glep.2009.9.1.146

Socol, A., Ivan, O. R., Danuletiu, A. E., Cioca, I. C., Botar, C. F., & Virdea, D. E. (2025). The moderating role of governmental artificial intelligence in shaping green growth dynamics in the European Union. *Sustainability (Basel)*, *17*(22), 10329. DOI: 10.3390/su172210329

Sofia. (2018). *Commissioner Malmström unveils 15-point plan to make EU trade and sustainable development chapters more effective*. Policy.Trade.Ec.Europa.Eu. https://policy.trade.ec.europa.eu/news/commissioner-malmstrom-unveils-15-point-plan-make-eu-trade-and-sustainable-development-chapters-more-2018-02-27_en

Sohag, K., Husain, S., & Soytas, U. (2024). Environmental policy stringency and ecological footprint linkage: Mitigation measures of renewable energy and innovation. *Energy Economics*, *136*(107721), 107721. Advance online publication. DOI: 10.1016/j.eneco.2024.107721

Sohag, K., Taskın, F. D., & Malik, M. N. (2019). Green economic growth, cleaner energy and militarization: Evidence from Turkey. *Resources Policy*, *63*, 101407. DOI: 10.1016/j.resourpol.2019.101407

Solarin, S. A., Al-Mulali, U., Musah, I., & Ozturk, I. (2017). Investigating the pollution haven hypothesis in Ghana: An empirical investigation. *Energy*, *124*, 706–719. DOI: 10.1016/j.energy.2017.02.089

Song, Y., Liu, T., Liang, D., Li, Y., & Song, X. (2019). A fuzzy stochastic model for carbon price prediction under the effect of demand-related policy in China's carbon market. *Ecological Economics*, *157*, 253–265. DOI: 10.1016/j.ecolecon.2018.10.001

Steinebach, Y. (2022). Instrument choice, implementation structures, and the effectiveness of environmental policies: A cross-national analysis. *Regulation & Governance*, *16*(1), 225–242. DOI: 10.1111/rego.12297

Stern, N. (2007), "Stern review on the economics of climate change", available at: https://webarchive. nationalarchives.gov.uk/20100407172811/http://www.hm-treasury.gov.uk/stern_review_report.htm

Stern, N., & Stiglitz, J. E. (2021). The social cost of carbon, risk, distribution, market failures: An alternative approach. SSRN Electronic Journal. DOI: 10.2139/ssrn.3785806

Stern, N. (2006). *The economics of climate change: The Stern review*. Cambridge University Press., DOI: 10.1017/CBO9780511817434

Stern, N. (2008). The economics of climate change: The Stern review. *The American Economic Review*, *98*(2), 1–37. DOI: 10.1257/aer.98.2.1

Steuer, S., & Troger, T. H. (2022). The role of disclosure in green finance. *Journal of Financial Regulation*, *8*(1), 1–50. DOI: 10.1093/jfr/fjac001

Stevis, D., Krause, D., & Morena, E. (2021). Towards a just transition for all: Lessons from the pandemic. [Source details not provided].

Stiglitz, J. E., Stern, N., Duan, M., Edenhofer, O., Giraud, G., Heal, G., La Rovere, E., Moyer, E., Mari Pangestu, P., Shukla, P., Sokona, Y., & Winkler, H. (2017). Report of the High-Level Commission on Carbon Prices. DOI: 10.13140/RG.2.2.26038.09288

Sun, C., Zhang, F., & Xu, M. (2017). Investigation of pollution haven hypothesis for China: An ARDL approach with breakpoint unit root tests. *Journal of Cleaner Production*, *161*, 153–164. DOI: 10.1016/j.jclepro.2017.05.119

Sun, J., Li, P., & Wang, Y. (2024). Policy tools for sustainability: Evaluating the effectiveness of fiscal measures in natural resource efficiency. *Resources Policy*, *89*, 104575. DOI: 10.1016/j.resourpol.2023.104575

Sun, Y., & Stephen, E. (2025). Sustainable Development Pathways: How Fiscal Policy, Green Innovation, and Environmental Governance Shape Ecological Footprints in G-20 Economies? *Sustainable Development*. Advance online publication. DOI: 10.1002/sd.70310

Tang, C. F., & Tan, B. W. (2015). The impact of energy consumption, income and foreign direct investment on carbon dioxide emissions in Vietnam. *Energy, 79*, 447–454. DOI: 10.1016/j.energy.2014.11.033

Tawiah, V., Zakari, A., & Adedoyin, F. F. (2021). Determinants of green growth in developed and developing countries. *Environmental Science and Pollution Research International, 28*(29), 39227–39242. DOI: 10.1007/s11356-021-13429-0

Taylor, P., Bays, J., Bradshaw, M., Webb, J., Britton, J., Bolton, R., Chaudry, M., Qadrdan, M., Wu, J., Anable, J., Brand, C., Rattle, I., Gailani, A., Bell, K., Poulter, H., Halliday, C., Shepherd, A., Watson, S., Lovett, A., & Hastings, A. (2023). Review of energy policy 2023. DOI: 10.5286/UKERC.EDC.000967

Terzani, S., & Turzo, T. (2021). Religious social norms and corporate sustainability: The effect of religiosity on environmental, social, and governance disclosure. *Corporate Social Responsibility and Environmental Management, 28*(1), 485–496. DOI: 10.1002/csr.2063

The World Bank. (2012). *Inclusive Green Growth: The Pathway to Sustainable Development*. The World Bank. https://documents1.worldbank.org/curated/en/368361468313515918/pdf/691250PUB0Publ067902B09780821395516.pdf

The World Bank. (2025). *State and Trends of Carbon Pricing 2025*. The World Bank. https://www.worldbank.org/en/publication/state-and-trends-of-carbon-pricing

Tobler, W. R. (1970). A computer movie simulating urban growth in the Detroit region. *Economic Geography, 46*(2), 234–240. DOI: 10.2307/143141

Tolliver, C., Keeley, A. R., & Managi, S. (2019). Green bonds for the Paris agreement and sustainable development goals. *Environmental Research Letters, 14*(6), 64009. DOI: 10.1088/1748-9326/ab1118

Tost, M., Hitch, M., Lutter, S., Feiel, S., & Moser, P. (2020). Carbon prices for meeting the Paris Agreement and their impact on key metals. *The Extractive Industries and Society, 7*(2), 593–599. DOI: 10.1016/j.exis.2020.01.012

Trading Economics. (2026). *EU Carbon Permits*. https://tradingeconomics.com/commodity/carbon

Tripathi, V., & Kaur, A. (2022). Does socially responsible investing pay in developing countries? A comparative study across select developed and developing markets. *FIIB Business Review, 11*(2), 189–205. DOI: 10.1177/2319714520980288

Truant, E., Corazza, L., & Scagnelli, S. D. (2017). Sustainability & risk disclosure: An exploratory study on sustainability reports. In *Preprints*. https://doi.org/DOI: 10.20944/preprints201704.0021.v1

Tu, Q., Betz, R., Mo, J., Fan, Y., & Liu, Y. (2019). Achieving grid parity of wind power in China—Present levelized cost of electricity and future evolution. *Applied Energy*, *250*, 1053–1064. DOI: 10.1016/j.apenergy.2019.05.039

Ulfah, I. F., Sukmana, R., Laila, N., & Sulaeman, S. (2024). A structured literature review on green sukuk (Islamic bonds): Implications for government policy and future studies. *Journal of Islamic Accounting and Business Research*, *15*(7), 1118–1133. DOI: 10.1108/JIABR-10-2022-0255

UN. (2026). *United Nations Framework Convention on Climate Change (UNFCCC) and Climate, Peace and Security*. https://www.un.org/climatesecuritymechanism/en/united-nations-framework-convention-climate-change-unfccc-and-climate-peace-and-security

UNCTAD. (2021). *Trade and development report 2021: From recovery to resilience. United Nations Conference on Trade and Development*. DOI: 10.18356/9789210010276

UNCTADstat. (2026). UNCTADstat Data centre [Data set]. https://unctadstat.unctad.org

UNFCCC. (2015). *Paris agreement*. United Nations.

UNFCCC. (2026). *The Paris Agreement*. Unfccc.Int. https://unfccc.int/process-and-meetings/the-paris-agreement

United Nations. (1987). *Report of the World Commission on Environment and Development*. https://digitallibrary.un.org/record/139811?v=pdf

United Nations. (2019). *Global Sustainable Development Report 2019*. United Nations. https://www.un.org/en/desa/global-sustainable-development-report-2019

United Nations. (2023). *Trade and Development Report 2023 Growth, Debt and Climate: Realigning the Global Financial Architecture*. United Nations Publications. https://unctad.org/system/files/official-document/tdr2023_en.pdf

Unruh, G. C. (2000). Understanding carbon lock-in. *Energy Policy*, *28*(12), 817–830. DOI: 10.1016/S0301-4215(00)00070-7

USGS. (2026). International Minerals Statistics and Information [Data set]. https://www.usgs.gov/centers/national-minerals-information-center/international-minerals-statistics-and-information

Vallee-Dubois, F. (2023). Government spending preferences over the life cycle. *Journal of Public Policy*, *43*(3), 468–489. DOI: 10.1017/S0143814X23000065

Vanhala, L. (2017). Process tracing in the study of environmental politics. *Global Environmental Politics*, *17*(4), 88–105. DOI: 10.1162/GLEP_a_00434

Veeravel, V., Hiremath, R. B., & Panda, P. (2025). Does internal carbon pricing improve firm performance? Evidence from Indian listed companies. *Finance Research Letters*, *86*, 108780. Advance online publication. DOI: 10.1016/j.frl.2025.108780

Verbruggen, A. (2021). *Pricing Carbon Emissions: Economic Reality and Utopia*. Routledge., DOI: 10.4324/9781003173816

Vićentijević, A., Parežanin, M., & Jednak, S. (2024). Assessing Serbian Iron and Steel Exports to the EU under CBAM. In *Proceedings of 19th International Symposium Unlocking the Hidden Potentials of Organization Through Merging of Humans and Digitals*. University of Belgrade – Faculty of Organizational Sciences.

Vidovic, D., Marmier, A., Zore, L. & Moya, J. A. (2023). *Greenhouse gas emission intensities of the steel, fertilisers, aluminium and cement industries in the EU and its main trading partners*. JRC Technical Report, Luxembourg. DOI: .DOI: 10.2760/359533

Vishali, M., & Shafi, M. K. M. (2024). Emerging paradigms in socially responsible investment (SRI)—A study with focus on ESG mutual funds in India. *Environment and Social Psychology*, *9*(4). Advance online publication. DOI: 10.54517/esp.v9i4.2006

Vitali, S., Tedeschi, G., & Gallegati, M. (2013). The impact of classes of innovators on technology, financial fragility, and economic growth. *Industrial and Corporate Change*, *22*(4), 1069–1091. DOI: 10.1093/icc/dtt024

von Malmborg, F. (2025). At the controls: Politics and policy entrepreneurs in EU policy to decarbonize maritime transport. *The Review of Policy Research*, *42*(5), 1243–1276. DOI: 10.1111/ropr.12609

Vongpatchim, P., Rangsungnoen, G., & Chainirun, P. (2025). Organizational management to achieve sustainable financial stability: A case study of the company in Thailand. *International Journal of Analysis and Applications*, *23*, 128. DOI: 10.28924/2291-8639-23-2025-128

Vrontisi, Z., Fragkiadakis, K., Kannavou, M., & Capros, P. (2020). Energy system transition and macroeconomic impacts of a European decarbonization action towards a below 2 °C climate stabilization. *Climatic Change*, *162*(4), 1857–1875. DOI: 10.1007/s10584-019-02440-7

Wackernagel, M., & Rees, W. E. (1997). Perceptual and structural barriers to investing in natural capital: Economics from an ecological footprint perspective. *Ecological Economics*, *20*(1), 3–24. DOI: 10.1016/S0921-8009(96)00077-8

Wan Zahari, W. M. Z. (2025). Operationalising Green Sukuk within the World Bank environmental and social framework. *Discover Environment*, *3*(1), 288. DOI: 10.1007/s44274-025-00490-6

Wang, D., Dong, L., & Mei, J. (2023). An advanced review of climate change mitigation policies in Germany, France, and the Netherlands. *Environmental Research Letters*, *18*(10), 103001. DOI: 10.1088/1748-9326/acf58f

Wang, K., Yan, M., Wang, Y., & Chang, C.-P. (2020). The impact of environmental policy stringency on air quality. *Atmospheric Environment*, *231*(117522), 117522. Advance online publication. DOI: 10.1016/j.atmosenv.2020.117522

Wang, Q. J., Sharma, S. S., Ni, G. H., & Chang, C. P. (2024). Governance, energy utilization and environmental protection: Role of extreme events. *Energy Economics*, *136*, 107765. Advance online publication. DOI: 10.1016/j.eneco.2024.107765

Wang, R., Chua, W. F., Simnett, R., & Zhou, S. (2024). Is greater connectivity of financial and non-financial information in annual reports valued by market participants? *The British Accounting Review*, *56*(6), 101407. DOI: 10.1016/j.bar.2024.101407

Wang, R., Wijen, F., & Heugens, P. P. M. A. R. (2018). Government's green grip: Multifaceted state influence on corporate environmental actions in China. *Strategic Management Journal*, *39*(2), 403–428. DOI: 10.1002/smj.2714

Wang, S., Sun, L., & Iqbal, S. (2022). Green financing role on renewable energy dependence and energy transition in E7 economies. *Renewable Energy*, *200*, 1561–1572. DOI: 10.1016/j.renene.2022.10.067

Wang, X., & Shao, Q. (2019). Non-linear effects of heterogeneous environmental regulations on green growth in G20 countries: Evidence from panel threshold regression. *The Science of the Total Environment*, *660*, 1346–1354. DOI: 10.1016/j.scitotenv.2019.01.094

Wang, Y., Han, L., Sun, J., & Sun, Z. (2024). Financing the green transition: Mobilizing resources for efficient natural resource management. *Resources Policy*, *89*, 104522. Advance online publication. DOI: 10.1016/j.resourpol.2023.104522

Wang, Y., & Yuan, G. (2026). Natural resource exploitation and productive capacity as drivers of ecological footprint: The roles of technology and economic policy uncertainty. *Geoscience Frontiers*, *17*(2), 102247. DOI: 10.1016/j.gsf.2026.102247

Waris, A. (2024). A Principled Approach to Financial Resource Collection and Allocation for the Realization of Human Rights in Creating a Global Fiscal Institution. *Bulletin for International Taxation, 78*(9–10), 388–393. DOI: 10.59403/36t1v90

Wei, J., Zhang, X., & Tamamine, T. (2024). Digital transformation in supply chains: Assessing the spillover effects on midstream firm innovation Jiangying. *Journal of Innovation & Knowledge, 9*(2), 1–11. DOI: 10.1016/j.jik.2024.100483

Wei, S., Jiandong, W., & Saleem, H. (2023). The impact of renewable energy transition, green growth, green trade and green innovation on environmental quality: Evidence from top 10 green future countries. *Frontiers in Environmental Science, 10*, 1076859. DOI: 10.3389/fenvs.2022.1076859

Welford, R., & Starkey, R. (1996). *Business and the Environment: A Reader*. Taylor & Francis. https://books.google.co.id/books/about/Business_and_the_Environment.html?id=i7UDHlOGfPEC&redir_esc=y

Welsch, H., 2004. Corruption, growth, and the environment: a cross-country analysis. Environ. Dev. Econ. 9 (5), 663e693. .DOI: 10.1017/S1355770X04001500

Wenjuan, S., & Zhao, K. (2023). Balancing fiscal expenditure competition and long-term innovation investment: Exploring trade-offs and policy implications for local governments. *PLoS One, 18*(11), e0293158. DOI: 10.1371/journal.pone.0293158 PMID: 38032928

Wibowo, M., Setiawan, H., Dewianawati, D., Setiawan, E., & Judijanto, L. (2025). The role of ESG criteria in sustainable financial project scope management: A systematic literature review. *Jurnal Ilmiah Manajemen Kesatuan, 13*(6), 5115–5126. DOI: 10.37641/jimkes.v13i6.4048

Widjanarko, A. P., & Gultom, Y. M. L. (2024). A Changing Landscape: Exploring the Relationship between Clean and Clear Status Policy, Coal Mining, and Deforestation. *Jurnal Manajemen Hutan Tropika, 30*(1), 94–106. DOI: 10.7226/jtfm.30.1.97

Wirdyansyah, D. (2025). Carbon Border Adjustment Mechanism (CBAM) and its implications for developing economies: A systematic literature review. *Indonesian Journal of Energy, 8*(2), 162–176. DOI: 10.33116/ije.v8i2.292

WMO. (2025). *State of the climate update for COP30.* https://library.wmo.int/records/item/69674-state-of-the-climate-update-for-cop30

Wolde-Rufael, Y., & Mulat-Weldemeskel, E. (2021). Do environmental taxes and environmental stringency policies reduce CO_2 emissions? Evidence from 7 emerging economies. *Environmental Science and Pollution Research International, 28*(18), 22392–22408. DOI: 10.1007/s11356-020-11475-8 PMID: 33417133

World Bank Group. (2020). *World Development Report 2020: Trading For Development in The Age Of Global Value Chains*. The World Bank. https://www.worldbank.org/en/publication/wdr2020

World Bank. (2010). *World development report 2010: Development and climate change*. World Bank.

World Bank. (2024). *State and trends of carbon pricing 2024*. World Bank.

World Bank. (2026). *World Development Indicators*. https://databank.worldbank.org/source/world-development-indicators

World Trade Law. (n.d.). *Uruguay Round Agreements*. Worldtradelaw.Net. Retrieved January 27, 2026, from https://www.worldtradelaw.net/static.php?type=public&page=uragreements

WTO. (2020). *World trade report 2020: Government policies to promote innovation in the digital age* (`). World Trade Organization. https://digitallibrary.un.org/record/4038629?v=pdf

Wu, J., Lodorfos, G., Dean, A., & Gioulmpaxiotis, G. (2017). The market performance of socially responsible investment during periods of the economic cycle – illustrated using the case of FTSE: Investment performance of SRI in an economic cycle. *MDE. Managerial and Decision Economics*, *38*(2), 238–251. DOI: 10.1002/mde.2772

Wu, W., Cheng, Y., Lin, X., & Yao, X. (2019). How does the implementation of the policy of electricity substitution influence green economic growth in China? *Energy Policy*, *131*, 251–261. DOI: 10.1016/j.enpol.2019.04.043

Wu, Y., & Tian, Y. (2022). The price of carbon risk: Evidence from China's bond market. *China Journal of Accounting Research*, *15*(2), 100245. DOI: 10.1016/j.cjar.2022.100245

Xhindole, C., Tarquinio, L., & Sierra-García, L. (2025). Climate change and Task Force on Climate-related Financial Disclosures (TCFD) reports: A comparison between Italy and Spain. *Journal of Accounting & Organizational Change*, *21*(7), 1–28. DOI: 10.1108/JAOC-05-2024-0172

Xiao, Z., Peng, H., & Pan, Z. (2022). Innovation, external technological environment and the total factor productivity of enterprises. *Accounting and Finance*, *62*(1), 3–29. DOI: 10.1111/acfi.12779

Xie, R., & Teo, T. S. H. (2022). Green technology innovation, environmental externality, and the cleaner upgrading of industrial structure in China — Considering the moderating effect of environmental regulation. *Technological Forecasting and Social Change, 184*, 1–15. DOI: 10.1016/j.techfore.2022.122020

Xie, S., & Wang, J. (2022). Evaluating the effect of China's carbon emission trading policy on energy efficiency of the construction industry based on a difference-in-differences method. *Advances in Civil Engineering, 2022*(1), 1–12. DOI: 10.1155/2022/6096435

Xu, D., Corbet, S., Lang, C., & Hu, Y. (2024). Understanding dynamic return connectedness and portfolio strategies among international sustainable exchange-traded funds. *Economic Modelling, 141*(106864), 106864. DOI: 10.1016/j.econmod.2024.106864

Xu, H. T., Pan, X. F., Li, J. M., Feng, S. H., & Guo, S. C. (2023). Comparing the impacts of carbon tax and carbon emission trading, which regulation is more effective? *Journal of Environmental Management, 330*, 117156. DOI: 10.1016/j.jenvman.2022.117156

Xu, H., Li, Y., Lin, W., & Li, Y. (2024). Government fiscal decentralization and haze and carbon reduction: Evidence from the fiscal Province-Managing-County reform. *Environmental Research, 252*, 119020. Advance online publication. DOI: 10.1016/j.envres.2024.119020

Xu, W., Sun, Z., & Ni, H. (2024). Transparency pays: How carbon emission disclosure lowers cost of capital. *Economic Analysis and Policy, 83*, 165–177. DOI: 10.1016/j.eap.2024.05.020

Yan, F., Chen, L., & Jia, F. (2024). Environmental, social, and governance disclosure in supply chains: A systematic literature review. *Production Planning and Control*, •••, 1–22. DOI: 10.1080/09537287.2024.2434147

Yang, F., Li, T., & Qi, Y. (2025). The impact of upgrading in the global value chain on embodied carbon emissions: Does technological progress matter? *Finance Research Letters, 84*, 1–12. DOI: 10.1016/j.frl.2025.107763

Yang, X., Li, N., Mu, H., Ahmad, M., & Meng, X. (2022). Population aging, renewable energy budgets and environmental sustainability: Does health expenditures matter? *Gondwana Research, 106*, 303–314. DOI: 10.1016/j.gr.2022.02.003

Yan, J., Guo, Y., & Wen, F. (2025). Carbon risk and the cost of equity capital: Evidence from China. *International Review of Economics & Finance, 99*, 103975. DOI: 10.1016/j.iref.2025.103975

Yatzkan, O., Cohen, R., Yaniv, E., & Rotem-Mindali, O. (2025). Urban Energy Transitions: A Systematic Review. *Land (Basel)*, *14*(3), 566. DOI: 10.3390/land14030566

Yenipazarli, A. (2016). Managing new and remanufactured products to mitigate environmental damage under emissions regulation. *European Journal of Operational Research*, *249*(1), 117–130. DOI: 10.1016/j.ejor.2015.08.020

Yen, M.-F., Shiu, Y.-M., & Wang, C.-F. (2019). Socially responsible investment returns and news: Evidence from Asia. *Corporate Social Responsibility and Environmental Management*, *26*(6), 1565–1578. DOI: 10.1002/csr.1833

Yilmaz, S. (2025). The Impact of Environmental Protection Expenditures on Reducing Greenhouse Gas Emissions. *Sustainability (Basel)*, *17*(7), 1–17. DOI: 10.3390/su17073192

Yin, X., Wang, D., Lu, J., & Liu, L. (2023). Does green credit policy promote corporate green innovation? Evidence from China. *Economic Change and Restructuring*, *56*(5), 3187–3215. DOI: 10.1007/s10644-023-09521-9

Yirong, Q. (2022). Does environmental policy stringency reduce CO_2 emissions? Evidence from high-polluted economies. *Journal of Cleaner Production*, *341*(130648), 130648. Advance online publication. DOI: 10.1016/j.jclepro.2022.130648

York University. (2026). *Data*. https://footprint.info.yorku.ca/data/

Yuan, J., Na, C., Lei, Q., Xiong, M., Guo, J., & Hu, Z. (2018). Coal use for power generation in China. *Resources, Conservation and Recycling*, *129*, 443–453. DOI: 10.1016/j.resconrec.2016.03.021

Zahroh, U. A., & Najicha, F. U. (2022). Problems and Challenges on Environmental Law Enforcement in Indonesia: AMDAL in the Context of Administrative Law. *Indonesian State Law Review*, *5*(2), 53–66. DOI: 10.15294/islrev.v5i2.46511

Zaman, K., Abdullah, A., Khan, A., Nasir, M. R. M., Hamzah, T. A. A. T., & Hussain, S. (2016). Dynamic linkages among energy consumption, environment, health and wealth in BRICS countries: Green growth key to sustainable development. *Renewable & Sustainable Energy Reviews*, *56*, 1263–1271. DOI: 10.1016/j.rser.2015.12.010

Zambrano-Monserrate, M. A., Ruano, M. A., Ormeño-Candelario, V., & Sanchez-Loor, D. A. (2020). Global ecological footprint and spatial dependence between countries. *Journal of Environmental Management*, *272*(111069), 111069. Advance online publication. DOI: 10.1016/j.jenvman.2020.111069 PMID: 32854881

Zarnic, Z., Varga, J., Labat, A., & Conte, A. (2010). What is the growth potential of green innovation? An assessment of EU climate policy options. SSRN *Electronic Journal*. DOI: 10.2139/ssrn.1728703

Zarrinpoor, N., & Khani, A. (2021). Designing a sustainable biofuel supply chain by considering carbon policies: A case study in Iran. *Energy, Sustainability and Society*, *11*(38), 1–22. DOI: 10.1186/s13705-021-00314-4

Zatti, A. (2020). Environmental taxes and subsidies: Some insights from the Italian experience. *Environment and Ecology*, *11*(1), 39–53. DOI: 10.21511/ee.11(1).2020.04

Zhang, C., Li, Y., & Liang, S. (2025). Climate change attention and systemic financial risk: A TENET analysis. *Finance Research Letters*, *72*, 106555. DOI: 10.1016/j.frl.2024.106555

Zhang, D. (2024). Eco-friendly revenues for healthcare: Assessing the relationship between green taxation, public health expenditures, and life expectancy in China. *Frontiers in Public Health*, *12*, 1358730. DOI: 10.3389/fpubh.2024.1358730 PMID: 38841673

Zhang, G., & Bi, S. (2023). Inhibition or promotion: the impact of carbon emission trading on market structure: evidence from China. *Frontiers in Energy Research*, *11*, 1238416. Advance online publication. DOI: 10.3389/fenrg.2023.1238416

Zhang, J., Tang, H., & Bao, M. (2023). Can environmental protection policies promote regional innovation efficiency: A difference-in-differences approach with continuous treatment. *Environmental Science and Pollution Research International*, *30*(1), 1357–1373. DOI: 10.1007/s11356-022-22280-w

Zhang, W., & Liu, L. (2019). Investment decisions of fired power plants on carbon utilization under the imperfect carbon emission trading schemes in China. *Processes (Basel, Switzerland)*, *7*(11), 828. DOI: 10.3390/pr7110828

Zhang, W., Zhu, B., Li, Y., & Yan, D. (2024). Revisiting the Porter hypothesis: A multi-country meta-analysis of the relationship between environmental regulation and green innovation. *Humanities & Social Sciences Communications*, *11*(232), 1–15. DOI: 10.1057/s41599-024-02671-9

Zhang, X., Loeschel, A., Lewis, J., Zhang, D., & Yan, J. (2020). Emissions trading systems for global low carbon energy and economic transformation. *Applied Energy*, *279*, 115858. DOI: 10.1016/j.apenergy.2020.115858

Zhang, Y., Shi, X., Wu, H., & Wu, Y. (2025). The synergetic effects of government concerns and public awareness on environmental protection. *Applied Economics*, 1–20. Advance online publication. DOI: 10.1080/00036846.2025.2606187

Zhang, Z., Ma, C., & Wang, A. (2023). Environmental governance, public health expenditure, and economic growth: Analysis in an OLG model. *International Journal of Environmental Research and Public Health*, *20*(4), 3033. DOI: 10.3390/ijerph20043033 PMID: 36833725

Zhang, Z., & Zhou, Y. (2025). Economic growth vs environmental sustainability: Examining resource extraction in the World's largest economies. *Frontiers in Environmental Science*, *13*, 1586619. Advance online publication. DOI: 10.3389/fenvs.2025.1586619

Zhao, Y., Dou, S., Li, J., Cheng, J., & Xu, D. (2025). The economic inequality effect of environmental policies—A case from China's "authoritarian environmentalism" actions. *Journal of Environmental Management*, *374*, 123926. Advance online publication. DOI: 10.1016/j.jenvman.2024.123926

Zhong, J., & Pei, J. (2022). Beggar thy neighbor? On the competitiveness and welfare impacts of the EU's proposed carbon border adjustment mechanism. *Energy Policy*, *162*, 112802. DOI: 10.1016/j.enpol.2022.112802

Zhong, J., & Pei, J. (2024). Carbon border adjustment mechanism : A systematic literature review of the latest developments. *Climate Policy*, *24*(2), 228–242. DOI: 10.1080/14693062.2023.2190074

Živanović, Z., Popović, V., Djordjević, A., Protić, B., Šećerov, V., & Jeftić, M. (2026). "Signs by the Roadside": On the Road to Just Green Transitions in Serbia. In Berisha, E., Moodie, J., Allkja, L., & Jeftić, M. (Eds.), *The Palgrave Handbook of Just Green Transitions in the Western Balkans and Beyond* (pp. 265–282). Palgrave Macmillan. DOI: 10.1007/978-3-031-95075-9_15

Zou, P., Wang, Q., Xie, J., & Zhou, C. (2020). Does doing good lead to doing better in emerging markets? Stock market responses to the SRI index announcements in Brazil, China, and South Africa. *Journal of the Academy of Marketing Science*, *48*(5), 966–986. DOI: 10.1007/s11747-019-00651-z

Zumente, I., & Bistrova, J. (2021). Do Baltic investors care about environmental, social and governance (ESG)? *Journal of Entrepreneurship and Sustainability Issues*, *8*(4), 349–362. DOI: 10.9770/jesi.2021.8.4(20)

Zvezdanović Lobanova, J., Kračun, D., & Kavkler, A. (2018). Effects of cross-border mergers and acquisitions on GDP per capita and domestic investment in transition countries. *Journal of Business Economics and Management*, *19*(1), 124–137. DOI: 10.3846/16111699.2017.1408677

Zvezdanović Lobanova, J., & Lobanov, M. (2023). Problems and perspectives of the European Green Deal with the focus on the SEE countries and Serbia. *The Review of International Affairs*, *LXXIV*(1188), 51–77. DOI: 10.18485/iipe_ria.2023.74.1188.3

About the Contributors

Mohieddine Rahmouni, Ph.D., is an Associate Professor of Economics at the Applied College, King Faisal University (Al-Ahsa, Saudi Arabia), and at the High School of Economic and Commercial Sciences of Tunis (ESSECT), University of Tunis, Tunisia. He earned his Ph.D. in Economics through a joint doctoral program between the University of Montesquieu Bordeaux IV (now the University of Bordeaux), France, and the University of Tunis. His research lies at the intersection of innovation economics, applied econometrics, productivity analysis, and industrial dynamics, with a particular focus on economic development and structural transformation in emerging economies. Dr. Rahmouni's scholarly work has been published in reputable international journals such as Structural Change and Economic Dynamics, the Journal of Industrial and Business Economics, and the International Journal of Innovation and Technology Management. His research explores the role of external knowledge sources, the determinants of innovation performance, and the policy mechanisms that influence firm-level productivity and competitiveness. Through rigorous empirical analysis, he contributes to advancing the understanding of how innovation systems and policy frameworks shape economic growth and industrial development in transitioning and emerging markets.

***

Lawal Abdulwahab Olamilekan is a dedicated academic with a PhD in Economics from the Universiti Brunei Darussalam, School of Business and Economics (AACSB-accredited). He holds a Master's degree in Health Economics and a Bachelor's in Economics Education from Taraba State University, Nigeria. His research interests include natural resource economics, health economics, development, and macroeconomics, especially in Africa and emerging economies. With over six years of academic experience, he has taught and supervised students across Nigeria, Somalia, Somaliland, and Brunei. His teaching expertise covers economics, management, and public health, while his research contributions include conference papers, journal articles, and book chapters. Lawal's proficiency in quantitative and qualitative methodologies, coupled with his advanced skills in econometric modelling and using software such as Stata, SPSS, and EViews, instills confidence in his technical abilities. He is a member of the World Economics Association and the Institute of Chartered Economists of Nigeria. His active engagement in collaborative research that bridges health policy, governance, and economic development to provide evidence-based insights for sustainable growth is truly inspiring.

Muhammad Agus Irawan is a student at the Faculty of Islamic Economics and Business, State Islamic University of Sunan Kudus (UIN Sunan Kudus), Indonesia. His academic interests focus on Islamic economics, sharia finance, and sustainable business practices.

K. Balaji is an Assistant Professor in Business and Management, Christ University, Bangalore. He did Ph.D. from KLU Business School, KL University,Vijayawada. He is having 12 years of teaching experience. He has to his credit 23 Research Articles published in reputed National and International Journals. He has participated and presented more than 12 papers in both National and International Seminars/Conferences and also attended more than 50 workshops/ FDPS organized by various reputed organizations. He has also participated in more than 50 seminars / webinars organized by various reputed organizations. He has also attended in 6 Short Term Training programs.He has successfully conducted 3 webinars, one 5 day FDP and one International Conference on Reimaging marketing in New Normal. He is a ratified as Assistant Professor by both JNTUH, JNTU Anantapur and Sri Venkateswara University,Tirupati. His specialized areas include, Accounting and Financial management, Marketing Management, Retailing Management, Consumer Behavior studies, Entrepreneurship and Business Laws.

Rajashree K. C is a Biomedical Engineer with a Master's in Business Administration from Saveetha University, specializing in Hospital Management and Marketing, and holds a Ph.D. in Healthcare Management. An energetic and enthusiastic professor, she excels in academics and as a multitasker, organizing seminars, workshops, cultural programs, and other extra-curricular activities. She serves as the Coordinator of NSS Unit of Saveetha School of Management, leading them to achieve multiple accolades including the Best Club award. A prominent researcher with publications in Web of Science, Scopus, and UGC-listed journals, she actively enhances her expertise through conferences, workshops, MOOCs, and certifications, including Quality Coordination in Hospitals. Awarded the

"Young Academician Award" and "Young Teacher Award," she is passionate about innovation, student skill development, and inspiring young minds through exemplary teaching and mentorship.

Bayu Tri Cahya, S.E., M.Si. is a lecturer at the State Islamic University of Sunan Kudus, specializing in economics and accounting, with a strong focus on Islamic economics, sharia finance, and sustainable development. He is actively engaged in research and publications at both national and international levels.

Aarti Chopra is a seasoned academician with over 20 years of teaching and administrative experience in higher education. She is an admired teacher and an efficient administrator. Besides her Masters and Doctorate in Business Administration, she also holds a professional law degree. Currently, she is working as an Associate Professor in MBA department at Poornima University, Jaipur and resource person at Lady Shri Ram College, New Delhi. She is the national gold medalist in the Public Relation Program. She is the author of several books and research papers on various topics related to Commerce and Management. She is also an active member of an NGO working actively for the promotion of Khadi and sustainable fashion. She is a member of many professional organisations and the joint secretary of a leading research organisation. She has 2 national and 1 international patents to her credit. Dr Chopra is the former student union president of Kanoria Mahila Mahavidyalaya and Vice President of KMM alumni association. She is the recipient of many awards such as Education Icon Award, Excellence in Academics Award and Mahila Shakti Award. She is also a SHRM certified corporate trainer and PoSH trainer having trained over 5000 industry professionals at various Banks and PSUs as Punjab National Bank, Rajasthan Rajya Vidyut Nigam, Rajasthan Electronics and Instruments Ltd, etc.

Monika Handayani is a distinguished academic and consultant with a strong focus on sustainability reporting. She currently serves as a lecturer and senate member at Politeknik Negeri Banjarmasin, as well as an Internal Quality Assurance System Auditor. In addition, she is an Assurer for Sustainability Reporting at the National Center for Sustainability Reporting in Jakarta, specializing in the evaluation of sustainability reports for mining, oil, and gas companies across Indonesia. Her academic qualifications are extensive, including a Bachelor's degree in Economics and Accounting, a Master's degree in Governmental Management Accounting, and a Doctorate in Accounting from Universitas Brawijaya, Malang. Monika Handayani is also a certified specialist in sustainability reporting, quality management auditing, chartered accountancy, and export management, holding several prestigious certifications such as Certified Sustainability Reporting Specialist (CSRS), Certified

Sustainability Reporting Assurance (CSRA), Certified Accountant (CA), and Certified International Internal Quality

Umi Hanifah, M.Acc., is a lecturer in the Accounting Undergraduate Program at Universitas Duta Bangsa Surakarta. She has a strong academic focus in accounting and finance, and is active in developing capital market literacy among students.

Baljit Kaur is an Associate Professor and Head at Punjab School of Economics, Guru Nanak Dev University, Amritsar, Punjab. Her research centres on public expenditure, health economics and development economics. She has worked on three projects: "Pradhan Mantri Mudra Yojana" commissioned under ICSSR ; Third Party Evaluation Study of 100 clusters of Phase 1 under Shyama Prasad Rurban Mission for zone 1' Commissioned by Ministry of Rural Development, New Delhi and 'Role of Dairy Farming in Rural Development of Punjab' commissioned under UGC-SAP. She has been a member of various academic bodies and has actively participated in research, with publications in both national as well as international journals

Fibriyani Nur Khairin is a distinguished academic and practitioner with a profound expertise in the evolving landscape of modern accounting. She currently serves as the Coordinator of the Accounting Undergraduate Program at the Faculty of Economics and Business, Universitas Mulawarman, where she plays a strategic role in shaping the curriculum and ensuring academic excellence. Her academic contributions are centered on a diverse range of research interests, including Sustainability Accounting, Social Enterprise, and Behavioral & Management Accounting. Fibriyani is particularly recognized for her proficiency in Qualitative Accounting Research, employing nuanced methodologies to explore the human and social dimensions of financial practices. Her professional standing is underpinned by a robust set of credentials, holding prestigious certifications such as Chartered Accountant (CA), Certified Sustainability Reporting Specialist (CSRS), Certified Sustainability Reporting Assurer (CSRA), and Certified International Qualitative Researcher (CIQaR). Beyond the classroom, she possesses significant practical experience as a sustainability practitioner, where she actively serves as both a preparer and an assessor of Sustainability Reports, helping organizations align their operations with global environmental and social standards. Through her combined roles as an educator, researcher, and consultant, she remains dedicated to advancing the accountability and social impact of the accounting profession in Indonesia.

Mikhail Lobanov is Deputy Director for Research and a Senior Research Fellow at the Institute of Economics, Russian Academy of Sciences in Moscow. His main fields of research are problems of socio-economic and political development in Central-Eastern and South-Eastern Europe, evolution of the world economy, regional economics and regional economic policy in Russia and abroad, the EU enlargement and processes of integration in Eurasia, functional and territorial organization of industry and agriculture, varieties of capitalist relations, development of trade and investment relation ships between Russia, CIS and Eastern European countries, complex country studies (with the focus on the Balkan countries).

Kafila Md is a dynamic academic leader currently serving as Associate Professor and Assistant Dean (Academics) at the School of Business, SR University. She holds a Ph.D. in Finance and brings over two decades of experience in teaching, research, academic mentoring, and institutional leadership. Her areas of expertise include Finance, Human Resource Management, Financial Analytics, and Career Skills Development. She is a passionate advocate of experiential learning and industry-academia collaboration, having actively facilitated internship opportunities, MoUs with industry partners, and student projects with real-world relevance. Dr. Kafila is also a prolific researcher—recently authoring a Scopus-indexed paper on predictive modeling in health insurance (XANNLight: A Novel Hybrid Ensemble Model), and mentoring research scholars who have published in Springer (Q2) journals. Beyond research, she shares thought leadership through LinkedIn, regularly posting about career-readiness, remote internships, employability skills, and academic innovation. Her content often focuses on bridging the gap between campus and corporate, empowering students and early-career professionals with knowledge and confidence. She also engages in interdisciplinary research and digital transformation initiatives, and often collaborates with startup ecosystems to prepare students for the evolving demands of business and technology landscapes.

Rifki Muhammad Bintang is a master student in the Master's Program of Public Administration at Universitas Brawijaya, Indonesia. He holds a Bachelor's degree in Government Studies from Universitas Muhammadiyah Malang. His academic interests focus on public policy, governance, community empowerment, and sustainable development. He has experience as a research assistant and is actively involved in policy-oriented research, particularly in the areas of public sector management and data-driven policy analysis. His work aims to contribute to evidence-based policymaking and the advancement of effective and inclusive public governance.

P. Praveen Kumar holds an MCom, MBA, and PhD in Finance from Pondicherry University. He secured the University 1st Rank in his Under Graduation. His teaching interests include Financial Accounting, Financial Management, Mergers & Acquisitions, Security Analysis & Portfolio Management, and other finance-related courses. His research interests extend to interdisciplinary areas.

Ravikumar R. Natarajan is an experienced academician with over 12+ years of teaching and research expertise across institutions in India, the UAE, and the Maldives. He currently serves as an Assistant Professor at Marwadi University, Rajkot, specializing in Machine Learning, Recommender Systems, and AI-driven applications in healthcare and security. He holds a Ph.D. in Machine Learning and Recommender Systems from Amity University, Jaipur, a Master of Engineering in CSE from VMRF University, Salem, and a Bachelor of Engineering in CSE from Anna University. He also has a MiniMBA from the Swiss eLearning Institute. Dr. Ravikumar has authored more than 8+ multiple SCIE/Scopus-indexed journal articles, 25+ IEEE/Springer conference papers, and co-authored a book on Artificial Intelligence. He has also published 9 patents and contributed 75+ book chapters in emerging domains such as Federated Learning, Blockchain, and Digital Twins for IGI Global, Wiley and Springer publisher. He actively mentors students through initiatives like the Research Activities Club (RAC) and Student Research Internship Training (SRIT), promoting innovation and research culture.

Rismawati Rismawati is a distinguished academic and consultant with a robust focus on sustainability reporting. She currently holds the position of lecturer and Head of the Quality Assurance Institute at Universitas Muhammadiyah Palopo, where she has been pivotal in ensuring the quality of university processes and outputs since February 2020. Additionally, she serves as an Assurer for Sustainability Reporting at the National Center for Sustainability Reporting in Jakarta, specializing in the evaluation of sustainability reports for mining companies across Indonesia. Her academic qualifications are extensive, comprising a Bachelor's degree in Economics and Accounting, a Master's degree in Accounting Science, and a Doctorate in Accounting from Universitas Brawijaya, Malang. Rismawati is also a certified specialist in sustainability reporting, risk management, and tax planning, holding several prestigious certifications including Certified Sustainability Reporting Specialist (CSRS), Certified Risk Management Practitioner (CRMP), Certified Management Accountant (CMA) and Certified Enterprise Risk Analysis (CERA). In her professional capacity, she has provided consultancy services in financial management and tax compliance for companies such as PT. Reski Barito Timur and PT. Helay Raya. Furthermore, she has authored multiple publications on Social Accounting, Sustainability Accounting, Management Accounting and CSR, contributing significantly to the academic community. Her interests in reading, writing, and travel reflect her commitment to lifelong learning and professional growth in her field.

Ali Roziqin is a Lecturer in the Department of Government Studies, Universitas Muhammadiyah Malang, Indonesia. He obtained his bachelor's degree from the

Department of Public Administration at Universitas Diponegoro, Indonesia. He holds a Master of Public Administration from the Universitas Gadjah Mada, Indonesia. His research interests are in bureaucracy, public policy and administration, and public sector innovation. He has published papers in the reputable international journals like Sustainability (MDPI), Local Environment (Taylor and Francis), Tourism Critiques, Public Administration Quarterly, Atlantic Journal of Communication, Frontiers in Communication, Journal of Science and Technology Policy Management, Journal of the Knowledge Economy, Frontiers in Communication and Public Administration and Policy: An Asia-Pacific Journal, as well as in the IGI Global

Aarthi S is a dedicated Assistant Professor in Computer Science with over six years of teaching experience. She is currently pursuing her Ph.D. at Marwadi University, Gujarat, and holds an M.Phil. and MCA from Bharathiar University, Tamil Nadu. Throughout her academic career, Aarthi has specialized in programming languages such as C++, Java, and C, and contributed to research in recommender systems and AI-related data privacy. She has published journal articles, contributed to book chapters, and actively participated in technical workshops. Known for her student mentorship and engagement in academic events, Aarthi remains committed to fostering innovation and excellence in computer science education.

Susenohaji is Lecturer in the Faculty of Vocational Studies, University of Brawijaya, Indonesia. He has research interest are in digital innovation, public finance, and rural government.

Ambati Suvarna is a full-time research scholar at SR University, focusing on Performance Appraisal of SRI Funds: A Comparative Analysis of Selective Public and Private Sector Companies. With 16 years of teaching experience in HR and finance subjects, she has established herself as an experienced educator and researcher. Her academic contributions include three conference papers published in ISBN books, one paper in SR University & conference proceedings, and another presented at an international conference at Shinawatra University, Thailand. Additionally, she has authored multiple book chapters and published two research papers in academic journals. Her extensive teaching background, combined with ongoing research, demonstrates her commitment to academia and expertise in financial analysis and human resource management. Her work contributes valuable insights to the field of sustainable and responsible investing (SRI) through comparative corporate performance analysis.

Jelena Zvezdanović Lobanova holds a Ph.D. in Economics from the University of Maribor and works as a Senior Research Associate at the Institute of Social Sciences in Belgrade. Her scientific research area includes macro and microeconomic issues related to international capital flows, foreign direct investment, cross-border mergers and acquisitions, the institutional environment, climate change, and green transition.

Index